Texas Penal Code

2010 Edition

WITH TABLES AND INDEX

As Amended through the 2009 First Called Session of the 81st Legislature

WEST®
A Thomson Reuters business

Mat #40723390

ISBN 978–0–31498–810–2

PREFACE

This Pamphlet contains the text of the Texas Penal Code, Subtitle C, Title 6 of the Health and Safety Code, on substance abuse regulation and crimes, Chapters 704, 705, 724 and 729 of the Transportation Code, relating to selected motor vehicle offenses, and Subchapter H of Chapter 411 of the Government Code, governing concealed handgun licenses. The laws are current through the 2009 First Called Session of the 81st Legislature.

The Penal Code as enacted included the Chapter and Section headings that appear herein. The analyses of these headings at the beginning of the Code and of each chapter, coupled with an editorially prepared Index, provide a quick and easy means of finding particular provisions of the Code. A Table of Sections Affected indicates sections of the Penal Code affected through the 2009 First Called Session of the 81st Legislature.

Table 1, Disposition, and Table 2, Derivation, are furnished, providing a means of tracing repealed subject matter into the Code and of searching out the source of the Code Sections.

Pursuant to section 5 of Chapter 399, the Texas Legislative Council has compiled a table showing the disposition of unrepealed articles of the Penal Code of 1925, which is also included herein as Table 3.

WEST

September, 2009

*

RELATED PRODUCTS FROM WEST

TEXAS PRACTICE SERIES

Guide to the Texas Rules of Evidence
Steven Goode, Olin Guy Wellborn III, and M. Michael Sharlot

Courtroom Handbook on Texas Evidence
Steven Goode, Olin Guy Wellborn III, and M. Michael Sharlot

Texas Land Titles and Title Examination
Aloysius A. Leopold

Texas Criminal Law
Michael B. Charlton

Texas Criminal Forms and Trial Manual
Michael J. McCormick, Thomas D. Blackwell and Betty Blackwell

Texas Law of Wills
Gerry W. Beyer

Texas Methods of Practice
Frank W. Elliott, John E. Krahmer, Hal M. Bateman and Nancy Saint-Paul

Texas Foreclosure: Law and Practice
Mike Baggett

Texas Probate and Decedents' Estates
M. K. Woodward and Ernest E. Smith III

Texas Business Organizations
Robert W. Hamilton, Elizabeth S. Miller and Robert A. Ragazzo

Texas Property Taxes
Jay D. Howell, Jr.

Texas Municipal Law and Practice
David B. Brooks

Texas Consumer Rights and Remedies
Stephen G. Cochran

Texas Consumer Law Handbook
Stephen G. Cochran

Texas Juvenile Law and Practice
Thomas S. Morgan and Harold C. Gaither, Jr.

Handbook of Texas Family Law
Don Koons

RELATED PRODUCTS

The Jury Charge in Texas Civil Litigation
T. Ray Guy

Texas County and Special District Law
David B. Brooks

Texas Workers' Compensation Law and Practice
Karen A. Lerner

Texas Marital Property and Homesteads
Aloysius A. Leopold

Texas Criminal Practice and Procedure
George E. Dix and Robert O. Dawson

Texas Medical Malpractice
Michael P. Penick

Texas Environmental Law
Jeff Civins, Jimmy Alan Hall and Mark K. Sahs

Handbook on Texas Discovery Practice
Alex Wilson Albright, Charles Herring, Jr. and Robert H. Pemberton

Handbook of Texas Lawyer and Judicial Ethics
Robert P. Schuwerk and Lillian B. Hardwick

Texas Contract Law
David R. Dow and Craig Smyser

Texas Elder Law
Molly Dear Abshire, H. Clyde Farrell, Patricia Flora Sitchler, and Wesley E. Wright

Texas DWI Law and Practice Handbook
Julie Kay Baker and Kyle C. Simpson

WEST'S TEXAS FORMS

Texas Creditors' Remedies and Debtors' Rights
Allen E. Smith

Texas Administrative Practice
Steven L. Martin

Texas Business Litigation—Forms and Commentary
Glidden Partners

Texas Minerals, Oil and Gas
John S. Lowe

Texas Business Entities
Ben Bateman and Nancy Saint–Paul

RELATED PRODUCTS

Texas Civil Trial and Appellate Practice
Frank W. Elliott

Texas Estate Planning
Donald J. Malouf and Henry J. Lischer

Administration of Decedents' Estates and Guardianships
Aloysius A. Leopold and Gerry W. Beyer

Texas Real Property
Gerry W. Beyer

Texas Family Law
John F. Elder

STATUTES, CODES AND RULES

Vernon's Texas Codes Annotated

Vernon's Texas Rules Annotated—Civil Procedure, Evidence and Appellate Procedure

Texas Administrative Code

Texas Rules of Court—State, Federal and Local

Texas Business and Commerce Code

Texas Civil Practice and Remedies Code

Texas Corporation and Partnership Laws

Texas Criminal and Motor Vehicle Code

Texas Criminal Procedure—Code and Rules

Texas Environmental Laws

Texas Family Code

Texas Finance Code

Texas Insurance Code

Texas Local Government Code

Texas Penal Code

Texas Probate Code

Texas Property Code

TEXAS ANNOTATED CODE SERIES

Anderson, Bartlett & East's Texas Uniform Commercial Code Annotated

Beyer's Texas Property Code Annotated

RELATED PRODUCTS

Carlson's Texas Employment Laws Annotated

Cooper, Hensley & Marshall's Texas Rules of Civil Procedure Annotated

Elliott & Morris' Texas Tax Code Annotated

Gaba's Texas Environmental Laws Annotated

Hanby's Texas Rules of Appellate Procedure Annotated

Johanson's Texas Probate Code Annotated

Kinkeade & McColloch's Texas Penal Code Annotated

McGehee's Texas Civil Practice and Remedies Code Annotated

Roach's Texas Rules of Evidence Annotated

Sampson & Tindall's Texas Family Code Annotated

Texas Business Statutes Annotated

Texas Civil Practice Statutes and Rules Annotated

CASES

Texas Cases: Covering Southwestern 1st

Texas Cases: Covering Southwestern 2d

Texas Cases: Covering Southwestern 3d

FORMS

Vernon's Texas Code Forms Annotated–UCC Forms

Texas Forms: Legal and Business

Texas Jurisprudence Pleading and Practice Forms 2d

West's Texas Forms

Texas Legal Practice Forms 2d

DIGESTS & ENCYCLOPEDIAS

Texas Jurisprudence 3d

West's Texas Digest (1840–1934)

West's Texas Digest 2d (1935–date)

Texas Encyclopedia of Criminal Law

OTHER RESEARCH TOOLS FOR TEXAS

Texas Practice Guide

Texas Family Law Service

RELATED PRODUCTS

West's Complete Texas Family Law (CD–ROM)

Texas Lawdesk Library (CD–ROM)

Texas Litigation Library (CD–ROM)

Texas Practice Series

McDonald & Carlson Texas Civil Practice 2d

Westlaw & KeyCite

Texas Digest

Texas Law Finder

Westlaw®

Westcheck.com™

West CD–ROM Libraries™

Many of these products are also available on CD–ROM and online via Westlaw.

To order any of these Texas practice tools,
call your West Representative or
1–800–328–9352.

NEED RESEARCH HELP?

You can get quality research results with free help—call the West Reference Attorneys when you have questions concerning Westlaw or West Publications at **1–800–REF–ATTY (1–800–733–2889)**.

INTERNET ACCESS

Contact the West Editorial Department directly with your questions and suggestions by e-mail at west.editor@thomson.com.
Visit West's home page at
west.thomson.com

*

TABLE OF CONTENTS

TEXAS PENAL CODE

Section Analysis, see beginning of each Chapter.

TITLE 1. INTRODUCTORY PROVISIONS

TITLE 2. GENERAL PRINCIPLES OF CRIMINAL RESPONSIBILITY

TITLE 3. PUNISHMENTS

TABLE OF CONTENTS

TITLE 4. INCHOATE OFFENSES

TITLE 5. OFFENSES AGAINST THE PERSON

TITLE 6. OFFENSES AGAINST THE FAMILY

TITLE 7. OFFENSES AGAINST PROPERTY

TITLE 8. OFFENSES AGAINST PUBLIC ADMINISTRATION

TABLE OF CONTENTS

TABLE OF CONTENTS

TRANSPORTATION CODE
TITLE 7. VEHICLES AND TRAFFIC

INDEX

EFFECTIVE DATES

The following table shows the date of adjournment and the effective date of ninety day bills enacted at sessions of the legislature beginning with the year 1945:

Year	Leg.	Session	Adjournment Date	Effective Date
1945	49	Regular	June 5, 1945	September 4, 1945
1947	50	Regular	June 6, 1947	September 5, 1947
1949	51	Regular	June 6, 1949	September 5, 1949
1951	52	Regular	June 8, 1951	September 7, 1951
1953	53	Regular	May 27, 1953	August 26, 1953
1954	53	1st C.S.	May 13, 1954	August 12, 1954
1955	54	Regular	June 7, 1955	September 6, 1955
1957	55	Regular	May 23, 1957	August 22, 1957
1957	55	1st C.S.	November 12, 1957	February 11, 1958
1957	55	2nd C.S.	December 3, 1957	March 4, 1958
1959	56	Regular	May 12, 1959	August 11, 1959
1959	56	1st C.S.	June 16, 1959	September 15, 1959
1959	56	2nd C.S.	July 16, 1959	October 15, 1959
1959	56	3rd C.S.	August 6, 1959	November 5, 1959
1961	57	Regular	May 29, 1961	August 28, 1961
1961	57	1st C.S.	August 8, 1961	November 7, 1961
1961	57	2nd C.S.	August 14, 1961	November 13, 1961
1962	57	3rd C.S.	February 1, 1962	May 3, 1962
1963	58	Regular	May 24, 1963	August 23, 1963
1965	59	Regular	May 31, 1965	August 30, 1965
1966	59	1st C.S.	February 23, 1966	*
1967	60	Regular	May 29, 1967	August 28, 1967
1968	60	1st C.S.	July 3, 1968	*
1969	61	Regular	June 2, 1969	September 1, 1969
1969	61	1st C.S.	August 26, 1969	*
1969	61	2nd C.S.	September 9, 1969	December 9, 1969
1971	62	Regular	May 31, 1971	August 30, 1971
1971	62	1st C.S.	June 4, 1971	September 3, 1971
1972	62	2nd C.S.	March 30, 1972	June 29, 1972
1972	62	3rd C.S.	July 7, 1972	*
1972	62	4th C.S.	October 17, 1972	January 16, 1973
1973	63	Regular	May 28, 1973	August 27, 1973
1973	63	1st C.S.	December 20, 1973	*
1975	64	Regular	June 2, 1975	September 1, 1975
1977	65	Regular	May 30, 1977	August 29, 1977
1977	65	1st C.S.	July 21, 1977	*
1978	65	2nd C.S.	August 8, 1978	November 7, 1978
1979	66	Regular	May 28, 1979	August 27, 1979

EFFECTIVE DATES

Year	Leg.	Session	Adjournment Date	Effective Date
1981	67	Regular	June 1, 1981	August 31, 1981
1981	67	1st C.S.	August 11, 1981	November 10, 1981
1982	67	2nd C.S.	May 28, 1982	*
1982	67	3rd C.S.	September 9, 1982	*
1983	68	Regular	May 30, 1983	August 29, 1983
1983	68	1st C.S.	June 25, 1983	September 23, 1983
1984	68	2nd C.S.	July 3, 1984	October 2, 1984
1985	69	Regular	May 27, 1985	August 26, 1985
1985	69	1st C.S.	May 30, 1985	August 29, 1985
1986	69	2nd C.S.	September 4, 1986	December 4, 1986
1986	69	3rd C.S.	September 30, 1986	December 30, 1986
1987	70	Regular	June 1, 1987	August 31, 1987
1987	70	1st C.S.	June 3, 1987	September 2, 1987
1987	70	2nd C.S.	July 21, 1987	October 20, 1987
1989	71	Regular	May 29, 1989	August 28, 1989
1989	71	1st C.S.	July 19, 1989	October 18, 1989
1989	71	2nd C.S.	December 12, 1989	*
1990	71	3rd C.S.	March 28, 1990	*
1990	71	4th C.S.	May 1, 1990	*
1990	71	5th C.S.	May 30, 1990	*
1990	71	6th C.S.	June 7, 1990	September 6, 1990
1991	72	Regular	May 27, 1991	August 26, 1991
1991	72	1st C.S.	August 13, 1991	November 12, 1991
1991	72	2nd C.S.	August 25, 1991	November 24, 1991
1992	72	3rd C.S.	January 8, 1992	April 8, 1992
1992	72	4th C.S.	December 3, 1992	*
1993	73	Regular	May 31, 1993	August 30, 1993
1995	74	Regular	May 29, 1995	August 28, 1995
1997	75	Regular	June 2, 1997	September 1, 1997
1999	76	Regular	May 31, 1999	August 30, 1999
2001	77	Regular	May 28, 2001	September 1, 2001
2003	78	Regular	June 2, 2003	September 1, 2003
2003	78	1st C.S.	July 28, 2003	November 1, 2003
2003	78	2nd C.S.	August 26, 2003	*
2005	79	2nd C.S.	August 19, 2005	November 18, 2005
2006	79	3rd C.S.	May 16, 2006	August 15, 2006
2007	80	Regular	May 28, 2007	August 27, 2007
2009	81	Regular	June 1, 2009	August 31, 2009
2009	81	1st C.S.	July 2, 2009	*

* No legislation for which the ninety day effective date is applicable.

DISPOSITION TABLE

PENAL CODE

TABLE 1
Disposition

Showing where provisions of former articles of Vernon's Annotated Penal Code are covered in the Penal Code as originally enacted or in other units of Vernon's Texas Statutes and Codes.

See Table 3 for Disposition of unrepealed articles of the Penal Code of 1925, as amended.

Vernon's Ann.P.C. Article	V.T.C.A. Penal Code Section
1, 2	1.02
3	1.03(a)
4, 5	1.05(b)
6	1.02
7	1.05(a)
8	1.05(b)
9	2.01
10	1.03
11	——
12	8.03
13 to 18	——
19	1.05(b)
	1.07(a)(17)
20, 21	1.05(b)
22	1.07(a)(27)
23	1.07(a)(2)
24 to 26	——
27	1.07(a)(22)
28	——
29	1.04(a)
30	8.07
31	8.07
32	8.05
33	——
34	8.01
35	——
36	8.04
37	9.21
38	8.05
39	6.01
40	8.03
41	8.02
42 to 44	6.04
45	2.05
46	2.03
	2.04
47	12.02
	12.03
	12.04
48	12.03
49, 50	——
51	12.01(c)
52	12.03
53 to 60	——
61	12.43
62 to 64	12.42
65	7.01
	7.02
66 to 71	7.02
72	7.01
73	6.04
74 to 76	——
77 to 79	38.05
80	7.03(2)
81	38.05
83 to 85	——
86, 87	39.01
88	——
89 to 91	39.01
92	1.07(a)(30)
93 to 96	39.01
98, 99	——
100, 101	39.01
107f	39.01
108	39.01
109	——
110	39.01
111	——
112 to 119	39.01
120	36.03
	39.01
121 to 131	——
132 to 139	——
141	——
142, 143	39.01
144	39.03
145, 146	39.01
147, 147c	37.11
147d § 2	——
148	42.09
149	——
152	42.09
153 to 157	——
158 to 160	36.02
160–a to 165	36.02
166, 167	32.43
168 to 174	36.02
177 to 178a	36.02

DISPOSITION TABLE

Vernon's Ann.P.C. Article	V.T.C.A. Penal Code Section
178b	32.44
184 to 187	——
188 to 197	36.02
198 to 200a	——
201 to 205	——
253	42.02
254	36.03
	42.02
255	42.01
	42.02
256	36.03
257	46.04(a)(2)
258	36.03
261	39.02
281	42.01
	42.05
282 to 287	——
302	37.02
	37.03
303	37.02
	37.03
304	37.07
305	37.01
306	37.03
307	37.03
	37.04
308	37.02
	37.03
309	——
310	37.02
311	37.01
312 to 314	——
315	7.02
316	36.05
317 to 322	38.08
323, 324	39.01
325	——
326	38.08
	38.10
327	38.08
	38.10
328 to 330	38.08
331 to 333a	25.03
334	38.08
335	38.05
336, 337	——
338, 339	38.03
340	——
341	38.03
	38.04
342 to 345	——
346	1.07(a)(25)
347	1.07(a)(11)
348	——
349	39.02
350 to 352	——
353	39.02
353a, 353b	38.07
353d	38.07
354 to 364	37.10
365 to 371	39.01
372	36.08
373	——
379, 380	——
381 to 383	39.01
384 to 395	39.01
396 to 403	39.01
407 to 414	39.01
415 to 418	39.01
418a	——
419	39.01
420 to 422	39.01
423	39.01
425	39.01
426, 427	39.01
427c	——
428	38.06
428a	36.05
429	37.11
430	38.12
438c, 438d	37.10
439	42.02
440, 441	36.03
442 to 446	38.07
	38.08
447, 448	36.03
449 to 452	42.02
453, 454	42.04
454a to 454g	——
455, 456	42.02
457	36.03
	42.02
458 to 463	38.06
	42.02
464	42.02
465	42.01
	42.02
466	42.02
466a	42.01
467 to 470	2.02
471	——
472	42.04
472a	42.02
	42.03
473	42.01
474	42.01
	42.03
	42.05
475, 475a	42.01
476	42.07
477	42.08
478	——
479	30.05
480	42.01
480a	42.12
481	——
482, 482a	42.01
483	46.02
484	46.03
485	42.01
	46.04
486	46.03
	46.04
487	——
488	46.02
489	46.06

DISPOSITION TABLE

Vernon's Ann.P.C. Article	V.T.C.A. Penal Code Section
	46.07
489a	——
489b	46.06
489c	46.05
489d	46.08
490 to 491	25.01
494	25.01
495	25.02
498 to 509	——
510 to 512	43.04
513	43.21
	43.22
	43.24
514	43.03
515	43.04
516	43.05
517, 518	——
519	43.03
	to
	43.05
520	1.04
521	43.06
522	43.04
523	——
524	21.04
	to
	21.06
525	43.03
	43.04
527	43.21
	to
	43.23
528, 528a	42.09
529, 530	42.10
534b	43.24
535	25.03
	25.04
535a	——
535b	25.04
535c, 535d	21.11
560	32.45
565	32.35
567	32.45
567b	31.06
	32.41
602	25.05
602–A	25.05
603	1.04
	C.C.P. 13.16
604	25.05
605	25.05
	C.C.P. 38.11
606	——
607 §§ (1) to (8)	——
§ (9)	43.02
§§ (10) to (13)	——
§ (14)	43.02
	43.03
§ (15)	43.03
§ (16)	21.07
	43.02
§§ (17), (18)	43.02
§ (19)	43.03

Vernon's Ann.P.C. Article	V.T.C.A. Penal Code Section
§ (20)	43.02
§ (21)	43.06
607a	43.02
608	——
609	C.C.P. 14.03
610 to 612	——
613	42.11
614	——
614b	——
615 to 618	47.02
619 to 621	47.06
	47.07
622	——
623	——
624	47.02
625	47.04
	47.06
	47.07
626 to 629	47.04
630	47.04
	47.06
631	——
632	——
633	C.C.P. ch. 18
634	R.C.S. 4667
635	——
636 to 638	C.C.P. 18.18
639	47.09
640, 641	39.01
642	——
642a to 642c	47.02 to 47.07
642c	47.09
643, 643a	47.02
644	——
645	47.01
646	47.02
646a to 648–2	47.02 to 47.04
649	47.04
650	47.03
	47.04
651	47.02
652	47.09
652a	47.02 to 47.07
654, 655	47.02 to 47.04
655a, 655b	——
695, 696	——
698c	Water Code
	§§ 21.551
	to
	21.564
	C.C.P. 17A.02
	to
	C.C.P. 17A.07
698d § 7	C.C.P. 17A.02
§ 8	C.C.P. 17A.03
§ 9	C.C.P. 17A.04
§ 10	C.C.P. 17A.06
§ 11	C.C.P. 17A.07
§ 12	——
699	——
701	——
702, 703	——
710 to 713	32.42

DISPOSITION TABLE

Vernon's Ann.P.C. Article	V.T.C.A. Penal Code Section
714 to 716	——
718	32.42
755 to 758	——
784	42.03
785, 786	42.03
790	——
791	9.22
796 to 797b	——
799	——
800, 801	——
802a	——
802a–1	19.05
802c	19.05
803	C.C.P. 14.03
813 to 817	——
831, 832	39.01
856	30.05
857	42.03
858	30.05
859	28.03
860	——
861	30.03
862	28.03
864	28.03
978o	31.04
979 to 993	32.21
995, 996	32.21
997	16.01
998	32.21
999	——
1000, 1001	32.46
1002	32.21
	32.47
	37.10
1002a	32.21
	32.47
	37.10
1003	32.46
1004	32.21
1005	3.01
	to
	3.04
1006 to 1008	32.21
1009	1.04
1010, 1011	32.21
1012 to 1017	32.21
1026	32.21
1030	32.42
1041	39.01
1042	——
1044, 1045	32.42
1050, 1051	32.42
1053	32.42
1056	31.04
1057	——
1094 to 1100	——
1106a	32.42
1111b	28.03
1111m	——
1117	——
1118 to 1121	37.03
1123	32.21
1137e, 1137e–1	31.04

Vernon's Ann.P.C. Article		V.T.C.A. Penal Code Section
1137f		28.03
		28.04
1137g		31.04
1137j		——
1138 to 1141		22.01
1142,	subd. 1	9.61
		to
		9.63
	subd. 2	9.21
	subd. 3	9.22
		9.32
	subd. 4	9.41
		to
		9.43
	subd. 5	9.51
	subd. 6	9.31
		9.33
		9.43
	subd. 7	9.31
1143		9.31
1144, 1145		22.01
1146		22.01
		22.07
		42.01
1146a		22.01
		22.05
1147		1.07(a)(11)
		22.02
		22.03
		22.04
1148		22.02
1148a		22.04
1149		22.02
1150		——
1151		22.02
1157		39.01
		39.02
1158		39.01
		39.02
1159		15.01
		22.01
		22.02
1160		15.01
		19.02
		22.01
		22.02
1160a		15.01
		19.02
		22.03
1161		46.01
1162		15.01
		21.02
1163		15.01
		29.02
1164		15.01
		30.02
1165		15.01
1166		22.02
1167		22.01
		22.02
1168		22.02
1169 to 1172		20.02
1173		9.03

DISPOSITION TABLE

Vernon's Ann.P.C. Article	V.T.C.A. Penal Code Section
1174	20.02
1175, 1176	39.02
1177	20.02
	20.03
	25.03
1177a	20.04
1178	20.03
1179 to 1182	20.02
	43.05
1183 to 1186	21.02
	21.03
	21.09
1187	21.01
1188	8.07
1189	21.02
	21.03
	21.09
1190	15.01
	21.02
1197 to 1200	—
1201	19.01
1202, 1203	6.04
	19.01
1204, 1205	—
1206	6.04
1207	9.32
1208 to 1211	9.21
1212	9.21
	9.51
	9.52
1213	—
1214 to 1218	9.21
	9.51
	9.52
1219	9.32
	9.33
1220	—
1221	9.32
1222	9.32
	9.33
	9.42
1223	—
1224 to 1226	9.32
	9.33
	9.41
1227	9.41
	to
	9.44
1228	6.01
	to
	6.04
1229	6.01
	to
	6.04
	9.61
	to
	9.63
1230	19.07
1231	19.07
1232	6.03
1233	6.03
1234, 1235	19.05
1236	6.04

Vernon's Ann.P.C. Article	V.T.C.A. Penal Code Section
	19.05
1237 to 1243	19.05
1256, 1257	19.02
1257a	19.06
1257b	—
1257c	19.04
	19.05
1258	19.06
1259 to 1260a	19.02
	19.04
	22.01
	22.02
1265, 1266	22.07
1267	9.04
	22.07
1268, 1268a	22.07
1269, 1270	—
1271	32.21
1272 to 1294	—
1295, 1296	42.07
1297	—
1298	31.03
	38.12
1299	37.08
1300 to 1303	—
1304 to 1309	28.02
1310, 1311	9.22
1312	28.02
1313	28.05
1314, 1315	28.02
1316	15.01
	28.02
1317 to 1321b	28.03
	28.04
1322	31.03
1323	28.03
	28.04
1324	—
1325	19.02
1326	15.01
1329	—
1331	19.02
	28.03
1332	19.02
	28.03
1333	31.07
1334	28.03
1335	19.02
	42.03
1336, 1337	28.03
1338	28.03
	28.04
1339	22.01
	22.02
	22.05
1339b	42.01
1340	—
1341, 1342	31.07
1343	28.03
1347	22.05
	28.03
	42.03
1348, 1349	31.03

DISPOSITION TABLE

Vernon's Ann.P.C. Article	V.T.C.A. Penal Code Section
1350	28.03
	28.04
	32.47
1350a	28.03
	28.04
1351	28.03
	30.05
1352 to 1355	28.03
	28.04
1358	28.03
	28.04
1359	28.03
	28.04
1364 to 1366	28.03
	28.04
1367	31.04
1368	28.03
	30.05
1372	28.03
	28.04
1373	28.03
	28.04
	42.11
1373–a	28.03
	28.04
	42.11
1374 to 1376	42.11
1377a	42.11
1377b	30.05
1377c	30.05
1379	28.03
	28.04
	31.03
1379a	28.03
	28.04
1380, 1381	——
1382	31.03
1383	28.03
	28.04
1384	28.03
	28.04
	31.03
1388a	28.03
	28.04
1388b–1	15.01
	28.03
	28.04
1389 to 1400	30.02
1401	31.03
1402	15.01
	30.02
1402a	30.03
1402b	16.01
1403	30.04
1404	30.04
1404–a	15.01
	30.02
1404b	30.04
1405, 1406	30.02
1407	31.03
1407a	30.05
1408	29.02
	29.03
1409	29.02

Vernon's Ann.P.C. Article	V.T.C.A. Penal Code Section
	29.03
	31.03
1410	31.03
1411	31.01
1412 to 1414	31.03
1415	1.07(a)(28)
	31.01
1416, 1417	31.03
1418, 1419	31.01
1420 to 1423	31.03
1424	——
1425	31.01
1426 to 1426c	31.03
1427	31.03
	32.47
	37.09
	37.10
1428 to 1430	31.03
1436b	31.03
1436c	31.03
1436e to 1436g	31.03
1437, 1438	31.03
1439	15.01
	31.03
1440 to 1442c	31.03
1443, 1444	31.03
1445	31.03
1458, 1459	31.03
1462 to 1466	31.03
1467, 1468	28.03
1469	31.03
	32.21
1470	31.03
1534 to 1536	31.03
1537	32.34
1538	31.03
1539 to 1541	31.03
	39.01
1542, 1543	31.03
1544	31.01
1544a	31.03
1544b	31.03
	39.01
1545	31.03
	31.04
1546	31.03
1546a	31.03
	32.32
1547	31.01
1548 to 1550	31.03
1551	31.04
1553a	31.04
1555	——
1555b, 1555c	32.31
1556	32.33
1559	1.04
	31.03
1560	1.04
	31.03
1621b	42.02
1622 to 1627	15.02
1628	1.04
	15.02
1629	1.04
	15.02

DISPOSITION TABLE

Vernon's Ann.P.C. Article	V.T.C.A. Penal Code Section
1673	30.03
	31.03
1723	46.02
1723a, 1724	42.06

TABLE 2
Derivation

Showing where provisions of the Penal Code, and other Codes and Statutes, were formerly covered in Vernon's Annotated Penal Code.

V.T.C.A. Penal Code Section	Vernon's Ann.P.C. Article
1.01	New
1.02	1
	2
	6
1.03	3
	10
1.04	29
	520
	603
	1009
	1559
	1560
	1628
	1629
1.05(a)	7
1.05(b)	4
	5
	8
	19
	to
	21
1.06	New
1.07(a)(2)	23
1.07(a)(11)	347
	1147
1.07(a)(17)	19
1.07(a)(22)	27
1.07(a)(25)	346
1.07(a)(27)	22
1.07(a)(28)	1415
1.07(a)(30)	92
1.08	New
2.01	9
2.02	—
2.03	46
2.04	46
2.05	45
2.06	New
3.01	
to	
3.04	1005
6.01	39
	1228
	1229
6.02	1228
	1229
6.03	39
	1228
	1229
	1232
	1233
6.04	42
	to
	44
	73
	1202
	1203
	1206
	1228
	1229
	1236
7.01	65
	72
7.02	65
	to
	71
	315
7.03(1)	New
7.03(2)	80
7.21	
to	
7.24	New
8.01	34
8.02	41
8.03	12
	40
8.04	36
8.05	32
	38
8.06	New
8.07	30
	31
	1188
9.01	New
9.02	New
9.03	1173
9.04	1267
9.05	New
9.21	37
	1142, subd. 2
	1208
	to
	1212
	1214
	to

DERIVATION TABLE

V.T.C.A. Penal Code Section	Vernon's Ann.P.C. Article
	1218
9.22	791
	1142, subd. 3
	1310
	1311
9.31	1142, subd. 6
	1142, subd. 7
	1143
9.32	1142, subds. 3, 4
	1207
	1219
9.33	1142, subd. 6
	1219
	1226
9.34	New
9.41	1142, subd. 4
	1224 to 1227
9.42	1142, subd. 4
	1222
	1227
9.43	1142, subd. 4
	1142, subd. 6
	1227
9.44	1227
9.51	1142, subd. 5
	1212
9.52	1212
	1214 to 1218
9.61	1142, subd. 1
	1229
9.62	1142, subd. 1
	1229
9.63	1142, subd. 1
	1229
12.01(a)	New
12.01(b)	New
12.01(c)	51
12.02	47
12.03	47
	48
	52
12.04	47
12.21 to 12.23	New
12.31 to 12.33	New
12.41	New
12.42	62 to 64
12.43	61
12.44	New
12.45	New
12.51	New
15.01	1162 to 1165
	1190
	1316
	1326
	1388b–1
	1402
	1404–a
	1439
15.02	1622 to 1629
15.03 to 15.05	New
16.01	997
	1402b
19.01	1201 to 1203
19.02	1160
	1160a
	1256
	1257
	1259 to 1260a
	1325
	1331
	1332
	1335
19.03	New
19.04	1257c
	1259 to 1260a
19.05	802a–1
	802c
	1234 to 1243
	1257c
	1260a
19.06	1257a
	1258
19.07	1230
	1231
20.01	New
20.02	1169 to 1172

DERIVATION TABLE

V.T.C.A. Penal Code Section	Vernon's Ann.P.C. Article
	1174
	1177
	1179
	to
	1182
20.03	1177
	1178
20.04	1177a
21.01	1187
21.02	1162
	1183
	to
	1186
	1189
	1190
21.03	1183
	to
	1186
	1189
21.04	
to	
21.06	524
21.07	607, § (16)
21.08	New
21.09	1183
	to
	1186
	1189
21.10	New
21.11	535c
	535d
21.12	New
22.01	1138
	to
	1141
	1144
	to
	1146a
	1159
	1160
	1167
	1259
	to
	1260a
	1339
22.02	1147
	1148
	1149
	1151
	1159
	1160
	1166
	1167
	1168
	1259
	to
	1260a
	1339
22.03	1147
	1160a
22.04	1147
	1148a
22.05	1146a
	1339
	1347
22.06	New
22.07	1146
	1265
	to
	1268
22.08	New
25.01	490
	to
	491
	494
25.02	495
25.03	331
	to
	333a
	535
	1177
25.04	331
	to
	333a
	535
	535b
25.05	602
	602–A
	604
	605
28.01	1305
28.02	1304
	to
	1309
	1312
	1314
	to
	1316
28.03	859
	862
	864
	1111b
	1137f
	1317
	to
	1321b
	1323
	1331
	1332
	1334
	1336
	1337
	1338
	1343
	1347
	1350
	1350a
	1351
	1352
	to
	1355
	1358
	1359
	1364
	to
	1366

DERIVATION TABLE

V.T.C.A. Penal Code Section	Vernon's Ann.P.C. Article
	1368
	1372
	to
	1373–a
	1379
	1379a
	1383
	1384
	1388a
	1388b–1
	1467
	1468
28.04	1137f
	1317
	to
	1321b
	1323
	1338
	1350
	1350a
	1352
	to
	1355
	1358
	1359
	1364
	to
	1366
	1372
	to
	1373–a
	1379
	1379a
	1383
	1384
	1388a
	1388b–1
28.05	1313
28.06	New
29.01	New
29.02	1163
	1408
	1409
29.03	1408
	1409
30.01	New
30.02	1164
	1389
	to
	1400
	1402
	to
	1406
30.03	861
	1402a
	1673
30.04	1403
	1404
	1404b
30.05	479
	856
	858
	1351

V.T.C.A. Penal Code Section	Vernon's Ann.P.C. Article
	1368
	1377b
	1377c
	1407a
31.01	1411
	1415
	1418
	1419
	1424
	1547
31.02	New
31.03	1298
	1322
	1348
	1349
	1379
	1382
	1384
	1401
	1407
	1409
	1410
	1412
	to
	1414
	1416
	1417
	1420
	to
	1423
	1426
	to
	1430
	1436b
	1436c
	1436e
	to
	1436g
	1437
	to
	1442c
	1443
	to
	1445
	1458
	1459
	1462
	to
	1466
	1469
	1470
	1534
	to
	1536
	1538
	to
	1546a
	1548
	to
	1550
	1559
	1560
	1673

DERIVATION TABLE

V.T.C.A. Penal Code Section	Vernon's Ann.P.C. Article
31.04	978*o*
	1056
	1137e
	1137e–1
	1137g
	1367
	1545
	1551
	1553a
31.05	New
31.06	567b
31.07	1333
	1341
	1342
31.08	
to	
31.10	New
32.01	
to	
32.03	New
32.21	979
	to
	993
	995
	996
	998
	1002
	1002a
	1004
	1006
	to
	1008
	1010
	1011
	1012
	to
	1017
	1026
	1123
	1271
	1469
32.22	New
32.31	1555b
	1555c
32.32	1546a
32.33	1556
32.34	1537
32.35	565
32.41	567b
32.42	710
	to
	713
	718
	1030
	1044
	1045
	1050
	1051
	1053
	1106a
32.43	166
	167
32.44	178b

V.T.C.A. Penal Code Section	Vernon's Ann.P.C. Article
32.45	560
	567
32.46	1000
	1001
	1003
32.47	1002
	1002a
	1350
	1427
32.48	New
36.01	New
36.02	158
	to
	165
	168
	to
	174
	177
	to
	178a
	188
	to
	197
36.03	120
	254
	256
	258
	440
	441
	447
	448
	457
36.04	New
36.05	316
	428a
36.06	New
36.07	New
36.08	372
36.09	New
36.10	New
37.01	305
	311
37.02	302
	303
	308
	310
37.03	302
	303
	306
	to
	308
	1118
	to
	1121
37.04	307
37.05	New
37.06	New
37.07	304
37.08	1299
37.09	1427
37.10	354
	to
	364

DERIVATION TABLE

V.T.C.A. Penal Code Section	Vernon's Ann.P.C. Article
	438c
	438d
	1002
	1002a
	1427
37.11	147
	147c
	429
38.01	New
38.02	New
38.03	338
	339
	341
38.04	341
38.05	77
	to
	79
	81
	335
38.06	428
	458
	to
	463
38.07	353a
	353b
	353d
	442
	to
	446
38.08	317
	to
	322
	326
	to
	330
	334
38.09	New
38.10	326
	327
38.11	C.C.P. 22.01a
38.12	430
	1298
38.13	New
39.01	86
	87
	89
	to
	91
	to
	93
	96
	107f
	108
	110
	112
	to
	120
	142
	143
	145
	146
	323
	324
	365
	to
	371
	381
	to
	403
	407
	to
	423
	425
	to
	427
	640
	641
	831
	832
	1041
	1157
	1158
	1539
	to
	1541
	1544b
39.02	261
	349
	353
	1157
	1158
	1175
	1176
39.03	144
42.01	255
	281
	465
	466a
	473
	to
	475a
	480
	482
	482a
	485
	1146
	1339b
42.02	253
	254
	255
	439
	449
	to
	452
	455
	to
	470
	472a
	1621b
42.03	472a
	474
	784
	to
	786
	857
	1335

DERIVATION TABLE

V.T.C.A. Penal Code Section	Vernon's Ann.P.C. Article
	1347
42.04	453
	454
	472
42.05	281
	474
42.06	1723a
	1724
42.07	476
	1295
	1296
42.08	477
42.09	148
	152
	528
	528a
42.10	529
	530
42.11	613
	1373
	1373–a
	1374
	to
	1377a
42.12	480a
43.01	New
	607, § (9)
	607, § (14)
	607, § (16)
	to
	607, § (18)
	607, § (20)
	607a
43.03	514
	to
	516
	519
	525
	607, § (14)
	607, § (15)
	607, § (19)
43.04	510
	to
	512
	514
	to
	516
	519
	522
	525
43.05	514
	to
	516
	519
	1179
	to
	1182
43.06	521
	607, § (21)
43.21	513
	527
43.22	513
	527
43.23	527
43.24	513
	534b
46.01	1161
46.02	483
	488
	1723
46.03	484
	486
46.04	485
	486
46.04(a)(1)	New
46.04(a)(2)	257
46.04(b)	New
46.04(c)	New
46.05	489c
46.06	489
	489b
46.07	489
46.08	489d
47.01	645
47.02	615
	to
	618
	624
	642a
	to
	642c
	643
	643a
	646
	646a
	to
	648–2
	651
	652a
	654
	655
47.03	642a
	to
	642c
	646a
	to
	648–2
	650
	652a
	654
	655
47.04	625
	to
	630
	642a
	to
	642c
	646a
	to
	648–2
	649
	650
	652a
	654
	655
47.05	642a
	to
	642c

V.T.C.A. Penal Code Section	Vernon's Ann.P.C. Article
	652a
	654
	655
47.06	619
	to
	621
	625
	630
	642a
	to
	642c
	652a
	654
	655
47.07	619
	to
	621
	625
	642a
	to
	642c
	652a
	654
	655
47.08	New
47.09	639
	642c
	652

DERIVATION TABLE

Showing where provisions of Vernon's Annotated Civil Statutes, V.T.C.A. Water Code and Vernon's Annotated Code of Criminal Procedure were formerly covered in Vernon's Annotated Penal Code.

Vernon's Ann. Civ.St. Article	Vernon's Ann. P.C. Article
4667	634

V.T.C.A. Water Code Section	Vernon's Ann. P.C. Article
21.551 to 21.564	698c

Vernon's Ann. C.C.P. Article	Vernon's Ann. P.C. Article
13.16	603
14.03	609
	803
17A.02(a)	698c § 8
	698d § 7
17A.03	698c § 9
	698d § 8
17A.04	698c § 10
	698d § 9
17A.06	698c § 11
	698d § 10
17A.07	698c § 12
	698d § 11
Ch. 18	633
18.18	636 to 638
38.11	605

TABLE 3
Disposition of Unrepealed Articles of the Texas Penal Code of 1925 and Vernon's Texas Penal Code

Pursuant to the authority granted by Section 5 of Chapter 399, Acts of the 63rd Legislature, the Texas Legislative Council compiled the following table showing the official citations of unrepealed articles of the 1925 Texas Penal Code and the classifications of unrepealed statutes compiled as articles of Vernon's Texas Penal Code. Unless otherwise indicated, the citations or classifications are to the Civil Statutes of Texas. Footnotes have been dropped where the Council felt explanatory comments might be helpful.

Former Penal Code Article Number	New Article Number
107e	[1]
108a	630c, § 1
108b	630c, § 2
108c	630c, § 3
108d	630c, § 4
131a	Tax.-Gen. 3.12
131c-1, § 16–a	[2]
§ 19	[3]
§ 25	[4]
§ 26	[5]
§ 26a	[6]
§ 27	[5]
§§ 28, 29	[7]
141e	Tax.-Gen. 12.10A
141f	7164b
142a	5421r
146a	6252–21
147d, §§ 1, 3	6252–22
167a	5428b
183–2	6252–23

Former Penal Code Article Number	New Election Code Section	V.A.T.S. Election Code Article Number
200a–1	301	15.01 [8]
200a–3	302	15.02 [8]
205a	303	15.03 [8]
206	311	15.11
207	312	15.12
208	313	15.13
209	314	15.14
210	315	15.15
212	316	15.16
212a	—	15.16a
213	317	15.17
215	321	15.21
216	322	15.22
217	323	15.23
218	324	15.24
219	325	15.25
220	326	15.26
221	327	15.27
222	328	15.28
223	329	15.29
225	330	15.30
226	331	15.31
227	332	15.32
228	333	15.33
229	334	15.34
230	335	15.35
231	336	15.36
231a	—	15.36a
231b	—	15.36b
232	341	15.41
233	342	15.42
234	343	15.43
235	344	15.44
236	345	15.45
237	346	15.46
238	347	15.47
239	348	15.48
240	349	15.49
241	350	15.50
242	351	15.51
243	352	15.52
244	361	15.61
245	362	15.62
246	363	15.63
246a	—	15.63a
247	364	15.64
248	365	15.65
249	366	15.66
250	367	15.67
259	371	15.71
260	372	15.72

Former Penal Code Article Number	New Article Number
286a	9001
353c	6184m
380a	6252–24
383a	2558a, § 15
414a	4388a
414b	689a–21

DISPOSITION TABLE

Former Penal Code Article Number	New Article Number
422b	4413a–24
427b	974a, § 7
427c–1	6674s, § 19
431	1302–5.05, § B
432 to 438	5996a to 5996g
454h	9002
454i	9003
531	4590.1
534	2338–1a
534a	2338–1b
561	548c
562	548d
563	548e
564	548f
566	548g
568	21.02–1
569	21.02–2
570	21.02–3
570a	21.07A [9]
570b	21.15–1
571	21.51
571a	5.12–1
572	21.15–2
573	21.15–3
574	21.15–4
575	3.56–1
576	21.15–5
577	3.67–1
578	21.21A
579	19.10–1
580	5.68–1
580a	14.37–1
580b	21.21B
581	10.41
582	10.42
583	10.43
584	10.44
585	10.45
586	11.18–1
588	14.56–1
589	15.19–1
590	15.19–2
591	18.01–1
592	18.03–1
593	18.11–1
594	18.16–1
595	18.22–1
596	5.41–1
597	5.48–1
597a	5.43–1
598	5.48–2
601	15.20–1
602	[10]
602–A	[10]
602–B	[10]
606a	695a, §§ 6, 7
614–1 to 614–17c	8501–1 to 8501–17c
656 to 664	8651 to 8659

Former Penal Code Article Number	New Article Number
666–1 to 666–58	[11]
667–1 to 667–33	[11]
696a	6674v–2
696a–1	4477–9
698d, §§ 1 to 6, §§ 13, 14	4477–5b
700b	4476–9
701a	4442a, § 7
704	4445, § 10
705b–1	912a–26a
705d	4476–10
713a	4474a
719	4476–1a
719a	118c
719b	118a, § 20
719c–1	118b–1
719e	4476–3a
725e	4476–11
725f	4476–15
726–2	4476–12
726–3	4476–13
726d, §§ 1 to 6, §§ 8 to 15A	4476–14
727	4476–16
728 to 734a	8401 to 8407a
734c	8451a
739	4498.1
740	4504a
741	4510a
742	4510b
742–a	4590c, § 17
742–b	4590c, § 18
742–c	4590c, § 19
743	4498a, § 2
744	4501a
744–a	4590c, § 20
744–b	4590c, § 21
745	4499.1
746	4441a
747	4548a
748	4548b
749	4546a
750	4548c
751	4548d
751a	4551h
752	4548e
752a	4548f
752b	4548g
752c	4548h
753	4551b–1
754	4548i
754a	4551a–1
754b	4548j
754c	4551g–1
758a	4542a, § 21
763 to 772	4457a to 4457j
773	4505a
774	4505b
775	4505c
778	4567b

DISPOSITION TABLE

Former Penal Code Article Number	New Article Number
779	4567c
780	4567d
781	4477b
781a	4477c
782	4477d
782a	4420b
782b	4420a
782c	4447p
782d	4447q
784a–1	6701d–4, § 1
784a–2	§ 2
784a–3	§ 3
787	6701d–5
788	6701d–6
792	6701d–7 [12]
799a	6687–12
802	6701*l*–1
802b	6701*l*–2
802d	6701*l*–3
802e	6701*l*–4
802f	6701*l*–5
803a	6701d–8
803b	6701d–9
804	6675b–1
805	6675b–2
806	6675b–3
806a	6687–11
807a, § 14f	6675a–16a
807b	6675a–3e
808	6675b–4
809	6675b–5
811	6675b–6
812	6675b–7
821	6701m–1
821a	6701m–2
826	6701d–10
827	4008b
827a	6701d–11
827a–2 to 827a–8	6701d–12 to 6701d–18
827aa	2372a–2
827b	6675a–6e
827c	6701d–19
827c–1	118b–2
827d	911j
827e	6701d–20 [13]
827f	6701d–21
827g	6701d–22
833	6674*o*–1
836	6711b
837	6712a
853	[14]
854	6799a
855	6799b
861a	678e–1
861b	678f–1
863	678e–2
865 to 868	3954–1 to 3954–4
869	3972.1
870	3972.2
871 to 978n–2	[15]
1027	5679a–1 [16]
1027a	5679a, §§ 9, 10
1028	5679d
1029	5679e
1031	5679f
1032	5679g
1033	5679h
1034	74a
1035	5722a
1036	5727a
1037	5726a
1038	5726b
1039	5726c
1040	5726d
1042b	5733a
1043	5736–1 [17]
1046	110a
1047	5680a
1048	5696a
1049	5698a
1052	5693a
1054	1440a
1055	5707a
1057a	1124a, § 5
1057b	5736b
1057c	5736c
1057d	5714
1067	5924.1
1068	5925a
1069	5927a
1070	5927b
1084	2485a
1085	2486a
1086	2489a
1087	2490a
1088	2495a
1089	2496a
1090	2497a
1091	2498a
1092	2499a
1093	2499b
1101 to 1106	8601 to 8606
1107 to 1111	8607 to 8611
1111a–1	6032d
1111c	6049f
1111c–1	9201
1112	9004
1112b	6049g
1116	9005
1117a	Ins.Code 15.21
1122	9006
1124	5195a
1125	1275a
1125a	1287a, §§ 9 to 12
1131	700a
1137	1528h
1137b	46f–2
1137b–1	46f–3
1137e–2	1446b
1137h	6626c

DISPOSITION TABLE

Former Penal Code Article Number	New Article Number
1137i–1	9007
1137k	9008
1137l–10	9009
1137n	9010
1137*o*	6573b
1137q	9011
1137r	9012
1167a	9013
1176a	6252–25
1191 to 1196	4512.1 to 4512.6
1333A	9206a [18]
1334a	1432a
1351a	6942a
1369	6946a
1370	6946b
1370a	6971a
1371	192–2
1371a	192–3
1378a	192b, §§ 11 to 13
1384a	6143.1
1385	7361a
1386	7362a
1387	7363.1
1388	7363b
1430a	9014
1432 to 1435	6687–3 to 6687–6
1435a	6687–8
1436	6687–7
1436–1	6687–1
1436–2	6687–2
1436–3	6687–9
1436a	9015
1436d	6687–10
1444a	6983b
1446	6905a
1447	6908f–1
1448	6908f–2
1449	6904a
1450	6908b
1451	6908a
1452	6908c
1453	6908g
1454	6908d
1455	6909a
1456	6910a
1456a	6908e
1457	6907a
1460	6890a
1461	6890b
1471	6985a
1472	6978a
1473	6978b
1474	6978c
1475	6978d
1476	6998a
1477	6987a
1478	6990a
1479	6990b
1480	6986a
1481	6983a
1482	6984a
1483	6984b
1484	6997a
1485	6890c
1486	6898a
1487	6990c
1488	7005–2
1499	1281a
1500	1282a
1501	1286a
1502	1286b
1503	1285a
1505	7009b [19]
1505a	7014c
1505b	7014d
1512 to 1515	7014e–2 to 7014e–5
1518 to 1521	7014f–2 to 7014f–5
1522	7014b
1523 to 1525	7014f–6 to 7014f–8
1525a	7014e–1
1525b	7014f–1
1525b–1 to 1525b–3	7014f–9 to 7014f–11
1525c	7014g–1
1525d to 1525f	7014f–12 to 7014f–14
1525g	7014g–2
1533	564a
1546b	9016
1552	4596b
1553	4596c
1555a	67a, § 6
1561	5145a
1562	5150a
1563	5147a
1564	5151b
1565	5148a
1566	5151c
1567	5178a
1568	5179a
1573 to 1578b	5181a to 5181h
1579 to 1581	5165.1 to 5165.3
1581a	5159a, §§ 5, 6
1582	5182–1
1583a	1269o
1583b	CCP 1041b
1583–1	1269p
1583–2	1269q
1583–3	1269r
1594	5901b
1595	5901a
1596	5904a

DISPOSITION TABLE

Former Penal Code Article Number	New Article Number
1597	5906a
1598	5907a
1599	5908a
1600	5905a
1601	5909a
1602	5910a
1603	5911a
1604	5912a
1605	5913a
1606	5914a
1607	5914b
1608	5915a
1609	5917a
1610	5918a
1611	5919a
1612	5920a
1613	5196a
1614	5196b
1615	5201a
1616 to 1620	5196c to 5196g
1621	5205a
1630	6057a
1631	6057b
1631a	6020b
1645 to 1648	178a to 178d
1648a	9017
1649	6559g–1
1650	6559g–2
1651	4005a
1652	4006a
1653	4006b
1654	4013a
1655 to 1658	4015a to 4015d
1658a	4015e
1661	4015f
1661a	6145c
1662 to 1672	6559h–1 to 6559h–11
1684 to 1690	6559i–1 to 6559i–7
1690a	911a, § 14
1690b	911b, § 16
1690d	[20]
1690e	911h
1690f	911i
1691	123a
1692	126a
1693	127a
1694	127b
1695	119a
1696	129a
1697	126b
1698	135.1
1699	127c
1700	127d
1700a–1	135a–1, § 9
1700a–2	118b–3
1700a–3	118b, § 21
1701 to 1708	93d–1[21] to 93d–8
1720a	695c–3
1721	9202
1721A	9203
1722	9204
1722a	9206
1725	9205

[1] This article was repealed by Acts 1951, 52nd Leg., p. 362, ch. 228, § 1.

[2] Repealed; see, now, V.A.T.S. Tax.-Gen. arts. 7.25, 7.26.

[3] Repealed; see, now, V.A.T.S. Tax.-Gen. art. 7.29.

[4] Repealed; see, now, V.A.T.S. Tax.-Gen. art. 7.36.

[5] Repealed; see, now, V.A.T.S. Tax.-Gen. art. 7.37.

[6] Expired.

[7] Repealed; see, now, V.A.T.S. Tax.-Gen. art. 7.38.

[8] This article was probably impliedly repealed by Acts 1966, 59th Leg., 1st C.S., p. 1, ch. 1, § 4 (the voter registration law of 1966).

[9] This article was probably superseded and impliedly repealed by Insurance Code, art. 21.07, § 12.

[10] See V.T.C.A. Penal Code, § 25.05 note.

[11] These articles were repealed by § 2 of Acts 1977, 65th Leg., p. 557, ch. 194, enacting the Alcoholic Beverage Code as a unit of the Texas Legislative Council's statutory revision program (see V.A.C.S. art. 5429b–1).

[12] This article was probably impliedly repealed by virtue of the express repeal of arts. 790 and 791, to which it refers.

[13] This article was probably impliedly repealed by the Uniform Act Regulating Traffic on Highways (V.A.C.S., art. 6701d).

[14] V.A.T.S. Water Auxiliary Laws, art. 7849a.

[15] These articles were repealed by § 2(a)(1) of Acts 1975, 64th Leg., p. 1804, ch. 545, enacting the Parks and Wildlife Code as a unit of the Texas Legislative Council's statutory revision program (see V.A.C.S. art. 5429b–1).

[16] This article was probably impliedly repealed by Acts 1931, 42nd Leg., ch. 68 (V.A.C.S. art. 5679a). The penal provisions of Chapter 68 were originally designated as art. 1027a, V.T.P.C., but have now been incorporated in V.A.C.S. art. 5679a.

[17] This article was probably impliedly repealed when art. 1042, Penal Code of Texas, 1925, to which it is an exception, was repealed by Acts 1973, 63rd Leg., ch. 399, § 3 (adopting the new Penal Code).

[18] This article was probably impliedly repealed by V.T.P.C., art. 1722a, § 24(d); see, now, V.T.C.S., art. 9206, § 24(d).

[19] This article was probably impliedly repealed by Acts 1959, 56th Leg., ch. 192 (V.A.C.S. art. 7009a).

[20] Deleted; identical to V.A.C.S. art. 911d, § 15.

[21] These articles were probably impliedly repealed by Acts 1929, 41st Leg., ch. 304; see, now, V.A.C.S. art. 93b, the Texas Seed Law.

Submitted by
ROBERT E. FREEMAN
Revisor of Statutes
Texas Legislative Council

Austin, Texas
October, 1973

PENAL CODE
TABLE OF SECTIONS AFFECTED BY THE 81st LEGISLATURE, REGULAR AND FIRST CALLED SESSION

Sec.	Effect	Acts 2009 Ch.	Sec.
1.07(a)(27)	Repealed	87	25.144
1.07(a)(46–a)	Added	421	1
3.03(b)	Amended	1130	21
3.03(b–1)	Added	1130	21
3.03 note	—	1130	26
8.07(a)	Amended	311	5
12.31	Amended	765	1
12.31(a)	Amended	87	25.145
12.31 note	—	765	3
12.32(a)	Amended	87	25.146
12.33(a)	Amended	87	25.147
12.34(a)	Amended	87	25.148
12.41	Amended	87	25.149
12.42(d)	Amended	87	25.150
12.50	Added	731	1
12.50 note	—	731	2
15.031(e)	Amended	1130	2
15.031 note	—	1130	9
16.02(e–1)	Added	1169	9
16.02 note	—	1169	10
16.06(d)	Amended	1122	1
16.06(e)	Added	1122	1
16.06 note	—	1122	2
20A.02(a)	Amended	1002	7
20A.02(b)	Amended	1002	7
20A.02 note	—	1002	10
21.11(a)	Amended	260	1
21.11(b–1)	Added	260	1
21.11 note	—	260	6
21.12(a)	Amended	260	2
21.12(b–1)	Added	260	2
22.01(b)	Amended	427	1
		665	2
22.01(b–1)	Added	427	1
22.01(f)	Amended	427	1
22.01(g)	Added	427	1
22.01 note	—	427	2
22.011(c)(1)	Amended	260	3
22.011(e)	Amended	260	4
22.015	Repealed	435	3
22.02(b)	Amended	594	2
22.04(f)	Amended	284	38
22.04 note	—	284	48(a)
25.02(c)	Amended	673	1
25.02 note	—	673	2
25.07(a)	Reenacted and amended	87	19.001
25.11	Added	665	1
25.11 note	—	665	3
28.02(a–2)	Added	1168	1
28.02(f)	Amended	1168	1
28.02(g)	Amended	1168	1
28.02 note	—	1168	2
28.03(b)	Amended	638	1
28.03 note	—	638	2
28.08(a)	Amended	639	4
30.05(a)	Amended	1138	1

Sec.	Effect	Acts 2009 Ch.	Sec.
30.05(b)(8)	Added	1138	2
30.05(b)(9)	Added	1138	2
30.05(b)(10)	Added	1138	2
30.05(b)(11)	Added	1138	2
30.05(c)	Repealed	1138	4
30.05(d)	Amended	1138	3
30.05(e)	Amended	1138	3
30.05(j)	Repealed	1138	4
30.05 note	—	1138	5
31.03(c)	Amended	933	3J.01
31.03(e)	Amended	70	1
		105	1
		139	1
		295	1
31.03(f)	Amended	903	1
31.03(h)(3)	Added	903	2
31.03 note	—	70	2
		139	2
		295	2
		903	3
31.11(b)	Amended	933	3J.02
32.21(c)	Amended	670	1
32.21(e–1)	Added	670	1
32.21 note	—	670	4
32.31(d)	Amended	670	2
32.32 heading	Amended	709	4
32.32(b–1)	Added	709	5
32.32(d)	Amended	709	5
32.51(b)	Reenacted	87	19.002
32.51(c–1)	Added	670	3
33.05(f)	Added	503	1
33.07	Added	911	1
37.10(c)(2)	Amended	73	1
37.10(j)	Added	1130	31
37.10 note	—	73	2
		1130	35
38.04(b)	Amended	1400	4
38.11	Reenacted and amended	1169	1
38.11 note	—	1169	10
38.12(d)	Amended	1252	1
38.12 note	—	1252	2
38.14 heading	Amended	394	1
		942	1
38.14(a)(3)	Added	942	2
38.14(b)	Amended	394	2
		942	3
38.14(c)	Amended	394	2
		942	3
38.14(d)	Amended	394	2
		942	3
38.14(e)	Amended	394	2
38.14 note	—	394	3
		942	4
38.152	Added	1222	1
39.02(e)	Added	82	1
39.02(f)	Added	82	1
39.02 note	—	82	2
39.04(b)	Reenacted and amended	87	19.003
39.04(f)	Amended	260	5
39.04(h)	Added	260	5
42.10(a)	Amended	1357	1

Sec.	Effect	Acts 2009 Ch.	Sec.
42.10(b)	Amended	1357	1
42.10(e)	Amended	1357	1
42.10 note	—	1357	5
43.02(d)	Added	1002	8
43.02 note	—	1002	10
43.05(a)	Amended	1002	9
43.05 note	—	1002	10
46.01(11)	Amended	1199	1
46.01 note	—	1199	2
46.03(d)	Amended	1146	4B.21
46.035(k)	Added	687	1
46.035 note	—	687	2
46.04(f)	Added	1146	11.24
46.04(g)	Added	1146	11.24
46.04 note	—	1146	11.30
46.07	Amended	280	1
46.14	Added	153	1
46.15(a)	Reenacted and amended	87	19.004
		794	4
46.15(b)	Reenacted and amended	87	19.005
		1146	4B.22
46.15(g)	Added	299	1
71.02(a)	Amended	153	2
		1130	1
		1357	2
71.02 note	—	153	5
		1130	9
71.022 heading	Amended	435	1
71.022(a–1)	Added	435	2
71.022(d)	Added	435	2
71.022 note	—	435	4(a)
71.023	Added	1130	3
71.028	Added	1130	3
71.028 note	—	1130	9
71.029	Added	1130	3

*

PENAL CODE

TITLE 1. INTRODUCTORY PROVISIONS

TITLE 2. GENERAL PRINCIPLES OF CRIMINAL RESPONSIBILITY

TITLE 3. PUNISHMENTS

TITLE 4. INCHOATE OFFENSES

TITLE 5. OFFENSES AGAINST THE PERSON

TITLE 6. OFFENSES AGAINST THE FAMILY

TITLE 7. OFFENSES AGAINST PROPERTY

TITLE 8. OFFENSES AGAINST PUBLIC ADMINISTRATION

TITLE 9. OFFENSES AGAINST PUBLIC ORDER AND DECENCY

TITLE 10. OFFENSES AGAINST PUBLIC HEALTH, SAFETY, AND MORALS

TITLE 11. ORGANIZED CRIME

Enactment

Acts 1973, 63rd Leg., p. 883, ch. 399, § 1, enacted the new Texas Penal Code, effective January 1, 1974. Section 2 thereof made various conforming amendments in the Texas Civil Statutes and Codes and § 3 repealed articles of the Texas Penal Code of 1925 and Vernon's Texas Penal Code, as amended.

Sections 4 to 7 of the 1973 Act provided:

"Sec. 4. Effective date. This Act takes effect on January 1, 1974.

"Sec. 5. Disposition of unrepealed articles. (a) The purpose of this section is to provide for transfer of articles of the Penal Code of Texas, 1925, which are not repealed by this Act to the civil statutes or other appropriate places within the framework of Texas statute law, without reenactment and without altering the meaning or effect of the unrepealed articles, so that when this Act takes effect there will be only one Texas Penal Code without the confusion that would result if remnants of the old Penal Code were allowed to continue to exist in that form in the statute books.

"(b) In order to carry out the purpose of this section, the Texas Legislative Council shall prepare and submit to the secretary of state, for publication with the Acts of the 63rd Legislature, Regular Session, 1973, an appendix listing the unrepealed articles of the Penal Code of Texas, 1925, as amended, and prescribing for each unrepealed title, chapter, or article a new official citation. The council may include in the appendix

any comments that may be helpful to users of the statute books.

"(c) In order that the five-volume Vernon's Texas Penal Code Annotated may be completely replaced, the council in the appendix authorized by Subsection (b) of this section may also recommend transfer and reclassification of statutes which were not enacted as part of the Penal Code of Texas, 1925, but were compiled as articles of Vernon's Texas Penal Code.

"(d) Nothing in this section or done under its authority alters the meaning or effect of any statute of this state.

"Sec. 6. Saving provisions. (a) Except as provided in Subsections (b) and (c) of this section, this Act applies only to offenses committed on or after its effective date, and a criminal action for an offense committed before this Act's effective date is governed by the law existing before the effective date, which law is continued in effect for this purpose, as if this Act were not in force. For purposes of this section, an offense is committed on or after the effective date of this Act if any element of the offense occurs on or after the effective date.

"(b) Conduct constituting an offense under existing law that is repealed by this Act and that does not constitute an offense under this Act may not be prosecuted after the effective date of this Act. If, on the effective date of this Act, a criminal action is pending for conduct that was an offense under the laws repealed by this Act and that does not constitute an offense under this Act, the action is dismissed on the effective date of this Act. However, a conviction existing on the effective date of this Act for conduct constituting an offense under laws repealed by this Act is valid and unaffected by this Act. For purposes of this section, "conviction" means a finding of guilt in a court of competent jurisdiction, and it is of no consequence that the conviction is not final.

"(c) In a criminal action pending on or commenced on or after the effective date of this Act, for an offense committed before the effective date, the defendant, if adjudged guilty, shall be assessed punishment under this Act if he so elects by written motion filed with the trial court before the sentencing hearing begins.

"Sec. 7. Severability. If any provision of this Act or the application thereof to any person or circumstance is held invalid, such invalidity shall not affect other provisions or applications of the Act which can be given effect without the invalid provision or application, and to this end the provisions of this Act are declared to be severable."

Tables

Table 1, Disposition, and Table 2, Derivation, are provided at the front of this volume, providing a means of tracing repealed subject matter into the Code and of searching out the source of the Code sections.

Pursuant to Acts 1973, 63rd Leg., p. 995, ch. 399, § 5, the Texas Legislative Council has compiled a table showing the disposition of unrepealed articles of the Texas Penal Code of 1925 and Vernon's Texas Penal Code, which is also included herein as Table 3.

TITLE 1. INTRODUCTORY PROVISIONS

CHAPTER 1. GENERAL PROVISIONS

Section

§ 1.01. Short Title

This code shall be known and may be cited as the Penal Code.

Acts 1973, 63rd Leg., p. 883, ch. 399, § 1, eff. Jan. 1, 1974. Amended by Acts 1993, 73rd Leg., ch. 900, § 1.01, eff. Sept. 1, 1994.

§ 1.02. Objectives of Code

The general purposes of this code are to establish a system of prohibitions, penalties, and correctional measures to deal with conduct that unjustifiably and inexcusably causes or threatens harm to those individual or public interests for which state protection is appropriate. To this end, the provisions of this code are intended, and shall be construed, to achieve the following objectives:

(1) to insure the public safety through:

(A) the deterrent influence of the penalties hereinafter provided;

(B) the rehabilitation of those convicted of violations of this code; and

(C) such punishment as may be necessary to prevent likely recurrence of criminal behavior;

(2) by definition and grading of offenses to give fair warning of what is prohibited and of the consequences of violation;

(3) to prescribe penalties that are proportionate to the seriousness of offenses and that permit recognition of differences in rehabilitation possibilities among individual offenders;

(4) to safeguard conduct that is without guilt from condemnation as criminal;

(5) to guide and limit the exercise of official discretion in law enforcement to prevent arbitrary or oppressive treatment of persons suspected, accused, or convicted of offenses; and

(6) to define the scope of state interest in law enforcement against specific offenses and to systematize the exercise of state criminal jurisdiction.

Acts 1973, 63rd Leg., p. 883, ch. 399, § 1, eff. Jan. 1, 1974. Amended by Acts 1993, 73rd Leg., ch. 900, § 1.01, eff. Sept. 1, 1994.

§ 1.03. Effect of Code

(a) Conduct does not constitute an offense unless it is defined as an offense by statute, municipal ordinance, order of a county commissioners court, or rule authorized by and lawfully adopted under a statute.

(b) The provisions of Titles 1, 2, and 3 apply to offenses defined by other laws, unless the statute defining the offense provides otherwise; however, the punishment affixed to an offense defined outside this code shall be applicable unless the punishment is classified in accordance with this code.

(c) This code does not bar, suspend, or otherwise affect a right or liability to damages, penalty, forfeiture, or other remedy authorized by law to be recovered or enforced in a civil suit for conduct this code defines as an offense, and the civil injury is not merged in the offense.

Acts 1973, 63rd Leg., p. 883, ch. 399, § 1, eff. Jan. 1, 1974. Amended by Acts 1993, 73rd Leg., ch. 900, § 1.01, eff. Sept. 1, 1994.

§ 1.04. Territorial Jurisdiction

(a) This state has jurisdiction over an offense that a person commits by his own conduct or the conduct of another for which he is criminally responsible if:

(1) either the conduct or a result that is an element of the offense occurs inside this state;

(2) the conduct outside this state constitutes an attempt to commit an offense inside this state;

(3) the conduct outside this state constitutes a conspiracy to commit an offense inside this state, and an act in furtherance of the conspiracy occurs inside this state; or

(4) the conduct inside this state constitutes an attempt, solicitation, or conspiracy to commit, or establishes criminal responsibility for the commission of, an offense in another jurisdiction that is also an offense under the laws of this state.

(b) If the offense is criminal homicide, a "result" is either the physical impact causing death or the death itself. If the body of a criminal homicide victim is found in this state, it is presumed that the death occurred in this state. If death alone is the basis for jurisdiction, it is a defense to the exercise of jurisdiction by this state that the conduct that constitutes the offense is not made criminal in the jurisdiction where the conduct occurred.

(c) An offense based on an omission to perform a duty imposed on an actor by a statute of this state is committed inside this state regardless of the location of the actor at the time of the offense.

(d) This state includes the land and water and the air space above the land and water over which this state has power to define offenses.

Acts 1973, 63rd Leg., p. 883, ch. 399, § 1, eff. Jan. 1, 1974. Amended by Acts 1993, 73rd Leg., ch. 900, § 1.01, eff. Sept. 1, 1994.

§ 1.05. Construction of Code

(a) The rule that a penal statute is to be strictly construed does not apply to this code. The provisions of this code shall be construed according to the fair import of their terms, to promote justice and effect the objectives of the code.

(b) Unless a different construction is required by the context, Sections 311.011, 311.012, 311.014, 311.015, and 311.021 through 311.032 of Chapter 311, Government Code (Code Construction Act), apply to the construction of this code.

(c) In this code:

(1) a reference to a title, chapter, or section without further identification is a reference to a title, chapter, or section of this code; and

(2) a reference to a subchapter, subsection, subdivision, paragraph, or other numbered or lettered unit without further identification is a reference to a unit of the next-larger unit of this code in which the reference appears.

Acts 1973, 63rd Leg., p. 883, ch. 399, § 1, eff. Jan. 1, 1974. Amended by Acts 1985, 69th Leg., ch. 479, § 69, eff. Sept. 1, 1985; Acts 1993, 73rd Leg., ch. 900, § 1.01, eff. Sept. 1, 1994.

§ 1.06. Computation of Age

A person attains a specified age on the day of the anniversary of his birthdate.

Acts 1973, 63rd Leg., p. 883, ch. 399, § 1, eff. Jan. 1, 1974. Amended by Acts 1993, 73rd Leg., ch. 900, § 1.01, eff. Sept. 1, 1994.

§ 1.07. Definitions

(a) In this code:

(1) "Act" means a bodily movement, whether voluntary or involuntary, and includes speech.

(2) "Actor" means a person whose criminal responsibility is in issue in a criminal action. Whenever the term "suspect" is used in this code, it means "actor."

(3) "Agency" includes authority, board, bureau, commission, committee, council, department, district, division, and office.

(4) "Alcoholic beverage" has the meaning assigned by Section 1.04, Alcoholic Beverage Code.

(5) "Another" means a person other than the actor.

(6) "Association" means a government or governmental subdivision or agency, trust, partnership, or two or more persons having a joint or common economic interest.

(7) "Benefit" means anything reasonably regarded as economic gain or advantage, including benefit to any other person in whose welfare the beneficiary is interested.

(8) "Bodily injury" means physical pain, illness, or any impairment of physical condition.

(9) "Coercion" means a threat, however communicated:

(A) to commit an offense;

(B) to inflict bodily injury in the future on the person threatened or another;

(C) to accuse a person of any offense;

(D) to expose a person to hatred, contempt, or ridicule;

(E) to harm the credit or business repute of any person; or

(F) to take or withhold action as a public servant, or to cause a public servant to take or withhold action.

(10) "Conduct" means an act or omission and its accompanying mental state.

(11) "Consent" means assent in fact, whether express or apparent.

(12) "Controlled substance" has the meaning assigned by Section 481.002, Health and Safety Code.

(13) "Corporation" includes nonprofit corporations, professional associations created pursuant to statute, and joint stock companies.

(14) "Correctional facility" means a place designated by law for the confinement of a person arrested for, charged with, or convicted of a criminal offense. The term includes:

(A) a municipal or county jail;

(B) a confinement facility operated by the Texas Department of Criminal Justice;

(C) a confinement facility operated under contract with any division of the Texas Department of Criminal Justice; and

(D) a community corrections facility operated by a community supervision and corrections department.

(15) "Criminal negligence" is defined in Section 6.03 (Culpable Mental States).

(16) "Dangerous drug" has the meaning assigned by Section 483.001, Health and Safety Code.

(17) "Deadly weapon" means:

(A) a firearm or anything manifestly designed, made, or adapted for the purpose of inflicting death or serious bodily injury; or

(B) anything that in the manner of its use or intended use is capable of causing death or serious bodily injury.

(18) "Drug" has the meaning assigned by Section 481.002, Health and Safety Code.

(19) "Effective consent" includes consent by a person legally authorized to act for the owner. Consent is not effective if:

(A) induced by force, threat, or fraud;

(B) given by a person the actor knows is not legally authorized to act for the owner;

(C) given by a person who by reason of youth, mental disease or defect, or intoxication is known by the actor to be unable to make reasonable decisions; or

(D) given solely to detect the commission of an offense.

(20) "Electric generating plant" means a facility that generates electric energy for distribution to the public.

(21) "Electric utility substation" means a facility used to switch or change voltage in connection with the transmission of electric energy for distribution to the public.

(22) "Element of offense" means:

(A) the forbidden conduct;

(B) the required culpability;

(C) any required result; and

(D) the negation of any exception to the offense.

(23) "Felony" means an offense so designated by law or punishable by death or confinement in a penitentiary.

(24) "Government" means:

(A) the state;

(B) a county, municipality, or political subdivision of the state; or

(C) any branch or agency of the state, a county, municipality, or political subdivision.

(25) "Harm" means anything reasonably regarded as loss, disadvantage, or injury, including harm to another person in whose welfare the person affected is interested.

(26) "Individual" means a human being who is alive, including an unborn child at every stage of gestation from fertilization until birth.

(27) Repealed by Acts 2009, 81st Leg., ch. 87, § 25.

(28) "Intentional" is defined in Section 6.03 (Culpable Mental States).

(29) "Knowing" is defined in Section 6.03 (Culpable Mental States).

(30) "Law" means the constitution or a statute of this state or of the United States, a written opinion of a court of record, a municipal ordinance, an order of a county commissioners court, or a rule authorized by and lawfully adopted under a statute.

(31) "Misdemeanor" means an offense so designated by law or punishable by fine, by confinement in jail, or by both fine and confinement in jail.

(32) "Oath" includes affirmation.

(33) "Official proceeding" means any type of administrative, executive, legislative, or judicial proceeding that may be conducted before a public servant.

(34) "Omission" means failure to act.

(35) "Owner" means a person who:

(A) has title to the property, possession of the property, whether lawful or not, or a greater right to possession of the property than the actor; or

(B) is a holder in due course of a negotiable instrument.

(36) "Peace officer" means a person elected, employed, or appointed as a peace officer under Article 2.12, Code of Criminal Procedure, Section 51.212 or 51.214, Education Code, or other law.

(37) "Penal institution" means a place designated by law for confinement of persons arrested for, charged with, or convicted of an offense.

(38) "Person" means an individual, corporation, or association.

(39) "Possession" means actual care, custody, control, or management.

(40) "Public place" means any place to which the public or a substantial group of the public has access and includes, but is not limited to, streets, highways, and the common areas of schools, hospitals, apartment houses, office buildings, transport facilities, and shops.

(41) "Public servant" means a person elected, selected, appointed, employed, or otherwise designated as one of the following, even if he has not yet qualified for office or assumed his duties:

(A) an officer, employee, or agent of government;

(B) a juror or grand juror; or

(C) an arbitrator, referee, or other person who is authorized by law or private written agreement to hear or determine a cause or controversy; or

(D) an attorney at law or notary public when participating in the performance of a governmental function; or

(E) a candidate for nomination or election to public office; or

(F) a person who is performing a governmental function under a claim of right although he is not legally qualified to do so.

(42) "Reasonable belief" means a belief that would be held by an ordinary and prudent man in the same circumstances as the actor.

(43) "Reckless" is defined in Section 6.03 (Culpable Mental States).

(44) "Rule" includes regulation.

(45) "Secure correctional facility" means:

(A) a municipal or county jail; or

(B) a confinement facility operated by or under a contract with any division of the Texas Department of Criminal Justice.

(46) "Serious bodily injury" means bodily injury that creates a substantial risk of death or that causes death, serious permanent disfigurement, or protracted loss or impairment of the function of any bodily member or organ.

(46–a) "Sight order" means a written or electronic instruction to pay money that is authorized by the person giving the instruction and that is payable on demand or at a definite time by the person being instructed to pay. The term includes a check, an electronic debit, or an automatic bank draft.

(47) "Swear" includes affirm.

(48) "Unlawful" means criminal or tortious or both and includes what would be criminal or tortious but for a defense not amounting to justification or privilege.

(49) "Death" includes, for an individual who is an unborn child, the failure to be born alive.

(b) The definition of a term in this code applies to each grammatical variation of the term.

Acts 1973, 63rd Leg., p. 883, ch. 399, § 1, eff. Jan. 1, 1974. Amended by Acts 1975, 64th Leg., p. 912, ch. 342, § 1, eff. Sept. 1, 1975; Acts 1977, 65th Leg., p. 2123, ch. 848, § 1, eff. Aug. 29, 1977; Acts 1979, 66th Leg., p. 1113, ch. 530, § 1, eff. Aug. 27, 1979; Acts 1979, 66th Leg., p. 1520, ch. 655, § 1, eff. Sept. 1, 1979; Acts 1987, 70th Leg., ch. 167, § 5.01(a)(43), eff. Sept. 1, 1987; Acts 1989, 71st Leg., ch. 997, § 1, eff. Aug. 28, 1989; Acts 1991, 72nd Leg., ch. 543, § 1, eff. Sept. 1, 1991; Acts 1993, 73rd Leg., ch. 900, § 1.01, eff. Sept. 1, 1994; Acts 2003, 78th Leg., ch. 822, § 2.01, eff. Sept. 1, 2003; Acts 2009, 81st Leg., ch. 87, § 25.144, eff. Sept. 1, 2009; Acts 2009, 81st Leg., ch. 421, § 1, eff. Sept. 1, 2009.

§ 1.08. Preemption

No governmental subdivision or agency may enact or enforce a law that makes any conduct covered by this code an offense subject to a criminal penalty. This section shall apply only as long as the law governing the conduct proscribed by this code is legally enforceable.

Acts 1973, 63rd Leg., p. 883, ch. 399, § 1, eff. Jan. 1, 1974. Amended by Acts 1993, 73rd Leg., ch. 900, § 1.01, eff. Sept. 1, 1994.

§ 1.09. Concurrent Jurisdiction Under This Code to Prosecute Offenses That Involve State Property

With the consent of the appropriate local county or district attorney, the attorney general has concurrent jurisdiction with that consenting local prosecutor to prosecute under this code any offense an element of which occurs on state property or any offense that involves the use, unlawful appropriation, or misapplication of state property, including state funds.

Added by Acts 2007, 80th Leg., ch. 378, § 1, eff. June 15, 2007.

CHAPTER 2. BURDEN OF PROOF

Section

§ 2.01. Proof Beyond a Reasonable Doubt

All persons are presumed to be innocent and no person may be convicted of an offense unless each element of the offense is proved beyond a reasonable doubt. The fact that he has been arrested, confined, or indicted for, or otherwise charged with, the offense gives rise to no inference of guilt at his trial.

Acts 1973, 63rd Leg., p. 883, ch. 399, § 1, eff. Jan. 1, 1974. Amended by Acts 1993, 73rd Leg., ch. 900, § 1.01, eff. Sept. 1, 1994.

§ 2.02. Exception

(a) An exception to an offense in this code is so labeled by the phrase: "It is an exception to the application of . . . ."

(b) The prosecuting attorney must negate the existence of an exception in the accusation charging commission of the offense and prove beyond a reasonable doubt that the defendant or defendant's conduct does not fall within the exception.

(c) This section does not affect exceptions applicable to offenses enacted prior to the effective date of this code.

Acts 1973, 63rd Leg., p. 883, ch. 399, § 1, eff. Jan. 1, 1974. Amended by Acts 1993, 73rd Leg., ch. 900, § 1.01, eff. Sept. 1, 1994.

§ 2.03. Defense

(a) A defense to prosecution for an offense in this code is so labeled by the phrase: "It is a defense to prosecution . . . ."

(b) The prosecuting attorney is not required to negate the existence of a defense in the accusation charging commission of the offense.

(c) The issue of the existence of a defense is not submitted to the jury unless evidence is admitted supporting the defense.

(d) If the issue of the existence of a defense is submitted to the jury, the court shall charge that a reasonable doubt on the issue requires that the defendant be acquitted.

(e) A ground of defense in a penal law that is not plainly labeled in accordance with this chapter has the procedural and evidentiary consequences of a defense.

Acts 1973, 63rd Leg., p. 883, ch. 399, § 1, eff. Jan. 1, 1974. Amended by Acts 1993, 73rd Leg., ch. 900, § 1.01, eff. Sept. 1, 1994.

§ 2.04. Affirmative Defense

(a) An affirmative defense in this code is so labeled by the phrase: "It is an affirmative defense to prosecution . . . ."

(b) The prosecuting attorney is not required to negate the existence of an affirmative defense in the accusation charging commission of the offense.

(c) The issue of the existence of an affirmative defense is not submitted to the jury unless evidence is admitted supporting the defense.

(d) If the issue of the existence of an affirmative defense is submitted to the jury, the court shall charge that the defendant must prove the affirmative defense by a preponderance of evidence.

Acts 1973, 63rd Leg., p. 883, ch. 399, § 1, eff. Jan. 1, 1974. Amended by Acts 1993, 73rd Leg., ch. 900, § 1.01, eff. Sept. 1, 1994.

§ 2.05. Presumption

(a) Except as provided by Subsection (b), when this code or another penal law establishes a presumption with respect to any fact, it has the following consequences:

(1) if there is sufficient evidence of the facts that give rise to the presumption, the issue of the existence of the presumed fact must be submitted to the jury, unless the court is satisfied that the evidence as a whole clearly precludes a finding beyond a reasonable doubt of the presumed fact; and

(2) if the existence of the presumed fact is submitted to the jury, the court shall charge the jury, in terms of the presumption and the specific element to which it applies, as follows:

(A) that the facts giving rise to the presumption must be proven beyond a reasonable doubt;

(B) that if such facts are proven beyond a reasonable doubt the jury may find that the element of the offense sought to be presumed exists, but it is not bound to so find;

(C) that even though the jury may find the existence of such element, the state must prove beyond a reasonable doubt each of the other elements of the offense charged; and

(D) if the jury has a reasonable doubt as to the existence of a fact or facts giving rise to the presumption, the presumption fails and the jury shall not consider the presumption for any purpose.

(b) When this code or another penal law establishes a presumption in favor of the defendant with respect to any fact, it has the following consequences:

(1) if there is sufficient evidence of the facts that give rise to the presumption, the issue of the existence of the presumed fact must be submitted to the jury unless the court is satisfied that the evidence as a whole clearly precludes a finding beyond a reasonable doubt of the presumed fact; and

(2) if the existence of the presumed fact is submitted to the jury, the court shall charge the jury, in terms of the presumption, that:

(A) the presumption applies unless the state proves beyond a reasonable doubt that the facts giving rise to the presumption do not exist;

(B) if the state fails to prove beyond a reasonable doubt that the facts giving rise to the presumption do not exist, the jury must find that the presumed fact exists;

(C) even though the jury may find that the presumed fact does not exist, the state must prove beyond a reasonable doubt each of the elements of the offense charged; and

(D) if the jury has a reasonable doubt as to whether the presumed fact exists, the presumption applies and the jury must consider the presumed fact to exist.

Acts 1973, 63rd Leg., p. 883, ch. 399, § 1, eff. Jan. 1, 1974. Amended by Acts 1975, 64th Leg., p. 912, ch. 342, § 2, eff. Sept. 1, 1975; Acts 1993, 73rd Leg., ch. 900, § 1.01, eff. Sept. 1, 1994; Acts 2005, 79th Leg., ch. 288, § 2, eff. Sept. 1, 2005.

CHAPTER 3. MULTIPLE PROSECUTIONS

§ 3.01. Definition

In this chapter, "criminal episode" means the commission of two or more offenses, regardless of whether the harm is directed toward or inflicted upon more than one person or item of property, under the following circumstances:

(1) the offenses are committed pursuant to the same transaction or pursuant to two or more transactions that are connected or constitute a common scheme or plan; or

(2) the offenses are the repeated commission of the same or similar offenses.

Acts 1973, 63rd Leg., p. 883, ch. 399, § 1, eff. Jan. 1, 1974. Amended by Acts 1987, 70th Leg., ch. 387, § 1, eff. Sept. 1, 1987; Acts 1993, 73rd Leg., ch. 900, § 1.01, eff. Sept. 1, 1994.

§ 3.02. Consolidation and Joinder of Prosecutions

(a) A defendant may be prosecuted in a single criminal action for all offenses arising out of the same criminal episode.

(b) When a single criminal action is based on more than one charging instrument within the jurisdiction of the trial court, the state shall file written notice of the action not less than 30 days prior to the trial.

(c) If a judgment of guilt is reversed, set aside, or vacated, and a new trial ordered, the state may not prosecute in a single criminal action in the new trial any offense not joined in the former prosecution unless evidence to establish probable guilt for that offense was not known to the appropriate prosecuting official at the time the first prosecution commenced.

Acts 1973, 63rd Leg., p. 883, ch. 399, § 1, eff. Jan. 1, 1974. Amended by Acts 1993, 73rd Leg., ch. 900, § 1.01, eff. Sept. 1, 1994.

§ 3.03. Sentences for Offenses Arising Out of Same Criminal Episode

(a) When the accused is found guilty of more than one offense arising out of the same criminal episode prosecuted in a single criminal action, a sentence for each offense for which he has been found guilty shall be pronounced. Except as provided by Subsection (b), the sentences shall run concurrently.

(b) If the accused is found guilty of more than one offense arising out of the same criminal episode, the sentences may run concurrently or consecutively if each sentence is for a conviction of:

(1) an offense:

(A) under Section 49.07 or 49.08, regardless of whether the accused is convicted of violations of the same section more than once or is convicted of violations of both sections; or

(B) for which a plea agreement was reached in a case in which the accused was charged with more than one offense listed in Paragraph (A), regardless of whether the accused is charged with violations of the same section more than once or is charged with violations of both sections;

(2) an offense:

(A) under Section 33.021 or an offense under Section 21.02, 21.11, 22.011, 22.021, 25.02, or 43.25 committed against a victim younger than 17 years of age at the time of the commission of the offense regardless of whether the accused is convicted of violations of the same section more than once or is convicted of violations of more than one section; or

(B) for which a plea agreement was reached in a case in which the accused was charged with more than one offense listed in Paragraph (A) committed against a victim younger than 17 years of age at the time of the commission of the offense regardless of whether the accused is charged with violations of the same section more than once or is charged with violations of more than one section;

(3) an offense:

(A) under Section 21.15 or 43.26, regardless of whether the accused is convicted of violations of the same section more than once or is convicted of violations of both sections; or

(B) for which a plea agreement was reached in a case in which the accused was charged with more than one offense listed in Paragraph (A), regardless of whether the accused is charged with violations of the same section more than once or is charged with violations of both sections; or

(4) an offense for which the judgment in the case contains an affirmative finding under Article 42.0197, Code of Criminal Procedure.

(b–1) Subsection (b)(4) does not apply to a defendant whose case was transferred to the court under Section 54.02, Family Code.

Acts 1973, 63rd Leg., p. 883, ch. 399, § 1, eff. Jan. 1, 1974. Amended by Acts 1993, 73rd Leg., ch. 900, § 1.01, eff. Sept. 1, 1994; Acts 1995, 74th Leg., ch. 596, § 1, eff. Sept. 1, 1995; Acts 1997, 75th Leg., ch. 667, § 2, eff. Sept. 1, 1997; Acts 2005, 79th Leg., ch. 527, § 1, eff. Sept. 1, 2005; Acts 2007, 80th Leg., ch. 593, § 3.47, eff. Sept. 1, 2007; Acts 2007, 80th Leg., ch. 1291, § 6, eff. Sept. 1, 2007; Acts 2009, 81st Leg., ch. 1130, § 21, eff. Sept. 1, 2009.

Section 11 of Acts 2007, 80th Leg., ch. 1291 provides:

"Subsection (b), Section 3.03, and Subsection (f), Section 33.021, Penal Code, as amended by this Act, apply only to an offense committed on or after September 1, 2007. An offense committed before September 1, 2007, is covered by the law in effect when the offense was committed, and the former law is continued in effect for that purpose. For the purposes of this section, an offense was committed before September 1, 2007, if any element of the offense occurred before that date."

Section 26 of Acts 2009, 81st Leg., ch. 1130 provides:

"Section 3.03(b), Penal Code, as amended by this Act, applies only to an offense committed on or after the effective date [Sept. 1, 2009] of this Act. An offense committed before the effective date of this Act is covered by the law in effect when the offense was committed, and the former law is continued in effect for that purpose. For purposes of this section, an offense was committed before the effective date of this Act if any element of the offense occurred before that date."

§ 3.04. Severance

(a) Whenever two or more offenses have been consolidated or joined for trial under Section 3.02, the defendant shall have a right to a severance of the offenses.

(b) In the event of severance under this section, the provisions of Section 3.03 do not apply, and the court in its discretion may order the sentences to run either concurrently or consecutively.

(c) The right to severance under this section does not apply to a prosecution for offenses described by Section 3.03(b) unless the court determines that the defendant or the state would be unfairly prejudiced by a joinder of offenses, in which event the judge may order the offenses to be tried separately or may order other relief as justice requires.

Acts 1973, 63rd Leg., p. 883, ch. 399, § 1, eff. Jan. 1, 1974. Amended by Acts 1993, 73rd Leg., ch. 900, § 1.01, eff. Sept. 1, 1994; Acts 1997, 75th Leg., ch. 667, § 3, eff. Sept. 1, 1997; Acts 2005, 79th Leg., ch. 527, § 2, eff. Sept. 1, 2005.

TITLE 2. GENERAL PRINCIPLES OF CRIMINAL RESPONSIBILITY

CHAPTER 6. CULPABILITY GENERALLY

Section

§ 6.01. Requirement of Voluntary Act or Omission

(a) A person commits an offense only if he voluntarily engages in conduct, including an act, an omission, or possession.

(b) Possession is a voluntary act if the possessor knowingly obtains or receives the thing possessed or is aware of his control of the thing for a sufficient time to permit him to terminate his control.

(c) A person who omits to perform an act does not commit an offense unless a law as defined by Section 1.07 provides that the omission is an offense or otherwise provides that he has a duty to perform the act.

Acts 1973, 63rd Leg., p. 883, ch. 399, § 1, eff. Jan. 1, 1974. Amended by Acts 1975, 64th Leg., p. 913, ch. 342, § 3, eff. Sept. 1, 1975; Acts 1993, 73rd Leg., ch. 3, § 1, eff. Feb. 25, 1993; Acts 1993, 73rd Leg., ch. 900, § 1.01, eff. Sept. 1, 1994.

§ 6.02. Requirement of Culpability

(a) Except as provided in Subsection (b), a person does not commit an offense unless he intentionally, knowingly, recklessly, or with criminal negligence engages in conduct as the definition of the offense requires.

(b) If the definition of an offense does not prescribe a culpable mental state, a culpable mental state is nevertheless required unless the definition plainly dispenses with any mental element.

(c) If the definition of an offense does not prescribe a culpable mental state, but one is nevertheless required under Subsection (b), intent, knowledge, or recklessness suffices to establish criminal responsibility.

(d) Culpable mental states are classified according to relative degrees, from highest to lowest, as follows:

(1) intentional;

(2) knowing;

(3) reckless;

(4) criminal negligence.

(e) Proof of a higher degree of culpability than that charged constitutes proof of the culpability charged.

(f) An offense defined by municipal ordinance or by order of a county commissioners court may not dispense with the requirement of a culpable mental state if the offense is punishable by a fine exceeding the amount authorized by Section 12.23.

Acts 1973, 63rd Leg., p. 883, ch. 399, § 1, eff. Jan. 1, 1974. Amended by Acts 1993, 73rd Leg., ch. 900, § 1.01, eff. Sept. 1, 1994; Acts 2005, 79th Leg., ch. 1219, § 1, eff. Sept. 1, 2005.

§ 6.03. Definitions of Culpable Mental States

(a) A person acts intentionally, or with intent, with respect to the nature of his conduct or to a result of his conduct when it is his conscious objective or desire to engage in the conduct or cause the result.

(b) A person acts knowingly, or with knowledge, with respect to the nature of his conduct or to circumstances surrounding his conduct when he is aware of the nature of his conduct or that the circumstances exist. A person acts knowingly, or with knowledge, with respect to a result of his conduct when he is aware that his conduct is reasonably certain to cause the result.

(c) A person acts recklessly, or is reckless, with respect to circumstances surrounding his conduct or the result of his conduct when he is aware of but consciously disregards a substantial and unjustifiable risk that the circumstances exist or the result will occur. The risk must be of such a nature and degree that its disregard constitutes a gross deviation from the standard of care that an ordinary person would exercise under all the circumstances as viewed from the actor's standpoint.

(d) A person acts with criminal negligence, or is criminally negligent, with respect to circumstances surrounding his conduct or the result of his conduct when he ought to be aware of a substantial and unjustifiable risk that the circumstances exist or the result will occur. The risk must be of such a nature and degree that the failure to perceive it constitutes a gross deviation from the standard of care that an ordinary person would exercise under all the circumstances as viewed from the actor's standpoint.

Acts 1973, 63rd Leg., p. 883, ch. 399, § 1, eff. Jan. 1, 1974. Amended by Acts 1993, 73rd Leg., ch. 900, § 1.01, eff. Sept. 1, 1994.

§ 6.04. Causation: Conduct and Results

(a) A person is criminally responsible if the result would not have occurred but for his conduct, operating either alone or concurrently with another cause, unless the concurrent cause was clearly sufficient to produce the result and the conduct of the actor clearly insufficient.

(b) A person is nevertheless criminally responsible for causing a result if the only difference between what actually occurred and what he desired, contemplated, or risked is that:

(1) a different offense was committed; or

(2) a different person or property was injured, harmed, or otherwise affected.

Acts 1973, 63rd Leg., p. 883, ch. 399, § 1, eff. Jan. 1, 1974. Amended by Acts 1993, 73rd Leg., ch. 900, § 1.01, eff. Sept. 1, 1994.

CHAPTER 7. CRIMINAL RESPONSIBILITY FOR CONDUCT OF ANOTHER

SUBCHAPTER A. COMPLICITY

Section

SUBCHAPTER B. CORPORATIONS AND ASSOCIATIONS

SUBCHAPTER A. COMPLICITY

§ 7.01. Parties to Offenses

(a) A person is criminally responsible as a party to an offense if the offense is committed by his own conduct, by the conduct of another for which he is criminally responsible, or by both.

(b) Each party to an offense may be charged with commission of the offense.

(c) All traditional distinctions between accomplices and principals are abolished by this section, and each party to an offense may be charged and convicted without alleging that he acted as a principal or accomplice.

Acts 1973, 63rd Leg., p. 883, ch. 399, § 1, eff. Jan. 1, 1974. Amended by Acts 1993, 73rd Leg., ch. 900, § 1.01, eff. Sept. 1, 1994.

§ 7.02. Criminal Responsibility for Conduct of Another

(a) A person is criminally responsible for an offense committed by the conduct of another if:

(1) acting with the kind of culpability required for the offense, he causes or aids an innocent or nonresponsible person to engage in conduct prohibited by the definition of the offense;

(2) acting with intent to promote or assist the commission of the offense, he solicits, encourages, directs, aids, or attempts to aid the other person to commit the offense; or

(3) having a legal duty to prevent commission of the offense and acting with intent to promote or assist its commission, he fails to make a reasonable effort to prevent commission of the offense.

(b) If, in the attempt to carry out a conspiracy to commit one felony, another felony is committed by one of the conspirators, all conspirators are guilty of the felony actually committed, though having no intent to commit it, if the offense was committed in furtherance of the unlawful purpose and was one that should have been anticipated as a result of the carrying out of the conspiracy.

Acts 1973, 63rd Leg., p. 883, ch. 399, § 1, eff. Jan. 1, 1974. Amended by Acts 1993, 73rd Leg., ch. 900, § 1.01, eff. Sept. 1, 1994.

§ 7.03. Defenses Excluded

In a prosecution in which an actor's criminal responsibility is based on the conduct of another, the actor may be convicted on proof of commission of the offense and that he was a party to its commission, and it is no defense:

(1) that the actor belongs to a class of persons that by definition of the offense is legally incapable of committing the offense in an individual capacity; or

(2) that the person for whose conduct the actor is criminally responsible has been acquitted, has not been prosecuted or convicted, has been convicted of a different offense or of a different type or class of offense, or is immune from prosecution.

Acts 1973, 63rd Leg., p. 883, ch. 399, § 1, eff. Jan. 1, 1974. Amended by Acts 1993, 73rd Leg., ch. 900, § 1.01, eff. Sept. 1, 1994.

SUBCHAPTER B. CORPORATIONS AND ASSOCIATIONS

§ 7.21. Definitions

In this subchapter:

(1) "Agent" means a director, officer, employee, or other person authorized to act in behalf of a corporation or association.

(2) "High managerial agent" means:

(A) a partner in a partnership;

(B) an officer of a corporation or association;

(C) an agent of a corporation or association who has duties of such responsibility that his conduct reasonably may be assumed to represent the policy of the corporation or association.

Acts 1973, 63rd Leg., p. 883, ch. 399, § 1, eff. Jan. 1, 1974. Amended by Acts 1993, 73rd Leg., ch. 900, § 1.01, eff. Sept. 1, 1994.

§ 7.22. Criminal Responsibility of Corporation or Association

(a) If conduct constituting an offense is performed by an agent acting in behalf of a corporation or association and within the scope of his office or employment, the corporation or association is criminally responsible for an offense defined:

(1) in this code where corporations and associations are made subject thereto;

(2) by law other than this code in which a legislative purpose to impose criminal responsibility on corporations or associations plainly appears; or

(3) by law other than this code for which strict liability is imposed, unless a legislative purpose not to impose criminal responsibility on corporations or associations plainly appears.

(b) A corporation or association is criminally responsible for a felony offense only if its commission was authorized, requested, commanded, performed, or recklessly tolerated by:

(1) a majority of the governing board acting in behalf of the corporation or association; or

(2) a high managerial agent acting in behalf of the corporation or association and within the scope of his office or employment.

Acts 1973, 63rd Leg., p. 883, ch. 399, § 1, eff. Jan. 1, 1974. Amended by Acts 1975, 64th Leg., p. 913, ch. 342, § 4, eff. Sept. 1, 1975; Acts 1993, 73rd Leg., ch. 900, § 1.01, eff. Sept. 1, 1994.

§ 7.23. Criminal Responsibility of Person for Conduct in Behalf of Corporation or Association

(a) An individual is criminally responsible for conduct that he performs in the name of or in behalf of a corporation or association to the same extent as if the conduct were performed in his own name or behalf.

(b) An agent having primary responsibility for the discharge of a duty to act imposed by law on a corporation or association is criminally responsible for omission to discharge the duty to the same extent as if the duty were imposed by law directly on him.

(c) If an individual is convicted of conduct constituting an offense performed in the name of or on behalf of a corporation or association, he is subject to the sentence authorized by law for an individual convicted of the offense.

Acts 1973, 63rd Leg., p. 883, ch. 399, § 1, eff. Jan. 1, 1974. Amended by Acts 1993, 73rd Leg., ch. 900, § 1.01, eff. Sept. 1, 1994.

§ 7.24. Defense to Criminal Responsibility of Corporation or Association

It is an affirmative defense to prosecution of a corporation or association under Section 7.22(a)(1) or (a)(2) that the high managerial agent having supervisory responsibility over the subject matter of the offense employed due diligence to prevent its commission.

Acts 1973, 63rd Leg., p. 883, ch. 399, § 1, eff. Jan. 1, 1974. Amended by Acts 1975, 64th Leg., p. 913, ch. 342, § 5, eff. Sept. 1, 1975; Acts 1993, 73rd Leg., ch. 900, § 1.01, eff. Sept. 1, 1994.

CHAPTER 8. GENERAL DEFENSES TO CRIMINAL RESPONSIBILITY

Section

§ 8.01. Insanity

(a) It is an affirmative defense to prosecution that, at the time of the conduct charged, the actor, as a result of severe mental disease or defect, did not know that his conduct was wrong.

(b) The term "mental disease or defect" does not include an abnormality manifested only by repeated criminal or otherwise antisocial conduct.

Acts 1973, 63rd Leg., p. 883, ch. 399, § 1, eff. Jan. 1, 1974. Amended by Acts 1983, 68th Leg., p. 2640, ch. 454, § 1, eff. Aug. 29, 1983; Acts 1993, 73rd Leg., ch. 900, § 1.01, eff. Sept. 1, 1994.

§ 8.02. Mistake of Fact

(a) It is a defense to prosecution that the actor through mistake formed a reasonable belief about a matter of fact if his mistaken belief negated the kind of culpability required for commission of the offense.

(b) Although an actor's mistake of fact may constitute a defense to the offense charged, he may nevertheless be convicted of any lesser included offense of which he would be guilty if the fact were as he believed.

Acts 1973, 63rd Leg., p. 883, ch. 399, § 1, eff. Jan. 1, 1974. Amended by Acts 1993, 73rd Leg., ch. 900, § 1.01, eff. Sept. 1, 1994.

§ 8.03. Mistake of Law

(a) It is no defense to prosecution that the actor was ignorant of the provisions of any law after the law has taken effect.

(b) It is an affirmative defense to prosecution that the actor reasonably believed the conduct charged did not constitute a crime and that he acted in reasonable reliance upon:

(1) an official statement of the law contained in a written order or grant of permission by an administrative agency charged by law with responsibility for interpreting the law in question; or

(2) a written interpretation of the law contained in an opinion of a court of record or made by a public official charged by law with responsibility for interpreting the law in question.

(c) Although an actor's mistake of law may constitute a defense to the offense charged, he may nevertheless be convicted of a lesser included offense of which he would be guilty if the law were as he believed.

Acts 1973, 63rd Leg., p. 883, ch. 399, § 1, eff. Jan. 1, 1974. Amended by Acts 1993, 73rd Leg., ch. 900, § 1.01, eff. Sept. 1, 1994.

§ 8.04. Intoxication

(a) Voluntary intoxication does not constitute a defense to the commission of crime.

(b) Evidence of temporary insanity caused by intoxication may be introduced by the actor in mitigation of the penalty attached to the offense for which he is being tried.

(c) When temporary insanity is relied upon as a defense and the evidence tends to show that such insanity was caused by intoxication, the court shall charge the jury in accordance with the provisions of this section.

(d) For purposes of this section "intoxication" means disturbance of mental or physical capacity resulting from the introduction of any substance into the body.

Acts 1973, 63rd Leg., p. 883, ch. 399, § 1, eff. Jan. 1, 1974. Amended by Acts 1993, 73rd Leg., ch. 900, § 1.01, eff. Sept. 1, 1994.

§ 8.05. Duress

(a) It is an affirmative defense to prosecution that the actor engaged in the proscribed conduct because he was compelled to do so by threat of imminent death or serious bodily injury to himself or another.

(b) In a prosecution for an offense that does not constitute a felony, it is an affirmative defense to prosecution that the actor engaged in the proscribed conduct because he was compelled to do so by force or threat of force.

(c) Compulsion within the meaning of this section exists only if the force or threat of force would render a person of reasonable firmness incapable of resisting the pressure.

(d) The defense provided by this section is unavailable if the actor intentionally, knowingly, or recklessly placed himself in a situation in which it was probable that he would be subjected to compulsion.

(e) It is no defense that a person acted at the command or persuasion of his spouse, unless he acted under compulsion that would establish a defense under this section.

Acts 1973, 63rd Leg., p. 883, ch. 399, § 1, eff. Jan. 1, 1974. Amended by Acts 1993, 73rd Leg., ch. 900, § 1.01, eff. Sept. 1, 1994.

§ 8.06. Entrapment

(a) It is a defense to prosecution that the actor engaged in the conduct charged because he was induced to do so by a law enforcement agent using persuasion or other means likely to cause persons to commit the offense. Conduct merely affording a person an opportunity to commit an offense does not constitute entrapment.

(b) In this section "law enforcement agent" includes personnel of the state and local law enforcement agencies as well as of the United States and any person acting in accordance with instructions from such agents.

Acts 1973, 63rd Leg., p. 883, ch. 399, § 1, eff. Jan. 1, 1974. Amended by Acts 1993, 73rd Leg., ch. 900, § 1.01, eff. Sept. 1, 1994.

§ 8.07. Age Affecting Criminal Responsibility

(a) A person may not be prosecuted for or convicted of any offense that the person committed when younger than 15 years of age except:

(1) perjury and aggravated perjury when it appears by proof that the person had sufficient discretion to understand the nature and obligation of an oath;

(2) a violation of a penal statute cognizable under Chapter 729, Transportation Code, except for conduct for which the person convicted may be sentenced to imprisonment or confinement in jail;

(3) a violation of a motor vehicle traffic ordinance of an incorporated city or town in this state;

(4) a misdemeanor punishable by fine only;

(5) a violation of a penal ordinance of a political subdivision;

(6) a violation of a penal statute that is, or is a lesser included offense of, a capital felony, an aggravated controlled substance felony, or a felony of the first degree for which the person is transferred to the court under Section 54.02, Family Code, for prosecution if the person committed the offense when 14 years of age or older; or

(7) a capital felony or an offense under Section 19.02 for which the person is transferred to the court under Section 54.02(j)(2)(A), Family Code.

(b) Unless the juvenile court waives jurisdiction under Section 54.02, Family Code, and certifies the individual for criminal prosecution or the juvenile court has previously waived jurisdiction under that section and certified the individual for criminal prosecution, a person may not be prosecuted for or convicted of any offense committed before reaching 17 years of age except an offense described by Subsections (a)(1)–(5).

(c) No person may, in any case, be punished by death for an offense committed while the person was younger than 18 years.

Acts 1973, 63rd Leg., p. 883, ch. 399, § 1, eff. Jan. 1, 1974. Amended by Acts 1975, 64th Leg., p. 2158, ch. 693, § 24, eff. Sept. 1, 1975; Acts 1987, 70th Leg., ch. 1040, § 26, eff. Sept. 1, 1987; Acts 1989, 71st Leg., ch. 1245, § 3, eff. Sept. 1, 1989; Acts 1991, 72nd Leg., ch. 169, § 3, eff. Sept. 1, 1991; Acts 1993, 73rd Leg., ch. 900, § 1.01, eff. Sept. 1, 1994. Amended by Acts 1995, 74th Leg., ch. 262, § 77, eff. Jan. 1, 1996; Acts 1997, 75th Leg., ch. 165, § 30.236, eff. Sept. 1, 1997; Acts 1997, 75th Leg., ch. 822, § 4, eff. Sept. 1, 1997; Acts 1997, 75th Leg., ch. 1086, § 42, eff. Sept. 1, 1997; Acts 2001, 77th Leg., ch. 1297, § 68, eff. Sept. 1, 2001; Acts 2003, 78th Leg., ch. 283, § 52, eff. Sept. 1, 2003; Acts 2005, 79th Leg., ch. 787, § 2, eff. Sept. 1, 2005; Acts 2005, 79th Leg., ch. 949, § 45, eff. Sept. 1, 2005; Acts 2009, 81st Leg., ch. 311, § 5, eff. Sept. 1, 2009.

Section 6 of Acts 2009, 81st Leg., ch. 311 provides:

"The change in law made by this Act applies only to conduct that occurs on or after the effective date [Sept. 1, 2009] of this Act. Conduct that occurs before the effective date of this Act is covered by the law in effect at the time the conduct occurred, and the former law is continued in effect for that purpose. For the purposes of this section, conduct violating a penal law of this state occurs before the effective date of this Act if any element of the violation occurred before that date."

CHAPTER 9. JUSTIFICATION EXCLUDING CRIMINAL RESPONSIBILITY

SUBCHAPTER A. GENERAL PROVISIONS

§ 9.01. Definitions

In this chapter:

(1) "Custody" has the meaning assigned by Section 38.01.

(2) "Escape" has the meaning assigned by Section 38.01.

(3) "Deadly force" means force that is intended or known by the actor to cause, or in the manner of its use or intended use is capable of causing, death or serious bodily injury.

(4) "Habitation" has the meaning assigned by Section 30.01.

(5) "Vehicle" has the meaning assigned by Section 30. 01.

Acts 1973, 63rd Leg., p. 883, ch. 399, § 1, eff. Jan. 1, 1974. Amended by Acts 1993, 73rd Leg., ch. 900, § 1.01, eff. Sept. 1, 1994; Acts 1997, 75th Leg., ch. 293, § 1, eff. Sept. 1, 1997; Acts 2007, 80th Leg., ch. 1, § 1, eff. Sept. 1, 2007.

§ 9.02. Justification as a Defense

It is a defense to prosecution that the conduct in question is justified under this chapter.

Acts 1973, 63rd Leg., p. 883, ch. 399, § 1, eff. Jan. 1, 1974. Amended by Acts 1993, 73rd Leg., ch. 900, § 1.01, eff. Sept. 1, 1994.

§ 9.03. Confinement as Justifiable Force

Confinement is justified when force is justified by this chapter if the actor takes reasonable measures to terminate the confinement as soon as he knows he safely can unless the person confined has been arrested for an offense.

Acts 1973, 63rd Leg., p. 883, ch. 399, § 1, eff. Jan. 1, 1974. Amended by Acts 1993, 73rd Leg., ch. 900, § 1.01, eff. Sept. 1, 1994.

§ 9.04. Threats as Justifiable Force

The threat of force is justified when the use of force is justified by this chapter. For purposes of this section, a threat to cause death or serious bodily injury by the production of a weapon or otherwise, as long as the actor's purpose is limited to creating an apprehension that he will use deadly force if necessary, does not constitute the use of deadly force.

Acts 1973, 63rd Leg., p. 883, ch. 399, § 1, eff. Jan. 1, 1974. Amended by Acts 1993, 73rd Leg., ch. 900, § 1.01, eff. Sept. 1, 1994.

§ 9.05. Reckless Injury of Innocent Third Person

Even though an actor is justified under this chapter in threatening or using force or deadly force against another, if in doing so he also recklessly injures or kills an innocent third person, the justification afforded by this chapter is unavailable in a prosecution for the reckless injury or killing of the innocent third person.

Acts 1973, 63rd Leg., p. 883, ch. 399, § 1, eff. Jan. 1, 1974. Amended by Acts 1993, 73rd Leg., ch. 900, § 1.01, eff. Sept. 1, 1994.

§ 9.06. Civil Remedies Unaffected

The fact that conduct is justified under this chapter does not abolish or impair any remedy for the conduct that is available in a civil suit.

Acts 1973, 63rd Leg., p. 883, ch. 399, § 1, eff. Jan. 1, 1974. Amended by Acts 1993, 73rd Leg., ch. 900, § 1.01, eff. Sept. 1, 1994.

SUBCHAPTER B. JUSTIFICATION GENERALLY

§ 9.21. Public Duty

(a) Except as qualified by Subsections (b) and (c), conduct is justified if the actor reasonably believes the conduct is required or authorized by law, by the judgment or order of a competent court or other governmental tribunal, or in the execution of legal process.

(b) The other sections of this chapter control when force is used against a person to protect persons (Subchapter C),[1] to protect property (Subchapter D),[2] for law enforcement (Subchapter E),[3] or by virtue of a special relationship (Subchapter F).[4]

(c) The use of deadly force is not justified under this section unless the actor reasonably believes the deadly force is specifically required by statute or unless it occurs in the lawful conduct of war. If deadly force is so justified, there is no duty to retreat before using it.

(d) The justification afforded by this section is available if the actor reasonably believes:

(1) the court or governmental tribunal has jurisdiction or the process is lawful, even though the court or governmental tribunal lacks jurisdiction or the process is unlawful; or

(2) his conduct is required or authorized to assist a public servant in the performance of his official duty, even though the servant exceeds his lawful authority.

Acts 1973, 63rd Leg., p. 883, ch. 399, § 1, eff. Jan. 1, 1974. Amended by Acts 1993, 73rd Leg., ch. 900, § 1.01, eff. Sept. 1, 1994.

[1] V.T.C.A., Penal Code § 9.31 et seq.
[2] V.T.C.A., Penal Code § 9.41 et seq.
[3] V.T.C.A., Penal Code § 9.51 et seq.
[4] V.T.C.A., Penal Code § 9.61 et seq.

§ 9.22. Necessity

Conduct is justified if:

(1) the actor reasonably believes the conduct is immediately necessary to avoid imminent harm;

(2) the desirability and urgency of avoiding the harm clearly outweigh, according to ordinary standards of reasonableness, the harm sought to be prevented by the law proscribing the conduct; and

(3) a legislative purpose to exclude the justification claimed for the conduct does not otherwise plainly appear.

Acts 1973, 63rd Leg., p. 883, ch. 399, § 1, eff. Jan. 1, 1974. Amended by Acts 1993, 73rd Leg., ch. 900, § 1.01, eff. Sept. 1, 1994.

SUBCHAPTER C. PROTECTION OF PERSONS

§ 9.31. Self-Defense

(a) Except as provided in Subsection (b), a person is justified in using force against another when and to the degree the actor reasonably believes the force is immediately necessary to protect the actor against the other's use or attempted use of unlawful force. The actor's belief that the force was immediately necessary as described by this subsection is presumed to be reasonable if the actor:

(1) knew or had reason to believe that the person against whom the force was used:

(A) unlawfully and with force entered, or was attempting to enter unlawfully and with force, the actor's occupied habitation, vehicle, or place of business or employment;

(B) unlawfully and with force removed, or was attempting to remove unlawfully and with force, the actor from the actor's habitation, vehicle, or place of business or employment; or

(C) was committing or attempting to commit aggravated kidnapping, murder, sexual assault, aggravated sexual assault, robbery, or aggravated robbery;

(2) did not provoke the person against whom the force was used; and

(3) was not otherwise engaged in criminal activity, other than a Class C misdemeanor that is a violation of a law or ordinance regulating traffic at the time the force was used.

(b) The use of force against another is not justified:

(1) in response to verbal provocation alone;

(2) to resist an arrest or search that the actor knows is being made by a peace officer, or by a person acting in a peace officer's presence and at his direction, even though the arrest or search is unlawful, unless the resistance is justified under Subsection (c);

(3) if the actor consented to the exact force used or attempted by the other;

(4) if the actor provoked the other's use or attempted use of unlawful force, unless:

(A) the actor abandons the encounter, or clearly communicates to the other his intent to do so reasonably believing he cannot safely abandon the encounter; and

(B) the other nevertheless continues or attempts to use unlawful force against the actor; or

(5) if the actor sought an explanation from or discussion with the other person concerning the actor's differences with the other person while the actor was:

(A) carrying a weapon in violation of Section 46.02; or

(B) possessing or transporting a weapon in violation of Section 46.05.

(c) The use of force to resist an arrest or search is justified:

(1) if, before the actor offers any resistance, the peace officer (or person acting at his direction) uses or attempts to use greater force than necessary to make the arrest or search; and

(2) when and to the degree the actor reasonably believes the force is immediately necessary to protect himself against the peace officer's (or other person's) use or attempted use of greater force than necessary.

(d) The use of deadly force is not justified under this subchapter except as provided in Sections 9.32, 9.33, and 9.34.

(e) A person who has a right to be present at the location where the force is used, who has not provoked the person against whom the force is used, and who is not engaged in criminal activity at the time the force is used is not required to retreat before using force as described by this section.

(f) For purposes of Subsection (a), in determining whether an actor described by Subsection (e) reasonably believed that the use of force was necessary, a finder of fact may not consider whether the actor failed to retreat.

Acts 1973, 63rd Leg., p. 883, ch. 399, § 1, eff. Jan. 1, 1974. Amended by Acts 1993, 73rd Leg., ch. 900, § 1.01, eff. Sept. 1, 1994; Acts 1995, 74th Leg., ch. 190, § 1, eff. Sept. 1, 1995; Acts 2007, 80th Leg., ch. 1, § 2, eff. Sept. 1, 2007.

Section 5(a) of Acts 2007, 80th Leg., ch. 1 provides:

"Sections 9.31 and 9.32, Penal Code, as amended by this Act, apply only to an offense committed on or after the effective date of this Act. An offense committed before the effective date of this Act is covered by the law in effect when the offense was committed, and the former law is continued in effect for this purpose. For the purposes of this subsection, an offense is committed before the effective date of this Act if any element of the offense occurs before the effective date."

§ 9.32. Deadly Force in Defense of Person

(a) A person is justified in using deadly force against another:

(1) if the actor would be justified in using force against the other under Section 9.31; and

(2) when and to the degree the actor reasonably believes the deadly force is immediately necessary:

(A) to protect the actor against the other's use or attempted use of unlawful deadly force; or

(B) to prevent the other's imminent commission of aggravated kidnapping, murder, sexual assault, aggravated sexual assault, robbery, or aggravated robbery.

(b) The actor's belief under Subsection (a)(2) that the deadly force was immediately necessary as described by that subdivision is presumed to be reasonable if the actor:

(1) knew or had reason to believe that the person against whom the deadly force was used:

(A) unlawfully and with force entered, or was attempting to enter unlawfully and with force, the actor's occupied habitation, vehicle, or place of business or employment;

(B) unlawfully and with force removed, or was attempting to remove unlawfully and with force, the actor from the actor's habitation, vehicle, or place of business or employment; or

(C) was committing or attempting to commit an offense described by Subsection (a)(2)(B);

(2) did not provoke the person against whom the force was used; and

(3) was not otherwise engaged in criminal activity, other than a Class C misdemeanor that is a violation of a law or ordinance regulating traffic at the time the force was used.

(c) A person who has a right to be present at the location where the deadly force is used, who has not provoked the person against whom the deadly force is used, and who is not engaged in criminal activity at the time the deadly force is used is not required to retreat before using deadly force as described by this section.

(d) For purposes of Subsection (a)(2), in determining whether an actor described by Subsection (c) reasonably believed that the use of deadly force was necessary, a finder of fact may not consider whether the actor failed to retreat.

Acts 1973, 63rd Leg., p. 883, ch. 399, § 1, eff. Jan. 1, 1974. Amended by Acts 1983, 68th Leg., p. 5316, ch. 977, § 5, eff. Sept. 1, 1983; Acts 1993, 73rd Leg., ch. 900, § 1.01, eff. Sept. 1, 1994; Acts 1995, 74th Leg., ch. 235, § 1, eff. Sept. 1, 1995; Acts 2007, 80th Leg., ch. 1, § 3, eff. Sept. 1, 2007.

Section 5(a) of Acts 2007, 80th Leg., ch. 1 provides:

"Sections 9.31 and 9.32, Penal Code, as amended by this Act, apply only to an offense committed on or after the effective date of this Act. An offense committed before the effective date of this Act is covered by the law in effect when the offense was committed, and the former law is continued in effect for this purpose. For the purposes of this subsection, an offense is committed before the effective date of this Act if any element of the offense occurs before the effective date."

§ 9.33. Defense of Third Person

A person is justified in using force or deadly force against another to protect a third person if:

(1) under the circumstances as the actor reasonably believes them to be, the actor would be justified under Section 9.31 or 9.32 in using force or deadly force to protect himself against the unlawful force or unlawful deadly force he reasonably believes to be threatening the third person he seeks to protect; and

(2) the actor reasonably believes that his intervention is immediately necessary to protect the third person.

Acts 1973, 63rd Leg., p. 883, ch. 399, § 1, eff. Jan. 1, 1974. Amended by Acts 1993, 73rd Leg., ch. 900, § 1.01, eff. Sept. 1, 1994.

§ 9.34. Protection of Life or Health

(a) A person is justified in using force, but not deadly force, against another when and to the degree he reasonably believes the force is immediately necessary to prevent the other from committing suicide or inflicting serious bodily injury to himself.

(b) A person is justified in using both force and deadly force against another when and to the degree he reasonably believes the force or deadly force is immediately necessary to preserve the other's life in an emergency.

Acts 1973, 63rd Leg., p. 883, ch. 399, § 1, eff. Jan. 1, 1974. Amended by Acts 1993, 73rd Leg., ch. 900, § 1.01, eff. Sept. 1, 1994.

SUBCHAPTER D. PROTECTION OF PROPERTY

§ 9.41. Protection of One's Own Property

(a) A person in lawful possession of land or tangible, movable property is justified in using force against another when and to the degree the actor reasonably believes the force is immediately necessary to prevent or terminate the other's trespass on the land or unlawful interference with the property.

(b) A person unlawfully dispossessed of land or tangible, movable property by another is justified in using force against the other when and to the degree the actor reasonably believes the force is immediately necessary to reenter the land or recover the property if the actor uses the force immediately or in fresh pursuit after the dispossession and:

(1) the actor reasonably believes the other had no claim of right when he dispossessed the actor; or

(2) the other accomplished the dispossession by using force, threat, or fraud against the actor.

Acts 1973, 63rd Leg., p. 883, ch. 399, § 1, eff. Jan. 1, 1974. Amended by Acts 1993, 73rd Leg., ch. 900, § 1.01, eff. Sept. 1, 1994.

§ 9.42. Deadly Force to Protect Property

A person is justified in using deadly force against another to protect land or tangible, movable property:

(1) if he would be justified in using force against the other under Section 9.41; and

(2) when and to the degree he reasonably believes the deadly force is immediately necessary:

(A) to prevent the other's imminent commission of arson, burglary, robbery, aggravated robbery, theft during the nighttime, or criminal mischief during the nighttime; or

(B) to prevent the other who is fleeing immediately after committing burglary, robbery, aggravated robbery, or theft during the nighttime from escaping with the property; and

(3) he reasonably believes that:

(A) the land or property cannot be protected or recovered by any other means; or

(B) the use of force other than deadly force to protect or recover the land or property would expose the actor or another to a substantial risk of death or serious bodily injury.

Acts 1973, 63rd Leg., p. 883, ch. 399, § 1, eff. Jan. 1, 1974. Amended by Acts 1993, 73rd Leg., ch. 900, § 1.01, eff. Sept. 1, 1994.

§ 9.43. Protection of Third Person's Property

A person is justified in using force or deadly force against another to protect land or tangible, movable property of a third person if, under the circumstances as he reasonably believes them to be, the actor would be justified under Section 9.41 or 9.42 in using force or deadly force to protect his own land or property and:

(1) the actor reasonably believes the unlawful interference constitutes attempted or consummated theft of or criminal mischief to the tangible, movable property; or

(2) the actor reasonably believes that:

(A) the third person has requested his protection of the land or property;

(B) he has a legal duty to protect the third person's land or property; or

(C) the third person whose land or property he uses force or deadly force to protect is the actor's spouse, parent, or child, resides with the actor, or is under the actor's care.

Acts 1973, 63rd Leg., p. 883, ch. 399, § 1, eff. Jan. 1, 1974. Amended by Acts 1993, 73rd Leg., ch. 900, § 1.01, eff. Sept. 1, 1994.

§ 9.44. Use of Device to Protect Property

The justification afforded by Sections 9.41 and 9.43 applies to the use of a device to protect land or tangible, movable property if:

(1) the device is not designed to cause, or known by the actor to create a substantial risk of causing, death or serious bodily injury; and

(2) use of the device is reasonable under all the circumstances as the actor reasonably believes them to be when he installs the device.

Acts 1973, 63rd Leg., p. 883, ch. 399, § 1, eff. Jan. 1, 1974. Amended by Acts 1975, 64th Leg., p. 913, ch. 342, § 6, eff. Sept. 1, 1975. Acts 1993, 73rd Leg., ch. 900, § 1.01, eff. Sept. 1, 1994.

SUBCHAPTER E. LAW ENFORCEMENT

§ 9.51. Arrest and Search

(a) A peace officer, or a person acting in a peace officer's presence and at his direction, is justified in using force against another when and to the degree the actor reasonably believes the force is immediately necessary to make or assist in making an arrest or search, or to prevent or assist in preventing escape after arrest, if:

(1) the actor reasonably believes the arrest or search is lawful or, if the arrest or search is made under a warrant, he reasonably believes the warrant is valid; and

(2) before using force, the actor manifests his purpose to arrest or search and identifies himself as a peace officer or as one acting at a peace officer's direction, unless he reasonably believes his purpose and identity are already known by or cannot reasonably be made known to the person to be arrested.

(b) A person other than a peace officer (or one acting at his direction) is justified in using force against another when and to the degree the actor reasonably believes the force is immediately necessary to make or assist in making a lawful arrest, or to prevent or assist in preventing escape after lawful arrest if, before using force, the actor manifests his purpose to and the reason for the arrest or reasonably believes his purpose and the reason are already known by or cannot reasonably be made known to the person to be arrested.

(c) A peace officer is justified in using deadly force against another when and to the degree the peace officer reasonably believes the deadly force is immediately necessary to make an arrest, or to prevent escape after arrest, if the use of force would have been justified under Subsection (a) and:

(1) the actor reasonably believes the conduct for which arrest is authorized included the use or attempted use of deadly force; or

(2) the actor reasonably believes there is a substantial risk that the person to be arrested will cause death or serious bodily injury to the actor or another if the arrest is delayed.

(d) A person other than a peace officer acting in a peace officer's presence and at his direction is justified in using deadly force against another when and to the degree the person reasonably believes the deadly force is immediately necessary to make a lawful arrest, or to prevent escape after a lawful arrest, if the use of force would have been justified under Subsection (b) and:

(1) the actor reasonably believes the felony or offense against the public peace for which arrest is authorized included the use or attempted use of deadly force; or

(2) the actor reasonably believes there is a substantial risk that the person to be arrested will cause death or serious bodily injury to another if the arrest is delayed.

(e) There is no duty to retreat before using deadly force justified by Subsection (c) or (d).

(f) Nothing in this section relating to the actor's manifestation of purpose or identity shall be construed as conflicting with any other law relating to the issuance, service, and execution of an arrest or search warrant either under the laws of this state or the United States.

(g) Deadly force may only be used under the circumstances enumerated in Subsections (c) and (d).

Acts 1973, 63rd Leg., p. 883, ch. 399, § 1, eff. Jan. 1, 1974. Amended by Acts 1993, 73rd Leg., ch. 900, § 1.01, eff. Sept. 1, 1994.

§ 9.52. Prevention of Escape From Custody

The use of force to prevent the escape of an arrested person from custody is justifiable when the force could have been employed to effect the arrest under which the person is in custody, except that a guard employed by a correctional facility or a peace officer is justified in using any force, including deadly force, that he reasonably believes to be immediately necessary to prevent the escape of a person from the correctional facility.

Acts 1973, 63rd Leg., p. 883, ch. 399, § 1, eff. Jan. 1, 1974. Amended by Acts 1993, 73rd Leg., ch. 900, § 1.01, eff. Sept. 1, 1994.

§ 9.53. Maintaining Security in Correctional Facility

An officer or employee of a correctional facility is justified in using force against a person in custody when and to the degree the officer or employee reasonably believes the force is necessary to maintain the security of the correctional facility, the safety or security of other persons in custody or employed by the correctional facility, or his own safety or security.

Added by Acts 1987, 70th Leg., ch. 512, § 1, eff. Sept. 1, 1987. Amended by Acts 1993, 73rd Leg., ch. 900, § 1.01, eff. Sept. 1, 1994.

SUBCHAPTER F. SPECIAL RELATIONSHIPS

§ 9.61. Parent-Child

(a) The use of force, but not deadly force, against a child younger than 18 years is justified:

(1) if the actor is the child's parent or stepparent or is acting in loco parentis to the child; and

(2) when and to the degree the actor reasonably believes the force is necessary to discipline the child or to safeguard or promote his welfare.

(b) For purposes of this section, "in loco parentis" includes grandparent and guardian, any person acting by, through, or under the direction of a court with jurisdiction over the child, and anyone who has express or implied consent of the parent or parents.

Acts 1973, 63rd Leg., p. 883, ch. 399, § 1, eff. Jan. 1, 1974. Amended by Acts 1993, 73rd Leg., ch. 900, § 1.01, eff. Sept. 1, 1994.

§ 9.62. Educator-Student

The use of force, but not deadly force, against a person is justified:

(1) if the actor is entrusted with the care, supervision, or administration of the person for a special purpose; and

(2) when and to the degree the actor reasonably believes the force is necessary to further the special purpose or to maintain discipline in a group.

Acts 1973, 63rd Leg., p. 883, ch. 399, § 1, eff. Jan. 1, 1974. Amended by Acts 1993, 73rd Leg., ch. 900, § 1.01, eff. Sept. 1, 1994.

§ 9.63. Guardian-Incompetent

The use of force, but not deadly force, against a mental incompetent is justified:

(1) if the actor is the incompetent's guardian or someone similarly responsible for the general care and supervision of the incompetent; and

(2) when and to the degree the actor reasonably believes the force is necessary:

(A) to safeguard and promote the incompetent's welfare; or

(B) if the incompetent is in an institution for his care and custody, to maintain discipline in the institution.

Acts 1973, 63rd Leg., p. 883, ch. 399, § 1, eff. Jan. 1, 1974. Amended by Acts 1993, 73rd Leg., ch. 900, § 1.01, eff. Sept. 1, 1994.

TITLE 3. PUNISHMENTS

CHAPTER 12. PUNISHMENTS

SUBCHAPTER A. GENERAL PROVISIONS

SUBCHAPTER A. GENERAL PROVISIONS

§ 12.01. Punishment in Accordance With Code

(a) A person adjudged guilty of an offense under this code shall be punished in accordance with this chapter and the Code of Criminal Procedure.

(b) Penal laws enacted after the effective date of this code shall be classified for punishment purposes in accordance with this chapter.

(c) This chapter does not deprive a court of authority conferred by law to forfeit property, dissolve a corporation, suspend or cancel a license or permit, remove a person from office, cite for contempt, or impose any other civil penalty. The civil penalty may be included in the sentence.

Acts 1973, 63rd Leg., p. 883, ch. 399, § 1, eff. Jan. 1, 1974. Amended by Acts 1993, 73rd Leg., ch. 900, § 1.01, eff. Sept. 1, 1994.

§ 12.02. Classification of Offenses

Offenses are designated as felonies or misdemeanors.

Acts 1973, 63rd Leg., p. 883, ch. 399, § 1, eff. Jan. 1, 1974. Amended by Acts 1993, 73rd Leg., ch. 900, § 1.01, eff. Sept. 1, 1994.

§ 12.03. Classification of Misdemeanors

(a) Misdemeanors are classified according to the relative seriousness of the offense into three categories:

(1) Class A misdemeanors;

(2) Class B misdemeanors;

(3) Class C misdemeanors.

(b) An offense designated a misdemeanor in this code without specification as to punishment or category is a Class C misdemeanor.

(c) Conviction of a Class C misdemeanor does not impose any legal disability or disadvantage.

Acts 1973, 63rd Leg., p. 883, ch. 399, § 1, eff. Jan. 1, 1974. Amended by Acts 1993, 73rd Leg., ch. 900, § 1.01, eff. Sept. 1, 1994.

§ 12.04. Classification of Felonies

(a) Felonies are classified according to the relative seriousness of the offense into five categories:

(1) capital felonies;

(2) felonies of the first degree;

(3) felonies of the second degree;

(4) felonies of the third degree; and

(5) state jail felonies.

(b) An offense designated a felony in this code without specification as to category is a state jail felony.

Acts 1973, 63rd Leg., p. 883, ch. 399, § 1, eff. Jan. 1, 1974. Amended by Acts 1973, 63rd Leg., p. 1125, ch. 426, art. 2, § 3, eff. Jan. 1, 1974; Acts 1993, 73rd Leg., ch. 900, § 1.01, eff. Sept. 1, 1994.

SUBCHAPTER B. ORDINARY MISDEMEANOR PUNISHMENTS

§ 12.21. Class A Misdemeanor

An individual adjudged guilty of a Class A misdemeanor shall be punished by:

(1) a fine not to exceed $4,000;

(2) confinement in jail for a term not to exceed one year; or

(3) both such fine and confinement.

Acts 1973, 63rd Leg., p. 883, ch. 399, § 1, eff. Jan. 1, 1974. Amended by Acts 1991, 72nd Leg., ch. 108, § 1, eff. Sept. 1, 1991; Acts 1993, 73rd Leg., ch. 900, § 1.01, eff. Sept. 1, 1994.

§ 12.22. Class B Misdemeanor

An individual adjudged guilty of a Class B misdemeanor shall be punished by:

(1) a fine not to exceed $2,000;

(2) confinement in jail for a term not to exceed 180 days; or

(3) both such fine and confinement.

Acts 1973, 63rd Leg., p. 883, ch. 399, § 1, eff. Jan. 1, 1974. Amended by Acts 1991, 72nd Leg., ch. 108, § 1, eff. Sept. 1, 1991; Acts 1993, 73rd Leg., ch. 900, § 1.01, eff. Sept. 1, 1994.

§ 12.23. Class C Misdemeanor

An individual adjudged guilty of a Class C misdemeanor shall be punished by a fine not to exceed $500.

Acts 1973, 63rd Leg., p. 883, ch. 399, § 1, eff. Jan. 1, 1974. Amended by Acts 1991, 72nd Leg., ch. 108, § 1, eff. Sept. 1, 1991; Acts 1993, 73rd Leg., ch. 900, § 1.01, eff. Sept. 1, 1994.

SUBCHAPTER C. ORDINARY FELONY PUNISHMENTS

§ 12.31. Capital Felony

(a) An individual adjudged guilty of a capital felony in a case in which the state seeks the death penalty shall be punished by imprisonment in the Texas Department of Criminal Justice for life without parole or by death. An individual adjudged guilty of a capital felony in a case in which the state does not seek the death penalty shall be punished by imprisonment in the Texas Department of Criminal Justice for:

(1) life, if the individual's case was transferred to the court under Section 54.02, Family Code; or

(2) life without parole.

(b) In a capital felony trial in which the state seeks the death penalty, prospective jurors shall be informed that a sentence of life imprisonment without parole or death is mandatory on conviction of a capital felony. In a capital felony trial in which the state does not seek the death penalty, prospective jurors shall be informed that the state is not seeking the death penalty and that:

(1) a sentence of life imprisonment is mandatory on conviction of the capital felony, if the case was transferred to the court under Section 54.02, Family Code; or

(2) a sentence of life imprisonment without parole is mandatory on conviction of the capital felony.

Added by Acts 1973, 63rd Leg., p. 1124, ch. 426, art. 2, § 2, eff. Jan. 1, 1974. Amended by Acts 1991, 72nd Leg., ch. 652, § 12, eff. Sept. 1, 1991; Acts 1991, 72nd Leg., ch. 838, § 4, eff. Sept. 1, 1991; Acts 1993, 73rd Leg., ch. 900, § 1.01, eff. Sept. 1, 1994; Acts 2005, 79th Leg., ch. 787, § 1, eff. Sept. 1, 2005; Acts 2009, 81st Leg., ch. 87, § 25.145, eff. Sept. 1, 2009; Acts 2009, 81st Leg., ch. 765, § 1, eff. Sept. 1, 2009.

Section 3 of Acts 2009, 81st Leg., ch. 765 provides:

"The change in law made by this Act applies only to an offense committed on or after the effective date [Sept. 1, 2009] of this Act.

An offense committed before the effective date of this Act is covered by the law in effect when the offense was committed, and the former law is continued in effect for that purpose. For purposes of this section, an offense was committed before the effective date of this Act if any element of the offense occurred before that date."

§ 12.32. First Degree Felony Punishment

(a) An individual adjudged guilty of a felony of the first degree shall be punished by imprisonment in the Texas Department of Criminal Justice for life or for any term of not more than 99 years or less than 5 years.

(b) In addition to imprisonment, an individual adjudged guilty of a felony of the first degree may be punished by a fine not to exceed $10,000.

Acts 1973, 63rd Leg., p. 883, ch. 399, § 1, eff. Jan. 1, 1974. Renumbered from V.T.C.A., Penal Code § 12.31 by Acts 1973, 63rd Leg., p. 1124, ch. 426, art. 2, § 2, eff. Jan. 1, 1974. Amended by Acts 1979, 66th Leg., p. 1058, ch. 488, § 1, eff. Sept. 1, 1979; Acts 1993, 73rd Leg., ch. 900, § 1.01, eff. Sept. 1, 1994; Acts 2009, 81st, ch. 87, § 25.146, eff. Sept. 1, 2009.

§ 12.33. Second Degree Felony Punishment

(a) An individual adjudged guilty of a felony of the second degree shall be punished by imprisonment in the Texas Department of Criminal Justice for any term of not more than 20 years or less than 2 years.

(b) In addition to imprisonment, an individual adjudged guilty of a felony of the second degree may be punished by a fine not to exceed $10,000.

Acts 1973, 63rd Leg., p. 883, ch. 399, § 1, eff. Jan. 1, 1974. Renumbered from V.T.C.A., Penal Code § 12.32 by Acts 1973, 63rd Leg., p. 1124, ch. 426, art. 2, § 2, eff. Jan. 1, 1974. Amended by Acts 1993, 73rd Leg., ch. 900, § 1.01, eff. Sept. 1, 1994; Acts 2009, 81st Leg., ch. 87, § 25.147, eff. Sept. 1, 2009.

§ 12.34. Third Degree Felony Punishment

(a) An individual adjudged guilty of a felony of the third degree shall be punished by imprisonment in the Texas Department of Criminal Justice for any term of not more than 10 years or less than 2 years.

(b) In addition to imprisonment, an individual adjudged guilty of a felony of the third degree may be punished by a fine not to exceed $10,000.

Acts 1973, 63rd Leg., p. 883, ch. 399, § 1, eff. Jan. 1, 1974. Renumbered from V.T.C.A., Penal Code § 12.33 by Acts 1973, 63rd Leg., p. 1124, ch. 426, art. 2, § 2, eff. Jan. 1,1974. Amended by Acts 1989, 71st Leg., ch. 785, § 4.01, eff. Sept. 1, 1989; Acts 1990, 71st Leg., 6th C.S., ch. 25, § 7, eff. June 18, 1990; Acts 1993, 73rd Leg., ch. 900, § 1.01, eff. Sept. 1, 1994; Acts 2009, 81st Leg., ch. 87, § 25.148, eff. Sept. 1, 2009.

§ 12.35. State Jail Felony Punishment

(a) Except as provided by Subsection (c), an individual adjudged guilty of a state jail felony shall be punished by confinement in a state jail for any term of not more than two years or less than 180 days.

(b) In addition to confinement, an individual adjudged guilty of a state jail felony may be punished by a fine not to exceed $10,000.

(c) An individual adjudged guilty of a state jail felony shall be punished for a third degree felony if it is shown on the trial of the offense that:

(1) a deadly weapon as defined by Section 1.07 was used or exhibited during the commission of the offense or during immediate flight following the commission of the offense, and that the individual used or exhibited the deadly weapon or was a party to the offense and knew that a deadly weapon would be used or exhibited; or

(2) the individual has previously been finally convicted of any felony:

(A) under Section 21.02 or listed in Section 3g(a)(1), Article 42.12, Code of Criminal Procedure; or

(B) for which the judgment contains an affirmative finding under Section 3g(a)(2), Article 42.12, Code of Criminal Procedure.

Added by Acts 1993, 73rd Leg., ch. 900, § 1.01, eff. Sept. 1, 1994. Amended by Acts 2007, 80th Leg., ch. 593, § 3.48, eff. Sept. 1, 2007.

SUBCHAPTER D. EXCEPTIONAL SENTENCES

§ 12.41 Classification of Offenses Outside this Code

For purposes of this subchapter, any conviction not obtained from a prosecution under this code shall be classified as follows:

(1) "felony of the third degree" if imprisonment in the Texas Department of Criminal Justice or another penitentiary is affixed to the offense as a possible punishment;

(2) "Class B misdemeanor" if the offense is not a felony and confinement in a jail is affixed to the offense as a possible punishment;

(3) "Class C misdemeanor" if the offense is punishable by fine only.

Acts 1973, 63rd Leg., p. 883, ch. 399, § 1, eff. Jan. 1, 1974. Amended by Acts 1993, 73rd Leg., ch. 900, § 1.01, eff. Sept. 1, 1994; Acts 2009, 81st Leg., ch. 87, § 25.149, eff. Sept. 1, 2009.

§ 12.42. Penalties for Repeat and Habitual Felony Offenders

(a)(1) If it is shown on the trial of a state jail felony punishable under Section 12.35(a) that the defendant has previously been finally convicted of two state jail felonies, on conviction the defendant shall be punished for a third-degree felony.

(2) If it is shown on the trial of a state jail felony punishable under Section 12.35(a) that the defendant has previously been finally convicted of two felonies, and the second previous felony conviction is for an offense that occurred subsequent to the first previous conviction having become final, on conviction the defendant shall be punished for a second-degree felony.

(3) Except as provided by Subsection (c)(2), if it is shown on the trial of a state jail felony punishable under Section 12.35(c) or on the trial of a third-degree felony that the defendant has been once before convicted of a felony, on conviction he shall be punished for a second-degree felony.

(b) Except as provided by Subsection (c)(2), if it is shown on the trial of a second-degree felony that the defendant has been once before convicted of a felony, on conviction he shall be punished for a first-degree felony.

(c)(1) If it is shown on the trial of a first-degree felony that the defendant has been once before convicted of a felony, on conviction he shall be punished by imprisonment in the Texas Department of Criminal Justice for life, or for any term of not more than 99 years or less than 15 years. In addition to imprisonment, an individual may be punished by a fine not to exceed $10,000.

(2) Notwithstanding Subdivision (1), a defendant shall be punished by imprisonment in the Texas Department of Criminal Justice for life if:

(A) the defendant is convicted of an offense:

(i) under Section 21.11(a)(1), 22.021, or 22.011, Penal Code;

(ii) under Section 20.04(a)(4), Penal Code, if the defendant committed the offense with the intent to violate or abuse the victim sexually; or

(iii) under Section 30.02, Penal Code, punishable under Subsection (d) of that section, if the defendant committed the offense with the intent to commit a felony described by Subparagraph (i) or (ii) or a felony under Section 21.11, Penal Code; and

(B) the defendant has been previously convicted of an offense:

(i) under Section 43.25 or 43.26, Penal Code, or an offense under Section 43.23, Penal Code, punishable under Subsection (h) of that section;

(ii) under Section 21.02, 21.11, 22.011, 22.021, or 25.02, Penal Code;

(iii) under Section 20.04(a)(4), Penal Code, if the defendant committed the offense with the intent to violate or abuse the victim sexually;

(iv) under Section 30.02, Penal Code, punishable under Subsection (d) of that section, if the defendant committed the offense with the intent to commit a felony described by Subparagraph (ii) or (iii); or

(v) under the laws of another state containing elements that are substantially similar to the elements of an offense listed in Subparagraph (i), (ii), (iii), or (iv).

(3) Notwithstanding Subdivision (1) or (2), a defendant shall be punished for a capital felony if it is shown on the trial of an offense under Section 22.021 otherwise punishable under Subsection (f) of that section that the defendant has previously been finally convicted of:

(A) an offense under Section 22.021 that was committed against a victim described by Section 22.021(f)(1) or was committed against a victim described by Section 22.021(f)(2) and in a manner described by Section 22.021(a)(2)(A); or

(B) an offense that was committed under the laws of another state that:

(i) contains elements that are substantially similar to the elements of an offense under Section 22.021; and

(ii) was committed against a victim described by Section 22.021(f)(1) or was committed against a victim described by Section 22.021(f)(2) and in a manner substantially similar to a manner described by Section 22.021(a)(2)(A).

(4) Notwithstanding Subdivision (1) or (2), a defendant shall be punished by imprisonment in the Texas Department of Criminal Justice for life without parole if it is shown on the trial of an offense under Section 21.02 that the defendant has previously been finally convicted of:

(A) an offense under Section 21.02; or

(B) an offense that was committed under the laws of another state and that contains elements that are substantially similar to the elements of an offense under Section 21.02.

(d) Except as provided by Subsection (c)(2), if it is shown on the trial of a felony offense other than a state jail felony punishable under Section 12.35(a) that the defendant has previously been finally convicted of two felony offenses, and the second previous felony conviction is for an offense that occurred subsequent to the first previous conviction having become final, on conviction he shall be punished by imprisonment in the Texas Department of Criminal Justice for life, or for any term of not more than 99 years or less than 25 years.

(e) A previous conviction for a state jail felony punished under Section 12.35(a) may not be used for enhancement purposes under Subsection (b), (c), or (d).

(f) For the purposes of Subsections (a), (b), (c)(1), and (e), an adjudication by a juvenile court under Section 54.03, Family Code, that a child engaged in delinquent conduct on or after January 1, 1996, constituting a felony offense for which the child is committed to the Texas Youth Commission under Section 54.04(d)(2), (d)(3), or (m), Family Code, or Section 54.05(f), Family Code, is a final felony conviction.

(g) For the purposes of Subsection (c)(2):

(1) a defendant has been previously convicted of an offense listed under Subsection (c)(2)(B) if the defendant was adjudged guilty of the offense or entered a plea of guilty or nolo contendere in return for a grant of deferred adjudication, regardless of whether the sentence for the offense was ever imposed or whether the sentence was probated and the defendant was subsequently discharged from community supervision; and

(2) a conviction under the laws of another state for an offense containing elements that are substantially similar to the elements of an offense listed under Subsection (c)(2)(B) is a conviction of an offense listed under Subsection (c)(2)(B).

Acts 1973, 63rd Leg., p. 883, ch. 399, § 1, eff. Jan. 1, 1974. Amended by Acts 1983, 68th Leg., p. 1750, ch. 339, § 1, eff. Sept. 1, 1983; Acts 1985, 69th Leg., ch. 582, § 1, eff. Sept. 1, 1985; Acts 1993, 73rd Leg., ch. 900, § 1.01, eff. Sept. 1, 1994; Acts 1995, 74th Leg., ch. 250, § 1, eff. Sept. 1, 1995; Acts 1995, 74th Leg., ch. 262, § 78, eff. Jan. 1, 1996; Acts 1995, 74th Leg., ch. 318, § 1, eff. Jan. 1, 1996; Acts 1997, 75th Leg., ch. 665, §§ 1, 2, eff. Sept. 1, 1997; Acts 1997, 75th Leg., ch. 667, § 4, eff. Sept. 1, 1997; Acts 1999, 76th Leg., ch. 62, § 15.01, eff. Sept. 1, 1999; Acts 2003, 78th Leg., ch. 283, § 53, eff. Sept. 1, 2003; Acts 2003, 78th Leg., ch. 1005, § 2, eff. Sept. 1, 2003; Acts 2007, 80th Leg., ch. 340, §§ 1 to 4, eff. Sept. 1, 2007; Acts 2007, 80th Leg., ch. 593, §§ 1.14 to 1.16, eff. Sept. 1, 2007; Acts 2009, 81st Leg., ch. 87, § 25.150, eff. Sept. 1, 2009.

§ 12.422. Deleted by Acts 1993, 73rd Leg., ch. 900, § 1.01, eff. Sept. 1, 1993

§ 12.43. Penalties for Repeat and Habitual Misdemeanor Offenders

(a) If it is shown on the trial of a Class A misdemeanor that the defendant has been before convicted of a Class A misdemeanor or any degree of felony, on conviction he shall be punished by:

(1) a fine not to exceed $4,000;

(2) confinement in jail for any term of not more than one year or less than 90 days; or

(3) both such fine and confinement.

(b) If it is shown on the trial of a Class B misdemeanor that the defendant has been before convicted of a Class A or Class B misdemeanor or any degree of felony, on conviction he shall be punished by:

(1) a fine not to exceed $2,000;

(2) confinement in jail for any term of not more than 180 days or less than 30 days; or

(3) both such fine and confinement.

(c) If it is shown on the trial of an offense punishable as a Class C misdemeanor under Section 42.01 or 49.02 that the defendant has been before convicted under either of those sections three times or three times for any combination of those offenses and each prior offense was committed in the 24 months preceding the date of commission of the instant offense, the defendant shall be punished by:

(1) a fine not to exceed $2,000;

(2) confinement in jail for a term not to exceed 180 days; or

(3) both such fine and confinement.

(d) If the punishment scheme for an offense contains a specific enhancement provision increasing punishment for a defendant who has previously been convicted of the offense, the specific enhancement provision controls over this section.

Acts 1973, 63rd Leg., p. 883, ch. 399, § 1, eff. Jan. 1, 1974. Amended by Acts 1993, 73rd Leg., ch. 900, § 1.01, eff. Sept. 1, 1994; Acts 1995, 74th Leg., ch. 318, § 2, eff. Sept. 1, 1995; Acts 1999, 76th Leg., ch. 564, § 1, eff. Sept. 1, 1999.

§ 12.44. Reduction of State Jail Felony Punishment to Misdemeanor Punishment

(a) A court may punish a defendant who is convicted of a state jail felony by imposing the confinement permissible as punishment for a Class A misdemeanor if, after considering the gravity and circumstances of the felony committed and the history, character, and rehabilitative needs of the defendant, the court finds that such punishment would best serve the ends of justice.

(b) At the request of the prosecuting attorney, the court may authorize the prosecuting attorney to prosecute a state jail felony as a Class A misdemeanor.

Acts 1973, 63rd Leg., p. 883, ch. 399, § 1, eff. Jan. 1, 1974. Amended by Acts 1989, 71st Leg., ch. 785, § 4.02, eff. Sept. 1, 1989; Acts 1993, 73rd Leg., ch. 900, § 1.01, eff. Sept. 1, 1994; Acts 1995, 74th Leg., ch. 318, § 3, eff. Sept. 1, 1995; Acts 2005, 79th Leg., ch. 1276, § 1, eff. Sept. 1, 2005.

§ 12.45. Admission of Unadjudicated Offense

(a) A person may, with the consent of the attorney for the state, admit during the sentencing hearing his guilt of one or more unadjudicated offenses and request the court to take each into account in determining sentence for the offense or offenses of which he stands adjudged guilty.

(b) Before a court may take into account an admitted offense over which exclusive venue lies in another county or district, the court must obtain permission from the prosecuting attorney with jurisdiction over the offense.

(c) If a court lawfully takes into account an admitted offense, prosecution is barred for that offense.

Acts 1973, 63rd Leg., p. 883, ch. 399, § 1, eff. Jan. 1, 1974. Amended by Acts 1983, 68th Leg., p. 4131, ch. 649, § 1, eff. Aug. 29, 1983; Acts 1993, 73rd Leg., ch. 900, § 1.01, eff. Sept. 1, 1994.

§ 12.46. Use of Prior Convictions

The use of a conviction for enhancement purposes shall not preclude the subsequent use of such conviction for enhancement purposes.

Added by Acts 1979, 66th Leg., p. 1027, ch. 459, § 1, eff. June 7, 1979. Amended by Acts 1993, 73rd Leg., ch. 900, § 1.01, eff. Sept. 1, 1994.

§ 12.47. Penalty if Offense Committed Because of Bias or Prejudice

(a) If an affirmative finding under Article 42.014, Code of Criminal Procedure, is made in the trial of an offense other than a first degree felony or a Class A misdemeanor, the punishment for the offense is increased to the punishment prescribed for the next highest category of offense. If the offense is a Class A misdemeanor, the minimum term of confinement for the offense is increased to 180 days. This section does not apply to the trial of an offense of injury to a disabled individual under § 22.04, if the affirmative finding in the case under Article 42.014, Code of Criminal Procedure, shows that the defendant intentionally selected the victim because the victim was disabled.

(b) The attorney general, if requested to do so by a prosecuting attorney, may assist the prosecuting attorney in the investigation or prosecution of an offense committed because of bias or prejudice. The attorney general shall designate one individual in the division of the attorney general's office that assists in the prosecution of criminal cases to coordinate responses to requests made under this subsection.

Added by Acts 1993, 73rd Leg., ch. 987, § 1, eff. Sept. 1, 1993. Amended by Acts 1997, 75th Leg., ch. 751, § 1, eff. Sept. 1, 1997; Acts 2001, 77th Leg., ch. 85, § 1.01, eff. Sept. 1, 2001.

§ 12.48. Certain Offenses Resulting in Loss to Nursing and Convalescent Homes

If it is shown on the trial of an offense under Chapter 31 or 32 that, as a result of a loss incurred because of the conduct charged, a trustee was appointed and emergency assistance funds, other than funds used to pay the expenses of the trustee, were used for a nursing or convalescent home under Subchapter D, Chapter 242, Health and Safety Code,[1] the punishment for the offense is increased to the punishment prescribed for the next higher category of offense except that a felony of the first degree is punished as a felony of the first degree.

Added by Acts 1999, 76th Leg., ch. 439, § 4, eff. Sept. 1, 1999.

[1] V.T.C.A., Health and Safety Code § 242.091 et seq.

§ 12.49. Penalty if Controlled Substance Used to Commit Offense

If the court makes an affirmative finding under Article 42.012, Code of Criminal Procedure, in the punishment phase of the trial of an offense under Chapter 29, Chapter 31, or Title 5,[1] other than a first degree felony or a Class A misdemeanor, the punishment for the offense is increased to the punishment prescribed for the next highest category of offense. If the offense is a Class A misdemeanor, the minimum term of confinement for the offense is increased to 180 days.

Added by Acts 1999, 76th Leg., ch. 417, § 2(a), eff. Sept. 1, 1999. Renumbered from V.T.C.A., Penal Code § 12.48 and amended by Acts 2001, 77th Leg., ch. 1420, §§ 21.001(93), 21.002(15), eff. Sept. 1, 2001.

[1] V.T.C.A., Penal Code § 25.01 et seq.

§ 12.50. Penalty if Offense Committed in Disaster Area or Evacuated Area

(a) Subject to Subsection (c), the punishment for an offense described by Subsection (b) is increased to the punishment prescribed for the next higher category of offense if it is shown on the trial of the offense that the offense was committed in an area that was, at the time of the offense:

(1) subject to a declaration of a state of disaster made by:

(A) the president of the United States under the Robert T. Stafford Disaster Relief and Emergency Assistance Act (42 U.S.C. Section 5121 et seq.);

(B) the governor under Section 418.014, Government Code; or

(C) the presiding officer of the governing body of a political subdivision under Section 418.108, Government Code; or

(2) subject to an emergency evacuation order.

(b) The increase in punishment authorized by this section applies only to an offense under:

(1) Section 22.01;

(2) Section 29.02;

(3) Section 30.02; and

(4) Section 31.03.

(c) If an offense listed under Subsection (b)(1) or (4) is punishable as a Class A misdemeanor, the minimum term of confinement for the offense is increased to 180 days. If an offense listed under Subsection (b)(3) or (4) is punishable as a felony of the first degree, the punishment for that offense may not be increased under this section.

(d) It is a defense to a charge under Subsection (b)(4) that the conduct in question meets the elements of necessity outlined in Section 9.22.

(e) For purposes of this section, "emergency evacuation order" means an official statement issued by the governing body of this state or a political subdivision of this state to recommend or require the evacuation of all or part of the population of an area stricken or threatened with a disaster.

Added by Acts 2009, 81st Leg., ch. 731, § 1, eff. Sept. 1, 2009.

Section 2 of Acts 2009, 81st Leg., ch. 731 provides:

"The change in law made by this Act applies only to an offense committed on or after the effective date of this Act. An offense committed before the effective date of this Act is governed by the law in effect at the time the offense was committed, and the former law is continued in effect for that purpose. For purposes of this section, an offense was committed before the effective date of this Act if any element of the offense occurred before that date."

SUBCHAPTER E. CORPORATIONS AND ASSOCIATIONS

§ 12.51. Authorized Punishments for Corporations and Associations

(a) If a corporation or association is adjudged guilty of an offense that provides a penalty consisting of a fine only, a court may sentence the corporation or association to pay a fine in an amount fixed by the court, not to exceed the fine provided by the offense.

(b) If a corporation or association is adjudged guilty of an offense that provides a penalty including imprisonment, or that provides no specific penalty, a court may sentence the corporation or association to pay a fine in an amount fixed by the court, not to exceed:

(1) $20,000 if the offense is a felony of any category;

(2) $10,000 if the offense is a Class A or Class B misdemeanor;

(3) $2,000 if the offense is a Class C misdemeanor; or

(4) $50,000 if, as a result of an offense classified as a felony or Class A misdemeanor, an individual suffers serious bodily injury or death.

(c) In lieu of the fines authorized by Subsections (a), (b)(1), (b)(2), and (b)(4), if a court finds that the corporation or association gained money or property or caused personal injury or death, property damage, or other loss through the commission of a felony or Class A or Class B misdemeanor, the court may sentence the corporation or association to pay a fine in an amount fixed by the court, not to exceed double the amount gained or caused by the corporation or association to be lost or damaged, whichever is greater.

(d) In addition to any sentence that may be imposed by this section, a corporation or association that has been adjudged guilty of an offense may be ordered by the court to give notice of the conviction to any person the court deems appropriate.

(e) On conviction of a corporation or association, the court shall notify the attorney general of that fact.

Acts 1973, 63rd Leg., p. 883, ch. 399, § 1, eff. Jan. 1, 1974. Amended by Acts 1977, 65th Leg., p. 1917, ch. 768, § 1, eff. June 16, 1977; Acts 1987, 70th Leg., ch. 1085, § 1, eff. Sept. 1, 1987; Acts 1993, 73rd Leg., ch. 900, § 1.01, eff. Sept. 1, 1994.

TITLE 4. INCHOATE OFFENSES

CHAPTER 15. PREPARATORY OFFENSES

§ 15.01. Criminal Attempt

(a) A person commits an offense if, with specific intent to commit an offense, he does an act amounting to more than mere preparation that tends but fails to effect the commission of the offense intended.

(b) If a person attempts an offense that may be aggravated, his conduct constitutes an attempt to commit the aggravated offense if an element that aggravates the offense accompanies the attempt.

(c) It is no defense to prosecution for criminal attempt that the offense attempted was actually committed.

(d) An offense under this section is one category lower than the offense attempted, and if the offense attempted is a state jail felony, the offense is a Class A misdemeanor.

Acts 1973, 63rd Leg., p. 883, ch. 399, § 1, eff. Jan. 1, 1974. Amended by Acts 1975, 64th Leg., p. 478, ch. 203, § 4, eff. Sept. 1, 1975; Acts 1993, 73rd Leg., ch. 900, § 1.01, eff. Sept. 1, 1994.

§ 15.02. Criminal Conspiracy

(a) A person commits criminal conspiracy if, with intent that a felony be committed:

(1) he agrees with one or more persons that they or one or more of them engage in conduct that would constitute the offense; and

(2) he or one or more of them performs an overt act in pursuance of the agreement.

(b) An agreement constituting a conspiracy may be inferred from acts of the parties.

(c) It is no defense to prosecution for criminal conspiracy that:

(1) one or more of the coconspirators is not criminally responsible for the object offense;

(2) one or more of the coconspirators has been acquitted, so long as two or more coconspirators have not been acquitted;

(3) one or more of the coconspirators has not been prosecuted or convicted, has been convicted of a different offense, or is immune from prosecution;

(4) the actor belongs to a class of persons that by definition of the object offense is legally incapable of committing the object offense in an individual capacity; or

(5) the object offense was actually committed.

(d) An offense under this section is one category lower than the most serious felony that is the object of the conspiracy, and if the most serious felony that is the object of the conspiracy is a state jail felony, the offense is a Class A misdemeanor.

Acts 1973, 63rd Leg., p. 883, ch. 399, § 1, eff. Jan. 1, 1974. Amended by Acts 1993, 73rd Leg., ch. 900, § 1.01, eff. Sept. 1, 1994.

§ 15.03. Criminal Solicitation

(a) A person commits an offense if, with intent that a capital felony or felony of the first degree be committed, he requests, commands, or attempts to induce another to engage in specific conduct that, under the circumstances surrounding his conduct as the actor believes them to be, would constitute the felony or make the other a party to its commission.

(b) A person may not be convicted under this section on the uncorroborated testimony of the person allegedly solicited and unless the solicitation is made under circumstances strongly corroborative of both the solicitation itself and the actor's intent that the other person act on the solicitation.

(c) It is no defense to prosecution under this section that:

(1) the person solicited is not criminally responsible for the felony solicited;

(2) the person solicited has been acquitted, has not been prosecuted or convicted, has been convicted of a different offense or of a different type or class of offense, or is immune from prosecution;

(3) the actor belongs to a class of persons that by definition of the felony solicited is legally incapable of committing the offense in an individual capacity; or

(4) the felony solicited was actually committed.

(d) An offense under this section is:

(1) a felony of the first degree if the offense solicited is a capital offense; or

(2) a felony of the second degree if the offense solicited is a felony of the first degree.

Acts 1973, 63rd Leg., p. 883, ch. 399, § 1, eff. Jan. 1, 1974. Amended by Acts 1993, 73rd Leg., ch. 462, § 1, eff. Sept. 1, 1993; Acts 1993, 73rd Leg., ch. 900, § 1.01, eff. Sept. 1, 1994.

§ 15.031. Criminal Solicitation of a Minor

(a) A person commits an offense if, with intent that an offense listed by Section 3g(a)(1), Article 42.12, Code of Criminal Procedure, be committed, the person requests, commands, or attempts to induce a minor to engage in specific conduct that, under the circumstances surrounding the actor's conduct as the actor believes them to be, would constitute an offense listed by Section 3g(a)(1), Article 42.12, or make the minor a party to the commission of an offense listed by Section 3g(a)(1), Article 42.12.

(b) A person commits an offense if, with intent that an offense under Section 21.02, 21.11, 22.011, 22.021, or 43.25 be committed, the person by any means requests, commands, or attempts to induce a minor or another whom the person believes to be a minor to engage in specific conduct that, under the circumstances surrounding the actor's conduct as the actor believes them to be, would constitute an offense under one of those sections or would make the minor or other believed by the person to be a minor a party to the commission of an offense under one of those sections.

(c) A person may not be convicted under this section on the uncorroborated testimony of the minor allegedly solicited unless the solicitation is made under circumstances strongly corroborative of both the solicitation itself and the actor's intent that the minor act on the solicitation.

(d) It is no defense to prosecution under this section that:

(1) the minor solicited is not criminally responsible for the offense solicited;

(2) the minor solicited has been acquitted, has not been prosecuted or convicted, has been convicted of a different offense or of a different type or class of offense, or is immune from prosecution;

(3) the actor belongs to a class of persons that by definition of the offense solicited is legally incapable of committing the offense in an individual capacity; or

(4) the offense solicited was actually committed.

(e) An offense under this section is one category lower than the solicited offense, except that an offense under this section is the same category as the solicited offense if it is shown on the trial of the offense that the actor:

(1) was at the time of the offense 17 years of age or older and a member of a criminal street gang, as defined by Section 71.01; and

(2) committed the offense with the intent to:

(A) further the criminal activities of the criminal street gang; or

(B) avoid detection as a member of a criminal street gang.

(f) In this section, "minor" means an individual younger than 17 years of age.

Added by Acts 1995, 74th Leg., ch. 262, § 79, eff. Jan. 1, 1996. Amended by Acts 1999, 76th Leg., ch. 1415, § 22(a), eff. Sept. 1, 1999; Acts 2007, 80th Leg., ch. 593, § 3.49, eff. Sept. 1, 2007; Acts 2009, 81st Leg., ch. 1130, § 2, eff. Sept. 1, 2009.

Section 9 of Acts 2009, 81st Leg., ch. 1130 provides:

"Section 15.031(e) and Section 71.02(a), Penal Code, as amended by this Act, and Section 71.028, Penal Code, as added by this Act, apply only to an offense committed on or after the effective date [Sept. 1, 2009] of this Act. An offense committed before the effective date of this Act is covered by the law in effect when the offense was committed, and the former law is continued in effect for that purpose. For purposes of this section, an offense was committed before the effective date of this Act if any element of the offense occurred before that date."

§ 15.04. Renunciation Defense

(a) It is an affirmative defense to prosecution under Section 15.01 that under circumstances manifesting a voluntary and complete renunciation of his criminal objective the actor avoided commission of the offense attempted by abandoning his criminal conduct or, if abandonment was insufficient to avoid commission of the offense, by taking further affirmative action that prevented the commission.

(b) It is an affirmative defense to prosecution under Section 15.02 or 15.03 that under circumstances manifesting a voluntary and complete renunciation of his criminal objective the actor countermanded his solicitation or withdrew from the conspiracy before commission of the object offense and took further affirmative action that prevented the commission of the object offense.

(c) Renunciation is not voluntary if it is motivated in whole or in part:

(1) by circumstances not present or apparent at the inception of the actor's course of conduct that

increase the probability of detection or apprehension or that make more difficult the accomplishment of the objective; or

(2) by a decision to postpone the criminal conduct until another time or to transfer the criminal act to another but similar objective or victim.

(d) Evidence that the defendant renounced his criminal objective by abandoning his criminal conduct, countermanding his solicitation, or withdrawing from the conspiracy before the criminal offense was committed and made substantial effort to prevent the commission of the object offense shall be admissible as mitigation at the hearing on punishment if he has been found guilty of criminal attempt, criminal solicitation, or criminal conspiracy; and in the event of a finding of renunciation under this subsection, the punishment shall be one grade lower than that provided for the offense committed.

Acts 1973, 63rd Leg., p. 883, ch. 399, § 1, eff. Jan. 1, 1974. Amended by Acts 1993, 73rd Leg., ch. 900, § 1.01, eff. Sept. 1, 1994.

§ 15.05. No Offense

Attempt or conspiracy to commit, or solicitation of, a preparatory offense defined in this chapter is not an offense.

Acts 1973, 63rd Leg., p. 883, ch. 399, § 1, eff. Jan. 1, 1974. Amended by Acts 1993, 73rd Leg., ch. 900, § 1.01, eff. Sept. 1, 1994.

CHAPTER 16. CRIMINAL INSTRUMENTS, INTERCEPTION OF WIRE OR ORAL COMMUNICATION, AND INSTALLATION OF TRACKING DEVICE

Section

§ 16.01. Unlawful Use of Criminal Instrument

(a) A person commits an offense if:

(1) he possesses a criminal instrument with intent to use it in the commission of an offense; or

(2) with knowledge of its character and with intent to use or aid or permit another to use in the commission of an offense, he manufactures, adapts, sells, installs, or sets up a criminal instrument.

(b) For the purpose of this section, "criminal instrument" means anything, the possession, manufacture, or sale of which is not otherwise an offense, that is specially designed, made, or adapted for use in the commission of an offense.

(c) An offense under Subsection (a)(1) is one category lower than the offense intended. An offense under Subsection (a)(2) is a state jail felony.

Acts 1973, 63rd Leg., p. 883, ch. 399, § 1, eff. Jan. 1, 1974. Amended by Acts 1975, 64th Leg., p. 913, ch. 342, § 7, eff. Sept. 1, 1975; Acts 1993, 73rd Leg., ch. 900, § 1.01, eff. Sept. 1, 1994.

§ 16.02. Unlawful Interception, Use, or Disclosure of Wire, Oral, or Electronic Communications

(a) In this section, "computer trespasser," "covert entry," "communication common carrier," "contents," "electronic communication," "electronic, mechanical, or other device," "immediate life-threatening situation," "intercept," "investigative or law enforcement officer," "member of a law enforcement unit specially trained to respond to and deal with life-threatening situations," "oral communication," "protected computer," "readily accessible to the general public," and "wire communication" have the meanings given those terms in Article 18.20, Code of Criminal Procedure.

(b) A person commits an offense if the person:

(1) intentionally intercepts, endeavors to intercept, or procures another person to intercept or endeavor to intercept a wire, oral, or electronic communication;

(2) intentionally discloses or endeavors to disclose to another person the contents of a wire, oral, or electronic communication if the person knows or has reason to know the information was obtained through the interception of a wire, oral, or electronic communication in violation of this subsection;

(3) intentionally uses or endeavors to use the contents of a wire, oral, or electronic communication if the person knows or is reckless about whether the information was obtained through the interception of a wire, oral, or electronic communication in violation of this subsection;

(4) knowingly or intentionally effects a covert entry for the purpose of intercepting wire, oral, or electronic communications without court order or authorization; or

(5) intentionally uses, endeavors to use, or procures any other person to use or endeavor to use any electronic, mechanical, or other device to intercept any oral communication when the device:

(A) is affixed to, or otherwise transmits a signal through a wire, cable, or other connection used in wire communications; or

(B) transmits communications by radio or interferes with the transmission of communications by radio.

(c) It is an affirmative defense to prosecution under Subsection (b) that:

(1) an operator of a switchboard or an officer, employee, or agent of a communication common carrier whose facilities are used in the transmission of a wire or electronic communication intercepts a communication or discloses or uses an intercepted communication in the normal course of employment while engaged in an activity that is a necessary incident to the rendition of service or to the protection of the rights or property of the carrier of the communication, unless the interception results from the communication common carrier's use of service observing or random monitoring for purposes other than mechanical or service quality control checks;

(2) an officer, employee, or agent of a communication common carrier provides information, facilities, or technical assistance to an investigative or law enforcement officer who is authorized as provided by this section to intercept a wire, oral, or electronic communication;

(3) a person acting under color of law intercepts:

(A) a wire, oral, or electronic communication, if the person is a party to the communication or if one of the parties to the communication has given prior consent to the interception;

(B) a wire, oral, or electronic communication, if the person is acting under the authority of Article 18.20, Code of Criminal Procedure; or

(C) a wire or electronic communication made by a computer trespasser and transmitted to, through, or from a protected computer, if:

(i) the interception did not acquire a communication other than one transmitted to or from the computer trespasser;

(ii) the owner of the protected computer consented to the interception of the computer trespasser's communications on the protected computer; and

(iii) actor was lawfully engaged in an ongoing criminal investigation and the actor had reasonable suspicion to believe that the contents of the computer trespasser's communications likely to be obtained would be material to the investigation;

(4) a person not acting under color of law intercepts a wire, oral, or electronic communication, if:

(A) the person is a party to the communication; or

(B) one of the parties to the communication has given prior consent to the interception, unless the communication is intercepted for the purpose of committing an unlawful act;

(5) a person acting under color of law intercepts a wire, oral, or electronic communication if:

(A) oral or written consent for the interception is given by a magistrate before the interception;

(B) an immediate life-threatening situation exists;

(C) the person is a member of a law enforcement unit specially trained to:

(i) respond to and deal with life-threatening situations; or

(ii) install electronic, mechanical, or other devices; and

(D) the interception ceases immediately on termination of the life-threatening situation;

(6) an officer, employee, or agent of the Federal Communications Commission intercepts a communication transmitted by radio or discloses or uses an intercepted communication in the normal course of employment and in the discharge of the monitoring responsibilities exercised by the Federal Communications Commission in the enforcement of Chapter 5, Title 47, United States Code; [1]

(7) a person intercepts or obtains access to an electronic communication that was made through an electronic communication system that is configured to permit the communication to be readily accessible to the general public;

(8) a person intercepts radio communication, other than a cordless telephone communication that is transmitted between a cordless telephone handset and a base unit, that is transmitted:

(A) by a station for the use of the general public;

(B) to ships, aircraft, vehicles, or persons in distress;

(C) by a governmental, law enforcement, civil defense, private land mobile, or public safety communications system that is readily accessible to the general public, unless the radio communication is transmitted by a law enforcement representative to or from a mobile data terminal;

(D) by a station operating on an authorized frequency within the bands allocated to the amateur, citizens band, or general mobile radio services; or

(E) by a marine or aeronautical communications system;

(9) a person intercepts a wire or electronic communication the transmission of which causes harmful interference to a lawfully operating station or consumer electronic equipment, to the extent necessary to identify the source of the interference;

(10) a user of the same frequency intercepts a radio communication made through a system that uses frequencies monitored by individuals engaged in the provision or the use of the system, if the communication is not scrambled or encrypted; or

(11) a provider of electronic communications service records the fact that a wire or electronic communication was initiated or completed in order to protect the provider, another provider furnishing service towards the completion of the communication, or a user of that service from fraudulent, unlawful, or abusive use of the service.

(d) A person commits an offense if the person:

(1) intentionally manufactures, assembles, possesses, or sells an electronic, mechanical, or other device knowing or having reason to know that the device is designed primarily for nonconsensual interception of wire, electronic, or oral communications and that the device or a component of the device has been or will be used for an unlawful purpose; or

(2) places in a newspaper, magazine, handbill, or other publication an advertisement of an electronic, mechanical, or other device:

(A) knowing or having reason to know that the device is designed primarily for nonconsensual interception of wire, electronic, or oral communications;

(B) promoting the use of the device for the purpose of nonconsensual interception of wire, electronic, or oral communications; or

(C) knowing or having reason to know that the advertisement will promote the use of the device for the purpose of nonconsensual interception of wire, electronic, or oral communications.

(e) It is an affirmative defense to prosecution under Subsection (d) that the manufacture, assembly, possession, or sale of an electronic, mechanical, or other device that is designed primarily for the purpose of nonconsensual interception of wire, electronic, or oral communication is by:

(1) a communication common carrier or a provider of wire or electronic communications service or an officer, agent, or employee of or a person under contract with a communication common carrier or provider acting in the normal course of the provider's or communication carrier's business;

(2) an officer, agent, or employee of a person under contract with, bidding on contracts with, or doing business with the United States or this state acting in the normal course of the activities of the United States or this state;

(3) a member of the Department of Public Safety who is specifically trained to install wire, oral, or electronic communications intercept equipment; or

(4) a member of a local law enforcement agency that has an established unit specifically designated to respond to and deal with life-threatening situations.

(e–1) It is a defense to prosecution under Subsection (d)(1) that the electronic, mechanical, or other device is possessed by a person authorized to possess the device under Section 500.008, Government Code, or Section 61.0455, Human Resources Code.

(f) An offense under this section is a felony of the second degree, unless the offense is committed under Subsection (d) or (g), in which event the offense is a state jail felony.

(g) A person commits an offense if, knowing that a government attorney or an investigative or law enforcement officer has been authorized or has applied for authorization to intercept wire, electronic, or oral communications, the person obstructs, impedes, prevents, gives notice to another of, or attempts to give notice to another of the interception.

(h) Repealed by Acts 2005, 79th Leg., ch. 889, § 1.

Added by Acts 1981, 67th Leg., p. 738, ch. 275, § 2, eff. Aug. 31, 1981. Amended by Acts 1983, 68th Leg., p. 4878, ch. 864, §§ 1 to 3, eff. June 19, 1983; Acts 1989, 71st Leg., ch. 1166, § 16, eff. Sept. 1, 1989; Acts 1993, 73rd Leg., ch. 790, § 16, eff. Sept. 1, 1993; Acts 1993, 73rd Leg., ch. 900, § 1.01, eff. Sept. 1, 1994; Acts 1997, 75th Leg., ch. 1051, § 9, eff. Sept. 1, 1997; Acts 2001, 77th Leg., ch. 1270, § 11, eff. Sept. 1, 2001; Acts 2003, 78th Leg., ch. 678, § 1, eff. Sept. 1, 2003; Acts 2005, 79th Leg., ch. 889, § 1, eff. June 17, 2005; Acts 2009, 81st Leg., ch. 1169, § 9, eff. Sept. 1, 2009.

[1] 47 U.S.C.A. § 151.

Section 10 of Acts 2009, 81st Leg., ch. 1169 provides:

"The changes in law made by this Act with respect to Sections 16.02 and 38.11, Penal Code, apply only to an offense committed on or after the effective date [Sept. 1, 2009] of this Act. An offense committed before the effective date of this Act is governed by the law in effect when the offense was committed, and the former law is continued in effect for that purpose. For purposes of this section, an offense was committed before the effective date of this Act if any element of the offense occurred before that date."

§ 16.021. Deleted by Acts 1993, 73rd Leg., ch. 900, § 1.01, eff. Sept. 1, 1994

§ 16.03. Unlawful Use of Pen Register or Trap and Trace Device

(a) A person commits an offense if the person knowingly installs or uses a pen register or trap and trace device to record or decode electronic or other impulses for the purpose of identifying telephone numbers dialed or otherwise transmitted on a telephone line.

(b) In this section, "authorized peace officer," "communications common carrier," "pen register," and "trap and trace device" have the meanings assigned by Article 18.21, Code of Criminal Procedure.

(c) It is an affirmative defense to prosecution under Subsection (a) that the actor is:

(1) an officer, employee, or agent of a communications common carrier and the actor installs or uses a device or equipment to record a number dialed from or to a telephone instrument in the normal course of business of the carrier for purposes of:

(A) protecting property or services provided by the carrier; or

(B) assisting another who the actor reasonably believes to be a peace officer authorized to install or use a pen register or trap and trace device under Article 18.21, Code of Criminal Procedure;

(2) an officer, employee, or agent of a lawful enterprise and the actor installs or uses a device or equipment while engaged in an activity that:

(A) is a necessary incident to the rendition of service or to the protection of property of or services provided by the enterprise; and

(B) is not made for the purpose of gathering information for a law enforcement agency or private investigative agency, other than information related to the theft of communication or information services provided by the enterprise; or

(3) a person authorized to install or use a pen register or trap and trace device under Article 18.21, Code of Criminal Procedure.

(d) An offense under this section is a state jail felony.

Added by Acts 1985, 69th Leg., ch. 587, § 6, eff. Aug. 26, 1985. Amended by Acts 1989, 71st Leg., ch. 958, § 2, eff. Sept. 1, 1989; Acts 1993, 73rd Leg., ch. 900, § 1.01, eff. Sept. 1, 1994; Acts 1997, 75th Leg., ch. 1051, § 10, eff. Sept. 1, 1997.

§ 16.04. Unlawful Access to Stored Communications

(a) In this section, "electronic communication," "electronic storage," "user," and "wire communication" have the meanings assigned to those terms in Article 18.21, Code of Criminal Procedure.

(b) A person commits an offense if the person obtains, alters, or prevents authorized access to a wire or electronic communication while the communication is in electronic storage by:

(1) intentionally obtaining access without authorization to a facility through which a wire or electronic communications service is provided; or

(2) intentionally exceeding an authorization for access to a facility through which a wire or electronic communications service is provided.

(c) Except as provided by Subsection (d), an offense under Subsection (b) is a Class A misdemeanor.

(d) If committed to obtain a benefit or to harm another, an offense is a state jail felony.

(e) It is an affirmative defense to prosecution under Subsection (b) that the conduct was authorized by:

(1) the provider of the wire or electronic communications service;

(2) the user of the wire or electronic communications service;

(3) the addressee or intended recipient of the wire or electronic communication; or

(4) Article 18.21, Code of Criminal Procedure.

Added by Acts 1989, 71st Leg., ch. 958, § 3, eff. Sept. 1, 1989. Amended by Acts 1993, 73rd Leg., ch. 900, § 1.01, eff. Sept. 1, 1994; Acts 1997, 75th Leg., ch. 1051, § 11, eff. Sept. 1, 1997.

§ 16.05. Illegal Divulgence of Public Communications

(a) In this section, "electronic communication," "electronic communications service," and "electronic communications system" have the meanings given those terms in Article 18.20, Code of Criminal Procedure.

(b) A person who provides electronic communications service to the public commits an offense if the person knowingly divulges the contents of a communication to another who is not the intended recipient of the communication.

(c) It is an affirmative defense to prosecution under Subsection (b) that the actor divulged the contents of the communication:

(1) as authorized by federal or state law;

(2) to a person employed, authorized, or whose facilities are used to forward the communication to the communication's destination; or

(3) to a law enforcement agency if the contents reasonably appear to pertain to the commission of a crime.

(d) Except as provided by Subsection (e), an offense under Subsection (b) that involves a scrambled or encrypted radio communication is a state jail felony.

(e) If committed for a tortious or illegal purpose or to gain a benefit, an offense under Subsection (b) that involves a radio communication that is not scrambled or encrypted:

(1) is a Class A misdemeanor if the communication is not a public land mobile radio service communication or a paging service communication; or

(2) is a Class C misdemeanor if the communication is a public land mobile radio service communication or a paging service communication.

(f) Repealed by Acts 1997, 75th Leg., ch. 1051, § 13, eff. Sept. 1, 1997.

Added by Acts 1989, 71st Leg., ch. 1166, § 17, eff. Sept. 1, 1989. Renumbered from V.T.C.A., Penal Code § 16.04 by Acts 1990, 71st Leg., 6th C.S., ch. 12, § 2(24), eff. Sept. 6, 1990. Amended by Acts 1993, 73rd Leg., ch. 900, § 1.01, eff. Sept. 1, 1994; Acts 1997, 75th Leg., ch. 1051, §§ 12, 13, eff. Sept. 1, 1997.

§ 16.06. Unlawful Installation of Tracking Device

(a) In this section:

(1) "Electronic or mechanical tracking device" means a device capable of emitting an electronic frequency or other signal that may be used by a person to identify, monitor, or record the location of another person or object.

(2) "Motor vehicle" has the meaning assigned by Section 501.002, Transportation Code.

(b) A person commits an offense if the person knowingly installs an electronic or mechanical tracking device on a motor vehicle owned or leased by another person.

(c) An offense under this section is a Class A misdemeanor.

(d) It is an affirmative defense to prosecution under this section that the person:

(1) obtained the effective consent of the owner or lessee of the motor vehicle before the electronic or mechanical tracking device was installed;

(2) assisted another whom the person reasonably believed to be a peace officer authorized to install the device in the course of a criminal investigation or pursuant to an order of a court to gather information for a law enforcement agency; or

(3) was a private investigator licensed under Chapter 1702, Occupations Code, who installed the device:

(A) with written consent:

(i) to install the device given by the owner or lessee of the motor vehicle; and

(ii) to enter private residential property, if that entry was necessary to install the device, given by the owner or lessee of the property; or

(B) pursuant to an order of or other authorization from a court to gather information.

(e) This section does not apply to a peace officer who installed the device in the course of a criminal investigation or pursuant to an order of a court to gather information for a law enforcement agency.

Added by Acts 1999, 76th Leg., ch. 728, § 1, eff. Sept. 1, 1999. Amended by Acts 2001, 77th Leg., ch. 1420, § 14.828, eff. Sept. 1, 2001; Acts 2009, 81st Leg., ch. 1122, § 1, eff. Sept. 1, 2009.

Section 2 of Acts 2009, 81st Leg., ch. 1122 provides:

"The change in law made by this Act applies only to an offense committed on or after the effective date [Sept. 1, 2009] of this Act. An offense committed before the effective date of this Act is governed by the law in effect at the time the offense was committed, and the former law is continued in effect for that purpose. For purposes of this section, an offense was committed before the effective date of this Act if any element of the offense occurred before that date."

TITLE 5. OFFENSES AGAINST THE PERSON

CHAPTER 19. CRIMINAL HOMICIDE

Section

§ 19.01. Types of Criminal Homicide

(a) A person commits criminal homicide if he intentionally, knowingly, recklessly, or with criminal negligence causes the death of an individual.

(b) Criminal homicide is murder, capital murder, manslaughter, or criminally negligent homicide.

Acts 1973, 63rd Leg., p. 883, ch. 399, § 1, eff. Jan. 1, 1974. Amended by Acts 1973, 63rd Leg., p. 1123, ch. 426, art. 2, § 1, eff. Jan. 1, 1974; Acts 1993, 73rd Leg., ch. 900, § 1.01, eff. Sept. 1, 1994.

§ 19.02. Murder

(a) In this section:

(1) "Adequate cause" means cause that would commonly produce a degree of anger, rage, resentment, or terror in a person of ordinary temper, sufficient to render the mind incapable of cool reflection.

(2) "Sudden passion" means passion directly caused by and arising out of provocation by the individual killed or another acting with the person killed which passion arises at the time of the offense and is not solely the result of former provocation.

(b) A person commits an offense if he:

(1) intentionally or knowingly causes the death of an individual;

(2) intends to cause serious bodily injury and commits an act clearly dangerous to human life that causes the death of an individual; or

(3) commits or attempts to commit a felony, other than manslaughter, and in the course of and in furtherance of the commission or attempt, or in immediate flight from the commission or attempt, he commits or attempts to commit an act clearly dangerous to human life that causes the death of an individual.

(c) Except as provided by Subsection (d), an offense under this section is a felony of the first degree.

(d) At the punishment stage of a trial, the defendant may raise the issue as to whether he caused the death under the immediate influence of sudden passion arising from an adequate cause. If the defendant proves the issue in the affirmative by a preponderance of the evidence, the offense is a felony of the second degree.

Acts 1973, 63rd Leg., p. 883, ch. 399, § 1, eff. Jan. 1, 1974. Amended by Acts 1973, 63rd Leg., p. 1123, ch. 426, art. 2, § 1, eff. Jan. 1, 1974; Acts 1993, 73rd Leg., ch. 900, § 1.01, eff. Sept. 1, 1994.

§ 19.03. Capital Murder

(a) A person commits an offense if the person commits murder as defined under Section 19.02(b)(1) and:

(1) the person murders a peace officer or fireman who is acting in the lawful discharge of an official duty and who the person knows is a peace officer or fireman;

(2) the person intentionally commits the murder in the course of committing or attempting to commit kidnapping, burglary, robbery, aggravated sexual assault, arson, obstruction or retaliation, or terroristic threat under Section 22.07(a)(1), (3), (4), (5), or (6);

(3) the person commits the murder for remuneration or the promise of remuneration or employs another to commit the murder for remuneration or the promise of remuneration;

(4) the person commits the murder while escaping or attempting to escape from a penal institution;

(5) the person, while incarcerated in a penal institution, murders another:

(A) who is employed in the operation of the penal institution; or

(B) with the intent to establish, maintain, or participate in a combination or in the profits of a combination;

(6) the person:

(A) while incarcerated for an offense under this section or Section 19.02, murders another; or

(B) while serving a sentence of life imprisonment or a term of 99 years for an offense under Section 20.04, 22.021, or 29.03, murders another;

(7) the person murders more than one person:

(A) during the same criminal transaction; or

(B) during different criminal transactions but the murders are committed pursuant to the same scheme or course of conduct;

(8) the person murders an individual under six years of age; or

(9) the person murders another person in retaliation for or on account of the service or status of the other person as a judge or justice of the supreme

court, the court of criminal appeals, a court of appeals, a district court, a criminal district court, a constitutional county court, a statutory county court, a justice court, or a municipal court.

(b) An offense under this section is a capital felony.

(c) If the jury or, when authorized by law, the judge does not find beyond a reasonable doubt that the defendant is guilty of an offense under this section, he may be convicted of murder or of any other lesser included offense.

Added by Acts 1973, 63rd Leg., p. 1123, ch. 426, art. 2, § 1, eff. Jan. 1, 1974. Amended by Acts 1983, 68th Leg., p. 5317, ch. 977, § 6, eff. Sept. 1, 1983; Acts 1985, 69th Leg., ch. 44, § 1, eff. Sept. 1, 1985; Acts 1991, 72nd Leg., ch. 652, § 13, eff. Sept. 1, 1991; Acts 1993, 73rd Leg., ch. 715, § 1, eff. Sept. 1, 1993; Acts 1993, 73rd Leg., ch. 887, § 1, eff. Sept. 1, 1993; Acts 1993, 73rd Leg., ch. 900, § 1.01, eff. Sept. 1, 1994; Acts 2003, 78th Leg., ch. 388, § 1, eff. Sept. 1, 2003; Acts 2005, 79th Leg., ch. 428, § 1, eff. Sept. 1, 2005.

§ 19.04. Manslaughter

(a) A person commits an offense if he recklessly causes the death of an individual.

(b) An offense under this section is a felony of the second degree.

Acts 1973, 63rd Leg., p. 883, ch. 399, § 1, eff. Jan. 1, 1974. Renumbered from V.T.C.A., Penal Code § 19.04 by Acts 1973, 63rd Leg., p. 1123, ch. 426, art. 2, § 1, eff. Jan. 1, 1974. Amended by Acts 1987, 70th Leg., ch. 307, § 1, eff. Sept. 1, 1987. Renumbered from V.T.C.A., Penal Code § 19.05 and amended by Acts 1993, 73rd Leg., ch. 900, § 1.01, eff. Sept. 1, 1994.

§ 19.05. Criminally Negligent Homicide

(a) A person commits an offense if he causes the death of an individual by criminal negligence.

(b) An offense under this section is a state jail felony.

Acts 1973, 63rd Leg., p. 883, ch. 399, § 1, eff. Jan. 1, 1974. Renumbered from V.T.C.A., Penal Code § 19.06 by Acts 1973, 63rd Leg., p. 1123, ch. 426, art. 2, § 1, eff. Jan. 1, 1974. Renumbered from V.T.C.A., Penal Code § 19.07 and amended by Acts 1993, 73rd Leg., ch. 900, § 1.01, eff. Sept. 1, 1994.

§ 19.06. Applicability to Certain Conduct

This chapter does not apply to the death of an unborn child if the conduct charged is:

(1) conduct committed by the mother of the unborn child;

(2) a lawful medical procedure performed by a physician or other licensed health care provider with the requisite consent, if the death of the unborn child was the intended result of the procedure;

(3) a lawful medical procedure performed by a physician or other licensed health care provider with the requisite consent as part of an assisted reproduction as defined by Section 160.102, Family Code; or

(4) the dispensation of a drug in accordance with law or administration of a drug prescribed in accordance with law.

Added by Acts 2003, 78th Leg., ch. 822, § 2.02, eff. Sept. 1, 2003.

§ 19.07. Renumbered as V.T.C.A., Penal Code § 19.05 by Acts 1993, 73rd Leg., ch. 900, § 1.01, eff. Sept. 1, 1994

CHAPTER 20. KIDNAPPING AND UNLAWFUL RESTRAINT

Section

§ 20.01. Definitions

In this chapter:

(1) "Restrain" means to restrict a person's movements without consent, so as to interfere substantially with the person's liberty, by moving the person from one place to another or by confining the person. Restraint is "without consent" if it is accomplished by:

(A) force, intimidation, or deception; or

(B) any means, including acquiescence of the victim, if:

(i) the victim is a child who is less than 14 years of age or an incompetent person and the parent, guardian, or person or institution acting in loco parentis has not acquiesced in the movement or confinement; or

(ii) the victim is a child who is 14 years of age or older and younger than 17 years of age, the victim is taken outside of the state and outside a 120-mile radius from the victim's residence, and the parent, guardian, or person or institution acting in loco parentis has not acquiesced in the movement.

(2) "Abduct" means to restrain a person with intent to prevent his liberation by:

(A) secreting or holding him in a place where he is not likely to be found; or

(B) using or threatening to use deadly force.

(3) "Relative" means a parent or stepparent, ancestor, sibling, or uncle or aunt, including an adoptive relative of the same degree through marriage or adoption.

(4) "Person" means an individual, corporation, or association.

(5) Notwithstanding Section 1.07, "individual" means a human being who has been born and is alive.

Acts 1973, 63rd Leg., p. 883, ch. 399, § 1, eff. Jan. 1, 1974. Amended by Acts 1993, 73rd Leg., ch. 900, § 1.01, eff. Sept. 1, 1994; Acts 1999, 76th Leg., ch. 790, § 1, eff. Sept. 1, 1999; Acts 2003, 78th Leg., ch. 822, § 2.03, eff. Sept. 1, 2003.

§ 20.02. Unlawful Restraint

(a) A person commits an offense if he intentionally or knowingly restrains another person.

(b) It is an affirmative defense to prosecution under this section that:

(1) the person restrained was a child younger than 14 years of age;

(2) the actor was a relative of the child; and

(3) the actor's sole intent was to assume lawful control of the child.

(c) An offense under this section is a Class A misdemeanor, except that the offense is:

(1) a state jail felony if the person restrained was a child younger than 17 years of age; or

(2) a felony of the third degree if:

(A) the actor recklessly exposes the victim to a substantial risk of serious bodily injury;

(B) the actor restrains an individual the actor knows is a public servant while the public servant is lawfully discharging an official duty or in retaliation or on account of an exercise of official power or performance of an official duty as a public servant; or

(C) the actor while in custody restrains any other person.

(d) It is no offense to detain or move another under this section when it is for the purpose of effecting a lawful arrest or detaining an individual lawfully arrested.

(e) It is an affirmative defense to prosecution under this section that:

(1) the person restrained was a child who is 14 years of age or older and younger than 17 years of age;

(2) the actor does not restrain the child by force, intimidation, or deception; and

(3) the actor is not more than three years older than the child.

Acts 1973, 63rd Leg., p. 883, ch. 399, § 1, eff. Jan. 1, 1974. Amended by Acts 1993, 73rd Leg., ch. 900, § 1.01, eff. Sept. 1, 1994; Acts 1997, 75th Leg., ch. 707, §§ 1(b), 2, eff. Sept. 1, 1997; Acts 1999, 76th Leg., ch. 790, § 2, eff. Sept. 1, 1999; Acts 2001, 77th Leg., ch. 524, § 1, eff. Sept. 1, 2001.

§ 20.03. Kidnapping

(a) A person commits an offense if he intentionally or knowingly abducts another person.

(b) It is an affirmative defense to prosecution under this section that:

(1) the abduction was not coupled with intent to use or to threaten to use deadly force;

(2) the actor was a relative of the person abducted; and

(3) the actor's sole intent was to assume lawful control of the victim.

(c) An offense under this section is a felony of the third degree.

Acts 1973, 63rd Leg., p. 883, ch. 399, § 1, eff. Jan. 1, 1974. Amended by Acts 1993, 73rd Leg., ch. 900, § 1.01, eff. Sept. 1, 1994.

§ 20.04. Aggravated Kidnapping

(a) A person commits an offense if he intentionally or knowingly abducts another person with the intent to:

(1) hold him for ransom or reward;

(2) use him as a shield or hostage;

(3) facilitate the commission of a felony or the flight after the attempt or commission of a felony;

(4) inflict bodily injury on him or violate or abuse him sexually;

(5) terrorize him or a third person; or

(6) interfere with the performance of any governmental or political function.

(b) A person commits an offense if the person intentionally or knowingly abducts another person and uses or exhibits a deadly weapon during the commission of the offense.

(c) Except as provided by Subsection (d), an offense under this section is a felony of the first degree.

(d) At the punishment stage of a trial, the defendant may raise the issue as to whether he voluntarily released the victim in a safe place. If the defendant proves the issue in the affirmative by a preponderance of the evidence, the offense is a felony of the second degree.

Acts 1973, 63rd Leg., p. 883, ch. 399, § 1, eff. Jan. 1, 1974. Amended by Acts 1993, 73rd Leg., ch. 900, § 1.01, eff. Sept. 1, 1994; Acts 1995, 74th Leg., ch. 318, § 4, eff. Sept. 1, 1995.

§ 20.05. Unlawful Transport

(a) A person commits an offense if the person for pecuniary benefit transports an individual in a manner that:

(1) is designed to conceal the individual from local, state, or federal law enforcement authorities; and

(2) creates a substantial likelihood that the individual will suffer serious bodily injury or death.

(b) An offense under this section is a state jail felony.

Added by Acts 1999, 76th Leg., ch. 1014, § 1, eff. Sept. 1, 1999.

CHAPTER 20A. TRAFFICKING OF PERSONS

§ 20A.01. Definitions

In this chapter:

(1) "Forced labor or services" means labor or services, including conduct that constitutes an offense under Section 43.02, that are performed or provided by another person and obtained through an actor's:

(A) causing or threatening to cause bodily injury to the person or another person or otherwise causing the person performing or providing labor or services to believe that the person or another person will suffer bodily injury;

(B) restraining or threatening to restrain the person or another person in a manner described by Section 20.01(1) or causing the person performing or providing labor or services to believe that the person or another person will be restrained;

(C) knowingly destroying, concealing, removing, confiscating, or withholding from the person or another person, or threatening to destroy, conceal, remove, confiscate, or withhold from the person or another person, the person's actual or purported:

(i) government records;

(ii) identifying information; or

(iii) personal property;

(D) threatening the person with abuse of the law or the legal process in relation to the person or another person;

(E) threatening to report the person or another person to immigration officials or other law enforcement officials or otherwise blackmailing or extorting the person or another person;

(F) exerting financial control over the person or another person by placing the person or another person under the actor's control as security for a debt to the extent that:

(i) the value of the services provided by the person or another person as reasonably assessed is not applied toward the liquidation of the debt;

(ii) the duration of the services provided by the person or another person is not limited and the nature of the services provided by the person or another person is not defined; or

(iii) the principal amount of the debt does not reasonably reflect the value of the items or services for which the debt was incurred; or

(G) using any scheme, plan, or pattern intended to cause the person to believe that the person or another person will be subjected to serious harm or restraint if the person does not perform or provide the labor or services.

(2) "Traffic" means to transport, entice, recruit, harbor, provide, or otherwise obtain another person by any means.

Added by Acts 2003, 78th Leg., ch. 641, § 2, eff. Sept. 1, 2003. Amended by Acts 2007, 80th Leg., ch. 258, § 16.01, eff. Sept. 1, 2007; Acts 2007, 80th Leg., ch. 849, § 4, eff. June 15, 2007.

Section 16.06 of Acts 2007, 80th Leg., ch. 258 provides:

"Sections 20A.01 and 20A.02, Penal Code, as amended by this article apply only to an offense committed on or after the effective date of this article. An offense committed before the effective date of this article is governed by the law in effect when the offense was committed, and the former law is continued in effect for that purpose. For purposes of this section, an offense is committed before the effective date of this article if any element of the offense occurs before the effective date.

Sections 9 and 11 of Acts 2007, 80th Leg., ch. 849 provide:

"Sec. 9. Sections 20A.01 and 20A.02, Penal Code, as amended by this Act, apply only to an offense committed on or after the effective date of this Act. An offense committed before the effective date of this Act is governed by the law in effect when the offense was committed, and the former law is continued in effect for that purpose. For purposes of this section, an offense is committed before the effective date of this Act if any element of the offense occurs before the effective date."

"Sec. 11. The change in law made by this Act applies only to a judgment of conviction entered on or after the effective date of this Act, a grant of deferred adjudication made on or after the effective date of this Act, or a disposition of delinquent conduct made on or after the effective date of this Act."

§ 20A.02. Trafficking of Persons

(a) A person commits an offense if the person knowingly:

(1) traffics another person with the intent or knowledge that the trafficked person will engage in forced labor or services; or

(2) benefits from participating in a venture that involves an activity described by Subdivision (1), including by receiving labor or services the person knows are forced labor or services.

(b) Except as otherwise provided by this subsection, an offense under this section is a felony of the second degree. An offense under this section is a felony of the first degree if:

(1) the applicable conduct constitutes an offense under Section 43.05 or 43.25 and the person who is trafficked is a child younger than 18 years of age at the time of the offense, regardless of whether the actor knows the age of the child at the time the actor commits the offense; or

(2) the commission of the offense results in the death of the person who is trafficked.

(c) If conduct constituting an offense under this section also constitutes an offense under another section of this code, the actor may be prosecuted under either section or under both sections.

Added by Acts 2003, 78th Leg., ch. 641, § 2, eff. Sept. 1, 2003. Amended by Acts 2007, 80th Leg., ch. 258, § 16.02, eff. Sept. 1, 2007; Acts 2007, 80th Leg. ch. 849, § 5, eff. June 15, 2007; Acts 2009, 81st Leg., ch. 1002, § 7, eff. Sept. 1, 2009.

Section 16.06 of Acts 2007, 80th Leg., ch. 258 provides:

"Sections 20A.01 and 20A.02, Penal Code, as amended by this article apply only to an offense committed on or after the effective date of this article. An offense committed before the effective date of this article is governed by the law in effect when the offense was committed, and the former law is continued in effect for that purpose. For purposes of this section, an offense is committed before the effective date of this article if any element of the offense occurs before the effective date."

Sections 9 and 11 of Acts 2007, 80th Leg., ch. 849 provide:

"Sec. 9. Sections 20A.01 and 20A.02, Penal Code, as amended by this Act, apply only to an offense committed on or after the effective date of this Act. An offense committed before the effective date of this Act is governed by the law in effect when the offense was committed, and the former law is continued in effect for that purpose. For purposes of this section, an offense is committed before the effective date of this Act if any element of the offense occurs before the effective date."

"Sec. 11. The change in law made by this Act applies only to a judgment of conviction entered on or after the effective date of this Act, a grant of deferred adjudication made on or after the effective date of this Act, or a disposition of delinquent conduct made on or after the effective date of this Act."

Section 10(d) of Acts 2009, 81st Leg., ch. 1002 provides:

"(d) The changes in law made by this Act to Sections 20A.02, 43.02, and 43. 05, Penal Code, apply only to an offense committed on or after the effective date [Sept. 1, 2009] of this Act. An offense committed before the effective date of this Act is covered by the law in effect when the offense was committed, and the former law is continued in effect for that purpose. For purposes of this section, an offense was committed before the effective date of this Act if any element of the offense was committed before that date."

CHAPTER 21. SEXUAL OFFENSES

Section

§ 21.01. Definitions

In this chapter:

(1) "Deviate sexual intercourse" means:

(A) any contact between any part of the genitals of one person and the mouth or anus of another person; or

(B) the penetration of the genitals or the anus of another person with an object.

(2) "Sexual contact" means, except as provided by Section 21.11, any touching of the anus, breast, or any part of the genitals of another person with intent to arouse or gratify the sexual desire of any person.

(3) "Sexual intercourse" means any penetration of the female sex organ by the male sex organ.

(4) "Spouse" means a person to whom a person is legally married under Subtitle A, Title 1, Family Code, or a comparable law of another jurisdiction.

Acts 1973, 63rd Leg., p. 883, ch. 399, § 1, eff. Jan. 1, 1974. Amended by Acts 1979, 66th Leg., p. 373, ch. 168, § 1, eff. Aug. 27, 1979; Acts 1981, 67th Leg., p. 203, ch. 96, § 3, eff. Sept. 1, 1981; Acts 1993, 73rd Leg., ch. 900, § 1.01, eff. Sept. 1, 1994; Acts 2001, 77th Leg., ch. 739, § 1, eff. Sept. 1, 2001; Acts 2005, 79th Leg., ch. 268, § 1.124, eff. Sept. 1, 2005.

§ 21.02. Continuous Sexual Abuse of Young Child or Children

(a) In this section, "child" has the meaning assigned by Section 22.011(c).

(b) A person commits an offense if:

(1) during a period that is 30 or more days in duration, the person commits two or more acts of sexual abuse, regardless of whether the acts of sexual abuse are committed against one or more victims; and

(2) at the time of the commission of each of the acts of sexual abuse, the actor is 17 years of age or older and the victim is a child younger than 14 years of age.

(c) For purposes of this section, "act of sexual abuse" means any act that is a violation of one or more of the following penal laws:

(1) aggravated kidnapping under Section 20.04(a)(4), if the actor committed the offense with the intent to violate or abuse the victim sexually;

(2) indecency with a child under Section 21.11(a)(1), if the actor committed the offense in a manner other than by touching, including touching through clothing, the breast of a child;

(3) sexual assault under Section 22.011;

(4) aggravated sexual assault under Section 22.021;

(5) burglary under Section 30.02, if the offense is punishable under Subsection (d) of that section and the actor committed the offense with the intent to commit an offense listed in Subdivisions (1)–(4); and

(6) sexual performance by a child under Section 43.25.

(d) If a jury is the trier of fact, members of the jury are not required to agree unanimously on which specific acts of sexual abuse were committed by the defendant or the exact date when those acts were committed. The jury must agree unanimously that the defendant, during a period that is 30 or more days in duration, committed two or more acts of sexual abuse.

(e) A defendant may not be convicted in the same criminal action of an offense listed under Subsection (c) the victim of which is the same victim as a victim of the offense alleged under Subsection (b) unless the offense listed in Subsection (c):

(1) is charged in the alternative;

(2) occurred outside the period in which the offense alleged under Subsection (b) was committed; or

(3) is considered by the trier of fact to be a lesser included offense of the offense alleged under Subsection (b).

(f) A defendant may not be charged with more than one count under Subsection (b) if all of the specific acts of sexual abuse that are alleged to have been committed are alleged to have been committed against a single victim.

(g) It is an affirmative defense to prosecution under this section that the actor:

(1) was not more than five years older than:

(A) the victim of the offense, if the offense is alleged to have been committed against only one victim; or

(B) the youngest victim of the offense, if the offense is alleged to have been committed against more than one victim;

(2) did not use duress, force, or a threat against a victim at the time of the commission of any of the acts of sexual abuse alleged as an element of the offense; and

(3) at the time of the commission of any of the acts of sexual abuse alleged as an element of the offense:

(A) was not required under Chapter 62, Code of Criminal Procedure, to register for life as a sex offender; or

(B) was not a person who under Chapter 62 had a reportable conviction or adjudication for an offense under this section or an act of sexual abuse as described by Subsection (c).

(h) An offense under this section is a felony of the first degree, punishable by imprisonment in the Texas Department of Criminal Justice for life, or for any term of not more than 99 years or less than 25 years.

Added by Acts 2007, 80th Leg., ch. 593, § 1.17, eff. Sept. 1, 2007.

§§ 21.03 to 21.05. Repealed by Acts 1983, 68th Leg., ch. 997, § 12, eff. Sept. 1, 1983

See, now, V.T.C.A. Penal Code, §§ 22.011 and 22.021.

§ 21.06. Homosexual Conduct

(a) A person commits an offense if he engages in deviate sexual intercourse with another individual of the same sex.

(b) An offense under this section is a Class C misdemeanor.

Acts 1973, 63rd Leg., p. 883, ch. 399, § 1, eff. Jan. 1, 1974. Amended by Acts 1993, 73rd Leg., ch. 900, § 1.01, eff. Sept. 1, 1994.

This section was declared unconstitutional by Lawrence v. Texas, 539 U.S. 558, 123 S.Ct. 2472.

§ 21.07. Public Lewdness

(a) A person commits an offense if he knowingly engages in any of the following acts in a public place or, if not in a public place, he is reckless about whether another is present who will be offended or alarmed by his:

(1) act of sexual intercourse;

(2) act of deviate sexual intercourse;

(3) act of sexual contact; or

(4) act involving contact between the person's mouth or genitals and the anus or genitals of an animal or fowl.

(b) An offense under this section is a Class A misdemeanor.

Acts 1973, 63rd Leg., p. 883, ch. 399, § 1, eff. Jan. 1, 1974. Amended by Acts 1993, 73rd Leg., ch. 900, § 1.01, eff. Sept. 1, 1994.

§ 21.08. Indecent Exposure

(a) A person commits an offense if he exposes his anus or any part of his genitals with intent to arouse or gratify the sexual desire of any person, and he is reckless about whether another is present who will be offended or alarmed by his act.

(b) An offense under this section is a Class B misdemeanor.

Acts 1973, 63rd Leg., p. 883, ch. 399, § 1, eff. Jan. 1, 1974. Amended by Acts 1983, 68th Leg., p. 509, ch. 924, § 1, eff. Sept. 1, 1983; Acts 1993, 73rd Leg., ch. 900, § 1.01, eff. Sept. 1, 1994.

§§ 21.09, 21.10. Repealed by Acts 1983, 68th Leg., ch. 977, § 12, eff. Sept. 1, 1983

See, now, §§ 22.011 and 22.021.

§ 21.11. Indecency With a Child

(a) A person commits an offense if, with a child younger than 17 years of age, whether the child is of the same or opposite sex, the person:

(1) engages in sexual contact with the child or causes the child to engage in sexual contact; or

(2) with intent to arouse or gratify the sexual desire of any person:

(A) exposes the person's anus or any part of the person's genitals, knowing the child is present; or

(B) causes the child to expose the child's anus or any part of the child's genitals.

(b) It is an affirmative defense to prosecution under this section that the actor:

(1) was not more than three years older than the victim and of the opposite sex;

(2) did not use duress, force, or a threat against the victim at the time of the offense; and

(3) at the time of the offense:

(A) was not required under Chapter 62, Code of Criminal Procedure, to register for life as a sex offender; or

(B) was not a person who under Chapter 62 had a reportable conviction or adjudication for an offense under this section.

(b–1) It is an affirmative defense to prosecution under this section that the actor was the spouse of the child at the time of the offense.

(c) In this section, "sexual contact" means the following acts, if committed with the intent to arouse or gratify the sexual desire of any person:

(1) any touching by a person, including touching through clothing, of the anus, breast, or any part of the genitals of a child; or

(2) any touching of any part of the body of a child, including touching through clothing, with the anus, breast, or any part of the genitals of a person.

(d) An offense under Subsection (a)(1) is a felony of the second degree and an offense under Subsection (a)(2) is a felony of the third degree.

Acts 1973, 63rd Leg., p. 883, ch. 399, § 1, eff. Jan. 1, 1974. Amended by Acts 1981, 67th Leg., p. 472, ch. 202, § 3, eff. Sept. 1, 1981; Acts 1987, 70th Leg., ch. 1028, § 1, eff. Sept. 1, 1987; Acts 1993, 73rd Leg., ch. 900, § 1.01, eff. Sept. 1, 1994; Acts 1999, 76th Leg., ch. 1415, § 23, eff. Sept. 1, 1999; Acts 2001, 77th Leg., ch. 739, § 2, eff. Sept. 1, 2001; Acts 2009, 81st Leg., ch. 260, § 1, eff. Sept. 1, 2009.

Section 6 of Acts 2009, 81st Leg., ch. 260 provides:

"The change in law made by this Act applies only to an offense committed on or after the effective date [Sept. 1, 2009] of this Act. An offense committed before the effective date of this Act is covered by the law in effect when the offense was committed, and the former law is continued in effect for that purpose. For purposes of this section, an offense was committed before the effective date of this Act if any element of the offense occurred before that date."

§ 21.12. Improper Relationship Between Educator and Student

(a) An employee of a public or private primary or secondary school commits an offense if the employee engages in:

(1) sexual contact, sexual intercourse, or deviate sexual intercourse with a person who is enrolled in a public or private primary or secondary school at which the employee works; or

(2) conduct described by Section 33.021, with a person described by Subdivision (1), regardless of the age of that person.

(b) An offense under this section is a felony of the second degree.

(b–1) It is an affirmative defense to prosecution under this section that the actor was the spouse of the enrolled person at the time of the offense.

(c) If conduct constituting an offense under this section also constitutes an offense under another section of this code, the actor may be prosecuted under either section or both sections.

(d) The name of a person who is enrolled in a public or private primary or secondary school and involved in an improper relationship with an educator as provided by Subsection (a) may not be released to the public and is not public information under Chapter 552, Government Code.

Added by Acts 2003, 78th Leg., ch. 224, § 1, eff. Sept. 1, 2003. Amended by Acts 2007, 80th Leg., ch. 610, § 1, eff. Sept. 1, 2007; Acts 2007, 80th Leg., ch. 772, § 1, eff. Sept. 1, 2007; Acts 2009, 81st Leg., ch. 260, § 2, eff. Sept. 1, 2009.

Section 3 of Acts 2007, 80th Leg., ch. 610 provides:

"The change in law made by this Act applies only to an offense committed on or after the effective date of this Act. An offense committed before the effective date of this Act is covered by the law in effect when the offense was committed, and the former law is continued in effect for that purpose. For the purposes of this section, an offense was committed before the effective date of this Act if any element of the offense was committed before that date."

Section 6 of Acts 2009, 81st Leg., ch. 260 provides:

"The change in law made by this Act applies only to an offense committed on or after the effective date [Sept. 1, 2009] of this Act. An offense committed before the effective date of this Act is covered by the law in effect when the offense was committed, and the former law is continued in effect for that purpose. For purposes of this section, an offense was committed before the effective date of this Act if any element of the offense occurred before that date."

§ 21.13. Renumbered as V.T.C.A., Penal Code § 22.065 by Acts 1983, 68th Leg., ch. 977, § 4, eff. Sept. 1, 1983

§ 21.14. Deleted by Acts 1993, 73rd Leg., ch. 900, § 1.01, eff. Sept. 1, 1994

§ 21.15. Improper Photography or Visual Recording

(a) In this section, "promote" has the meaning assigned by Section 43.21.

(b) A person commits an offense if the person:

(1) photographs or by videotape or other electronic means records, broadcasts, or transmits a visual image of another at a location that is not a bathroom or private dressing room:

(A) without the other person's consent; and

(B) with intent to arouse or gratify the sexual desire of any person;

(2) photographs or by videotape or other electronic means records, broadcasts, or transmits a visual image of another at a location that is a bathroom or private dressing room:

(A) without the other person's consent; and

(B) with intent to:

(i) invade the privacy of the other person; or

(ii) arouse or gratify the sexual desire of any person; or

(3) knowing the character and content of the photograph, recording, broadcast, or transmission, promotes a photograph, recording, broadcast, or transmission described by Subdivision (1) or (2).

(c) An offense under this section is a state jail felony.

(d) If conduct that constitutes an offense under this section also constitutes an offense under any other law, the actor may be prosecuted under this section or the other law.

(e) For purposes of Subsection (b)(2), a sign or signs posted indicating that the person is being photographed or that a visual image of the person is being recorded, broadcast, or transmitted is not sufficient to establish the person's consent under that subdivision.

Added by Acts 2001, 77th Leg., ch. 458, § 1, eff. Sept. 1, 2001. Amended by Acts 2003, 78th Leg., ch. 500, § 1, eff. Sept. 1, 2003; Acts 2007, 80th Leg., ch. 306, § 1, eff. Sept. 1, 2007.

Section 2 of Acts 2007, 80th Leg., ch. 306 provides:

"The change in law made by this Act applies only to an offense committed on or after the effective date of this Act. An offense committed before the effective date of this Act is governed by the law in effect when the offense was committed, and the former law is continued in effect for that purpose. For the purposes of this section, an offense is committed before the effective date of this Act if any element of the offense was committed before that date."

CHAPTER 22. ASSAULTIVE OFFENSES

§ 22.01. Assault

(a) A person commits an offense if the person:

(1) intentionally, knowingly, or recklessly causes bodily injury to another, including the person's spouse;

(2) intentionally or knowingly threatens another with imminent bodily injury, including the person's spouse; or

(3) intentionally or knowingly causes physical contact with another when the person knows or should reasonably believe that the other will regard the contact as offensive or provocative.

(b) An offense under Subsection (a)(1) is a Class A misdemeanor, except that the offense is a felony of the third degree if the offense is committed against:

(1) a person the actor knows is a public servant while the public servant is lawfully discharging an official duty, or in retaliation or on account of an exercise of official power or performance of an official duty as a public servant;

(2) a person whose relationship to or association with the defendant is described by Section 71.0021(b), 71.003, or 71.005, Family Code, if:

(A) it is shown on the trial of the offense that the defendant has been previously convicted of an offense under this chapter, Chapter 19, or Section 20.03, 20.04 21.11, or 25.11 against a person whose relationship to or association with the defendant is described by Section 71.0021(b), 71.003, or 71.005, Family Code; or

(B) the offense is committed by intentionally, knowingly, or recklessly impeding the normal breathing or circulation of the blood of the person by applying pressure to the person's throat or neck or by blocking the person's nose or mouth;

(3) a person who contracts with government to perform a service in a facility as defined by Section 1.07(a)(14), Penal Code, or Section 51.02(13) or (14), Family Code, or an employee of that person:

(A) while the person or employee is engaged in performing a service within the scope of the contract, if the actor knows the person or employee is authorized by government to provide the service; or

(B) in retaliation for or on account of the person's or employee's performance of a service within the scope of the contract;

(4) a person the actor knows is a security officer while the officer is performing a duty as a security officer; or

(5) a person the actor knows is emergency services personnel while the person is providing emergency services.

(b–1) Notwithstanding Subsection (b)(2), an offense under Subsection (a)(1) is a felony of the second degree if:

(1) the offense is committed against a person whose relationship to or association with the defendant is described by Section 71.0021(b), 71.003, or 71.005, Family Code;

(2) it is shown on the trial of the offense that the defendant has been previously convicted of an offense under this chapter, Chapter 19, or Section 20.03, 20.04, or 21.11 against a person whose relationship to or association with the defendant is

described by Section 71.0021(b), 71.003, or 71.005, Family Code; and

(3) the offense is committed by intentionally, knowingly, or recklessly impeding the normal breathing or circulation of the blood of the person by applying pressure to the person's throat or neck or by blocking the person's nose or mouth.

(c) An offense under Subsection (a)(2) or (3) is a Class C misdemeanor, except that the offense is:

(1) a Class A misdemeanor if the offense is committed under Subsection (a)(3) against an elderly individual or disabled individual, as those terms are defined by Section 22.04; or

(2) a Class B misdemeanor if the offense is committed by a person who is not a sports participant against a person the actor knows is a sports participant either:

(A) while the participant is performing duties or responsibilities in the participant's capacity as a sports participant; or

(B) in retaliation for or on account of the participant's performance of a duty or responsibility within the participant's capacity as a sports participant.

(d) For purposes of Subsection (b), the actor is presumed to have known the person assaulted was a public servant, a security officer, or emergency services personnel if the person was wearing a distinctive uniform or badge indicating the person's employment as a public servant or status as a security officer or emergency services personnel.

(e) In this section:

(1) "Emergency services personnel" includes firefighters, emergency medical services personnel as defined by Section 773.003, Health and Safety Code, and other individuals who, in the course and scope of employment or as a volunteer, provide services for the benefit of the general public during emergency situations.

(2) Repealed by Acts 2005, 79th Leg., ch. 788, § 6.

(3) "Security officer" means a commissioned security officer as defined by Section 1702.002, Occupations Code, or a noncommissioned security officer registered under Section 1702.221, Occupations Code.

(4) "Sports participant" means a person who participates in any official capacity with respect to an interscholastic, intercollegiate, or other organized amateur or professional athletic competition and includes an athlete, referee, umpire, linesman, coach, instructor, administrator, or staff member.

(f) For the purposes of Subsections (b)(2)(A) and (b–1)(2):

(1) a defendant has been previously convicted of an offense listed in those subsections committed against a person whose relationship to or association with the defendant is described by Section 71.0021(b), 71.003, or 71.005, Family Code, if the defendant was adjudged guilty of the offense or entered a plea of guilty or nolo contendere in return for a grant of deferred adjudication, regardless of whether the sentence for the offense was ever imposed or whether the sentence was probated and the defendant was subsequently discharged from community supervision; and

(2) a conviction under the laws of another state for an offense containing elements that are substantially similar to the elements of an offense listed in those subsections is a conviction of the offense listed.

(g) If conduct constituting an offense under this section also constitutes an offense under another section of this code, the actor may be prosecuted under either section or both sections.

Acts 1973, 63rd Leg., p. 883, ch. 399, § 1, eff. Jan. 1, 1974. Amended by Acts 1977, 65th Leg., 1st C.S., p. 55, ch. 2, §§ 12, 13, eff. July 22, 1977; Acts 1979, 66th Leg., p. 260, ch. 135, §§ 1, 2, eff. Aug. 27, 1979; Acts 1979, 66th Leg., p. 367, ch. 164, § 2, eff. Sept. 1, 1979; Acts 1983, 68th Leg., p. 5311, ch. 977, § 1, eff. Sept. 1, 1983; Acts 1987, 70th Leg., ch. 1052, § 2.08, eff. Sept. 1, 1987; Acts 1989, 71st Leg., ch. 739, §§ 1 to 3, eff. Sept. 1, 1989; Acts 1991, 72nd Leg., ch. 14, § 284(23) to (26), eff. Sept. 1, 1991; Acts 1991, 72nd Leg., ch. 334, § 1, eff. Sept. 1, 1991; Acts 1991, 72nd Leg., ch. 366, § 1, eff. Sept. 1, 1991; Acts 1993, 73rd Leg., ch. 900, § 1.01, eff. Sept. 1, 1994; Acts 1997, 75th Leg., ch. 165, § 27.01, eff. Sept. 1, 1997; Acts 1995, 74th Leg., ch. 318, § 5, eff. Sept. 1, 1995; Acts 1995, 74th Leg., ch. 659, § 1, eff. Sept. 1, 1995; Acts 1997, 75th Leg., ch. 165, §§ 27.01, 31.01(68), eff. Sept. 1, 1997; Acts 1999, 76th Leg., ch. 62, § 15.02(a), eff. Sept. 1, 1999; Acts 1999, 76th Leg., ch. 1158, § 1, eff. Sept. 1, 1999; Acts 2003, 78th Leg., ch. 294, § 1, eff. Sept. 1, 2003; Acts 2003, 78th Leg., ch. 1019, §§ 1, 2, eff. Sept. 1, 2003; Acts 2003, 78th Leg., ch. 1028, § 1, eff. Sept. 1, 2003; Acts 2005, 79th Leg., ch. 728, §§ 16.001, 16.002, eff. Sept. 1, 2005; Acts 2005, 79th Leg., ch. 788, §§ 1, 2, 6, eff. Sept. 1, 2005; Acts 2007, 80th Leg., ch. 623, §§ 1, 2, eff. Sept. 1, 2007; Acts 2009, 81st Leg., ch. 427, § 1, eff. Sept. 1, 2009; Acts 2009, 81st Leg., ch. 665, § 2, eff. Sept. 1, 2009.

Section 3 of Acts 2007, 80th Leg., ch. 623 provides:

"The change in law made by this Act applies only to an offense committed on or after the effective date of this Act. An offense committed before the effective date of this Act is governed by the law in effect when the offense was committed, and the former law is continued in effect for that purpose. For purposes of this section, an offense was committed before the effective date of this Act if any element of the offense was committed before that date."

Section 2 of Acts 2009, 81st Leg., ch. 427 provides:

"The change in law made by this Act applies only to an offense committed on or after the effective date [Sept. 1, 2009] of this Act. An offense committed before the effective date of this Act is covered by the law in effect when the offense was committed, and the former law is continued in effect for that purpose. For purposes of this section, an offense was committed before the effective date of this Act if any element of the offense occurred before that date."

Section 3 of Acts 2009, 81st Leg., ch. 665 provides:

"The change in law made by this Act applies only to an offense committed on or after the effective date [Sept. 1, 2009] of this Act. An offense committed before the effective date of this Act is covered by the law in effect when the offense was committed, and the former law is continued in effect for that purpose. For purposes of this section, an offense was committed before the effective date of this Act if any element of the offense occurred before that date."

§ 22.011. Sexual Assault

(a) A person commits an offense if the person:

(1) intentionally or knowingly:

(A) causes the penetration of the anus or sexual organ of another person by any means, without that person's consent;

(B) causes the penetration of the mouth of another person by the sexual organ of the actor, without that person's consent; or

(C) causes the sexual organ of another person, without that person's consent, to contact or penetrate the mouth, anus, or sexual organ of another person, including the actor; or

(2) intentionally or knowingly:

(A) causes the penetration of the anus or sexual organ of a child by any means;

(B) causes the penetration of the mouth of a child by the sexual organ of the actor;

(C) causes the sexual organ of a child to contact or penetrate the mouth, anus, or sexual organ of another person, including the actor;

(D) causes the anus of a child to contact the mouth, anus, or sexual organ of another person, including the actor; or

(E) causes the mouth of a child to contact the anus or sexual organ of another person, including the actor.

(b) A sexual assault under Subsection (a)(1) is without the consent of the other person if:

(1) the actor compels the other person to submit or participate by the use of physical force or violence;

(2) the actor compels the other person to submit or participate by threatening to use force or violence against the other person, and the other person believes that the actor has the present ability to execute the threat;

(3) the other person has not consented and the actor knows the other person is unconscious or physically unable to resist;

(4) the actor knows that as a result of mental disease or defect the other person is at the time of the sexual assault incapable either of appraising the nature of the act or of resisting it;

(5) the other person has not consented and the actor knows the other person is unaware that the sexual assault is occurring;

(6) the actor has intentionally impaired the other person's power to appraise or control the other person's conduct by administering any substance without the other person's knowledge;

(7) the actor compels the other person to submit or participate by threatening to use force or violence against any person, and the other person believes that the actor has the ability to execute the threat;

(8) the actor is a public servant who coerces the other person to submit or participate;

(9) the actor is a mental health services provider or a health care services provider who causes the other person, who is a patient or former patient of the actor, to submit or participate by exploiting the other person's emotional dependency on the actor;

(10) the actor is a clergyman who causes the other person to submit or participate by exploiting the other person's emotional dependency on the clergyman in the clergyman's professional character as spiritual adviser; or

(11) the actor is an employee of a facility where the other person is a resident, unless the employee and resident are formally or informally married to each other under Chapter 2, Family Code.

(c) In this section:

(1) "Child" means a person younger than 17 years of age.

(2) "Spouse" means a person who is legally married to another.

(3) "Health care services provider" means:

(A) a physician licensed under Subtitle B, Title 3, Occupations Code;[1]

(B) a chiropractor licensed under Chapter 201, Occupations Code;

(C) a physical therapist licensed under Chapter 453, Occupations Code;

(D) a physician assistant licensed under Chapter 204, Occupations Code; or

(E) a registered nurse, a vocational nurse, or an advanced practice nurse licensed under Chapter 301, Occupations Code.

(4) "Mental health services provider" means an individual, licensed or unlicensed, who performs or purports to perform mental health services, including a:

(A) licensed social worker as defined by Section 505.002, Occupations Code;

(B) chemical dependency counselor as defined by Section 504.001, Occupations Code;

(C) licensed professional counselor as defined by Section 503.002, Occupations Code;

(D) licensed marriage and family therapist as defined by Section 502.002, Occupations Code;

(E) member of the clergy;

(F) psychologist offering psychological services as defined by Section 501.003, Occupations Code; or

(G) special officer for mental health assignment certified under Section 1701.404, Occupations Code.

(5) "Employee of a facility" means a person who is an employee of a facility defined by Section 250.001, Health and Safety Code, or any other person who provides services for a facility for compensation, including a contract laborer.

(d) It is a defense to prosecution under Subsection (a)(2) that the conduct consisted of medical care for the child and did not include any contact between the anus or sexual organ of the child and the mouth, anus, or sexual organ of the actor or a third party.

(e) It is an affirmative defense to prosecution under Subsection (a)(2):

(1) that the actor was the spouse of the child at the time of the offense; or

(2) that:

(A) the actor was not more than three years older than the victim and at the time of the offense:

(i) was not required under Chapter 62, Code of Criminal Procedure, to register for life as a sex offender; or

(ii) was not a person who under Chapter 62, Code of Criminal Procedure, had a reportable conviction or adjudication for an offense under this section; and

(B) the victim:

(i) was a child of 14 years of age or older; and

(ii) was not a person whom the actor was prohibited from marrying or purporting to marry or with whom the actor was prohibited from living under the appearance of being married under Section 25.01.

(f) An offense under this section is a felony of the second degree, except that an offense under this section is a felony of the first degree if the victim was a person whom the actor was prohibited from marrying or purporting to marry or with whom the actor was prohibited from living under the appearance of being married under Section 25.01.

Added by Acts 1983, 68th Leg., p. 5312, ch. 977, § 3, eff. Sept. 1, 1983. Amended by Acts 1985, 69th Leg., ch. 557, § 1, eff. Sept. 1, 1985; Acts 1987, 70th Leg., ch. 1029, § 1, eff. Sept. 1, 1987; Acts 1991, 72nd Leg., ch. 662, § 1, eff. Sept. 1, 1991; Acts 1993, 73rd Leg., ch. 900, § 1.01, eff. Sept. 1, 1994; Acts 1995, 74th Leg., ch. 273, § 1, eff. Sept. 1, 1995; Acts 1995, 74th Leg., ch. 318, § 6, eff. Sept. 1, 1995; Acts 1997, 75th Leg., ch. 1031, §§ 1, 2, eff. Sept. 1, 1997; Acts 1997, 75th Leg., ch. 1286, § 1, eff. Sept. 1, 1997; Acts 1999, 76th Leg., ch. 1102, § 3, eff. Sept. 1, 1999; Acts 1999, 76th Leg., ch. 1415, § 24, eff. Sept. 1, 1999; Acts 2001, 77th Leg., ch. 1420, § 14.829, eff. Sept. 1, 2001; Acts 2003, 78th Leg., ch. 155, §§ 1, 2, eff. Sept. 1, 2003; Acts 2003, 78th Leg., ch. 528, § 1, eff. Sept. 1, 2003; Acts 2003, 78th Leg., ch. 553, § 2.017, eff. Feb. 1, 2004; Acts 2005, 79th Leg., ch. 268, § 4.02, eff. Sept. 1, 2005; Acts 2009, 81st Leg., ch. 260, §§ 3, 4, eff. Sept. 1, 2009.

[1] V.T.C.A., Occupations Code § 151.001 et seq.

Section 6 of Acts 2009, 81st Leg., ch. 260 provides:

"The change in law made by this Act applies only to an offense committed on or after the effective date [Sept. 1, 2009] of this Act. An offense committed before the effective date of this Act is covered by the law in effect when the offense was committed, and the former law is continued in effect for that purpose. For purposes of this section, an offense was committed before the effective date of this Act if any element of the offense occurred before that date."

§ 22.012. Deleted by Acts 1993, 73rd Leg., ch. 900, § 1.01, eff. Sept. 1, 1994

§ 22.015. Repealed by Acts 2009, 81st Leg., ch. 435 § 3, eff. Sept. 1, 2009

§ 22.02. Aggravated Assault

(a) A person commits an offense if the person commits assault as defined in § 22.01 and the person:

(1) causes serious bodily injury to another, including the person's spouse; or

(2) uses or exhibits a deadly weapon during the commission of the assault.

(b) An offense under this section is a felony of the second degree, except that the offense is a felony of the first degree if:

(1) the actor uses a deadly weapon during the commission of the assault and causes serious bodily

injury to a person whose relationship to or association with the defendant is described by Section 71.0021(b), 71.003, or 71.005, Family Code;

(2) regardless of whether the offense is committed under Subsection (a)(1) or (a)(2), the offense is committed:

(A) by a public servant acting under color of the servant's office or employment;

(B) against a person the actor knows is a public servant while the public servant is lawfully discharging an official duty, or in retaliation or on account of an exercise of official power or performance of an official duty as a public servant;

(C) in retaliation against or on account of the service of another as a witness, prospective witness, informant, or person who has reported the occurrence of a crime; or

(D) against a person the actor knows is a security officer while the officer is performing a duty as a security officer; or

(3) the actor is in a motor vehicle, as defined by Section 501.002, Transportation Code, and:

(A) knowingly discharges a firearm at or in the direction of a habitation, building, or vehicle;

(B) is reckless as to whether the habitation, building, or vehicle is occupied; and

(C) in discharging the firearm, causes serious bodily injury to any person.

(c) The actor is presumed to have known the person assaulted was a public servant or a security officer if the person was wearing a distinctive uniform or badge indicating the person's employment as a public servant or status as a security officer.

(d) In this section, "security officer" means a commissioned security officer as defined by Section 1702.002, Occupations Code, or a noncommissioned security officer registered under Section 1702.221, Occupations Code.

Acts 1973, 63rd Leg., p. 883, ch. 399, § 1, eff. Jan. 1, 1974. Amended by Acts 1979, 66th Leg., p. 367, ch. 164, § 2, eff. Sept. 1, 1979; Acts 1979, 66th Leg., p. 1521, ch. 655, § 2, eff. Sept. 1, 1979; Acts 1983, 68th Leg., p. 349, ch. 79, § 1, eff. Sept. 1, 1983; Acts 1983, 68th Leg., p. 5311, ch. 977, § 2, eff. Sept. 1, 1983; Acts 1985, 69th Leg., ch. 223, § 1, eff. Sept. 1, 1985; Acts 1987, 70th Leg., ch. 18, § 3, eff. April 14, 1987; Acts 1987, 70th Leg., ch. 1101, § 12, eff. Sept. 1, 1987; Acts 1989, 71st Leg., ch. 939, §§ 1 to 3, eff. Sept. 1, 1989; Acts 1991, 72nd Leg., ch. 334, § 2, eff. Sept. 1, 1991; Acts 1991, 72nd Leg., ch. 903, § 1, eff. Sept. 1, 1991; Acts 1993, 73rd Leg., ch. 900, § 1.01, eff. Sept. 1, 1994; Acts 2003, 78th Leg., ch. 1019, § 3, eff. Sept. 1, 2003; Acts 2005, 79th Leg., ch. 788, § 3, eff. Sept. 1, 2005; Acts 2009, 81st Leg., ch. 594, § 2, eff. Sept. 1, 2009.

Section 3 of Acts 2009, 81st Leg., ch. 594 provides:

"The change in law made by this Act applies only to an offense committed on or after the effective date of this Act. An offense committed before the effective date of this Act is covered by the law in effect immediately before the effective date of this Act, and the former law is continued in effect for that purpose. For purposes of this section, an offense was committed before the effective date of this Act if any element of the offense was committed before that date."

§ 22.021. Aggravated Sexual Assault

(a) A person commits an offense:

(1) if the person:

(A) intentionally or knowingly:

(i) causes the penetration of the anus or sexual organ of another person by any means, without that person's consent;

(ii) causes the penetration of the mouth of another person by the sexual organ of the actor, without that person's consent; or

(iii) causes the sexual organ of another person, without that person's consent, to contact or penetrate the mouth, anus, or sexual organ of another person, including the actor; or

(B) intentionally or knowingly:

(i) causes the penetration of the anus or sexual organ of a child by any means;

(ii) causes the penetration of the mouth of a child by the sexual organ of the actor;

(iii) causes the sexual organ of a child to contact or penetrate the mouth, anus, or sexual organ of another person, including the actor;

(iv) causes the anus of a child to contact the mouth, anus, or sexual organ of another person, including the actor; or

(v) causes the mouth of a child to contact the anus or sexual organ of another person, including the actor; and

(2) if:

(A) the person:

(i) causes serious bodily injury or attempts to cause the death of the victim or another person in the course of the same criminal episode;

(ii) by acts or words places the victim in fear that death, serious bodily injury, or kidnapping will be imminently inflicted on any person;

(iii) by acts or words occurring in the presence of the victim threatens to cause the death, serious bodily injury, or kidnapping of any person;

(iv) uses or exhibits a deadly weapon in the course of the same criminal episode;

(v) acts in concert with another who engages in conduct described by Subdivision (1) directed toward the same victim and occurring during the course of the same criminal episode; or

(vi) administers or provides flunitrazepam, otherwise known as rohypnol, gamma hydroxybutyrate, or ketamine to the victim of the offense with the intent of facilitating the commission of the offense;

(B) the victim is younger than 14 years of age; or

(C) the victim is an elderly individual or a disabled individual.

(b) In this section:

(1) "Child" has the meaning assigned by Section 22.011(c).

(2) "Elderly individual" and "disabled individual" have the meanings assigned by Section 22.04(c).

(c) An aggravated sexual assault under this section is without the consent of the other person if the aggravated sexual assault occurs under the same circumstances listed in Section 22.011(b).

(d) The defense provided by Section 22.011(d) applies to this section.

(e) An offense under this section is a felony of the first degree.

(f) The minimum term of imprisonment for an offense under this section is increased to 25 years if:

(1) the victim of the offense is younger than six years of age at the time the offense is committed; or

(2) the victim of the offense is younger than 14 years of age at the time the offense is committed and the actor commits the offense in a manner described by Subsection (a)(2)(A).

Added by Acts 1983, 68th Leg., p. 5312, ch. 977, § 3, eff. Sept. 1, 1983. Amended by Acts 1987, 70th Leg., ch. 573, § 1, eff. Sept. 1, 1987; Acts 1987, 70th Leg., 2nd C.S., ch. 16, § 1, eff. Sept. 1, 1987; Acts 1993, 73rd Leg., ch. 900, § 1.01, eff. Sept. 1, 1994; Acts 1995, 74th Leg., ch. 318, § 7, eff. Sept. 1, 1995; Acts 1997, 75th Leg., ch. 1286, § 2, eff. Sept. 1, 1997; Acts 1999, 76th Leg., ch. 417, § 1, eff. Sept. 1, 1999; Acts 2001, 77th Leg., ch. 459, § 5, eff. Sept. 1, 2001; Acts 2003, 78th Leg., ch. 528, § 2, eff. Sept. 1, 2003; Acts 2003, 78th Leg., ch. 896, § 1, eff. Sept. 1, 2003; Acts 2007, 80th Leg., ch. 593, § 1.18, eff. Sept. 1, 2007.

§ 22.03. Deleted by Acts 1993, 73rd Leg., ch. 900, § 1.01, eff. Sept. 1, 1994

§ 22.04. Injury to a Child, Elderly Individual, or Disabled Individual

(a) A person commits an offense if he intentionally, knowingly, recklessly, or with criminal negligence, by act or intentionally, knowingly, or recklessly by omission, causes to a child, elderly individual, or disabled individual:

(1) serious bodily injury;

(2) serious mental deficiency, impairment, or injury; or

(3) bodily injury.

(a–1) A person commits an offense if the person is an owner, operator, or employee of a group home, nursing facility, assisted living facility, intermediate care facility for persons with mental retardation, or other institutional care facility and the person intentionally, knowingly, recklessly, or with criminal negligence by omission causes to a child, elderly individual, or disabled individual who is a resident of that group home or facility:

(1) serious bodily injury;

(2) serious mental deficiency, impairment, or injury;

(3) bodily injury; or

(4) exploitation.

(b) An omission that causes a condition described by Subsection (a)(1), (2), or (3) or (a–1)(1), (2), (3), or (4) is conduct constituting an offense under this section if:

(1) the actor has a legal or statutory duty to act; or

(2) the actor has assumed care, custody, or control of a child, elderly individual, or disabled individual.

(c) In this section:

(1) "Child" means a person 14 years of age or younger.

(2) "Elderly individual" means a person 65 years of age or older.

(3) "Disabled individual" means a person older than 14 years of age who by reason of age or physical or mental disease, defect, or injury is substantially unable to protect himself from harm or to provide food, shelter, or medical care for himself.

(4) "Exploitation" means the illegal or improper use of an individual or of the resources of the individual for monetary or personal benefit, profit, or gain.

(d) For purposes of an omission that causes a condition described by Subsection (a)(1), (2), or (3), the actor has assumed care, custody, or control if he has by act, words, or course of conduct acted so as to cause a reasonable person to conclude that he has accepted responsibility for protection, food, shelter, and medical care for a child, elderly individual, or disabled individual. For purposes of an omission that causes a condition described by Subsection (a–1)(1), (2), (3), or (4), the actor acting during the actor's capacity as owner, operator, or employee of a group home or facility described by Subsection (a–1) is considered to have accepted responsibility for protection, food, shelter, and medical care for the child, elderly individual, or disabled individual who is a resident of the group home or facility.

(e) An offense under Subsection (a)(1) or (2) or (a–1)(1) or (2) is a felony of the first degree when the conduct is committed intentionally or knowingly. When the conduct is engaged in recklessly, the offense is a felony of the second degree.

(f) An offense under Subsection (a)(3) or (a–1)(3) or (4) is a felony of the third degree when the conduct is committed intentionally or knowingly, except that an offense under Subsection (a)(3) is a felony of the second degree when the conduct is committed intentionally or knowingly and the victim is a disabled individual residing in a center, as defined by Section 555.001, Health and Safety Code, or in a facility licensed under Chapter 252, Health and Safety Code, and the actor is an employee of the center or facility whose employment involved providing direct care for the victim. When the conduct is engaged in recklessly, the offense is a state jail felony.

(g) An offense under Subsection (a) is a state jail felony when the person acts with criminal negligence. An offense under Subsection (a–1) is a state jail felony when the person, with criminal negligence and by omission, causes a condition described by Subsection (a–1)(1), (2), (3), or (4).

(h) A person who is subject to prosecution under both this section and another section of this code may be prosecuted under either or both sections. Section 3.04 does not apply to criminal episodes prosecuted under both this section and another section of this code. If a criminal episode is prosecuted under both this section and another section of this code and sentences are assessed for convictions under both sections, the sentences shall run concurrently.

(i) It is an affirmative defense to prosecution under Subsection (b)(2) that before the offense the actor:

(1) notified in person the child, elderly individual, or disabled individual that he would no longer provide any of the care described by Subsection (d); and

(2) notified in writing the parents or person other than himself acting in loco parentis to the child, elderly individual, or disabled individual that he would no longer provide any of the care described by Subsection (d); or

(3) notified in writing the Department of Protective and Regulatory Services that he would no longer provide any of the care set forth in Subsection (d).

(j) Written notification under Subsection (i)(2) or (i)(3) is not effective unless it contains the name and address of the actor, the name and address of the child, elderly individual, or disabled individual, the type of care provided by the actor, and the date the care was discontinued.

(k) It is a defense to prosecution under this section that the act or omission consisted of:

(1) reasonable medical care occurring under the direction of or by a licensed physician; or

(2) emergency medical care administered in good faith and with reasonable care by a person not licensed in the healing arts.

(*l*) It is an affirmative defense to prosecution under this section:

(1) that the act or omission was based on treatment in accordance with the tenets and practices of a recognized religious method of healing with a generally accepted record of efficacy;

(2) for a person charged with an act of omission causing to a child, elderly individual, or disabled individual a condition described by Subsection (a)(1), (2), or (3) that:

(A) there is no evidence that, on the date prior to the offense charged, the defendant was aware of an incident of injury to the child, elderly individual, or disabled individual and failed to report the incident; and

(B) the person:

(i) was a victim of family violence, as that term is defined by Section 71.004, Family Code, committed by a person who is also charged with an offense against the child, elderly individual, or disabled individual under this section or any other section of this title;

(ii) did not cause a condition described by Subsection (a)(1), (2), or (3); and

(iii) did not reasonably believe at the time of the omission that an effort to prevent the person also charged with an offense against the child, elderly individual, or disabled individual from committing the offense would have an effect; or

(3) that:

(A) the actor was not more than three years older than the victim at the time of the offense; and

(B) the victim was a child at the time of the offense.

Acts 1973, 63rd Leg., p. 883, ch. 399, § 1, eff. Jan. 1, 1974. Amended by Acts 1977, 65th Leg., p. 2067, ch. 819, § 1, eff. Aug. 29, 1977; Acts 1979, 66th Leg., p. 365, ch. 162, § 1, eff. Aug. 27, 1979; Acts 1981, 67th Leg., p. 472, ch. 202, § 4, eff. Sept. 1, 1981; Acts 1981, 67th Leg., p. 2397, ch. 604, § 1, eff. Sept. 1, 1981; Acts 1989, 71st Leg., ch. 357, § 1, eff. Sept. 1, 1989; Acts 1991, 72nd Leg., ch. 497, § 1, eff. Sept. 1, 1991; Acts 1993, 73rd Leg., ch. 900, § 1.01, eff. Sept. 1, 1994; Acts 1995, 74th Leg., ch. 76, § 8.139, eff. Sept. 1, 1995; Acts 1999, 76th Leg., ch. 62, § 15.02(b), eff. Sept. 1, 1999; Acts 2005, 79th Leg., ch. 268, § 1.125(a), eff. Sept. 1, 2005; Acts 2005, 79th Leg., ch. 949, § 46, eff. Sept. 1, 2005; Acts 2009, 81st Leg., ch. 284, § 38, eff. June 11, 2009.

Section 48(a) of Acts 2009, 81st Leg., ch. 284 provides:

"(a) The changes in law made by this Act to Section 261.109, Family Code, Section 48.052, Human Resources Code, and Section 22.04, Penal Code, apply only to an offense committed on or after the effective date [June 11, 2009] of this Act. An offense committed before the effective date of this Act is governed by the law in effect when the offense was committed, and the former law is continued in effect for that purpose. For purposes of this section, an offense was committed before the effective date of this Act if any element of the offense occurred before that date."

§ 22.041. Abandoning or Endangering Child

(a) In this section, "abandon" means to leave a child in any place without providing reasonable and necessary care for the child, under circumstances under which no reasonable, similarly situated adult would leave a child of that age and ability.

(b) A person commits an offense if, having custody, care, or control of a child younger than 15 years, he intentionally abandons the child in any place under circumstances that expose the child to an unreasonable risk of harm.

(c) A person commits an offense if he intentionally, knowingly, recklessly, or with criminal negligence, by act or omission, engages in conduct that places a child younger than 15 years in imminent danger of death, bodily injury, or physical or mental impairment.

(c–1) For purposes of Subsection (c), it is presumed that a person engaged in conduct that places a child in imminent danger of death, bodily injury, or physical or mental impairment if:

(1) the person manufactured, possessed, or in any way introduced into the body of any person the controlled substance methamphetamine in the presence of the child;

(2) the person's conduct related to the proximity or accessibility of the controlled substance methamphetamine to the child and an analysis of a specimen of the child's blood, urine, or other bodily substance indicates the presence of methamphetamine in the child's body; or

(3) the person injected, ingested, inhaled, or otherwise introduced a controlled substance listed in Penalty Group 1, Section 481.102, Health and Safety Code, into the human body when the person was not in lawful possession of the substance as defined by Section 481.002(24) of that code.

(d) Except as provided by Subsection (e), an offense under Subsection (b) is:

(1) a state jail felony if the actor abandoned the child with intent to return for the child; or

(2) a felony of the third degree if the actor abandoned the child without intent to return for the child.

(e) An offense under Subsection (b) is a felony of the second degree if the actor abandons the child under circumstances that a reasonable person would believe would place the child in imminent danger of death, bodily injury, or physical or mental impairment.

(f) An offense under Subsection (c) is a state jail felony.

(g) It is a defense to prosecution under Subsection (c) that the act or omission enables the child to practice for or participate in an organized athletic event and that appropriate safety equipment and procedures are employed in the event.

(h) It is an exception to the application of this section that the actor voluntarily delivered the child to a designated emergency infant care provider under Section 262.302, Family Code.

Added by Acts 1985, 69th Leg., ch. 791, § 1, eff. Sept. 1, 1985. Amended by Acts 1989, 71st Leg., ch. 904, § 1, eff. Sept. 1, 1989; Acts 1993, 73rd Leg., ch. 900, § 1.01, eff. Sept. 1, 1994; Acts 1997, 75th Leg., ch. 687, § 1, eff. Sept. 1, 1997; Acts 1999, 76th Leg., ch. 1087, § 3, eff. Sept. 1, 1999; Acts 2001, 77th Leg., ch. 809, § 7, eff. Sept. 1, 2001; Acts 2005, 79th Leg., ch. 282, § 10, eff. Aug. 1, 2005; Acts 2007, 80th Leg., ch. 840, § 2, eff. Sept. 1, 2007.

Section 3 of Acts 2007, 80th Leg., ch. 840 provides:

"The change in law made by this Act applies only to an offense committed on or after the effective date [Sept. 1, 2007] of this Act. An offense committed before the effective date of this Act is governed by the law in effect when the offense was committed, and the former law is continued in effect for that purpose. For purposes of this section, an offense was committed before the effective date of this Act if any element of the offense was committed before that date."

§ 22.05. Deadly Conduct

(a) A person commits an offense if he recklessly engages in conduct that places another in imminent danger of serious bodily injury.

(b) A person commits an offense if he knowingly discharges a firearm at or in the direction of:

(1) one or more individuals; or

(2) a habitation, building, or vehicle and is reckless as to whether the habitation, building, or vehicle is occupied.

(c) Recklessness and danger are presumed if the actor knowingly pointed a firearm at or in the direction of another whether or not the actor believed the firearm to be loaded.

(d) For purposes of this section, "building," "habitation," and "vehicle" have the meanings assigned those terms by Section 30.01.

(e) An offense under Subsection (a) is a Class A misdemeanor. An offense under Subsection (b) is a felony of the third degree.

Acts 1973, 63rd Leg., p. 883, ch. 399, § 1, eff. Jan. 1, 1974. Amended by Acts 1993, 73rd Leg., ch. 900, § 1.01, eff. Sept. 1, 1994.

§ 22.06. Consent as Defense to Assaultive Conduct

(a) The victim's effective consent or the actor's reasonable belief that the victim consented to the actor's conduct is a defense to prosecution under Section 22.01 (Assault), 22.02 (Aggravated Assault), or 22.05 (Deadly Conduct) if:

(1) the conduct did not threaten or inflict serious bodily injury; or

(2) the victim knew the conduct was a risk of:

(A) his occupation;

(B) recognized medical treatment; or

(C) a scientific experiment conducted by recognized methods.

(b) The defense to prosecution provided by Subsection (a) is not available to a defendant who commits an offense described by Subsection (a) as a condition of the defendant's or the victim's initiation or continued membership in a criminal street gang, as defined by Section 71.01.

Acts 1973, 63rd Leg., p. 883, ch. 399, § 1, eff. Jan. 1, 1974. Amended by Acts 1993, 73rd Leg., ch. 900, § 1.01, eff. Sept. 1, 1994; Acts 2007, 80th Leg., ch. 273, § 1, eff. Sept. 1, 2007.

Section 2 of Acts 2007, 80th Leg., ch. 273 provides:

"The change in law made by this Act applies only to an offense committed on or after the effective date of this Act. An offense committed before the effective date of this Act is covered by the law in effect when the offense was committed, and the former law is continued in effect for that purpose. For purposes of this section, an offense is committed before the effective date of this Act if any element of the offense occurs before the effective date."

§ 22.065. Repealed by Texas Rules of Criminal Evidence effective September 1, 1986 [Acts 1985, 69th Leg., ch. 685, § 9(b)]

By order of the Court of Criminal Appeals dated December 18, 1985, effective September 1, 1986 adopting the Texas Rules of Criminal Evidence, this section is deemed to be repealed as it relates to criminal cases and criminal law matters pursuant to Acts 1985, 69th Leg., ch. 685, effective August 26, 1985, classified as Vernon's Ann. Civ.St. art. 1811f. The repeal is effective simultaneously with the effective date of the comprehensive body of rules of evidence promulgated by the Court of Criminal Appeals.

See, now, Vernon's Ann.Texas Rule Evid., rule 412.

§ 22.07. Terroristic Threat

(a) A person commits an offense if he threatens to commit any offense involving violence to any person or property with intent to:

(1) cause a reaction of any type to his threat by an official or volunteer agency organized to deal with emergencies;

(2) place any person in fear of imminent serious bodily injury;

(3) prevent or interrupt the occupation or use of a building, room, place of assembly, place to which the public has access, place of employment or occupation, aircraft, automobile, or other form of conveyance, or other public place;

(4) cause impairment or interruption of public communications, public transportation, public water, gas, or power supply or other public service;

(5) place the public or a substantial group of the public in fear of serious bodily injury; or

(6) influence the conduct or activities of a branch or agency of the federal government, the state, or a political subdivision of the state.

(b) An offense under Subsection (a)(1) is a Class B misdemeanor.

(c) An offense under Subsection (a)(2) is a Class B misdemeanor, except that the offense is a Class A misdemeanor if the offense:

(1) is committed against a member of the person's family or household or otherwise constitutes family violence; or

(2) is committed against a public servant.

(d) An offense under Subsection (a)(3) is a Class A misdemeanor, unless the actor causes pecuniary loss of $1,500 or more to the owner of the building, room, place, or conveyance, in which event the offense is a state jail felony.

(e) An offense under Subsection (a)(4), (a)(5), or (a)(6) is a felony of the third degree.

(f) In this section:

(1) "Family" has the meaning assigned by Section 71.003, Family Code.

(2) "Family violence" has the meaning assigned by Section 71.004, Family Code.

(3) "Household" has the meaning assigned by Section 71.005, Family Code.

(g) For purposes of Subsection (d), the amount of pecuniary loss is the amount of economic loss suffered by the owner of the building, room, place, or conveyance as a result of the prevention or interruption of the occupation or use of the building, room, place, or conveyance.

Acts 1973, 63rd Leg., p. 883, ch. 399, § 1, eff. Jan. 1, 1974. Amended by Acts 1979, 66th Leg., p. 1114, ch. 530, § 2, eff. Aug. 27, 1979; Acts 1993, 73rd Leg., ch. 900, § 1.01, eff. Sept. 1, 1994; Acts 2003, 78th Leg., ch. 139, § 1, eff. Sept. 1, 2003; Acts 2003, 78th Leg., ch. 388, § 2, eff. Sept. 1, 2003; Acts 2003, 78th Leg., ch. 446, § 1, eff. Sept. 1, 2003; Acts 2005, 79th Leg., ch. 728, § 16.003, eff. Sept. 1, 2005.

§ 22.08. Aiding Suicide

(a) A person commits an offense if, with intent to promote or assist the commission of suicide by another, he aids or attempts to aid the other to commit or attempt to commit suicide.

(b) An offense under this section is a Class C misdemeanor unless the actor's conduct causes suicide or attempted suicide that results in serious bodily injury, in which event the offense is a state jail felony.

Acts 1973, 63rd Leg., p. 883, ch. 399, § 1, eff. Jan. 1, 1974. Amended by Acts 1993, 73rd Leg., ch. 900, § 1.01, eff. Sept. 1, 1994.

§ 22.09. Tampering With Consumer Product

(a) In this section:

(1) "Consumer Product" means any product offered for sale to or for consumption by the public and includes "food" and "drugs" as those terms are defined in Section 431.002, Health and Safety Code.

(2) "Tamper" means to alter or add a foreign substance to a consumer product to make it probable that the consumer product will cause serious bodily injury.

(b) A person commits an offense if he knowingly or intentionally tampers with a consumer product knowing that the consumer product will be offered for sale to the public or as a gift to another.

(c) A person commits an offense if he knowingly or intentionally threatens to tamper with a consumer product with the intent to cause fear, to affect the sale of the consumer product, or to cause bodily injury to any person.

(d) An offense under Subsection (b) is a felony of the second degree unless a person suffers serious bodily injury, in which event it is a felony of the first degree. An offense under Subsection (c) is a felony of the third degree.

Added by Acts 1983, 68th Leg., p. 2812, ch. 481, § 1, eff. Sept. 1, 1983. Amended by Acts 1989, 71st Leg., ch. 1008, § 1, eff. Sept. 1, 1989; Acts 1991, 72nd Leg., ch. 14, § 284(32), eff. Sept. 1, 1991; Acts 1993, 73rd Leg., ch. 900, § 1.01, eff. Sept. 1, 1994.

§ 22.10. Leaving a Child in a Vehicle

(a) A person commits an offense if he intentionally or knowingly leaves a child in a motor vehicle for longer than five minutes, knowing that the child is:

(1) younger than seven years of age; and

(2) not attended by an individual in the vehicle who is 14 years of age or older.

(b) An offense under this section is a Class C misdemeanor.

Added by Acts 1984, 68th Leg., 2nd C.S., ch. 24, § 1, eff. Oct. 2, 1984. Amended by Acts 1993, 73rd Leg., ch. 900, § 1.01, eff. Sept. 1, 1994.

§ 22.11. Harassment By Persons in Certain Correctional Facilities; Harassment of Public Servant.

(a) A person commits an offense if, with the intent to assault, harass, or alarm, the person:

(1) while imprisoned or confined in a correctional or detention facility, causes another person to contact the blood, seminal fluid, vaginal fluid, saliva, urine, or feces of the actor, any other person, or an animal; or

(2) causes another person the actor knows to be a public servant to contact the blood, seminal fluid, vaginal fluid, saliva, urine, or feces of the actor, any other person, or an animal while the public servant is lawfully discharging an official duty or in retaliation or on account of an exercise of the public servant's official power or performance of an official duty.

(b) An offense under this section is a felony of the third degree.

(c) If conduct constituting an offense under this section also constitutes an offense under another section of this code, the actor may be prosecuted under either section.

(d) In this section, "correctional or detention facility" means:

(1) a secure correctional facility; or

(2) a "secure correctional facility" or a "secure detention facility" as defined by Section 51.02, Family Code, operated by or under contract with a juvenile board or the Texas Youth Commission or any other facility operated by or under contract with that commission.

(e) For purposes of Subsection (a)(2), the actor is presumed to have known the person was a public servant if the person was wearing a distinctive uniform or badge indicating the person's employment as a public servant.

Added by Acts 1999, 76th Leg., ch. 335, § 1, eff. Sept. 1, 1999. Amended by Acts 2003, 78th Leg., ch. 878, § 1, eff. Sept. 1, 2003; Acts 2003, 78th Leg., ch. 1006, § 1, eff. Sept. 1, 2003; Acts 2005, 79th Leg., ch. 543, §§ 1, 2, eff. Sept. 1, 2005.

§ 22.12. Applicability to Certain Conduct

This chapter does not apply to conduct charged as having been committed against an individual who is an unborn child if the conduct is:

(1) committed by the mother of the unborn child;

(2) a lawful medical procedure performed by a physician or other health care provider with the requisite consent;

(3) a lawful medical procedure performed by a physician or other licensed health care provider with the requisite consent as part of an assisted reproduction as defined by Section 160.102, Family Code; or

(4) the dispensation of a drug in accordance with law or administration of a drug prescribed in accordance with law.

Added by Acts 2003, 78th Leg., ch. 822, § 2.04, eff. Sept. 1, 2003.

TITLE 6. OFFENSES AGAINST THE FAMILY

CHAPTER 25. OFFENSES AGAINST THE FAMILY

§ 25.01. Bigamy

(a) An individual commits an offense if:

(1) he is legally married and he:

(A) purports to marry or does marry a person other than his spouse in this state, or any other state or foreign country, under circumstances that would, but for the actor's prior marriage, constitute a marriage; or

(B) lives with a person other than his spouse in this state under the appearance of being married; or

(2) he knows that a married person other than his spouse is married and he:

(A) purports to marry or does marry that person in this state, or any other state or foreign country, under circumstances that would, but for the person's prior marriage, constitute a marriage; or

(B) lives with that person in this state under the appearance of being married.

(b) For purposes of this section, "under the appearance of being married" means holding out that the parties are married with cohabitation and an intent to be married by either party.

(c) It is a defense to prosecution under Subsection (a)(1) that the actor reasonably believed at the time of the commission of the offense that the actor and the person whom the actor married or purported to marry or with whom the actor lived under the appearance of being married were legally eligible to be married because the actor's prior marriage was void or had been dissolved by death, divorce, or annulment. For purposes of this subsection, an actor's belief is reasonable if the belief is substantiated by a certified copy of a death certificate or other signed document issued by a court.

(d) For the purposes of this section, the lawful wife or husband of the actor may testify both for or against the actor concerning proof of the original marriage.

(e) An offense under this section is a felony of the third degree, except that if at the time of the commission of the offense, the person whom the actor marries or purports to marry or with whom the actor lives under the appearance of being married is:

(1) 16 years of age or older, the offense is a felony of the second degree; or

(2) younger than 16 years of age, the offense is a felony of the first degree.

Acts 1973, 63rd Leg., p. 883, ch. 399, § 1, eff. Jan. 1, 1974. Amended by Acts 1993, 73rd Leg., ch. 900, § 1.01, eff. Sept. 1, 1994; Acts 2005, 79th Leg., ch. 268, § 4.03, eff. Sept. 1, 2005.

§ 25.02. Prohibited Sexual Conduct

(a) A person commits an offense if the person engages in sexual intercourse or deviate sexual intercourse with another person the actor knows to be, without regard to legitimacy:

(1) the actor's ancestor or descendant by blood or adoption;

(2) the actor's current or former stepchild or stepparent;

(3) the actor's parent's brother or sister of the whole or half blood;

(4) the actor's brother or sister of the whole or half blood or by adoption;

(5) the children of the actor's brother or sister of the whole or half blood or by adoption; or

(6) the son or daughter of the actor's aunt or uncle of the whole or half blood or by adoption.

(b) For purposes of this section:

(1) "Deviate sexual intercourse" means any contact between the genitals of one person and the mouth or anus of another person with intent to arouse or gratify the sexual desire of any person.

(2) "Sexual intercourse" means any penetration of the female sex organ by the male sex organ.

(c) An offense under this section is a felony of the third degree, unless the offense is committed under Subsection (a)(1), in which event the offense is a felony of the second degree.

Acts 1973, 63rd Leg., p. 883, ch. 399, § 1, eff. Jan. 1, 1974. Amended by Acts 1993, 73rd Leg., ch. 900, § 1.01, eff. Sept. 1, 1994; Acts 2005, 79th Leg., ch. 268, § 4.04, eff. Sept. 1, 2005; Acts 2009, 81st Leg., ch. 673, § 1, eff. Sept. 1, 2009.

Section 2 of Acts 2009, 81st Leg., ch. 673 provides:

"The change in law made by this Act applies only to an offense committed on or after the effective date [Sept. 1, 2009] of this Act. An offense committed before the effective date of this Act is covered by the law in effect when the offense was committed, and the former law is continued in effect for that purpose. For purposes of this section, an offense was committed before the effective date of this Act if any element of the offense was committed before that date."

§ 25.03. Interference With Child Custody

(a) A person commits an offense if the person takes or retains a child younger than 18 years when the person:

(1) knows that the person's taking or retention violates the express terms of a judgment or order, including a temporary order, of a court disposing of the child's custody; or

(2) has not been awarded custody of the child by a court of competent jurisdiction, knows that a suit for divorce or a civil suit or application for habeas corpus to dispose of the child's custody has been filed, and takes the child out of the geographic area of the counties composing the judicial district if the court is a district court or the county if the court is a statutory county court, without the permission of the court and with the intent to deprive the court of authority over the child.

(b) A noncustodial parent commits an offense if, with the intent to interfere with the lawful custody of a child younger than 18 years, the noncustodial parent knowingly entices or persuades the child to leave the custody of the custodial parent, guardian, or person standing in the stead of the custodial parent or guardian of the child.

(c) It is a defense to prosecution under Subsection (a)(2) that the actor returned the child to the geographic area of the counties composing the judicial district if the court is a district court or the county if the court is a statutory county court, within three days after the date of the commission of the offense.

(d) An offense under this section is a state jail felony.

Acts 1973, 63rd Leg., p. 883, ch. 399, § 1, eff. Jan. 1, 1974. Amended by Acts 1979, 66th Leg., p. 1111, ch. 527, § 1, eff. Aug. 27, 1979; Acts 1987, 70th Leg., ch. 444, § 1, eff. Sept. 1, 1987; Acts 1989, 71st Leg., ch. 830, § 1, eff. Sept. 1, 1989; Acts 1993, 73rd Leg., ch. 900, § 1.01, eff. Sept. 1, 1994; Acts 2001, 77th Leg., ch. 332, § 1, eff. May 24, 2001; Acts 2007, 80th Leg., ch. 272, § 1, eff. Sept. 1, 2007.

Section 3 of Acts 2007, 80th Leg., ch. 272 provides:

"The change in law made by this Act applies only to an offense committed on or after the effective date of this Act. An offense committed before the effective date of this Act is governed by the law in effect when the offense was committed, and the former law is continued in effect for that purpose. For purposes of this section, an offense was committed before the effective date of this Act if any element of the offense was committed before that date."

§ 25.031. Agreement to Abduct From Custody

(a) A person commits an offense if the person agrees, for remuneration or the promise of remuneration, to abduct a child younger than 18 years of age by force, threat of force, misrepresentation, stealth, or unlawful entry, knowing that the child is under the care and control of a person having custody or physical possession of the child under a court order, including a temporary order, or under the care and control of another person who is exercising care and control with the consent of a person having custody or physical possession under a court order, including a temporary order.

(b) An offense under this section is a state jail felony.

Added by Acts 1987, 70th Leg., ch. 444, § 3, eff. Sept. 1, 1987. Amended by Acts 1993, 73rd Leg., ch. 900, § 1.01, eff. Sept. 1, 1994; Acts 2007, 80th Leg., ch. 272, § 2, eff. Sept. 1, 2007.

§ 25.04. Enticing a Child

(a) A person commits an offense if, with the intent to interfere with the lawful custody of a child younger than 18 years, he knowingly entices, persuades, or takes the child from the custody of the parent or guardian or person standing in the stead of the parent or guardian of such child.

(b) An offense under this section is a Class B misdemeanor, unless it is shown on the trial of the offense that the actor intended to commit a felony against the child, in which event an offense under this section is a felony of the third degree.

Acts 1973, 63rd Leg., p. 883, ch. 399, § 1, eff. Jan. 1, 1974. Amended by Acts 1993, 73rd Leg., ch. 900, § 1.01, eff. Sept. 1, 1994; Acts 1999, 76th Leg., ch. 685, § 7, eff. Sept. 1, 1999.

§ 25.05. Criminal Nonsupport

(a) An individual commits an offense if the individual intentionally or knowingly fails to provide support for the individual's child younger than 18 years of age, or for the individual's child who is the subject of a court order requiring the individual to support the child.

(b) For purposes of this section, "child" includes a child born out of wedlock whose paternity has either been acknowledged by the actor or has been established in a civil suit under the Family Code or the law of another state.

(c) Under this section, a conviction may be had on the uncorroborated testimony of a party to the offense.

(d) It is an affirmative defense to prosecution under this section that the actor could not provide support for the actor's child.

(e) The pendency of a prosecution under this section does not affect the power of a court to enter an order for child support under the Family Code.

(f) An offense under this section is a state jail felony.

Acts 1973, 63rd Leg., p. 883, ch. 399, § 1, eff. Jan. 1, 1974. Amended by Acts 1987, 70th Leg., 2nd C.S., ch. 73, § 13, eff. Nov. 1, 1987; Acts 1993, 73rd Leg., ch. 900, § 1.01, eff. Sept. 1, 1994; Acts 2001, 77th Leg., ch. 375, § 1, eff. May 25, 2001.

Subsection (d) [formerly subsec. (f)] of this section was declared unconstitutional by Lowry v. State, 671 S.W.2d 601.

§ 25.06. Harboring Runaway Child

(a) A person commits an offense if he knowingly harbors a child and he is criminally negligent about whether the child:

(1) is younger than 18 years; and

(2) has escaped from the custody of a peace officer, a probation officer, the Texas Youth Council, or a detention facility for children, or is voluntarily absent from the child's home without the consent of the child's parent or guardian for a substantial length of time or without the intent to return.

(b) It is a defense to prosecution under this section that the actor was related to the child within the second degree by consanguinity or affinity, as determined under Chapter 573, Government Code.

(c) It is a defense to prosecution under this section that the actor notified:

(1) the person or agency from which the child escaped or a law enforcement agency of the presence of the child within 24 hours after discovering that the child had escaped from custody; or

(2) a law enforcement agency or a person at the child's home of the presence of the child within 24 hours after discovering that the child was voluntarily absent from home without the consent of the child's parent or guardian.

(d) An offense under this section is a Class A misdemeanor.

(e) On the receipt of a report from a peace officer, probation officer, the Texas Youth Council, a foster home, or a detention facility for children that a child has escaped its custody or upon receipt of a report from a parent, guardian, conservator, or legal custodian that a child is missing, a law enforcement agency shall immediately enter a record of the child into the National Crime Information Center.

Added by Acts 1979, 66th Leg., p. 1155, ch. 558, § 1, eff. Sept. 1, 1979. Amended by Acts 1983, 68th Leg., p. 4750, ch. 831, p. 4750, § 1, eff. Sept. 1, 1983; Acts 1991, 72nd Leg., ch. 561, § 40, eff. Aug. 26, 1991. Renumbered from V.T.C.A., Penal Code § 25.07 by Acts 1993, 73rd Leg., ch. 900, § 1.01, eff. Sept. 1, 1994. Amended by Acts 1995, 74th Leg., ch. 76, § 5.95(27), eff. Sept. 1, 1995.

Another § 25.06, added by Acts 1977, 65th Leg., p. 81, ch. 38, § 1, and amended by Acts 1981, 67th Leg., p. 2211, ch. 514, § 1, was renumbered as § 25.11 by Acts 1987, 70th Leg., ch. 167, § 5.01(a)(44).

§ 25.07. Violation of Certain Court Orders or Conditions of Bond in a Family Violence Case

(a) A person commits an offense if, in violation of a condition of bond set in a family violence case and related to the safety of the victim or the safety of the community, an order issued under Article 17.292, Code of Criminal Procedure, an order issued under Section 6.504, Family Code, Chapter 83, Family Code, if the temporary ex parte order has been served on the person, or Chapter 85, Family Code, or an order issued by another jurisdiction as provided by Chapter 88, Family Code, the person knowingly or intentionally:

(1) commits family violence or an act in furtherance of an offense under Section 22.011, 22.021, or 42.072;

(2) communicates:

(A) directly with a protected individual or a member of the family or household in a threatening or harassing manner;

(B) a threat through any person to a protected individual or a member of the family or household; or

(C) in any manner with the protected individual or a member of the family or household except through the person's attorney or a person appointed by the court, if the violation is of an order described by this subsection and the order prohibits any communication with a protected individual or a member of the family or household;

(3) goes to or near any of the following places as specifically described in the order or condition of bond:

(A) the residence or place of employment or business of a protected individual or a member of the family or household; or

(B) any child care facility, residence, or school where a child protected by the order or condition of bond normally resides or attends; or

(4) possesses a firearm.

(b) For the purposes of this section:

(1) "Family violence," " family," "household," and "member of a household" have the meanings assigned by Chapter 71, Family Code.

(2) "Firearm" has the meaning assigned by Chapter 46.

(c) If conduct constituting an offense under this section also constitutes an offense under another section of this code, the actor may be prosecuted under either section or under both sections.

(d) Reconciliatory actions or agreements made by persons affected by an order do not affect the validity of the order or the duty of a peace officer to enforce this section.

(e) A peace officer investigating conduct that may constitute an offense under this section for a violation of an order may not arrest a person protected by that order for a violation of that order.

(f) It is not a defense to prosecution under this section that certain information has been excluded, as provided by Section 85.007, Family Code, or Article 17.292, Code of Criminal Procedure, from an order to which this section applies.

(g) An offense under this section is a Class A misdemeanor unless it is shown on the trial of the offense that the defendant has previously been convicted under this section two or more times or has violated the order or condition of bond by committing an assault or the offense of stalking, in which event the offense is a third degree felony.

Added by Acts 1983, 68th Leg., p. 4049, ch. 631, § 3, eff. Sept. 1, 1983. Amended by Acts 1985, 69th Leg., ch. 583, § 3, eff. Sept. 1, 1985; Acts 1987, 70th Leg., ch. 170, § 1, eff. Sept. 1, 1987; Acts 1987, 70th Leg., ch. 677, § 8, eff. Sept. 1, 1987; Acts 1989, 71st Leg., ch. 614, §§ 23 to 26, eff. Sept. 1, 1989; Acts 1989, 71st Leg., ch. 739, §§ 4 to 7, eff. Sept. 1, 1989; Acts 1991, 72nd Leg., ch. 366, § 2, eff. Sept. 1, 1991. Renumbered from V.T.C.A., Penal Code § 25.08 and amended by Acts 1993, 73rd Leg., ch. 900, § 1.01, eff. Sept. 1, 1994. Amended by Acts 1995, 74th Leg., ch. 658, §§ 2, 3, eff. June 14, 1995; Acts 1995, 74th Leg., ch. 660, §§ 1, 2, eff. Sept. 1, 1995; Acts 1995, 74th Leg., ch. 1024, § 23, eff. Sept. 1, 1995; Acts 1997, 75th Leg., ch. 1, § 2, eff. Jan. 28, 1997; Acts 1997, 75th Leg., ch. 1193, § 21, eff. Sept. 1, 1997; Acts 1999, 76th Leg., ch. 62, § 15.02(c), eff. Sept. 1, 1999; Acts 2001, 77th Leg., ch. 23, § 1, eff. Sept. 1, 2001; Acts 2003, 78th Leg., ch. 134, § 1, eff. Sept. 1, 2003; Acts 2007, 80th Leg., ch. 66, § 2, eff. May 11, 2007; Acts 2007, 80th Leg., ch. 1113, §§ 1, 2; Acts 2009, 81st Leg., ch. 87, § 19.001, eff. Sept. 1, 2009.

Section 3 of Acts 2007, 80th Leg., ch. 66 provides:

"The change in law made by this Act applies only to a defendant arrested on or after the effective date of this Act. A defendant arrested before the effective date of this Act is covered by the law in effect on the date the defendant was arrested, and the former law is continued in effect for that purpose."

Sections 8 and 9 of Acts 2007, 80th Leg., ch. 1113 provide:

"Sec. 8. This Act applies only to an offense committed on or after the effective date of this Act [Jan. 1, 2008]. An offense committed before the effective date of this Act is governed by the law in effect at the time the offense was committed, and the former law is continued in effect for that purpose. For purposes of this section, an offense was committed before the effective date of this Act if any element of the offense was committed before that date.

"Sec. 9. This Act takes effect January 1, 2008, but only if the constitutional amendment proposed by the 80th Legislature, Regular Session, 2007, authorizing the denial of bail to a person who violates certain court orders or conditions of release in a felony or family violence case is approved by the voters. If that constitutional amendment is not approved by the voters, this Act has no effect."

§ 25.071. Violation of Protective Order Preventing Offense Caused by Bias or Prejudice

(a) A person commits an offense if, in violation of an order issued under Article 6.08, Code of Criminal Procedure, the person knowingly or intentionally:

(1) commits an offense under Title 5[1] or Section 28.02, 28.03, or 28.08 and commits the offense because of bias or prejudice as described by Article 42.014, Code of Criminal Procedure;

(2) communicates:

(A) directly with a protected individual in a threatening or harassing manner;

(B) a threat through any person to a protected individual; or

(C) in any manner with the protected individual, if the order prohibits any communication with a protected individual; or

(3) goes to or near the residence or place of employment or business of a protected individual.

(b) If conduct constituting an offense under this section also constitutes an offense under another section of this code, the actor may be prosecuted under either section or under both sections.

(c) A peace officer investigating conduct that may constitute an offense under this section for a violation of an order may not arrest a person protected by that order for a violation of that order.

(d) An offense under this section is a Class A misdemeanor unless it is shown on the trial of the offense that the defendant has previously been convicted under this section two or more times or has violated the protective order by committing an assault, in which event the offense is a third degree felony.

Added by Acts 2001, 77th Leg., ch. 85, § 3.02, eff. Sept. 1, 2001.

[1] V.T.C.A., Penal Code § 25.01 et seq.

§ 25.08. Sale or Purchase of Child

(a) A person commits an offense if he:

(1) possesses a child younger than 18 years of age or has the custody, conservatorship, or guardianship of a child younger than 18 years of age, whether or not he has actual possession of the child, and he offers to accept, agrees to accept, or accepts a thing of value for the delivery of the child to another or for the possession of the child by another for purposes of adoption; or

(2) offers to give, agrees to give, or gives a thing of value to another for acquiring or maintaining the possession of a child for the purpose of adoption.

(b) It is an exception to the application of this section that the thing of value is:

(1) a fee or reimbursement paid to a child-placing agency as authorized by law;

(2) a fee paid to an attorney, social worker, mental health professional, or physician for services rendered in the usual course of legal or medical practice or in providing adoption counseling;

(3) a reimbursement of legal or medical expenses incurred by a person for the benefit of the child; or

(4) a necessary pregnancy-related expense paid by a child-placing agency for the benefit of the

child's parent during the pregnancy or after the birth of the child as permitted by the minimum standards for child-placing agencies and Department of Protective and Regulatory Services rules.

(c) An offense under this section is a felony of the third degree, except that the offense is a felony of the second degree if the actor commits the offense with intent to commit an offense under Section 43.25.

Added by Acts 1977, 65th Leg., p. 81, ch. 38, § 1, eff. March 30, 1977. Amended by Acts 1981, 67th Leg., p. 2211, ch. 514, § 1, eff. Sept. 1, 1981. Renumbered from V.T.C.A., Penal Code § 25.06 by Acts 1987, 70th Leg., ch. 167, § 5.01(a)(44). Renumbered from V.T.C.A., Penal Code § 25.11 and amended by Acts 1993, 73rd Leg., ch. 900, § 1.01, eff. Sept. 1, 1994. Amended by Acts 2001, 77th Leg., ch. 134, § 1, eff. Sept. 1, 2001; Acts 2003, 78th Leg., ch. 1005, § 3, eff. Sept. 1, 2003.

§ 25.09. Advertising for Placement of Child

(a) A person commits an offense if the person advertises in the public media that the person will place a child for adoption or will provide or obtain a child for adoption.

(b) This section does not apply to a licensed child-placing agency that is identified in the advertisement as a licensed child-placing agency.

(c) An offense under this section is a Class A misdemeanor unless the person has been convicted previously under this section, in which event the offense is a felony of the third degree.

(d) In this section:

(1) "Child" has the meaning assigned by Section 101.003, Family Code.

(2) "Public media" has the meaning assigned by Section 38.01. The term also includes communications through the use of the Internet or another public computer network.

Added by Acts 1997, 75th Leg., ch. 561, § 31, eff. Sept. 1, 1997.

§ 25.10. Interference with Rights of Guardian of the Person

(a) In this section:

(1) "Possessory right" means the right of a guardian of the person to have physical possession of a ward and to establish the ward's legal domicile, as provided by Section 767(1), Texas Probate Code.

(2) "Ward" has the meaning assigned by Section 601, Texas Probate Code.

(b) A person commits an offense if the person takes, retains, or conceals a ward when the person knows that the person's taking, retention, or concealment interferes with a possessory right with respect to the ward.

(c) An offense under this section is a state jail felony.

(d) This section does not apply to a governmental entity where the taking, retention, or concealment of the ward was authorized by Subtitle E, Title 5, Family Code, or Chapter 48, Human Resources Code.

Added by Acts 2003, 78th Leg., ch. 549, § 32, eff. Sept. 1, 2003.

§ 25.11. Continuous Violence Against the Family

(a) A person commits an offense if, during a period that is 12 months or less in duration, the person two or more times engages in conduct that constitutes an offense under Section 22.01(a)(1) against another person or persons whose relationship to or association with the defendant is described by Section 71. 0021(b), 71.003, or 71.005, Family Code.

(b) If the jury is the trier of fact, members of the jury are not required to agree unanimously on the specific conduct in which the defendant engaged that constituted an offense under Section 22.01(a)(1) against the person or persons described by Subsection (a) or the exact date when that conduct occurred. The jury must agree unanimously that the defendant, during a period that is 12 months or less in duration, two or more times engaged in conduct that constituted an offense under Section 22.01(a)(1) against the person or persons described by Subsection (a).

(c) A defendant may not be convicted in the same criminal action of another offense the victim of which is an alleged victim of the offense under Subsection (a) and an element of which is any conduct that is alleged as an element of the offense under Subsection (a) unless the other offense:

(1) is charged in the alternative;

(2) occurred outside the period in which the offense alleged under Subsection (a) was committed; or

(3) is considered by the trier of fact to be a lesser included offense of the offense alleged under Subsection (a).

(d) A defendant may not be charged with more than one count under Subsection (a) if all of the specific conduct that is alleged to have been engaged in is alleged to have been committed against a single victim or members of the same household, as defined by Section 71.005, Family Code.

(e) An offense under this section is a felony of the third degree.

Added by Acts 2009, 81st Leg., ch. 665, § 1, eff. Sept. 1, 2009.

Section 3 of Acts 2009, 81st Leg., ch. 665 provides:

"The change in law made by this Act applies only to an offense committed on or after the effective date [Sept. 1, 2009] of this Act. An offense committed before the effective date of this Act is covered by the law in effect when the offense was committed, and the former law is continued in effect for that purpose. For purposes of this section, an offense was committed before the effective date of this Act if any element of the offense occurred before that date."

TITLE 7. OFFENSES AGAINST PROPERTY

CHAPTER 28. ARSON, CRIMINAL MISCHIEF, AND OTHER PROPERTY DAMAGE OR DESTRUCTION

Section

§ 28.01. Definitions

In this chapter:

(1) "Habitation" means a structure or vehicle that is adapted for the overnight accommodation of persons and includes:

(A) each separately secured or occupied portion of the structure or vehicle; and

(B) each structure appurtenant to or connected with the structure or vehicle.

(2) "Building" means any structure or enclosure intended for use or occupation as a habitation or for some purpose of trade, manufacture, ornament, or use.

(3) "Property" means:

(A) real property;

(B) tangible or intangible personal property, including anything severed from land; or

(C) a document, including money, that represents or embodies anything of value.

(4) "Vehicle" includes any device in, on, or by which any person or property is or may be propelled, moved, or drawn in the normal course of commerce or transportation.

(5) "Open-space land" means real property that is undeveloped for the purpose of human habitation.

(6) "Controlled burning" means the burning of unwanted vegetation with the consent of the owner of the property on which the vegetation is located and in such a manner that the fire is controlled and limited to a designated area.

Acts 1973, 63rd Leg., p. 883, ch. 399, § 1, eff. Jan. 1, 1974. Amended by Acts 1979, 66th Leg., p. 1216, ch. 588, § 1, eff. Sept. 1, 1979; Acts 1989, 71st Leg., ch. 31, § 1, eff. Sept. 1, 1989; Acts 1993, 73rd Leg., ch. 900, § 1.01, eff. Sept. 1, 1994.

§ 28.02. Arson

(a) A person commits an offense if the person starts a fire, regardless of whether the fire continues after ignition, or causes an explosion with intent to destroy or damage:

(1) any vegetation, fence, or structure on open-space land; or

(2) any building, habitation, or vehicle:

(A) knowing that it is within the limits of an incorporated city or town;

(B) knowing that it is insured against damage or destruction;

(C) knowing that it is subject to a mortgage or other security interest;

(D) knowing that it is located on property belonging to another;

(E) knowing that it has located within it property belonging to another; or

(F) when the person is reckless about whether the burning or explosion will endanger the life of some individual or the safety of the property of another.

(a–1) A person commits an offense if the person recklessly starts a fire or causes an explosion while manufacturing or attempting to manufacture a controlled substance and the fire or explosion damages any building, habitation, or vehicle.

(a–2) A person commits an offense if the person intentionally starts a fire or causes an explosion and in so doing:

(1) recklessly damages or destroys a building belonging to another; or

(2) recklessly causes another person to suffer bodily injury or death.

(b) It is an exception to the application of Subsection (a)(1) that the fire or explosion was a part of the controlled burning of open-space land.

(c) It is a defense to prosecution under Subsection (a)(2)(A) that prior to starting the fire or causing the explosion, the actor obtained a permit or other written authorization granted in accordance with a city ordinance, if any, regulating fires and explosions.

(d) An offense under Subsection (a) is a felony of the second degree, except that the offense is a felony of the first degree if it is shown on the trial of the offense that:

(1) bodily injury or death was suffered by any person by reason of the commission of the offense; or

(2) the property intended to be damaged or destroyed by the actor was a habitation or a place of assembly or worship.

(e) An offense under Subsection (a–1) is a state jail felony, except that the offense is a felony of the third degree if it is shown on the trial of the offense that bodily injury or death was suffered by any person by reason of the commission of the offense.

(f) An offense under Subsection (a–2) is a state jail felony.

(g) If conduct that constitutes an offense under Subsection (a–1) or that constitutes an offense under Subsection (a–2) also constitutes an offense under another subsection of this section or another section of this code, the actor may be prosecuted under Subsection (a–1) or Subsection (a–2), under the other subsection of this section, or under the other section of this code.

Acts 1973, 63rd Leg., p. 883, ch. 399, § 1, eff. Jan. 1, 1974. Amended by Acts 1979, 66th Leg., p. 1216, ch. 588, § 2, eff. Sept. 1, 1979; Acts 1981, 67th Leg., p. 1837, ch. 425, § 1, eff. Sept. 1, 1981; Acts 1989, 71st Leg., ch. 31, § 2, eff. Sept. 1, 1989; Acts 1993, 73rd Leg., ch. 900, § 1.01, eff. Sept. 1, 1994; Acts 1997, 75th Leg., ch. 1006, § 1, eff. Sept. 1, 1997; Acts 2001, 77th Leg., ch. 976, § 1, eff. Sept. 1, 2001; Acts 2005, 79th Leg., ch. 960, § 1, eff. Sept. 1, 2005; Acts 2009, 81st Leg., ch. 1168, § 1, eff. Sept. 1, 2009.

Section 2 of Acts 2009, 81st Leg., ch. 1168 provides:

"The change in law made by this Act applies only to an offense committed on or after the effective date [Sept. 1, 2009] of this Act. An offense committed before the effective date of this Act is covered by the law in effect when the offense was committed, and the former law is continued in effect for that purpose. For purposes of this section, an offense was committed before the effective date of this Act if any element of the offense occurred before that date."

§ 28.03. Criminal Mischief

(a) A person commits an offense if, without the effective consent of the owner:

(1) he intentionally or knowingly damages or destroys the tangible property of the owner;

(2) he intentionally or knowingly tampers with the tangible property of the owner and causes pecuniary loss or substantial inconvenience to the owner or a third person; or

(3) he intentionally or knowingly makes markings, including inscriptions, slogans, drawings, or paintings, on the tangible property of the owner.

(b) Except as provided by Subsections (f) and (h), an offense under this section is:

(1) a Class C misdemeanor if:

(A) the amount of pecuniary loss is less than $50; or

(B) except as provided in Subdivision (3)(A) or (3)(B), it causes substantial inconvenience to others;

(2) a Class B misdemeanor if the amount of pecuniary loss is $50 or more but less than $500;

(3) a Class A misdemeanor if:

(A) the amount of pecuniary loss is $500 or more but less than $1,500; or

(B) the actor causes in whole or in part impairment or interruption of any public water supply, or causes to be diverted in whole, in part, or in any manner, including installation or removal of any device for any such purpose, any public water supply, regardless of the amount of the pecuniary loss;

(4) a state jail felony if the amount of pecuniary loss is:

(A) $1,500 or more but less than $20,000;

(B) less than $1,500, if the property damaged or destroyed is a habitation and if the damage or destruction is caused by a firearm or explosive weapon;

(C) less than $1,500, if the property was a fence used for the production or containment of:

(i) cattle, bison, horses, sheep, swine, goats, exotic livestock, or exotic poultry; or

(ii) game animals as that term is defined by Section 63.001, Parks and Wildlife Code; or

(D) less than $20,000 and the actor causes wholly or partly impairment or interruption of public communications, public transportation, public gas or power supply, or other public service, or causes to be diverted wholly, partly, or in any manner, including installation or removal of any device for any such purpose, any public communications or public gas or power supply;

(5) a felony of the third degree if the amount of the pecuniary loss is $20,000 or more but less than $100,000;

(6) a felony of the second degree if the amount of pecuniary loss is $100,000 or more but less than $200,000; or

(7) a felony of the first degree if the amount of pecuniary loss is $200,000 or more.

(c) For the purposes of this section, it shall be presumed that a person who is receiving the economic benefit of public communications, public water, gas, or power supply, has knowingly tampered with the tangible property of the owner if the communication or supply has been:

(1) diverted from passing through a metering device; or

(2) prevented from being correctly registered by a metering device; or

(3) activated by any device installed to obtain public communications, public water, gas, or power supply without a metering device.

(d) The terms "public communication, public transportation, public gas or power supply, or other public service" and "public water supply" shall mean, refer to, and include any such services subject to regulation by the Public Utility Commission of Texas, the Railroad Commission of Texas, or the Texas Natural Resource Conservation Commission or any such services enfranchised by the State of Texas or any political subdivision thereof.

(e) When more than one item of tangible property, belonging to one or more owners, is damaged, destroyed, or tampered with in violation of this section pursuant to one scheme or continuing course of conduct, the conduct may be considered as one offense, and the amounts of pecuniary loss to property resulting from the damage to, destruction of, or tampering with the property may be aggregated in determining the grade of the offense.

(f) An offense under this section is a state jail felony if the damage or destruction is inflicted on a place of worship or human burial, a public monument, or a community center that provides medical, social, or educational programs and the amount of the pecuniary loss to real property or to tangible personal property is less than $20,000.

(g) In this section:

(1) "Explosive weapon" means any explosive or incendiary device that is designed, made, or adapted for the purpose of inflicting serious bodily injury, death, or substantial property damage, or for the principal purpose of causing such a loud report as to cause undue public alarm or terror, and includes:

(A) an explosive or incendiary bomb, grenade, rocket, and mine;

(B) a device designed, made, or adapted for delivering or shooting an explosive weapon; and

(C) a device designed, made, or adapted to start a fire in a time-delayed manner.

(2) "Firearm" has the meaning assigned by Section 46.01.

(3) "Institution of higher education" has the meaning assigned by Section 61.003, Education Code.

(4) "Aluminum wiring" means insulated or noninsulated wire or cable that consists of at least 50 percent aluminum, including any tubing or conduit attached to the wire or cable.

(5) "Bronze wiring" means insulated or noninsulated wire or cable that consists of at least 50 percent bronze, including any tubing or conduit attached to the wire or cable.

(6) "Copper wiring" means insulated or noninsulated wire or cable that consists of at least 50 percent copper, including any tubing or conduit attached to the wire or cable.

(7) "Transportation communications equipment" means:

(A) an official traffic-control device, railroad sign or signal, or traffic-control signal, as those terms are defined by Section 541.304, Transportation Code; or

(B) a sign, signal, or device erected by a railroad, public body, or public officer to direct the movement of a railroad train, as defined by Section 541.202, Transportation Code.

(8) "Transportation communications device" means any item attached to transportation communications equipment, including aluminum wiring, bronze wiring, and copper wiring.

(h) An offense under this section is a state jail felony if the amount of the pecuniary loss to real property or to tangible personal property is $1,500 or more but less than $20,000 and the damage or destruction is inflicted on a public or private elementary school, secondary school, or institution of higher education.

(*i*) Notwithstanding Subsection (b), an offense under this section is a felony of the first degree if the property is livestock and the damage is caused by introducing bovine spongiform encephalopathy, commonly known as mad cow disease, or a disease described by Section 161.041(a), Agriculture Code. In this subsection, "livestock" has the meaning assigned by Section 161.001, Agriculture Code.

(j) Notwithstanding Subsection (b), an offense under this section is a felony of the third degree if:

(1) the tangible property damaged, destroyed, or tampered with is transportation communications equipment or a transportation communications device; and

(2) the amount of the pecuniary loss to the tangible property is less than $100,000.

Acts 1973, 63rd Leg., p. 883, ch. 399, § 1, eff. Jan. 1, 1974. Amended by Acts 1981, 67th Leg., p. 66, ch. 29, § 1, eff. Aug. 31, 1981; Acts 1983, 68th Leg., p. 2917, ch. 497, § 1, eff. Sept. 1, 1983; Acts 1985, 69th Leg., ch. 352, § 1, eff. Sept. 1, 1985; Acts 1989, 71st Leg., ch. 559, § 1, eff. June 14, 1989; Acts 1989, 71st Leg., ch. 1253, § 1, eff. Sept. 1, 1989; Acts 1989, 71st Leg., 1st C.S., ch. 42, § 1, eff. Sept. 1, 1989; Acts 1993, 73rd Leg., ch. 900, § 1.01, eff. Sept. 1, 1994; Acts 1995, 74th Leg., ch. 76, § 11.280, eff. Sept. 1, 1995; Acts 1997, 75th Leg., ch. 1083, § 1, eff. Sept. 1, 1997; Acts 1999, 76th Leg., ch. 686, § 1, eff. Sept. 1, 1999; Acts 2001, 77th Leg., ch. 747, § 1, eff. Sept. 1, 2001; Acts 2001, 77th Leg., ch. 976, § 2, eff. Sept. 1, 2001; Acts 2003, 78th Leg., ch. 1280, § 1, eff. Sept. 1, 2003; Acts 2007, 80th Leg., ch. 690, §§ 1, 2, eff. Sept. 1, 2007; Acts 2009, 81st Leg., ch. 638, § 1, eff. Sept. 1, 2009.

Section 3 of Acts 2007, 80th Leg., ch. 690 provides:

"The change in law made by this Act applies only to an offense committed on or after the effective date of this Act. An offense committed before the effective date [Sept. 1, 2007] of this Act is covered by the law in effect when the offense was committed, and the former law is continued in effect for that purpose. For purposes of this section, an offense was committed before the effective date of this Act if any element of the offense was committed before that date."

Section 2 of Acts 2009, 81st Leg., ch. 638 provides:

"The change in law made by this Act in amending Section 28.03(b), Penal Code, applies only to an offense committed on or after the effective date [Sept. 1, 2009] of this Act. An offense committed before the effective date of this Act is covered by the law in effect when the offense was committed, and the former law is continued in effect for that purpose. For purposes of this section, an offense is committed before the effective date of this Act if any element of the offense occurred before that date."

§ 28.04. Reckless Damage or Destruction

(a) A person commits an offense if, without the effective consent of the owner, he recklessly damages or destroys property of the owner.

(b) An offense under this section is a Class C misdemeanor.

Acts 1973, 63rd Leg., p. 883, ch. 399, § 1, eff. Jan. 1, 1974. Amended by Acts 1993, 73rd Leg., ch. 900, § 1.01, eff. Sept. 1, 1994.

§ 28.05. Actor's Interest in Property

It is no defense to prosecution under this chapter that the actor has an interest in the property damaged or destroyed if another person also has an interest that the actor is not entitled to infringe.

Acts 1973, 63rd Leg., p. 883, ch. 399, § 1, eff. Jan. 1, 1974. Amended by Acts 1993, 73rd Leg., ch. 900, § 1.01, eff. Sept. 1, 1994.

§ 28.06. Amount of Pecuniary Loss

(a) The amount of pecuniary loss under this chapter, if the property is destroyed, is:

(1) the fair market value of the property at the time and place of the destruction; or

(2) if the fair market value of the property cannot be ascertained, the cost of replacing the property within a reasonable time after the destruction.

(b) The amount of pecuniary loss under this chapter, if the property is damaged, is the cost of repairing or restoring the damaged property within a reasonable time after the damage occurred.

(c) The amount of pecuniary loss under this chapter for documents, other than those having a readily ascertainable market value, is:

(1) the amount due and collectible at maturity less any part that has been satisfied, if the document constitutes evidence of a debt; or

(2) the greatest amount of economic loss that the owner might reasonably suffer by virtue of the destruction or damage if the document is other than evidence of a debt.

(d) If the amount of pecuniary loss cannot be ascertained by the criteria set forth in Subsections (a) through (c), the amount of loss is deemed to be greater than $500 but less than $1,500.

(e) If the actor proves by a preponderance of the evidence that he gave consideration for or had a legal interest in the property involved, the value of the interest so proven shall be deducted from:

(1) the amount of pecuniary loss if the property is destroyed; or

(2) the amount of pecuniary loss to the extent of an amount equal to the ratio the value of the interest bears to the total value of the property, if the property is damaged.

Acts 1973, 63rd Leg., p. 883, ch. 399, § 1, eff. Jan. 1, 1974. Amended by Acts 1983, 68th Leg., p. 2918, ch. 497, § 2, eff. Sept. 1, 1983; Acts 1993, 73rd Leg., ch. 900, § 1.01, eff. Sept. 1, 1994.

§ 28.07. Interference With Railroad Property

(a) In this section:

(1) "Railroad property" means:

(A) a train, locomotive, railroad car, caboose, work equipment, rolling stock, safety device, switch, or connection that is owned, leased, operated, or possessed by a railroad; or

(B) a railroad track, rail, bridge, trestle, or right-of-way owned or used by a railroad.

(2) "Tamper" means to move, alter, or interfere with railroad property.

(b) A person commits an offense if the person:

(1) throws an object or discharges a firearm or weapon at a train or rail-mounted work equipment; or

(2) without the effective consent of the owner:

(A) enters or remains on railroad property, knowing that it is railroad property;

(B) tampers with railroad property;

(C) places an obstruction on a railroad track or right-of-way; or

(D) causes in any manner the derailment of a train, railroad car, or other railroad property that moves on tracks.

(c) An offense under Subsection (b)(1) is a Class B misdemeanor unless the person causes bodily injury to another, in which event the offense is a felony of the third degree.

(d) An offense under Subsection (b)(2)(A) is a Class C misdemeanor.

(e) An offense under Subsection (b)(2)(B), (b)(2)(C), or (b)(2)(D) is a Class C misdemeanor unless the person causes pecuniary loss, in which event the offense is:

(1) a Class B misdemeanor if the amount of pecuniary loss is $20 or more but less than $500;

(2) a Class A misdemeanor if the amount of pecuniary loss is $500 or more but less than $1,500;

(3) a state jail felony if the amount of pecuniary loss is $1,500 or more but less than $20,000;

(4) a felony of the third degree if the amount of the pecuniary loss is $20,000 or more but less than $100,000;

(5) a felony of the second degree if the amount of pecuniary loss is $100,000 or more but less than $200,000; or

(6) a felony of the first degree if the amount of the pecuniary loss is $200,000 or more.

(f) The conduct described in Subsection (b)(2)(A) is not an offense under this section if it is undertaken by an employee of the railroad or by a representative of a labor organization which represents or is seeking to represent the employees of the railroad as long as the employee or representative has a right to engage in such conduct under the Railway Labor Act (45 U.S.C. Section 151 et seq.).

Added by Acts 1989, 71st Leg., ch. 908, § 1, eff. Sept. 1, 1989. Amended by Acts 1993, 73rd Leg., ch. 900, § 1.01, eff. Sept. 1, 1994.

§ 28.08. Graffiti

(a) A person commits an offense if, without the effective consent of the owner, the person intentionally or knowingly makes markings, including inscriptions, slogans, drawings, or paintings, on the tangible property of the owner with:

(1) paint;

(2) an indelible marker; or

(3) an etching or engraving device.

(b) Except as provided by Subsection (d), an offense under this section is:

(1) a Class B misdemeanor if the amount of pecuniary loss is less than $500;

(2) a Class A misdemeanor if the amount of pecuniary loss is $500 or more but less than $1,500;

(3) a state jail felony if the amount of pecuniary loss is $1,500 or more but less than $20,000;

(4) a felony of the third degree if the amount of pecuniary loss is $20,000 or more but less than $100,000;

(5) a felony of the second degree if the amount of pecuniary loss is $100,000 or more but less than $200,000; or

(6) a felony of the first degree if the amount of pecuniary loss is $200,000 or more.

(c) When more than one item of tangible property, belonging to one or more owners, is marked in violation of this section pursuant to one scheme or continuing course of conduct, the conduct may be considered as one offense, and the amounts of pecuniary loss to property resulting from the marking of the property may be aggregated in determining the grade of the offense.

(d) An offense under this section is a state jail felony if:

(1) the marking is made on a school, an institution of higher education, a place of worship or human burial, a public monument, or a community center that provides medical, social, or educational programs; and

(2) the amount of the pecuniary loss to real property or to tangible personal property is less than $20,000.

(e) In this section:

(1) "Aerosol paint" means an aerosolized paint product.

(2) "Etching or engraving device" means a device that makes a delineation or impression on tangible property, regardless of the manufacturer's intended use for that device.

(3) "Indelible marker" means a device that makes a mark with a paint or ink product that is specifically formulated to be more difficult to erase, wash out, or remove than ordinary paint or ink products.

(4) "Institution of higher education" has the meaning assigned by Section 481.134, Health and Safety Code.

(5) "School" means a private or public elementary or secondary school.

Added by Acts 1997, 75th Leg., ch. 593, § 1, eff. Sept. 1, 1997. Amended by Acts 1999, 76th Leg., ch. 166, §§ 1, 2, eff. Sept. 1, 1999; Acts 1999, 76th Leg., ch. 695, § 1, eff. Sept. 1, 1999; Acts 2001, 77th Leg., ch. 1420, § 16.001, eff. Sept. 1, 2001; Acts 2009, 81st Leg., ch. 639, § 4, eff. Sept. 1, 2009.

Section 5 of Acts 2009, 81st Leg., ch. 639 provides:

"The change in law made by this Act applies only to an offense that is committed or conduct that occurs on or after the effective date [Sept. 1, 2009] of this Act. An offense that is committed or conduct that occurs before the effective date of this Act is covered by the law in effect when the offense was committed or the conduct occurred, and the former law is continued in effect for that purpose. For purposes of this section, an offense was committed or conduct occurred before the effective date of this Act if any element of the offense or conduct occurred before that date."

CHAPTER 29. ROBBERY

Section

§ 29.01. Definitions

In this chapter:

(1) "In the course of committing theft" means conduct that occurs in an attempt to commit, during the commission, or in immediate flight after the attempt or commission of theft.

(2) "Property" means:

(A) tangible or intangible personal property including anything severed from land; or

(B) a document, including money, that represents or embodies anything of value.

Acts 1973, 63rd Leg., p. 883, ch. 399, § 1, eff. Jan. 1, 1974. Amended by Acts 1993, 73rd Leg., ch. 900, § 1.01, eff. Sept. 1, 1994.

§ 29.02. Robbery

(a) A person commits an offense if, in the course of committing theft as defined in Chapter 31 and with intent to obtain or maintain control of the property, he:

(1) intentionally, knowingly, or recklessly causes bodily injury to another; or

(2) intentionally or knowingly threatens or places another in fear of imminent bodily injury or death.

(b) An offense under this section is a felony of the second degree.

Acts 1973, 63rd Leg., p. 883, ch. 399, § 1, eff. Jan. 1, 1974. Amended by Acts 1993, 73rd Leg., ch. 900, § 1.01, eff. Sept. 1, 1994.

§ 29.03. Aggravated Robbery

(a) A person commits an offense if he commits robbery as defined in Section 29.02, and he:

(1) causes serious bodily injury to another;

(2) uses or exhibits a deadly weapon; or

(3) causes bodily injury to another person or threatens or places another person in fear of imminent bodily injury or death, if the other person is:

(A) 65 years of age or older; or

(B) a disabled person.

(b) An offense under this section is a felony of the first degree.

(c) In this section, "disabled person" means an individual with a mental, physical, or developmental disability who is substantially unable to protect himself from harm.

Acts 1973, 63rd Leg., p. 883, ch. 399, § 1, eff. Jan. 1, 1974. Amended by Acts 1989, 71st Leg., ch. 357, § 2, eff. Sept. 1, 1989; Acts 1993, 73rd Leg., ch. 900, § 1.01, eff. Sept. 1, 1994.

CHAPTER 30. BURGLARY AND CRIMINAL TRESPASS

§ 30.01. Definitions

In this chapter:

(1) "Habitation" means a structure or vehicle that is adapted for the overnight accommodation of persons, and includes:

(A) each separately secured or occupied portion of the structure or vehicle; and

(B) each structure appurtenant to or connected with the structure or vehicle.

(2) "Building" means any enclosed structure intended for use or occupation as a habitation or for some purpose of trade, manufacture, ornament, or use.

(3) "Vehicle" includes any device in, on, or by which any person or property is or may be propelled, moved, or drawn in the normal course of commerce or transportation, except such devices as are classified as "habitation."

Acts 1973, 63rd Leg., p. 883, ch. 399, § 1, eff. Jan. 1, 1974. Amended by Acts 1993, 73rd Leg., ch. 900, § 1.01, eff. Sept. 1, 1994.

§ 30.02. Burglary

(a) A person commits an offense if, without the effective consent of the owner, the person:

(1) enters a habitation, or a building (or any portion of a building) not then open to the public, with intent to commit a felony, theft, or an assault; or

(2) remains concealed, with intent to commit a felony, theft, or an assault, in a building or habitation; or

(3) enters a building or habitation and commits or attempts to commit a felony, theft, or an assault.

(b) For purposes of this section, "enter" means to intrude:

(1) any part of the body; or

(2) any physical object connected with the body.

(c) Except as provided in Subsection (d), an offense under this section is a:

(1) state jail felony if committed in a building other than a habitation; or

(2) felony of the second degree if committed in a habitation.

(d) An offense under this section is a felony of the first degree if:

(1) the premises are a habitation; and

(2) any party to the offense entered the habitation with intent to commit a felony other than felony theft or committed or attempted to commit a felony other than felony theft.

Acts 1973, 63rd Leg., p. 883, ch. 399, § 1, eff. Jan. 1, 1974. Amended by Acts 1993, 73rd Leg., ch. 900, § 1.01, eff. Sept. 1, 1994; Acts 1995, 74th Leg., ch. 318, § 8, eff. Sept. 1, 1995; Acts 1999, 76th Leg., ch. 727, § 1, eff. Sept. 1, 1999.

§ 30.03. Burglary of Coin-Operated or Coin Collection Machines

(a) A person commits an offense if, without the effective consent of the owner, he breaks or enters into any coin-operated machine, coin collection machine, or other coin-operated or coin collection receptacle, contrivance, apparatus, or equipment used for the purpose of providing lawful amusement, sales of goods, services, or other valuable things, or telecommunications with intent to obtain property or services.

(b) For purposes of this section, "entry" includes every kind of entry except one made with the effective consent of the owner.

(c) An offense under this section is a Class A misdemeanor.

Acts 1973, 63rd Leg., p. 883, ch. 399, § 1, eff. Jan. 1, 1974. Amended by Acts 1987, 70th Leg., ch. 62, § 1, eff. Sept. 1, 1987; Acts 1993, 73rd Leg., ch. 900, § 1.01, eff. Sept. 1, 1994.

§ 30.04. Burglary of Vehicles

(a) A person commits an offense if, without the effective consent of the owner, he breaks into or enters a vehicle or any part of a vehicle with intent to commit any felony or theft.

(b) For purposes of this section, "enter" means to intrude:

(1) any part of the body; or

(2) any physical object connected with the body.

(c) For purposes of this section, a container or trailer carried on a rail car is a part of the rail car.

(d) An offense under this section is a Class A misdemeanor, except that:

(1) the offense is a Class A misdemeanor with a minimum term of confinement of six months if it is shown on the trial of the offense that the defendant has been previously convicted of an offense under this section; and

(2) the offense is a state jail felony if:

(A) it is shown on the trial of the offense that the defendant has been previously convicted two or more times of an offense under this section; or

(B) the vehicle or part of the vehicle broken into or entered is a rail car.

(d–1) For the purposes of Subsection (d), a defendant has been previously convicted under this section if the defendant was adjudged guilty of the offense or entered a plea of guilty or nolo contendere in return for a grant of deferred adjudication, regardless of whether the sentence for the offense was ever imposed or whether the sentence was probated and the defendant was subsequently discharged from community supervision.

(e) It is a defense to prosecution under this section that the actor entered a rail car or any part of a rail car and was at that time an employee or a representative of employees exercising a right under the Railway Labor Act (45 U.S.C. Section 151 et seq.).

Acts 1973, 63rd Leg., p. 883, ch. 399, § 1, eff. Jan. 1, 1974. Amended by Acts 1993, 73rd Leg., ch. 900, § 1.01, eff. Sept. 1, 1994; Acts 1999, 76th Leg., ch. 916, § 1, eff. Sept. 1, 1999; Acts 2007, 80th Leg., ch. 308, § 1, eff. Sept. 1, 2007.

§ 30.05. Criminal Trespass

(a) A person commits an offense if the person enters or remains on or in property of another, including residential land, agricultural land, a recreational vehicle park, a building, or an aircraft or other vehicle, without effective consent and the person:

(1) had notice that the entry was forbidden; or

(2) received notice to depart but failed to do so.

(b) For purposes of this section:

(1) "Entry" means the intrusion of the entire body.

(2) "Notice" means:

(A) oral or written communication by the owner or someone with apparent authority to act for the owner;

(B) fencing or other enclosure obviously designed to exclude intruders or to contain livestock;

(C) a sign or signs posted on the property or at the entrance to the building, reasonably likely to come to the attention of intruders, indicating that entry is forbidden;

(D) the placement of identifying purple paint marks on trees or posts on the property, provided that the marks are:

(i) vertical lines of not less than eight inches in length and not less than one inch in width;

(ii) placed so that the bottom of the mark is not less than three feet from the ground or more than five feet from the ground; and

(iii) placed at locations that are readily visible to any person approaching the property and no more than:

(a) 100 feet apart on forest land; or

(b) 1,000 feet apart on land other than forest land; or

(E) the visible presence on the property of a crop grown for human consumption that is under cultivation, in the process of being harvested, or marketable if harvested at the time of entry.

(3) "Shelter center" has the meaning assigned by Section 51.002, Human Resources Code.

(4) "Forest land" means land on which the trees are potentially valuable for timber products.

(5) "Agricultural land" has the meaning assigned by Section 75.001, Civil Practice and Remedies Code.

(6) "Superfund site" means a facility that:

(A) is on the National Priorities List established under Section 105 of the federal Comprehensive Environmental Response, Compensation, and Liability Act of 1980 (42 U.S.C. Section 9605); or

(B) is listed on the state registry established under Section 361.181, Health and Safety Code.

(7) "Critical infrastructure facility" means one of the following, if completely enclosed by a fence or

other physical barrier that is obviously designed to exclude intruders:

(A) a chemical manufacturing facility;

(B) a refinery;

(C) an electrical power generating facility, substation, switching station, electrical control center, or electrical transmission or distribution facility;

(D) a water intake structure, water treatment facility, wastewater treatment plant, or pump station;

(E) a natural gas transmission compressor station;

(F) a liquid natural gas terminal or storage facility;

(G) a telecommunications central switching office;

(H) a port, railroad switching yard, trucking terminal, or other freight transportation facility;

(I) a gas processing plant, including a plant used in the processing, treatment, or fractionation of natural gas; or

(J) a transmission facility used by a federally licensed radio or television station.

(8) "Protected freshwater area" has the meaning assigned by Section 90.001, Parks and Wildlife Code.

(9) "Recognized state" means another state with which the attorney general of this state, with the approval of the governor of this state, negotiated an agreement after determining that the other state:

(A) has firearm proficiency requirements for peace officers; and

(B) fully recognizes the right of peace officers commissioned in this state to carry weapons in the other state.

(10) "Recreational vehicle park" means a tract of land that has rental spaces for two or more recreational vehicles, as defined by Section 522.004, Transportation Code.

(11) "Residential land" means real property improved by a dwelling and zoned for or otherwise authorized for single-family or multifamily use.

(c) Repealed by Acts 2009, 81st Leg., ch. 1138, § 4.

(d) An offense under this section is:

(1) a Class B misdemeanor, except as provided by Subdivisions (2) and (3);

(2) a Class C misdemeanor, except as provided by Subdivision (3), if the offense is committed:

(A) on agricultural land and within 100 feet of the boundary of the land; or

(B) on residential land and within 100 feet of a protected freshwater area; and

(3) a Class A misdemeanor if:

(A) the offense is committed:

(i) in a habitation or a shelter center;

(ii) on a Superfund site; or

(iii) on or in a critical infrastructure facility; or

(B) the person carries a deadly weapon during the commission of the offense.

(e) It is a defense to prosecution under this section that the actor at the time of the offense was:

(1) a firefighter or emergency medical services personnel, as defined by Section 773.003, Health and Safety Code, acting in the lawful discharge of an official duty under exigent circumstances;

(2) a person who was:

(A) an employee or agent of:

(i) an electric utility, as defined by Section 31.002, Utilities Code;

(ii) a telecommunications provider, as defined by Section 51.002, Utilities Code;

(iii) a video service provider or cable service provider, as defined by Section 66.002, Utilities Code;

(iv) a gas utility, as defined by Section 101.003 or 121.001, Utilities Code; or

(v) a pipeline used for the transportation or sale of oil, gas, or related products; and

(B) performing a duty within the scope of that employment or agency; or

(3) a person who was:

(A) employed by or acting as agent for an entity that had, or that the person reasonably believed had, effective consent or authorization provided by law to enter the property; and

(B) performing a duty within the scope of that employment or agency.

(f) It is a defense to prosecution under this section that:

(1) the basis on which entry on the property or land or in the building was forbidden is that entry with a handgun was forbidden; and

(2) the person was carrying a concealed handgun and a license issued under Subchapter H, Chapter 411, Government Code, to carry a concealed handgun of the same category the person was carrying.

(g) It is a defense to prosecution under this section that the actor entered a railroad switching yard or any part of a railroad switching yard and was at that time an employee or a representative of employees exercising a right under the Railway Labor Act (45 U.S.C. Section 151 et seq.).

(h) At the punishment stage of a trial in which the attorney representing the state seeks the increase in punishment provided by Subsection (d)(1)(C), the defendant may raise the issue as to whether the defendant entered or remained on or in a critical infrastructure facility as part of a peaceful or lawful assembly, including an attempt to exercise rights guaranteed by state or federal labor laws. If the defendant proves the issue in the affirmative by a preponderance of the evidence, the increase in punishment provided by Subsection (d)(1)(C) does not apply.

(i) This section does not apply if:

(1) the basis on which entry on the property or land or in the building was forbidden is that entry with a handgun or other weapon was forbidden; and

(2) the actor at the time of the offense was a peace officer, including a commissioned peace officer of a recognized state, or a special investigator under Article 2.122, Code of Criminal Procedure, regardless of whether the peace officer or special investigator was engaged in the actual discharge of an official duty while carrying the weapon.

(j) Repealed by Acts 2009, 81st Leg., ch. 1138, § 4.

Acts 1973, 63rd Leg., p. 883, ch. 399, § 1, eff. Jan. 1, 1974. Amended by Acts 1979, 66th Leg., p. 1114, ch. 530, § 3, eff. Aug. 27, 1979; Acts 1981, 67th Leg., p. 2385, ch. 596, § 1, eff. Sept. 1, 1981; Acts 1989, 71st Leg., ch. 139, § 1, eff. Sept. 1, 1989; Acts 1991, 72nd Leg., ch. 308, § 1, eff. Sept. 1, 1991; Acts 1993, 73rd Leg., ch. 24, § 1, eff. Sept. 1, 1993; Acts 1993, 73rd Leg., ch. 900, § 1.01, eff. Sept. 1, 1994; Acts 1997, 75th Leg., ch. 1229, §§ 1, 2, eff. Sept. 1, 1997; Acts 1999, 76th Leg., ch. 161, § 1, eff. Sept. 1, 1999; Acts 1999, 76th Leg., ch. 169, §§ 1, 2, eff. Sept. 1, 1999; Acts 1999, 76th Leg., ch. 765, §§ 1, 2, eff. Sept. 1, 1999; Acts 2001, 77th Leg., ch. 1420, §§ 16.002, 21.001(94), eff. Sept. 1, 2001; Acts 2003, 78th Leg., ch. 1078, § 1, eff. Sept. 1, 2003; Acts 2003, 78th Leg., ch. 1178, § 1, eff. Sept. 1, 2003; Acts 2003, 78th Leg., ch. 1276, § 14B.001, eff. Sept. 1, 2003; Acts 2005, 79th Leg., ch. 1093, § 3, eff. Sept. 1, 2005; Acts 2005, 79th Leg., ch. 1337, §§ 20, 21, eff. June 18, 2005; Acts 2007, 80th Leg., ch. 921, §§ 17.001(61), 17.002(13), eff. Sept. 1, 2007; Acts 2009, 81st Leg., ch. 1138, §§ 1 to 4, eff. Sept. 1, 2009.

Section 5 of Acts 2009, 81st Leg., ch. 1138 provides:

"The change in law made by this Act applies only to an offense committed on or after the effective date [Sept. 1, 2009] of this Act. An offense committed before the effective date of this Act is covered by the law in effect when the offense was committed, and the former law is continued in effect for that purpose. For purposes of this section, an offense was committed before the effective date of this Act if any element of the offense was committed before that date."

§ 30.06. Trespass by Holder of License to Carry Concealed Handgun

(a) A license holder commits an offense if the license holder:

(1) carries a handgun under the authority of Subchapter H, Chapter 411, Government Code,[1] on property of another without effective consent; and

(2) received notice that:

(A) entry on the property by a license holder with a concealed handgun was forbidden; or

(B) remaining on the property with a concealed handgun was forbidden and failed to depart.

(b) For purposes of this section, a person receives notice if the owner of the property or someone with apparent authority to act for the owner provides notice to the person by oral or written communication.

(c) In this section:

(1) "Entry" has the meaning assigned by Section 30.05(b).

(2) "License holder" has the meaning assigned by Section 46.035(f).

(3) "Written communication" means:

(A) a card or other document on which is written language identical to the following: "Pursuant to Section 30.06, Penal Code (trespass by holder of license to carry a concealed handgun), a person licensed under Subchapter H, Chapter 411, Government Code (concealed handgun law), may not enter this property with a concealed handgun"; or

(B) a sign posted on the property that:

(i) includes the language described by Paragraph (A) in both English and Spanish;

(ii) appears in contrasting colors with block letters at least one inch in height; and

(iii) is displayed in a conspicuous manner clearly visible to the public.

(d) An offense under this section is a Class A misdemeanor.

(e) It is an exception to the application of this section that the property on which the license holder carries a handgun is owned or leased by a governmental entity and is not a premises or other place on which the license holder is prohibited from carrying the handgun under Section 46.03 or 46.035.

Added by Acts 1997, 75th Leg., ch. 1261, § 23, eff. Sept. 1, 1997. Amended by Acts 1999, 76th Leg., ch. 62, § 9.24, eff. Sept. 1, 1999; Acts 2003, 78th Leg., ch. 1178, § 2, eff. Sept. 1, 2003.

[1] V.T.C.A., Government Code § 411.001 et seq.

CHAPTER 31. THEFT

§ 31.01. Definitions

In this chapter:

(1) "Deception" means:

(A) creating or confirming by words or conduct a false impression of law or fact that is likely to affect the judgment of another in the transaction, and that the actor does not believe to be true;

(B) failing to correct a false impression of law or fact that is likely to affect the judgment of another in the transaction, that the actor previously created or confirmed by words or conduct, and that the actor does not now believe to be true;

(C) preventing another from acquiring information likely to affect his judgment in the transaction;

(D) selling or otherwise transferring or encumbering property without disclosing a lien, security interest, adverse claim, or other legal impediment to the enjoyment of the property, whether the lien, security interest, claim, or impediment is or is not valid, or is or is not a matter of official record; or

(E) promising performance that is likely to affect the judgment of another in the transaction and that the actor does not intend to perform or knows will not be performed, except that failure to perform the promise in issue without other evidence of intent or knowledge is not sufficient proof that the actor did not intend to perform or knew the promise would not be performed.

(2) "Deprive" means:

(A) to withhold property from the owner permanently or for so extended a period of time that a major portion of the value or enjoyment of the property is lost to the owner;

(B) to restore property only upon payment of reward or other compensation; or

(C) to dispose of property in a manner that makes recovery of the property by the owner unlikely.

(3) "Effective consent" includes consent by a person legally authorized to act for the owner. Consent is not effective if:

(A) induced by deception or coercion;

(B) given by a person the actor knows is not legally authorized to act for the owner;

(C) given by a person who by reason of youth, mental disease or defect, or intoxication is known by the actor to be unable to make reasonable property dispositions;

(D) given solely to detect the commission of an offense; or

(E) given by a person who by reason of advanced age is known by the actor to have a diminished capacity to make informed and rational decisions about the reasonable disposition of property.

(4) "Appropriate" means:

(A) to bring about a transfer or purported transfer of title to or other nonpossessory interest in property, whether to the actor or another; or

(B) to acquire or otherwise exercise control over property other than real property.

(5) "Property" means:

(A) real property;

(B) tangible or intangible personal property including anything severed from land; or

(C) a document, including money, that represents or embodies anything of value.

(6) "Service" includes:

(A) labor and professional service;

(B) telecommunication, public utility, or transportation service;

(C) lodging, restaurant service, and entertainment; and

(D) the supply of a motor vehicle or other property for use.

(7) "Steal" means to acquire property or service by theft.

(8) "Certificate of title" has the meaning assigned by Section 501.002, Transportation Code.

(9) "Used or secondhand motor vehicle" means a used motor vehicle, as that term is defined by Section 501.002, Transportation Code.

(10) "Elderly individual" has the meaning assigned by Section 22.04(c).

Acts 1973, 63rd Leg., p. 883, ch. 399, § 1, eff. Jan. 1, 1974. Amended by Acts 1975, 64th Leg., p. 914, ch. 342, § 9, eff. Sept. 1, 1975; Acts 1985, 69th Leg., ch. 901, § 2, eff. Sept. 1, 1985; Acts 1993, 73rd Leg., ch. 900, § 1.01, eff. Sept. 1, 1994; Acts 1997, 75th Leg., ch. 165, § 30.237, eff. Sept. 1, 1997; Acts 2003, 78th Leg., ch. 432, § 1, eff. Sept. 1, 2003.

§ 31.02. Consolidation of Theft Offenses

Theft as defined in Section 31.03 constitutes a single offense superseding the separate offenses previously known as theft, theft by false pretext, conversion by a bailee, theft from the person, shoplifting, acquisition of property by threat, swindling, swindling by worthless check, embezzlement, extortion, receiving or concealing embezzled property, and receiving or concealing stolen property.

Acts 1973, 63rd Leg., p. 883, ch. 399, § 1, eff. Jan. 1, 1974. Amended by Acts 1993, 73rd Leg., ch. 900, § 1.01, eff. Sept. 1, 1994.

§ 31.03. Theft

(a) A person commits an offense if he unlawfully appropriates property with intent to deprive the owner of property.

(b) Appropriation of property is unlawful if:

(1) it is without the owner's effective consent;

(2) the property is stolen and the actor appropriates the property knowing it was stolen by another; or

(3) property in the custody of any law enforcement agency was explicitly represented by any law enforcement agent to the actor as being stolen and the actor appropriates the property believing it was stolen by another.

(c) For purposes of Subsection (b):

(1) evidence that the actor has previously participated in recent transactions other than, but similar to, that which the prosecution is based is admissible for the purpose of showing knowledge or intent and the issues of knowledge or intent are raised by the actor's plea of not guilty;

(2) the testimony of an accomplice shall be corroborated by proof that tends to connect the actor to the crime, but the actor's knowledge or intent may be established by the uncorroborated testimony of the accomplice;

(3) an actor engaged in the business of buying and selling used or secondhand personal property, or lending money on the security of personal property deposited with the actor, is presumed to know upon receipt by the actor of stolen property (other than a motor vehicle subject to Chapter 501, Transportation Code) that the property has been previously stolen from another if the actor pays for or loans against the property $25 or more (or consideration of equivalent value) and the actor knowingly or recklessly:

(A) fails to record the name, address, and physical description or identification number of the seller or pledgor;

(B) fails to record a complete description of the property, including the serial number, if reasonably available, or other identifying characteristics; or

(C) fails to obtain a signed warranty from the seller or pledgor that the seller or pledgor has the right to possess the property. It is the express intent of this provision that the presumption arises unless the actor complies with each of the numbered requirements;

(4) for the purposes of Subdivision (3)(A), "identification number" means driver's license number, military identification number, identification certificate, or other official number capable of identifying an individual;

(5) stolen property does not lose its character as stolen when recovered by any law enforcement agency;

(6) an actor engaged in the business of obtaining abandoned or wrecked motor vehicles or parts of an abandoned or wrecked motor vehicle for resale, disposal, scrap, repair, rebuilding, demolition, or other form of salvage is presumed to know on receipt by the actor of stolen property that the property has been previously stolen from another if the actor knowingly or recklessly:

(A) fails to maintain an accurate and legible inventory of each motor vehicle component part purchased by or delivered to the actor, including the date of purchase or delivery, the name, age, address, sex, and driver's license number of the seller or person making the delivery, the license plate number of the motor vehicle in which the part was delivered, a complete description of the part, and the vehicle identification number of the motor vehicle from which the part was removed, or in lieu of maintaining an inventory, fails to record the name and certificate of inventory number of the person who dismantled the motor vehicle from which the part was obtained;

(B) fails on receipt of a motor vehicle to obtain a certificate of authority, sales receipt, or transfer document as required by Chapter 683, Transportation Code, or a certificate of title showing that the motor vehicle is not subject to a lien or that all recorded liens on the motor vehicle have been released; or

(C) fails on receipt of a motor vehicle to immediately remove an unexpired license plate from the motor vehicle, to keep the plate in a secure and locked place, or to maintain an inventory, on forms provided by the Texas Department of Motor Vehicles, of license plates kept under this paragraph, including for each plate or set of plates the license plate number and the make, motor number, and vehicle identification number of the motor vehicle from which the plate was removed;

(7) an actor who purchases or receives a used or secondhand motor vehicle is presumed to know on receipt by the actor of the motor vehicle that the motor vehicle has been previously stolen from another if the actor knowingly or recklessly:

(A) fails to report to the Texas Department of Motor Vehicles the failure of the person who sold or delivered the motor vehicle to the actor to deliver to the actor a properly executed certificate of title to the motor vehicle at the time the motor vehicle was delivered; or

(B) fails to file with the county tax assessor-collector of the county in which the actor received the motor vehicle, not later than the 20th day after the date the actor received the motor vehicle, the registration license receipt and certificate of title or evidence of title delivered to the actor in accordance with Subchapter D, Chapter 520, Transportation Code,[1] at the time the motor vehicle was delivered;

(8) an actor who purchases or receives from any source other than a licensed retailer or distributor of pesticides a restricted-use pesticide or a state-limited-use pesticide or a compound, mixture, or preparation containing a restricted-use or state-limited-use pesticide is presumed to know on receipt by the actor of the pesticide or compound, mixture, or preparation that the pesticide or compound, mixture, or preparation has been previously stolen from another if the actor:

(A) fails to record the name, address, and physical description of the seller or pledgor;

(B) fails to record a complete description of the amount and type of pesticide or compound, mixture, or preparation purchased or received; and

(C) fails to obtain a signed warranty from the seller or pledgor that the seller or pledgor has the right to possess the property; and

(9) an actor who is subject to Section 409, Packers and Stockyards Act (7 U.S.C. Section 228b), that obtains livestock from a commission merchant by representing that the actor will make prompt payment is presumed to have induced the commission merchant's consent by deception if the actor fails to make full payment in accordance with Section 409, Packers and Stockyards Act (7 U.S.C. Section 228b).

(d) It is not a defense to prosecution under this section that:

(1) the offense occurred as a result of a deception or strategy on the part of a law enforcement agency, including the use of an undercover operative or peace officer;

(2) the actor was provided by a law enforcement agency with a facility in which to commit the offense or an opportunity to engage in conduct constituting the offense; or

(3) the actor was solicited to commit the offense by a peace officer, and the solicitation was of a type that would encourage a person predisposed to commit the offense to actually commit the offense, but would not encourage a person not predisposed to commit the offense to actually commit the offense.

(e) Except as provided by Subsection (f), an offense under this section is:

(1) a Class C misdemeanor if the value of the property stolen is less than:

(A) $50; or

(B) $20 and the defendant obtained the property by issuing or passing a check or similar sight order in a manner described by Section 31.06;

(2) a Class B misdemeanor if:

(A) the value of the property stolen is:

(i) $50 or more but less than $500; or

(ii) $20 or more but less than $500 and the defendant obtained the property by issuing or passing a check or similar sight order in a manner described by Section 31.06;

(B) the value of the property stolen is less than:

(i) $50 and the defendant has previously been convicted of any grade of theft; or

(ii) $20, the defendant has previously been convicted of any grade of theft, and the defendant obtained the property by issuing or passing a check or similar sight order in a manner described by Section 31.06; or

(C) the property stolen is a driver's license, commercial driver's license, or personal identification certificate issued by this state or another state;

(3) a Class A misdemeanor if the value of the property stolen is $500 or more but less than $1,500;

(4) a state jail felony if:

(A) the value of the property stolen is $1,500 or more but less than $20,000, or the property is less than 10 head of sheep, swine, or goats or any part thereof under the value of $20,000;

(B) regardless of value, the property is stolen from the person of another or from a human corpse or grave, including property that is a military grave marker;

(C) the property stolen is a firearm, as defined by Section 46.01;

(D) the value of the property stolen is less than $1,500 and the defendant has been previously convicted two or more times of any grade of theft;

(E) the property stolen is an official ballot or official carrier envelope for an election; or

(F) the value of the property stolen is less than $20,000 and the property stolen is insulated or noninsulated tubing, rods, water gate stems, wire, or cable that consists of at least 50 percent:

(i) aluminum;

(ii) bronze; or

(iii) copper;

(5) a felony of the third degree if the value of the property stolen is $20,000 or more but less than $100,000, or the property is:

(A) cattle, horses, or exotic livestock or exotic fowl as defined by Section 142.001, Agriculture Code, stolen during a single transaction and having an aggregate value of less than $100,000; or

(B) 10 or more head of sheep, swine, or goats stolen during a single transaction and having an aggregate value of less than $100,000;

(6) a felony of the second degree if the value of the property stolen is $100,000 or more but less than $200,000; or

(7) a felony of the first degree if the value of the property stolen is $200,000 or more.

(f) An offense described for purposes of punishment by Subsections (e)(1)–(6) is increased to the next higher category of offense if it is shown on the trial of the offense that:

(1) the actor was a public servant at the time of the offense and the property appropriated came into the actor's custody, possession, or control by virtue of his status as a public servant;

(2) the actor was in a contractual relationship with government at the time of the offense and the property appropriated came into the actor's custody, possession, or control by virtue of the contractual relationship;

(3) the owner of the property appropriated was at the time of the offense:

(A) an elderly individual; or

(B) a nonprofit organization; or

(4) the actor was a Medicare provider in a contractual relationship with the federal government at the time of the offense and the property appropriated came into the actor's custody, possession, or control by virtue of the contractual relationship.

(g) For the purposes of Subsection (a), a person is the owner of exotic livestock or exotic fowl as defined by Section 142.001, Agriculture Code, only if the person qualifies to claim the animal under Section 142.0021, Agriculture Code, if the animal is an estray.

(h) In this section:

(1) "Restricted-use pesticide" means a pesticide classified as a restricted-use pesticide by the administrator of the Environmental Protection Agency under 7 U.S.C. Section 136a, as that law existed on January 1, 1995, and containing an active ingredient

listed in the federal regulations adopted under that law (40 C.F.R. Section 152.175) and in effect on that date.

(2) "State-limited-use pesticide" means a pesticide classified as a state-limited-use pesticide by the Department of Agriculture under Section 76.003, Agriculture Code, as that section existed on January 1, 1995, and containing an active ingredient listed in the rules adopted under that section (4 TAC Section 7.24) as that section existed on that date.

(3) "Nonprofit organization" means an organization that is exempt from federal income taxation under Section 501(a), Internal Revenue Code of 1986, by being described as an exempt organization by Section 501(c)(3) of that code.

(i) For purposes of Subsection (c)(9), "livestock" and "commission merchant" have the meanings assigned by Section 147.001, Agriculture Code.

(j) With the consent of the appropriate local county or district attorney, the attorney general has concurrent jurisdiction with that consenting local prosecutor to prosecute an offense under this section that involves the state Medicaid program.

Acts 1973, 63rd Leg., p. 883, ch. 399, § 1, eff. Jan. 1, 1974. Amended by Acts 1975, 64th Leg., p. 914, ch. 342, § 10, eff. Sept. 1, 1975; Acts 1977, 65th Leg., p. 937, ch. 349, § 1, eff. Aug. 29, 1977; Acts 1981, 67th Leg., p. 849, ch. 298, § 1, eff. Sept. 1, 1981; Acts 1981, 67th Leg., p. 2065, ch. 455, § 1, eff. June 11, 1981; Acts 1983, 68th Leg., p. 2918, ch. 497, § 3, eff. Sept. 1, 1983; Acts 1983, 68th Leg., p. 3244, ch. 558, § 11, eff. Sept. 1, 1983; Acts 1983, 68th Leg., p. 4523, ch. 741, § 1, eff. Sept. 1, 1983; Acts 1985, 69th Leg., ch. 599, § 1, eff. Sept. 1, 1985; Acts 1985, 69th Leg., ch. 901, § 1, eff. Sept. 1, 1985; Acts 1987, 70th Leg., ch. 167, § 5.01(a)(45), eff. Sept. 1, 1987; Acts 1989, 71st Leg., ch. 245, § 1, eff. Sept. 1, 1989; Acts 1989, 71st Leg., ch. 724, §§ 2, 3, eff. Sept. 1, 1989; Acts 1991, 72nd Leg., ch. 14, § 284(80), eff. Sept. 1, 1991; Acts 1991, 72nd Leg., ch. 565, § 1, eff. Sept. 1, 1991; Acts 1993, 73rd Leg., ch. 203, §§ 4, 5, eff. Sept. 1, 1993; Acts 1993, 73rd Leg., ch. 900, § 1.01, eff. Sept. 1, 1994; Acts 1995, 74th Leg., ch. 318, § 9, eff. Sept. 1, 1995; Acts 1995, 74th Leg., ch. 734, § 1, eff. Sept. 1, 1995; Acts 1995, 74th Leg., ch. 843, § 1, eff. Sept. 1, 1995; Acts 1997, 75th Leg., ch. 165, §§ 30.238, 31.01(69), eff. Sept. 1, 1997; Acts 1997, 75th Leg., ch. 1153, § 7.01, eff. Sept. 1, 1997; Acts 2001, 77th Leg., ch. 1276, § 1, eff. Sept. 1, 2001; Acts 2003, 78th Leg., ch. 198, § 2.136, eff. Sept. 1, 2003; Acts 2003, 78th Leg., ch. 257, § 13, eff. Sept. 1, 2003; Acts 2003, 78th Leg., ch. 393, § 20, eff. Sept. 1, 2003; Acts 2003, 78th Leg., ch. 432, § 2, eff. Sept. 1, 2003; Acts 2007, 80th Leg., ch. 304, § 1, eff. Sept. 1, 2007; Acts 2009, 81st Leg., ch. 70, § 1, eff. Sept. 1, 2009; Acts 2009, 81st Leg., ch. 105, § 1, eff. May 23, 2009; Acts 2009, 81st Leg., ch. 139, § 1, eff. Sept. 1, 2009; Acts 2009, 81st Leg., ch. 295, § 1, eff. Sept. 1, 2009; Acts 2009, 81st Leg., ch. 903, §§ 1, 2, eff. Sept. 1, 2009; Acts 2009, 81st Leg., ch. 933, § 3J.01, eff. Sept. 1, 2009.

[1] V.T.C.A., Transportation Code § 520.031 et seq.

Section 2 of Acts 2007, 80th Leg., ch. 304 provides:

"The change in law made by this Act applies only to an offense committed on or after the effective date of this Act. An offense committed before the effective date [Sept. 1, 2007] of this Act is governed by the law in effect when the offense was committed, and the former law is continued in effect for that purpose. For the purposes of this section, an offense is committed before the effective date of this Act if any element of the offense occurs before that date."

Section 2 of Acts 2009, 81st Leg., ch. 70 provides:

"The change in law made by this Act applies only to an offense committed on or after the effective date [Sept. 1, 2009] of this Act. An offense committed before the effective date of this Act is covered by the law in effect when the offense was committed, and the former law is continued in effect for that purpose. For purposes of this section, an offense was committed before the effective date of this Act if any element of the offense occurred before that date."

Section 2 of Acts 2009, 81st Leg., ch. 139 provides:

"The change in law made by this Act applies only to an offense committed on or after the effective date [Sept. 1, 2009] of this Act. An offense committed before the effective date of this Act is covered by the law in effect when the offense was committed, and the former law is continued in effect for that purpose. For purposes of this section, an offense was committed before the effective date of this Act if any element of the offense occurred before that date."

Section 2 of Acts 2009, 81st Leg., ch. 295 provides:

"The change in law made by this Act applies only to an offense committed on or after the effective date [Sept. 1, 2009] of this Act. An offense committed before the effective date of this Act is governed by the law in effect when the offense was committed, and the former law is continued in effect for that purpose. For the purposes of this section, an offense is committed before the effective date of this Act if any element of the offense occurs before that date."

Section 3 of Acts 2009, 81st Leg., ch. 903 provides:

"The change in law made by this Act applies only to an offense committed on or after the effective date of this Act. An offense committed before the effective date of this Act is covered by the law in effect when the offense was committed, and the former law is continued in effect for that purpose. For purposes of this section, an offense was committed before the effective date of this Act if any element of the offense was committed before that date."

§ 31.04. Theft of Service

(a) A person commits theft of service if, with intent to avoid payment for service that he knows is provided only for compensation:

(1) he intentionally or knowingly secures performance of the service by deception, threat, or false token;

(2) having control over the disposition of services of another to which he is not entitled, he intentionally or knowingly diverts the other's services to his own benefit or to the benefit of another not entitled to them;

(3) having control of personal property under a written rental agreement, he holds the property beyond the expiration of the rental period without the effective consent of the owner of the property, thereby depriving the owner of the property of its use in further rentals; or

(4) he intentionally or knowingly secures the performance of the service by agreeing to provide compensation and, after the service is rendered, fails to make payment after receiving notice demanding payment.

(b) For purposes of this section, intent to avoid payment is presumed if:

(1) the actor absconded without paying for the service or expressly refused to pay for the service in circumstances where payment is ordinarily made immediately upon rendering of the service, as in hotels, campgrounds, recreational vehicle parks, restaurants, and comparable establishments;

(2) the actor failed to make payment under a service agreement within 10 days after receiving notice demanding payment;

(3) the actor returns property held under a rental agreement after the expiration of the rental agreement and fails to pay the applicable rental charge for the property within 10 days after the date on which the actor received notice demanding payment; or

(4) the actor failed to return the property held under a rental agreement:

(A) within five days after receiving notice demanding return, if the property is valued at less than $1,500; or

(B) within three days after receiving notice demanding return, if the property is valued at $1,500 or more.

(c) For purposes of Subsections (a)(4), (b)(2), and (b)(4), notice shall be notice in writing, sent by registered or certified mail with return receipt requested or by telegram with report of delivery requested, and addressed to the actor at his address shown on the rental agreement or service agreement.

(d) If written notice is given in accordance with Subsection (c), it is presumed that the notice was received no later than five days after it was sent.

(e) An offense under this section is:

(1) a Class C misdemeanor if the value of the service stolen is less than $20;

(2) a Class B misdemeanor if the value of the service stolen is $20 or more but less than $500;

(3) a Class A misdemeanor if the value of the service stolen is $500 or more but less than $1,500;

(4) a state jail felony if the value of the service stolen is $1,500 or more but less than $20,000;

(5) a felony of the third degree if the value of the service stolen is $20,000 or more but less than $100,000;

(6) a felony of the second degree if the value of the service stolen is $100,000 or more but less than $200,000; or

(7) a felony of the first degree if the value of the service stolen is $200,000 or more.

(f) Notwithstanding any other provision of this code, any police or other report of stolen vehicles by a political subdivision of this state shall include on the report any rental vehicles whose renters have been shown to such reporting agency to be in violation of Subsection (b)(2) and shall indicate that the renting agency has complied with the notice requirements demanding return as provided in this section.

(g) It is a defense to prosecution under this section that:

(1) the defendant secured the performance of the service by giving a post-dated check or similar sight order to the person performing the service; and

(2) the person performing the service or any other person presented the check or sight order for payment before the date on the check or sight order.

Acts 1973, 63rd Leg., p. 883, ch. 399, § 1, eff. Jan. 1, 1974. Amended by Acts 1977, 65th Leg., p. 1138, ch. 429, § 1, eff. Aug. 29, 1977; Acts 1983, 68th Leg., p. 2920, ch. 497, § 4, eff. Sept. 1, 1983; Acts 1991, 72nd Leg., ch. 565, § 15, eff. Sept. 1, 1991; Acts 1993, 73rd Leg., ch. 900, § 1.01, eff. Sept. 1, 1994; Acts 1995, 74th Leg., ch. 479, § 1, eff. Aug. 28, 1995; Acts 1999, 76th Leg., ch. 843, § 1, eff. Sept. 1, 1999; Acts 2001, 77th Leg., ch. 1245, §§ 1, 2, eff. Sept. 1, 2001; Acts 2003, 78th Leg., ch. 419, § 1, eff. Sept. 1, 2003.

§ 31.05. Theft of Trade Secrets

(a) For purposes of this section:

(1) "Article" means any object, material, device, or substance or any copy thereof, including a writing, recording, drawing, sample, specimen, prototype, model, photograph, microorganism, blueprint, or map.

(2) "Copy" means a facsimile, replica, photograph, or other reproduction of an article or a note, drawing, or sketch made of or from an article.

(3) "Representing" means describing, depicting, containing, constituting, reflecting, or recording.

(4) "Trade secret" means the whole or any part of any scientific or technical information, design, process, procedure, formula, or improvement that

has value and that the owner has taken measures to prevent from becoming available to persons other than those selected by the owner to have access for limited purposes.

(b) A person commits an offense if, without the owner's effective consent, he knowingly:

(1) steals a trade secret;

(2) makes a copy of an article representing a trade secret; or

(3) communicates or transmits a trade secret.

(c) An offense under this section is a felony of the third degree.

Acts 1973, 63rd Leg., p. 883, ch. 399, § 1, eff. Jan. 1, 1974. Amended by Acts 1993, 73rd Leg., ch. 900, § 1.01, eff. Sept. 1, 1994.

§ 31.06. Presumption for Theft by Check

(a) If the actor obtained property or secured performance of service by issuing or passing a check or similar sight order for the payment of money, when the issuer did not have sufficient funds in or on deposit with the bank or other drawee for the payment in full of the check or order as well as all other checks or orders then outstanding, it is prima facie evidence of his intent to deprive the owner of property under Section 31.03 (Theft) including a drawee or third-party holder in due course who negotiated the check or to avoid payment for service under Section 31.04 (Theft of Service) (except in the case of a postdated check or order) if:

(1) he had no account with the bank or other drawee at the time he issued the check or order; or

(2) payment was refused by the bank or other drawee for lack of funds or insufficient funds, on presentation within 30 days after issue, and the issuer failed to pay the holder in full within 10 days after receiving notice of that refusal.

(b) For purposes of Subsection (a)(2) or (f)(3), notice may be actual notice or notice in writing that:

(1) is sent by:

(A) first class mail, evidenced by an affidavit of service; or

(B) registered or certified mail with return receipt requested;

(2) is addressed to the issuer at the issuer's address shown on:

(A) the check or order;

(B) the records of the bank or other drawee; or

(C) the records of the person to whom the check or order has been issued or passed; and

(3) contains the following statement:

"This is a demand for payment in full for a check or order not paid because of a lack of funds or insufficient funds. If you fail to make payment in full within 10 days after the date of receipt of this notice, the failure to pay creates a presumption for committing an offense, and this matter may be referred for criminal prosecution."

(c) If written notice is given in accordance with Subsection (b), it is presumed that the notice was received no later than five days after it was sent.

(d) Nothing in this section prevents the prosecution from establishing the requisite intent by direct evidence.

(e) Partial restitution does not preclude the presumption of the requisite intent under this section.

(f) If the actor obtained property by issuing or passing a check or similar sight order for the payment of money, the actor's intent to deprive the owner of the property under Section 31.03 (Theft) is presumed, except in the case of a postdated check or order, if:

(1) the actor ordered the bank or other drawee to stop payment on the check or order;

(2) the bank or drawee refused payment to the holder on presentation of the check or order within 30 days after issue;

(3) the owner gave the actor notice of the refusal of payment and made a demand to the actor for payment or return of the property; and

(4) the actor failed to:

(A) pay the holder within 10 days after receiving the demand for payment; or

(B) return the property to the owner within 10 days after receiving the demand for return of the property.

Acts 1973, 63rd Leg., p. 883, ch. 399, § 1, eff. Jan. 1, 1974. Amended by Acts 1991, 72nd Leg., ch. 543, § 2, eff. Sept. 1, 1991; Acts 1993, 73rd Leg., ch. 900, § 1.01, eff. Sept. 1, 1994; Acts 1995, 74th Leg., ch. 753, § 1, eff. Sept. 1, 1995; Acts 2007, 80th Leg., ch. 976, § 1, eff. Sept. 1, 2007.

Section 5 of Acts 2007, 80th Leg., ch. 976 provides:

"The change in law made by this Act applies only to an offense committed on or after the effective date [Sept. 1, 2007] of this Act. An offense committed before the effective date of this Act is covered by the law in effect when the offense was committed, and the former law is continued in effect for that purpose. For purposes of this section, an offense was committed before the effective date of this Act if any element of the offense was committed before that date."

§ 31.07. Unauthorized Use of a Vehicle

(a) A person commits an offense if he intentionally or knowingly operates another's boat, airplane, or motor-propelled vehicle without the effective consent of the owner.

(b) An offense under this section is a state jail felony.

Acts 1973, 63rd Leg., p. 883, ch. 399, § 1, eff. Jan. 1, 1974. Amended by Acts 1993, 73rd Leg., ch. 900, § 1.01, eff. Sept. 1, 1994.

§ 31.08. Value

(a) Subject to the additional criteria of Subsections (b) and (c), value under this chapter is:

(1) the fair market value of the property or service at the time and place of the offense; or

(2) if the fair market value of the property cannot be ascertained, the cost of replacing the property within a reasonable time after the theft.

(b) The value of documents, other than those having a readily ascertainable market value, is:

(1) the amount due and collectible at maturity less that part which has been satisfied, if the document constitutes evidence of a debt; or

(2) the greatest amount of economic loss that the owner might reasonably suffer by virtue of loss of the document, if the document is other than evidence of a debt.

(c) If property or service has value that cannot be reasonably ascertained by the criteria set forth in Subsections (a) and (b), the property or service is deemed to have a value of $500 or more but less than $1,500.

(d) If the actor proves by a preponderance of the evidence that he gave consideration for or had a legal interest in the property or service stolen, the amount of the consideration or the value of the interest so proven shall be deducted from the value of the property or service ascertained under Subsection (a), (b), or (c) to determine value for purposes of this chapter.

Acts 1973, 63rd Leg., p. 883, ch. 399, § 1, eff. Jan. 1, 1974. Amended by Acts 1983, 68th Leg., p. 2920, ch. 497, § 5, eff. Sept. 1, 1983; Acts 1993, 73rd Leg., ch. 900, § 1.01, eff. Sept. 1, 1994.

§ 31.09. Aggregation of Amounts Involved in Theft

When amounts are obtained in violation of this chapter pursuant to one scheme or continuing course of conduct, whether from the same or several sources, the conduct may be considered as one offense and the amounts aggregated in determining the grade of the offense.

Acts 1973, 63rd Leg., p. 883, ch. 399, § 1, eff. Jan. 1, 1974. Amended by Acts 1993, 73rd Leg., ch. 900, § 1.01, eff. Sept. 1, 1994.

§ 31.10. Actor's Interest in Property

It is no defense to prosecution under this chapter that the actor has an interest in the property or service stolen if another person has the right of exclusive possession of the property.

Acts 1973, 63rd Leg., p. 883, ch. 399, § 1, eff. Jan. 1, 1974. Amended by Acts 1993, 73rd Leg., ch. 900, § 1.01, eff. Sept. 1, 1994.

§ 31.11. Tampering With Identification Numbers

(a) A person commits an offense if the person:

(1) knowingly or intentionally removes, alters, or obliterates the serial number or other permanent identification marking on tangible personal property; or

(2) possesses, sells, or offers for sale tangible personal property and:

(A) the actor knows that the serial number or other permanent identification marking has been removed, altered, or obliterated; or

(B) a reasonable person in the position of the actor would have known that the serial number or other permanent identification marking has been removed, altered, or obliterated.

(b) It is an affirmative defense to prosecution under this section that the person was:

(1) the owner or acting with the effective consent of the owner of the property involved;

(2) a peace officer acting in the actual discharge of official duties; or

(3) acting with respect to a number assigned to a vehicle by the Texas Department of Transportation or the Texas Department of Motor Vehicles, as applicable, and the person was:

(A) in the actual discharge of official duties as an employee or agent of the department; or

(B) in full compliance with the rules of the department as an applicant for an assigned number approved by the department.

(c) Property involved in a violation of this section may be treated as stolen for purposes of custody and disposition of the property.

(d) An offense under this section is a Class A misdemeanor.

(e) In this section, "vehicle" has the meaning given by Section 541.201, Transportation Code.

Added by Acts 1979, 66th Leg., p. 417, ch. 191, § 1, eff. Sept. 1, 1979. Amended by Acts 1983, 68th Leg., p. 4525, ch. 741, § 2, eff. Sept. 1, 1983; Acts 1991, 72nd Leg., ch. 113, § 1, eff. Sept. 1, 1991; Acts 1993, 73rd Leg., ch. 900, § 1.01, eff. Sept. 1, 1994; Acts 1997, 75th Leg., ch. 165, § 30.239, eff. Sept. 1, 1997; Acts 2009, 81st Leg., ch. 933, § 3J.02, eff. Sept. 1, 2009.

§ 31.12. Theft of or Tampering With Multichannel Video or Information Services

(a) A person commits an offense if, without the authorization of the multichannel video or information services provider, the person intentionally or knowingly:

(1) makes or maintains a connection, whether physically, electrically, electronically, or inductively, to:

(A) a cable, wire, or other component of or media attached to a multichannel video or information services system; or

(B) a television set, videotape recorder, or other receiver attached to a multichannel video or information system;

(2) attaches, causes to be attached, or maintains the attachment of a device to:

(A) a cable, wire, or other component of or media attached to a multichannel video or information services system; or

(B) a television set, videotape recorder, or other receiver attached to a multichannel video or information services system;

(3) tampers with, modifies, or maintains a modification to a device installed by a multichannel video or information services provider; or

(4) tampers with, modifies, or maintains a modification to an access device or uses that access device or any unauthorized access device to obtain services from a multichannel video or information services provider.

(b) In this section:

(1) "Access device," "connection," and "device" mean an access device, connection, or device wholly or partly designed to make intelligible an encrypted, encoded, scrambled, or other nonstandard signal carried by a multichannel video or information services provider.

(2) "Encrypted, encoded, scrambled, or other nonstandard signal" means any type of signal or transmission not intended to produce an intelligible program or service without the use of a device, signal, or information provided by a multichannel video or information services provider.

(3) "Multichannel video or information services provider" means a licensed cable television system, video dialtone system, multichannel multipoint distribution services system, direct broadcast satellite system, or other system providing video or information services that are distributed by cable, wire, radio frequency, or other media.

(c) This section does not prohibit the manufacture, distribution, sale, or use of satellite receiving antennas that are otherwise permitted by state or federal law.

(d) An offense under this section is a Class C misdemeanor unless it is shown on the trial of the offense that the actor:

(1) has been previously convicted one time of an offense under this section, in which event the offense is a Class B misdemeanor, or convicted two or more times of an offense under this section, in which event the offense is a Class A misdemeanor; or

(2) committed the offense for remuneration, in which event the offense is a Class A misdemeanor, unless it is also shown on the trial of the offense that the actor has been previously convicted two or more times of an offense under this section, in which event the offense is a Class A misdemeanor with a minimum fine of $2,000 and a minimum term of confinement of 180 days.

(e) For the purposes of this section, each connection, attachment, modification, or act of tampering is a separate offense.

Added by Acts 1995, 74th Leg., ch. 318, § 10, eff. Sept. 1, 1995. Amended by Acts 1999, 76th Leg., ch. 858, § 1, eff. Sept. 1, 1999.

§ 31.13. Manufacture, Distribution, or Advertisement of Multichannel Video or Information Services Device

(a) A person commits an offense if the person for remuneration intentionally or knowingly manufactures, assembles, modifies, imports into the state, exports out of the state, distributes, advertises, or offers for sale, with an intent to aid in the commission of an offense under Section 31.12, a device, a kit or part for a device, or a plan for a system of components wholly or partly designed to make intelligible an encrypted, encoded, scrambled, or other nonstandard signal carried or caused by a multichannel video or information services provider.

(b) In this section, "device," "encrypted, encoded, scrambled, or other nonstandard signal," and "multichannel video or information services provider" have the meanings assigned by Section 31.12.

(c) This section does not prohibit the manufacture, distribution, advertisement, offer for sale, or use of satellite receiving antennas that are otherwise permitted by state or federal law.

(d) An offense under this section is a Class A misdemeanor.

Added by Acts 1995, 74th Leg., ch. 318, § 10, eff. Sept. 1, 1995. Amended by Acts 1999, 76th Leg., ch. 858, § 2, eff. Sept. 1, 1999.

§ 31.14. Sale or Lease of Multichannel Video or Information Services Device

(a) A person commits an offense if the person intentionally or knowingly sells or leases, with an intent to aid in the commission of an offense under Section 31.12, a device, a kit or part for a device, or a plan for a system of components wholly or partly designed to make intelligible an encrypted, encoded, scrambled, or other nonstandard signal carried or caused by a multichannel video or information services provider.

(b) In this section, "device," "encrypted, encoded, scrambled, or other nonstandard signal," and "multichannel video or information services provider" have the meanings assigned by Section 31.12.

(c) This section does not prohibit the sale or lease of satellite receiving antennas that are otherwise permitted by state or federal law without providing notice to the comptroller.

(d) An offense under this section is a Class A misdemeanor.

Added by Acts 1999, 76th Leg., ch. 858, § 3, eff. Sept. 1, 1999.

§ 31.15. Possession, Manufacture, or Distribution of Certain Instruments Used to Commit Retail Theft

(a) In this section:

(1) "Retail theft detector" means an electrical, mechanical, electronic, or magnetic device used to prevent or detect shoplifting and includes any article or component part essential to the proper operation of the device.

(2) "Shielding or deactivation instrument" means any item or tool designed, made, or adapted for the purpose of preventing the detection of stolen merchandise by a retail theft detector. The term includes a metal-lined or foil-lined shopping bag and any item used to remove a security tag affixed to retail merchandise.

(b) A person commits an offense if, with the intent to use the instrument to commit theft, the person:

(1) possesses a shielding or deactivation instrument; or

(2) knowingly manufactures, sells, offers for sale, or otherwise distributes a shielding or deactivation instrument.

(c) An offense under this section is a Class A misdemeanor.

Added by Acts 2001, 77th Leg., ch. 109, § 1, eff. Sept. 1, 2001.

§ 31.16. Organized Retail Theft

(a) In this section, "retail merchandise" means one or more items of tangible personal property displayed, held, stored, or offered for sale in a retail establishment.

(b) A person commits an offense if the person intentionally conducts, promotes, or facilitates an activity in which the person receives, possesses, conceals, stores, barters, sells, or disposes of a total value of not less than $1,500 of:

(1) stolen retail merchandise; or

(2) merchandise explicitly represented to the person as being stolen retail merchandise.

(c) An offense under this section is:

(1) a state jail felony if the total value of the merchandise involved in the activity is $1,500 or more but less than $20,000;

(2) a felony of the third degree if the total value of the merchandise involved in the activity is $20,000 or more but less than $100,000;

(3) a felony of the second degree if the total value of the merchandise involved in the activity is $100,000 or more but less than $200,000; or

(4) a felony of the first degree if the total value of the merchandise involved in the activity is $200,000 or more.

(d) An offense described for purposes of punishment by Subsections (c)(1)–(3) is increased to the next higher category of offense if it is shown on the trial of the offense that the person organized, supervised, financed, or managed one or more other persons engaged in an activity described by Subsection (b).

(e) For the purposes of punishment, an offense under this section or an offense described by Section 31.03(e)(1) or (2) is increased to the next highest category of offense if it is shown at the trial of the offense that the defendant, with the intent that a distraction from the commission of the offense be created, intentionally, knowingly, or recklessly caused an alarm to sound or otherwise become activated during the commission of the offense.

Added by Acts 2007, 80th Leg., ch. 1274, § 1, eff. Sept. 1, 2007.

Section 3 of Acts 2007, 80th Leg., ch. 1274 provides:

"The change in law made by this Act in adding section 31.16(e), Penal Code, applies only to an offense committed on or after the effective date of this Act. An offense committed before the effective date of this Act is governed by the law in effect at the time the offense was committed, and the former law is continued in effect for that purpose. For the purposes of this section, an offense is committed before the effective date of this Act if any element of the offense occurs before that date."

CHAPTER 32. FRAUD

SUBCHAPTER A. GENERAL PROVISIONS

SUBCHAPTER A. GENERAL PROVISIONS

§ 32.01. Definitions

In this chapter:

(1) "Financial institution" means a bank, trust company, insurance company, credit union, building and loan association, savings and loan association, investment trust, investment company, or any other organization held out to the public as a place for deposit of funds or medium of savings or collective investment.

(2) "Property" means:

(A) real property;

(B) tangible or intangible personal property including anything severed from land; or

(C) a document, including money, that represents or embodies anything of value.

(3) "Service" includes:

(A) labor and professional service;

(B) telecommunication, public utility, and transportation service;

(C) lodging, restaurant service, and entertainment; and

(D) the supply of a motor vehicle or other property for use.

(4) "Steal" means to acquire property or service by theft.

Acts 1973, 63rd Leg., p. 883, ch. 399, § 1, eff. Jan. 1, 1974. Amended by Acts 1993, 73rd Leg., ch. 900, § 1.01, eff. Sept. 1, 1994.

§ 32.02. Value

(a) Subject to the additional criteria of Subsections (b) and (c), value under this chapter is:

(1) the fair market value of the property or service at the time and place of the offense; or

(2) if the fair market value of the property cannot be ascertained, the cost of replacing the property within a reasonable time after the offense.

(b) The value of documents, other than those having a readily ascertainable market value, is:

(1) the amount due and collectible at maturity less any part that has been satisfied, if the document constitutes evidence of a debt; or

(2) the greatest amount of economic loss that the owner might reasonably suffer by virtue of loss of the document, if the document is other than evidence of a debt.

(c) If property or service has value that cannot be reasonably ascertained by the criteria set forth in Subsections (a) and (b), the property or service is deemed to have a value of $500 or more but less than $1,500.

(d) If the actor proves by a preponderance of the evidence that he gave consideration for or had a legal interest in the property or service stolen, the amount of the consideration or the value of the interest so proven shall be deducted from the value of the property or service ascertained under Subsection (a), (b), or (c) to determine value for purposes of this chapter.

Acts 1973, 63rd Leg., p. 883, ch. 399, § 1, eff. Jan. 1, 1974. Amended by Acts 1993, 73rd Leg., ch. 900, § 1.01, eff. Sept. 1, 1994.

§ 32.03. Aggregation of Amounts Involved in Fraud

When amounts are obtained in violation of this chapter pursuant to one scheme or continuing course of conduct, whether from the same or several sources, the conduct may be considered as one offense and the amounts aggregated in determining the grade of offense.

Acts 1973, 63rd Leg., p. 883, ch. 399, § 1, eff. Jan. 1, 1974. Amended by Acts 1993, 73rd Leg., ch. 900, § 1.01, eff. Sept. 1, 1994.

SUBCHAPTER B. FORGERY

§ 32.21. Forgery

(a) For purposes of this section:

(1) "Forge" means:

(A) to alter, make, complete, execute, or authenticate any writing so that it purports:

(i) to be the act of another who did not authorize that act;

(ii) to have been executed at a time or place or in a numbered sequence other than was in fact the case; or

(iii) to be a copy of an original when no such original existed;

(B) to issue, transfer, register the transfer of, pass, publish, or otherwise utter a writing that is forged within the meaning of Paragraph (A); or

(C) to possess a writing that is forged within the meaning of Paragraph (A) with intent to utter it in a manner specified in Paragraph (B).

(2) "Writing" includes:

(A) printing or any other method of recording information;

(B) money, coins, tokens, stamps, seals, credit cards, badges, and trademarks; and

(C) symbols of value, right, privilege, or identification.

(b) A person commits an offense if he forges a writing with intent to defraud or harm another.

(c) Except as provided by Subsections (d), (e), and (e–1), an offense under this section is a Class A misdemeanor.

(d) An offense under this section is a state jail felony if the writing is or purports to be a will, codicil, deed, deed of trust, mortgage, security instrument, security agreement, credit card, check, authorization to debit an account at a financial institution, or similar sight order for payment of money, contract, release, or other commercial instrument.

(e) An offense under this section is a felony of the third degree if the writing is or purports to be:

(1) part of an issue of money, securities, postage or revenue stamps;

(2) a government record listed in Section 37.01(2)(C); or

(3) other instruments issued by a state or national government or by a subdivision of either, or part

of an issue of stock, bonds, or other instruments representing interests in or claims against another person.

(e–1) An offense under this section is increased to the next higher category of offense if it is shown on the trial of the offense that the offense was committed against an elderly individual as defined by Section 22.04.

(f) A person is presumed to intend to defraud or harm another if the person acts with respect to two or more writings of the same type and if each writing is a government record listed in Section 37.01(2)(C).

Acts 1973, 63rd Leg., p. 883, ch. 399, § 1, eff. Jan. 1, 1974. Amended by Acts 1991, 72nd Leg., ch. 113, § 2, eff. Sept. 1, 1991; Acts 1993, 73rd Leg., ch. 900, § 1.01, eff. Sept. 1, 1994; Acts 1997, 75th Leg., ch. 189, § 1, eff. May 21, 1997; Acts 2003, 78th Leg., ch. 1104, § 1, eff. Sept. 1, 2003; Acts 2009, 81st Leg., ch. 670, § 1, eff. Sept. 1, 2009.

Section 4 of Acts 2009, 81st Leg., ch. 670 provides:

"The change in law made by this Act applies only to an offense committed on or after the effective date of this Act. An offense committed before the effective date [Sept. 1, 2009] of this Act is governed by the law in effect when the offense was committed, and the former law is continued in effect for that purpose. For the purposes of this section, an offense was committed before the effective date of this Act if any element of the offense occurred before that date."

§ 32.22. Criminal Simulation

(a) A person commits an offense if, with intent to defraud or harm another:

(1) he makes or alters an object, in whole or in part, so that it appears to have value because of age, antiquity, rarity, source, or authorship that it does not have;

(2) he possesses an object so made or altered, with intent to sell, pass, or otherwise utter it; or

(3) he authenticates or certifies an object so made or altered as genuine or as different from what it is.

(b) An offense under this section is a Class A misdemeanor.

Acts 1973, 63rd Leg., p. 883, ch. 399, § 1, eff. Jan. 1, 1974. Amended by Acts 1993, 73rd Leg., ch. 900, § 1.01, eff. Sept. 1, 1994.

§ 32.23. Trademark Counterfeiting

(a) In this section:

(1) "Counterfeit mark" means a mark that is identical to or substantially indistinguishable from a protected mark the use or production of which is not authorized by the owner of the protected mark.

(2) "Identification mark" means a data plate, serial number, or part identification number.

(3) "Protected mark" means a trademark or service mark or an identification mark that is:

(A) registered with the secretary of state;

(B) registered on the principal register of the United States Patent and Trademark Office;

(C) registered under the laws of another state; or

(D) protected by Section 16.30, Business & Commerce Code, or by 36 U.S.C. Section 371 et seq.

(4) "Retail value" means the actor's regular selling price for a counterfeit mark or an item or service that bears or is identified by a counterfeit mark, except that if an item bearing a counterfeit mark is a component of a finished product, the retail value means the actor's regular selling price of the finished product on or in which the component is used, distributed, or sold.

(5) "Service mark" has the meaning assigned by Section 16.01, Business & Commerce Code.

(6) "Trademark" has the meaning assigned by Section 16.01, Business & Commerce Code.

(b) A person commits an offense if the person intentionally manufactures, displays, advertises, distributes, offers for sale, sells, or possesses with intent to sell or distribute a counterfeit mark or an item or service that:

(1) bears or is identified by a counterfeit mark; or

(2) the person knows or should have known bears or is identified by a counterfeit mark.

(c) A state or federal certificate of registration of intellectual property is prima facie evidence of the facts stated in the certificate.

(d) For the purposes of Subsection (e), when items or services are the subject of counterfeiting in violation of this section pursuant to one scheme or continuing course of conduct, the conduct may be considered as one offense and the retail value of the items or services aggregated in determining the grade of offense.

(e) An offense under this section is a:

(1) Class C misdemeanor if the retail value of the item or service is less than $20;

(2) Class B misdemeanor if the retail value of the item or service is $20 or more but less than $500;

(3) Class A misdemeanor if the retail value of the item or service is $500 or more but less than $1,500;

(4) state jail felony if the retail value of the item or service is $1,500 or more but less than $20,000;

(5) felony of the third degree if the retail value of the item or service is $20,000 or more but less than $100,000;

(6) felony of the second degree if the retail value of the item or service is $100,000 or more but less than $200,000; or

(7) felony of the first degree if the retail value of the item or service is $200,000 or more.

Added by Acts 1997, 75th Leg., ch. 1161, § 2, eff. Sept. 1, 1997.

§ 32.24. Stealing or Receiving Stolen Check or Similar Sight Order

(a) A person commits an offense if the person steals an unsigned check or similar sight order or, with knowledge that an unsigned check or similar sight order has been stolen, receives the check or sight order with intent to use it, to sell it, or to transfer it to a person other than the person from whom the check or sight order was stolen.

(b) An offense under this section is a Class A misdemeanor.

Added by Acts 1999, 76th Leg., ch. 1413, § 1, eff. Sept. 1, 1999.

SUBCHAPTER C. CREDIT

§ 32.31. Credit Card or Debit Card Abuse

(a) For purposes of this section:

(1) "Cardholder" means the person named on the face of a credit card or debit card to whom or for whose benefit the card is issued.

(2) "Credit card" means an identification card, plate, coupon, book, number, or any other device authorizing a designated person or bearer to obtain property or services on credit. The term includes the number or description of the device if the device itself is not produced at the time of ordering or obtaining the property or service.

(3) "Expired credit card" means a credit card bearing an expiration date after that date has passed.

(4) "Debit card" means an identification card, plate, coupon, book, number, or any other device authorizing a designated person or bearer to communicate a request to an unmanned teller machine or a customer convenience terminal or obtain property or services by debit to an account at a financial institution. The term includes the number or description of the device if the device itself is not produced at the time of ordering or obtaining the benefit.

(5) "Expired debit card" means a debit card bearing as its expiration date a date that has passed.

(6) "Unmanned teller machine" means a machine, other than a telephone, capable of being operated by a customer, by which a customer may communicate to a financial institution a request to withdraw a benefit for himself or for another directly from the customer's account or from the customer's account under a line of credit previously authorized by the institution for the customer.

(7) "Customer convenience terminal" means an unmanned teller machine the use of which does not involve personnel of a financial institution.

(b) A person commits an offense if:

(1) with intent to obtain a benefit fraudulently, he presents or uses a credit card or debit card with knowledge that:

(A) the card, whether or not expired, has not been issued to him and is not used with the effective consent of the cardholder; or

(B) the card has expired or has been revoked or cancelled;

(2) with intent to obtain a benefit, he uses a fictitious credit card or debit card or the pretended number or description of a fictitious card;

(3) he receives a benefit that he knows has been obtained in violation of this section;

(4) he steals a credit card or debit card or, with knowledge that it has been stolen, receives a credit card or debit card with intent to use it, to sell it, or to transfer it to a person other than the issuer or the cardholder;

(5) he buys a credit card or debit card from a person who he knows is not the issuer;

(6) not being the issuer, he sells a credit card or debit card;

(7) he uses or induces the cardholder to use the cardholder's credit card or debit card to obtain property or service for the actor's benefit for which the cardholder is financially unable to pay;

(8) not being the cardholder, and without the effective consent of the cardholder, he possesses a credit card or debit card with intent to use it;

(9) he possesses two or more incomplete credit cards or debit cards that have not been issued to him with intent to complete them without the effective consent of the issuer. For purposes of this subdivision, a card is incomplete if part of the matter that an issuer requires to appear on the card before it can be used, other than the signature of the cardholder, has not yet been stamped, embossed, imprinted, or written on it;

(10) being authorized by an issuer to furnish goods or services on presentation of a credit card or debit card, he, with intent to defraud the issuer or the cardholder, furnishes goods or services on presentation of a credit card or debit card obtained or retained in violation of this section or a credit card or debit card that is forged, expired, or revoked; or

(11) being authorized by an issuer to furnish goods or services on presentation of a credit card or debit card, he, with intent to defraud the issuer or a cardholder, fails to furnish goods or services that he represents in writing to the issuer that he has furnished.

(c) It is presumed that a person who used a revoked, cancelled, or expired credit card or debit card had knowledge that the card had been revoked, cancelled, or expired if he had received notice of revocation, cancellation, or expiration from the issuer. For purposes of this section, notice may be either notice given orally in person or by telephone, or in writing by mail or by telegram. If written notice was sent by registered or certified mail with return receipt requested, or by telegram with report of delivery requested, addressed to the cardholder at the last address shown by the records of the issuer, it is presumed that the notice was received by the cardholder no later than five days after sent.

(d) An offense under this section is a state jail felony, except that the offense is a felony of the third degree if it is shown on the trial of the offense that the offense was committed against an elderly individual as defined by Section 22.04.

Acts 1973, 63rd Leg., p. 883, ch. 399, § 1, eff. Jan. 1, 1974. Amended by Acts 1993, 73rd Leg., ch. 900, § 1.01, eff. Sept. 1, 1994; Acts 2003, 78th Leg., ch. 1104, §§ 2, 3, eff. Sept. 1, 2003; Acts 2005, 79th Leg., ch. 1054, § 1, eff. Sept. 1, 2005; Acts 2009, 81st Leg., ch. 670, § 2, eff. Sept. 1, 2009.

Section 4 of Acts 2009, 81st Leg., ch. 670 provides:

"The change in law made by this Act applies only to an offense committed on or after the effective date of this Act. An offense committed before the effective date [Sept. 1, 2009] of this Act is governed by the law in effect when the offense was committed, and the former law is continued in effect for that purpose. For the purposes of this section, an offense was committed before the effective date of this Act if any element of the offense occurred before that date."

§ 32.32. False Statement to Obtain Property or Credit or in the Provision of Certain Services

(a) For purposes of this section, "credit" includes:

(1) a loan of money;

(2) furnishing property or service on credit;

(3) extending the due date of an obligation;

(4) comaking, endorsing, or guaranteeing a note or other instrument for obtaining credit;

(5) a line or letter of credit;

(6) a credit card, as defined in Section 32.31 (Credit Card or Debit Card Abuse); and

(7) a mortgage loan.

(b) A person commits an offense if he intentionally or knowingly makes a materially false or misleading written statement to obtain property or credit, including a mortgage loan.

(b–1) A person commits an offense if the person intentionally or knowingly makes a materially false or misleading written statement in providing an appraisal of real property for compensation.

(c) An offense under this section is:

(1) a Class C misdemeanor if the value of the property or the amount of credit is less than $50;

(2) a Class B misdemeanor if the value of the property or the amount of credit is $50 or more but less than $500;

(3) a Class A misdemeanor if the value of the property or the amount of credit is $500 or more but less than $1,500;

(4) a state jail felony if the value of the property or the amount of credit is $1,500 or more but less than $20,000;

(5) a felony of the third degree if the value of the property or the amount of credit is $20,000 or more but less than $100,000;

(6) a felony of the second degree if the value of the property or the amount of credit is $100,000 or more but less than $200,000; or

(7) a felony of the first degree if the value of the property or the amount of credit is $200,000 or more.

(d) The following agencies shall assist a prosecuting attorney of the United States or of a county or judicial district of this state, a county or state law enforcement agency of this state, or a federal law enforcement agency in the investigation of an offense under this section involving a mortgage loan:

(1) the office of the attorney general;

(2) the Department of Public Safety;

(3) the Texas Department of Insurance;

(4) the Office of Consumer Credit Commissioner;

(5) the Texas Department of Banking;

(6) the credit union department;

(7) the Department of Savings and Mortgage Lending;

(8) the Texas Real Estate Commission;

(9) the Texas Appraiser Licensing and Certification Board; and

(10) the Texas Department of Housing and Community Affairs.

(e) With the consent of the appropriate local county or district attorney, the attorney general has concurrent jurisdiction with that consenting local prosecutor to prosecute an offense under this section that involves a mortgage loan.

Acts 1973, 63rd Leg., p. 883, ch. 399, § 1, eff. Jan. 1, 1974. Amended by Acts 1993, 73rd Leg., ch. 900, § 1.01, eff. Sept. 1, 1994; Acts 1995, 74th Leg., ch. 76, § 14.50, eff. Sept. 1, 1995; Acts 2001, 77th Leg., ch. 1245, § 3, eff. Sept. 1, 2001; Acts 2007, 80th Leg., ch. 285, § 5, eff. Sept. 1, 2007; Acts 2009, 81st Leg., ch. 709, §§ 4, 5, eff. Sept. 1, 2009.

§ 32.33. Hindering Secured Creditors

(a) For purposes of this section:

(1) "Remove" means transport, without the effective consent of the secured party, from the state in which the property was located when the security interest or lien attached.

(2) "Security interest" means an interest in personal property or fixtures that secures payment or performance of an obligation.

(b) A person who has signed a security agreement creating a security interest in property or a mortgage or deed of trust creating a lien on property commits an offense if, with intent to hinder enforcement of that interest or lien, he destroys, removes, conceals, encumbers, or otherwise harms or reduces the value of the property.

(c) For purposes of this section, a person is presumed to have intended to hinder enforcement of the security interest or lien if, when any part of the debt secured by the security interest or lien was due, he failed:

(1) to pay the part then due; and

(2) if the secured party had made demand, to deliver possession of the secured property to the secured party.

(d) An offense under Subsection (b) is a:

(1) Class C misdemeanor if the value of the property destroyed, removed, concealed, encumbered, or otherwise harmed or reduced in value is less than $20;

(2) Class B misdemeanor if the value of the property destroyed, removed, concealed, encumbered, or otherwise harmed or reduced in value is $20 or more but less than $500;

(3) Class A misdemeanor if the value of the property destroyed, removed, concealed, encumbered, or otherwise harmed or reduced in value is $500 or more but less than $1,500;

(4) state jail felony if the value of the property destroyed, removed, concealed, encumbered, or otherwise harmed or reduced in value is $1,500 or more but less than $20,000;

(5) felony of the third degree if the value of the property destroyed, removed, concealed, encumbered, or otherwise harmed or reduced in value is $20,000 or more but less than $100,000;

(6) felony of the second degree if the value of the property destroyed, removed, concealed, encumbered, or otherwise harmed or reduced in value is $100,000 or more but less than $200,000; or

(7) felony of the first degree if the value of the property destroyed, removed, concealed, encumbered, or otherwise harmed or reduced in value is $200,000 or more.

(e) A person who is a debtor under a security agreement, and who does not have a right to sell or dispose of the secured property or is required to account to the secured party for the proceeds of a permitted sale or disposition, commits an offense if the person sells or otherwise disposes of the secured property, or does not account to the secured party for the proceeds of a sale or other disposition as required, with intent to appropriate (as defined in Chapter 31) the proceeds or value of the secured property. A person is presumed to have intended to appropriate proceeds if the person does not deliver the proceeds to the secured party or account to the secured party for the proceeds before the 11th day after the day that the secured party makes a lawful demand for the proceeds or account. An offense under this subsection is:

(1) a Class C misdemeanor if the proceeds obtained from the sale or other disposition are money or goods having a value of less than $20;

(2) a Class B misdemeanor if the proceeds obtained from the sale or other disposition are money or goods having a value of $20 or more but less than $500;

(3) a Class A misdemeanor if the proceeds obtained from the sale or other disposition are money or goods having a value of $500 or more but less than $1,500;

(4) a state jail felony if the proceeds obtained from the sale or other disposition are money or goods having a value of $1,500 or more but less than $20,000;

(5) a felony of the third degree if the proceeds obtained from the sale or other disposition are money or goods having a value of $20,000 or more but less than $100,000;

(6) a felony of the second degree if the proceeds obtained from the sale or other disposition are money or goods having a value of $100,000 or more but less than $200,000; or

(7) a felony of the first degree if the proceeds obtained from the sale or other disposition are money or goods having a value of $200,000 or more.

Acts 1973, 63rd Leg., p. 883, ch. 399, § 1, eff. Jan. 1, 1974. Amended by Acts 1979, 66th Leg., p. 501, ch. 232, § 1, eff. Sept. 1, 1979; Acts 1985, 69th Leg., ch. 914, § 5, eff. Sept. 1, 1985; Acts 1993, 73rd Leg., ch. 900, § 1.01, eff. Sept. 1, 1994.

§ 32.34. Fraudulent Transfer of a Motor Vehicle

(a) In this section:

(1) "Lease" means the grant of use and possession of a motor vehicle for consideration, whether or not the grant includes an option to buy the vehicle.

(2) "Motor vehicle" means a device in, on, or by which a person or property is or may be transported or drawn on a highway, except a device used exclusively on stationary rails or tracks.

(3) "Security interest" means an interest in personal property or fixtures that secures payment or performance of an obligation.

(4) "Third party" means a person other than the actor or the owner of the vehicle.

(5) "Transfer" means to transfer possession, whether or not another right is also transferred, by means of a sale, lease, sublease, lease assignment, or other property transfer.

(b) A person commits an offense if the person acquires, accepts possession of, or exercises control over the motor vehicle of another under a written or oral agreement to arrange for the transfer of the vehicle to a third party and:

(1) knowing the vehicle is subject to a security interest, lease, or lien, the person transfers the vehicle to a third party without first obtaining written authorization from the vehicle's secured creditor, lessor, or lienholder;

(2) intending to defraud or harm the vehicle's owner, the person transfers the vehicle to a third party;

(3) intending to defraud or harm the vehicle's owner, the person disposes of the vehicle in a manner other than by transfer to a third party; or

(4) the person does not disclose the location of the vehicle on the request of the vehicle's owner, secured creditor, lessor, or lienholder.

(c) For the purposes of Subsection (b)(2), the actor is presumed to have intended to defraud or harm the motor vehicle's owner if the actor does not take reasonable steps to determine whether or not the third party is financially able to pay for the vehicle.

(d) It is a defense to prosecution under Subsection (b)(1) that the entire indebtedness secured by or owed under the security interest, lease, or lien is paid or satisfied in full not later than the 30th day after the date that the transfer was made.

(e) It is not a defense to prosecution under Subsection (b)(1) that the motor vehicle's owner has violated a contract creating a security interest, lease, or lien in the motor vehicle.

(f) An offense under Subsection (b)(1), (b)(2), or (b)(3) is:

(1) a state jail felony if the value of the motor vehicle is less than $20,000; or

(2) a felony of the third degree if the value of the motor vehicle is $20,000 or more.

(g) An offense under Subsection (b)(4) is a Class A misdemeanor.

Added by Acts 1989, 71st Leg., ch. 954, § 1, eff. Sept. 1, 1989. Renumbered from V.T.C.A., Penal Code, § 32.36 and amended by Acts 1993, 73rd Leg., ch. 900, § 1.01, eff. Sept. 1, 1994.

§ 32.35. Credit Card Transaction Record Laundering

(a) In this section:

(1) "Agent" means a person authorized to act on behalf of another and includes an employee.

(2) "Authorized vendor" means a person authorized by a creditor to furnish property, service, or anything else of value upon presentation of a credit card by a cardholder.

(3) "Cardholder" means the person named on the face of a credit card to whom or for whose benefit the credit card is issued, and includes the named person's agents.

(4) "Credit card" means an identification card, plate, coupon, book, number, or any other device authorizing a designated person or bearer to obtain property or services on credit. It includes the number or description on the device if the device itself is not produced at the time of ordering or obtaining the property or service.

(5) "Creditor" means a person licensed under Chapter 342, Finance Code, a bank, savings and loan association, credit union, or other regulated financial institution that lends money or otherwise extends credit to a cardholder through a credit card and that authorizes other persons to honor the credit card.

(b) A person commits an offense if the person is an authorized vendor who, with intent to defraud the creditor or cardholder, presents to a creditor, for payment, a credit card transaction record of a sale that was not made by the authorized vendor or the vendor's agent.

(c) A person commits an offense if, without the creditor's authorization, the person employs, solicits, or otherwise causes an authorized vendor or the vendor's agent to present to a creditor, for payment, a credit card transaction record of a sale that was not made by the authorized vendor or the vendor's agent.

(d) It is presumed that a person is not the agent of an authorized vendor if a fee is paid or offered to be paid by the person to the authorized vendor in connection with the vendor's presentment to a creditor of a credit card transaction record.

(e) An offense under this section is a:

(1) Class C misdemeanor if the amount of the record of a sale is less than $20;

(2) Class B misdemeanor if the amount of the record of a sale is $20 or more but less than $500;

(3) Class A misdemeanor if the amount of the record of a sale is $500 or more but less than $1,500;

(4) state jail felony if the amount of the record of a sale is $1,500 or more but less than $20,000;

(5) felony of the third degree if the amount of the record of a sale is $20,000 or more but less than $100,000;

(6) felony of the second degree if the amount of the record of a sale is $100,000 or more but less than $200,000; or

(7) felony of the first degree if the amount of the record of a sale is $200,000 or more.

Added by Acts 1991, 72nd Leg., ch. 792, § 1, eff. Aug. 26, 1991. Renumbered from V.T.C.A., Penal Code § 32.37 and amended by Acts 1993, 73rd Leg., ch. 900, § 1.01, eff. Sept. 1, 1994. Amended by Acts 1997, 75th Leg., ch. 1396, § 38, eff. Sept. 1, 1997; Acts 1999, 76th Leg., ch. 62, § 7.83, eff. Sept. 1, 1999.

SUBCHAPTER D. OTHER DECEPTIVE PRACTICES

§ 32.41. Issuance of Bad Check

(a) A person commits an offense if he issues or passes a check or similar sight order for the payment of money knowing that the issuer does not have sufficient funds in or on deposit with the bank or other drawee for the payment in full of the check or order as well as all other checks or orders outstanding at the time of issuance.

(b) This section does not prevent the prosecution from establishing the required knowledge by direct evidence; however, for purposes of this section, the issuer's knowledge of insufficient funds is presumed (except in the case of a postdated check or order) if:

(1) he had no account with the bank or other drawee at the time he issued the check or order; or

(2) payment was refused by the bank or other drawee for lack of funds or insufficient funds on presentation within 30 days after issue and the issuer failed to pay the holder in full within 10 days after receiving notice of that refusal.

(c) Notice for purposes of Subsection (b)(2) may be actual notice or notice in writing that:

(1) is sent by:

(A) first class mail, evidenced by an affidavit of service; or

(B) registered or certified mail with return receipt requested;

(2) is addressed to the issuer at the issuer's address shown on:

(A) the check or order;

(B) the records of the bank or other drawee; or

(C) the records of the person to whom the check or order has been issued or passed; and

(3) contains the following statement:

"This is a demand for payment in full for a check or order not paid because of a lack of funds or insufficient funds. If you fail to make payment in full within 10 days after the date of receipt of this notice, the failure to pay creates a presumption for committing an offense, and this matter may be referred for criminal prosecution."

(d) If notice is given in accordance with Subsection (c), it is presumed that the notice was received no later than five days after it was sent.

(e) A person charged with an offense under this section may make restitution for the bad checks. Restitution shall be made through the prosecutor's office if collection and processing were initiated through that office. In other cases restitution may be, with the approval of the court in which the offense is filed:

(1) made through the court; or

(2) collected by a law enforcement agency if a peace officer of that agency executes a warrant against the person charged with the offense.

(f) Except as otherwise provided by this subsection, an offense under this section is a Class C misdemeanor. If the check or similar sight order that was issued or passed was for a child support payment the obligation for which is established under a court order, the offense is a Class B misdemeanor.

(g) An offense under this section is not a lesser included offense of an offense under Section 31.03 or 31.04.

Acts 1973, 63rd Leg., p. 883, ch. 399, § 1, eff. Jan. 1, 1974. Amended by Acts 1983, 68th Leg., p. 5050, ch. 911, § 1, eff. Aug. 29, 1983; Acts 1987, 70th Leg., ch. 687, § 2, eff. June 18, 1987; Acts 1989, 71st Leg., ch. 1038, § 1, eff. June 16, 1989; Acts 1993, 73rd Leg., ch. 900, § 1.01, eff. Sept. 1, 1994; Acts 1995, 74th Leg., ch. 753, § 2, eff. Sept. 1, 1995; Acts 1997, 75th Leg., ch. 702, § 14, eff. Sept. 1, 1997; Acts 2007, 80th Leg., ch. 976, § 2, eff. Sept. 1, 2007; Acts 2007, 80th Leg., ch. 1393, § 1, eff. Sept. 1, 2007.

Section 5 of Acts 2007, 80th Leg., ch. 976 provides:

"The change in law made by this Act applies only to an offense committed on or after the effective date [Sept. 1, 2007] of this Act. An offense committed before the effective date of this Act is covered by the law in effect when the offense was committed, and the former law is continued in effect for that purpose. For purposes of this section, an offense was committed before the effective date of this Act if any element of the offense was committed before that date."

Section 3(a) of Acts 2007, 80th Leg., ch. 1393 provides:

"(a) Section 32.41(e), Penal Code, as amended by this Act, applies only to a warrant executed by a peace officer on or after the effective date of this Act."

§ 32.42. Deceptive Business Practices

(a) For purposes of this section:

(1) "Adulterated" means varying from the standard of composition or quality prescribed by law or set by established commercial usage.

(2) "Business" includes trade and commerce and advertising, selling, and buying service or property.

(3) "Commodity" means any tangible or intangible personal property.

(4) "Contest" includes sweepstake, puzzle, and game of chance.

(5) "Deceptive sales contest" means a sales contest:

(A) that misrepresents the participant's chance of winning a prize;

(B) that fails to disclose to participants on a conspicuously displayed permanent poster (if the contest is conducted by or through a retail outlet) or on each card game piece, entry blank, or other paraphernalia required for participation in the contest (if the contest is not conducted by or through a retail outlet):

(i) the geographical area or number of outlets in which the contest is to be conducted;

(ii) an accurate description of each type of prize;

(iii) the minimum number and minimum amount of cash prizes; and

(iv) the minimum number of each other type of prize; or

(C) that is manipulated or rigged so that prizes are given to predetermined persons or retail establishments. A sales contest is not deceptive if the total value of prizes to each retail outlet is in a uniform ratio to the number of game pieces distributed to that outlet.

(6) "Mislabeled" means varying from the standard of truth or disclosure in labeling prescribed by law or set by established commercial usage.

(7) "Prize" includes gift, discount, coupon, certificate, gratuity, and any other thing of value awarded in a sales contest.

(8) "Sales contest" means a contest in connection with the sale of a commodity or service by which a person may, as determined by drawing, guessing, matching, or chance, receive a prize and which is not regulated by the rules of a federal regulatory agency.

(9) "Sell" and "sale" include offer for sale, advertise for sale, expose for sale, keep for the purpose of sale, deliver for or after sale, solicit and offer to buy, and every disposition for value.

(b) A person commits an offense if in the course of business he intentionally, knowingly, recklessly, or with criminal negligence commits one or more of the following deceptive business practices:

(1) using, selling, or possessing for use or sale a false weight or measure, or any other device for falsely determining or recording any quality or quantity;

(2) selling less than the represented quantity of a property or service;

(3) taking more than the represented quantity of property or service when as a buyer the actor furnishes the weight or measure;

(4) selling an adulterated or mislabeled commodity;

(5) passing off property or service as that of another;

(6) representing that a commodity is original or new if it is deteriorated, altered, rebuilt, reconditioned, reclaimed, used, or secondhand;

(7) representing that a commodity or service is of a particular style, grade, or model if it is of another;

(8) advertising property or service with intent:

(A) not to sell it as advertised, or

(B) not to supply reasonably expectable public demand, unless the advertising adequately discloses a time or quantity limit;

(9) representing the price of property or service falsely or in a way tending to mislead;

(10) making a materially false or misleading statement of fact concerning the reason for, existence of, or amount of a price or price reduction;

(11) conducting a deceptive sales contest; or

(12) making a materially false or misleading statement:

(A) in an advertisement for the purchase or sale of property or service; or

(B) otherwise in connection with the purchase or sale of property or service.

(c) An offense under Subsections (b)(1), (b)(2), (b)(3), (b)(4), (b)(5), and (b)(6) is:

(1) a Class C misdemeanor if the actor commits an offense with criminal negligence and if he has not previously been convicted of a deceptive business practice; or

(2) a Class A misdemeanor if the actor commits an offense intentionally, knowingly, recklessly or if he has been previously convicted of a Class B or C misdemeanor under this section.

(d) An offense under Subsections (b)(7), (b)(8), (b)(9), (b)(10), (b)(11), and (b)(12) is a Class A misdemeanor.

Acts 1973, 63rd Leg., p. 883, ch. 399, § 1, eff. Jan. 1, 1974. Amended by Acts 1975, 64th Leg., p. 1350, ch. 508, §§ 1, 2, eff. Sept. 1, 1975; Acts 1993, 73rd Leg., ch. 900, § 1.01, eff. Sept. 1, 1994.

§ 32.43. Commercial Bribery

(a) For purposes of this section:

(1) "Beneficiary" means a person for whom a fiduciary is acting.

(2) "Fiduciary" means:

(A) an agent or employee;

(B) a trustee, guardian, custodian, administrator, executor, conservator, receiver, or similar fiduciary;

(C) a lawyer, physician, accountant, appraiser, or other professional advisor; or

(D) an officer, director, partner, manager, or other participant in the direction of the affairs of a corporation or association.

(b) A person who is a fiduciary commits an offense if, without the consent of his beneficiary, he intentionally or knowingly solicits, accepts, or agrees to accept any benefit from another person on agreement or understanding that the benefit will influence the conduct of the fiduciary in relation to the affairs of his beneficiary.

(c) A person commits an offense if he offers, confers, or agrees to confer any benefit the acceptance of which is an offense under Subsection (b).

(d) An offense under this section is a state jail felony.

(e) In lieu of a fine that is authorized by Subsection (d), and in addition to the imprisonment that is authorized by that subsection, if the court finds that an individual who is a fiduciary gained a benefit through the commission of an offense under Subsection (b), the court may sentence the individual to pay a fine in an amount fixed by the court, not to exceed double the value of the benefit gained. This subsection does not affect the application of Section 12.51(c) to an offense under this section committed by a corporation or association.

Acts 1973, 63rd Leg., p. 883, ch. 399, § 1, eff. Jan. 1, 1974. Amended by Acts 1983, 68th Leg., p. 1942, ch. 357, § 1, eff. Sept. 1, 1983; Acts 1993, 73rd Leg., ch. 900, § 1.01, eff. Sept. 1, 1994.

§ 32.44. Rigging Publicly Exhibited Contest

(a) A person commits an offense if, with intent to affect the outcome (including the score) of a publicly exhibited contest:

(1) he offers, confers, or agrees to confer any benefit on, or threatens harm to:

(A) a participant in the contest to induce him not to use his best efforts; or

(B) an official or other person associated with the contest; or

(2) he tampers with a person, animal, or thing in a manner contrary to the rules of the contest.

(b) A person commits an offense if he intentionally or knowingly solicits, accepts, or agrees to accept any benefit the conferring of which is an offense under Subsection (a).

(c) An offense under this section is a Class A misdemeanor.

Acts 1973, 63rd Leg., p. 883, ch. 399, § 1, eff. Jan. 1, 1974. Amended by Acts 1993, 73rd Leg., ch. 900, § 1.01, eff. Sept. 1, 1994.

§ 32.441. Illegal Recruitment of an Athlete

(a) A person commits an offense if, without the consent of the governing body or a designee of the governing body of an institution of higher education, the person intentionally or knowingly solicits, accepts, or agrees to accept any benefit from another on an agreement or understanding that the benefit will influence the conduct of the person in enrolling in the institution and participating in intercollegiate athletics.

(b) A person commits an offense if he offers, confers, or agrees to confer any benefit the acceptance of which is an offense under Subsection (a).

(c) It is an exception to prosecution under this section that the person offering, conferring, or agreeing to confer a benefit and the person soliciting, accepting, or agreeing to accept a benefit are related within the second degree of consanguinity or affinity, as determined under Chapter 573, Government Code.

(d) It is an exception to prosecution under Subsection (a) that, not later than the 60th day after the date the person accepted or agreed to accept a benefit, the person contacted a law enforcement agency and furnished testimony or evidence about the offense.

(e) An offense under this section is a:

(1) Class C misdemeanor if the value of the benefit is less than $20;

(2) Class B misdemeanor if the value of the benefit is $20 or more but less than $500;

(3) Class A misdemeanor if the value of the benefit is $500 or more but less than $1,500;

(4) state jail felony if the value of the benefit is $1,500 or more but less than $20,000;

(5) felony of the third degree if the value of the benefit is $20,000 or more but less than $100,000;

(6) felony of the second degree if the value of the benefit is $100,000 or more but less than $200,000; or

(7) felony of the first degree if the value of the benefit is $200,000 or more.

Added by Acts 1989, 71st Leg., ch. 125, § 1, eff. Sept. 1, 1989. Amended by Acts 1991, 72nd Leg., ch. 561, § 41, eff. Aug. 26, 1991; Acts 1993, 73rd Leg., ch. 900, § 1.01, eff. Sept. 1, 1994; Acts 1995, 74th Leg., ch. 76, § 5.95(27), eff. Sept. 1, 1995.

§ 32.45. Misapplication of Fiduciary Property or Property of Financial Institution

(a) For purposes of this section:

(1) "Fiduciary" includes:

(A) a trustee, guardian, administrator, executor, conservator, and receiver;

(B) an attorney in fact or agent appointed under a durable power of attorney as provided by Chapter XII, Texas Probate Code;

(C) any other person acting in a fiduciary capacity, but not a commercial bailee unless the commercial bailee is a party in a motor fuel sales agreement with a distributor or supplier, as those terms are defined by Section 153.001, Tax Code; and

(D) an officer, manager, employee, or agent carrying on fiduciary functions on behalf of a fiduciary.

(2) "Misapply" means deal with property contrary to:

(A) an agreement under which the fiduciary holds the property; or

(B) a law prescribing the custody or disposition of the property.

(b) A person commits an offense if he intentionally, knowingly, or recklessly misapplies property he holds as a fiduciary or property of a financial institution in a manner that involves substantial risk of loss to the owner of the property or to a person for whose benefit the property is held.

(c) An offense under this section is:

(1) a Class C misdemeanor if the value of the property misapplied is less than $20;

(2) a Class B misdemeanor if the value of the property misapplied is $20 or more but less than $500;

(3) a Class A misdemeanor if the value of the property misapplied is $500 or more but less than $1,500;

(4) a state jail felony if the value of the property misapplied is $1,500 or more but less than $20,000;

(5) a felony of the third degree if the value of the property misapplied is $20,000 or more but less than $100,000;

(6) a felony of the second degree if the value of the property misapplied is $100,000 or more but less than $200,000; or

(7) a felony of the first degree if the value of the property misapplied is $200,000 or more.

(d) An offense described for purposes of punishment by Subsections (c)(1)–(6) is increased to the next higher category of offense if it is shown on the trial of the offense that the offense was committed against an elderly individual as defined by Section 22.04.

(e) With the consent of the appropriate local county or district attorney, the attorney general has concurrent jurisdiction with that consenting local prosecutor to prosecute an offense under this section that involves the state Medicaid program.

Acts 1973, 63rd Leg., p. 883, ch. 399, § 1, eff. Jan. 1, 1974. Amended by Acts 1991, 72nd Leg., ch. 565, § 2, eff. Sept. 1, 1991; Acts 1993, 73rd Leg., ch. 900, § 1.01, eff. Sept. 1, 1994; Acts 1997, 75th Leg., ch. 1036, § 14, eff. Sept. 1, 1997; Acts 2001, 77th Leg., ch. 1047, § 1, eff. Sept. 1, 2001; Acts 2003, 78th Leg., ch. 198, § 2.137, eff. Sept. 1, 2003; Acts 2003, 78th Leg., ch. 257, § 14, eff. Sept. 1, 2003; Acts 2003, 78th Leg., ch. 432, § 3, eff. Sept. 1, 2003; Acts 2005, 79th Leg., ch. 728, § 23.001(77), eff. Sept. 1, 2005.

§ 32.46. Securing Execution of Document by Deception

(a) A person commits an offense if, with intent to defraud or harm any person, he, by deception:

(1) causes another to sign or execute any document affecting property or service or the pecuniary interest of any person; or

(2) causes or induces a public servant to file or record any purported judgment or other document purporting to memorialize or evidence an act, an order, a directive, or process of:

(A) a purported court that is not expressly created or established under the constitution or the laws of this state or of the United States;

(B) a purported judicial entity that is not expressly created or established under the constitution or laws of this state or of the United States; or

(C) a purported judicial officer of a purported court or purported judicial entity described by Paragraph (A) or (B).

(b) An offense under Subsection (a)(1) is a:

(1) Class C misdemeanor if the value of the property, service, or pecuniary interest is less than $20;

(2) Class B misdemeanor if the value of the property, service, or pecuniary interest is $20 or more but less than $500;

(3) Class A misdemeanor if the value of the property, service, or pecuniary interest is $500 or more but less than $1,500;

(4) state jail felony if the value of the property, service, or pecuniary interest is $1,500 or more but less than $20,000;

(5) felony of the third degree if the value of the property, service, or pecuniary interest is $20,000 or more but less than $100,000;

(6) felony of the second degree if the value of the property, service, or pecuniary interest is $100,000 or more but less than $200,000; or

(7) felony of the first degree if the value of the property, service, or pecuniary interest is $200,000 or more.

(c) An offense under Subsection (a)(2) is a state jail felony.

(c–1) An offense described for purposes of punishment by Subsections (b)(1)–(6) and (c) is increased to the next higher category of offense if it is shown on the trial of the offense that the offense was committed against an elderly individual as defined by Section 22.04 or involves the state Medicaid program.

(d) In this section, "deception" has the meaning assigned by Section 31.01.

(e) With the consent of the appropriate local county or district attorney, the attorney general has concurrent jurisdiction with that consenting local prosecutor to prosecute an offense under this section that involves the state Medicaid program.

Acts 1973, 63rd Leg., p. 883, ch. 399, § 1, eff. Jan. 1, 1974. Amended by Acts 1993, 73rd Leg., ch. 900, § 1.01, eff. Sept. 1, 1994; Acts 1997, 75th Leg., ch. 189, § 2, eff. May 21, 1997; Acts 2003, 78th Leg., ch. 198, § 2.138, eff. Sept. 1, 2003; Acts 2003, 78th Leg., ch. 257, § 15, eff. Sept. 1, 2003; Acts 2003, 78th Leg., ch. 432, § 4, eff. Sept. 1, 2003; Acts 2007, 80th Leg., ch. 127, § 4, eff. Sept. 1, 2007.

§ 32.47. Fraudulent Destruction, Removal, or Concealment of Writing

(a) A person commits an offense if, with intent to defraud or harm another, he destroys, removes, conceals, alters, substitutes, or otherwise impairs the verity, legibility, or availability of a writing, other than a governmental record.

(b) For purposes of this section, "writing" includes:

(1) printing or any other method of recording information;

(2) money, coins, tokens, stamps, seals, credit cards, badges, trademarks;

(3) symbols of value, right, privilege, or identification; and

(4) universal product codes, labels, price tags, or markings on goods.

(c) Except as provided in Subsection (d), an offense under this section is a Class A misdemeanor.

(d) An offense under this section is a state jail felony if the writing:

(1) is a will or codicil of another, whether or not the maker is alive or dead and whether or not it has been admitted to probate; or

(2) is a deed, mortgage, deed of trust, security instrument, security agreement, or other writing for which the law provides public recording or filing, whether or not the writing has been acknowledged.

Acts 1973, 63rd Leg., p. 883, ch. 399, § 1, eff. Jan. 1, 1974. Amended by Acts 1993, 73rd Leg., ch. 900, § 1.01, eff. Sept. 1, 1994; Acts 2001, 77th Leg., ch. 21, § 1, eff. Sept. 1, 2001.

§ 32.48. Simulating Legal Process

(a) A person commits an offense if the person recklessly causes to be delivered to another any document that simulates a summons, complaint, judgment, or other court process with the intent to:

(1) induce payment of a claim from another person; or

(2) cause another to:

(A) submit to the putative authority of the document; or

(B) take any action or refrain from taking any action in response to the document, in compliance with the document, or on the basis of the document.

(b) Proof that the document was mailed to any person with the intent that it be forwarded to the intended recipient is a sufficient showing that the document was delivered.

(c) It is not a defense to prosecution under this section that the simulating document:

(1) states that it is not legal process; or

(2) purports to have been issued or authorized by a person or entity who did not have lawful authority to issue or authorize the document.

(d) If it is shown on the trial of an offense under this section that the simulating document was filed with, presented to, or delivered to a clerk of a court or an employee of a clerk of a court created or established under the constitution or laws of this state, there is a rebuttable presumption that the document was delivered with the intent described by Subsection (a).

(e) Except as provided by Subsection (f), an offense under this section is a Class A misdemeanor.

(f) If it is shown on the trial of an offense under this section that the defendant has previously been convicted of a violation of this section, the offense is a state jail felony.

Added by Acts 1997, 75th Leg., ch. 189, § 3, eff. May 21, 1997.

§ 32.49. Refusal to Execute Release of Fraudulent Lien or Claim

(a) A person commits an offense if, with intent to defraud or harm another, the person:

(1) owns, holds, or is the beneficiary of a purported lien or claim asserted against real or personal property or an interest in real or personal property

that is fraudulent, as described by Section 51.901(c), Government Code; and

(2) not later than the 21st day after the date of receipt of actual or written notice sent by either certified or registered mail, return receipt requested, to the person's last known address, or by telephonic document transfer to the recipient's current telecopier number, requesting the execution of a release of the fraudulent lien or claim, refuses to execute the release on the request of:

(A) the obligor or debtor; or

(B) any person who owns any interest in the real or personal property described in the document or instrument that is the basis for the lien or claim.

(b) A person who fails to execute a release of the purported lien or claim within the period prescribed by Subsection (a)(2) is presumed to have had the intent to harm or defraud another.

(c) An offense under this section is a Class A misdemeanor.

Added by Acts 1997, 75th Leg., ch. 189, § 4, eff. May 21, 1997.

§ 32.50. Deceptive Preparation and Marketing of Academic Product

(a) For purposes of this section:

(1) "Academic product" means a term paper, thesis, dissertation, essay, report, recording, work of art, or other written, recorded, pictorial, or artistic product or material submitted or intended to be submitted by a person to satisfy an academic requirement of the person.

(2) "Academic requirement" means a requirement or prerequisite to receive course credit or to complete a course of study or degree, diploma, or certificate program at an institution of higher education.

(3) "Institution of higher education" means an institution of higher education or private or independent institution of higher education as those terms are defined by Section 61.003, Education Code, or a private postsecondary educational institution as that term is defined by Section 61.302, Education Code.

(b) A person commits an offense if, with intent to make a profit, the person prepares, sells, offers or advertises for sale, or delivers to another person an academic product when the person knows, or should reasonably have known, that a person intends to submit or use the academic product to satisfy an academic requirement of a person other than the person who prepared the product.

(c) A person commits an offense if, with intent to induce another person to enter into an agreement or obligation to obtain or have prepared an academic product, the person knowingly makes or disseminates a written or oral statement that the person will prepare or cause to be prepared an academic product to be sold for use in satisfying an academic requirement of a person other than the person who prepared the product.

(d) It is a defense to prosecution under this section that the actor's conduct consisted solely of action taken as an employee of an institution of higher education in providing instruction, counseling, or tutoring in research or writing to students of the institution.

(e) It is a defense to prosecution under this section that the actor's conduct consisted solely of offering or providing tutorial or editing assistance to another person in connection with the other person's preparation of an academic product to satisfy the other person's academic requirement, and the actor does not offer or provide substantial preparation, writing, or research in the production of the academic product.

(f) It is a defense to prosecution under this section that the actor's conduct consisted solely of typing, transcribing, or reproducing a manuscript for a fee, or of offering to do so.

(g) An offense under this section is a Class C misdemeanor.

Added by Acts 1997, 75th Leg., ch. 730, § 1, eff. Sept. 1, 1997. Renumbered from V.T.C.A., Penal Code § 32.49 by Acts 1999, 76th Leg., ch. 62, § 19.01(87), (88), eff. Sept. 1, 1999.

§ 32.51. Fraudulent Use or Possession of Identifying Information

(a) In this section:

(1) "Identifying information" means information that alone or in conjunction with other information identifies a person, including a person's:

(A) name and social security number, date of birth, or government-issued identification number;

(B) unique biometric data, including the person's fingerprint, voice print, or retina or iris image;

(C) unique electronic identification number, address, routing code, or financial institution account number; and

(D) telecommunication identifying information or access device.

(2) "Telecommunication access device" means a card, plate, code, account number, personal identification number, electronic serial number, mobile identification number, or other telecommunications service, equipment, or instrument identifier or means of account access that alone or in conjunction with another telecommunication access device may be used to:

(A) obtain money, goods, services, or other thing of value; or

(B) initiate a transfer of funds other than a transfer originated solely by paper instrument.

(b) A person commits an offense if the person, with the intent to harm or defraud another, obtains, possesses, transfers, or uses an item of:

(1) identifying information of another person without the other person's consent;

(2) information concerning a deceased natural person, including a stillborn infant or fetus, that would be identifying information of that person were that person alive, if the item of information is obtained, possessed, transferred, or used without legal authorization; or

(3) identifying information of a child younger than 18 years of age.

(b–1) For the purposes of Subsection (b), the actor is presumed to have the intent to harm or defraud another if the actor possesses:

(1) the identifying information of three or more other persons;

(2) information described by Subsection (b)(2) concerning three or more deceased persons; or

(3) information described by Subdivision (1) or (2) concerning three or more persons or deceased persons.

(b–2) The presumption established under Subsection (b–1) does not apply to a business or other commercial entity or a government agency that is engaged in a business activity or governmental function that does not violate a penal law of this state.

(c) An offense under this section is:

(1) a state jail felony if the number of items obtained, possessed, transferred, or used is less than five;

(2) a felony of the third degree if the number of items obtained, possessed, transferred, or used is five or more but less than 10;

(3) a felony of the second degree if the number of items obtained, possessed, transferred, or used is 10 or more but less than 50; or

(4) a felony of the first degree if the number of items obtained, possessed, transferred, or used is 50 or more.

(c–1) An offense described for purposes of punishment by Subsections (c)(1)–(3) is increased to the next higher category of offense if it is shown on the trial of the offense that the offense was committed against an elderly individual as defined by Section 22.04.

(d) If a court orders a defendant convicted of an offense under this section to make restitution to the victim of the offense, the court may order the defendant to reimburse the victim for lost income or other expenses, other than attorney's fees, incurred as a result of the offense.

(e) If conduct that constitutes an offense under this section also constitutes an offense under any other law, the actor may be prosecuted under this section, the other law, or both.

Added by Acts 1999, 76th Leg., ch. 1159, § 1, eff. Sept. 1, 1999. Amended by Acts 2003, 78th Leg., ch. 1104, § 4, eff. Sept. 1, 2003; Acts 2007, 80th Leg., ch. 631, § 1, eff. Sept. 1, 2007; Acts 2007, 80th Leg., ch. 1163, § 1, eff. Sept. 1, 2007; Acts 2007, 80th Leg., ch. 1173, §§ 1, 2, eff. Sept. 1, 2007; Acts 2009, 81st Leg., ch. 87, § 19.002, eff. Sept. 1, 2009; Acts 2009, 81st Leg., ch. 670, § 3, eff. Sept. 1, 2009.

Section 2 of Acts 2007, 80th Leg., ch. 631 provides:

"The change in law made by this Act applies only to an offense committed on or after the effective date of this Act. An offense committed before the effective date of this Act is governed by the law in effect when the offense was committed, and the former law is continued in effect for that purpose. For purposes of this section, an offense was committed before the effective date of this Act if any element of the offense occurred before that date."

Section 3 of Acts 2007, 80th Leg., ch. 1163 provides:

"This Act applies only to an offense committed on or after the effective date [Sept. 1, 2007] of this Act. An offense committed before the effective date of this Act is covered by the law in effect at the time the offense was committed, and the former law is continued in effect for that purpose. For the purposes of this section, an offense was committed before the effective date of this Act if any element of the offense was committed before that date."

Section 3 of Acts 2007, 80th Leg., ch. 1173 provides:

"The change in law made by this Act applies only to an offense committed on or after the effective date [Sept. 1, 2007] of this Act. An offense committed before the effective date of this Act is covered by the law in effect when the offense was committed, and the former law is continued in effect for that purpose. For purposes of this section, an offense was committed before the effective date of this Act if any element of the offense was committed before that date."

Section 4 of Acts 2009, 81st Leg., ch. 670 provides:

"The change in law made by this Act applies only to an offense committed on or after the effective date [Sept. 1, 2009] of this Act. An offense committed before the effective date of this Act is governed by the law in effect when the offense was committed, and the former law is continued in effect for that purpose. For the purposes of this section, an offense was committed before the effective date of this Act if any element of the offense occurred before that date."

§ 32.52. Fraudulent, Substandard, or Fictitious Degree

(a) In this section, "fraudulent or substandard degree" has the meaning assigned by Section 61.302, Education Code.

(b) A person commits an offense if the person:

(1) uses or claims to hold a postsecondary degree that the person knows:

(A) is a fraudulent or substandard degree;

(B) is fictitious or has otherwise not been granted to the person; or

(C) has been revoked; and

(2) uses or claims to hold that degree:

(A) in a written or oral advertisement or other promotion of a business; or

(B) with the intent to:

(i) obtain employment;

(ii) obtain a license or certificate to practice a trade, profession, or occupation;

(iii) obtain a promotion, a compensation or other benefit, or an increase in compensation or other benefit, in employment or in the practice of a trade, profession, or occupation;

(iv) obtain admission to an educational program in this state; or

(v) gain a position in government with authority over another person, regardless of whether the actor receives compensation for the position.

(c) An offense under this section is a Class B misdemeanor.

(d) If conduct that constitutes an offense under this section also constitutes an offense under any other law, the actor may be prosecuted under this section or the other law.

Added by Acts 2005, 79th Leg., ch. 1039, § 8, eff. Sept. 1, 2005.

§§ 32.53 to 32.54. Deleted by Acts 1993, 73rd Leg., ch. 900, § 1.01, eff. Sept. 1, 1994

§ 32.55. Deleted by Acts 1993, 73rd Leg., ch. 900, § 13.02

SUBCHAPTER E. SAVINGS AND LOAN ASSOCIATIONS [DELETED]

§§ 32.71, 32.72. Deleted by Acts 1993, 73rd Leg., ch. 900, § 1.01, eff. Sept. 1, 1994

CHAPTER 33. COMPUTER CRIMES

§ 33.01. Definitions

In this chapter:

(1) "Access" means to approach, instruct, communicate with, store data in, retrieve or intercept data from, alter data or computer software in, or otherwise make use of any resource of a computer, computer network, computer program, or computer system.

(2) "Aggregate amount" means the amount of:

(A) any direct or indirect loss incurred by a victim, including the value of money, property, or service stolen or rendered unrecoverable by the offense; or

(B) any expenditure required by the victim to verify that a computer, computer network, computer program, or computer system was not altered, acquired, damaged, deleted, or disrupted by the offense.

(3) "Communications common carrier" means a person who owns or operates a telephone system in this state that includes equipment or facilities for the conveyance, transmission, or reception of communications and who receives compensation from persons who use that system.

(4) "Computer" means an electronic, magnetic, optical, electrochemical, or other high-speed data processing device that performs logical, arithmetic, or memory functions by the manipulations of electronic or magnetic impulses and includes all input,

output, processing, storage, or communication facilities that are connected or related to the device.

(5) "Computer network" means the interconnection of two or more computers or computer systems by satellite, microwave, line, or other communication medium with the capability to transmit information among the computers.

(6) "Computer program" means an ordered set of data representing coded instructions or statements that when executed by a computer cause the computer to process data or perform specific functions.

(7) "Computer services" means the product of the use of a computer, the information stored in the computer, or the personnel supporting the computer, including computer time, data processing, and storage functions.

(8) "Computer system" means any combination of a computer or computer network with the documentation, computer software, or physical facilities supporting the computer or computer network.

(9) "Computer software" means a set of computer programs, procedures, and associated documentation related to the operation of a computer, computer system, or computer network.

(10) "Computer virus" means an unwanted computer program or other set of instructions inserted into a computer's memory, operating system, or program that is specifically constructed with the ability to replicate itself or to affect the other programs or files in the computer by attaching a copy of the unwanted program or other set of instructions to one or more computer programs or files.

(11) "Data" means a representation of information, knowledge, facts, concepts, or instructions that is being prepared or has been prepared in a formalized manner and is intended to be stored or processed, is being stored or processed, or has been stored or processed in a computer. Data may be embodied in any form, including but not limited to computer printouts, magnetic storage media, laser storage media, and punchcards, or may be stored internally in the memory of the computer.

(12) "Effective consent" includes consent by a person legally authorized to act for the owner. Consent is not effective if:

(A) induced by deception, as defined by Section 31.01, or induced by coercion;

(B) given by a person the actor knows is not legally authorized to act for the owner;

(C) given by a person who by reason of youth, mental disease or defect, or intoxication is known by the actor to be unable to make reasonable property dispositions;

(D) given solely to detect the commission of an offense; or

(E) used for a purpose other than that for which the consent was given.

(13) "Electric utility" has the meaning assigned by Section 31.002, Utilities Code.

(14) "Harm" includes partial or total alteration, damage, or erasure of stored data, interruption of computer services, introduction of a computer virus, or any other loss, disadvantage, or injury that might reasonably be suffered as a result of the actor's conduct.

(15) "Owner" means a person who:

(A) has title to the property, possession of the property, whether lawful or not, or a greater right to possession of the property than the actor;

(B) has the right to restrict access to the property; or

(C) is the licensee of data or computer software.

(16) "Property" means:

(A) tangible or intangible personal property including a computer, computer system, computer network, computer software, or data; or

(B) the use of a computer, computer system, computer network, computer software, or data.

Added by Acts 1985, 69th Leg., ch. 600, § 1, eff. Sept. 1, 1985. Amended by Acts 1989, 71st Leg., ch. 306, § 1, eff. Sept. 1, 1989; Acts 1993, 73rd Leg., ch. 900, § 1.01, eff. Sept. 1, 1994; Acts 1997, 75th Leg., ch. 306, § 1, eff. Sept. 1, 1997; Acts 1999, 76th Leg., ch. 62, § 18.44, eff. Sept. 1, 1999.

§ 33.02. Breach of Computer Security

(a) A person commits an offense if the person knowingly accesses a computer, computer network, or computer system without the effective consent of the owner.

(b) An offense under this section is a Class B misdemeanor unless in committing the offense the actor knowingly obtains a benefit, defrauds or harms another, or alters, damages, or deletes property, in which event the offense is:

(1) a Class A misdemeanor if the aggregate amount involved is less than $1,500;

(2) a state jail felony if:

(A) the aggregate amount involved is $1,500 or more but less than $20,000; or

(B) the aggregate amount involved is less than $1,500 and the defendant has been previously convicted two or more times of an offense under this chapter;

(3) a felony of the third degree if the aggregate amount involved is $20,000 or more but less than $100,000;

(4) a felony of the second degree if the aggregate amount involved is $100,000 or more but less than $200,000; or

(5) a felony of the first degree if the aggregate amount involved is $200,000 or more.

(c) When benefits are obtained, a victim is defrauded or harmed, or property is altered, damaged, or deleted in violation of this section, whether or not in a single incident, the conduct may be considered as one offense and the value of the benefits obtained and of the losses incurred because of the fraud, harm, or alteration, damage, or deletion of property may be aggregated in determining the grade of the offense.

(d) A person who his [1] subject to prosecution under this section and any other section of this code may be prosecuted under either or both sections.

Added by Acts 1985, 69th Leg., ch. 600, § 1, eff. Sept. 1, 1985. Amended by Acts 1989, 71st Leg., ch. 306, § 2, eff. Sept. 1, 1989; Acts 1993, 73rd Leg., ch. 900, § 1.01, eff. Sept. 1, 1994; Acts 1997, 75th Leg., ch. 306, § 2, eff. Sept. 1, 1997; Acts 2001, 77th Leg., ch. 1411, § 1, eff. Sept. 1, 2001.

[1] So in enrolled bill.

§ 33.021. Online Solicitation of a Minor

(a) In this section:

(1) "Minor" means:

(A) an individual who represents himself or herself to be younger than 17 years of age; or

(B) an individual whom the actor believes to be younger than 17 years of age.

(2) "Sexual contact," "sexual intercourse," and "deviate sexual intercourse" have the meanings assigned by Section 21.01.

(3) "Sexually explicit" means any communication, language, or material, including a photographic or video image, that relates to or describes sexual conduct, as defined by Section 43.25.

(b) A person who is 17 years of age or older commits an offense if, with the intent to arouse or gratify the sexual desire of any person, the person, over the Internet, by electronic mail or text message or other electronic message service or system, or through a commercial online service, intentionally:

(1) communicates in a sexually explicit manner with a minor; or

(2) distributes sexually explicit material to a minor.

(c) A person commits an offense if the person, over the Internet, by electronic mail or text message or other electronic message service or system, or through a commercial online service, knowingly solicits a minor to meet another person, including the actor, with the intent that the minor will engage in sexual contact, sexual intercourse, or deviate sexual intercourse with the actor or another person.

(d) It is not a defense to prosecution under Subsection (c) that:

(1) the meeting did not occur;

(2) the actor did not intend for the meeting to occur; or

(3) the actor was engaged in a fantasy at the time of commission of the offense.

(e) It is a defense to prosecution under this section that at the time conduct described by Subsection (b) or (c) was committed:

(1) the actor was married to the minor; or

(2) the actor was not more than three years older than the minor and the minor consented to the conduct.

(f) An offense under Subsection (b) is a felony of the third degree, except that the offense is a felony of the second degree if the minor is younger than 14 years of age or is an individual whom the actor believes to be younger than 14 years of age at the time of the commission of the offense. An offense under Subsection (c) is a felony of the second degree.

(g) If conduct that constitutes an offense under this section also constitutes an offense under any other law, the actor may be prosecuted under this section, the other law, or both.

Added by Acts 2005, 79th Leg., ch. 1273, § 1, eff. June 18, 2005. Amended by Acts 2007, 80th Leg., ch. 610, § 2, eff. Sept. 1, 2007; Acts 2007, 80th Leg., ch. 1291, § 7, eff. Sept. 1, 2007.

Section 3 of Acts 2007, 80th Leg., ch. 610 provides:

"The change in law made by this Act applies only to an offense committed on or after the effective date of this Act. An offense committed before the effective date of this Act is covered by the law in effect when the offense was committed, and the former law is continued in effect for that purpose. For the purposes of this section, an offense was committed before the effective date of this Act if any element of the offense was committed before that date."

Section 11 of Acts 2007, 80th Leg., ch. 1291 provides:

"Subsection (b), Section 3.03, and Subsection (f), Section 33.021, Penal Code, as amended by this Act, apply only to an offense committed on or after September 1, 2007. An offense committed before September 1, 2007, is covered by the law in effect when the offense was committed, and the former law is continued in effect for that purpose. For the purposes of this section, an offense was committed before September 1, 2007, if any element of the offense occurred before that date."

§ 33.03. Defenses

It is an affirmative defense to prosecution under Section 33.02 that the actor was an officer, employee, or agent of a communications common carrier or electric utility and committed the proscribed act or acts in the course of employment while engaged in an activity that is a necessary incident to the rendition of service or to the protection of the rights or property of the communications common carrier or electric utility.

Added by Acts 1985, 69th Leg., ch. 600, § 1, eff. Sept. 1, 1985. Renumbered from V.T.C.A., Penal Code § 33.04 and amended by Acts 1993, 73rd Leg., ch. 900, § 1.01, eff. Sept. 1, 1994.

§ 33.04. Assistance by Attorney General

The attorney general, if requested to do so by a prosecuting attorney, may assist the prosecuting attorney in the investigation or prosecution of an offense under this chapter or of any other offense involving the use of a computer.

Added by Acts 1985, 69th Leg., ch. 600, § 1, eff. Sept. 1, 1985. Renumbered from V.T.C.A., Penal Code § 33.05 by Acts 1993, 73rd Leg., ch. 900, § 1.01, eff. Sept. 1, 1994.

§ 33.05. Tampering With Direct Recording Electronic Voting Machine

(a) In this section:

(1) "Direct recording electronic voting machine" has the meaning assigned by Section 121.003, Election Code.

(2) "Measure" has the meaning assigned by Section 1.005, Election Code.

(b) A person commits an offense if the person knowingly accesses a computer, computer network, computer program, computer software, or computer system that is a part of a voting system that uses direct recording electronic voting machines and by means of that access:

(1) prevents a person from lawfully casting a vote;

(2) changes a lawfully cast vote;

(3) prevents a lawfully cast vote from being counted; or

(4) causes a vote that was not lawfully cast to be counted.

(c) An offense under this section does not require that the votes as affected by the person's actions described by Subsection (b) actually be the votes used in the official determination of the outcome of the election.

(d) An offense under this section is a felony of the first degree.

(e) Notwithstanding Section 15.01(d), an offense under Section 15.01(a) is a felony of the third degree if the offense the actor intends to commit is an offense under this section.

(f) With the consent of the appropriate local county or district attorney, the attorney general has concurrent jurisdiction with that consenting local prosecutor to investigate or prosecute an offense under this section.

Added by Acts 2005, 79th Leg., ch. 470, § 1, eff. Sept. 1, 2005. Amended by Acts 2009, 81st Leg., ch. 503, § 1, eff. Sept. 1, 2009.

§ 33.07. Online Harassment

(a) A person commits an offense if the person uses the name or persona of another person to create a web page on or to post one or more messages on a commercial social networking site:

(1) without obtaining the other person's consent; and

(2) with the intent to harm, defraud, intimidate, or threaten any person.

(b) A person commits an offense if the person sends an electronic mail, instant message, text message, or similar communication that references a name, domain address, phone number, or other item of identifying information belonging to any person:

(1) without obtaining the other person's consent;

(2) with the intent to cause a recipient of the communication to reasonably believe that the other person authorized or transmitted the communication; and

(3) with the intent to harm or defraud any person.

(c) An offense under Subsection (a) is a felony of the third degree. An offense under Subsection (b) is a Class A misdemeanor, except that the offense is a felony of the third degree if the actor commits the offense with the intent to solicit a response by emergency personnel.

(d) If conduct that constitutes an offense under this section also constitutes an offense under any other law, the actor may be prosecuted under this section, the other law, or both.

(e) It is a defense to prosecution under this section that the actor is any of the following entities or that the actor's conduct consisted solely of action taken as an employee of any of the following entities:

(1) a commercial social networking site;

(2) an Internet service provider;

(3) an interactive computer service, as defined by 47 U.S.C. Section 230;

(4) a telecommunications provider, as defined by Section 51.002, Utilities Code; or

(5) a video service provider or cable service provider, as defined by Section 66.002, Utilities Code.

(f) In this section:

(1) "Commercial social networking site" means any business, organization, or other similar entity operating a website that permits persons to become registered users for the purpose of establishing personal relationships with other users through direct or real-time communication with other users or the creation of web pages or profiles available to the public or to other users. The term does not include an electronic mail program or a message board program.

(2) "Identifying information" has the meaning assigned by Section 32.51.

Added by Acts 2009, 81st Leg., ch. 911, § 1, eff. Sept. 1, 2009.

CHAPTER 33A. TELECOMMUNICATIONS CRIMES

Section

§ 33A.01. Definitions

In this chapter:

(1) "Counterfeit telecommunications access device" means a telecommunications access device that is false, fraudulent, not issued to a legitimate telecommunications access device subscriber account, or otherwise unlawful or invalid.

(2) "Counterfeit telecommunications device" means a telecommunications device that has been altered or programmed alone or with another telecommunications device to acquire, intercept, receive, or otherwise facilitate the use of a telecommunications service without the authority or consent of the telecommunications service provider and includes a clone telephone, clone microchip, tumbler telephone, tumbler microchip, or wireless scanning device capable of acquiring, intercepting, receiving, or otherwise facilitating the use of a telecommunications service without immediate detection.

(3) "Deliver" means to actually or constructively sell, give, loan, or otherwise transfer a telecommunications device, or a counterfeit telecommunications device or any telecommunications plans, instructions, or materials, to another person.

(4) "Publish" means to communicate information or make information available to another person orally, in writing, or by means of telecommunications and includes communicating information on a computer bulletin board or similar system.

(5) "Telecommunications" means the origination, emission, transmission, or reception of data, images, signals, sounds, or other intelligence or equivalence of intelligence over a communications system by any method, including an electronic, magnetic, optical, digital, or analog method.

(6) "Telecommunications access device" means an instrument, device, card, plate, code, account number, personal identification number, electronic serial number, mobile identification number, counterfeit number, or financial transaction device that alone or with another telecommunications access device can acquire, intercept, provide, receive, use, or otherwise facilitate the use of a telecommunications device, counterfeit telecommunications device, or telecommunications service.

(7) "Telecommunications device" means any instrument, equipment, machine, or device that facilitates telecommunications and includes a computer, computer chip or circuit, telephone, pager, personal communications device, transponder, receiver, radio, modem, or device that enables use of a modem.

(8) "Telecommunications service" means the provision, facilitation, or generation of telecommunications through the use of a telecommunications device or telecommunications access device over a telecommunications system.

(9) "Value of the telecommunications service obtained or attempted to be obtained" includes the value of:

(A) a lawful charge for telecommunications service avoided or attempted to be avoided;

(B) money, property, or telecommunications service lost, stolen, or rendered unrecoverable by an offense; and

(C) an expenditure incurred by a victim to verify that a telecommunications device or telecommunications access device or telecommunications service was not altered, acquired, damaged, or disrupted as a result of an offense.

Added by Acts 1997, 75th Leg., ch. 306, § 3, eff. Sept. 1, 1997.

§ 33A.02. Unauthorized Use of Telecommunications Service

(a) A person commits an offense if the person is an officer, shareholder, partner, employee, agent, or independent contractor of a telecommunications service provider and the person knowingly and without authority uses or diverts telecommunications service for the person's own benefit or to the benefit of another.

(b) An offense under this section is:

(1) a Class B misdemeanor if the value of the telecommunications service used or diverted is less than $500;

(2) a Class A misdemeanor if:

(A) the value of the telecommunications service used or diverted is $500 or more but less than $1,500; or

(B) the value of the telecommunications service used or diverted is less than $500 and the defendant has been previously convicted of an offense under this chapter;

(3) a state jail felony if:

(A) the value of the telecommunications service used or diverted is $1,500 or more but less than $20,000; or

(B) the value of the telecommunications service used or diverted is less than $1,500 and the defendant has been previously convicted two or more times of an offense under this chapter;

(4) a felony of the third degree if the value of the telecommunications service used or diverted is $20,000 or more but less than $100,000;

(5) a felony of the second degree if the value of the telecommunications service used or diverted is $100,000 or more but less than $200,000; or

(6) a felony of the first degree if the value of the telecommunications service used or diverted is $200,000 or more.

(c) When telecommunications service is used or diverted in violation of this section pursuant to one scheme or continuing course of conduct, whether or not in a single incident, the conduct may be considered as one offense and the values of the service used or diverted may be aggregated in determining the grade of the offense.

Added by Acts 1997, 75th Leg., ch. 306, § 3, eff. Sept. 1, 1997.

§ 33A.03. Manufacture, Possession, or Delivery of Unlawful Telecommunications Device

(a) A person commits an offense if the person manufactures, possesses, delivers, offers to deliver, or advertises:

(1) a counterfeit telecommunications device; or

(2) a telecommunications device that is intended to be used to:

(A) commit an offense under Section 33A.04; or

(B) conceal the existence or place of origin or destination of a telecommunications service.

(b) A person commits an offense if the person delivers, offers to deliver, or advertises plans, instructions, or materials for manufacture of:

(1) a counterfeit telecommunications device; or

(2) a telecommunications device that is intended to be used to commit an offense under Subsection (a).

(c) An offense under this section is a felony of the third degree.

(d) It is a defense to prosecution under this section that the person was an officer, agent, or employee of a telecommunications service provider who engaged in the conduct for the purpose of gathering information for a law enforcement investigation related to an offense under this chapter.

Added by Acts 1997, 75th Leg., ch. 306, § 3, eff. Sept. 1, 1997.

§ 33A.04. Theft of Telecommunications Service

(a) A person commits an offense if the person knowingly obtains or attempts to obtain telecommunications service to avoid or cause another person to avoid a lawful charge for that service by using:

(1) a telecommunications access device without the authority or consent of the subscriber or lawful holder of the device or pursuant to an agreement for an exchange of value with the subscriber or lawful holder of the device to allow another person to use the device;

(2) a counterfeit telecommunications access device;

(3) a telecommunications device or counterfeit telecommunications device; or

(4) a fraudulent or deceptive scheme, pretense, method, or conspiracy, or other device or means, including a false, altered, or stolen identification.

(b) An offense under this section is:

(1) a Class B misdemeanor if the value of the telecommunications service obtained or attempted to be obtained is less than $500;

(2) a Class A misdemeanor if:

(A) the value of the telecommunications service obtained or attempted to be obtained is $500 or more but less than $1,500; or

(B) the value of the telecommunications service obtained or attempted to be obtained is less than $500 and the defendant has been previously convicted of an offense under this chapter;

(3) a state jail felony if:

(A) the value of the telecommunications service obtained or attempted to be obtained is $1,500 or more but less than $20,000; or

(B) the value of the telecommunications service obtained or attempted to be obtained is less than $1,500 and the defendant has been previously convicted two or more times of an offense under this chapter;

(4) a felony of the third degree if the value of the telecommunications service obtained or attempted to be obtained is $20,000 or more but less than $100,000;

(5) a felony of the second degree if the value of the telecommunications service obtained or attempted to be obtained is $100,000 or more but less than $200,000; or

(6) a felony of the first degree if the value of the telecommunications service obtained or attempted to be obtained is $200,000 or more.

(c) When telecommunications service is obtained or attempted to be obtained in violation of this section pursuant to one scheme or continuing course of conduct, whether or not in a single incident, the conduct may be considered as one offense and the values of the service obtained or attempted to be obtained may be aggregated in determining the grade of the offense.

Added by Acts 1997, 75th Leg., ch. 306, § 3, eff. Sept. 1, 1997.

§ 33A.05. Publication of Telecommunications Access Device

(a) A person commits an offense if the person with criminal negligence publishes a telecommunications access device or counterfeit telecommunications access device that is designed to be used to commit an offense under Section 33A.04.

(b) Except as otherwise provided by this subsection, an offense under this section is a Class A misdemeanor. An offense under this section is a felony of the third degree if the person has been previously convicted of an offense under this chapter.

Added by Acts 1997, 75th Leg., ch. 306, § 3, eff. Sept. 1, 1997.

§ 33A.06. Assistance by Attorney General

The attorney general, if requested to do so by a prosecuting attorney, may assist the prosecuting attorney in the investigation or prosecution of an offense under this chapter or of any other offense involving the use of telecommunications equipment, services, or devices.

Added by Acts 1997, 75th Leg., ch. 306, § 3, eff. Sept. 1, 1997.

CHAPTER 34. MONEY LAUNDERING

Section

§ 34.01. Definitions

In this chapter:

(1) "Criminal activity" means any offense, including any preparatory offense, that is:

(A) classified as a felony under the laws of this state or the United States; or

(B) punishable by confinement for more than one year under the laws of another state.

(2) "Funds" includes:

(A) coin or paper money of the United States or any other country that is designated as legal tender and that circulates and is customarily used and accepted as a medium of exchange in the country of issue;

(B) United States silver certificates, United States Treasury notes, and Federal Reserve System notes;

(C) an official foreign bank note that is customarily used and accepted as a medium of exchange in a foreign country and a foreign bank draft; and

(D) currency or its equivalent, including an electronic fund, personal check, bank check, traveler's check, money order, bearer negotiable instrument, bearer investment security, bearer security, or certificate of stock in a form that allows title to pass on delivery.

(3) "Financial institution" has the meaning assigned by Section 32.01.

(4) "Proceeds" means funds acquired or derived directly or indirectly from, produced through, or realized through an act.

Added by Acts 1993, 73rd Leg., ch. 761, § 2, eff. Sept. 1, 1993. Amended by Acts 2005, 79th Leg., ch. 1162, § 1, eff. Sept. 1, 2005.

§ 34.02. Money Laundering

(a) A person commits an offense if the person knowingly:

(1) acquires or maintains an interest in, conceals, possesses, transfers, or transports the proceeds of criminal activity;

(2) conducts, supervises, or facilitates a transaction involving the proceeds of criminal activity;

(3) invests, expends, or receives, or offers to invest, expend, or receive, the proceeds of criminal activity or funds that the person believes are the proceeds of criminal activity; or

(4) finances or invests or intends to finance or invest funds that the person believes are intended to further the commission of criminal activity.

(a–1) Knowledge of the specific nature of the criminal activity giving rise to the proceeds is not required to establish a culpable mental state under this section.

(b) For purposes of this section, a person is presumed to believe that funds are the proceeds of or are intended to further the commission of criminal activity if a peace officer or a person acting at the direction of a peace officer represents to the person that the funds are proceeds of or are intended to further the commission of criminal activity, as applicable, regardless of whether the peace officer or person acting at the peace officer's direction discloses the person's status as a peace officer or that the person is acting at the direction of a peace officer.

(c) It is a defense to prosecution under this section that the person acted with intent to facilitate the lawful seizure, forfeiture, or disposition of funds or other legitimate law enforcement purpose pursuant to the laws of this state or the United States.

(d) It is a defense to prosecution under this section that the transaction was necessary to preserve a person's right to representation as guaranteed by the Sixth Amendment of the United States Constitution and by Article 1, Section 10, of the Texas Constitution or that the funds were received as bona fide legal fees by a licensed attorney and at the time of their receipt, the attorney did not have actual knowledge that the funds were derived from criminal activity.

(e) An offense under this section is:

(1) a state jail felony if the value of the funds is $1,500 or more but less than $20,000;

(2) a felony of the third degree if the value of the funds is $20,000 or more but less than $100,000;

(3) a felony of the second degree if the value of the funds is $100,000 or more but less than $200,000; or

(4) a felony of the first degree if the value of the funds is $200,000 or more.

(f) For purposes of this section, if proceeds of criminal activity are related to one scheme or continuing course of conduct, whether from the same or several sources, the conduct may be considered as one offense and the value of the proceeds aggregated in determining the classification of the offense.

(g) For purposes of this section, funds on deposit at a branch of a financial institution are considered the property of that branch and any other branch of the financial institution.

(h) If conduct that constitutes an offense under this section also constitutes an offense under any other law, the actor may be prosecuted under this section, the other law, or both.

Added by Acts 1993, 73rd Leg., ch. 761, § 2, eff. Sept. 1, 1993. Amended by Acts 2005, 79th Leg., ch. 1162, § 2, eff. Sept. 1, 2005.

§ 34.021. Protection From Civil Liability

Notwithstanding Section 1.03(c), a financial institution or an agent of the financial institution acting in a manner described by Section 34.02(c) is not liable for civil damages to a person who:

(1) claims an ownership interest in funds involved in an offense under Section 34.02; or

(2) conducts with the financial institution or an insurer, as defined by Article 1.02, Insurance Code, a transaction concerning funds involved in an offense under Section 34.02.

Added by Acts 2005, 79th Leg., ch. 1162, § 3, eff. Sept. 1, 2005.

§ 34.03. Assistance by Attorney General

The attorney general, if requested to do so by a prosecuting attorney, may assist in the prosecution of an offense under this chapter.

Added by Acts 1993, 73rd Leg., ch. 761, § 2, eff. Sept. 1, 1993.

CHAPTER 35. INSURANCE FRAUD

§ 35.01. Definitions

In this chapter:

(1) "Insurance policy" means a written instrument in which is provided the terms of any certificate of insurance, binder of coverage, contract of insurance, benefit plan, nonprofit hospital service plan, motor club service plan, surety bond, cash bond, or any other alternative to insurance authorized by Chapter 601, Transportation Code. The term includes any instrument authorized to be regulated by the Texas Department of Insurance.

(2) "Insurer" has the meaning assigned by Article 1.02, Insurance Code.

(3) "Statement" means an oral or written communication or a record or documented representation of fact made to an insurer. The term includes computer-generated information.

(4) "Value of the claim" means the total dollar amount of a claim for payment under an insurance policy or, as applicable, the value of the claim determined under Section 35.025.

Added by Acts 1995, 74th Leg., ch. 621, § 1, eff. Sept. 1, 1995. Amended by Acts 2001, 77th Leg., ch. 1420, § 14.830, eff. Sept. 1, 2001; Acts 2003, 78th Leg., ch. 1276, § 10A.541, eff. Sept. 1, 2003; Acts 2005, 79th Leg., ch. 1162, § 4, eff. Sept. 1, 2005.

§ 35.015. Materiality

A statement is material for the purposes of this chapter, regardless of the admissibility of the statement at trial, if the statement could have affected:

(1) the eligibility for coverage or amount of the payment on a claim for payment under an insurance policy; or

(2) the decision of an insurer whether to issue an insurance policy.

Added by Acts 2005, 79th Leg., ch. 1162, § 4, eff. Sept. 1, 2005.

§ 35.02. Insurance Fraud

(a) A person commits an offense if, with intent to defraud or deceive an insurer, the person, in support of a claim for payment under an insurance policy:

(1) prepares or causes to be prepared a statement that:

(A) the person knows contains false or misleading material information; and

(B) is presented to an insurer; or

(2) presents or causes to be presented to an insurer a statement that the person knows contains false or misleading material information.

(a–1) A person commits an offense if the person, with intent to defraud or deceive an insurer and in support of an application for an insurance policy:

(1) prepares or causes to be prepared a statement that:

(A) the person knows contains false or misleading material information; and

(B) is presented to an insurer; or

(2) presents or causes to be presented to an insurer a statement that the person knows contains false or misleading material information.

(b) A person commits an offense if, with intent to defraud or deceive an insurer, the person solicits, offers, pays, or receives a benefit in connection with the furnishing of goods or services for which a claim for payment is submitted under an insurance policy.

(c) An offense under Subsection (a) or (b) is:

(1) a Class C misdemeanor if the value of the claim is less than $50;

(2) a Class B misdemeanor if the value of the claim is $50 or more but less than $500;

(3) a Class A misdemeanor if the value of the claim is $500 or more but less than $1,500;

(4) a state jail felony if the value of the claim is $1,500 or more but less than $20,000;

(5) a felony of the third degree if the value of the claim is $20,000 or more but less than $100,000;

(6) a felony of the second degree if the value of the claim is $100,000 or more but less than $200,000; or

(7) a felony of the first degree if:

(A) the value of the claim is $200,000 or more; or

(B) an act committed in connection with the commission of the offense places a person at risk of death or serious bodily injury.

(d) An offense under Subsection (a–1) is a state jail felony.

(e) The court shall order a defendant convicted of an offense under this section to pay restitution, including court costs and attorney's fees, to an affected insurer.

(f) If conduct that constitutes an offense under this section also constitutes an offense under any other law, the actor may be prosecuted under this section, the other law, or both.

(g) For purposes of this section, if the actor proves by a preponderance of the evidence that a portion of the claim for payment under an insurance policy resulted from a valid loss, injury, expense, or service covered by the policy, the value of the claim is equal to the difference between the total claim amount and the amount of the valid portion of the claim.

(h) If it is shown on the trial of an offense under this section that the actor submitted a bill for goods or services in support of a claim for payment under an insurance policy to the insurer issuing the policy, a rebuttable presumption exists that the actor caused the claim for payment to be prepared or presented.

Added by Acts 1995, 74th Leg., ch. 621, § 1, eff. Sept. 1, 1995. Amended by Acts 2003, 78th Leg., ch. 605, § 1, eff. Sept. 1, 2003; Acts 2005, 79th Leg., ch. 1162, § 4, eff. Sept. 1, 2005.

§ 35.025. Value of Claim

(a) Except as provided by Subsection (b) and subject to Subsection (c), for the purposes of Section 35.02(c), if the value of a claim is not readily ascertainable, the value of the claim is:

(1) the fair market value, at the time and place of the offense, of the goods or services that are the subject of the claim; or

(2) the cost of replacing the goods or services that are the subject of the claim within a reasonable time after the claim.

(b) If goods or services that are the subject of a claim cannot be reasonably ascertained under Subsection (a), the goods or services are considered to have a value of $500 or more but less than $1,500.

(c) If the actor proves by a preponderance of the evidence that a portion of the claim for payment under an insurance policy resulted from a valid loss, injury, expense, or service covered by the policy, the value of the claim is equal to the difference between the total claim amount and the amount of the valid portion of the claim.

Added by Acts 2005, 79th Leg., ch. 1162, § 4, eff. Sept. 1, 2005.

§ 35.03. Aggregation and Multiple Offenses

(a) When separate claims in violation of this chapter are communicated to an insurer or group of insurers pursuant to one scheme or continuing course of conduct, the conduct may be considered as one offense and the value of the claims aggregated in determining the classification of the offense. If claims are aggregated under this subsection, Subsection (b) shall not apply.

(b) When three or more separate claims in violation of this chapter are communicated to an insurer or group of insurers pursuant to one scheme or continuing course of conduct, the conduct may be considered as one offense, and the classification of the offense shall be one category higher than the most serious single offense proven from the separate claims, except that if the most serious offense is a felony of the first degree, the offense is a felony of the first degree.

This subsection shall not be applied if claims are aggregated under Subsection (a).

Added by Acts 1995, 74th Leg., ch. 621, § 1, eff. Sept. 1, 1995.

§ 35.04. Jurisdiction of Attorney General

(a) The attorney general may offer to an attorney representing the state in the prosecution of an offense under Section 35.02 the investigative, technical, and litigation assistance of the attorney general's office.

(b) The attorney general may prosecute or assist in the prosecution of an offense under Section 35.02 on the request of the attorney representing the state described by Subsection (a).

Added by Acts 1995, 74th Leg., ch. 621, § 1, eff. Sept. 1, 1995.

CHAPTER 35A. MEDICAID FRAUD

Section

§ 35A.01. Definitions

In this chapter:

(1) "Claim" has the meaning assigned by Section 36.001, Human Resources Code.

(2) "Fiscal agent" has the meaning assigned by Section 36.001, Human Resources Code.

(3) "Health care practitioner" has the meaning assigned by Section 36.001, Human Resources Code.

(4) "Managed care organization" has the meaning assigned by Section 36.001, Human Resources Code.

(5) "Medicaid program" has the meaning assigned by Section 36.001, Human Resources Code.

(6) "Medicaid recipient" has the meaning assigned by Section 36.001, Human Resources Code.

(7) "Physician" has the meaning assigned by Section 36.001, Human Resources Code.

(8) "Provider" has the meaning assigned by Section 36.001, Human Resources Code.

(9) "Service" has the meaning assigned by Section 36.001, Human Resources Code.

Added by Acts 2005, 79th Leg., ch. 806, § 16, eff. Sept. 1, 2005.

§ 35A.02. Medicaid Fraud

(a) A person commits an offense if the person:

(1) knowingly makes or causes to be made a false statement or misrepresentation of a material fact to permit a person to receive a benefit or payment under the Medicaid program that is not authorized or that is greater than the benefit or payment that is authorized;

(2) knowingly conceals or fails to disclose information that permits a person to receive a benefit or payment under the Medicaid program that is not authorized or that is greater than the benefit or payment that is authorized;

(3) knowingly applies for and receives a benefit or payment on behalf of another person under the Medicaid program and converts any part of the benefit or payment to a use other than for the benefit of the person on whose behalf it was received;

(4) knowingly makes, causes to be made, induces, or seeks to induce the making of a false statement or misrepresentation of material fact concerning:

(A) the conditions or operation of a facility in order that the facility may qualify for certification or recertification required by the Medicaid program, including certification or recertification as:

(i) a hospital;

(ii) a nursing facility or skilled nursing facility;

(iii) a hospice;

(iv) an intermediate care facility for the mentally retarded;

(v) an assisted living facility; or

(vi) a home health agency; or

(B) information required to be provided by a federal or state law, rule, regulation, or provider agreement pertaining to the Medicaid program;

(5) except as authorized under the Medicaid program, knowingly pays, charges, solicits, accepts, or receives, in addition to an amount paid under the Medicaid program, a gift, money, a donation, or other consideration as a condition to the provision of a service or product or the continued provision of a service or product if the cost of the service or product is paid for, in whole or in part, under the Medicaid program;

(6) knowingly presents or causes to be presented a claim for payment under the Medicaid program for a product provided or a service rendered by a person who:

(A) is not licensed to provide the product or render the service, if a license is required; or

(B) is not licensed in the manner claimed;

(7) knowingly makes a claim under the Medicaid program for:

(A) a service or product that has not been approved or acquiesced in by a treating physician or health care practitioner;

(B) a service or product that is substantially inadequate or inappropriate when compared to generally recognized standards within the particular discipline or within the health care industry; or

(C) a product that has been adulterated, debased, mislabeled, or that is otherwise inappropriate;

(8) makes a claim under the Medicaid program and knowingly fails to indicate the type of license and the identification number of the licensed health care provider who actually provided the service;

(9) knowingly enters into an agreement, combination, or conspiracy to defraud the state by obtaining or aiding another person in obtaining an unauthorized payment or benefit from the Medicaid program or a fiscal agent;

(10) is a managed care organization that contracts with the Health and Human Services Commission or other state agency to provide or arrange to provide health care benefits or services to individuals eligible under the Medicaid program and knowingly:

(A) fails to provide to an individual a health care benefit or service that the organization is required to provide under the contract;

(B) fails to provide to the commission or appropriate state agency information required to be provided by law, commission or agency rule, or contractual provision; or

(C) engages in a fraudulent activity in connection with the enrollment of an individual eligible under the Medicaid program in the organization's managed care plan or in connection with marketing the organization's services to an individual eligible under the Medicaid program;

(11) knowingly obstructs an investigation by the attorney general of an alleged unlawful act under this section or under Section 32.039, 32.0391, or 36.002, Human Resources Code; or

(12) knowingly makes, uses, or causes the making or use of a false record or statement to conceal, avoid, or decrease an obligation to pay or transmit money or property to this state under the Medicaid program.

(b) An offense under this section is:

(1) a Class C misdemeanor if the amount of any payment or the value of any monetary or in-kind benefit provided or claim for payment made under the Medicaid program, directly or indirectly, as a result of the conduct is less than $50;

(2) a Class B misdemeanor if the amount of any payment or the value of any monetary or in-kind benefit provided or claim for payment made under the Medicaid program, directly or indirectly, as a result of the conduct is $50 or more but less than $500;

(3) a Class A misdemeanor if the amount of any payment or the value of any monetary or in-kind benefit provided or claim for payment made under the Medicaid program, directly or indirectly, as a result of the conduct is $500 or more but less than $1,500;

(4) a state jail felony if:

(A) the amount of any payment or the value of any monetary or in-kind benefit provided or claim for payment made under the Medicaid program, directly or indirectly, as a result of the conduct is $1,500 or more but less than $20,000;

(B) the offense is committed under Subsection (a)(11); or

(C) it is shown on the trial of the offense that the amount of the payment or value of the benefit described by this subsection cannot be reasonably ascertained;

(5) a felony of the third degree if the amount of any payment or the value of any monetary or in-kind benefit provided or claim for payment made under the Medicaid program, directly or indirectly, as a result of the conduct is $20,000 or more but less than $100,000;

(6) a felony of the second degree if the amount of any payment or the value of any monetary or in-kind benefit provided or claim for payment made under the Medicaid program, directly or indirectly, as a result of the conduct is $100,000 or more but less than $200,000; or

(7) a felony of the first degree if the amount of any payment or the value of any monetary or in-kind benefit provided or claim for payment made under the Medicaid program, directly or indirectly, as a result of the conduct is $200,000 or more.

(c) If conduct constituting an offense under this section also constitutes an offense under another section of this code or another provision of law, the actor may be prosecuted under either this section or the other section or provision.

(d) When multiple payments or monetary or in-kind benefits are provided under the Medicaid program as a result of one scheme or continuing course of conduct, the conduct may be considered as one offense and the amounts of the payments or monetary or in-kind benefits aggregated in determining the grade of the offense.

Added by Acts 2005, 79th Leg., ch. 806, § 16, eff. Sept. 1, 2005. Amended by Acts 2007, 80th Leg., ch. 127, § 5, eff. Sept. 1, 2007.

TITLE 8. OFFENSES AGAINST PUBLIC ADMINISTRATION

CHAPTER 36. BRIBERY AND CORRUPT INFLUENCE

Section

§ 36.01. Definitions

In this chapter:

(1) "Custody" means:

(A) detained or under arrest by a peace officer; or

(B) under restraint by a public servant pursuant to an order of a court.

(2) "Party official" means a person who holds any position or office in a political party, whether by election, appointment, or employment.

(3) "Benefit" means anything reasonably regarded as pecuniary gain or pecuniary advantage, including benefit to any other person in whose welfare the beneficiary has a direct and substantial interest.

(4) "Vote" means to cast a ballot in an election regulated by law.

Acts 1973, 63rd Leg., p. 883, ch. 399, § 1, eff. Jan. 1, 1974. Amended by Acts 1975, 64th Leg., p. 915, ch. 342, § 11, eff. Sept. 1, 1975; Acts 1983, 68th Leg., p. 3237, ch. 558, § 1, eff. Sept. 1, 1983; Acts 1989, 71st Leg., ch. 67, § 2, eff. Sept. 1, 1989; Acts 1991, 72nd Leg., ch. 304, § 4.01, eff. Jan. 1, 1992; Acts 1991, 72nd Leg., ch. 565, § 3, eff. Sept. 1, 1991; Acts 1993, 73rd Leg., ch. 900, § 1.01, eff. Sept. 1, 1994.

§ 36.02. Bribery

(a) A person commits an offense if he intentionally or knowingly offers, confers, or agrees to confer on another, or solicits, accepts, or agrees to accept from another:

(1) any benefit as consideration for the recipient's decision, opinion, recommendation, vote, or other exercise of discretion as a public servant, party official, or voter;

(2) any benefit as consideration for the recipient's decision, vote, recommendation, or other exercise of official discretion in a judicial or administrative proceeding;

(3) any benefit as consideration for a violation of a duty imposed by law on a public servant or party official; or

(4) any benefit that is a political contribution as defined by Title 15, Election Code,[1] or that is an expenditure made and reported in accordance with Chapter 305, Government Code, if the benefit was offered, conferred, solicited, accepted, or agreed to pursuant to an express agreement to take or withhold a specific exercise of official discretion if such exercise of official discretion would not have been taken or withheld but for the benefit; notwithstanding any rule of evidence or jury instruction allowing factual inferences in the absence of certain evidence, direct evidence of the express agreement shall be required in any prosecution under this subdivision.

(b) It is no defense to prosecution under this section that a person whom the actor sought to influence was not qualified to act in the desired way whether because he had not yet assumed office or he lacked jurisdiction or for any other reason.

(c) It is no defense to prosecution under this section that the benefit is not offered or conferred or that the benefit is not solicited or accepted until after:

(1) the decision, opinion, recommendation, vote, or other exercise of discretion has occurred; or

(2) the public servant ceases to be a public servant.

(d) It is an exception to the application of Subdivisions (1), (2), and (3) of Subsection (a) that the benefit is a political contribution as defined by Title 15, Election Code, or an expenditure made and reported in accordance with Chapter 305, Government Code.

(e) An offense under this section is a felony of the second degree.

Acts 1973, 63rd Leg., p. 883, ch. 399, § 1, eff. Jan. 1, 1974. Amended by Acts 1975, 64th Leg., p. 915, ch. 342, § 11, eff. Sept. 1, 1975; Acts 1983, 68th Leg., p. 3237, ch. 558, § 2, eff. Sept. 1, 1983; Acts 1991, 72nd Leg., ch. 304, § 4.02, eff. Jan. 1, 1992; Acts 1993, 73rd Leg., ch. 900, § 1.01, eff. Sept. 1, 1994.

[1] V.T.C.A., Election Code § 251.001 et seq.

§ 36.03. Coercion of Public Servant or Voter

(a) A person commits an offense if by means of coercion he:

(1) influences or attempts to influence a public servant in a specific exercise of his official power or a specific performance of his official duty or influences or attempts to influence a public servant to violate the public servant's known legal duty; or

(2) influences or attempts to influence a voter not to vote or to vote in a particular manner.

(b) An offense under this section is a Class A misdemeanor unless the coercion is a threat to commit a felony, in which event it is a felony of the third degree.

(c) It is an exception to the application of Subsection (a)(1) of this section that the person who influences or attempts to influence the public servant is a member of the governing body of a governmental entity, and that the action that influences or attempts to influence the public servant is an official action taken by the member of the governing body. For the purposes of this subsection, the term "official action" includes deliberations by the governing body of a governmental entity.

Acts 1973, 63rd Leg., p. 883, ch. 399, § 1, eff. Jan. 1, 1974. Amended by Acts 1989, 71st Leg., ch. 67, §§ 1, 3, eff. Sept. 1, 1989; Acts 1993, 73rd Leg., ch. 900, § 1.01, eff. Sept. 1, 1994.

§ 36.04. Improper Influence

(a) A person commits an offense if he privately addresses a representation, entreaty, argument, or other communication to any public servant who exercises or will exercise official discretion in an adjudicatory proceeding with an intent to influence the outcome of the proceeding on the basis of considerations other than those authorized by law.

(b) For purposes of this section, "adjudicatory proceeding" means any proceeding before a court or any other agency of government in which the legal rights, powers, duties, or privileges of specified parties are determined.

(c) An offense under this section is a Class A misdemeanor.

Acts 1973, 63rd Leg., p. 883, ch. 399, § 1, eff. Jan. 1, 1974. Amended by Acts 1993, 73rd Leg., ch. 900, § 1.01, eff. Sept. 1, 1994.

§ 36.05. Tampering With Witness

(a) A person commits an offense if, with intent to influence the witness, he offers, confers, or agrees to confer any benefit on a witness or prospective witness in an official proceeding or coerces a witness or prospective witness in an official proceeding:

(1) to testify falsely;

(2) to withhold any testimony, information, document, or thing;

(3) to elude legal process summoning him to testify or supply evidence;

(4) to absent himself from an official proceeding to which he has been legally summoned; or

(5) to abstain from, discontinue, or delay the prosecution of another.

(b) A witness or prospective witness in an official proceeding commits an offense if he knowingly solicits, accepts, or agrees to accept any benefit on the representation or understanding that he will do any of the things specified in Subsection (a).

(c) It is a defense to prosecution under Subsection (a)(5) that the benefit received was:

(1) reasonable restitution for damages suffered by the complaining witness as a result of the offense; and

(2) a result of an agreement negotiated with the assistance or acquiescence of an attorney for the state who represented the state in the case.

(d) An offense under this section is a state jail felony.

Acts 1973, 63rd Leg., p. 883, ch. 399, § 1, eff. Jan. 1, 1974. Amended by Acts 1993, 73rd Leg., ch. 900, § 1.01, eff. Sept. 1, 1994; Acts 1997, 75th Leg., ch. 721, § 1, eff. Sept. 1, 1997.

§ 36.06. Obstruction or Retaliation

(a) A person commits an offense if he intentionally or knowingly harms or threatens to harm another by an unlawful act:

(1) in retaliation for or on account of the service or status of another as a:

(A) public servant, witness, prospective witness, or informant; or

(B) person who has reported or who the actor knows intends to report the occurrence of a crime; or

(2) to prevent or delay the service of another as a:

(A) public servant, witness, prospective witness, or informant; or

(B) person who has reported or who the actor knows intends to report the occurrence of a crime.

(b) In this section:

(1) "Honorably retired peace officer" means a peace officer who:

(A) did not retire in lieu of any disciplinary action;

(B) was eligible to retire from a law enforcement agency or was ineligible to retire only as a result of an injury received in the course of the officer's employment with the agency; and

(C) is entitled to receive a pension or annuity for service as a law enforcement officer or is not entitled to receive a pension or annuity only because the law enforcement agency that employed the officer does not offer a pension or annuity to its employees.

(2) "Informant" means a person who has communicated information to the government in connection with any governmental function.

(3) "Public servant" includes an honorably retired peace officer.

(c) An offense under this section is a felony of the third degree unless the victim of the offense was harmed or threatened because of the victim's service or status as a juror, in which event the offense is a felony of the second degree.

Acts 1973, 63rd Leg., p. 883, ch. 399, § 1, eff. Jan. 1, 1974. Amended by Acts 1983, 68th Leg., p. 3238, ch. 558, § 4, eff. Sept. 1, 1983; Acts 1989, 71st Leg., ch. 557, § 1, eff. Sept. 1, 1989; Acts 1993, 73rd Leg., ch. 900, § 1.01, eff. Sept. 1, 1994; Acts 1997, 75th Leg., ch. 239, § 1, eff. Sept. 1, 1997; Acts 2001, 77th Leg., ch. 835, § 1, eff. Sept. 1, 2001; Acts 2003, 78th Leg., ch. 246, § 1, eff. Sept. 1, 2003.

§ 36.07. Acceptance of Honorarium

(a) A public servant commits an offense if the public servant solicits, accepts, or agrees to accept an honorarium in consideration for services that the public servant would not have been requested to provide but for the public servant's official position or duties.

(b) This section does not prohibit a public servant from accepting transportation and lodging expenses in connection with a conference or similar event in which the public servant renders services, such as addressing an audience or engaging in a seminar, to the extent that those services are more than merely perfunctory, or from accepting meals in connection with such an event.

(c) An offense under this section is a Class A misdemeanor.

Added by Acts 1991, 72nd Leg., ch. 304, § 4.03, eff. Jan. 1, 1992. Amended by Acts 1993, 73rd Leg., ch. 900, § 1.01, eff. Sept. 1, 1994.

§ 36.08. Gift to Public Servant by Person Subject to His Jurisdiction

(a) A public servant in an agency performing regulatory functions or conducting inspections or investigations commits an offense if he solicits, accepts, or agrees to accept any benefit from a person the public servant knows to be subject to regulation, inspection, or investigation by the public servant or his agency.

(b) A public servant in an agency having custody of prisoners commits an offense if he solicits, accepts, or agrees to accept any benefit from a person the public servant knows to be in his custody or the custody of his agency.

(c) A public servant in an agency carrying on civil or criminal litigation on behalf of government commits an offense if he solicits, accepts, or agrees to accept any benefit from a person against whom the public servant knows litigation is pending or contemplated by the public servant or his agency.

(d) A public servant who exercises discretion in connection with contracts, purchases, payments, claims, or other pecuniary transactions of government commits an offense if he solicits, accepts, or agrees to accept any benefit from a person the public servant knows is interested in or likely to become interested in any contract, purchase, payment, claim, or transaction involving the exercise of his discretion.

(e) A public servant who has judicial or administrative authority, who is employed by or in a tribunal having judicial or administrative authority, or who participates in the enforcement of the tribunal's decision, commits an offense if he solicits, accepts, or agrees to accept any benefit from a person the public servant knows is interested in or likely to become interested in any matter before the public servant or tribunal.

(f) A member of the legislature, the governor, the lieutenant governor, or a person employed by a member of the legislature, the governor, the lieutenant governor, or an agency of the legislature commits an offense if he solicits, accepts, or agrees to accept any benefit from any person.

(g) A public servant who is a hearing examiner employed by an agency performing regulatory functions and who conducts hearings in contested cases commits an offense if the public servant solicits, accepts, or agrees to accept any benefit from any person who is appearing before the agency in a contested case, who is doing business with the agency, or who the public servant knows is interested in any matter before the public servant. The exception provided by § 36.10(b) does not apply to a benefit under this subsection.

(h) An offense under this section is a Class A misdemeanor.

(i) A public servant who receives an unsolicited benefit that the public servant is prohibited from accepting under this section may donate the benefit to a governmental entity that has the authority to accept the gift or may donate the benefit to a recognized tax-exempt charitable organization formed for educational, religious, or scientific purposes.

Acts 1973, 63rd Leg., p. 883, ch. 399, § 1, eff. Jan. 1, 1974. Amended by Acts 1975, 64th Leg., p. 915, ch. 342, § 11, eff. Sept. 1, 1975; Acts 1983, 68th Leg., p. 3238, ch. 558, § 5, eff. Sept. 1, 1983; Acts 1991, 72nd Leg., ch. 304, § 4.04, eff. Jan. 1, 1992; Acts 1993, 73rd Leg., ch. 900, § 1.01, eff. Sept. 1, 1994.

§ 36.09. Offering Gift to Public Servant

(a) A person commits an offense if he offers, confers, or agrees to confer any benefit on a public servant that he knows the public servant is prohibited by law from accepting.

(b) An offense under this section is a Class A misdemeanor.

Acts 1973, 63rd Leg., p. 883, ch. 399, § 1, eff. Jan. 1, 1974. Amended by Acts 1993, 73rd Leg., ch. 900, § 1.01, eff. Sept. 1, 1994.

§ 36.10. Non-Applicable

(a) Sections 36.08 (Gift to Public Servant) and 36.09 (Offering Gift to Public Servant) do not apply to:

(1) a fee prescribed by law to be received by a public servant or any other benefit to which the public servant is lawfully entitled or for which he gives legitimate consideration in a capacity other than as a public servant;

(2) a gift or other benefit conferred on account of kinship or a personal, professional, or business relationship independent of the official status of the recipient; or

(3) a benefit to a public servant required to file a statement under Chapter 572, Government Code, or a report under Title 15, Election Code,[1] that is derived from a function in honor or appreciation of the recipient if:

(A) the benefit and the source of any benefit in excess of $50 is reported in the statement; and

(B) the benefit is used solely to defray the expenses that accrue in the performance of duties or activities in connection with the office which are nonreimbursable by the state or political subdivision;

(4) a political contribution as defined by Title 15, Election Code;

(5) a gift, award, or memento to a member of the legislative or executive branch that is required to be reported under Chapter 305, Government Code;

(6) an item with a value of less than $50, excluding cash or a negotiable instrument as described by Section 3.104, Business & Commerce Code; or

(7) an item issued by a governmental entity that allows the use of property or facilities owned, leased, or operated by the governmental entity.

(b) Section 36.08 (Gift to Public Servant) does not apply to food, lodging, transportation, or entertainment accepted as a guest and, if the donee is required by law to report those items, reported by the donee in accordance with that law.

(c) Section 36.09 (Offering Gift to Public Servant) does not apply to food, lodging, transportation, or entertainment accepted as a guest and, if the donor is required by law to report those items, reported by the donor in accordance with that law.

(d) Section 36.08 (Gift to Public Servant) does not apply to a gratuity accepted and reported in accordance with Section 11.0262, Parks and Wildlife Code. Section 36.09 (Offering Gift to Public Servant) does not apply to a gratuity that is offered in accordance with Section 11.0262, Parks and Wildlife Code.

Acts 1973, 63rd Leg., p. 883, ch. 399, § 1, eff. Jan. 1, 1974. Amended by Acts 1975, 64th Leg., p. 915, ch. 342, § 11, eff. Sept. 1, 1975; Acts 1981, 67th Leg., p. 2707, ch. 738, § 1, eff. Jan. 1, 1982; Acts 1983, 68th Leg., p. 3240, ch. 558, § 6, eff. Sept. 1, 1983; Acts 1987, 70th Leg., ch. 472, § 60, eff. Sept. 1, 1987; Acts 1991, 72nd Leg., ch. 304, § 4.05, eff. Jan. 1, 1992; Acts 1993, 73rd Leg., ch. 900, § 1.01, eff. Sept. 1, 1994; Acts 1995, 74th Leg., ch. 76, § 5.95(38), eff. Sept. 1, 1995; Acts 2005, 79th Leg., ch. 639, § 2, eff. Sept. 1, 2005.

[1] V.T.C.A., Election Code § 251.001 et seq.

CHAPTER 37. PERJURY AND OTHER FALSIFICATION

§ 37.01. Definitions

In this chapter:

(1) "Court record" means a decree, judgment, order, subpoena, warrant, minutes, or other document issued by a court of:

(A) this state;

(B) another state;

(C) the United States;

(D) a foreign country recognized by an act of congress or a treaty or other international convention to which the United States is a party;

(E) an Indian tribe recognized by the United States; or

(F) any other jurisdiction, territory, or protectorate entitled to full faith and credit in this state under the United States Constitution.

(2) "Governmental record" means:

(A) anything belonging to, received by, or kept by government for information, including a court record;

(B) anything required by law to be kept by others for information of government;

(C) a license, certificate, permit, seal, title, letter of patent, or similar document issued by government, by another state, or by the United States;

(D) a standard proof of motor vehicle liability insurance form described by Section 601.081, Transportation Code, a certificate of an insurance company described by Section 601.083 of that code, a document purporting to be such a form or certificate that is not issued by an insurer authorized to write motor vehicle liability insurance in this state, an electronic submission in a form described by Section 502.153(i), Transportation Code, or an evidence of financial responsibility described by Section 601.053 of that code;

(E) an official ballot or other election record; or

(F) the written documentation a mobile food unit is required to obtain under Section 437.0074, Health and Safety Code.

(3) "Statement" means any representation of fact.

Acts 1973, 63rd Leg., p. 883, ch. 399, § 1, eff. Jan. 1, 1974. Amended by Acts 1991, 72nd Leg., ch. 113, § 3, eff. Sept. 1, 1991; Acts 1993, 73rd Leg., ch. 900, § 1.01, eff. Sept. 1, 1994; Acts 1997, 75th Leg., ch. 189, § 5, eff. May 21, 1997; Acts 1997, 75th Leg., ch. 823, § 3, eff. Sept. 1, 1997; Acts 1999, 76th Leg., ch. 659, § 1, eff. Sept. 1, 1999; Acts 2003, 78th Leg., ch. 393, § 21, eff. Sept. 1, 2003; Acts 2007, 80th Leg., ch. 1276, § 2, eff. Sept. 1, 2007.

§ 37.02. Perjury

(a) A person commits an offense if, with intent to deceive and with knowledge of the statement's meaning:

(1) he makes a false statement under oath or swears to the truth of a false statement previously made and the statement is required or authorized by law to be made under oath; or

(2) he makes a false unsworn declaration under Chapter 132, Civil Practice and Remedies Code.

(b) An offense under this section is a Class A misdemeanor.

Acts 1973, 63rd Leg., p. 883, ch. 399, § 1, eff. Jan. 1, 1974. Amended by Acts 1993, 73rd Leg., ch. 900, § 1.01, eff. Sept. 1, 1994.

§ 37.03. Aggravated Perjury

(a) A person commits an offense if he commits perjury as defined in Section 37.02, and the false statement:

(1) is made during or in connection with an official proceeding; and

(2) is material.

(b) An offense under this section is a felony of the third degree.

Acts 1973, 63rd Leg., p. 883, ch. 399, § 1, eff. Jan. 1, 1974. Amended by Acts 1993, 73rd Leg., ch. 900, § 1.01, eff. Sept. 1, 1994.

§ 37.04. Materiality

(a) A statement is material, regardless of the admissibility of the statement under the rules of evidence, if it could have affected the course or outcome of the official proceeding.

(b) It is no defense to prosecution under Section 37.03 (Aggravated Perjury) that the declarant mistakenly believed the statement to be immaterial.

(c) Whether a statement is material in a given factual situation is a question of law.

Acts 1973, 63rd Leg., p. 883, ch. 399, § 1, eff. Jan. 1, 1974. Amended by Acts 1993, 73rd Leg., ch. 900, § 1.01, eff. Sept. 1, 1994.

§ 37.05. Retraction

It is a defense to prosecution under Section 37.03 (Aggravated Perjury) that the actor retracted his false statement:

(1) before completion of the testimony at the official proceeding; and

(2) before it became manifest that the falsity of the statement would be exposed.

Acts 1973, 63rd Leg., p. 883, ch. 399, § 1, eff. Jan. 1, 1974. Amended by Acts 1993, 73rd Leg., ch. 900, § 1.01, eff. Sept. 1, 1994.

§ 37.06. Inconsistent Statements

An information or indictment for perjury under Section 37.02 or aggravated perjury under Section 37.03 that alleges that the declarant has made statements under oath, both of which cannot be true, need not allege which statement is false. At the trial the prosecution need not prove which statement is false.

Acts 1973, 63rd Leg., p. 883, ch. 399, § 1, eff. Jan. 1, 1974. Amended by Acts 1993, 73rd Leg., ch. 900, § 1.01, eff. Sept. 1, 1994.

§ 37.07. Irregularities No Defense

(a) It is no defense to prosecution under Section 37.02 (Perjury) or 37.03 (Aggravated Perjury) that the oath was administered or taken in an irregular manner, or that there was some irregularity in the appointment or qualification of the person who administered the oath.

(b) It is no defense to prosecution under Section 37.02 (Perjury) or 37.03 (Aggravated Perjury) that a document was not sworn to if the document contains a recital that it was made under oath, the declarant was aware of the recital when he signed the document, and the document contains the signed jurat of a public servant authorized to administer oaths.

Acts 1973, 63rd Leg., p. 883, ch. 399, § 1, eff. Jan. 1, 1974. Amended by Acts 1993, 73rd Leg., ch. 900, § 1.01, eff. Sept. 1, 1994.

§ 37.08. False Report to Peace Officer or Law Enforcement Employee

(a) A person commits an offense if, with intent to deceive, he knowingly makes a false statement that is material to a criminal investigation and makes the statement to:

(1) a peace officer conducting the investigation; or

(2) any employee of a law enforcement agency that is authorized by the agency to conduct the investigation and that the actor knows is conducting the investigation.

(b) In this section, "law enforcement agency" has the meaning assigned by Article 59.01, Code of Criminal Procedure.

(c) An offense under this section is a Class B misdemeanor.

Acts 1973, 63rd Leg., p. 883, ch. 399, § 1, eff. Jan. 1, 1974. Amended by Acts 1993, 73rd Leg., ch. 900, § 1.01, eff. Sept. 1, 1994; Acts 1997, 75th Leg., ch. 925, § 1, eff. Sept. 1, 1997.

§ 37.081. False Report Regarding Missing Child or Missing Person

(a) A person commits an offense if, with intent to deceive, the person knowingly:

(1) files a false report of a missing child or missing person with a law enforcement officer or agency; or

(2) makes a false statement to a law enforcement officer or other employee of a law enforcement agency relating to a missing child or missing person.

(b) An offense under this section is a Class C misdemeanor.

Added by Acts 1999, 76th Leg., ch. 200, § 3, eff. Sept. 1, 1999.

§ 37.09. Tampering With or Fabricating Physical Evidence

(a) A person commits an offense if, knowing that an investigation or official proceeding is pending or in progress, he:

(1) alters, destroys, or conceals any record, document, or thing with intent to impair its verity, legibility, or availability as evidence in the investigation or official proceeding; or

(2) makes, presents, or uses any record, document, or thing with knowledge of its falsity and with intent to affect the course or outcome of the investigation or official proceeding.

(b) This section shall not apply if the record, document, or thing concealed is privileged or is the work product of the parties to the investigation or official proceeding.

(c) An offense under Subsection (a) or Subsection (d)(1) is a felony of the third degree, unless the thing altered, destroyed, or concealed is a human corpse, in which case the offense is a felony of the second degree. An offense under Subsection (d)(2) is a Class A misdemeanor.

(d) A person commits an offense if the person:

(1) knowing that an offense has been committed, alters, destroys, or conceals any record, document, or thing with intent to impair its verity, legibility, or availability as evidence in any subsequent investigation of or official proceeding related to the offense; or

(2) observes a human corpse under circumstances in which a reasonable person would believe that an offense had been committed, knows or reasonably should know that a law enforcement agency is not aware of the existence of or location of the corpse, and fails to report the existence of and location of the corpse to a law enforcement agency.

(e) In this section, "human corpse" has the meaning assigned by Section 42.08.

Acts 1973, 63rd Leg., p. 883, ch. 399, § 1, eff. Jan. 1, 1974. Amended by Acts 1991, 72nd Leg., ch. 565, § 4, eff. Sept. 1, 1991; Acts 1993, 73rd Leg., ch. 900, § 1.01, eff. Sept. 1, 1994; Acts 1997, 75th Leg., ch. 1284, § 1, eff. Sept. 1, 1997; Acts 2007, 80th Leg., ch. 287, § 1, eff. September 1, 2007.

§ 37.10. Tampering With Governmental Record

(a) A person commits an offense if he:

(1) knowingly makes a false entry in, or false alteration of, a governmental record;

(2) makes, presents, or uses any record, document, or thing with knowledge of its falsity and with intent that it be taken as a genuine governmental record;

(3) intentionally destroys, conceals, removes, or otherwise impairs the verity, legibility, or availability of a governmental record;

(4) possesses, sells, or offers to sell a governmental record or a blank governmental record form with intent that it be used unlawfully;

(5) makes, presents, or uses a governmental record with knowledge of its falsity; or

(6) possesses, sells, or offers to sell a governmental record or a blank governmental record form with knowledge that it was obtained unlawfully.

(b) It is an exception to the application of Subsection (a)(3) that the governmental record is destroyed pursuant to legal authorization or transferred under Section 441.204, Government Code. With regard to the destruction of a local government record, legal authorization includes compliance with the provisions of Subtitle C, Title 6, Local Government Code.[1]

(c)(1) Except as provided by Subdivisions (2), (3), and (4) and by Subsection (d), an offense under this section is a Class A misdemeanor unless the actor's intent is to defraud or harm another, in which event the offense is a state jail felony.

(2) An offense under this section is a felony of the third degree if it is shown on the trial of the offense that the governmental record was:

(A) a public school record, report, or assessment instrument required under Chapter 39, Education Code, or was a license, certificate, permit, seal, title, letter of patent, or similar document issued by government, by another state, or by the United States, unless the actor's intent is to defraud or harm another, in which event the offense is a felony of the second degree;

(B) a written report of a medical, chemical, toxicological, ballistic, or other expert examination or test performed on physical evidence for the purpose of determining the connection or relevance of the evidence to a criminal action; or

(C) a written report of the certification, inspection, or maintenance record of an instrument, apparatus, implement, machine, or other similar device used in the course of an examination or test performed on physical evidence for the purpose of determining the connection or relevance of the evidence to a criminal action.

(3) An offense under this section is a Class C misdemeanor if it is shown on the trial of the offense that the governmental record is a govern-

mental record that is required for enrollment of a student in a school district and was used by the actor to establish the residency of the student.

(4) An offense under this section is a Class B misdemeanor if it is shown on the trial of the offense that the governmental record is a written appraisal filed with an appraisal review board under Section 41.43(a–1), Tax Code, that was performed by a person who had a contingency interest in the outcome of the appraisal review board hearing.

(d) An offense under this section, if it is shown on the trial of the offense that the governmental record is described by Section 37.01(2)(D), is:

(1) a Class B misdemeanor if the offense is committed under Subsection (a)(2) or Subsection (a)(5) and the defendant is convicted of presenting or using the record;

(2) a felony of the third degree if the offense is committed under:

(A) Subsection (a)(1), (3), (4), or (6); or

(B) Subsection (a)(2) or (5) and the defendant is convicted of making the record; and

(3) a felony of the second degree, notwithstanding Subdivisions (1) and (2), if the actor's intent in committing the offense was to defraud or harm another.

(e) It is an affirmative defense to prosecution for possession under Subsection (a)(6) that the possession occurred in the actual discharge of official duties as a public servant.

(f) It is a defense to prosecution under Subsection (a)(1), (a)(2), or (a)(5) that the false entry or false information could have no effect on the government's purpose for requiring the governmental record.

(g) A person is presumed to intend to defraud or harm another if the person acts with respect to two or more of the same type of governmental records or blank governmental record forms and if each governmental record or blank governmental record form is a license, certificate, permit, seal, title, or similar document issued by government.

(h) If conduct that constitutes an offense under this section also constitutes an offense under Section 32.48 or 37.13, the actor may be prosecuted under any of those sections.

(i) With the consent of the appropriate local county or district attorney, the attorney general has concurrent jurisdiction with that consenting local prosecutor to prosecute an offense under this section that involves the state Medicaid program.

(j) It is not a defense to prosecution under Subsection (a)(2) that the record, document, or thing made, presented, or used displays or contains the statement "NOT A GOVERNMENT DOCUMENT" or another substantially similar statement intended to alert a person to the falsity of the record, document, or thing, unless the record, document, or thing displays the statement diagonally printed clearly and indelibly on both the front and back of the record, document, or thing in solid red capital letters at least one-fourth inch in height.

Acts 1973, 63rd Leg., p. 883, ch. 399, § 1, eff. Jan. 1, 1974. Amended by Acts 1989, 71st Leg., ch. 1248, § 66, eff. Sept. 1, 1989; Acts 1991, 72nd Leg., ch. 113, § 4, eff. Sept. 1, 1991; Acts 1991, 72nd Leg., ch. 565, § 5, eff. Sept. 1, 1991; Acts 1993, 73rd Leg., ch. 900, § 1.01, eff. Sept. 1, 1994; Acts 1997, 75th Leg., ch. 189, § 6, eff. May 21, 1997; Acts 1997, 75th Leg., ch. 823, § 4, eff. Sept. 1, 1997; Acts 1999, 76th Leg., ch. 659, § 2, eff. Sept. 1, 1999; Acts 1999, 76th Leg., ch. 718, § 1, eff. Sept. 1, 1999; Acts 2001, 77th Leg., ch. 771, § 3, eff. June 13, 2001; Acts 2003, 78th Leg., ch. 198, § 2.139, eff. Sept. 1, 2003; Acts 2003, 78th Leg., ch. 257, § 16, eff. Sept. 1, 2003; Acts 2005, 79th Leg., ch. 1364, § 1, eff. June 18, 2005; Acts 2007, 80th Leg., ch. 1085, § 2, eff. Sept. 1, 2007; Acts 2009, 81st Leg., ch. 73, § 1, eff. Sept. 1, 2009; Acts 2009, 81st Leg., ch. 1130, § 31, eff. Sept. 1, 2009.

[1] V.T.C.A., Local Government Code § 201.001 et seq.

Section 3(b) of Acts 2007, 80th Leg., ch. 1085 provides:

"(b) The change in law made by Section 2 of this Act applies only to an offense committed on or after the effective date [Sept. 1, 2007] of this Act. An offense committed before the effective date of this Act is governed by the law in effect at the time the offense was committed, and the former law is continued in effect for that purpose. For the purposes of this subsection, an offense was committed before the effective date of this Act if any element of the offense occurred before that date."

Section 2 of Acts 2009, 81st Leg., ch. 73 provides:

"The change in law made by this Act applies only to an offense committed on or after the effective date [Sept. 1, 2009] of this Act. An offense committed before the effective date of this Act is governed by the law in effect when the offense was committed, and the former law is continued in effect for that purpose. For purposes of this section, an offense was committed before the effective date of this Act if any element of the offense occurred before that date."

Section 35 of Acts 2009, 81st Leg., ch. 1130 provides:

"Section 37.10(j), Penal Code, and Sections 521.454(d), 521.455(c), and 521.456(e), Transportation Code, as added by this Act, apply only to an offense committed on or after the effective date [Sept. 1, 2009] of this Act. An offense committed before the effective date of this Act is covered by the law in effect when the offense was committed, and the former law is continued in effect for that purpose. For purposes of this section, an offense was committed before the effective date of this Act if any element of the offense occurred before that date."

§ 37.101. Fraudulent Filing of Financing Statement

(a) A person commits an offense if the person knowingly presents for filing or causes to be presented for filing a financing statement that the person knows:

(1) is forged;

(2) contains a material false statement; or

(3) is groundless.

(b) An offense under Subsection (a)(1) is a felony of the third degree, unless it is shown on the trial of the offense that the person had previously been convicted under this section on two or more occasions, in which event the offense is a felony of the second degree. An offense under Subsection (a)(2) or (a)(3) is a Class A misdemeanor, unless the person commits the offense with the intent to defraud or harm another, in which event the offense is a state jail felony.

Added by Acts 1997, 75th Leg., ch. 189, § 10, eff. May 21, 1997.

§ 37.11. Impersonating Public Servant

(a) A person commits an offense if he:

(1) impersonates a public servant with intent to induce another to submit to his pretended official authority or to rely on his pretended official acts; or

(2) knowingly purports to exercise any function of a public servant or of a public office, including that of a judge and court, and the position or office through which he purports to exercise a function of a public servant or public office has no lawful existence under the constitution or laws of this state or of the United States.

(b) An offense under this section is a felony of the third degree.

Acts 1973, 63rd Leg., p. 883, ch. 399, § 1, eff. Jan. 1, 1974. Amended by Acts 1993, 73rd Leg., ch. 900, § 1.01, eff. Sept. 1, 1994; Acts 1997, 75th Leg., ch. 189, § 7, eff. May 21, 1997.

§ 37.12. False Identification as Peace Officer; Misrepresentation of Property

(a) A person commits an offense if:

(1) the person makes, provides to another person, or possesses a card, document, badge, insignia, shoulder emblem, or other item bearing an insignia of a law enforcement agency that identifies a person as a peace officer or a reserve law enforcement officer; and

(2) the person who makes, provides, or possesses the item bearing the insignia knows that the person so identified by the item is not commissioned as a peace officer or reserve law enforcement officer as indicated on the item.

(b) It is a defense to prosecution under this section that:

(1) the card, document, badge, insignia, shoulder emblem, or other item bearing an insignia of a law enforcement agency clearly identifies the person as an honorary or junior peace officer or reserve law enforcement officer, or as a member of a junior posse;

(2) the person identified as a peace officer or reserve law enforcement officer by the item bearing the insignia was commissioned in that capacity when the item was made; or

(3) the item was used or intended for use exclusively for decorative purposes or in an artistic or dramatic presentation.

(c) In this section, "reserve law enforcement officer" has the same meaning as is given that term in Section 1701.001, Occupations Code.

(d) A person commits an offense if the person intentionally or knowingly misrepresents an object as property belonging to a law enforcement agency.

(e) An offense under this section is a Class B misdemeanor.

Added by Acts 1983, 68th Leg., p. 5672, ch. 1075, § 1, eff. Sept. 1, 1983. Amended by Acts 1987, 70th Leg., ch. 514, § 1, eff. Sept. 1, 1987; Acts 1993, 73rd Leg., ch. 900, § 1.01, eff. Sept. 1, 1994; Acts 2001, 77th Leg., ch. 1420, § 14.831, eff. Sept. 1, 2001.

§ 37.13. Record of a Fraudulent Court

(a) A person commits an offense if the person makes, presents, or uses any document or other record with:

(1) knowledge that the document or other record is not a record of a court created under or established by the constitution or laws of this state or of the United States; and

(2) the intent that the document or other record be given the same legal effect as a record of a court created under or established by the constitution or laws of this state or of the United States.

(b) An offense under this section is a Class A misdemeanor, except that the offense is a felony of the third degree if it is shown on the trial of the offense that the defendant has previously been convicted under this section on two or more occasions.

(c) If conduct that constitutes an offense under this section also constitutes an offense under Section 32.48 or 37.10, the actor may be prosecuted under any of those sections.

Added by Acts 1997, 75th Leg., ch. 189, § 8, eff. May 21, 1997.

CHAPTER 38. OBSTRUCTING GOVERNMENTAL OPERATION

§ 38.01. Definitions

In this chapter:

(1) "Custody" means:

(A) under arrest by a peace officer or under restraint by a public servant pursuant to an order of a court of this state or another state of the United States; or

(B) under restraint by an agent or employee of a facility that is operated by or under contract with the United States and that confines persons arrested for, charged with, or convicted of criminal offenses.

(2) "Escape" means unauthorized departure from custody or failure to return to custody following temporary leave for a specific purpose or limited period or leave that is part of an intermittent sentence, but does not include a violation of conditions of community supervision or parole other than conditions that impose a period of confinement in a secure correctional facility.

(3) "Economic benefit" means anything reasonably regarded as an economic gain or advantage, including accepting or offering to accept employment for a fee, accepting or offering to accept a fee, entering into a fee contract, or accepting or agreeing to accept money or anything of value.

(4) "Finance" means to provide funds or capital or to furnish with necessary funds.

(5) "Fugitive from justice" means a person for whom a valid arrest warrant has been issued.

(6) "Governmental function" includes any activity that a public servant is lawfully authorized to undertake on behalf of government.

(7) "Invest funds" means to commit money to earn a financial return.

(8) "Member of the family" means anyone related within the third degree of consanguinity or affinity, as determined under Chapter 573, Government Code.

(9) "Qualified nonprofit organization" means a nonprofit organization that meets the following conditions:

(A) the primary purposes of the organization do not include the rendition of legal services or education regarding legal services;

(B) the recommending, furnishing, paying for, or educating persons regarding legal services is incidental and reasonably related to the primary purposes of the organization;

(C) the organization does not derive a financial benefit from the rendition of legal services by a lawyer; and

(D) the person for whom the legal services are rendered, and not the organization, is recognized as the client of a lawyer.

(10) "Public media" means a telephone directory or legal directory, newspaper or other periodical, billboard or other sign, radio or television broadcast, recorded message the public may access by dialing a telephone number, or a written communication not prohibited by Section 38.12(d).

(11) "Solicit employment" means to communicate in person or by telephone with a prospective client or a member of the prospective client's family concerning professional employment within the scope of a professional's license, registration, or certification arising out of a particular occurrence or event, or series of occurrences or events, or concerning an existing problem of the prospective client within the scope of the professional's license, registration, or certification, for the purpose of providing professional services to the prospective client, when neither the person receiving the communication nor anyone acting on that person's behalf has requested the communication. The term does not include a communication initiated by a family member of the person receiving a communication, a communication by a professional who has a prior or existing professional-client relationship with the person receiving the communication, or communication by an attorney for a qualified nonprofit organization with the organization's members for the purpose of educating the organization's members to understand the law, to recognize legal problems, to make intelligent selection of legal counsel, or to use available legal services. The term does not include an advertisement by a professional through public media.

(12) "Professional" means an attorney, chiropractor, physician, surgeon, private investigator, or any other person licensed, certified, or registered by a state agency that regulates a health care profession.

Acts 1973, 63rd Leg., p. 883, ch. 399, § 1, eff. Jan. 1, 1974. Amended by Acts 1989, 71st Leg., ch. 866, § 1, eff. Sept. 1, 1989; Acts 1991, 72nd Leg., ch. 14, § 284(14), eff. Sept. 1, 1991; Acts 1991, 72nd Leg., ch. 561, § 42, eff. Aug. 26, 1991; Acts 1993, 73rd Leg., ch. 723, § 1, eff. Sept. 1, 1993; Acts 1993, 73rd Leg., ch. 900, § 1.01, eff. Sept. 1, 1994; Acts 1995, 74th Leg., ch. 76, § 5.95(27), eff. Sept. 1, 1995; Acts 1995, 74th Leg., ch. 321, § 1.103, eff. Sept. 1, 1995; Acts 1997, 75th Leg., ch. 293, § 2, eff. Sept. 1, 1997; Acts 1997, 75th Leg., ch. 750, § 1, eff. Sept. 1, 1997.

§ 38.03. Resisting Arrest, Search, or Transportation

(a) A person commits an offense if he intentionally prevents or obstructs a person he knows is a peace officer or a person acting in a peace officer's presence and at his direction from effecting an arrest, search, or transportation of the actor or another by using force against the peace officer or another.

(b) It is no defense to prosecution under this section that the arrest or search was unlawful.

(c) Except as provided in Subsection (d), an offense under this section is a Class A misdemeanor.

(d) An offense under this section is a felony of the third degree if the actor uses a deadly weapon to resist the arrest or search.

Acts 1973, 63rd Leg., p. 883, ch. 399, § 1, eff. Jan. 1, 1974. Acts 1991, 72nd Leg., ch. 277, §§ 1, 2, eff. Sept. 1, 1991; Acts 1993, 73rd Leg., ch. 900, § 1.01, eff. Sept. 1, 1994.

§ 38.04. Evading Arrest or Detention

(a) A person commits an offense if he intentionally flees from a person he knows is a peace officer attempting lawfully to arrest or detain him.

(b) An offense under this section is a Class A misdemeanor, except that the offense is:

(1) a state jail felony if:

(A) the actor has been previously convicted under this section; or

(B) the actor uses a vehicle while the actor is in flight and the actor has not been previously convicted under this section;

(2) a felony of the third degree if:

(A) the actor uses a vehicle while the actor is in flight and the actor has been previously convicted under this section; or

(B) another suffers serious bodily injury as a direct result of an attempt by the officer from whom the actor is fleeing to apprehend the actor while the actor is in flight; or

(3) a felony of the second degree if another suffers death as a direct result of an attempt by the officer from whom the actor is fleeing to apprehend the actor while the actor is in flight.

(c) In this section, "vehicle" has the meaning assigned by Section 541.201, Transportation Code.

(d) A person who is subject to prosecution under both this section and another law may be prosecuted under either or both this section and the other law.

Acts 1973, 63rd Leg., p. 883, ch. 399, § 1, eff. Jan. 1, 1974. Amended by Acts 1987, 70th Leg., ch. 504, § 1, eff. Sept. 1, 1987. Acts 1989, 71st Leg., ch. 126, § 1, eff. Sept. 1, 1989; Acts 1993, 73rd Leg., ch. 900, § 1.01, eff. Sept. 1, 1994; Acts 1995, 74th Leg., ch. 708, § 1, eff. Sept. 1, 1995; Acts 1997, 75th Leg., ch. 165, § 30.240, eff. Sept. 1, 1997; Acts 2001, 77th Leg., ch. 1334, § 3, eff. Sept. 1, 2001; Acts 2001, 77th Leg., ch. 1480, § 1, eff. Sept. 1, 2001; Acts 2009, 81st Leg., ch. 1400, § 4, eff. Sept. 1, 2009.

Section 7 of Acts 2009, 81st Leg., ch. 1400 provides:

"The change in law made by this Act applies only to an offense committed on or after the effective date [Sept. 1, 2009] of this Act. An offense committed before the effective date of this Act is covered by the law in effect when the offense was committed, and the former law is continued in effect for that purpose. For purposes of this section, an offense was committed before the effective date of this Act if any element of the offense was committed before that date."

§ 38.05. Hindering Apprehension or Prosecution

(a) A person commits an offense if, with intent to hinder the arrest, prosecution, conviction, or punishment of another for an offense or, with intent to hinder the arrest, detention, adjudication, or disposition of a child for engaging in delinquent conduct that violates a penal law of the state, or with intent to hinder the arrest of another under the authority of a warrant or capias, he:

(1) harbors or conceals the other;

(2) provides or aids in providing the other with any means of avoiding arrest or effecting escape; or

(3) warns the other of impending discovery or apprehension.

(b) It is a defense to prosecution under Subsection (a)(3) that the warning was given in connection with an effort to bring another into compliance with the law.

(c) Except as provided by Subsection (d), an offense under this section is a Class A misdemeanor.

(d) An offense under this section is a felony of the third degree if the person who is harbored, concealed, provided with a means of avoiding arrest or effecting escape, or warned of discovery or apprehension is under arrest for, charged with, or convicted of a felony, including an offense under Section 62.102, Code of Criminal Procedure, or is in custody or detention for, is alleged in a petition to have engaged in, or has been adjudicated as having engaged in delinquent conduct that violates a penal law of the grade of felony, including an offense under Section 62.102, Code of Criminal Procedure, and the person charged under this section knew that the person they harbored, concealed, provided with a means of avoiding arrest or effecting escape, or warned of discovery or apprehension is under arrest for, charged with, or convicted of a felony, or is in custody or detention for, is alleged in a petition to have engaged in, or has been adjudicated as having engaged in delinquent conduct that violates a penal law of the grade of felony.

Acts 1973, 63rd Leg., p. 883, ch. 399, § 1, eff. Jan. 1, 1974. Amended by Acts 1991, 72nd Leg., ch. 748, § 1, eff. Sept. 1, 1991; Acts 1993, 73rd Leg., ch. 900, § 1.01, eff. Sept. 1, 1994; Acts 1995, 74th Leg., ch. 318, § 11, eff. Sept. 1, 1995; Acts 2005, 79th Leg., ch. 607, § 1, eff. Sept. 1, 2005; Acts 2007, 80th Leg., ch. 593, § 1.19, eff. Sept. 1, 2007.

§ 38.06. Escape

(a) A person commits an offense if he escapes from custody when he is:

(1) under arrest for, charged with, or convicted of an offense;

(2) in custody pursuant to a lawful order of a court;

(3) detained in a secure detention facility, as that term is defined by Section 51.02, Family Code; or

(4) in the custody of a juvenile probation officer for violating an order imposed by the juvenile court under Section 52.01, Family Code.

(b) Except as provided in Subsections (c), (d), and (e), an offense under this section is a Class A misdemeanor.

(c) An offense under this section is a felony of the third degree if the actor:

(1) is under arrest for, charged with, or convicted of a felony;

(2) is confined in a secure correctional facility; or

(3) is committed to a secure correctional facility, as defined by Section 51.02, Family Code, other than a halfway house, operated by or under contract with the Texas Youth Commission.

(d) An offense under this section is a felony of the second degree if the actor to effect his escape causes bodily injury.

(e) An offense under this section is a felony of the first degree if to effect his escape the actor:

(1) causes serious bodily injury; or

(2) uses or threatens to use a deadly weapon.

Acts 1973, 63rd Leg., p. 883, ch. 399, § 1, eff. Jan. 1, 1974. Amended by Acts 1985, 69th Leg., ch. 328, § 1, eff. Sept. 1, 1985. Renumbered from V.T.C.A., Penal Code § 38.07 and amended by Acts 1993, 73rd Leg., ch. 900, § 1.01, eff. Sept. 1, 1994. Amended by Acts 1999, 76th Leg., ch. 526, § 1, eff. Sept. 1, 1999; Acts 2007, 80th Leg., ch. 908, § 38, eff. Sept. 1, 2007.

§ 38.07. Permitting or Facilitating Escape

(a) An official or employee of a correctional facility commits an offense if he knowingly permits or facilitates the escape of a person in custody.

(b) A person commits an offense if he knowingly causes or facilitates the escape of one who is in custody pursuant to:

(1) an allegation or adjudication of delinquency; or

(2) involuntary commitment for mental illness under Subtitle C, Title 7, Health and Safety Code,[1] or for chemical dependency under Chapter 462, Health and Safety Code.

(c) Except as provided in Subsections (d) and (e), an offense under this section is a Class A misdemeanor.

(d) An offense under this section is a felony of the third degree if the person in custody:

(1) was under arrest for, charged with, or convicted of a felony; or

(2) was confined in a correctional facility other than a secure correctional facility after conviction of a felony.

(e) An offense under this section is a felony of the second degree if:

(1) the actor or the person in custody used or threatened to use a deadly weapon to effect the escape; or

(2) the person in custody was confined in a secure correctional facility after conviction of a felony.

(f) In this section, "correctional facility" means:

(1) any place described by Section 1.07(a)(14); or

(2) a "secure correctional facility" or "secure detention facility" as those terms are defined by Section 51.02, Family Code.

Acts 1973, 63rd Leg., p. 883, ch. 399, § 1, eff. Jan. 1, 1974. Renumbered from V.T.C.A., Penal Code § 38.08 and amended by Acts 1993, 73rd Leg., ch. 900, § 1.01, eff. Sept. 1, 1994; Acts 2007, 80th Leg., ch. 908, § 39, eff. Sept. 1, 2007.

[1] V.T.C.A., Health & Safety Code § 531.001 et seq.

§ 38.08. Effect of Unlawful Custody

It is no defense to prosecution under Section 38.06 or 38.07 that the custody was unlawful.

Acts 1973, 63rd Leg., p. 883, ch. 399, § 1, eff. Jan. 1, 1974. Renumbered from V.T.C.A., Penal Code § 38.09 and amended by Acts 1993, 73rd Leg., ch. 900, § 1.01, eff. Sept. 1, 1994.

§ 38.09. Implements for Escape

(a) A person commits an offense if, with intent to facilitate escape, he introduces into a correctional facility, or provides a person in custody or an inmate with, a deadly weapon or anything that may be useful for escape.

(b) An offense under this section is a felony of the third degree unless the actor introduced or provided a deadly weapon, in which event the offense is a felony of the second degree.

(c) In this section, "correctional facility" means:

(1) any place described by Section 1.07(a)(14); or

(2) a "secure correctional facility" or "secure detention facility" as those terms are defined by Section 51.02, Family Code.

Acts 1973, 63rd Leg., p. 883, ch. 399, § 1, eff. Jan. 1, 1974. Renumbered from V.T.C.A., Penal Code § 38.10 and amended by Acts 1993, 73rd Leg., ch. 900, § 1.01, eff. Sept. 1, 1994; Acts 2007, 80th Leg., ch. 908, § 40, eff. Sept. 1, 2007.

§ 38.10. Bail Jumping and Failure to Appear

(a) A person lawfully released from custody, with or without bail, on condition that he subsequently appear commits an offense if he intentionally or knowingly fails to appear in accordance with the terms of his release.

(b) It is a defense to prosecution under this section that the appearance was incident to community supervision, parole, or an intermittent sentence.

(c) It is a defense to prosecution under this section that the actor had a reasonable excuse for his failure to appear in accordance with the terms of his release.

(d) Except as provided in Subsections (e) and (f), an offense under this section is a Class A misdemeanor.

(e) An offense under this section is a Class C misdemeanor if the offense for which the actor's appearance was required is punishable by fine only.

(f) An offense under this section is a felony of the third degree if the offense for which the actor's appearance was required is classified as a felony.

Acts 1973, 63rd Leg., p. 883, ch. 399, § 1, eff. Jan. 1, 1974. Renumbered from V.T.C.A., Penal Code § 38.11 and amended by Acts 1993, 73rd Leg., ch. 900, § 1.01, eff. Sept. 1, 1994.

§ 38.11. Prohibited Substances and Items in Correctional Facility

(a) A person commits an offense if the person provides, or possesses with the intent to provide:

(1) an alcoholic beverage, controlled substance, or dangerous drug to a person in the custody of a correctional facility, except on the prescription of a practitioner;

(2) a deadly weapon to a person in the custody of a correctional facility;

(3) a cellular telephone or other wireless communications device or a component of one of those devices to a person in the custody of a correctional facility;

(4) money to a person confined in a correctional facility; or

(5) a cigarette or tobacco product to a person confined in a correctional facility, except that if the facility is a local jail regulated by the Commission on Jail Standards, the person commits an offense only if providing the cigarette or tobacco product violates a rule or regulation adopted by the sheriff or jail administrator that:

(A) prohibits the possession of a cigarette or tobacco product by a person confined in the jail; or

(B) places restrictions on:

(i) the possession of a cigarette or tobacco product by a person confined in the jail; or

(ii) the manner in which a cigarette or tobacco product may be provided to a person confined in the jail.

(b) A person commits an offense if the person takes an alcoholic beverage, controlled substance, or dangerous drug into a correctional facility.

(c) A person commits an offense if the person takes a controlled substance or dangerous drug on property owned, used, or controlled by a correctional facility.

(d) A person commits an offense if the person:

(1) possesses a controlled substance or dangerous drug while in a correctional facility or on property owned, used, or controlled by a correctional facility; or

(2) possesses a deadly weapon while in a correctional facility.

(e) It is an affirmative defense to prosecution under Subsection (b), (c), or (d)(1) that the person possessed the alcoholic beverage, controlled substance, or dangerous drug pursuant to a prescription issued by a practitioner or while delivering the beverage, substance, or drug to a warehouse, pharmacy, or practitioner on property owned, used, or controlled by the correctional facility. It is an affirmative defense to prosecution under Subsection (d)(2) that the person possessing the deadly weapon is a peace officer or is an officer or employee of the correctional facility who is authorized to possess the deadly weapon while on duty or traveling to or from the person's place of assignment.

(f) In this section:

(1) "Practitioner" has the meaning assigned by Section 481.002, Health and Safety Code.

(2) "Prescription" has the meaning assigned by Section 481.002, Health and Safety Code.

(3) "Cigarette" has the meaning assigned by Section 154.001, Tax Code.

(4) "Tobacco product" has the meaning assigned by Section 155.001, Tax Code.

(5) "Component" means any item necessary for the current, ongoing, or future operation of a cellular telephone or other wireless communications device, including a subscriber identity module card or functionally equivalent portable memory chip, a battery or battery charger, and any number of minutes that have been purchased or for which a contract has been entered into and during which a cellular telephone or other wireless communications device is capable of transmitting or receiving communications.

(6) "Correctional facility" means:

(A) any place described by Section 1.07(a)(14)(A), (B), or (C); or

(B) a secure correctional facility or secure detention facility, as defined by Section 51.02, Family Code.

(g) An offense under this section is a felony of the third degree.

(h) Notwithstanding Section 15.01(d), if a person commits the offense of criminal attempt to commit an offense under Subsection (a), (b), or (c), the offense committed under Section 15.01 is a felony of the third degree.

(i) It is an affirmative defense to prosecution under Subsection (b) that the actor:

(1) is a duly authorized member of the clergy with rights and privileges granted by an ordaining authority that includes administration of a religious ritual or ceremony requiring the presence or consumption of an alcoholic beverage; and

(2) takes four ounces or less of an alcoholic beverage into the correctional facility and personally consumes all of the alcoholic beverage or departs from the facility with any portion of the beverage not consumed.

(j) A person commits an offense if the person, while confined in a correctional facility, possesses a cellular telephone or other wireless communications device or a component of one of those devices.

(k) A person commits an offense if, with the intent to provide to or make a cellular telephone or other wireless communications device or a component of one of those devices available for use by a person in the custody of a correctional facility, the person:

(1) acquires a cellular telephone or other wireless communications device or a component of one of those devices to be delivered to the person in custody;

(2) provides a cellular telephone or other wireless communications device or a component of one of those devices to another person for delivery to the person in custody; or

(3) makes a payment to a communication common carrier, as defined by Article 18.20, Code of Criminal Procedure, or to any communication service that provides to its users the ability to send or receive wire or electronic communications.

Added by Acts 1991, 72nd Leg., 2nd C.S., ch. 10, § 5.01, eff. Oct. 1, 1991. Renumbered from V.T.C.A., Penal Code § 38.112 and amended by Acts 1993, 73rd Leg., ch. 900, § 1.01, eff. Sept. 1, 1994. Amended by Acts 1999, 76th Leg., ch. 362, § 1, eff. Sept. 1, 1999; Acts 1999, 76th Leg., ch. 649, § 1, eff. Sept. 1, 1999; Acts 2003, 78th Leg., ch. 470, §§ 1 to 3, eff. Sept. 1, 2003; Acts 2005, 79th Leg., ch. 499, § 1, eff. June 17, 2005; Acts 2005, 79th Leg., ch. 949, §§ 47, 48, eff. Sept. 1, 2005; Acts 2005, 79th Leg., ch. 1092, § 1, eff. Sept. 1, 2005; Acts 2009, 81st Leg., ch. 1169, § 1, eff. Sept. 1, 2009.

Section 10 of Acts 2009, 81st Leg., ch. 1169 provides:

"The changes in law made by this Act with respect to Sections 16.02 and 38.11, Penal Code, apply only to an offense committed on or after the effective date [Sept. 1, 2009] of this Act. An offense committed before the effective date of this Act is governed by the law in effect when the offense was committed, and the former law is continued in effect for that purpose. For purposes of this section, an offense was committed before the effective date of this Act if any element of the offense occurred before that date."

§ 38.111. Improper Contact With Victim

(a) A person commits an offense if the person, while confined in a correctional facility after being charged with or convicted of an offense listed in Article 62.001(5), Code of Criminal Procedure, contacts by letter, telephone, or any other means, either directly or through a third party, a victim of the offense or a member of the victim's family, if:

(1) the victim was younger than 17 years of age at the time of the commission of the offense for which the person is confined; and

(2) the director of the correctional facility has not, before the person makes contact with the victim:

(A) received written and dated consent to the contact from:

(i) a parent of the victim;

(ii) a legal guardian of the victim;

(iii) the victim, if the victim is 17 years of age or older at the time of giving the consent; or

(iv) a member of the victim's family who is 17 years of age or older; and

(B) provided the person with a copy of the consent.

(b) The person confined in a correctional facility may not give the written consent required under Subsection (a)(2)(A).

(c) It is an affirmative defense to prosecution under this section that the contact was:

(1) indirect contact made through an attorney representing the person in custody; and

(2) solely for the purpose of representing the person in a criminal proceeding.

(d) An offense under this section is a Class A misdemeanor unless the actor is confined in a correctional facility after being convicted of a felony described by Subsection (a), in which event the offense is a felony of the third degree.

(e) In this section, "correctional facility" means:

(1) any place described by Section 1.07(a)(14); or

(2) a "secure correctional facility" or "secure detention facility" as those terms are defined by Section 51.02, Family Code.

Added by Acts 2001, 77th Leg., ch. 1337, § 1, eff. Sept. 1, 2001. Amended by Acts 2005, 79th Leg., ch. 1008, § 2.11, eff. Sept. 1, 2005; Acts 2007, 80th Leg., ch. 908, § 41, eff. Sept. 1, 2007.

§ 38.112. Violation of Protective Order Issued on Basis of Sexual Assault

(a) A person commits an offense if, in violation of an order issued under Chapter 7A, Code of Criminal Procedure, the person knowingly:

(1) communicates directly or indirectly with the applicant or any member of the applicant's family or household in a threatening or harassing manner;

(2) goes to or near the residence, place of employment or business, or child-care facility or school of the applicant or any member of the applicant's family or household; or

(3) possesses a firearm.

(b) If conduct constituting an offense under this section also constitutes an offense under another section of this code, the actor may be prosecuted under either section or under both sections.

(c) An offense under this section is a Class A misdemeanor.

Added by Acts 2003, 78th Leg., ch. 836, § 3, eff. Sept. 1, 2003.

§ 38.113. Unauthorized Absence From Community Corrections Facility, County Correctional Center, or Assignment Site

(a) A person commits an offense if the person:

(1) is sentenced to or is required as a condition of community supervision or correctional programming to submit to a period of detention or treatment in a community corrections facility or county correctional center;

(2) fails to report to or leaves the facility, the center, or a community service assignment site as directed by the court, community supervision and corrections department supervising the person, or director of the facility or center in which the person is detained or treated, as appropriate; and

(3) in failing to report or leaving acts without the approval of the court, the community supervision and corrections department supervising the person, or the director of the facility or center in which the person is detained or treated.

(b) An offense under this section is a state jail felony.

Added by Acts 1993, 73rd Leg., ch. 900, § 1.01, eff. Sept. 1, 1994. Amended by Acts 1995, 74th Leg., ch. 318, § 12, eff. Sept. 1, 1995.

§ 38.114. Contraband in Correctional Facility

(a) A person commits an offense if the person:

(1) provides contraband to an inmate of a correctional facility;

(2) otherwise introduces contraband into a correctional facility; or

(3) possesses contraband while confined in a correctional facility.

(b) In this section, "contraband":

(1) means:

(A) any item not provided by or authorized by the operator of the correctional facility; or

(B) any item provided by or authorized by the operator of the correctional facility that has been altered to accommodate a use other than the originally intended use; and

(2) does not include any item specifically prohibited under Section 38. 11.

(c) An offense under this section is a Class C misdemeanor, unless the offense is committed by an employee or a volunteer of the correctional facility, in which event the offense is a Class B misdemeanor.

(d) In this section, "correctional facility" means:

(1) any place described by Section 1.07(a)(14); or

(2) a "secure correctional facility" or "secure detention facility" as those terms are defined by Section 51.02, Family Code.

Added by Acts 2005, 79th Leg., ch. 499, § 2, eff. June 17, 2005. Amended by Acts 2007, 80th Leg., ch. 908, § 42, eff. Sept. 1, 2007.

§ 38.12. Barratry and Solicitation of Professional Employment

(a) A person commits an offense if, with intent to obtain an economic benefit the person:

(1) knowingly institutes a suit or claim that the person has not been authorized to pursue;

(2) solicits employment, either in person or by telephone, for himself or for another;

(3) pays, gives, or advances or offers to pay, give, or advance to a prospective client money or anything of value to obtain employment as a professional from the prospective client;

(4) pays or gives or offers to pay or give a person money or anything of value to solicit employment;

(5) pays or gives or offers to pay or give a family member of a prospective client money or anything of value to solicit employment; or

(6) accepts or agrees to accept money or anything of value to solicit employment.

(b) A person commits an offense if the person:

(1) knowingly finances the commission of an offense under Subsection (a);

(2) invests funds the person knows or believes are intended to further the commission of an offense under Subsection (a); or

(3) is a professional who knowingly accepts employment within the scope of the person's license, registration, or certification that results from the solicitation of employment in violation of Subsection (a).

(c) It is an exception to prosecution under Subsection (a) or (b) that the person's conduct is authorized by the Texas Disciplinary Rules of Professional Conduct or any rule of court.

(d) A person commits an offense if the person:

(1) is an attorney, chiropractor, physician, surgeon, or private investigator licensed to practice in this state or any person licensed, certified, or registered by a health care regulatory agency of this state; and

(2) with the intent to obtain professional employment for the person or for another, provides or knowingly permits to be provided to an individual who has not sought the person's employment, legal representation, advice, or care a written communication or a solicitation, including a solicitation in person or by telephone, that:

(A) concerns an action for personal injury or wrongful death or otherwise relates to an accident or disaster involving the person to whom the communication or solicitation is provided or a relative of that person and that was provided before the 31st day after the date on which the accident or disaster occurred;

(B) concerns a specific matter and relates to legal representation and the person knows or reasonably should know that the person to whom the communication or solicitation is directed is represented by a lawyer in the matter;

(C) concerns an arrest of or issuance of a summons to the person to whom the communication or solicitation is provided or a relative of that person and that was provided before the 31st day after the date on which the arrest or issuance of the summons occurred;

(D) concerns a lawsuit of any kind, including an action for divorce, in which the person to whom the communication or solicitation is provided is a defendant or a relative of that person, unless the lawsuit in which the person is named as a defendant has been on file for more than 31 days before the date on which the communication or solicitation was provided;

(E) is provided or permitted to be provided by a person who knows or reasonably should know that the injured person or relative of the injured person has indicated a desire not to be contacted by or receive communications or solicitations concerning employment;

(F) involves coercion, duress, fraud, overreaching, harassment, intimidation, or undue influence; or

(G) contains a false, fraudulent, misleading, deceptive, or unfair statement or claim.

(e) For purposes of Subsection (d)(2)(E), a desire not to be contacted is presumed if an accident report reflects that such an indication has been made by an injured person or that person's relative.

(f) An offense under Subsection (a) or (b) is a felony of the third degree.

(g) Except as provided by Subsection (h), an offense under Subsection (d) is a Class A misdemeanor.

(h) An offense under Subsection (d) is a felony of the third degree if it is shown on the trial of the offense that the defendant has previously been convicted under Subsection (d).

(i) Final conviction of felony barratry is a serious crime for all purposes and acts, specifically including the State Bar Rules and the Texas Rules of Disciplinary Procedure.

Acts 1973, 63rd Leg., p. 883, ch. 399, § 1, eff. Jan. 1, 1974. Amended by Acts 1989, 71st Leg., ch. 866, § 2, eff. Sept. 1, 1989; Acts 1993, 73rd Leg., ch. 723, § 2, eff. Sept. 1, 1993; Acts 1993, 73rd Leg., ch. 900, § 1.01, eff. Sept. 1, 1994; Acts 1997, 75th Leg., ch. 750, § 2, eff. Sept. 1, 1997; Acts 2009, 81st Leg., ch. 1252, § 1, eff. Sept. 1, 2009.

Section 2 of Acts 2009, 81st Leg., ch. 1252 provides:

"The change in law made by this Act applies only to an offense committed on or after the effective date [Sept. 1, 2009] of this Act. An offense committed before the effective date of this Act is governed by the law in effect at the time the offense was committed, and the former law is continued in effect for that purpose. For purposes of this section, an offense was committed before the effective date of this Act if any element of the offense occurred before that date."

§ 38.122. Falsely Holding Oneself Out as a Lawyer

(a) A person commits an offense if, with intent to obtain an economic benefit for himself or herself, the person holds himself or herself out as a lawyer, unless he or she is currently licensed to practice law in this state, another state, or a foreign country and is in good standing with the State Bar of Texas and the state bar or licensing authority of any and all other states and foreign countries where licensed.

(b) An offense under Subsection (a) of this section is a felony of the third degree.

(c) Final conviction of falsely holding oneself out to be a lawyer is a serious crime for all purposes and acts, specifically including the State Bar Rules.

Added by Acts 1993, 73rd Leg., ch. 723, § 5, eff. Sept. 1, 1993.

§ 38.123. Unauthorized Practice of Law

(a) A person commits an offense if, with intent to obtain an economic benefit for himself or herself, the person:

(1) contracts with any person to represent that person with regard to personal causes of action for property damages or personal injury;

(2) advises any person as to the person's rights and the advisability of making claims for personal injuries or property damages;

(3) advises any person as to whether or not to accept an offered sum of money in settlement of claims for personal injuries or property damages;

(4) enters into any contract with another person to represent that person in personal injury or property damage matters on a contingent fee basis with an attempted assignment of a portion of the person's cause of action; or

(5) enters into any contract with a third person which purports to grant the exclusive right to select and retain legal counsel to represent the individual in any legal proceeding.

(b) This section does not apply to a person currently licensed to practice law in this state, another state, or a foreign country and in good standing with the State Bar of Texas and the state bar or licensing authority of any and all other states and foreign countries where licensed.

(c) Except as provided by Subsection (d) of this section, an offense under Subsection (a) of this section is a Class A misdemeanor.

(d) An offense under Subsection (a) of this section is a felony of the third degree if it is shown on the trial of the offense that the defendant has previously been convicted under Subsection (a) of this section.

Added by Acts 1993, 73rd Leg., ch. 723, § 5, eff. Sept. 1, 1993.

§ 38.13. Hindering Proceedings by Disorderly Conduct

(a) A person commits an offense if he intentionally hinders an official proceeding by noise or violent or tumultuous behavior or disturbance.

(b) A person commits an offense if he recklessly hinders an official proceeding by noise or violent or tumultuous behavior or disturbance and continues after explicit official request to desist.

(c) An offense under this section is a Class A misdemeanor.

Added by Acts 1973, 63rd Leg., p. 833, ch. 399, § 1, eff. Jan. 1, 1974. Amended by Acts 1993, 73rd Leg., ch. 900, § 1.01, eff. Sept. 1, 1994.

§ 38.14. Taking or Attempting to Take Weapon from Peace Officer, Employee or Official of Correctional Facility, Parole Officer, or Community Supervision and Corrections Department Officer; or Commissioned Security Officer

(a) In this section:

(1) "Firearm" has the meanings assigned by Section 46.01.

(2) "Stun gun" means a device designed to propel darts or other projectiles attached to wires that, on contact, will deliver an electrical pulse capable of incapacitating a person.

(3) "Commissioned security officer" has the meaning assigned by Section 1702.002(5), Occupations Code.

(b) A person commits an offense if the person intentionally or knowingly and with force takes or attempts to take from a peace officer, employee or official of a correctional facility, parole officer, community supervision and corrections department officer, or commissioned security officer the officer's, employee's, or official's firearm, nightstick, stun gun, or personal protection chemical dispensing device with the intention of harming the officer, employee, or official or a third person.

(c) The actor is presumed to have known that the peace officer, employee or official of a correctional facility, parole officer, community supervision and corrections department officer, or commissioned security officer was a peace officer, employee or official of a correctional facility, parole officer, community supervision and corrections department officer, or commissioned security officer if:

(1) the officer, employee, or official was wearing a distinctive uniform or badge indicating his employment; or

(2) the officer, employee, or official identified himself as a peace officer, employee or official of a correctional facility, parole officer, community supervision and corrections department officer, or commissioned security officer.

(d) It is a defense to prosecution under this section that the defendant took or attempted to take the weapon from a peace officer, employee or official of a correctional facility, parole officer, community supervision and corrections department officer, or commissioned security officer who was using force against the defendant or another in excess of the amount of force permitted by law.

(e) An offense under this section is:

(1) a felony of the third degree, if the defendant took a weapon described by Subsection (b) from an officer, employee, or official described by that subsection; and

(2) a state jail felony, if the defendant attempted to take a weapon described by Subsection (b) from an officer, employee, or official described by that subsection.

Added by Acts 1989, 71st Leg., ch. 986, § 1, eff. Sept. 1, 1989. Renumbered from V.T.C.A., Penal Code § 38.16 by Acts 1990, 71st Leg., 6th C.S., ch. 12, § 2(25), eff. Sept. 6, 1990. Renumbered from V.T.C.A., Penal Code § 38.17 and amended by Acts 1993, 73rd Leg., ch. 900, § 1.01, eff. Sept. 1, 1994. Amended by Acts 1999, 76th Leg., ch. 714, § 1, eff. Sept. 1, 1999; Acts 2001, 77th Leg., ch. 322, § 1, eff. Sept. 1, 2001; Acts 2005, 79th Leg., ch. 1201, § 1, eff. Sept. 1, 2005; Acts 2009, 81st Leg., ch. 394, §§ 1, 2, eff. Sept. 1, 2009; Acts 2009, 81st Leg., ch. 942, §§ 1 to 3, eff. Sept. 1, 2009.

Section 3 of Acts 2009, 81st Leg., ch. 394 provides:

"The change in law made by this Act applies only to an offense committed on or after the effective date [Sept. 1, 2009] of this Act. An offense committed before the effective date of this Act is governed by the law in effect at the time the offense was committed, and the former law is continued in effect for that purpose. For purposes of this section, an offense was committed before the effective date of this Act if any element of the offense occurred before that date."

Section 4 of Acts 2009, 81st Leg., ch. 942 provides:

"The change in law made by this Act applies only to an offense committed on or after the effective date [Sept. 1, 2009] of this Act. An offense committed before the effective date of this Act is governed by the law in effect at the time the offense was committed, and the former law is continued in effect for that purpose. For purposes of this section, an offense was committed before the effective date of this Act if any element of the offense occurred before that date."

§ 38.15. Interference With Public Duties

(a) A person commits an offense if the person with criminal negligence interrupts, disrupts, impedes, or otherwise interferes with:

(1) a peace officer while the peace officer is performing a duty or exercising authority imposed or granted by law;

(2) a person who is employed to provide emergency medical services including the transportation of ill or injured persons while the person is performing that duty;

(3) a fire fighter, while the fire fighter is fighting a fire or investigating the cause of a fire;

(4) an animal under the supervision of a peace officer, corrections officer, or jailer, if the person knows the animal is being used for law enforcement, corrections, prison or jail security, or investigative purposes;

(5) the transmission of a communication over a citizen's band radio channel, the purpose of which communication is to inform or inquire about an emergency;

(6) an officer with responsibility for animal control in a county or municipality, while the officer is performing a duty or exercising authority imposed or granted under Chapter 821 or 822, Health and Safety Code; or

(7) a person who:

(A) has responsibility for assessing, enacting, or enforcing public health, environmental, radiation, or safety measures for the state or a county or municipality;

(B) is investigating a particular site as part of the person's responsibilities under Paragraph (A);

(C) is acting in accordance with policies and procedures related to the safety and security of the site described by Paragraph (B); and

(D) is performing a duty or exercising authority imposed or granted under the Agriculture Code, Health and Safety Code, Occupations Code, or Water Code.

(b) An offense under this section is a Class B misdemeanor.

(c) It is a defense to prosecution under Subsection (a)(1) that the conduct engaged in by the defendant was intended to warn a person operating a motor vehicle of the presence of a peace officer who was enforcing Subtitle C, Title 7, Transportation Code.[1]

(d) It is a defense to prosecution under this section that the interruption, disruption, impediment, or interference alleged consisted of speech only.

(e) In this section, "emergency" means a condition or circumstance in which an individual is or is reasonably believed by the person transmitting the communication to be in imminent danger of serious bodily injury or in which property is or is reasonably believed by the person transmitting the communication to be in imminent danger of damage or destruction.

Added by Acts 1989, 71st Leg., ch. 1162, § 1, eff. Sept. 1, 1989. Renumbered from V.T.C.A., Penal Code § 38.16 by Acts 1990, 71st Leg., 6th C.S., ch. 12, § 2(26), eff. Sept. 6, 1990. Renumbered from V.T.C.A., Penal Code § 38.18 and amended by Acts 1993, 73rd Leg., ch. 900, § 1.01, eff. Sept. 1, 1994. Amended by Acts 1997, 75th Leg., ch. 165, § 30.241, eff. Sept. 1, 1997; Acts 2005, 79th Leg., ch. 1212, § 1, eff. Sept. 1, 2005; Acts 2007, 80th Leg., ch. 1251, § 1, eff. Sept. 1, 2007.

[1] V.T.C.A., Transportation Code § 541.001 et seq.

Section 2 of Acts 2007, 80th Leg., ch. 1251 provides:

"The change in law made by this Act applies only to an offense committed on or after the effective date [Sept. 1, 2007] of this Act. An offense committed before the effective date of this Act is covered by the law in effect when the offense was committed, and the former law is continued in effect for that purpose. For purposes of this section, an offense was committed before the effective date of this Act if any element of the offense was committed before that date."

§ 38.151. Interference With Police Service Animals

(a) In this section:

(1) "Area of control" includes a vehicle, trailer, kennel, pen, or yard.

(2) "Handler or rider" means a peace officer, corrections officer, or jailer who is specially trained to use a police service animal for law enforcement, corrections, prison or jail security, or investigative purposes.

(3) "Police service animal" means a dog, horse, or other domesticated animal that is specially trained for use by a handler or rider.

(b) A person commits an offense if the person recklessly:

(1) taunts, torments, or strikes a police service animal;

(2) throws an object or substance at a police service animal;

(3) interferes with or obstructs a police service animal or interferes with or obstructs the handler or rider of a police service animal in a manner that:

(A) inhibits or restricts the handler's or rider's control of the animal; or

(B) deprives the handler or rider of control of the animal;

(4) releases a police service animal from its area of control;

(5) enters the area of control of a police service animal without the effective consent of the handler or rider, including placing food or any other object or substance into that area;

(6) injures or kills a police service animal; or

(7) engages in conduct likely to injure or kill a police service animal, including administering or setting a poison, trap, or any other object or substance.

(c) An offense under this section is:

(1) a Class C misdemeanor if the person commits an offense under Subsection (b)(1);

(2) a Class B misdemeanor if the person commits an offense under Subsection (b)(2);

(3) a Class A misdemeanor if the person commits an offense under Subsection (b)(3), (4), or (5);

(4) except as provided by Subdivision (5), a state jail felony if the person commits an offense under Subsection (b)(6) or (7) by injuring a police service animal or by engaging in conduct likely to injure the animal; or

(5) a felony of the second degree if the person commits an offense under Subsection (b)(6) or (7) by:

(A) killing a police service animal or engaging in conduct likely to kill the animal;

(B) injuring a police service animal in a manner that materially and permanently affects the ability of the animal to perform as a police service animal; or

(C) engaging in conduct likely to injure a police service animal in a manner that would materially and permanently affect the ability of the animal to perform as a police service animal.

Added by Acts 2001, 77th Leg., ch. 979, § 1, eff. Sept. 1, 2001. Amended by Acts 2007, 80th Leg., ch. 1331, § 5, eff. Sept. 1, 2007.

Section 8 of Acts 2007, 80th Leg., ch. 1331 provides:

"The changes in law made to Subsection (c), Section 38.151, Penal Code, by this Act apply only to an offense committed on or after the effective date [Sept. 1, 2007] of this Act. An offense committed before the effective date of this Act is covered by the law in effect when the offense was committed, and the former law is continued in effect for that purpose. For purposes of this section, an offense was committed before the effective date of this Act if any element of the offense was committed before that date."

§ 38.152. Interference with Radio Frequency Licensed to Government Entity

(a) A person commits an offense if, without the effective consent of the law enforcement agency, fire department, or emergency medical services provider, the person intentionally interrupts, disrupts, impedes, jams, or otherwise interferes with a radio frequency that is licensed by the Federal Communications Commission to a government entity and is used by the law enforcement agency, fire department, or emergency medical services provider.

(b) An offense under this section is a Class A misdemeanor, except that the offense is a state jail felony if the actor committed the offense with the intent to:

(1) facilitate the commission of another offense; or

(2) interfere with the ability of a law enforcement agency, a fire department, or an emergency medical services provider to respond to an emergency.

(c) In this section:

(1) "Emergency" has the meaning assigned by Section 38.15.

(2) "Emergency medical services provider" has the meaning assigned by Section 773.003, Health and Safety Code.

(3) "Law enforcement agency" has the meaning assigned by Article 59.01, Code of Criminal Procedure.

(d) If conduct constituting an offense under this section also constitutes an offense under another section of this code, the actor may be prosecuted under either section or under both sections.

Added by Acts 2009, 81st Leg., ch. 1222, § 1, eff. Sept. 1, 2009.

§ 38.16. Preventing Execution of Civil Process

(a) A person commits an offense if he intentionally or knowingly by words or physical action prevents the execution of any process in a civil cause.

(b) It is an exception to the application of this section that the actor evaded service of process by avoiding detection.

(c) An offense under this section is a Class C misdemeanor.

Added by Acts 1995, 74th Leg., ch. 318, § 13, eff. Sept. 1, 1995.

§ 38.17. Failure to Stop or Report Aggravated Sexual Assault of Child

(a) A person, other than a person who has a relationship with a child described by Section 22.04(b), commits an offense if:

(1) the actor observes the commission or attempted commission of an offense prohibited by Section 21.02 or 22.021(a)(2)(B) under circumstances in which a reasonable person would believe that an offense of a sexual or assaultive nature was being committed or was about to be committed against the child;

(2) the actor fails to assist the child or immediately report the commission of the offense to a peace officer or law enforcement agency; and

(3) the actor could assist the child or immediately report the commission of the offense without placing the actor in danger of suffering serious bodily injury or death.

(b) An offense under this section is a Class A misdemeanor.

Added by Acts 1999, 76th Leg., ch. 1344, § 1, eff. Sept. 1, 1999. Amended by Acts 2007, 80th Leg., ch. 593, § 3.50, eff. Sept. 1, 2007.

§ 38.171. Failure to Report Felony

(a) A person commits an offense if the person:

(1) observes the commission of a felony under circumstances in which a reasonable person would believe that an offense had been committed in which serious bodily injury or death may have resulted; and

(2) fails to immediately report the commission of the offense to a peace officer or law enforcement agency under circumstances in which:

(A) a reasonable person would believe that the commission of the offense had not been reported; and

(B) the person could immediately report the commission of the offense without placing himself or herself in danger of suffering serious bodily injury or death.

(b) An offense under this section is a Class A misdemeanor.

Added by Acts 2003, 78th Leg., ch. 1009, § 2, eff. Sept. 1, 2003.

§ 38.18. Use of Accident Report Information and Other Information for Pecuniary Gain

(a) This section applies to:

(1) information described by Section 550.065(a), Transportation Code;

(2) information reported under Chapter 772, Health and Safety Code, other than information that is confidential under that chapter; and

(3) information contained in a dispatch log, a towing record, or a record of a 9–1–1 service provider, other than information that is confidential under Chapter 772, Health and Safety Code.

(b) A person commits an offense if:

(1) the person obtains information described by Subsection (a) from the Department of Public Safety of the State of Texas or other governmental entity; and

(2) the information is subsequently used for the direct solicitation of business or employment for pecuniary gain by:

(A) the person;

(B) an agent or employee of the person; or

(C) the person on whose behalf the information was requested.

(c) A person who employs or engages another to obtain information described by Subsection (a) from the Department of Public Safety or other governmental entity commits an offense if the person subsequently uses the information for direct solicitation of business or employment for pecuniary gain.

(d) An offense under this section is a Class B misdemeanor.

Added by Acts 2001, 77th Leg., ch. 1032, § 1, eff. Sept. 1, 2001.

A former § 38.18 was renumbered as V.T.C.A., Penal Code § 38.15 by Acts 1993, 73rd Leg., ch. 900, § 1.01, eff. Sept. 1, 1994.

§ 38.19. Failure to Provide Notice and Report of Death of Resident of Institution

(a) A superintendent or general manager of an institution commits an offense if, as required by Article 49.24 or 49.25, Code of Criminal Procedure, the person fails to:

(1) provide notice of the death of an individual under the care, custody, or control of or residing in the institution;

(2) submit a report on the death of the individual; or

(3) include in the report material facts known or discovered by the person at the time the report was filed.

(b) An offense under this section is a Class B misdemeanor.

Added by Acts 2003, 78th Leg., ch. 894, § 4, eff. Sept. 1, 2003.

CHAPTER 39. ABUSE OF OFFICE

§ 39.01. Definitions

In this chapter:

(1) "Law relating to a public servant's office or employment" means a law that specifically applies to a person acting in the capacity of a public servant and that directly or indirectly:

(A) imposes a duty on the public servant; or

(B) governs the conduct of the public servant.

(2) "Misuse" means to deal with property contrary to:

(A) an agreement under which the public servant holds the property;

(B) a contract of employment or oath of office of a public servant;

(C) a law, including provisions of the General Appropriations Act specifically relating to government property, that prescribes the manner of custody or disposition of the property; or

(D) a limited purpose for which the property is delivered or received.

Added by Acts 1993, 73rd Leg., ch. 900, § 1.01, eff. Sept. 1, 1994.

§ 39.015. Concurrent Jurisdiction to Prosecute Offenses Under This Chapter

With the consent of the appropriate local county or district attorney, the attorney general has concurrent jurisdiction with that consenting local prosecutor to prosecute an offense under this chapter.

Added by Acts 2007, 80th Leg., ch. 378, § 2, eff. June 15, 2007.

§ 39.02. Abuse of Official Capacity

(a) A public servant commits an offense if, with intent to obtain a benefit or with intent to harm or defraud another, he intentionally or knowingly:

(1) violates a law relating to the public servant's office or employment; or

(2) misuses government property, services, personnel, or any other thing of value belonging to the government that has come into the public servant's custody or possession by virtue of the public servant's office or employment.

(b) An offense under Subsection (a)(1) is a Class A misdemeanor.

(c) An offense under Subsection (a)(2) is:

(1) a Class C misdemeanor if the value of the use of the thing misused is less than $20;

(2) a Class B misdemeanor if the value of the use of the thing misused is $20 or more but less than $500 ;

(3) a Class A misdemeanor if the value of the use of the thing misused is $500 or more but less than $1,500;

(4) a state jail felony if the value of the use of the thing misused is $1,500 or more but less than $20,000;

(5) a felony of the third degree if the value of the use of the thing misused is $20,000 or more but less than $100,000;

(6) a felony of the second degree if the value of the use of the thing misused is $100,000 or more but less than $200,000; or

(7) a felony of the first degree if the value of the use of the thing misused is $200,000 or more.

(d) A discount or award given for travel, such as frequent flyer miles, rental car or hotel discounts, or food coupons, are not things of value belonging to the government for purposes of this section due to the administrative difficulty and cost involved in recapturing the discount or award for a governmental entity.

(e) If separate transactions that violate Subsection (a)(2) are conducted pursuant to one scheme or continuing course of conduct, the conduct may be considered as one offense and the value of the use of the things misused in the transactions may be aggregated in determining the classification of the offense.

(f) The value of the use of a thing of value misused under Subsection (a)(2) may not exceed:

(1) the fair market value of the thing at the time of the offense; or

(2) if the fair market value of the thing cannot be ascertained, the cost of replacing the thing within a reasonable time after the offense.

Acts 1973, 63rd Leg., p. 883, ch. 399, § 1, eff. Jan. 1, 1974. Amended by Acts 1983, 68th Leg., p. 3241, ch. 558, § 7, eff. Sept. 1, 1983. Renumbered from V.T.C.A., Penal Code § 39.01 and amended by Acts 1993, 73rd Leg., ch. 900, § 1.01, eff. Sept. 1, 1994; Acts 2009, 81st Leg., ch. 82, § 1, eff. Sept. 1, 2009.

Section 2 of Acts 2009, 81st Leg., ch. 82 provides:

"The change in law made by this Act applies only to an offense committed on or after the effective date of this Act. An offense committed before the effective date of this Act is covered by the law in effect when the offense was committed, and the former law is continued in effect for that purpose. For purposes of this section, an offense was committed before the effective date of this Act if any element of the offense occurred before that date."

§§ 39.021, 39.022. Renumbered as V.T.C.A., Penal Code §§ 39.04, 39.05 by Acts 1993, 73rd Leg., ch. 900, § 1.01, eff. Sept. 1, 1994

§ 39.03. Official Oppression

(a) A public servant acting under color of his office or employment commits an offense if he:

(1) intentionally subjects another to mistreatment or to arrest, detention, search, seizure, dispossession, assessment, or lien that he knows is unlawful;

(2) intentionally denies or impedes another in the exercise or enjoyment of any right, privilege, power, or immunity, knowing his conduct is unlawful; or

(3) intentionally subjects another to sexual harassment.

(b) For purposes of this section, a public servant acts under color of his office or employment if he acts or purports to act in an official capacity or takes advantage of such actual or purported capacity.

(c) In this section, "sexual harassment" means unwelcome sexual advances, requests for sexual favors, or other verbal or physical conduct of a sexual nature, submission to which is made a term or condition of a person's exercise or enjoyment of any right, privilege, power, or immunity, either explicitly or implicitly.

(d) An offense under this section is a Class A misdemeanor.

Acts 1973, 63rd Leg., p. 883, ch. 399, § 1, eff. Jan. 1, 1974. Amended by Acts 1989, 71st Leg., ch. 1217, § 1, eff. Sept. 1, 1989; Acts 1991, 72nd Leg., ch. 16, § 19.01(34), eff. Aug. 26, 1991. Renumbered from V.T.C.A., Penal Code § 39.02 by Acts 1993, 73rd Leg., ch. 900, § 1.01, eff. Sept. 1, 1994.

§ 39.04. Violations of the Civil Rights of Person in Custody; Improper Sexual Activity With Person in Custody

(a) An official of a correctional facility, an employee of a correctional facility, a person other than an employee who works for compensation at a correctional facility, a volunteer at a correctional facility, or a peace officer commits an offense if the person intentionally:

(1) denies or impedes a person in custody in the exercise or enjoyment of any right, privilege, or immunity knowing his conduct is unlawful; or

(2) engages in sexual contact, sexual intercourse, or deviate sexual intercourse with an individual in custody or, in the case of an individual in the custody of the Texas Youth Commission, employs, authorizes, or induces the individual to engage in sexual conduct or a sexual performance.

(b) An offense under Subsection (a)(1) is a Class A misdemeanor. An offense under Subsection (a)(2) is a state jail felony, except that an offense under Subsection (a)(2) is a felony of the second degree if the offense is committed against:

(1) an individual in the custody of the Texas Youth Commission; or

(2) a juvenile offender detained in or committed to a correctional facility the operation of which is financed primarily with state funds.

(c) This section shall not preclude prosecution for any other offense set out in this code.

(d) The Attorney General of Texas shall have concurrent jurisdiction with law enforcement agencies to investigate violations of this statute involving serious bodily injury or death.

(e) In this section:

(1) "Correctional facility" means:

(A) any place described by Section 1.07(a)(14); or

(B) a "secure correctional facility" or "secure detention facility" as defined by Section 51.02, Family Code.

(2) "Custody" means the detention, arrest, or confinement of an adult offender or the detention or the commitment of a juvenile offender to a facility operated by or under a contract with the Texas Youth Commission or a facility operated by or under contract with a juvenile board.

(3) "Sexual contact," "sexual intercourse," and "deviate sexual intercourse" have the meanings assigned by Section 21.01.

(4) "Sexual conduct" and "performance" have the meanings assigned by Section 43.25.

(5) "Sexual performance" means any performance or part thereof that includes sexual conduct by an individual.

(f) An employee of the Texas Department of Criminal Justice, the Texas Youth Commission, or a local juvenile probation department commits an offense if the employee engages in sexual contact, sexual intercourse, or deviate sexual intercourse with an individual who the employee knows is under the supervision of the department, commission, or probation department but not in the custody of the department, commission, or probation department.

(g) An offense under Subsection (f) is a state jail felony.

(h) It is an affirmative defense to prosecution under Subsection (f) that the actor was the spouse of the individual at the time of the offense.

Added by Acts 1979, 66th Leg., p. 1383, ch. 618, § 1, eff. Sept. 1, 1979. Amended by Acts 1983, 68th Leg., p. 3242, ch. 558, § 8, eff. Sept. 1, 1983; Acts 1987, 70th Leg., ch. 18, § 5, eff. April 15, 1987. Renumbered from V.T.C.A., Penal Code § 39.021 and amended by Acts 1993, 73rd Leg., ch. 900, § 1.01, eff. Sept. 1, 1994. Amended by Acts 1997, 75th Leg., ch. 1406, § 1, eff. Sept. 1, 1997; Acts 1999, 76th Leg., ch. 158, §§ 1 to 3, eff. Sept. 1, 1999; Acts 2001, 77th Leg., ch. 1070, § 1, eff. Sept. 1, 2001; Acts 2001, 77th Leg., ch. 1297, § 69, eff. Sept. 1, 2001; Acts 2007, 80th Leg., ch. 263, §§ 62, 63, eff. June 8, 2007; Acts 2007, 80th Leg., ch. 378, § 3, eff. June 15, 2007; Acts 2007, 80th Leg., ch. 908, § 43, eff. Sept. 1, 2007; Acts 2009, 81st Leg., ch. 87, § 19.003, eff. Sept. 1, 2009; Acts 2009, 81st Leg., ch. 260, § 5, eff. Sept. 1, 2009.

Section 68 of Acts 2007, 80th Leg., ch. 263 provides:

"The change in law made by this Act to Section 39.04, Penal Code, applies only to an offense committed on or after September 1, 2007. An offense committed before September 1, 2007, is governed by the law in effect when the offense was committed, and the former law is continued in effect for that purpose. For purposes of this section, an offense was committed before September 1, 2007, if any element of the offense occurred before that date."

Section 6 of Acts 2009, 81st Leg., ch. 260 provides:

"The change in law made by this Act applies only to an offense committed on or after the effective date [Sept. 1, 2009] of this Act. An offense committed before the effective date of this Act is covered by the law in effect when the offense was committed, and the former law is continued in effect for that purpose. For purposes of this section, an offense was committed before the effective date of this Act if any element of the offense occurred before that date."

§ 39.05. Failure to Report Death of Prisoner

(a) A person commits an offense if the person is required to conduct an investigation and file a report by Article 49.18, Code of Criminal Procedure, and the person fails to investigate the death, fails to file the report as required, or fails to include in a filed report facts known or discovered in the investigation.

(b) A person commits an offense if the person is required by Section 501.055, Government Code, to:

(1) give notice of the death of an inmate and the person fails to give the notice; or

(2) conduct an investigation and file a report and the person:

(A) fails to conduct the investigation or file the report; or

(B) fails to include in the report facts known to the person or discovered by the person in the investigation.

(c) An offense under this section is a Class B misdemeanor.

Added by Acts 1983, 68th Leg., p. 2510, ch. 441, § 2, eff. Sept. 1, 1983. Renumbered from V.T.C.A., Penal Code § 39.022 and amended by Acts 1993, 73rd Leg., ch. 900, § 1.01, eff. Sept. 1, 1994. Amended by Acts 1995, 74th Leg., ch. 321, § 1.104, eff. Sept. 1, 1995.

§ 39.06. Misuse of Official Information

(a) A public servant commits an offense if, in reliance on information to which he has access by virtue of his office or employment and that has not been made public, he:

(1) acquires or aids another to acquire a pecuniary interest in any property, transaction, or enterprise that may be affected by the information;

(2) speculates or aids another to speculate on the basis of the information; or

(3) as a public servant, including as a principal of a school, coerces another into suppressing or failing to report that information to a law enforcement agency.

(b) A public servant commits an offense if with intent to obtain a benefit or with intent to harm or defraud another, he discloses or uses information for a nongovernmental purpose that:

(1) he has access to by means of his office or employment; and

(2) has not been made public.

(c) A person commits an offense if, with intent to obtain a benefit or with intent to harm or defraud another, he solicits or receives from a public servant information that:

(1) the public servant has access to by means of his office or employment; and

(2) has not been made public.

(d) In this section, "information that has not been made public" means any information to which the public does not generally have access, and that is prohibited from disclosure under Chapter 552, Government Code.

(e) Except as provided by Subsection (f), an offense under this section is a felony of the third degree.

(f) An offense under Subsection (a)(3) is a Class C misdemeanor.

Acts 1973, 63rd Leg., p. 883, ch. 399, § 1, eff. Jan. 1, 1974. Amended by Acts 1983, 68th Leg., p. 3243, ch. 558, § 9, eff. Sept. 1, 1983; Acts 1987, 70th Leg., ch. 30, § 1, eff. Sept. 1, 1987; Acts 1987, 70th Leg., 2nd C.S., ch. 43, § 3, eff. Oct. 20, 1987; Acts 1989, 71st Leg., ch. 927, § 1, eff. Aug. 28, 1989. Renumbered from V.T.C.A., Penal Code § 39.03 and amended by Acts 1993, 73rd Leg., ch. 900, § 1.01, eff. Sept. 1, 1994. Amended by Acts 1995, 74th Leg., ch. 76, § 5.95(90), eff. Sept. 1, 1995; Acts 1995, 74th Leg., ch. 76, § 14.52, eff. Sept. 1, 1995.

TITLE 9. OFFENSES AGAINST PUBLIC ORDER AND DECENCY

CHAPTER 42. DISORDERLY CONDUCT AND RELATED OFFENSES

Section

§ 42.01. Disorderly Conduct

(a) A person commits an offense if he intentionally or knowingly:

(1) uses abusive, indecent, profane, or vulgar language in a public place, and the language by its very utterance tends to incite an immediate breach of the peace;

(2) makes an offensive gesture or display in a public place, and the gesture or display tends to incite an immediate breach of the peace;

(3) creates, by chemical means, a noxious and unreasonable odor in a public place;

(4) abuses or threatens a person in a public place in an obviously offensive manner;

(5) makes unreasonable noise in a public place other than a sport shooting range, as defined by Section 250.001, Local Government Code, or in or near a private residence that he has no right to occupy;

(6) fights with another in a public place;

(7) discharges a firearm in a public place other than a public road or a sport shooting range, as defined by Section 250.001, Local Government Code;

(8) displays a firearm or other deadly weapon in a public place in a manner calculated to alarm;

(9) discharges a firearm on or across a public road;

(10) exposes his anus or genitals in a public place and is reckless about whether another may be present who will be offended or alarmed by his act; or

(11) for a lewd or unlawful purpose:

(A) enters on the property of another and looks into a dwelling on the property through any window or other opening in the dwelling;

(B) while on the premises of a hotel or comparable establishment, looks into a guest room not the person's own through a window or other opening in the room; or

(C) while on the premises of a public place, looks into an area such as a restroom or shower stall or changing or dressing room that is designed to provide privacy to a person using the area.

(b) It is a defense to prosecution under Subsection (a)(4) that the actor had significant provocation for his abusive or threatening conduct.

(c) For purposes of this section:

(1) an act is deemed to occur in a public place or near a private residence if it produces its offensive or proscribed consequences in the public place or near a private residence; and

(2) a noise is presumed to be unreasonable if the noise exceeds a decibel level of 85 after the person making the noise receives notice from a magistrate or peace officer that the noise is a public nuisance.

(d) An offense under this section is a Class C misdemeanor unless committed under Subsection (a)(7) or (a)(8), in which event it is a Class B misdemeanor.

(e) It is a defense to prosecution for an offense under Subsection (a)(7) or (9) that the person who discharged the firearm had a reasonable fear of bodily injury to the person or to another by a dangerous wild animal as defined by Section 822.101, Health and Safety Code.

Acts 1973, 63rd Leg., p. 883, ch. 399, § 1, eff. Jan. 1, 1974. Amended by Acts 1977, 65th Leg., p. 181, ch. 89, §§ 1, 2, eff. Aug. 29, 1977; Acts 1983, 68th Leg., p. 4641, ch. 800, § 1, eff. Sept. 1, 1983; Acts 1991, 72nd Leg., ch. 145, § 2, eff. Aug. 26, 1991; Acts 1993, 73rd Leg., ch. 900, § 1.01, eff. Sept. 1, 1994; Acts 1995, 74th Leg., ch. 318, § 14, eff. Sept. 1, 1995; Acts 2001, 77th Leg., ch. 54, § 4, eff. Sept. 1, 2001; Acts 2003, 78th Leg., ch. 389, § 1, eff. Sept. 1, 2003.

§ 42.015. Deleted by Acts 1993, 73rd Leg., ch. 900, § 13.02

§ 42.02. Riot

(a) For the purpose of this section, "riot" means the assemblage of seven or more persons resulting in conduct which:

(1) creates an immediate danger of damage to property or injury to persons;

(2) substantially obstructs law enforcement or other governmental functions or services; or

(3) by force, threat of force, or physical action deprives any person of a legal right or disturbs any person in the enjoyment of a legal right.

(b) A person commits an offense if he knowingly participates in a riot.

(c) It is a defense to prosecution under this section that the assembly was at first lawful and when one of those assembled manifested an intent to engage in conduct enumerated in Subsection (a), the actor retired from the assembly.

(d) It is no defense to prosecution under this section that another who was a party to the riot has been acquitted, has not been arrested, prosecuted, or convicted, has been convicted of a different offense or of a different type or class of offense, or is immune from prosecution.

(e) Except as provided in Subsection (f), an offense under this section is a Class B misdemeanor.

(f) An offense under this section is an offense of the same classification as any offense of a higher grade committed by anyone engaged in the riot if the offense was:

(1) in the furtherance of the purpose of the assembly; or

(2) an offense which should have been anticipated as a result of the assembly.

Acts 1973, 63rd Leg., p. 883, ch. 399, § 1, eff. Jan. 1, 1974. Amended by Acts 1993, 73rd Leg., ch. 900, § 1.01, eff. Sept. 1, 1994.

§ 42.03. Obstructing Highway or Other Passageway

(a) A person commits an offense if, without legal privilege or authority, he intentionally, knowingly, or recklessly:

(1) obstructs a highway, street, sidewalk, railway, waterway, elevator, aisle, hallway, entrance, or exit to which the public or a substantial group of the public has access, or any other place used for the passage of persons, vehicles, or conveyances, regardless of the means of creating the obstruction and whether the obstruction arises from his acts alone or from his acts and the acts of others; or

(2) disobeys a reasonable request or order to move issued by a person the actor knows to be or is informed is a peace officer, a fireman, or a person with authority to control the use of the premises:

(A) to prevent obstruction of a highway or any of those areas mentioned in Subdivision (1); or

(B) to maintain public safety by dispersing those gathered in dangerous proximity to a fire, riot, or other hazard.

(b) For purposes of this section, "obstruct" means to render impassable or to render passage unreasonably inconvenient or hazardous.

(c) An offense under this section is a Class B misdemeanor.

Acts 1973, 63rd Leg., p. 883, ch. 399, § 1, eff. Jan. 1, 1974. Amended by Acts 1993, 73rd Leg., ch. 900, § 1.01, eff. Sept. 1, 1994.

§ 42.04. Defense When Conduct Consists of Speech or Other Expression

(a) If conduct that would otherwise violate Section 42.01(a)(5) (Unreasonable Noise), 42.03 (Obstructing Passageway), or 42.055 (Funeral Service Disruptions) consists of speech or other communication, of gathering with others to hear or observe such speech or communication, or of gathering with others to picket or otherwise express in a nonviolent manner a position on social, economic, political, or religious questions, the actor must be ordered to move, disperse, or otherwise remedy the violation prior to his arrest if he has not yet intentionally harmed the interests of others which those sections seek to protect.

(b) The order required by this section may be given by a peace officer, a fireman, a person with authority to control the use of the premises, or any person directly affected by the violation.

(c) It is a defense to prosecution under Section 42.01(a)(5), 42.03, or 42.055:

(1) that in circumstances in which this section requires an order no order was given;

(2) that an order, if given, was manifestly unreasonable in scope; or

(3) that an order, if given, was promptly obeyed.

Acts 1973, 63rd Leg., p. 883, ch. 399, § 1, eff. Jan. 1, 1974. Amended by Acts 1993, 73rd Leg., ch. 900, § 1.01, eff. Sept. 1, 1994; Acts 2006, 79th Leg., 3rd C.S., ch. 2, § 2, eff. May 19, 2006.

§ 42.05. Disrupting Meeting or Procession

(a) A person commits an offense if, with intent to prevent or disrupt a lawful meeting, procession, or gathering, he obstructs or interferes with the meeting, procession, or gathering by physical action or verbal utterance.

(b) An offense under this section is a Class B misdemeanor.

Acts 1973, 63rd Leg., p. 883, ch. 399, § 1, eff. Jan. 1, 1974. Amended by Acts 1993, 73rd Leg., ch. 900, § 1.01, eff. Sept. 1, 1994.

§ 42.055. Funeral Service Disruptions

(a) In this section:

(1) "Facility" means a building at which any portion of a funeral service takes place, including a funeral parlor, mortuary, private home, or established place of worship.

(2) "Funeral service" means a ceremony, procession, or memorial service, including a wake or viewing, held in connection with the burial or cremation of the dead.

(3) "Picketing" means:

(A) standing, sitting, or repeated walking, riding, driving, or other similar action by a person displaying or carrying a banner, placard, or sign;

(B) engaging in loud singing, chanting, whistling, or yelling, with or without noise amplification through a device such as a bullhorn or microphone; or

(C) blocking access to a facility or cemetery being used for a funeral service.

(b) A person commits an offense if, during the period beginning one hour before the service begins and ending one hour after the service is completed, the person engages in picketing within 1,000 feet of a facility or cemetery being used for a funeral service.

(c) An offense under this section is a Class B misdemeanor.

Added by Acts 2006, 79th Leg., 3rd C.S., ch. 2, § 1, eff. May 19, 2006. Amended by Acts 2007, 80th Leg., ch. 256, § 1, eff. June 4, 2007.

Section 2 of Acts 2007, 80th Leg., ch. 256 provides:

"The change in law made by this Act applies only to an offense committed on or after the effective date [June 4, 2007] of this Act. An offense committed before the effective date of this Act is covered by the law in effect when the offense was committed, and the former law is continued in effect for that purpose. For the purposes of this section, an offense is committed before the effective date of this Act if any element of the offense occurs before that date."

§ 42.06. False Alarm or Report

(a) A person commits an offense if he knowingly initiates, communicates or circulates a report of a present, past, or future bombing, fire, offense, or other emergency that he knows is false or baseless and that would ordinarily:

(1) cause action by an official or volunteer agency organized to deal with emergencies;

(2) place a person in fear of imminent serious bodily injury; or

(3) prevent or interrupt the occupation of a building, room, place of assembly, place to which the public has access, or aircraft, automobile, or other mode of conveyance.

(b) An offense under this section is a Class A misdemeanor unless the false report is of an emergency involving a public primary or secondary school, public communications, public transportation, public water, gas, or power supply or other public service, in which event the offense is a state jail felony.

Acts 1973, 63rd Leg., p. 883, ch. 399, § 1, eff. Jan. 1, 1974. Amended by Acts 1979, 66th Leg., p. 1114, ch. 530, § 4, eff. Aug. 27, 1979; Acts 1993, 73rd Leg., ch. 900, § 1.01, eff. Sept. 1, 1994.

§ 42.061. Silent or Abusive Calls to 9–1–1 Service

(a) In this section "9–1–1 service" and "public safety answering point" or "PSAP" have the meanings assigned by Section 772.001, Health and Safety Code.

(b) A person commits an offense if the person makes a telephone call to 9–1–1 when there is not an emergency and knowingly or intentionally:

(1) remains silent; or

(2) makes abusive or harassing statements to a PSAP employee.

(c) A person commits an offense if the person knowingly permits a telephone under the person's control to be used by another person in a manner described in Subsection (b).

(d) An offense under this section is a Class B misdemeanor.

Added by Acts 1989, 71st Leg., ch. 582, § 1, eff. Sept. 1, 1989. Amended by Acts 1991, 72nd Leg., ch. 14, § 284(2), eff. Sept. 1, 1991; Acts 1993, 73rd Leg., ch. 900, § 1.01, eff. Sept. 1, 1994.

§ 42.062. Interference With Emergency Telephone Call

(a) An individual commits an offense if the individual knowingly prevents or interferes with another individual's ability to place an emergency telephone call or to request assistance in an emergency from a law enforcement agency, medical facility, or other agency or entity the primary purpose of which is to provide for the safety of individuals.

(b) An individual commits an offense if the individual recklessly renders unusable a telephone that would otherwise be used by another individual to place an emergency telephone call or to request assistance in an emergency from a law enforcement agency, medical facility, or other agency or entity the primary purpose of which is to provide for the safety of individuals.

(c) An offense under this section is a Class A misdemeanor, except that the offense is a state jail felony if the actor has previously been convicted under this section.

(d) In this section, "emergency" means a condition or circumstance in which any individual is or is reasonably believed by the individual making a telephone call to be in fear of imminent assault or in which property is or is reasonably believed by the individual making the telephone call to be in imminent danger of damage or destruction.

Added by Acts 2001, 77th Leg., ch. 690, § 1, eff. Sept. 1, 2001. Amended by Acts 2003, 78th Leg., ch. 460, § 1, eff. Sept. 1, 2003; Acts 2003, 78th Leg., ch. 1164, § 1, eff. Sept. 1, 2003.

§ 42.07. Harassment

(a) A person commits an offense if, with intent to harass, annoy, alarm, abuse, torment, or embarrass another, he:

(1) initiates communication by telephone, in writing, or by electronic communication and in the course of the communication makes a comment, request, suggestion, or proposal that is obscene;

(2) threatens, by telephone, in writing, or by electronic communication, in a manner reasonably likely to alarm the person receiving the threat, to inflict bodily injury on the person or to commit a felony against the person, a member of his family or household, or his property;

(3) conveys, in a manner reasonably likely to alarm the person receiving the report, a false report, which is known by the conveyor to be false, that another person has suffered death or serious bodily injury;

(4) causes the telephone of another to ring repeatedly or makes repeated telephone communications anonymously or in a manner reasonably likely to harass, annoy, alarm, abuse, torment, embarrass, or offend another;

(5) makes a telephone call and intentionally fails to hang up or disengage the connection;

(6) knowingly permits a telephone under the person's control to be used by another to commit an offense under this section; or

(7) sends repeated electronic communications in a manner reasonably likely to harass, annoy, alarm, abuse, torment, embarrass, or offend another.

(b) In this section:

(1) "Electronic communication" means a transfer of signs, signals, writing, images, sounds, data, or intelligence of any nature transmitted in whole or in part by a wire, radio, electromagnetic, photoelectronic, or photo-optical system. The term includes:

(A) a communication initiated by electronic mail, instant message, network call, or facsimile machine; and

(B) a communication made to a pager.

(2) "Family" and "household" have the meaning assigned by Chapter 71, Family Code.

(3) "Obscene" means containing a patently offensive description of or a solicitation to commit an ultimate sex act, including sexual intercourse, masturbation, cunnilingus, fellatio, or anilingus, or a description of an excretory function.

(c) An offense under this section is a Class B misdemeanor, except that the offense is a Class A misdemeanor if the actor has previously been convicted under this section.

Acts 1973, 63rd Leg., p. 883, ch. 399, § 1, eff. Jan. 1, 1974. Amended by Acts 1983, 68th Leg., p. 2204, ch. 411, § 1, eff. Sept. 1, 1983; Acts 1993, 73rd Leg., ch. 10, § 1, eff. March 19, 1993; Acts 1993, 73rd Leg., ch. 900, § 1.01, eff. Sept. 1, 1994; Acts 1995, 74th Leg., ch. 657, § 1, eff. June 14, 1995; Acts 1999, 76th Leg., ch. 62, § 15.02(d), eff. Sept. 1, 1999; Acts 2001, 77th Leg., ch. 1222, § 1, eff. Sept. 1, 2001.

Subsection (a)(7) of this section was declared unconstitutional by Karenev v. State, 258 S.W.3d 210 (Tex.App.-Fort Worth, 2008)

§ 42.071. Repealed by Acts 1997, 75th Leg., ch. 1, § 10, eff. Jan. 28, 1997

§ 42.072. Stalking

(a) A person commits an offense if the person, on more than one occasion and pursuant to the same scheme or course of conduct that is directed specifically at another person, knowingly engages in conduct, including following the other person, that:

(1) the actor knows or reasonably believes the other person will regard as threatening:

(A) bodily injury or death for the other person;

(B) bodily injury or death for a member of the other person's family or household; or

(C) that an offense will be committed against the other person's property;

(2) causes the other person or a member of the other person's family or household to be placed in fear of bodily injury or death or fear that an offense will be committed against the other person's property; and

(3) would cause a reasonable person to fear:

(A) bodily injury or death for himself or herself;

(B) bodily injury or death for a member of the person's family or household; or

(C) that an offense will be committed against the person's property.

(b) An offense under this section is a felony of the third degree, except that the offense is a felony of the second degree if the actor has previously been convicted under this section.

(c) In this section, "family," "household," and "member of a household" have the meanings assigned by Chapter 71, Family Code.

Added by Acts 1997, 75th Leg., ch. 1, § 1, eff. Jan. 28, 1997. Amended by Acts 1999, 76th Leg., ch. 62, § 15.02(e), eff. Sept. 1, 1999; Acts 2001, 77th Leg., ch. 1222, § 2, eff. Sept. 1, 2001.

§ 42.08. Abuse of Corpse

(a) A person commits an offense if the person, without legal authority, knowingly:

(1) disinters, disturbs, damages, dissects, in whole or in part, carries away, or treats in an offensive manner a human corpse;

(2) conceals a human corpse knowing it to be illegally disinterred;

(3) sells or buys a human corpse or in any way traffics in a human corpse;

(4) transmits or conveys, or procures to be transmitted or conveyed, a human corpse to a place outside the state; or

(5) vandalizes, damages, or treats in an offensive manner the space in which a human corpse has been interred or otherwise permanently laid to rest.

(b) An offense under this section is a Class A misdemeanor.

(c) In this section, "human corpse" includes:

(1) any portion of a human corpse;

(2) the cremated remains of a human corpse; or

(3) any portion of the cremated remains of a human corpse.

(d) If conduct constituting an offense under this section also constitutes an offense under another section of this code, the actor may be prosecuted under either section or both sections.

(e) It is a defense to prosecution under this section that the actor:

(1) as a member or agent of a cemetery organization, removed or damaged anything that had been placed in or on any portion of the organization's cemetery in violation of the rules of the organization; or

(2) removed anything:

(A) placed in the cemetery in violation of the rules of the cemetery organization; or

(B) placed in the cemetery by or with the cemetery organization's consent but that, in the organization's judgment, had become wrecked, unsightly, or dilapidated.

(f) In this section, "cemetery" and "cemetery organization" have the meanings assigned by Section 711.001, Health and Safety Code.

Acts 1973, 63rd Leg., p. 883, ch. 399, § 1, eff. Jan. 1, 1974. Renumbered from V.T.C.A., Penal Code § 42.10 by Acts 1993, 73rd Leg., ch. 900, § 1.01, eff. Sept. 1, 1994. Amended by Acts 2005, 79th Leg., ch. 1025, § 1, eff. June 18, 2005.

§ 42.09. Cruelty to Livestock Animals

(a) A person commits an offense if the person intentionally or knowingly:

(1) tortures a livestock animal;

(2) fails unreasonably to provide necessary food, water, or care for a livestock animal in the person's custody;

(3) abandons unreasonably a livestock animal in the person's custody;

(4) transports or confines a livestock animal in a cruel and unusual manner;

(5) administers poison to a livestock animal, other than cattle, horses, sheep, swine, or goats, belonging to another without legal authority or the owner's effective consent;

(6) causes one livestock animal to fight with another livestock animal or with an animal as defined by Section 42.092;

(7) uses a live livestock animal as a lure in dog race training or in dog coursing on a racetrack;

(8) trips a horse; or

(9) seriously overworks a livestock animal.

(b) In this section:

(1) "Abandon" includes abandoning a livestock animal in the person's custody without making reasonable arrangements for assumption of custody by another person.

(2) "Cruel manner" includes a manner that causes or permits unjustified or unwarranted pain or suffering.

(3) "Custody" includes responsibility for the health, safety, and welfare of a livestock animal subject to the person's care and control, regardless of ownership of the livestock animal.

(4) "Depredation" has the meaning assigned by Section 71.001, Parks and Wildlife Code.

(5) "Livestock animal" means:

(A) cattle, sheep, swine, goats, ratites, or poultry commonly raised for human consumption;

(B) a horse, pony, mule, donkey, or hinny;

(C) native or nonnative hoofstock raised under agriculture practices; or

(D) native or nonnative fowl commonly raised under agricultural practices.

(6) "Necessary food, water, or care" includes food, water, or care provided to the extent required to maintain the livestock animal in a state of good health.

(7) "Torture" includes any act that causes unjustifiable pain or suffering.

(8) "Trip" means to use an object to cause a horse to fall or lose its balance.

(c) An offense under Subsection (a)(2), (3), (4), or (9) is a Class A misdemeanor, except that the offense is a state jail felony if the person has previously been convicted two times under this section, two times under Section 42.092, or one time under this section and one time under Section 42.092. An offense under Subsection (a)(1), (5), (6), (7), or (8) is a state jail felony, except that the offense is a felony of the third degree if the person has previously been convicted two times under this section, two times under Section 42.092, or one time under this section and one time under Section 42.092.

(d) It is a defense to prosecution under Subsection (a)(8) that the actor tripped the horse for the purpose of identifying the ownership of the horse or giving veterinary care to the horse.

(e) It is a defense to prosecution for an offense under this section that the actor was engaged in bona fide experimentation for scientific research.

(f) It is an exception to the application of this section that the conduct engaged in by the actor is a generally accepted and otherwise lawful:

(1) form of conduct occurring solely for the purpose of or in support of:

(A) fishing, hunting, or trapping; or

(B) wildlife management, wildlife or depredation control, or shooting preserve practices as regulated by state and federal law; or

(2) animal husbandry or agriculture practice involving livestock animals.

(g) This section does not create a civil cause of action for damages or enforcement of this section.

Acts 1973, 63rd Leg., p. 883, ch. 399, § 1, eff. Jan. 1, 1974. Amended by Acts 1975, 64th Leg., p. 917, ch. 342, § 12, eff. Sept. 1, 1975; Acts 1985, 69th Leg., ch. 549, § 1, eff. Sept. 1, 1985; Acts 1991, 72nd Leg., ch. 78, § 1, eff. Aug. 26, 1991. Renumbered from V.T.C.A., Penal Code § 42.11 and amended by Acts 1993, 73rd Leg., ch. 900, § 1.01, eff. Sept. 1, 1994. Amended by Acts 1995, 74th Leg., ch. 318, § 15, eff. Sept. 1, 1995; Acts 1997, 75th Leg., ch. 1283, § 1, eff. Sept. 1, 1997; Acts 2001, 77th Leg., ch. 54, § 3, eff. Sept. 1, 2001; Acts 2001, 77th Leg., ch. 450, § 1, eff. Sept. 1, 2001; Acts 2003, 78th Leg., ch. 1275, § 2(116), eff. Sept. 1, 2003; Acts 2007, 80th Leg., ch. 886, § 1, eff. Sept. 1, 2007.

Section 7 of Acts 2007, 80th Leg., ch. 886 provides:

"The change in law made by this Act applies only to an offense committed on or after the effective date of this Act. An offense committed before the effective date of this Act is governed by the law in effect when the offense was committed, and the former law is continued in effect for that purpose. For purposes of this section, an offense was committed before the effective date of this Act if any element of the offense was committed before that date."

§ 42.091. Attack on Assistance Animal

(a) A person commits an offense if the person intentionally, knowingly, or recklessly attacks, injures, or kills an assistance animal.

(b) A person commits an offense if the person intentionally, knowingly, or recklessly incites or permits an animal owned by or otherwise in the custody of the actor to attack, injure, or kill an assistance animal and, as a result of the person's conduct, the assistance animal is attacked, injured, or killed.

(c) An offense under this section is a:

(1) Class A misdemeanor if the actor or an animal owned by or otherwise in the custody of the actor attacks an assistance animal;

(2) state jail felony if the actor or an animal owned by or otherwise in the custody of the actor injures an assistance animal; or

(3) felony of the third degree if the actor or an animal owned by or otherwise in the custody of the actor kills an assistance animal.

(d) A court shall order a defendant convicted of an offense under Subsection (a) to make restitution to the owner of the assistance animal for:

(1) related veterinary or medical bills;

(2) the cost of:

(A) replacing the assistance animal; or

(B) retraining an injured assistance animal by an organization generally recognized by agencies involved in the rehabilitation of persons with disabilities as reputable and competent to provide special equipment for or special training to an animal to help a person with a disability; and

(3) any other expense reasonably incurred as a result of the offense.

(e) In this section:

(1) "Assistance animal" has the meaning assigned by Section 121.002, Human Resources Code.

(2) "Custody" has the meaning assigned by Section 42. 09.

Added by Acts 2003, 78th Leg., ch. 710, § 2, eff. Sept. 1, 2003.

§ 42.092. Cruelty to Nonlivestock Animals

(a) In this section:

(1) "Abandon" includes abandoning an animal in the person's custody without making reasonable arrangements for assumption of custody by another person.

(2) "Animal" means a domesticated living creature, including any stray or feral cat or dog, and a wild living creature previously captured. The term does not include an uncaptured wild living creature or a livestock animal.

(3) "Cruel manner" includes a manner that causes or permits unjustified or unwarranted pain or suffering.

(4) "Custody" includes responsibility for the health, safety, and welfare of an animal subject to the person's care and control, regardless of ownership of the animal.

(5) "Depredation" has the meaning assigned by Section 71.001, Parks and Wildlife Code.

(6) "Livestock animal" has the meaning assigned by Section 42.09.

(7) "Necessary food, water, care, or shelter" includes food, water, care, or shelter provided to the extent required to maintain the animal in a state of good health.

(8) "Torture" includes any act that causes unjustifiable pain or suffering.

(b) A person commits an offense if the person intentionally, knowingly, or recklessly:

(1) tortures an animal or in a cruel manner kills or causes serious bodily injury to an animal;

(2) without the owner's effective consent, kills, administers poison to, or causes serious bodily injury to an animal;

(3) fails unreasonably to provide necessary food, water, care, or shelter for an animal in the person's custody;

(4) abandons unreasonably an animal in the person's custody;

(5) transports or confines an animal in a cruel manner;

(6) without the owner's effective consent, causes bodily injury to an animal;

(7) causes one animal to fight with another animal, if either animal is not a dog;

(8) uses a live animal as a lure in dog race training or in dog coursing on a racetrack; or

(9) seriously overworks an animal.

(c) An offense under Subsection (b)(3), (4), (5), (6), or (9) is a Class A misdemeanor, except that the offense is a state jail felony if the person has previously been convicted two times under this section, two times under Section 42.09, or one time under this section and one time under Section 42.09. An offense under Subsection (b)(1), (2), (7), or (8) is a state jail felony, except that the offense is a felony of the third degree if the person has previously been convicted two times under this section, two times under Section 42.09, or one time under this section and one time under Section 42.09.

(d) It is a defense to prosecution under this section that:

(1) the actor had a reasonable fear of bodily injury to the actor or to another person by a dangerous wild animal as defined by Section 822.101, Health and Safety Code; or

(2) the actor was engaged in bona fide experimentation for scientific research.

(e) It is a defense to prosecution under Subsection (b)(2) or (6) that:

(1) the animal was discovered on the person's property in the act of or after injuring or killing the person's livestock animals or damaging the person's crops and that the person killed or injured the animal at the time of this discovery; or

(2) the person killed or injured the animal within the scope of the person's employment as a public servant or in furtherance of activities or operations associated with electricity transmission or distribution, electricity generation or operations associated with the generation of electricity, or natural gas delivery.

(f) It is an exception to the application of this section that the conduct engaged in by the actor is a generally accepted and otherwise lawful:

(1) form of conduct occurring solely for the purpose of or in support of:

(A) fishing, hunting, or trapping; or

(B) wildlife management, wildlife or depredation control, or shooting preserve practices as regulated by state and federal law; or

(2) animal husbandry or agriculture practice involving livestock animals.

(g) This section does not create a civil cause of action for damages or enforcement of the section.

Added by Acts 2007, 80th Leg., ch. 886, § 2, eff. Sept. 1, 2007.

Section 7 of Acts 2007, 80th Leg., ch. 886 provides:

"The change in law made by this Act applies only to an offense committed on or after the effective date of this Act. An offense committed before the effective date of this Act is governed by the law in effect when the offense was committed, and the former law is continued in effect for that purpose. For purposes of this section, an offense was committed before the effective date of this Act if any element of the offense was committed before that date."

§ 42.10. Dog Fighting

(a) A person commits an offense if the person intentionally or knowingly:

(1) causes a dog to fight with another dog;

(2) participates in the earnings of or operates a facility used for dog fighting;

(3) uses or permits another to use any real estate, building, room, tent, arena, or other property for dog fighting;

(4) owns or possesses dog-fighting equipment with the intent that the equipment be used to train a dog for dog fighting or in furtherance of dog fighting;

(5) owns or trains a dog with the intent that the dog be used in an exhibition of dog fighting; or

(6) attends as a spectator an exhibition of dog fighting.

(b) In this section:

(1) "Dog fighting" means any situation in which one dog attacks or fights with another dog.

(2) "Dog-fighting equipment" has the meaning assigned by Article 18.18(g), Code of Criminal Procedure.

(c) A conviction under Subsection (a)(2) or (3) may be had upon the uncorroborated testimony of a party to the offense.

(d) It is a defense to prosecution under Subsection (a)(1) that the actor caused a dog to fight with another dog to protect livestock, other property, or a person from the other dog, and for no other purpose.

(e) An offense under Subsection (a)(4), (5), or (6) is a Class A misdemeanor. An offense under Subsection (a)(1), (2), or (3) is a state jail felony.

Added by Acts 1983, 68th Leg., p. 1610, ch. 305, § 1, eff. Sept. 1, 1983. Renumbered from V.T.C.A., Penal Code § 42.111 and amended by Acts 1993, 73rd Leg., ch. 900, § 1.01, eff. Sept. 1, 1994; Acts 2007, 80th Leg., ch. 644, § 1, eff. Sept. 1, 2007; Acts 2009, 81st Leg., ch. 1357, § 1, eff. Sept. 1, 2009.

Section 2 of Acts 2007, 80th Leg., ch. 644 provides:

"The change in law made by this Act applies only to an offense committed on or after the effective date of this Act [Sept. 1, 2007]. An offense committed before the effective date of this Act is covered by the law in effect when the offense was committed, and the former law is continued in effect for that purpose. For purposes of this section, an offense was committed before the effective date of this Act if any element of the offense was committed before that date."

Section 5 of Acts 2009, 81st Leg., ch. 1357 provides:

"The changes in law made by this Act apply only to an offense committed on or after the effective date [Sept. 1, 2009] of this Act or to the forfeiture of property used in the commission of that offense. An offense committed before the effective date of this Act, or the forfeiture of property used in the commission of that offense, is governed by the law in effect when the offense was committed, and the former law is continued in effect for that purpose. For purposes of this section, an offense was committed before the effective date of this Act if any element of the offense occurred before that date."

§ 42.11. Destruction of Flag

(a) A person commits an offense if the person intentionally or knowingly damages, defaces, mutilates, or burns the flag of the United States or the State of Texas.

(b) In this section, "flag" means an emblem, banner, or other standard or a copy of an emblem, standard, or banner that is an official or commonly recognized depiction of the flag of the United States or of this state and is capable of being flown from a staff of any character or size. The term does not include a representation of a flag on a written or printed document, a periodical, stationery, a painting or photograph, or an article of clothing or jewelry.

(c) It is an exception to the application of this section that the act that would otherwise constitute an offense is done in conformity with statutes of the United States or of this state relating to the proper disposal of damaged flags.

(d) An offense under this section is a Class A misdemeanor.

Added by Acts 1989, 71st Leg., 1st C.S., ch. 27, § 1, eff. Sept. 1, 1989. Renumbered from V.T.C.A., Penal Code § 42.14 by Acts 1993, 73rd Leg., ch. 900, § 1.01, eff. Sept. 1, 1994.

§ 42.111. Renumbered as V.T.C.A., Penal Code § 42.10 by Acts 1993, 73rd Leg., ch. 900, § 1.01, eff. Sept. 1, 1994

§ 42.12. Discharge of Firearm in Certain Municipalities

(a) A person commits an offense if the person recklessly discharges a firearm inside the corporate limits of a municipality having a population of 100,000 or more.

(b) An offense under this section is a Class A misdemeanor.

(c) If conduct constituting an offense under this section also constitutes an offense under another section of this code, the person may be prosecuted under either section.

(d) Subsection (a) does not affect the authority of a municipality to enact an ordinance which prohibits the discharge of a firearm.

Added by Acts 1995, 74th Leg., ch. 663, § 1, eff. Sept. 1, 1995.

§ 42.13. Use of Laser Pointers

(a) A person commits an offense if the person knowingly directs a light from a laser pointer at a uniformed safety officer, including a peace officer, security guard, firefighter, emergency medical service worker, or other uniformed municipal, state, or federal officer.

(b) In this section, "laser pointer" means a device that emits a visible light amplified by the stimulated emission of radiation.

(c) An offense under this section is a Class C misdemeanor.

Added by Acts 2003, 78th Leg., ch. 467, § 1, eff. Sept. 1, 2003.

§ 42.14. Illumination of Aircraft by Intense Light

(a) A person commits an offense if:

(1) the person intentionally directs a light from a laser pointer or other light source at an aircraft; and

(2) the light has an intensity sufficient to impair the operator's ability to control the aircraft.

(b) It is an affirmative defense to prosecution under this section that the actor was using the light to send an emergency distress signal.

(c) An offense under this section is a Class C misdemeanor unless the intensity of the light impairs the operator's ability to control the aircraft, in which event the offense is a Class A misdemeanor.

(d) If conduct that constitutes an offense under this section also constitutes an offense under any other law, the actor may be prosecuted under this section or the other law.

(e) In this section, "laser pointer" has the meaning assigned by Section 42.13.

Added by Acts 2007, 80th Leg., ch. 680, § 1, eff. Sept. 1, 2007.

CHAPTER 43. PUBLIC INDECENCY

SUBCHAPTER A. PROSTITUTION

SUBCHAPTER A. PROSTITUTION

§ 43.01. Definitions

In this subchapter:

(1) "Deviate sexual intercourse" means any contact between the genitals of one person and the mouth or anus of another person.

(2) "Prostitution" means the offense defined in Section 43.02.

(3) "Sexual contact" means any touching of the anus, breast, or any part of the genitals of another person with intent to arouse or gratify the sexual desire of any person.

(4) "Sexual conduct" includes deviate sexual intercourse, sexual contact, and sexual intercourse.

(5) "Sexual intercourse" means any penetration of the female sex organ by the male sex organ.

Acts 1973, 63rd Leg., p. 883, ch. 399, § 1, eff. Jan. 1, 1974. Amended by Acts 1979, 66th Leg., p. 373, ch. 168, § 2, eff. Aug. 27, 1979; Acts 1993, 73rd Leg., ch. 900, § 1.01, eff. Sept. 1, 1994.

§ 43.02. Prostitution

(a) A person commits an offense if he knowingly:

(1) offers to engage, agrees to engage, or engages in sexual conduct for a fee; or

(2) solicits another in a public place to engage with him in sexual conduct for hire.

(b) An offense is established under Subsection (a)(1) whether the actor is to receive or pay a fee. An offense is established under Subsection (a)(2) whether the actor solicits a person to hire him or offers to hire the person solicited.

(c) An offense under this section is a Class B misdemeanor, unless the actor has previously been convicted one or two times of an offense under this section, in which event it is a Class A misdemeanor. If the actor has previously been convicted three or more times of an offense under this section, the offense is a state jail felony.

(d) It is a defense to prosecution under this section that the actor engaged in the conduct that constitutes the offense because the actor was the victim of conduct that constitutes an offense under Section 20A.02.

Acts 1973, 63rd Leg., p. 883, ch. 399, § 1, eff. Jan. 1, 1974. Amended by Acts 1977, 65th Leg., p. 757, ch. 286, § 1, eff. May 27, 1977; Acts 1993, 73rd Leg., ch. 900, § 1.01, eff. Sept. 1, 1994; Acts 2001, 77th Leg., ch. 987, § 1, eff. Sept. 1, 2001; Acts 2009, 81st Leg., ch. 1002, § 8, eff. Sept. 1, 2009.

Section 10(d) of Acts 2009, 81st Leg., ch. 1002 provides:

"(d) The changes in law made by this Act to Sections 20A.02, 43.02, and 43. 05, Penal Code, apply only to an offense committed on or after the effective date [Sept. 1, 2009] of this Act. An offense committed before the effective date of this Act is covered by the law in effect when the offense was committed, and the former law is continued in effect for that purpose. For purposes of this section, an offense was committed before the effective date of this Act if any element of the offense was committed before that date."

§ 43.03. Promotion of Prostitution

(a) A person commits an offense if, acting other than as a prostitute receiving compensation for personally rendered prostitution services, he or she knowingly:

(1) receives money or other property pursuant to an agreement to participate in the proceeds of prostitution; or

(2) solicits another to engage in sexual conduct with another person for compensation.

(b) An offense under this section is a Class A misdemeanor.

Acts 1973, 63rd Leg., p. 883, ch. 399, § 1, eff. Jan. 1, 1974. Amended by Acts 1977, 65th Leg., p. 758, ch. 287, § 1, eff. May 27, 1977; Acts 1993, 73rd Leg., ch. 900, § 1.01, eff. Sept. 1, 1994.

§ 43.04. Aggravated Promotion of Prostitution

(a) A person commits an offense if he knowingly owns, invests in, finances, controls, supervises, or manages a prostitution enterprise that uses two or more prostitutes.

(b) An offense under this section is a felony of the third degree.

Acts 1973, 63rd Leg., p. 883, ch. 399, § 1, eff. Jan. 1, 1974. Amended by Acts 1993, 73rd Leg., ch. 900, § 1.01, eff. Sept. 1, 1994.

§ 43.05. Compelling Prostitution

(a) A person commits an offense if the person knowingly:

(1) causes another by force, threat, or fraud to commit prostitution; or

(2) causes by any means a child younger than 18 years to commit prostitution, regardless of whether the actor knows the age of the child at the time the actor commits the offense.

(b) An offense under this section is a felony of the second degree.

Acts 1973, 63rd Leg., p. 883, ch. 399, § 1, eff. Jan. 1, 1974. Amended by Acts 1993, 73rd Leg., ch. 900, § 1.01, eff. Sept. 1, 1994; Acts 2009, 81st Leg., ch. 1002, § 9, eff. Sept. 1, 2009.

Section 10(d) of Acts 2009, 81st Leg., ch. 1002 provides:

"(d) The changes in law made by this Act to Sections 20A.02, 43.02, and 43. 05, Penal Code, apply only to an offense committed on or after the effective date [Sept. 1, 2009] of this Act. An offense committed before the effective date of this Act is covered by the law in effect when the offense was committed, and the former law is continued in effect for that purpose. For purposes of this section, an offense was committed before the effective date of this Act if any element of the offense was committed before that date."

§ 43.06. Accomplice Witness; Testimony and Immunity

(a) A party to an offense under this subchapter may be required to furnish evidence or testify about the offense.

(b) A party to an offense under this subchapter may not be prosecuted for any offense about which he is required to furnish evidence or testify, and the evidence and testimony may not be used against the party in any adjudicatory proceeding except a prosecution for aggravated perjury.

(c) For purposes of this section, "adjudicatory proceeding" means a proceeding before a court or any other agency of government in which the legal rights, powers, duties, or privileges of specified parties are determined.

(d) A conviction under this subchapter may be had upon the uncorroborated testimony of a party to the offense.

Acts 1973, 63rd Leg., p. 883, ch. 399, § 1, eff. Jan. 1, 1974. Amended by Acts 1993, 73rd Leg., ch. 900, § 1.01, eff. Sept. 1, 1994.

SUBCHAPTER B. OBSCENITY

§ 43.21. Definitions

(a) In this subchapter:

(1) "Obscene" means material or a performance that:

(A) the average person, applying contemporary community standards, would find that taken as a whole appeals to the prurient interest in sex;

(B) depicts or describes:

(i) patently offensive representations or descriptions of ultimate sexual acts, normal or perverted, actual or simulated, including sexual intercourse, sodomy, and sexual bestiality; or

(ii) patently offensive representations or descriptions of masturbation, excretory functions, sadism, masochism, lewd exhibition of the genitals, the male or female genitals in a state of sexual stimulation or arousal, covered male genitals in a discernibly turgid state or a device designed and marketed as useful primarily for stimulation of the human genital organs; and

(C) taken as a whole, lacks serious literary, artistic, political, and scientific value.

(2) "Material" means anything tangible that is capable of being used or adapted to arouse interest, whether through the medium of reading, observation, sound, or in any other manner, but does not include an actual three dimensional obscene device.

(3) "Performance" means a play, motion picture, dance, or other exhibition performed before an audience.

(4) "Patently offensive" means so offensive on its face as to affront current community standards of decency.

(5) "Promote" means to manufacture, issue, sell, give, provide, lend, mail, deliver, transfer, transmit, publish, distribute, circulate, disseminate, present, exhibit, or advertise, or to offer or agree to do the same.

(6) "Wholesale promote" means to manufacture, issue, sell, provide, mail, deliver, transfer, transmit, publish, distribute, circulate, disseminate, or to offer or agree to do the same for purpose of resale.

(7) "Obscene device" means a device including a dildo or artificial vagina, designed or marketed as useful primarily for the stimulation of human genital organs.

(b) If any of the depictions or descriptions of sexual conduct described in this section are declared by a court of competent jurisdiction to be unlawfully included herein, this declaration shall not invalidate this section as to other patently offensive sexual conduct included herein.

Acts 1973, 63rd Leg., p. 883, ch. 399, § 1, eff. Jan. 1, 1974. Amended by Acts 1975, 64th Leg., p. 372, ch. 163, § 1, eff. Sept. 1, 1975; Acts 1979, 66th Leg., p. 1974, ch. 778, § 1, eff. Sept. 1, 1979; Acts 1993, 73rd Leg., ch. 900, § 1.01, eff. Sept. 1, 1994.

This section has been declared unconstitutional by Reliable Consultants, Inc. v. Earle, 517 F.3d 738, C.A.5 (Tex.), 2008.

§ 43.22. Obscene Display or Distribution

(a) A person commits an offense if he intentionally or knowingly displays or distributes an obscene photograph, drawing, or similar visual representation or other obscene material and is reckless about whether a person is present who will be offended or alarmed by the display or distribution.

(b) An offense under this section is a Class C misdemeanor.

Acts 1973, 63rd Leg., p. 883, ch. 399, § 1, eff. Jan. 1, 1974. Amended by Acts 1993, 73rd Leg., ch. 900, § 1.01, eff. Sept. 1, 1994.

§ 43.23. Obscenity

(a) A person commits an offense if, knowing its content and character, he wholesale promotes or possesses with intent to wholesale promote any obscene material or obscene device.

(b) Except as provided by Subsection (h), an offense under Subsection (a) is a state jail felony.

(c) A person commits an offense if, knowing its content and character, he:

(1) promotes or possesses with intent to promote any obscene material or obscene device; or

(2) produces, presents, or directs an obscene performance or participates in a portion thereof that is obscene or that contributes to its obscenity.

(d) Except as provided by Subsection (h), an offense under Subsection (c) is a Class A misdemeanor.

(e) A person who promotes or wholesale promotes obscene material or an obscene device or possesses the same with intent to promote or wholesale promote it in the course of his business is presumed to do so with knowledge of its content and character.

(f) A person who possesses six or more obscene devices or identical or similar obscene articles is presumed to possess them with intent to promote the same.

(g) It is an affirmative defense to prosecution under this section that the person who possesses or promotes material or a device proscribed by this section does so for a bona fide medical, psychiatric, judicial, legislative, or law enforcement purpose.

(h) The punishment for an offense under Subsection (a) is increased to the punishment for a felony of the third degree and the punishment for an offense under Subsection (c) is increased to the punishment for a state jail felony if it is shown on the trial of the offense that obscene material that is the subject of the offense visually depicts activities described by Section 43.21(a)(1)(B) engaged in by:

(1) a child younger than 18 years of age at the time the image of the child was made;

(2) an image that to a reasonable person would be virtually indistinguishable from the image of a child younger than 18 years of age; or

(3) an image created, adapted, or modified to be the image of an identifiable child.

(i) In this section, "identifiable child" means a person, recognizable as an actual person by the person's face, likeness, or other distinguishing characteristic, such as a unique birthmark or other recognizable feature:

(1) who was younger than 18 years of age at the time the visual depiction was created, adapted, or modified; or

(2) whose image as a person younger than 18 years of age was used in creating, adapting, or modifying the visual depiction.

(j) An attorney representing the state who seeks an increase in punishment under Subsection (h)(3) is not required to prove the actual identity of an identifiable child.

Acts 1973, 63rd Leg., p. 883, ch. 399, § 1, eff. Jan. 1, 1974. Amended by Acts 1979, 66th Leg., p. 1975, ch. 778, § 2, eff. Sept. 1, 1979; Acts 1993, 73rd Leg., ch. 900, § 1.01, eff. Sept. 1, 1994; Acts 2003, 78th Leg., ch. 1005, § 1, eff. Sept. 1, 2003.

This section has been declared unconstitutional by Reliable Consultants, Inc. v. Earle, 517 F.3d 738, C.A.5 (Tex.), 2008.

§ 43.24. Sale, Distribution, or Display of Harmful Material to Minor

(a) For purposes of this section:

(1) "Minor" means an individual younger than 18 years.

(2) "Harmful material" means material whose dominant theme taken as a whole:

(A) appeals to the prurient interest of a minor, in sex, nudity, or excretion;

(B) is patently offensive to prevailing standards in the adult community as a whole with respect to what is suitable for minors; and

(C) is utterly without redeeming social value for minors.

(b) A person commits an offense if, knowing that the material is harmful:

(1) and knowing the person is a minor, he sells, distributes, exhibits, or possesses for sale, distribution, or exhibition to a minor harmful material;

(2) he displays harmful material and is reckless about whether a minor is present who will be offended or alarmed by the display; or

(3) he hires, employs, or uses a minor to do or accomplish or assist in doing or accomplishing any of the acts prohibited in Subsection (b)(1) or (b)(2).

(c) It is a defense to prosecution under this section that:

(1) the sale, distribution, or exhibition was by a person having scientific, educational, governmental, or other similar justification; or

(2) the sale, distribution, or exhibition was to a minor who was accompanied by a consenting parent, guardian, or spouse.

(d) An offense under this section is a Class A misdemeanor unless it is committed under Subsection (b)(3) in which event it is a felony of the third degree.

Acts 1973, 63rd Leg., p. 883, ch. 399, § 1, eff. Jan. 1, 1974. Amended by Acts 1993, 73rd Leg., ch. 900, § 1.01, eff. Sept. 1, 1994.

§ 43.25. Sexual Performance by a Child

(a) In this section:

(1) "Sexual performance" means any performance or part thereof that includes sexual conduct by a child younger than 18 years of age.

(2) "Sexual conduct" means sexual contact, actual or simulated sexual intercourse, deviate sexual intercourse, sexual bestiality, masturbation, sado-masochistic abuse, or lewd exhibition of the genitals, the anus, or any portion of the female breast below the top of the areola.

(3) "Performance" means any play, motion picture, photograph, dance, or other visual representation that can be exhibited before an audience of one or more persons.

(4) "Produce" with respect to a sexual performance includes any conduct that directly contributes to the creation or manufacture of the sexual performance.

(5) "Promote" means to procure, manufacture, issue, sell, give, provide, lend, mail, deliver, transfer, transmit, publish, distribute, circulate, disseminate, present, exhibit, or advertise or to offer or agree to do any of the above.

(6) "Simulated" means the explicit depiction of sexual conduct that creates the appearance of actual sexual conduct and during which a person engaging in the conduct exhibits any uncovered portion of the breasts, genitals, or buttocks.

(7) "Deviate sexual intercourse" and "sexual contact" have the meanings assigned by Section 43.01.

(b) A person commits an offense if, knowing the character and content thereof, he employs, authorizes, or induces a child younger than 18 years of age to engage in sexual conduct or a sexual performance. A parent or legal guardian or custodian of a child younger than 18 years of age commits an offense if he consents to the participation by the child in a sexual performance.

(c) An offense under Subsection (b) is a felony of the second degree, except that the offense is a felony of the first degree if the victim is younger than 14 years of age at the time the offense is committed.

(d) A person commits an offense if, knowing the character and content of the material, he produces, directs, or promotes a performance that includes sexual conduct by a child younger than 18 years of age.

(e) An offense under Subsection (d) is a felony of the third degree, except that the offense is a felony of the second degree if the victim is younger than 14 years of age at the time the offense is committed.

(f) It is an affirmative defense to a prosecution under this section that:

(1) the defendant was the spouse of the child at the time of the offense;

(2) the conduct was for a bona fide educational, medical, psychological, psychiatric, judicial, law enforcement, or legislative purpose; or

(3) the defendant is not more than two years older than the child.

(g) When it becomes necessary for the purposes of this section or Section 43.26 to determine whether a child who participated in sexual conduct was younger than 18 years of age, the court or jury may make this determination by any of the following methods:

(1) personal inspection of the child;

(2) inspection of the photograph or motion picture that shows the child engaging in the sexual performance;

(3) oral testimony by a witness to the sexual performance as to the age of the child based on the child's appearance at the time;

(4) expert medical testimony based on the appearance of the child engaging in the sexual performance; or

(5) any other method authorized by law or by the rules of evidence at common law.

Added by Acts 1977, 65th Leg., p. 1035, ch. 381, § 1, eff. June 10, 1977. Amended by Acts 1979, 66th Leg., p. 1976, ch. 779, § 1, eff. Sept. 1, 1979; Acts 1985, 69th Leg., ch. 530, § 1, eff. Sept. 1, 1985; Acts 1993, 73rd Leg., ch. 900, § 1.01, eff. Sept. 1, 1994; Acts 1999, 76th Leg., ch. 1415, § 22(b), eff. Sept. 1, 1999; Acts 2003, 78th Leg., ch. 1005, §§ 4, 5 eff. Sept. 1, 2003; Acts 2007, 80th Leg., ch. 593, § 1.20, eff. Sept. 1, 2007.

§ 43.251. Employment Harmful to Children

(a) In this section:

(1) "Child" means a person younger than 18 years of age.

(2) "Massage" has the meaning assigned to the term "massage therapy" by Section 455.001, Occupations Code.

(3) "Massage establishment" has the meaning assigned by Section 455.001, Occupations Code.

(4) "Nude" means a child who is:

(A) entirely unclothed; or

(B) clothed in a manner that leaves uncovered or visible through less than fully opaque clothing any portion of the breasts below the top of the areola of the breasts, if the child is female, or any portion of the genitals or buttocks.

(5) "Sexually oriented commercial activity" means a massage establishment, nude studio, modeling studio, love parlor, or other similar commercial enterprise the primary business of which is the offering of a service that is intended to provide sexual stimulation or sexual gratification to the customer.

(6) "Topless" means a female child clothed in a manner that leaves uncovered or visible through less than fully opaque clothing any portion of her breasts below the top of the areola.

(b) A person commits an offense if the person employs, authorizes, or induces a child to work:

(1) in a sexually oriented commercial activity; or

(2) in any place of business permitting, requesting, or requiring a child to work nude or topless.

(c) An offense under this section is a Class A misdemeanor.

Added by Acts 1987, 70th Leg., ch. 783, § 1, eff. Aug. 31, 1987. Amended by Acts 1993, 73rd Leg., ch. 900, § 1.01, eff. Sept. 1, 1994; Acts 2001, 77th Leg., ch. 1420, § 14.832, eff. Sept. 1, 2001.

§ 43.26. Possession or Promotion of Child Pornography

(a) A person commits an offense if:

(1) the person knowingly or intentionally possesses visual material that visually depicts a child younger than 18 years of age at the time the image of the child was made who is engaging in sexual conduct; and

(2) the person knows that the material depicts the child as described by Subdivision (1).

(b) In this section:

(1) "Promote" has the meaning assigned by Section 43.25.

(2) "Sexual conduct" has the meaning assigned by Section 43.25.

(3) "Visual material" means:

(A) any film, photograph, videotape, negative, or slide or any photographic reproduction that contains or incorporates in any manner any film, photograph, videotape, negative, or slide; or

(B) any disk, diskette, or other physical medium that allows an image to be displayed on a computer or other video screen and any image transmitted to a computer or other video screen by telephone line, cable, satellite transmission, or other method.

(c) The affirmative defenses provided by Section 43.25(f) also apply to a prosecution under this section.

(d) An offense under Subsection (a) is a felony of the third degree.

(e) A person commits an offense if:

(1) the person knowingly or intentionally promotes or possesses with intent to promote material described by Subsection (a)(1); and

(2) the person knows that the material depicts the child as described by Subsection (a)(1).

(f) A person who possesses visual material that contains six or more identical visual depictions of a child as described by Subsection (a)(1) is presumed to possess the material with the intent to promote the material.

(g) An offense under Subsection (e) is a felony of the second degree.

Added by Acts 1985, 69th Leg., ch. 530, § 2, eff. Sept. 1, 1985. Amended by Acts 1989, 71st Leg., ch. 361, § 1, eff. Sept. 1, 1989; Acts 1989, 71st Leg., ch. 968, § 1, eff. Sept. 1, 1989; Acts 1993, 73rd Leg., ch. 900, § 1.01, eff. Sept. 1, 1994; Acts 1995, 74th Leg., ch. 76, § 14.51, eff. Sept. 1, 1995; Acts 1997, 75th Leg., ch. 933, § 1, eff. Sept. 1, 1997; Acts 1999, 76th Leg., ch. 1415, § 22(c), eff. Sept. 1, 1999.

§ 43.27. Duty to Report

(a) For purposes of this section, "visual material" has the meaning assigned by Section 43.26.

(b) A business that develops or processes visual material and determines that the material may be evidence of a criminal offense under this subchapter shall report the existence of the visual material to a local law enforcement agency.

Added by Acts 2003, 78th Leg., ch. 1005, § 6, eff. Sept. 1, 2003.

TITLE 10. OFFENSES AGAINST PUBLIC HEALTH, SAFETY, AND MORALS

CHAPTER 46. WEAPONS

Section

§ 46.01. Definitions

In this chapter:

(1) "Club" means an instrument that is specially designed, made, or adapted for the purpose of inflicting serious bodily injury or death by striking a person with the instrument, and includes but is not limited to the following:

(A) blackjack;

(B) nightstick;

(C) mace;

(D) tomahawk.

(2) "Explosive weapon" means any explosive or incendiary bomb, grenade, rocket, or mine, that is designed, made, or adapted for the purpose of inflicting serious bodily injury, death, or substantial property damage, or for the principal purpose of causing such a loud report as to cause undue public alarm or terror, and includes a device designed, made, or adapted for delivery or shooting an explosive weapon.

(3) "Firearm" means any device designed, made, or adapted to expel a projectile through a barrel by using the energy generated by an explosion or burning substance or any device readily convertible to that use. Firearm does not include a firearm that may have, as an integral part, a folding knife blade or other characteristics of weapons made illegal by this chapter and that is:

(A) an antique or curio firearm manufactured before 1899; or

(B) a replica of an antique or curio firearm manufactured before 1899, but only if the replica does not use rim fire or center fire ammunition.

(4) "Firearm silencer" means any device designed, made, or adapted to muffle the report of a firearm.

(5) "Handgun" means any firearm that is designed, made, or adapted to be fired with one hand.

(6) "Illegal knife" means a:

(A) knife with a blade over five and one-half inches;

(B) hand instrument designed to cut or stab another by being thrown;

(C) dagger, including but not limited to a dirk, stiletto, and poniard;

(D) bowie knife;

(E) sword; or

(F) spear.

(7) "Knife" means any bladed hand instrument that is capable of inflicting serious bodily injury or death by cutting or stabbing a person with the instrument.

(8) "Knuckles" means any instrument that consists of finger rings or guards made of a hard substance and that is designed, made, or adapted for the purpose of inflicting serious bodily injury or death by striking a person with a fist enclosed in the knuckles.

(9) "Machine gun" means any firearm that is capable of shooting more than two shots automatically, without manual reloading, by a single function of the trigger.

(10) "Short-barrel firearm" means a rifle with a barrel length of less than 16 inches or a shotgun with a barrel length of less than 18 inches, or any weapon made from a shotgun or rifle if, as altered, it has an overall length of less than 26 inches.

(11) "Switchblade knife" means any knife that has a blade that folds, closes, or retracts into the handle or sheath and that opens automatically by pressure applied to a button or other device located on the handle or opens or releases a blade from the handle or sheath by the force of gravity or by the application of centrifugal force. The term does not include a knife that has a spring, detent, or other mechanism designed to create a bias toward closure and that requires exertion applied to the blade by hand, wrist, or arm to overcome the bias toward closure and open the knife.

(12) "Armor-piercing ammunition" means handgun ammunition that is designed primarily for the purpose of penetrating metal or body armor and to be used principally in pistols and revolvers.

(13) "Hoax bomb" means a device that:

(A) reasonably appears to be an explosive or incendiary device; or

(B) by its design causes alarm or reaction of any type by an official of a public safety agency or a volunteer agency organized to deal with emergencies.

(14) "Chemical dispensing device" means a device, other than a small chemical dispenser sold commercially for personal protection, that is designed, made, or adapted for the purpose of dispensing a substance capable of causing an adverse psychological or physiological effect on a human being.

(15) "Racetrack" has the meaning assigned that term by the Texas Racing Act (Article 179e, Vernon's Texas Civil Statutes).

(16) "Zip gun" means a device or combination of devices that was not originally a firearm and is adapted to expel a projectile through a smooth-bore or rifled-bore barrel by using the energy generated by an explosion or burning substance.

Acts 1973, 63rd Leg., p. 883, ch. 399, § 1, eff. Jan. 1, 1974. Amended by Acts 1975, 64th Leg., p. 917, ch. 342, § 13, eff. Sept. 1, 1975; Acts 1983, 68th Leg., p. 2650, ch. 457, § 1, eff. Sept. 1, 1983; Acts 1983, 68th Leg., p. 4830, ch. 852, § 1, eff. Sept. 1, 1983; Acts 1987, 70th Leg., ch. 167, § 5.01(a)(46), eff. Sept. 1, 1987; Acts 1989, 71st Leg., ch. 749, § 1, eff. Sept. 1, 1989; Acts 1991, 72nd Leg., ch. 229, § 1, eff. Sept. 1, 1991; Acts 1993, 73rd Leg., ch. 900, § 1.01, eff. Sept. 1, 1994; Acts 1999, 76th Leg., ch. 1445, § 1, eff. Sept. 1, 1999; Acts 2007, 80th Leg., ch. 921, § 12A.001, eff. Sept. 1, 2007; Acts 2009, 81st Leg., ch. 1199, § 1, eff. Sept. 1, 2009.

Section 2 of Acts 2009, 81st Leg., ch. 1199 provides:

"The change in law made by this Act applies only to an offense committed on or after the effective date [Sept. 1, 2009] of this Act. An offense committed before the effective date of this Act is covered by the law in effect when the offense was committed, and the former law is continued in effect for that purpose. For purposes of this section, an offense was committed before the effective date of this Act if any element of the offense was committed before that date."

§ 46.02. Unlawful Carrying Weapons

(a) A person commits an offense if the person intentionally, knowingly, or recklessly carries on or about his or her person a handgun, illegal knife, or club if the person is not:

(1) on the person's own premises or premises under the person's control; or

(2) inside of or directly en route to a motor vehicle that is owned by the person or under the person's control.

(a–1) A person commits an offense if the person intentionally, knowingly, or recklessly carries on or about his or her person a handgun in a motor vehicle that is owned by the person or under the person's control at any time in which:

(1) the handgun is in plain view; or

(2) the person is:

(A) engaged in criminal activity, other than a Class C misdemeanor that is a violation of a law or ordinance regulating traffic;

(B) prohibited by law from possessing a firearm; or

(C) a member of a criminal street gang, as defined by Section 71.01.

(a–2) For purposes of this section, "premises" includes real property and a recreational vehicle that is being used as living quarters, regardless of whether that use is temporary or permanent. In this subsection, "recreational vehicle" means a motor vehicle primarily designed as temporary living quarters or a vehicle that contains temporary living quarters and is designed to be towed by a motor vehicle. The term includes a travel trailer, camping trailer, truck camper, motor home, and horse trailer with living quarters.

(b) Except as provided by Subsection (c), an offense under this section is a Class A misdemeanor.

(c) An offense under this section is a felony of the third degree if the offense is committed on any premises licensed or issued a permit by this state for the sale of alcoholic beverages.

Acts 1973, 63rd Leg., p. 883, ch. 399, § 1, eff. Jan. 1, 1974. Amended by Acts 1975, 64th Leg., p. 109, ch. 49, § 1, eff. April 15, 1975; Acts 1975, 64th Leg., p. 918, ch. 342, § 14, eff. Sept. 1, 1975; Acts 1975, 64th Leg., p. 1330, ch. 494, § 2, eff. June 19, 1975; Acts 1977, 65th Leg., p. 1879, ch. 746, § 26, eff. Aug. 29, 1977; Acts 1981, 67th Leg., p. 2273, ch. 552, § 1, eff. Aug. 31, 1981; Acts 1983, 68th Leg., p. 5113, ch. 931, § 1, eff. Aug. 29, 1983; Acts 1987, 70th Leg., ch. 262, § 21, eff. Sept. 1, 1987; Acts 1987, 70th Leg., ch. 873, § 25, eff. Sept. 1, 1987; Acts 1991, 72nd Leg., ch. 168, § 1, eff. Sept. 1, 1991. Redesignated from V.T.C.A., Penal Code §§ 46.02, 46.03 and amended by Acts 1993, 73rd Leg., ch. 900, § 1.01, eff. Sept. 1, 1994. Amended by Acts 1995, 74th Leg., ch. 229, § 2, eff. Sept. 1, 1995; Acts 1995, 74th Leg., ch. 318, § 16, eff. Sept. 1, 1995; Acts 1995, 74th Leg., ch. 754, § 15, eff. Sept. 1, 1995; Acts 1995, 74th Leg., ch. 790, § 16, eff. Sept. 1, 1995; Acts 1995, 74th Leg., ch. 998, § 3, eff. Sept. 1, 1995; Acts 1997, 75th Leg., ch. 165, § 10.02, eff. Sept. 1, 1997; Acts 1997, 75th Leg., ch. 1221, § 1, eff. June 20, 1997; Acts 1997, 75th Leg., ch. 1261, § 24, eff. Sept. 1, 1997; Acts 2007, 80th Leg., ch. 693, § 1, eff. Sept. 1, 2007.

Section 4 of Acts 2007, 80th Leg., ch. 693 provides:

"The change in law made by this Act applies only to an offense committed on or after the effective date [Sept. 1, 2007] of this Act. An offense committed before the effective date of this Act is governed by the law in effect when the offense was committed, and the former law is continued in effect for that purpose. For purposes of this section, an offense was committed before the effective date of this Act if any element of the offense was committed before that date."

§ 46.03. Places Weapons Prohibited

(a) A person commits an offense if the person intentionally, knowingly, or recklessly possesses or goes with a firearm, illegal knife, club, or prohibited weapon listed in Section 46.05(a):

(1) on the physical premises of a school or educational institution, any grounds or building on which an activity sponsored by a school or educational institution is being conducted, or a passenger transportation vehicle of a school or educational institution, whether the school or educational institution is public or private, unless pursuant to written regulations or written authorization of the institution;

(2) on the premises of a polling place on the day of an election or while early voting is in progress;

(3) on the premises of any government court or offices utilized by the court, unless pursuant to written regulations or written authorization of the court;

(4) on the premises of a racetrack;

(5) in or into a secured area of an airport; or

(6) within 1,000 feet of premises the location of which is designated by the Texas Department of Criminal Justice as a place of execution under Article 43.19, Code of Criminal Procedure, on a day that a sentence of death is set to be imposed on the designated premises and the person received notice that:

(A) going within 1,000 feet of the premises with a weapon listed under this subsection was prohibited; or

(B) possessing a weapon listed under this subsection within 1,000 feet of the premises was prohibited.

(b) It is a defense to prosecution under Subsections (a)(1)–(4) that the actor possessed a firearm while in the actual discharge of his official duties as a member of the armed forces or national guard or a guard employed by a penal institution, or an officer of the court.

(c) In this section:

(1) "Premises" has the meaning assigned by Section 46.035.

(2) "Secured area" means an area of an airport terminal building to which access is controlled by the inspection of persons and property under federal law.

(d) It is a defense to prosecution under Subsection (a)(5) that the actor possessed a firearm or club while traveling to or from the actor's place of assignment or in the actual discharge of duties as:

(1) a member of the armed forces or national guard;

(2) a guard employed by a penal institution; or

(3) a security officer commissioned by the Texas Private Security Board if:

(A) the actor is wearing a distinctive uniform; and

(B) the firearm or club is in plain view; or

(4) a security officer who holds a personal protection authorization under Chapter 1702, Occupations Code, provided that the officer is either:

(A) wearing the uniform of a security officer, including any uniform or apparel described by Section 1702.323(d), Occupations Code, and carrying the officer's firearm in plain view; or

(B) not wearing the uniform of a security officer and carrying the officer's firearm in a concealed manner.

(e) It is a defense to prosecution under Subsection (a)(5) that the actor checked all firearms as baggage in accordance with federal or state law or regulations before entering a secured area.

(f) It is not a defense to prosecution under this section that the actor possessed a handgun and was licensed to carry a concealed handgun under Subchapter H, Chapter 411, Government Code.[1]

(g) An offense under this section is a third degree felony.

(h) It is a defense to prosecution under Subsection (a)(4) that the actor possessed a firearm or club while traveling to or from the actor's place of assignment or in the actual discharge of duties as a security officer commissioned by the Texas Board of Private Investigators and Private Security Agencies, if:

(1) the actor is wearing a distinctive uniform; and

(2) the firearm or club is in plain view.

(i) It is an exception to the application of Subsection (a)(6) that the actor possessed a firearm or club:

(1) while in a vehicle being driven on a public road; or

(2) at the actor's residence or place of employment.

Acts 1973, 63rd Leg., p. 883, ch. 399, § 1, eff. Jan. 1, 1974. Amended by Acts 1983, 68th Leg., p. 2962, ch. 508, § 1, eff. Aug. 29, 1983; Acts 1989, 71st Leg., ch. 749, § 2, eff. Sept. 1, 1989; Acts 1991, 72nd Leg., ch. 203, § 2.79; Acts 1991, 72nd Leg., ch. 386, § 71, eff. Aug. 26, 1991; Acts 1991, 72nd Leg., ch. 433, § 1, eff. Sept. 1, 1991; Acts 1991, 72nd Leg., ch. 554, § 50, eff. Sept. 1, 1991. Renumbered from V.T.C.A., Penal Code § 46.04 and amended by Acts 1993, 73rd Leg., ch. 900, § 1.01, eff. Sept. 1, 1994. Amended by Acts 1995, 74th Leg., ch. 229, § 3, eff. Sept. 1, 1995; Acts 1995, 74th Leg., ch. 260, § 42, eff. May 30, 1995; Acts 1995, 74th Leg., ch. 318, § 17, eff. Sept. 1, 1995; Acts 1995, 74th Leg., ch. 790, § 17, eff. Sept. 1, 1995; Acts 1997, 75th Leg., ch. 165, §§ 10.03, 31.01(70), eff. Sept. 1, 1997; Acts 1997, 75th Leg., ch. 1043, § 1, eff. Sept. 1, 1997; Acts 1997, 75th Leg., ch. 1221, §§ 2, 3, eff. June 20, 1997; Acts 1997, 75th Leg., ch. 1261, § 25, eff. Sept. 1, 1997; Acts 2001, 77th Leg., ch. 1060, §§ 1, 2 eff. Sept. 1, 2001; Acts 2003, 78th Leg., ch. 1178, § 3, eff. Sept. 1, 2003; Acts 2009, 81st Leg., ch. 1146, § 4B.21, eff. Sept. 1, 2009.

[1] V.T.C.A., Government Code § 411.001 et seq.

§ 46.035. Unlawful Carrying of Handgun by License Holder

(a) A license holder commits an offense if the license holder carries a handgun on or about the license holder's person under the authority of Subchapter H, Chapter 411, Government Code,[1] and intentionally fails to conceal the handgun.

(b) A license holder commits an offense if the license holder intentionally, knowingly, or recklessly carries a handgun under the authority of Subchapter H, Chapter 411, Government Code, regardless of whether the handgun is concealed, on or about the license holder's person:

(1) on the premises of a business that has a permit or license issued under Chapter 25, 28, 32, 69, or 74, Alcoholic Beverage Code, if the business derives 51 percent or more of its income from the sale or service of alcoholic beverages for on-premises consumption, as determined by the Texas Alcoholic Beverage Commission under Section 104.06, Alcoholic Beverage Code;

(2) on the premises where a high school, collegiate, or professional sporting event or interscholastic event is taking place, unless the license holder is a participant in the event and a handgun is used in the event;

(3) on the premises of a correctional facility;

(4) on the premises of a hospital licensed under Chapter 241, Health and Safety Code, or on the

premises of a nursing home licensed under Chapter 242, Health and Safety Code, unless the license holder has written authorization of the hospital or nursing home administration, as appropriate;

(5) in an amusement park; or

(6) on the premises of a church, synagogue, or other established place of religious worship.

(c) A license holder commits an offense if the license holder intentionally, knowingly, or recklessly carries a handgun under the authority of Subchapter H, Chapter 411, Government Code, regardless of whether the handgun is concealed, at any meeting of a governmental entity.

(d) A license holder commits an offense if, while intoxicated, the license holder carries a handgun under the authority of Subchapter H, Chapter 411, Government Code, regardless of whether the handgun is concealed.

(e) A license holder who is licensed as a security officer under Chapter 1702, Occupations Code, and employed as a security officer commits an offense if, while in the course and scope of the security officer's employment, the security officer violates a provision of Subchapter H, Chapter 411, Government Code.

(f) In this section:

(1) "Amusement park" means a permanent indoor or outdoor facility or park where amusement rides are available for use by the public that is located in a county with a population of more than one million, encompasses at least 75 acres in surface area, is enclosed with access only through controlled entries, is open for operation more than 120 days in each calendar year, and has security guards on the premises at all times. The term does not include any public or private driveway, street, sidewalk or walkway, parking lot, parking garage, or other parking area.

(2) "License holder" means a person licensed to carry a handgun under Subchapter H, Chapter 411, Government Code.

(3) "Premises" means a building or a portion of a building. The term does not include any public or private driveway, street, sidewalk or walkway, parking lot, parking garage, or other parking area.

(g) An offense under Subsection (a), (b), (c), (d), or (e) is a Class A misdemeanor, unless the offense is committed under Subsection (b)(1) or (b)(3), in which event the offense is a felony of the third degree.

(h) It is a defense to prosecution under Subsection (a) that the actor, at the time of the commission of the offense, displayed the handgun under circumstances in which the actor would have been justified in the use of deadly force under Chapter 9.

Text of subsec. (h–1) as added by Acts 2007, 80th Leg., ch. 1214, § 2

(h–1) It is a defense to prosecution under Subsections (b) and (c) that the actor, at the time of the commission of the offense, was:

(1) an active judicial officer, as defined by Section 411.201, Government Code; or

(2) a bailiff designated by the active judicial officer and engaged in escorting the officer.

Text of subsec. (h–1) as added by Acts 2007, 80th Leg., ch. 1222, § 5

(h–1) It is a defense to prosecution under Subsections (b)(1), (2), and (4)–(6), and (c) that at the time of the commission of the offense, the actor was:

(1) a judge or justice of a federal court;

(2) an active judicial officer, as defined by Section 411.201, Government Code; or

(3) a district attorney, assistant district attorney, criminal district attorney, assistant criminal district attorney, county attorney, or assistant county attorney.

(i) Subsections (b)(4), (b)(5), (b)(6), and (c) do not apply if the actor was not given effective notice under Section 30.06.

(j) Subsections (a) and (b)(1) do not apply to a historical reenactment performed in compliance with the rules of the Texas Alcoholic Beverage Commission.

(k) It is a defense to prosecution under Subsection (b)(1) that the actor was not given effective notice under Section 411.204, Government Code.

Added by Acts 1995, 74th Leg., ch. 229, § 4, eff. Sept. 1, 1995. Amended by Acts 1997, 75th Leg., ch. 165, § 10.04, eff. Sept. 1, 1997; Acts 1997, 75th Leg., ch. 1261, §§ 26, 27, eff. Sept. 1, 1997; Acts 2001, 77th Leg., ch. 1420, § 14.833, eff. Sept. 1, 2001; Acts 2005, 79th Leg., ch. 976, § 3, eff. Sept. 1, 2005; Acts 2007, 80th Leg., ch. 1214, § 2, eff. June 15, 2007; Acts 2007, 80th Leg., ch. 1222, § 5, eff. June 15, 2007; Acts 2009, 81st Leg., ch. 687, § 1, eff. Sept. 1, 2009.

[1] V.T.C.A., Government Code § 411.171 et seq.

Section 3 of Acts 2007, 80th Leg., ch. 1214 provides:

"The change in law made by this Act applies only to an offense committed on or after the effective date [month, day, 2007] of this Act. An offense committed before the effective date of this Act is covered by the law in effect when the offense was committed, and the former law is continued in effect for that purpose. For purposes of this section, an offense was committed before the effective date of this Act if any element of the offense was committed before that date."

Section 2 of Acts 2009, 81st Leg., ch. 687 provides:

"The change in law made by this Act applies only to an offense committed on or after the effective date of this Act. An offense committed before the effective date of this Act is governed by the law in effect at the time the offense was committed, and the former law is continued in effect for that purpose. For purposes of this section, an offense was committed before the effective date of this Act if any element of the offense occurred before that date."

§ 46.04. Unlawful Possession of Firearm

(a) A person who has been convicted of a felony commits an offense if he possesses a firearm:

(1) after conviction and before the fifth anniversary of the person's release from confinement following conviction of the felony or the person's release from supervision under community supervision, parole, or mandatory supervision, whichever date is later; or

(2) after the period described by Subdivision (1), at any location other than the premises at which the person lives.

(b) A person who has been convicted of an offense under Section 22.01, punishable as a Class A misdemeanor and involving a member of the person's family or household, commits an offense if the person possesses a firearm before the fifth anniversary of the later of:

(1) the date of the person's release from confinement following conviction of the misdemeanor; or

(2) the date of the person's release from community supervision following conviction of the misdemeanor.

(c) A person, other than a peace officer, as defined by Section 1.07, actively engaged in employment as a sworn, full-time paid employee of a state agency or political subdivision, who is subject to an order issued under Section 6.504 or Chapter 85, Family Code, under Article 17.292 or Chapter 7A, Code of Criminal Procedure, or by another jurisdiction as provided by Chapter 88, Family Code, commits an offense if the person possesses a firearm after receiving notice of the order and before expiration of the order.

(d) In this section, "family," "household," and "member of a household" have the meanings assigned by Chapter 71, Family Code.

(e) An offense under Subsection (a) is a felony of the third degree. An offense under Subsection (b) or (c) is a Class A misdemeanor.

(f) For the purposes of this section, an offense under the laws of this state, another state, or the United States is, except as provided by Subsection (g), a felony if, at the time it is committed, the offense:

(1) is designated by a law of this state as a felony;

(2) contains all the elements of an offense designated by a law of this state as a felony; or

(3) is punishable by confinement for one year or more in a penitentiary.

(g) An offense is not considered a felony for purposes of Subsection (f) if, at the time the person possesses a firearm, the offense:

(1) is not designated by a law of this state as a felony; and

(2) does not contain all the elements of any offense designated by a law of this state as a felony.

Acts 1973, 63rd Leg., p. 883, ch. 399, § 1, eff. Jan. 1, 1974. Renumbered from V.T.C.A., Penal Code § 46.05 and amended by Acts 1993, 73rd Leg., ch. 900, § 1.01, eff. Sept. 1, 1994. Amended by Acts 2001, 77th Leg., ch. 23, § 2, eff. Sept. 1, 2001; Acts 2003, 78th Leg., ch. 836, § 4, eff. Sept. 1, 2003; Acts 2009, 81st Leg., ch. 1146, § 11.24, eff. Sept. 1, 2009.

Section 11.30 of Acts 2009, 81st Leg., ch. 1146 provides:

"The change in law made by this Act in amending Section 46.04, Penal Code, applies only to an offense committed on or after the effective date [Sept. 1, 2009] of this Act. An offense committed before the effective date of this Act is covered by the law in effect when the offense was committed, and the former law is continued in effect for that purpose. For purposes of this section, an offense was committed before the effective date of this Act if any element of the offense occurred before that date."

§ 46.041. Unlawful Possession of Metal or Body Armor by Felon

(a) In this section, "metal or body armor" means any body covering manifestly designed, made, or adapted for the purpose of protecting a person against gunfire.

(b) A person who has been convicted of a felony commits an offense if after the conviction the person possesses metal or body armor.

(c) An offense under this section is a felony of the third degree.

Added by Acts 2001, 77th Leg., ch. 452, § 1, eff. Sept. 1, 2001.

§ 46.05. Prohibited Weapons

(a) A person commits an offense if he intentionally or knowingly possesses, manufactures, transports, repairs, or sells:

(1) an explosive weapon;

(2) a machine gun;

(3) a short-barrel firearm;

(4) a firearm silencer;

(5) a switchblade knife;

(6) knuckles;

(7) armor-piercing ammunition;

(8) a chemical dispensing device; or

(9) a zip gun.

(b) It is a defense to prosecution under this section that the actor's conduct was incidental to the performance of official duty by the armed forces or national guard, a governmental law enforcement agency, or a correctional facility.

(c) It is a defense to prosecution under this section that the actor's possession was pursuant to registration pursuant to the National Firearms Act,[1] as amended.

(d) It is an affirmative defense to prosecution under this section that the actor's conduct:

(1) was incidental to dealing with a switchblade knife, springblade knife, or short-barrel firearm solely as an antique or curio; or

(2) was incidental to dealing with armor-piercing ammunition solely for the purpose of making the ammunition available to an organization, agency, or institution listed in Subsection (b).

(e) An offense under this section is a felony of the third degree unless it is committed under Subsection (a)(5) or (a)(6), in which event, it is a Class A misdemeanor.

(f) It is a defense to prosecution under this section for the possession of a chemical dispensing device that the actor is a security officer and has received training on the use of the chemical dispensing device by a training program that is:

(1) provided by the Commission on Law Enforcement Officer Standards and Education; or

(2) approved for the purposes described by this subsection by the Texas Private Security Board of the Department of Public Safety.

(g) In Subsection (f), "security officer" means a commissioned security officer as defined by Section 1702.002, Occupations Code, or a noncommissioned security officer registered under Section 1702.221, Occupations Code.

Acts 1973, 63rd Leg., p. 883, ch. 399, § 1, eff. Jan. 1, 1974. Amended by Acts 1975, 64th Leg., p. 918, ch. 342, § 15, eff. Sept. 1, 1975; Acts 1983, 68th Leg., p. 2650, ch. 457, § 2, eff. Sept. 1, 1983; Acts 1983, 68th Leg., p. 4831, ch. 852, § 2, eff. Sept. 1, 1983; Acts 1987, 70th Leg., ch. 167, § 5.01(a)(47), eff. Sept. 1, 1987; Acts 1991, 72nd Leg., ch. 229, § 2, eff. Sept. 1, 1991; Renumbered from V.T.C.A., Penal Code § 46.06 and amended by Acts 1993, 73rd Leg., ch. 900, § 1.01, eff. Sept. 1, 1994; Acts 2003, 78th Leg., ch. 1071, § 1, eff. Sept. 1, 2003; Acts 2005, 79th Leg., ch. 1035, § 2.01, eff. Sept. 1, 2005; Acts 2005, 79th Leg., ch. 1278, § 7, eff. Sept. 1, 2005.

[1] 26 U.S.C.A. § 5801 et seq.

§ 46.06. Unlawful Transfer of Certain Weapons

(a) A person commits an offense if the person:

(1) sells, rents, leases, loans, or gives a handgun to any person knowing that the person to whom the handgun is to be delivered intends to use it unlawfully or in the commission of an unlawful act;

(2) intentionally or knowingly sells, rents, leases, or gives or offers to sell, rent, lease, or give to any child younger than 18 years any firearm, club, or illegal knife;

(3) intentionally, knowingly, or recklessly sells a firearm or ammunition for a firearm to any person who is intoxicated;

(4) knowingly sells a firearm or ammunition for a firearm to any person who has been convicted of a felony before the fifth anniversary of the later of the following dates:

(A) the person's release from confinement following conviction of the felony; or

(B) the person's release from supervision under community supervision, parole, or mandatory supervision following conviction of the felony;

(5) sells, rents, leases, loans, or gives a handgun to any person knowing that an active protective order is directed to the person to whom the handgun is to be delivered; or

(6) knowingly purchases, rents, leases, or receives as a loan or gift from another a handgun while an active protective order is directed to the actor.

(b) In this section:

(1) "Intoxicated" means substantial impairment of mental or physical capacity resulting from introduction of any substance into the body.

(2) "Active protective order" means a protective order issued under Title 4, Family Code,[1] that is in effect. The term does not include a temporary protective order issued before the court holds a hearing on the matter.

(c) It is an affirmative defense to prosecution under Subsection (a)(2) that the transfer was to a minor whose parent or the person having legal custody of the minor had given written permission for the sale or, if the transfer was other than a sale, the parent or person having legal custody had given effective consent.

(d) An offense under this section is a Class A misdemeanor, except that an offense under Subsection (a)(2) is a state jail felony if the weapon that is the subject of the offense is a handgun.

Acts 1973, 63rd Leg., p. 883, ch. 399, § 1, eff. Jan. 1, 1974. Amended by Acts 1985, 69th Leg., ch. 686, § 1, eff. Sept. 1, 1985. Renumbered from V.T.C.A., Penal Code § 46.07 and amended by Acts 1993, 73rd Leg., ch. 900, § 1.01, eff. Sept. 1, 1994. Amended by Acts 1995, 74th Leg., ch. 324, § 1, eff. Jan. 1, 1996; Acts 1997, 75th Leg., ch. 1193, § 22, eff. Sept. 1, 1997; Acts 1997, 75th Leg., ch. 1304, § 1, eff. Sept. 1, 1997; Acts 1999, 76th Leg., ch. 62, § 15.02(f), eff. Sept. 1, 1999.

[1] V.T.C.A., Family Code § 71.001 et seq.

§ 46.07. Interstate Purchase

A resident of this state may, if not otherwise precluded by law, purchase firearms, ammunition, reloading components, or firearm accessories in another state. This authorization is enacted in conformance with 18 U.S.C. Section 922(b)(3)(A).

Acts 1973, 63rd Leg., p. 883, ch. 399, § 1, eff. Jan. 1, 1974. Renumbered from V.T.C.A., Penal Code § 46.08 by Acts 1993, 73rd Leg., ch. 900, § 1.01, eff. Sept. 1, 1994. Amended by Acts 2009, 81st Leg., ch. 280, § 1, eff. May 30, 2009.

§ 46.08. Hoax Bombs

(a) A person commits an offense if the person knowingly manufactures, sells, purchases, transports, or possesses a hoax bomb with intent to use the hoax bomb to:

(1) make another believe that the hoax bomb is an explosive or incendiary device; or

(2) cause alarm or reaction of any type by an official of a public safety agency or volunteer agency organized to deal with emergencies.

(b) An offense under this section is a Class A misdemeanor.

Added by Acts 1983, 68th Leg., p. 4831, ch. 852, § 3, eff. Sept. 1, 1983. Renumbered from V.T.C.A., Penal Code § 46.09 by Acts 1993, 73rd Leg., ch. 900, § 1.01, eff. Sept. 1, 1994.

§ 46.09. Components of Explosives

(a) A person commits an offense if the person knowingly possesses components of an explosive weapon with the intent to combine the components into an explosive weapon for use in a criminal endeavor.

(b) An offense under this section is a felony of the third degree.

Added by Acts 1983, 68th Leg., p. 4832, ch. 852, § 4, eff. Sept. 1, 1983. Renumbered from V.T.C.A., Penal Code § 46.10 by Acts 1993, 73rd Leg., ch. 900, § 1.01, eff. Sept. 1, 1994.

§ 46.10. Deadly Weapon in Penal Institution

(a) A person commits an offense if, while confined in a penal institution, he intentionally, knowingly, or recklessly:

(1) carries on or about his person a deadly weapon; or

(2) possesses or conceals a deadly weapon in the penal institution.

(b) It is an affirmative defense to prosecution under this section that at the time of the offense the actor was engaged in conduct authorized by an employee of the penal institution.

(c) A person who is subject to prosecution under both this section and another section under this chapter may be prosecuted under either section.

(d) An offense under this section is a felony of the third degree.

Added by Acts 1985, 69th Leg., ch. 46, § 1, eff. Sept. 1, 1985. Amended by Acts 1987, 70th Leg., ch. 714, § 1, eff. Sept. 1, 1987. Renumbered from V.T.C.A., Penal Code § 46.11 by Acts 1993, 73rd Leg., ch. 900, § 1.01, eff. Sept. 1, 1994.

§ 46.11. Penalty if Offense Committed Within Weapon-Free School Zone

(a) Except as provided by Subsection (b), the punishment prescribed for an offense under this chapter is increased to the punishment prescribed for the next highest category of offense if it is shown beyond a reasonable doubt on the trial of the offense that the actor committed the offense in a place that the actor knew was:

(1) within 300 feet of the premises of a school; or

(2) on premises where:

(A) an official school function is taking place; or

(B) an event sponsored or sanctioned by the University Interscholastic League is taking place.

(b) This section does not apply to an offense under Section 46.03(a)(1).

(c) In this section:

(1) "Institution of higher education" and "premises" have the meanings assigned by Section 481.134, Health and Safety Code.

(2) "School" means a private or public elementary or secondary school.

Added by Acts 1995, 74th Leg., ch. 320, § 1, eff. Sept. 1, 1995. Amended by Acts 1997, 75th Leg., ch. 1063, § 10, eff. Sept. 1, 1997.

§ 46.12. Maps as Evidence of Location or Area

(a) In a prosecution of an offense for which punishment is increased under Section 46.11, a map produced or reproduced by a municipal or county engineer for the purpose of showing the location and boundaries of weapon-free zones is admissible in evidence and is prima facie evidence of the location or boundaries of those areas if the governing body of the municipality or county adopts a resolution or ordinance approving the map as an official finding and record of the location or boundaries of those areas.

(b) A municipal or county engineer may, on request of the governing body of the municipality or county, revise a map that has been approved by the governing body of the municipality or county as provided by Subsection (a).

(c) A municipal or county engineer shall file the original or a copy of every approved or revised map approved as provided by Subsection (a) with the county clerk of each county in which the area is located.

(d) This section does not prevent the prosecution from:

(1) introducing or relying on any other evidence or testimony to establish any element of an offense for which punishment is increased under Section 46.11; or

(2) using or introducing any other map or diagram otherwise admissible under the Texas Rules of Evidence.

Added by Acts 1995, 74th Leg., ch. 320, § 2, eff. Sept. 1, 1995. Amended by Acts 2005, 79th Leg., ch. 728, § 16.004, eff. Sept. 1, 2005.

§ 46.13. Making a Firearm Accessible to a Child

(a) In this section:

(1) "Child" means a person younger than 17 years of age.

(2) "Readily dischargeable firearm" means a firearm that is loaded with ammunition, whether or not a round is in the chamber.

(3) "Secure" means to take steps that a reasonable person would take to prevent the access to a readily dischargeable firearm by a child, including but not limited to placing a firearm in a locked container or temporarily rendering the firearm inoperable by a trigger lock or other means.

(b) A person commits an offense if a child gains access to a readily dischargeable firearm and the person with criminal negligence:

(1) failed to secure the firearm; or

(2) left the firearm in a place to which the person knew or should have known the child would gain access.

(c) It is an affirmative defense to prosecution under this section that the child's access to the firearm:

(1) was supervised by a person older than 18 years of age and was for hunting, sporting, or other lawful purposes;

(2) consisted of lawful defense by the child of people or property;

(3) was gained by entering property in violation of this code; or

(4) occurred during a time when the actor was engaged in an agricultural enterprise.

(d) Except as provided by Subsection (e), an offense under this section is a Class C misdemeanor.

(e) An offense under this section is a Class A misdemeanor if the child discharges the firearm and causes death or serious bodily injury to himself or another person.

(f) A peace officer or other person may not arrest the actor before the seventh day after the date on which the offense is committed if:

(1) the actor is a member of the family, as defined by Section 71.003, Family Code, of the child who discharged the firearm; and

(2) the child in discharging the firearm caused the death of or serious injury to the child.

(g) A dealer of firearms shall post in a conspicuous position on the premises where the dealer conducts business a sign that contains the following warning in block letters not less than one inch in height:

"IT IS UNLAWFUL TO STORE, TRANSPORT, OR ABANDON AN UNSECURED FIREARM IN A PLACE WHERE CHILDREN ARE LIKELY TO BE AND CAN OBTAIN ACCESS TO THE FIREARM."

Added by Acts 1995, 74th Leg., ch. 83, § 1, eff. Sept. 1, 1995. Amended by Acts 1999, 76th Leg., ch. 62, § 15.02(g), eff. Sept. 1, 1999.

§ 46.14. Firearm Smuggling

(a) A person commits an offense if the person knowingly engages in the business of transporting or transferring a firearm that the person knows was acquired in violation of the laws of any state or of the United States. For purposes of this subsection, a person is considered to engage in the business of transporting or transferring a firearm if the person engages in that conduct:

(1) on more than one occasion; or

(2) for profit or any other form of remuneration.

(b) An offense under this section is a felony of the third degree, unless it is shown on the trial of the offense that the offense was committed with respect to three or more firearms in a single criminal episode, in which event the offense is a felony of the second degree.

(c) This section does not apply to a peace officer who is engaged in the actual discharge of an official duty.

(d) If conduct that constitutes an offense under this section also constitutes an offense under any other law, the actor may be prosecuted under this section, the other law, or both.

Added by Acts 2009, 81st Leg., ch. 153, § 1, eff. Sept. 1, 2009.

§ 46.15. Nonapplicability

(a) Sections 46.02 and 46.03 do not apply to:

(1) peace officers or special investigators under Article 2.122, Code of Criminal Procedure, and neither section prohibits a peace officer or special investigator from carrying a weapon in this state, including in an establishment in this state serving the public, regardless of whether the peace officer or special investigator is engaged in the actual discharge of the officer's or investigator's duties while carrying the weapon;

(2) parole officers and neither section prohibits an officer from carrying a weapon in this state if the officer is:

(A) engaged in the actual discharge of the officer's duties while carrying the weapon; and

(B) in compliance with policies and procedures adopted by the Texas Department of Criminal Justice regarding the possession of a weapon by an officer while on duty;

(3) community supervision and corrections department officers appointed or employed under Section 76.004, Government Code, and neither section prohibits an officer from carrying a weapon in this state if the officer is:

(A) engaged in the actual discharge of the officer's duties while carrying the weapon; and

(B) authorized to carry a weapon under Section 76.0051, Government Code;

(4) a judge or justice of a federal court, the supreme court, the court of criminal appeals, a court of appeals, a district court, a criminal district court, a constitutional county court, a statutory county court, a justice court, or a municipal court who is licensed to carry a concealed handgun under Subchapter H, Chapter 411, Government Code[1];

(5) an honorably retired peace officer or federal criminal investigator who holds a certificate of proficiency issued under Section 1701.357, Occupations Code, and is carrying a photo identification that:

(A) verifies that the officer honorably retired after not less than 15 years of service as a commissioned officer; and

(B) is issued by a state or local law enforcement agency;

(6) a district attorney, criminal district attorney, county attorney, or municipal attorney who is licensed to carry a concealed handgun under Subchapter H, Chapter 411, Government Code;

(7) an assistant district attorney, assistant criminal district attorney, or assistant county attorney who is licensed to carry a concealed handgun under Subchapter H, Chapter 411, Government Code;

(8) a bailiff designated by an active judicial officer as defined by Section 411.201, Government Code, who is:

(A) licensed to carry a concealed handgun under Chapter 411, Government Code; and

(B) engaged in escorting the judicial officer; or

(9) a juvenile probation officer who is authorized to carry a firearm under Section 142.006, Human Resources Code.

(b) Section 46.02 does not apply to a person who:

(1) is in the actual discharge of official duties as a member of the armed forces or state military forces as defined by Section 431.001, Government Code, or as a guard employed by a penal institution;

(2) is traveling;

(3) is engaging in lawful hunting, fishing, or other sporting activity on the immediate premises where the activity is conducted, or is en route between the premises and the actor's residence or motor vehicle, if the weapon is a type commonly used in the activity;

(4) holds a security officer commission issued by the Texas Private Security Board, if the person is engaged in the performance of the person's duties as an officer commissioned under Chapter 1702, Occupations Code, or is traveling to or from the person's place of assignment and is wearing the officer's uniform and carrying the officer's weapon in plain view;

(5) acts as a personal protection officer and carries the person's security officer commission and personal protection officer authorization, if the person:

(A) is engaged in the performance of the person's duties as a personal protection officer under Chapter 1702, Occupations Code, or is traveling to or from the person's place of assignment; and

(B) is either:

(i) wearing the uniform of a security officer, including any uniform or apparel described by Section 1702.323(d), Occupations Code, and carrying the officer's weapon in plain view; or

(ii) not wearing the uniform of a security officer and carrying the officer's weapon in a concealed manner;

(6) is carrying a concealed handgun and a valid license issued under Subchapter H, Chapter 411, Government Code, to carry a concealed handgun of the same category as the handgun the person is carrying;

(7) holds an alcoholic beverage permit or license or is an employee of a holder of an alcoholic beverage permit or license if the person is supervising the operation of the permitted or licensed premises; or

(8) is a student in a law enforcement class engaging in an activity required as part of the class, if the weapon is a type commonly used in the activity and the person is:

(A) on the immediate premises where the activity is conducted; or

(B) en route between those premises and the person's residence and is carrying the weapon unloaded.

(c) The provision of Section 46.02 prohibiting the carrying of a club does not apply to a noncommissioned security guard at an institution of higher education who carries a nightstick or similar club, and who has undergone 15 hours of training in the proper use of the club, including at least seven hours of training in the use of the club for nonviolent restraint. For the purposes of this subsection, "nonviolent restraint" means the use of reasonable force, not intended and not likely to inflict bodily injury.

(d) The provisions of Section 46.02 prohibiting the carrying of a firearm or carrying of a club do not apply to a public security officer employed by the adjutant general under Section 431.029, Government Code, in performance of official duties or while traveling to or from a place of duty.

(e) The provisions of Section 46.02 prohibiting the carrying of an illegal knife do not apply to an individual carrying a bowie knife or a sword used in a historical demonstration or in a ceremony in which the knife or sword is significant to the performance of the ceremony.

(f) Section 46.03(a)(6) does not apply to a person who possesses a firearm or club while in the actual discharge of official duties as:

(1) a member of the armed forces or state military forces, as defined by Section 431.001, Government Code; or

(2) an employee of a penal institution.

(g) The provisions of Sections 46.02 and 46.03 prohibiting the possession or carrying of a club do not apply to an animal control officer who holds a certificate issued under Section 829.006, Health and Safety

Code, and who possesses or carries an instrument used specifically for deterring the bite of an animal while the officer is in the performance of official duties under the Health and Safety Code or is traveling to or from a place of duty.

(h) Repealed by Acts 2007, 80th Leg., ch. 693, § 3(1).

(i) Redesignated (j) by Acts 2007, 80th Leg., ch. 921, § 17.001(62).

(j) The provisions of Section 46.02 prohibiting the carrying of a handgun do not apply to an individual who carries a handgun as a participant in a historical reenactment performed in accordance with the rules of the Texas Alcoholic Beverage Commission.

Added by Acts 1995, 74th Leg., ch. 318, § 18, eff. Sept. 1, 1995. Amended by Acts 1997, 75th Leg., ch. 1221, § 4, eff. June 20, 1997; Acts 1997, 75th Leg., ch. 1261, § 28, eff. Sept. 1, 1997; Acts 1999, 76th Leg., ch. 62, § 9.25, eff. Sept. 1, 1999; Acts 1999, 76th Leg., ch. 1445, § 2, eff. Sept. 1, 1999; Acts 2001, 77th Leg., ch. 1060, § 3, eff. Sept. 1, 2001; Acts 2003, 78th Leg., ch. 325, § 2, eff. Sept. 1, 2003; Acts 2003, 78th Leg., ch. 421, § 1, eff. Sept. 1, 2003; Acts 2003, 78th Leg., ch. 795, § 1, eff. June 20, 2003; Acts 2005, 79th Leg., ch. 288, § 1, eff. Sept. 1, 2005; Acts 2005, 79th Leg., ch. 728, § 23.001(78), eff. Sept. 1, 2005; Acts 2005, 79th Leg., ch. 976, § 4, eff. Sept. 1, 2005; Acts 2005, 79th Leg., ch. 1093, § 1, eff. Sept. 1, 2005; Acts 2005, 79th Leg., ch. 1179, §§ 2, 3, eff. Sept. 1, 2005; Acts 2007, 80th Leg., ch. 647, § 1, eff. Sept. 1, 2007; Acts 2007, 80th Leg., ch. 693, §§ 2, 3, eff. Sept. 1, 2007; Acts 2007, 80th Leg., ch. 921, § 17.001(62), eff. Sept. 1, 2007; Acts. 2007, 80th Leg., ch. 1048, § 3, eff. Sept. 1, 2007; Acts 2007, 80th Leg., ch. 1214, § 1, eff. June 15, 2007; Acts 2007, 80th Leg., ch. 1222, § 6, eff. June 15, 2007; Acts 2009, 81st Leg., ch. 87, §§ 19.004, 19.005, eff. Sept. 1, 2009; Acts 2009, 81st Leg., ch. 299, § 1, eff. June 19, 2009; Acts 2009, 81st Leg., ch. 794, § 4, eff. June 19, 2009; Acts 2009, 81st Leg., ch. 1146, § 4B.22, eff. Sept. 1, 2009.

[1] V.T.C.A., Government Code § 411.001 et seq.

Section 2 of Acts 2007, 80th Leg., ch. 647 provides:

"The change in law made by this Act applies only to an offense committed on or after the effective date of this Act [Sept. 1, 2007]. An offense committed before the effective date of this Act is governed by the law in effect when the offense was committed, and the former law is continued in effect for that purpose. For purposes of this section, an offense was committed before the effective date of this Act if any element of the offense was committed before that date."

Section 4 of Acts 2007, 80th Leg., ch. 693 provides:

"The change in law made by this Act applies only to an offense committed on or after the effective date [Sept. 1, 2007] of this Act. An offense committed before the effective date of this Act is governed by the law in effect when the offense was committed, and the former law is continued in effect for that purpose. For purposes of this section, an offense was committed before the effective date of this Act if any element of the offense was committed before that date."

Section 3 of Acts 2007, 80th Leg., ch. 1214 provides:

"The change in law made by this Act applies only to an offense committed on or after the effective date [month, day, 2007] of this Act. An offense committed before the effective date of this Act is covered by the law in effect when the offense was committed, and the former law is continued in effect for that purpose. For purposes of this section, an offense was committed before the effective date of this Act if any element of the offense was committed before that date."

Section 4B.24 of Acts 2009, 81st Leg., ch. 1146 provides:

"To the extent of any conflict, this article prevails over another Act of the 81st Legislature, Regular Session, 2009, relating to nonsubstantive additions to and corrections in enacted codes."

CHAPTER 47. GAMBLING

Section

§ 47.01. Definitions

In this chapter:

(1) "Bet" means an agreement to win or lose something of value solely or partially by chance. A bet does not include:

(A) contracts of indemnity or guaranty, or life, health, property, or accident insurance;

(B) an offer of a prize, award, or compensation to the actual contestants in a bona fide contest for the determination of skill, speed, strength, or endurance or to the owners of animals, vehicles, watercraft, or aircraft entered in a contest; or

(C) an offer of merchandise, with a value not greater than $25, made by the proprietor of a bona fide carnival contest conducted at a carnival sponsored by a nonprofit religious, fraternal, school, law enforcement, youth, agricultural, or civic group, including any nonprofit agricultural or civic group incorporated by the state before 1955, if the person to receive the merchandise from the proprietor is the person who performs the carnival contest.

(2) "Bookmaking" means:

(A) to receive and record or to forward more than five bets or offers to bet in a period of 24 hours;

(B) to receive and record or to forward bets or offers to bet totaling more than $1,000 in a period of 24 hours; or

(C) a scheme by three or more persons to receive, record, or forward a bet or an offer to bet.

(3) "Gambling place" means any real estate, building, room, tent, vehicle, boat, or other property whatsoever, one of the uses of which is the making or settling of bets, bookmaking, or the conducting of a lottery or the playing of gambling devices.

(4) "Gambling device" means any electronic, electromechanical, or mechanical contrivance not excluded under Paragraph (B) that for a consideration affords the player an opportunity to obtain anything of value, the award of which is determined solely or partially by chance, even though accompanied by some skill, whether or not the prize is automatically paid by the contrivance. The term:

(A) includes, but is not limited to, gambling device versions of bingo, keno, blackjack, lottery, roulette, video poker, or similar electronic, electromechanical, or mechanical games, or facsimiles thereof, that operate by chance or partially so, that as a result of the play or operation of the game award credits or free games, and that record the number of free games or credits so awarded and the cancellation or removal of the free games or credits; and

(B) does not include any electronic, electromechanical, or mechanical contrivance designed, made, and adapted solely for bona fide amusement purposes if the contrivance rewards the player exclusively with noncash merchandise prizes, toys, or novelties, or a representation of value redeemable for those items, that have a wholesale value available from a single play of the game or device of not more than 10 times the amount charged to play the game or device once or $5, whichever is less.

(5) "Altered gambling equipment" means any contrivance that has been altered in some manner, including, but not limited to, shaved dice, loaded dice, magnetic dice, mirror rings, electronic sensors, shaved cards, marked cards, and any other equipment altered or designed to enhance the actor's chances of winning.

(6) "Gambling paraphernalia" means any book, instrument, or apparatus by means of which bets have been or may be recorded or registered; any record, ticket, certificate, bill, slip, token, writing, scratch sheet, or other means of carrying on bookmaking, wagering pools, lotteries, numbers, policy, or similar games.

(7) "Lottery" means any scheme or procedure whereby one or more prizes are distributed by chance among persons who have paid or promised consideration for a chance to win anything of value, whether such scheme or procedure is called a pool, lottery, raffle, gift, gift enterprise, sale, policy game, or some other name.

(8) "Private place" means a place to which the public does not have access, and excludes, among other places, streets, highways, restaurants, taverns, nightclubs, schools, hospitals, and the common areas of apartment houses, hotels, motels, office buildings, transportation facilities, and shops.

(9) "Thing of value" means any benefit, but does not include an unrecorded and immediate right of replay not exchangeable for value.

Acts 1973, 63rd Leg., p. 883, ch. 399, § 1, eff. Jan. 1, 1974. Amended by Acts 1987, 70th Leg., ch. 313, §§ 1, 2, eff. Sept. 1, 1987; Acts 1989, 71st Leg., ch. 396, § 1, eff. June 14, 1989; Acts 1993, 73rd Leg., ch. 774, § 1, eff. Aug. 30, 1993; Acts 1993, 73rd Leg., ch. 900, § 1.01, eff. Sept. 1, 1994; Acts 1995, 74th Leg., ch. 318, § 19, eff. Sept. 1, 1995.

§ 47.02. Gambling

(a) A person commits an offense if he:

(1) makes a bet on the partial or final result of a game or contest or on the performance of a participant in a game or contest;

(2) makes a bet on the result of any political nomination, appointment, or election or on the degree of success of any nominee, appointee, or candidate; or

(3) plays and bets for money or other thing of value at any game played with cards, dice, balls, or any other gambling device.

(b) It is a defense to prosecution under this section that:

(1) the actor engaged in gambling in a private place;

(2) no person received any economic benefit other than personal winnings; and

(3) except for the advantage of skill or luck, the risks of losing and the chances of winning were the same for all participants.

(c) It is a defense to prosecution under this section that the actor reasonably believed that the conduct:

(1) was permitted under Chapter 2001, Occupations Code;

(2) was permitted under Chapter 2002, Occupations Code;

(3) consisted entirely of participation in the state lottery authorized by the State Lottery Act (Chapter 466, Government Code);

(4) was permitted under the Texas Racing Act (Article 179e, Vernon's Texas Civil Statutes); or

(5) consisted entirely of participation in a drawing for the opportunity to participate in a hunting, fishing, or other recreational event conducted by the Parks and Wildlife Department.

(d) An offense under this section is a Class C misdemeanor.

(e) It is a defense to prosecution under this section that a person played for something of value other than money using an electronic, electromechanical, or mechanical contrivance excluded from the definition of "gambling device" under Section 47.01(4)(B).

Acts 1973, 63rd Leg., p. 883, ch. 399, § 1, eff. Jan. 1, 1974. Amended by Acts 1981, 67th Leg., 1st C.S., p. 101, ch. 11, § 43, eff. Nov. 10, 1981; Acts 1989, 71st Leg., ch. 957, § 2, eff. Jan. 1, 1990; Acts 1991, 72nd Leg., 1st C.S., ch. 6, § 3; Acts 1993, 73rd Leg., ch. 107, § 4.04, eff. Aug. 30, 1993; Acts 1993, 73rd Leg., ch. 774, § 2, eff. Aug. 30, 1993. Acts 1993, 73rd Leg., ch. 900, § 1.01, eff. Sept. 1, 1994; Acts 1995, 74th Leg., ch. 76, § 14.53, eff. Sept. 1, 1995; Acts 1995, 74th Leg., ch. 318, § 20, eff. Sept. 1, 1995; Acts 1995, 74th Leg., ch. 931, § 79, eff. June 16, 1995; Acts 1997, 75th Leg., ch. 1256, § 124, eff. Sept. 1, 1997; Acts 2001, 77th Leg., ch. 1420, § 14.834, eff. Sept. 1, 2001.

§ 47.03. Gambling Promotion

(a) A person commits an offense if he intentionally or knowingly does any of the following acts:

(1) operates or participates in the earnings of a gambling place;

(2) engages in bookmaking;

(3) for gain, becomes a custodian of anything of value bet or offered to be bet;

(4) sells chances on the partial or final result of or on the margin of victory in any game or contest or on the performance of any participant in any game or contest or on the result of any political nomination, appointment, or election or on the degree of success of any nominee, appointee, or candidate; or

(5) for gain, sets up or promotes any lottery or sells or offers to sell or knowingly possesses for transfer, or transfers any card, stub, ticket, check, or other device designed to serve as evidence of participation in any lottery.

(b) An offense under this section is a Class A misdemeanor.

Acts 1973, 63rd Leg., p. 883, ch. 399, § 1, eff. Jan. 1, 1974. Amended by Acts 1987, 70th Leg., ch. 313, § 3, eff. Sept. 1, 1987; Acts 1993, 73rd Leg., ch. 900, § 1.01, eff. Sept. 1, 1994.

§ 47.04. Keeping a Gambling Place

(a) A person commits an offense if he knowingly uses or permits another to use as a gambling place any real estate, building, room, tent, vehicle, boat, or other property whatsoever owned by him or under his control, or rents or lets any such property with a view or expectation that it be so used.

(b) It is an affirmative defense to prosecution under this section that:

(1) the gambling occurred in a private place;

(2) no person received any economic benefit other than personal winnings; and

(3) except for the advantage of skill or luck, the risks of losing and the chances of winning were the same for all participants.

(c) An offense under this section is a Class A misdemeanor.

Acts 1973, 63rd Leg., p. 883, ch. 399, § 1, eff. Jan. 1, 1974. Amended by Acts 1977, 65th Leg., p. 667, ch. 251, § 1, eff. Aug. 29, 1977. Acts 1989, 71st Leg., ch. 1030, § 1, eff. Sept. 1, 1989. Acts 1993, 73rd Leg., ch. 900, § 1.01, eff. Sept. 1, 1994.

§ 47.05. Communicating Gambling Information

(a) A person commits an offense if, with the intent to further gambling, he knowingly communicates information as to bets, betting odds, or changes in betting odds or he knowingly provides, installs, or maintains equipment for the transmission or receipt of such information.

(b) It is an exception to the application of Subsection (a) that the information communicated is intended for use in placing a lawful wager under Article 11, Texas Racing Act (Article 179e, Vernon's Texas Civil Statutes), and is not communicated in violation of Section 14.01 of that Act.

(c) An offense under this section is a Class A misdemeanor.

Acts 1973, 63rd Leg., p. 883, ch. 399, § 1, eff. Jan. 1, 1974. Amended by Acts 1993, 73rd Leg., ch. 900, § 1.01, eff. Sept. 1, 1994.

§ 47.06. Possession of Gambling Device, Equipment, or Paraphernalia

(a) A person commits an offense if, with the intent to further gambling, he knowingly owns, manufactures, transfers, or possesses any gambling device that he knows is designed for gambling purposes or any equipment that he knows is designed as a subassembly or essential part of a gambling device.

(b) A person commits an offense if, with the intent to further gambling, he knowingly owns, manufactures, transfers commercially, or possesses any altered gambling equipment that he knows is designed for gambling purposes or any equipment that he knows is designed as a subassembly or essential part of such device.

(c) A person commits an offense if, with the intent to further gambling, the person knowingly owns, manufactures, transfers commercially, or possesses gambling paraphernalia.

(d) It is a defense to prosecution under Subsections (a) and (c) that:

(1) the device, equipment, or paraphernalia is used for or is intended for use in gambling that is to occur entirely in a private place;

(2) a person involved in the gambling does not receive any economic benefit other than personal winnings; and

(3) except for the advantage of skill or luck, the chance of winning is the same for all participants.

(e) An offense under this section is a Class A misdemeanor.

(f) It is a defense to prosecution under Subsection (a) or (c) that the person owned, manufactured, transferred, or possessed the gambling device, equipment, or paraphernalia for the sole purpose of shipping it to another jurisdiction where the possession or use of the device, equipment, or paraphernalia was legal.

(g) A district or county attorney is not required to have a search warrant or subpoena to inspect a gambling device or gambling equipment or paraphernalia on an ocean-going vessel that enters the territorial waters of this state to call at a port in this state.

Acts 1973, 63rd Leg., p. 883, ch. 399, § 1, eff. Jan. 1, 1974. Amended by Acts 1977, 65th Leg., p. 668, ch. 251, § 2, eff. Aug. 29, 1977; Acts 1977, 65th Leg., p. 1865, ch. 741, § 1, eff. Aug. 29, 1977; Acts 1987, 70th Leg., ch. 167, § 5.01(a)(48), eff. Sept. 1, 1987; Acts 1987, 70th Leg., ch. 458, § 1, eff. Sept. 1, 1987; Acts 1989, 71st Leg., ch. 1030, § 2, eff. Sept. 1, 1989; Acts 1991, 72nd Leg., ch. 44, § 1, eff. Aug. 26, 1991; Acts 1991, 72nd Leg., ch. 315, § 1, eff. Sept. 1, 1991; Acts 1991, 72nd Leg., 1st C.S., ch. 6, § 4; Acts 1993, 73rd Leg., ch. 107, § 4.05, eff. Aug. 30, 1993; Acts 1993, 73rd Leg., ch. 284, § 30, eff. Sept. 1, 1993; Acts 1993, 73rd Leg., ch. 900, § 1.01, eff. Sept. 1, 1994.

§ 47.07. Evidence

In any prosecution under this chapter in which it is relevant to prove the occurrence of a sporting event, a published report of its occurrence in a daily newspaper, magazine, or other periodically printed publication of general circulation shall be admissible in evidence and is prima facie evidence that the event occurred.

Acts 1973, 63rd Leg., p. 883, ch. 399, § 1, eff. Jan. 1, 1974. Renumbered from V.T.C.A., Penal Code § 47.08 and amended by Acts 1993, 73rd Leg., ch. 900, § 1.01, eff. Sept. 1, 1994.

§ 47.08. Testimonial Immunity

(a) A party to an offense under this chapter may be required to furnish evidence or testify about the offense.

(b) A party to an offense under this chapter may not be prosecuted for any offense about which he is required to furnish evidence or testify, and the evidence and testimony may not be used against the party in any adjudicatory proceeding except a prosecution for aggravated perjury.

(c) For purposes of this section, "adjudicatory proceeding" means a proceeding before a court or any other agency of government in which the legal rights, powers, duties, or privileges of specified parties are determined.

(d) A conviction under this chapter may be had upon the uncorroborated testimony of a party to the offense.

Acts 1973, 63rd Leg., p. 883, ch. 399, § 1, eff. Jan. 1, 1974. Renumbered from V.T.C.A., Penal Code § 47.09 by Acts 1993, 73rd Leg., ch. 900, § 1.01, eff. Sept. 1, 1994.

§ 47.09. Other Defenses

(a) It is a defense to prosecution under this chapter that the conduct:

(1) was authorized under:

(A) Chapter 2001, Occupations Code;

(B) Chapter 2002, Occupations Code; or

(C) the Texas Racing Act (Article 179e, Vernon's Texas Civil Statutes);

(2) consisted entirely of participation in the state lottery authorized by Chapter 466, Government Code; or

(3) was a necessary incident to the operation of the state lottery and was directly or indirectly authorized by:

(A) Chapter 466, Government Code;

(B) the lottery division of the Texas Lottery Commission;

(C) the Texas Lottery Commission; or

(D) the director of the lottery division of the Texas Lottery Commission.

(b) It is an affirmative defense to prosecution under Sections 47.04, 47.06(a), and 47.06(c) that the gambling device, equipment, or paraphernalia is aboard an ocean-going vessel that enters the territorial waters of this state to call at a port in this state if:

(1) before the vessel enters the territorial waters of this state, the district attorney or, if there is no district attorney, the county attorney for the county in which the port is located receives notice of the existence of the device, equipment, or paraphernalia on board the vessel and of the anticipated dates on which the vessel will enter and leave the territorial waters of this state;

(2) at all times while the vessel is in the territorial waters of this state all devices, equipment, or paraphernalia are disabled, electronically or by another method, from a remote and secured area of the vessel in a manner that allows only the master or crew of the vessel to remove any disabling device;

(3) at all times while the vessel is in the territorial waters of this state any disabling device is not removed except for the purposes of inspecting or repairing the device, equipment, or paraphernalia; and

(4) the device, equipment, or paraphernalia is not used for gambling or other gaming purposes while the vessel is in the territorial waters of this state.

Added by Acts 1993, 73rd Leg., ch. 900, § 1.01, eff. Sept. 1, 1994. Amended by Acts 1995, 74th Leg., ch. 76, § 14.54, eff. Sept. 1, 1995; Acts 1997, 75th Leg., ch. 111, § 1, eff. May 16, 1997; Acts 1997, 75th Leg., ch. 1035, § 55, eff. June 19, 1997; Acts 1999, 76th Leg., ch. 844, § 1, eff. Sept. 1, 1999; Acts 2001, 77th Leg., ch. 1420, § 14.835, eff. Sept. 1, 2001.

§ 47.10. American Documentation of Vessel Required

If 18 U.S.C. Section 1082 is repealed, the affirmative defenses provided by Section 47.09(b) apply only if the vessel is documented under the laws of the United States.

Added by Acts 1989, 71st Leg., ch. 1030, § 4, eff. Sept. 1, 1989. Renumbered from V.T.C.A., Penal Code § 47.12 by Acts 1990, 71st Leg., 6th C.S., ch. 12, § 2(27), eff. Sept. 6, 1990. Renumbered from V.T.C.A., Penal Code § 47.13 and amended by Acts 1993, 73rd Leg., ch. 900, § 1.01, eff. Sept. 1, 1994.

§ 47.11. Deleted by Acts 1993, 73rd Leg., ch. 900, § 1.01, eff. Sept. 1, 1994

§ 47.111. Deleted by Acts 1993, 73rd Leg., ch. 900, § 13.02, eff. Sept. 1, 1994

§ 47.12. Deleted by Acts 1993, 73rd Leg., ch. 900, § 1.01, eff. Sept. 1, 1994

§ 47.13. Renumbered as V.T.C.A., Penal Code § 47.10 by Acts 1993, 73rd Leg., ch. 900, § 1.01, eff. Sept. 1, 1994

§ 47.14. Deleted by Acts 1993, 73rd Leg., ch. 900, § 1.01, eff. Sept. 1, 1994

CHAPTER 48. CONDUCT AFFECTING PUBLIC HEALTH

Section

§ 48.01. Smoking Tobacco

(a) A person commits an offense if he is in possession of a burning tobacco product or smokes tobacco in a facility of a public primary or secondary school or an elevator, enclosed theater or movie house, library, museum, hospital, transit system bus, or intrastate bus, as defined by Section 541.201, Transportation Code, plane, or train which is a public place.

(b) It is a defense to prosecution under this section that the conveyance or public place in which the offense takes place does not have prominently displayed a reasonably sized notice that smoking is prohibited by state law in such conveyance or public place and that an offense is punishable by a fine not to exceed $500.

(c) All conveyances and public places set out in Subsection (a) of Section 48.01 shall be equipped with facilities for extinguishment of smoking materials and it shall be a defense to prosecution under this section if the conveyance or public place within which the offense takes place is not so equipped.

(d) It is an exception to the application of Subsection (a) if the person is in possession of the burning tobacco product or smokes tobacco exclusively within an area designated for smoking tobacco or as a participant in an authorized theatrical performance.

(e) An area designated for smoking tobacco on a transit system bus or intrastate plane or train must also include the area occupied by the operator of the transit system bus, plane, or train.

(f) An offense under this section is punishable as a Class C misdemeanor.

Added by Acts 1975, 64th Leg., p. 744, ch. 290, § 1, eff. Sept. 1, 1975. Amended by Acts 1991, 72nd Leg., ch. 108, § 2, eff. Sept. 1, 1991; Acts 1993, 73rd Leg., ch. 900, § 1.01, eff. Sept. 1, 1994; Acts 1997, 75th Leg., ch. 165, § 30.242, eff. Sept. 1, 1997.

§ 48.015. Prohibitions Relating to Certain Cigarettes

(a) A person may not acquire, hold, own, possess, or transport for sale or distribution in this state or import or cause to be imported into this state for sale or distribution in this state:

(1) cigarettes that do not comply with all applicable requirements imposed by or under federal law and implementing regulations; or

(2) cigarettes to which stamps may not be affixed under Section 154.0415, Tax Code, other than cigarettes lawfully imported or brought into the state for personal use and cigarettes lawfully sold or intended to be sold as duty-free merchandise by a duty-free sales enterprise in accordance with 19 U.S.C. Section 1555(b), as amended.

(b) A person who commits an act prohibited by Subsection (a), knowing or having reason to know that the person is doing so, is guilty of a Class A misdemeanor.

Added by Acts 2001, 77th Leg., ch. 1104, § 6, eff. Sept. 1, 2001.

§ 48.02. Prohibition of the Purchase and Sale of Human Organs

(a) "Human organ" means the human kidney, liver, heart, lung, pancreas, eye, bone, skin, fetal tissue, or any other human organ or tissue, but does not include hair or blood, blood components (including plasma), blood derivatives, or blood reagents.

(b) A person commits an offense if he or she knowingly or intentionally offers to buy, offers to sell, acquires, receives, sells, or otherwise transfers any human organ for valuable consideration.

(c) It is an exception to the application of this section that the valuable consideration is: (1) a fee paid to a physician or to other medical personnel for services rendered in the usual course of medical practice or a fee paid for hospital or other clinical services; (2) reimbursement of legal or medical expenses incurred for the benefit of the ultimate receiver of the organ; or (3) reimbursement of expenses of travel, housing, and lost wages incurred by the donor of a human organ in connection with the donation of the organ.

(d) A violation of this section is a Class A misdemeanor.

Added by Acts 1985, 69th Leg., ch. 40, § 1, eff. Aug. 26, 1985. Amended by Acts 1993, 73rd Leg., ch. 900, § 1.01, eff. Sept. 1, 1994.

CHAPTER 49. INTOXICATION AND ALCOHOLIC BEVERAGE OFFENSES

Section

§ 49.01. Definitions

In this chapter:

(1) "Alcohol concentration" means the number of grams of alcohol per:

(A) 210 liters of breath;

(B) 100 milliliters of blood; or

(C) 67 milliliters of urine.

(2) "Intoxicated" means:

(A) not having the normal use of mental or physical faculties by reason of the introduction of alcohol, a controlled substance, a drug, a dangerous drug, a combination of two or more of those substances, or any other substance into the body; or

(B) having an alcohol concentration of 0.08 or more.

(3) "Motor vehicle" has the meaning assigned by Section 32.34(a).

(4) "Watercraft" means a vessel, one or more water skis, an aquaplane, or another device used for transporting or carrying a person on water, other than a device propelled only by the current of water.

(5) "Amusement ride" has the meaning assigned by Section 2151.002, Occupations Code.

(6) "Mobile amusement ride" has the meaning assigned by Section 2151.002, Occupations Code.

Added by Acts 1993, 73rd Leg., ch. 900, § 1.01, eff. Sept. 1, 1994. Amended by Acts 1999, 76th Leg., ch. 234, § 1, eff. Sept. 1, 1999; Acts 1999, 76th Leg., ch. 1364, § 8, eff. Jan. 1, 2000; Acts 2001, 77th Leg., ch. 1420, § 14.707, eff. Sept. 1, 2001.

§ 49.02. Public Intoxication

(a) A person commits an offense if the person appears in a public place while intoxicated to the degree that the person may endanger the person or another.

(a–1) For the purposes of this section, a premises licensed or permitted under the Alcoholic Beverage Code is a public place.

(b) It is a defense to prosecution under this section that the alcohol or other substance was administered for therapeutic purposes and as a part of the person's professional medical treatment by a licensed physician.

(c) Except as provided by Subsection (e), an offense under this section is a Class C misdemeanor.

(d) An offense under this section is not a lesser included offense under Section 49.04.

(e) An offense under this section committed by a person younger than 21 years of age is punishable in the same manner as if the minor committed an offense to which Section 106.071, Alcoholic Beverage Code, applies.

Added by Acts 1993, 73rd Leg., ch. 900, § 1.01, eff. Sept. 1, 1994. Amended by Acts 1997, 75th Leg., ch. 1013, § 12, eff. Sept. 1, 1997; Acts 2007, 80th Leg., ch. 68, § 25, eff. Sept. 1, 2007.

§ 49.03. Repealed by Acts 2001, 77th Leg., ch. 969, § 10, eff. Sept. 1, 2001

§ 49.031. Possession of Alcoholic Beverage in Motor Vehicle

(a) In this section:

(1) "Open container" means a bottle, can, or other receptacle that contains any amount of alcoholic beverage and that is open, that has been opened, that has a broken seal, or the contents of which are partially removed.

(2) "Passenger area of a motor vehicle" means the area of a motor vehicle designed for the seating of the operator and passengers of the vehicle. The term does not include:

(A) a glove compartment or similar storage container that is locked;

(B) the trunk of a vehicle; or

(C) the area behind the last upright seat of the vehicle, if the vehicle does not have a trunk.

(3) "Public highway" means the entire width between and immediately adjacent to the boundary lines of any public road, street, highway, interstate, or other publicly maintained way if any part is open for public use for the purpose of motor vehicle travel. The term includes the right-of-way of a public highway.

(b) A person commits an offense if the person knowingly possesses an open container in a passenger area of a motor vehicle that is located on a public highway, regardless of whether the vehicle is being operated or is stopped or parked. Possession by a person of one or more open containers in a single criminal episode is a single offense.

(c) It is an exception to the application of Subsection (b) that at the time of the offense the defendant was a passenger in:

(1) the passenger area of a motor vehicle designed, maintained, or used primarily for the transportation of persons for compensation, including a bus, taxicab, or limousine; or

(2) the living quarters of a motorized house coach or motorized house trailer, including a self-contained camper, a motor home, or a recreational vehicle.

(d) An offense under this section is a Class C misdemeanor.

(e) A peace officer charging a person with an offense under this section, instead of taking the person before a magistrate, shall issue to the person a written citation and notice to appear that contains the time and place the person must appear before a magistrate, the name and address of the person charged, and the offense charged. If the person makes a written promise to appear before the magistrate by signing in duplicate the citation and notice to appear issued by the officer, the officer shall release the person.

Added by Acts 2001, 77th Leg., ch. 969, § 2, eff. Sept. 1, 2001.

§ 49.04. Driving While Intoxicated

(a) A person commits an offense if the person is intoxicated while operating a motor vehicle in a public place.

(b) Except as provided by Subsection (c) and § 49.09, an offense under this section is a Class B misdemeanor, with a minimum term of confinement of 72 hours.

(c) If it is shown on the trial of an offense under this section that at the time of the offense the person operating the motor vehicle had an open container of alcohol in the person's immediate possession, the offense is a Class B misdemeanor, with a minimum term of confinement of six days.

Added by Acts 1993, 73rd Leg., ch. 900, § 1.01, eff. Sept. 1, 1994. Amended by Acts 1995, 74th Leg., ch. 76, § 14.55, eff. Sept. 1, 1995.

§ 49.045. Driving While Intoxicated With Child Passenger

(a) A person commits an offense if:

(1) the person is intoxicated while operating a motor vehicle in a public place; and

(2) the vehicle being operated by the person is occupied by a passenger who is younger than 15 years of age.

(b) An offense under this section is a state jail felony.

Added by Acts 2003, 78th Leg., ch. 787, § 1, eff. Sept. 1, 2003.

§ 49.05. Flying While Intoxicated

(a) A person commits an offense if the person is intoxicated while operating an aircraft.

(b) Except as provided by Section 49.09, an offense under this section is a Class B misdemeanor, with a minimum term of confinement of 72 hours.

Added by Acts 1993, 73rd Leg., ch. 900, § 1.01, eff. Sept. 1, 1994.

§ 49.06. Boating While Intoxicated

(a) A person commits an offense if the person is intoxicated while operating a watercraft.

(b) Except as provided by Section 49.09, an offense under this section is a Class B misdemeanor, with a minimum term of confinement of 72 hours.

Added by Acts 1993, 73rd Leg., ch. 900, § 1.01, eff. Sept. 1, 1994.

§ 49.065. Assembling or Operating an Amusement Ride While Intoxicated

(a) A person commits an offense if the person is intoxicated while operating an amusement ride or while assembling a mobile amusement ride.

(b) Except as provided by Subsection (c) and Section 49.09, an offense under this section is a Class B misdemeanor with a minimum term of confinement of 72 hours.

(c) If it is shown on the trial of an offense under this section that at the time of the offense the person operating the amusement ride or assembling the mobile amusement ride had an open container of alcohol in the person's immediate possession, the offense is a Class B misdemeanor with a minimum term of confinement of six days.

Added by Acts 1999, 76th Leg., ch. 1364, § 9, eff. Jan. 1, 2000.

§ 49.07. Intoxication Assault

(a) A person commits an offense if the person, by accident or mistake:

(1) while operating an aircraft, watercraft, or amusement ride while intoxicated, or while operating a motor vehicle in a public place while intoxicated, by reason of that intoxication causes serious bodily injury to another; or

(2) as a result of assembling a mobile amusement ride while intoxicated causes serious bodily injury to another.

(b) In this section, "serious bodily injury" means injury that creates a substantial risk of death or that causes serious permanent disfigurement or protracted loss or impairment of the function of any bodily member or organ.

(c) Except as provided by Section 49.09, an offense under this section is a felony of the third degree.

Added by Acts 1993, 73rd Leg., ch. 900, § 1.01, eff. Sept. 1, 1994. Amended by Acts 1999, 76th Leg., ch. 1364, § 10, eff. Jan. 1, 2000; Acts 2007, 80th Leg., ch. 662, § 2, eff. Sept. 1, 2007.

Sections 1 and 5 of Acts 2007, 80th Leg., ch. 662 provide:

"Sec. 1. This Act shall be known as the Darren Medlin and Dwayne Freeto Act."

"Sec. 5. The change in law made by this Act applies only to an offense committed on or after September 1, 2007. An offense committed before September 1, 2007, is covered by the law in effect when the offense was committed, and the former law is continued in effect for that purpose. For purposes of this section, an offense was committed before September 1, 2007, if any element of the offense was committed before that date."

§ 49.08. Intoxication Manslaughter

(a) A person commits an offense if the person:

(1) operates a motor vehicle in a public place, operates an aircraft, a watercraft, or an amusement ride, or assembles a mobile amusement ride; and

(2) is intoxicated and by reason of that intoxication causes the death of another by accident or mistake.

(b) Except as provided by Section 49.09, an offense under this section is a felony of the second degree.

Added by Acts 1993, 73rd Leg., ch. 900, § 1.01, eff. Sept. 1, 1994. Amended by Acts 1999, 76th Leg., ch. 1364, § 11, eff. Jan. 1, 2000; Acts 2007, 80th Leg., ch. 662, § 3, eff. Sept. 1, 2007.

Sections 1 and 5 of Acts 2007, 80th Leg., ch. 662 provide:

"Sec. 1. This Act shall be known as the Darren Medlin and Dwayne Freeto Act."

"Sec. 5. The change in law made by this Act applies only to an offense committed on or after September 1, 2007. An offense committed before September 1, 2007, is covered by the law in effect when the offense was committed, and the former law is continued in effect for that purpose. For purposes of this section, an offense was committed before September 1, 2007, if any element of the offense was committed before that date."

§ 49.09. Enhanced Offenses and Penalties

(a) Except as provided by Subsection (b), an offense under Section 49.04, 49.05, 49.06, or 49.065 is a Class A misdemeanor, with a minimum term of confinement of 30 days, if it is shown on the trial of the offense that the person has previously been convicted one time of an offense relating to the operating of a motor vehicle while intoxicated, an offense of operating an aircraft while intoxicated, an offense of operating a watercraft while intoxicated, or an offense of operating or assembling an amusement ride while intoxicated.

(b) An offense under Section 49.04, 49.05, 49.06, or 49.065 is a felony of the third degree if it is shown on the trial of the offense that the person has previously been convicted:

(1) one time of an offense under Section 49.08 or an offense under the laws of another state if the offense contains elements that are substantially similar to the elements of an offense under Section 49.08; or

(2) two times of any other offense relating to the operating of a motor vehicle while intoxicated, operating an aircraft while intoxicated, operating a watercraft while intoxicated, or operating or assembling an amusement ride while intoxicated.

(b–1) An offense under Section 49.07 is a felony of the second degree if it is shown on the trial of the offense that the person caused serious bodily injury to a peace officer, a firefighter, or emergency medical services personnel while in the actual discharge of an official duty.

(b–2) An offense under Section 49.08 is a felony of the first degree if it is shown on the trial of the offense that the person caused the death of a person described by Subsection (b–1).

(b–3) For the purposes of Subsection (b–1):

(1) "Emergency medical services personnel" has the meaning assigned by Section 773.003, Health and Safety Code.

(2) "Firefighter" means:

(A) an individual employed by this state or by a political or legal subdivision of this state who is subject to certification by the Texas Commission on Fire Protection; or

(B) a member of an organized volunteer firefighting unit that:

(i) renders fire-fighting services without remuneration; and

(ii) conducts a minimum of two drills each month, each at least two hours long.

(c) For the purposes of this section:

(1) "Offense relating to the operating of a motor vehicle while intoxicated" means:

(A) an offense under Section 49.04 or 49.045;

(B) an offense under Section 49.07 or 49.08, if the vehicle operated was a motor vehicle;

(C) an offense under Article 6701l–1, Revised Statutes, as that law existed before September 1, 1994;

(D) an offense under Article 6701l–2, Revised Statutes, as that law existed before January 1, 1984;

(E) an offense under Section 19.05(a)(2), as that law existed before September 1, 1994, if the vehicle operated was a motor vehicle; or

(F) an offense under the laws of another state that prohibit the operation of a motor vehicle while intoxicated.

(2) "Offense of operating an aircraft while intoxicated" means:

(A) an offense under Section 49.05;

(B) an offense under Section 49.07 or 49.08, if the vehicle operated was an aircraft;

(C) an offense under Section 1, Chapter 46, Acts of the 58th Legislature, Regular Session, 1963 (Article 46f–3, Vernon's Texas Civil Statutes), as that law existed before September 1, 1994;

(D) an offense under Section 19.05(a)(2), as that law existed before September 1, 1994, if the vehicle operated was an aircraft; or

(E) an offense under the laws of another state that prohibit the operation of an aircraft while intoxicated.

(3) "Offense of operating a watercraft while intoxicated" means:

(A) an offense under Section 49.06;

(B) an offense under Section 49.07 or 49.08, if the vehicle operated was a watercraft;

(C) an offense under Section 31.097, Parks and Wildlife Code, as that law existed before September 1, 1994;

(D) an offense under Section 19.05(a)(2), as that law existed before September 1, 1994, if the vehicle operated was a watercraft; or

(E) an offense under the laws of another state that prohibit the operation of a watercraft while intoxicated.

(4) "Offense of operating or assembling an amusement ride while intoxicated" means:

(A) an offense under Section 49.065;

(B) an offense under Section 49.07 or 49.08, if the offense involved the operation or assembly of an amusement ride; or

(C) an offense under the law of another state that prohibits the operation of an amusement ride while intoxicated or the assembly of a mobile amusement ride while intoxicated.

(d) For the purposes of this section, a conviction for an offense under Section 49.04, 49.045, 49.05, 49.06, 49.065, 49.07, or 49.08 that occurs on or after September 1, 1994, is a final conviction, whether the sentence for the conviction is imposed or probated.

(e) Repealed by Acts 2005, 79th Leg., ch. 996, § 3.

(f) Repealed by Acts 2005, 79th Leg., ch. 996, § 3.

(g) A conviction may be used for purposes of enhancement under this section or enhancement under Subchapter D, Chapter 12,[1] but not under both this section and Subchapter D.

(h) This subsection applies only to a person convicted of a second or subsequent offense relating to the operating of a motor vehicle while intoxicated committed within five years of the date on which the most recent preceding offense was committed. The court shall enter an order that requires the defendant to have a device installed, on each motor vehicle owned or operated by the defendant, that uses a deep-lung breath analysis mechanism to make impractical the operation of the motor vehicle if ethyl alcohol is detected in the breath of the operator, and that requires that before the first anniversary of the ending date of the period of license suspension under Section 521.344, Transportation Code, the defendant not operate any motor vehicle that is not equipped with that device. The court shall require the defendant to obtain the device at the defendant's own cost on or before that ending date, require the defendant to provide evidence to the court on or before that ending date that the device has been installed on each appropriate vehicle, and order the device to remain installed on each vehicle until the first anniversary of that ending date. If the court determines the offender is unable to pay for the device, the court may impose a reasonable payment schedule not to extend beyond the first anniversary of the date of installation. The Department of Public Safety shall approve devices for use under this subsection. Section 521.247, Transportation Code, applies to the approval of a device under this subsection and the consequences of that approval. Failure to comply with an order entered under this subsection is punishable by contempt. For the purpose of enforcing this subsection, the court that enters an order under this subsection retains jurisdiction over the defendant until the date on which the device is no longer required to remain installed. To the extent of a conflict between this subsection and Section 13(i), Article 42.12, Code of Criminal Procedure, this subsection controls.

Added by Acts 1993, 73rd Leg., ch. 900, § 1.01, eff. Sept. 1, 1994. Amended by Acts 1995, 74th Leg., ch. 76, § 14.56, eff. Sept. 1, 1995; Acts 1995, 74th Leg., ch. 318, § 21, eff. Sept. 1, 1995; Acts 1999, 76th Leg., ch. 1364, §§ 12, 13, eff. Jan. 1, 2000; Acts 2001, 77th Leg., ch. 648, §§ 1, 2, eff, Sept. 1, 2001; Acts 2001, 77th Leg., ch. 969, § 3, eff. Sept. 1, 2001; Acts 2003, 78th Leg., ch. 787, § 2, eff. Sept. 1, 2003; Acts 2003, 78th Leg., ch. 1275, § 2(117), eff. Sept. 1, 2003; Acts 2005, 79th Leg., ch. 996, §§ 1, 3 eff. Sept. 1, 2005; Acts 2007, 80th Leg., ch. 662, § 4, eff. Sept. 1, 2007.

[1] V.T.C.A., Penal Code § 12.41 et seq.

Sections 1 and 5 of Acts 2007, 80th Leg., ch. 662 provide:

"Sec. 1. This Act shall be known as the Darren Medlin and Dwayne Freeto Act."

"Sec. 5. The change in law made by this Act applies only to an offense committed on or after September 1, 2007. An offense committed before September 1, 2007, is covered by the law in effect when the offense was committed, and the former law is continued in effect for that purpose. For purposes of this section, an offense was committed before September 1, 2007, if any element of the offense was committed before that date."

§ 49.10. No Defense

In a prosecution under Section 49.03, 49.04, 49.045, 49.05, 49.06, 49.065, 49.07, or 49.08, the fact that the defendant is or has been entitled to use the alcohol, controlled substance, drug, dangerous drug, or other substance is not a defense.

Added by Acts 1993, 73rd Leg., ch. 900, § 1.01, eff. Sept. 1, 1994. Amended by Acts 1999, 76th Leg., ch. 1364, § 14, eff. Jan. 1, 2000; Acts 2003, 78th Leg., ch. 787, § 3, eff. Sept. 1, 2003.

§ 49.11. Proof of Mental State Unnecessary

(a) Notwithstanding Section 6.02(b), proof of a culpable mental state is not required for conviction of an offense under this chapter.

(b) Subsection (a) does not apply to an offense under Section 49.031.

Added by Acts 1995, 74th Leg., ch. 318, § 22, eff. Sept. 1, 1995. Amended by Acts 2001, 77th Leg., ch. 969, § 4, eff. Sept. 1, 2001.

§ 49.12. Applicability to Certain Conduct

Sections 49.07 and 49.08 do not apply to injury to or the death of an unborn child if the conduct charged is conduct committed by the mother of the unborn child.

Added by Acts 2003, 78th Leg., ch. 822, § 2.05, eff. Sept. 1, 2003.

TITLE 11. ORGANIZED CRIME

CHAPTER 71. ORGANIZED CRIME

Section

§ 71.01. Definitions

In this chapter,

(a) "Combination" means three or more persons who collaborate in carrying on criminal activities, although:

(1) participants may not know each other's identity;

(2) membership in the combination may change from time to time; and

(3) participants may stand in a wholesaler-retailer or other arm's-length relationship in illicit distribution operations.

(b) "Conspires to commit" means that a person agrees with one or more persons that they or one or more of them engage in conduct that would constitute the offense and that person and one or more of them perform an overt act in pursuance of the agreement. An agreement constituting conspiring to commit may be inferred from the acts of the parties.

(c) "Profits" means property constituting or derived from any proceeds obtained, directly or indirectly, from an offense listed in Section 71.02.

(d) "Criminal street gang" means three or more persons having a common identifying sign or symbol or an identifiable leadership who continuously or regularly associate in the commission of criminal activities.

Added by Acts 1977, 65th Leg., p. 922, ch. 346, § 1, eff. June 10, 1977. Amended by Acts 1989, 71st Leg., ch. 782, § 1, eff. Sept. 1, 1989; Acts 1991, 72nd Leg., ch. 555, § 1, eff. Sept. 1, 1991; Acts 1993, 73rd Leg., ch. 900, § 1.01, eff. Sept. 1, 1994; Acts 1995, 74th Leg., ch. 318, § 23, eff. Sept. 1, 1995.

§ 71.02. Engaging in Organized Criminal Activity

(a) A person commits an offense if, with the intent to establish, maintain, or participate in a combination or in the profits of a combination or as a member of a criminal street gang, the person commits or conspires to commit one or more of the following:

(1) murder, capital murder, arson, aggravated robbery, robbery, burglary, theft, aggravated kidnapping, kidnapping, aggravated assault, aggravated sexual assault, sexual assault, forgery, deadly conduct, assault punishable as a Class A misdemeanor, burglary of a motor vehicle, or unauthorized use of a motor vehicle;

(2) any gambling offense punishable as a Class A misdemeanor;

(3) promotion of prostitution, aggravated promotion of prostitution, or compelling prostitution;

(4) unlawful manufacture, transportation, repair, or sale of firearms or prohibited weapons;

(5) unlawful manufacture, delivery, dispensation, or distribution of a controlled substance or dangerous drug, or unlawful possession of a controlled substance or dangerous drug through forgery, fraud, misrepresentation, or deception;

(6) any unlawful wholesale promotion or possession of any obscene material or obscene device with the intent to wholesale promote the same;

(7) any offense under Subchapter B, Chapter 43,[1] depicting or involving conduct by or directed toward a child younger than 18 years of age;

(8) any felony offense under Chapter 32;

(9) any offense under Chapter 36;

(10) any offense under Chapter 34 or 35;

(11) any offense under Section 37.11(a);

(12) any offense under Chapter 20A;

(13) any offense under Section 37.10; or

(14) any offense under Section 38.06, 38.07, 38.09, 38.11, 42.10, 46.06(a)(1), or 46.14.

Text of subsection (b) as amended by Acts 1993, 73rd Leg., ch. 761, § 3

(b) Except as provided in Subsection (c) of this section, an offense under this section is one category higher than the most serious offense listed in Subdivisions (1) through (10) of Subsection (a) of this section that was committed, and if the most serious offense is a Class A misdemeanor, the offense is a felony of the third degree, except that if the most serious offense is a felony of the first degree, the offense is a felony of the first degree.

Text of subsection (b) as amended by Acts 1993, 73rd Leg., ch. 900, § 1.01

(b) Except as provided in Subsections (c) and (d), an offense under this section is one category higher than the most serious offense listed in Subsection (a) that was committed, and if the most serious offense is a Class A misdemeanor, the offense is a state jail felony, except that if the most serious offense is a felony of the first degree, the offense is a felony of the first degree.

Text of subsection (c) as amended by Acts 1993, 73rd Leg., ch. 761, § 3

(c) Conspiring to commit an offense under this section is of the same degree as the most serious offense listed in Subdivisions (1) through (10) of Subsection (a) of this section that the person conspired to commit.

Text of subsection (c) as amended by Acts 1993, 73rd Leg., ch. 900, § 1.01

(c) Conspiring to commit an offense under this section is of the same degree as the most serious offense listed in Subsection (a) that the person conspired to commit.

(d) At the punishment stage of a trial, the defendant may raise the issue as to whether in voluntary and complete renunciation of the offense he withdrew from the combination before commission of an offense listed in Subsection (a) and made substantial effort to prevent the commission of the offense. If the defendant proves the issue in the affirmative by a preponderance of the evidence the offense is the same category of offense as the most serious offense listed in Subsection (a) that is committed, unless the defendant is convicted of conspiring to commit the offense, in which event the offense is one category lower than the most serious offense that the defendant conspired to commit.

Added by Acts 1977, 65th Leg., p. 922, ch. 346, § 1, eff. June 10, 1977. Amended by Acts 1981, 67th Leg., p. 2373, ch. 587, §§ 1 to 3, eff. Sept. 1, 1981; Acts 1989, 71st Leg., ch. 782, § 2, eff. Sept. 1, 1989; Acts 1991, 72nd Leg., ch. 555, § 1, eff. Sept. 1, 1991; Acts 1993, 73rd Leg., ch. 761, § 3, eff. Sept. 1, 1993; Acts 1993, 73rd Leg., ch. 900, § 1.01, eff. Sept. 1, 1994; Acts 1995, 74th Leg., ch. 318, § 24, eff. Sept. 1, 1995; Acts 1997, 75th Leg., ch. 189, § 9, eff. May 21, 1997; Acts 1999, 76th Leg., ch. 685, § 8, eff. Sept. 1, 1999; Acts 2003, 78th Leg., ch. 641, § 3, eff. Sept. 1, 2003; Acts 2005, 79th Leg., ch. 1162, § 5, eff. Sept. 1, 2005; Acts 2007, 80th Leg., ch. 1163, § 2, eff. Sept. 1, 2007; Acts 2009, 81st Leg., ch. 153, § 2, eff. Sept. 1, 2009; Acts 2009, 81st Leg., ch. 1130, § 1, eff. Sept. 1, 2009; Acts 2009, 81st Leg., ch. 1357, § 2, eff. Sept. 1, 2009.

[1] V.T.C.A., Penal Code § 43.21 et seq.

Section 5 of Acts 2009, 81st Leg., ch. 153 provides:

"The change in law made by this Act in amending Subsection (a), Section 71.02, Penal Code, applies only to an offense committed on or after the effective date [Sept. 1, 2009] of this Act. An offense committed before the effective date of this Act is governed by the law in effect when the offense was committed, and the former law is continued in effect for that purpose. For purposes of this section, an offense was committed before the effective date of this Act if any element of the offense occurred before that date."

Section 9 of Acts 2009, 81st Leg., ch. 1130 provides:

"Section 15.031(e) and Section 71.02(a), Penal Code, as amended by this Act, and Section 71.028, Penal Code, as added by this Act, apply only to an offense committed on or after the effective date [Sept. 1, 2009] of this Act. An offense committed before the effective date of this Act is covered by the law in effect when the offense was committed, and the former law is continued in effect for that purpose. For purposes of this section, an offense was committed before the effective date of this Act if any element of the offense occurred before that date."

Section 5 of Acts 2009, 81st Leg., ch. 1357 provides:

"The changes in law made by this Act apply only to an offense committed on or after the effective date [Sept. 1, 2009] of this Act or to the forfeiture of property used in the commission of that offense. An offense committed before the effective date of this Act, or the forfeiture of property used in the commission of that offense, is governed by the law in effect when the offense was committed, and the former law is continued in effect for that purpose. For purposes of this section, an offense was committed before the effective date of this Act if any element of the offense occurred before that date."

§ 71.021. Violation of Court Order Enjoining Organized Criminal Activity

(a) A person commits an offense if the person knowingly violates a temporary or permanent order issued under Section 125.065(a) or (b), Civil Practice and Remedies Code.

(b) If conduct constituting an offense under this section also constitutes an offense under another section of this code, the actor may be prosecuted under either section or under both sections.

(c) An offense under this section is a Class A misdemeanor.

Added by Acts 1995, 74th Leg., ch. 584, § 1, eff. Sept. 1, 1995.

§ 71.022. Coercing, Inducing, or Soliciting Membership in a Criminal Street Gang

(a) A person commits an offense if the person knowingly causes, enables, encourages, recruits, or solicits another person to become a member of a criminal street gang which, as a condition of initiation, admission, membership, or continued membership, requires the commission of any conduct which constitutes an offense punishable as a Class A misdemeanor or a felony.

(a–1) A person commits an offense if, with intent to coerce, induce, or solicit a child to actively participate in the activities of a criminal street gang, the person:

(1) threatens the child or a member of the child's family with imminent bodily injury; or

(2) causes bodily injury to the child or a member of the child's family.

(b) Except as provided by Subsection (c), an offense under this section is a felony of the third degree.

(c) A second or subsequent offense under this section is a felony of the second degree.

(d) In this section:

(1) "Child" means an individual younger than 17 years of age.

(2) "Family" has the meaning assigned by Section 71.003, Family Code.

Added by Acts 1999, 76th Leg., ch. 1555, § 1, eff. Sept. 1, 1999. Amended by Acts 2009, 81st Leg., ch. 435, §§ 1, 2, eff. Sept. 1, 2009.

Section 4 (a) of Acts 2009, 81st Leg., ch. 435 provides:

"The change in law made by this Act in amending Section 71.022, Penal Code, applies only to an offense committed on or after the effective date of this Act. An offense committed before the effective date of this Act is covered by the law in effect when the offense was committed, and the former law is continued in effect for that purpose. For purposes of this section, an offense was committed before the effective date of this Act if any element of the offense occurred before that date."

§ 71.023. Directing Activities of Certain Criminal Street Gangs

(a) A person commits an offense if the person knowingly initiates, organizes, plans, finances, directs, manages, or supervises a criminal street gang or members of a criminal street gang with the intent to benefit, promote, or further the interests of the criminal street gang or to increase the person's standing, position, or status in the criminal street gang.

(b) An offense under this section is a felony of the first degree.

(c) Notwithstanding Section 71.01, in this section, "criminal street gang" means:

(1) an organization that:

(A) has more than 10 members whose names are included in an intelligence database under Chapter 61, Code of Criminal Procedure;

(B) has a hierarchical structure that has been documented in an intelligence database under Chapter 61, Code of Criminal Procedure;

(C) engages in profit-sharing among two or more members of the organization; and

(D) in one or more regions of this state served by different regional councils of government, continuously or regularly engages in conduct:

(i) that constitutes an offense listed in Section 3g(a)(1), Article 42. 12, Code of Criminal Procedure;

(ii) in which it is alleged that a deadly weapon is used or exhibited during the commission of or immediate flight from the commission of any felony offense; or

(iii) that is punishable as a felony of the first or second degree under Chapter 481, Health and Safety Code; or

(2) an organization that, in collaboration with an organization described by Subdivision (1), engages

in conduct or commits an offense or conspires to engage in conduct or commit an offense described by Subdivision (1)(D).

Added by Acts 2009, 81st Leg., ch. 1130, § 3, eff. Sept. 1, 2009.

§ 71.028. Gang–free Zones

(a) In this section:

(1) "Institution of higher education," "playground," "premises," "school," "video arcade facility," and "youth center" have the meanings assigned by Section 481.134, Health and Safety Code.

(2) "Shopping mall" means an enclosed public walkway or hall area that connects retail, service, or professional establishments.

(b) This section applies to an offense listed in Section 71.02(a)(1), (4), or (7), other than burglary, theft, burglary of a motor vehicle, or unauthorized use of a motor vehicle.

(c) Except as provided by Subsection (d), the punishment prescribed for an offense described by Subsection (b) is increased to the punishment prescribed for the next highest category of offense if the actor is 17 years of age or older and it is shown beyond a reasonable doubt on the trial of the offense that the actor committed the offense at a location that was:

(1) in, on, or within 1,000 feet of any:

(A) real property that is owned, rented, or leased by a school or school board;

(B) premises owned, rented, or leased by an institution of higher education;

(C) premises of a public or private youth center; or

(D) playground;

(2) in, on, or within 300 feet of any:

(A) shopping mall;

(B) movie theater;

(C) premises of a public swimming pool; or

(D) premises of a video arcade facility; or

(3) on a school bus.

(d) The punishment for an offense described by Subsection (b) may not be increased under this section if the offense is punishable under Section 71.02 as a felony of the first degree.

Added by Acts 2009, 81st Leg., ch. 1130, § 3, eff. Sept. 1, 2009.

Section 9 of Acts 2009, 81st Leg., ch. 1130 provides:

"Section 15.031(e) and Section 71.02(a), Penal Code, as amended by this Act, and Section 71.028, Penal Code, as added by this Act, apply only to an offense committed on or after the effective date [Sept. 1, 2009] of this Act. An offense committed before the effective date of this Act is covered by the law in effect when the offense was committed, and the former law is continued in effect for that purpose. For purposes of this section, an offense was committed before the effective date of this Act if any element of the offense occurred before that date."

§ 71.029. Maps as Evidence of Location or Area

(a) In a prosecution of an offense for which punishment is increased under Section 71. 028, a map produced or reproduced by a municipal or county engineer for the purpose of showing the location and boundaries of gang-free zones is admissible in evidence and is prima facie evidence of the location or boundaries of those zones if the governing body of the municipality or county adopts a resolution or ordinance approving the map as an official finding and record of the location or boundaries of those zones.

(b) A municipal or county engineer may, on request of the governing body of the municipality or county, revise a map that has been approved by the governing body of the municipality or county as provided by Subsection (a).

(c) A municipal or county engineer shall file the original or a copy of every approved or revised map approved as provided by Subsection (a) with the county clerk of each county in which the zone is located.

(d) This section does not prevent the prosecution from:

(1) introducing or relying on any other evidence or testimony to establish any element of an offense for which punishment is increased under Section 71.028; or

(2) using or introducing any other map or diagram otherwise admissible under the Texas Rules of Evidence.

Added by Acts 2009, 81st Leg., ch. 1130, § 3, eff. Sept. 1, 2009.

§ 71.03. Defenses Excluded

It is no defense to prosecution under Section 71.02 that:

(1) one or more members of the combination are not criminally responsible for the object offense;

(2) one or more members of the combination have been acquitted, have not been prosecuted or convicted, have been convicted of a different offense, or are immune from prosecution;

(3) a person has been charged with, acquitted, or convicted of any offense listed in Subsection (a) of Section 71.02; or

(4) once the initial combination of three or more persons is formed there is a change in the number or identity of persons in the combination as long as two or more persons remain in the combination and are involved in a continuing course of conduct constituting an offense under this chapter.

Added by Acts 1977, 65th Leg., p. 922, ch. 346, § 1, eff. June 10, 1977. Amended by Acts 1993, 73rd Leg., ch. 900, § 1.01, eff. Sept. 1, 1994.

§ 71.04. Testimonial Immunity

(a) A party to an offense under this chapter may be required to furnish evidence or testify about the offense.

(b) No evidence or testimony required to be furnished under the provisions of this section nor any information directly or indirectly derived from such evidence or testimony may be used against the witness in any criminal case, except a prosecution for aggravated perjury or contempt.

Added by Acts 1977, 65th Leg., p. 922, ch. 346, § 1, eff. June 10, 1977. Amended by Acts 1993, 73rd Leg., ch. 900, § 1.01, eff. Sept. 1, 1994.

§ 71.05. Renunciation Defense

Text of subsection (a) as amended by Acts 1993, 73rd Leg., ch. 761, § 3

(a) It is an affirmative defense to prosecution under Section 71.02 of this code that under circumstances manifesting a voluntary and complete renunciation of his criminal objective the actor withdrew from the combination before commission of an offense listed in Subdivisions (1) through (7) or Subdivision (10) of Subsection (a) of Section 71.02 of this code and took further affirmative action that prevented the commission of the offense.

Text of subsection (a) as amended by Acts 1993, 73rd Leg., ch. 900, § 1.01

(a) It is an affirmative defense to prosecution under Section 71.02 that under circumstances manifesting a voluntary and complete renunciation of his criminal objective the actor withdrew from the combination before commission of an offense listed in Subsection (a) of Section 71.02 and took further affirmative action that prevented the commission of the offense.

(b) For the purposes of this section and Subsection (d) of Section 71.02, renunciation is not voluntary if it is motivated in whole or in part:

(1) by circumstances not present or apparent at the inception of the actor's course of conduct that increase the probability of detection or apprehension or that make more difficult the accomplishment of the objective; or

(2) by a decision to postpone the criminal conduct until another time or to transfer the criminal act to another but similar objective or victim.

Text of subsection (c) as amended by Acts 1993, 73rd Leg., ch. 761, § 3

(c) Evidence that the defendant withdrew from the combination before commission of an offense listed in Subdivisions (1) through (7) or Subdivision (10) of Subsection (a) of Section 71.02 of this code and made substantial effort to prevent the commission of an offense listed in Subdivisions (1) through (7) or Subdivision (10) of Subsection (a) of Section 71.02 of this code shall be admissible as mitigation at the hearing on punishment if he has been found guilty under Section 71.02 of this code, and in the event of a finding of renunciation under this subsection, the punishment shall be one grade lower than that provided under Section 71.02 of this code.

Added by Acts 1977, 65th Leg., p. 922, ch. 346, § 1, eff. June 10, 1977. Amended by Acts 1981, 67th Leg., p. 2374, ch. 587, §§ 4, 5, eff. Sept. 1, 1981; Acts 1993, 73rd Leg., ch. 761, § 4, eff. Sept. 1, 1993; Acts 1993, 73rd Leg., ch. 900, § 1.01, eff. Sept. 1, 1994.

Deletion

Acts 1993, 73rd Leg., ch. 900, § 1.01 deleted subsec. (c).

GOVERNMENT CODE

TITLE 4. EXECUTIVE BRANCH

SUBTITLE B. LAW ENFORCEMENT AND PUBLIC PROTECTION

CHAPTER 411. DEPARTMENT OF PUBLIC SAFETY OF THE STATE OF TEXAS

SUBCHAPTER H. LICENSE TO CARRY A CONCEALED HANDGUN

SUBCHAPTER H. LICENSE TO CARRY A CONCEALED HANDGUN

§ 411.171. Definitions

In this subchapter:

(1) "Action" means single action, revolver, or semi-automatic action.

(2) "Chemically dependent person" means a person who frequently or repeatedly becomes intoxicated by excessive indulgence in alcohol or uses controlled substances or dangerous drugs so as to acquire a fixed habit and an involuntary tendency to become intoxicated or use those substances as often as the opportunity is presented.

(3) "Concealed handgun" means a handgun, the presence of which is not openly discernible to the ordinary observation of a reasonable person.

(4) "Convicted" means an adjudication of guilt or, except as provided in Section 411.1711, an order of deferred adjudication entered against a person by a court of competent jurisdiction whether or not the imposition of the sentence is subsequently probated and the person is discharged from community supervision. The term does not include an adjudication of guilt or an order of deferred adjudication that has been subsequently:

(A) expunged;

(B) pardoned under the authority of a state or federal official; or

(C) otherwise vacated, set aside, annulled, invalidated, voided, or sealed under any state or federal law.

(4–a) "Federal judge" means:

(A) a judge of a United States court of appeals;

(B) a judge of a United States district court;

(C) a judge of a United States bankruptcy court; or

(D) a magistrate judge of a United States district court.

(4–b) "State judge" means:

(A) the judge of an appellate court, a district court, or a county court at law of this state;

(B) an associate judge appointed under Chapter 201, Family Code; or

(C) a justice of the peace.

(5) "Handgun" has the meaning assigned by Section 46.01, Penal Code.

(6) "Intoxicated" has the meaning assigned by Section 49.01, Penal Code.

(7) "Qualified handgun instructor" means a person who is certified to instruct in the use of handguns by the department.

(8) Repealed by Acts 1999, 76th Leg., ch. 62, § 9.02(a), eff. Sept. 1, 1999.

Added by Acts 1997, 75th Leg., ch. 165, § 10.01(a), eff. Sept. 1, 1997. Amended by Acts 1999, 76th Leg., ch. 62, §§ 9.01(a), 9.02(a), eff. Sept. 1, 1999; Acts 2005, 79th Leg., ch. 1084, § 1, eff. Sept. 1, 2005; Acts 2007, 80th Leg., ch. 594, § 8, eff. Sept. 1, 2007; Acts 2009, 81st Leg., ch. 1146, §§ 6.06, 11.02, eff. Sept. 1, 2009; Acts 2009, 81st Leg., ch. 1259, § 2, eff. Sept. 1, 2009.

Section 11.26 of Acts 2009, 81st Leg., ch. 1146 provides:

"The changes in law made by Sections 411.171, 411.1711, 411.172, and 411.201(c), Government Code, as amended by this article, apply only to the eligibility of a person for the issuance, modification, or renewal of a license, the application for which is made on or after the effective date of this article. A holder of a license that was issued, modified, or renewed before the effective date of this article is not disqualified from holding that license solely by reason of this article."

§ 411.1711. Certain Exemptions From Convictions

A person is not convicted, as that term is defined by Section 411.171, if an order of deferred adjudication was entered against the person on a date not less than 10 years preceding the date of the person's application for a license under this subchapter unless the order of deferred adjudication was entered against the person for:

(1) a felony offense under:

(A) Title 5, Penal Code;

(B) Chapter 29, Penal Code;

(C) Section 25.07, Penal Code; or

(D) Section 30.02, Penal Code, if the offense is punishable under Subsection (c)(2) or (d) of that section; or

(2) an offense under the laws of another state if the offense contains elements that are substantially similar to the elements of an offense listed in Subdivision (1).

Added by Acts 2005, 79th Leg., ch. 1084, § 2, eff. Sept. 1, 2005. Amended by Acts 2009, 81st Leg., ch. 1146, § 11.01, eff. Sept. 1, 2009.

Section 11.26 of Acts 2009, 81st Leg., ch. 1146 provides:

"The changes in law made by Sections 411.171, 411.1711, 411.172, and 411.201(c), Government Code, as amended by this article, apply only to the eligibility of a person for the issuance, modification, or renewal of a license, the application for which is made on or after the effective date of this article. A holder of a license that was issued, modified, or renewed before the effective date of this article is not disqualified from holding that license solely by reason of this article."

§ 411.172. Eligibility

(a) A person is eligible for a license to carry a concealed handgun if the person:

(1) is a legal resident of this state for the six-month period preceding the date of application under this subchapter or is otherwise eligible for a license under Section 411.173(a);

(2) is at least 21 years of age;

(3) has not been convicted of a felony;

(4) is not charged with the commission of a Class A or Class B misdemeanor or equivalent offense, or of an offense under Section 42. 01, Penal Code, or equivalent offense, or of a felony under an information or indictment;

(5) is not a fugitive from justice for a felony or a Class A or Class B misdemeanor or equivalent offense;

(6) is not a chemically dependent person;

(7) is not incapable of exercising sound judgment with respect to the proper use and storage of a handgun;

(8) has not, in the five years preceding the date of application, been convicted of a Class A or Class B misdemeanor or equivalent offense or of an offense under Section 42.01, Penal Code, or equivalent offense;

(9) is fully qualified under applicable federal and state law to purchase a handgun;

(10) has not been finally determined to be delinquent in making a child support payment administered or collected by the attorney general;

(11) has not been finally determined to be delinquent in the payment of a tax or other money collected by the comptroller, the tax collector of a political subdivision of the state, or any agency or subdivision of the state;

(12) is not currently restricted under a court protective order or subject to a restraining order affecting the spousal relationship, other than a restraining order solely affecting property interests;

(13) has not, in the 10 years preceding the date of application, been adjudicated as having engaged in

delinquent conduct violating a penal law of the grade of felony; and

(14) has not made any material misrepresentation, or failed to disclose any material fact, in an application submitted pursuant to Section 411.174.

(b) For the purposes of this section, an offense under the laws of this state, another state, or the United States is:

(1) except as provided by Subsection (b–1), a felony if the offense, at the time the offense is committed:

(A) is designated by a law of this state as a felony;

(B) contains all the elements of an offense designated by a law of this state as a felony; or

(C) is punishable by confinement for one year or more in a penitentiary; and

(2) a Class A misdemeanor if the offense is not a felony and confinement in a jail other than a state jail felony facility is affixed as a possible punishment.

(b–1) An offense is not considered a felony for purposes of Subsection (b) if, at the time of a person's application for a license to carry a concealed handgun, the offense:

(1) is not designated by a law of this state as a felony; and

(2) does not contain all the elements of any offense designated by a law of this state as a felony.

(c) An individual who has been convicted two times within the 10-year period preceding the date on which the person applies for a license of an offense of the grade of Class B misdemeanor or greater that involves the use of alcohol or a controlled substance as a statutory element of the offense is a chemically dependent person for purposes of this section and is not qualified to receive a license under this subchapter. This subsection does not preclude the disqualification of an individual for being a chemically dependent person if other evidence exists to show that the person is a chemically dependent person.

(d) For purposes of Subsection (a)(7), a person is incapable of exercising sound judgment with respect to the proper use and storage of a handgun if the person:

(1) has been diagnosed by a licensed physician as suffering from a psychiatric disorder or condition that causes or is likely to cause substantial impairment in judgment, mood, perception, impulse control, or intellectual ability;

(2) suffers from a psychiatric disorder or condition described by Subdivision (1) that:

(A) is in remission but is reasonably likely to redevelop at a future time; or

(B) requires continuous medical treatment to avoid redevelopment;

(3) has been diagnosed by a licensed physician, determined by a review board or similar authority, or declared by a court to be incompetent to manage the person's own affairs; or

(4) has entered in a criminal proceeding a plea of not guilty by reason of insanity.

(e) The following constitutes evidence that a person has a psychiatric disorder or condition described by Subsection (d)(1):

(1) involuntary psychiatric hospitalization;

(2) psychiatric hospitalization;

(3) inpatient or residential substance abuse treatment in the preceding five-year period;

(4) diagnosis in the preceding five-year period by a licensed physician that the person is dependent on alcohol, a controlled substance, or a similar substance; or

(5) diagnosis at any time by a licensed physician that the person suffers or has suffered from a psychiatric disorder or condition consisting of or relating to:

(A) schizophrenia or delusional disorder;

(B) bipolar disorder;

(C) chronic dementia, whether caused by illness, brain defect, or brain injury;

(D) dissociative identity disorder;

(E) intermittent explosive disorder; or

(F) antisocial personality disorder.

(f) Notwithstanding Subsection (d), a person who has previously been diagnosed as suffering from a psychiatric disorder or condition described by Subsection (d) or listed in Subsection (e) is not because of that disorder or condition incapable of exercising sound judgment with respect to the proper use and storage of a handgun if the person provides the department with a certificate from a licensed physician whose primary practice is in the field of psychiatry stating that the psychiatric disorder or condition is in remission and is not reasonably likely to develop at a future time.

(g) Notwithstanding Subsection (a)(2), a person who is at least 18 years of age but not yet 21 years of age is eligible for a license to carry a concealed handgun if the person:

(1) is a member or veteran of the United States armed forces, including a member or veteran of the reserves or national guard;

(2) was discharged under honorable conditions, if discharged from the United States armed forces, reserves, or national guard; and

(3) meets the other eligibility requirements of Subsection (a) except for the minimum age required by federal law to purchase a handgun.

(h) The issuance of a license to carry a concealed handgun to a person eligible under Subsection (g) does not affect the person's ability to purchase a handgun or ammunition under federal law.

Added by Acts 1997, 75th Leg., ch. 165, § 10.01(a), eff. Sept. 1, 1997. Amended by Acts 1999, 76th Leg., ch. 62, §§ 9.03(a), 9.04(a), eff. Sept. 1, 1999; Acts 2003, 78th Leg., ch. 255, § 1, eff. Sept. 1, 2003; Acts 2005, 79th Leg., ch. 486, § 1, eff. Sept. 1, 2005; Acts 2009, 81st Leg., ch. 1146, § 11.03, eff. Sept. 1, 2009.

Section 11.26 of Acts 2009, 81st Leg., ch. 1146 provides:

"The changes in law made by Sections 411.171, 411.1711, 411.172, and 411.201(c), Government Code, as amended by this article, apply only to the eligibility of a person for the issuance, modification, or renewal of a license, the application for which is made on or after the effective date of this article. A holder of a license that was issued, modified, or renewed before the effective date of this article is not disqualified from holding that license solely by reason of this article."

§ 411.173. Nonresident License

(a) The department by rule shall establish a procedure for a person who meets the eligibility requirements of this subchapter other than the residency requirement established by Section 411.172(a)(1) to obtain a license under this subchapter if the person is a legal resident of another state or if the person relocates to this state with the intent to establish residency in this state. The procedure must include payment of a fee in an amount sufficient to recover the average cost to the department of obtaining a criminal history record check and investigation on a nonresident applicant. A license issued in accordance with the procedure established under this subsection:

(1) remains in effect until the license expires under Section 411.183; and

(2) may be renewed under Section 411.185.

(a–1) Repealed by Acts 2005, 79th Leg., ch. 915, § 4.

(b) The governor shall negotiate an agreement with any other state that provides for the issuance of a license to carry a concealed handgun under which a license issued by the other state is recognized in this state or shall issue a proclamation that a license issued by the other state is recognized in this state if the attorney general of the State of Texas determines that a background check of each applicant for a license issued by that state is initiated by state or local authorities or an agent of the state or local authorities before the license is issued. For purposes of this subsection, "background check" means a search of the National Crime Information Center database and the Interstate Identification Index maintained by the Federal Bureau of Investigation.

(c) The attorney general of the State of Texas shall annually:

(1) submit a report to the governor, lieutenant governor, and speaker of the house of representatives listing the states the attorney general has determined qualify for recognition under Subsection (b); and

(2) review the statutes of states that the attorney general has determined do not qualify for recognition under Subsection (b) to determine the changes to their statutes that are necessary to qualify for recognition under that subsection.

(d) The attorney general of the State of Texas shall submit the report required by Subsection (c)(1) not later than January 1 of each calendar year.

Added by Acts 1997, 75th Leg., ch. 165, § 10.01(a), eff. Sept. 1, 1997. Amended by Acts 1999, 76th Leg., ch. 62, § 9.05(a), eff. Sept. 1, 1999; Acts 2003, 78th Leg., ch. 255, § 2, eff. Sept. 1, 2003; Acts 2003, 78th Leg., ch. 752, § 1, eff. Sept. 1, 2003; Acts 2005, 79th Leg., ch. 915, §§ 1, 2, and 4, eff. Sept. 1, 2005.

§ 411.174. Application

(a) An applicant for a license to carry a concealed handgun must submit to the director's designee described by Section 411.176:

(1) a completed application on a form provided by the department that requires only the information listed in Subsection (b);

(2) one or more photographs of the applicant that meet the requirements of the department;

(3) a certified copy of the applicant's birth certificate or certified proof of age;

(4) proof of residency in this state;

(5) two complete sets of legible and classifiable fingerprints of the applicant taken by a person appropriately trained in recording fingerprints who is employed by a law enforcement agency or by a private entity designated by a law enforcement agency as an entity qualified to take fingerprints of an applicant for a license under this subchapter;

(6) a nonrefundable application and license fee of $140 paid to the department;

(7) evidence of handgun proficiency, in the form and manner required by the department;

(8) an affidavit signed by the applicant stating that the applicant:

(A) has read and understands each provision of this subchapter that creates an offense under the laws of this state and each provision of the laws of this state related to use of deadly force; and

(B) fulfills all the eligibility requirements listed under Section 411.172; and

(9) a form executed by the applicant that authorizes the director to make an inquiry into any noncriminal history records that are necessary to determine the applicant's eligibility for a license under Section 411.172(a).

(b) An applicant must provide on the application a statement of the applicant's:

(1) full name and place and date of birth;

(2) race and sex;

(3) residence and business addresses for the preceding five years;

(4) hair and eye color;

(5) height and weight;

(6) driver's license number or identification certificate number issued by the department;

(7) criminal history record information of the type maintained by the department under this chapter, including a list of offenses for which the applicant was arrested, charged, or under an information or indictment and the disposition of the offenses; and

(8) history, if any, of treatment received by, commitment to, or residence in:

(A) a drug or alcohol treatment center licensed to provide drug or alcohol treatment under the laws of this state or another state, but only if the treatment, commitment, or residence occurred during the preceding five years; or

(B) a psychiatric hospital.

(c) The department shall distribute on request a copy of this subchapter and application materials.

Added by Acts 1997, 75th Leg., ch. 165, § 10.01(a), eff. Sept. 1, 1997. Amended by Acts 1999, 76th Leg., ch. 62, § 9.06(a), eff. Sept. 1, 1999; Acts 2005, 79th Leg., ch. 486, § 2, eff. Sept. 1, 2005; Acts 2009, 81st Leg., ch. 1146, § 11.04, eff. Sept. 1, 2009.

Section 11.27 of Acts 2009, 81st Leg., ch. 1146 provides:

"The changes in law made by Sections 411.174, 411.176, 411.177, 411.184, 411.185, 411.188, 411.1882, and 411.201(d), Government Code, as amended by this article, and by the repeal of Sections 411.175 and 411.189, Government Code, apply only to an application for the issuance, modification, or renewal of a license that is submitted to the Department of Public Safety on or after the effective date of this article. An application submitted before the effective date of this article is governed by the law in effect when the application was submitted, and the former law is continued in effect for that purpose."

§ 411.175. Repealed by Acts 2009, 81st Leg., ch. 1146, § 11.25, eff. Sept. 1, 2009

§ 411.176. Review of Application Materials

(a) On receipt of application materials by the department at its Austin headquarters, the department shall conduct the appropriate criminal history record check of the applicant through its computerized criminal history system. Not later than the 30th day after the date the department receives the application materials, the department shall forward the materials to the director's designee in the geographical area of the applicant's residence so that the designee may conduct the investigation described by Subsection (b). For purposes of this section, the director's designee may be a noncommissioned employee of the department.

(b) The director's designee as needed shall conduct an additional criminal history record check of the applicant and an investigation of the applicant's local official records to verify the accuracy of the application materials. The director's designee may access any records necessary for purposes of this subsection. The scope of the record check and the investigation are at the sole discretion of the department, except that the director's designee shall complete the record check and investigation not later than the 60th day after the date the department receives the application materials. The department shall send a fingerprint card to the Federal Bureau of Investigation for a national criminal history check of the applicant. On completion of the investigation, the director's designee shall return all materials and the result of the investigation to the appropriate division of the department at its Austin headquarters.

(c) The director's designee may submit to the appropriate division of the department, at the department's Austin headquarters, along with the application materials a written recommendation for disapproval of the application, accompanied by an affidavit stating personal knowledge or naming persons with personal knowledge of a ground for denial under Section 411.172. The director's designee may also submit the application and the recommendation that the license be issued.

(d) On receipt at the department's Austin headquarters of the application materials and the result of the investigation by the director's designee, the department shall conduct any further record check or investigation the department determines is necessary if a question exists with respect to the accuracy of the application materials or the eligibility of the applicant, except that the department shall complete the record check and investigation not later than the 180th day after the date the department receives the application materials from the applicant.

Added by Acts 1997, 75th Leg., ch. 165, § 10.01(a), eff. Sept. 1, 1997. Amended by Acts 1999, 76th Leg., ch. 62, § 9.07(a), eff. Sept. 1, 1999; Acts 2009, 81st Leg., ch. 1146, § 11.05, eff. Sept. 1, 2009.

Section 11.27 of Acts 2009, 81st Leg., ch. 1146 provides:

"The changes in law made by Sections 411.174, 411.176, 411.177, 411.184, 411.185, 411.188, 411.1882, and 411.201(d), Government Code, as amended by this article, and by the repeal of Sections 411.175 and 411.189, Government Code, apply only to an application for the issuance, modification, or renewal of a license that is submitted to the Department of Public Safety on or after the effective date of this article. An application submitted before the effective date of this article is governed by the law in effect when the application was submitted, and the former law is continued in effect for that purpose."

§ 411.177. Issuance or Denial of License

(a) The department shall issue a license to carry a concealed handgun to an applicant if the applicant meets all the eligibility requirements and submits all the application materials. The department may issue a license to carry handguns only of the categories for which the applicant has demonstrated proficiency in the form and manner required by the department. The department shall administer the licensing procedures in good faith so that any applicant who meets all the eligibility requirements and submits all the application materials shall receive a license. The department may not deny an application on the basis of a capricious or arbitrary decision by the department.

(b) The department shall, not later than the 60th day after the date of the receipt by the director's designee of the completed application materials:

(1) issue the license;

(2) notify the applicant in writing that the application was denied:

(A) on the grounds that the applicant failed to qualify under the criteria listed in Section 411.172;

(B) based on the affidavit of the director's designee submitted to the department under Section 411.176(c); or

(C) based on the affidavit of the qualified handgun instructor submitted to the department under Section 411.188(k); or

(3) notify the applicant in writing that the department is unable to make a determination regarding the issuance or denial of a license to the applicant within the 60–day period prescribed by this subsection and include in that notification an explanation of the reason for the inability and an estimation of the amount of time the department will need to make the determination.

(c) Failure of the department to issue or deny a license for a period of more than 30 days after the department is required to act under Subsection (b) constitutes denial.

(d) A license issued under this subchapter is effective from the date of issuance.

Added by Acts 1997, 75th Leg., ch. 165, § 10.01(a), eff. Sept. 1, 1997. Amended by Acts 1999, 76th Leg., ch. 62, § 9.08(a), eff. Sept. 1, 1999; Acts 2009, 81st Leg., ch. 1146, § 11.06, eff. Sept. 1, 2009.

Section 11.27 of Acts 2009, 81st Leg., ch. 1146 provides:

"The changes in law made by Sections 411.174, 411.176, 411.177, 411.184, 411.185, 411.188, 411.1882, and 411.201(d), Government Code, as amended by this article, and by the repeal of Sections 411.175 and 411.189, Government Code, apply only to an application for the issuance, modification, or renewal of a license that is submitted to the Department of Public Safety on or after the effective date of this article. An application submitted before the effective date of this article is governed by the law in effect when the application was submitted, and the former law is continued in effect for that purpose."

§ 411.178. Notice to Local Law Enforcement

On request of a local law enforcement agency, the department shall notify the agency of the licenses that have been issued to license holders who reside in the county in which the agency is located.

Added by Acts 1997, 75th Leg., ch. 165, § 10.01(a), eff. Sept. 1, 1997. Amended by Acts 1999, 76th Leg., ch. 1189, § 14, eff. Sept. 1, 1999.

§ 411.179. Form of License

(a) The department by rule shall adopt the form of the license. A license must include:

(1) a number assigned to the license holder by the department;

(2) a statement of the period for which the license is effective;

(3) a statement of the category or categories of handguns the license holder may carry as provided by Subsection (b);

(4) a color photograph of the license holder;

(5) the license holder's full name, date of birth, hair and eye color, height, weight, and signature;

(6) the license holder's residence address or, as provided by Subsection (d), the street address of the courthouse in which the license holder or license holder's spouse serves as a federal judge or the license holder serves as a state judge; and

(7) the number of a driver's license or an identification certificate issued to the license holder by the department.

(b) A category of handguns contains handguns that are not prohibited by law and are of certain actions. The categories of handguns are:

(1) SA: any handguns, whether semi-automatic or not; and

(2) NSA: handguns that are not semi-automatic.

(c) In adopting the form of the license under Subsection (a), the department shall establish a procedure for the license of a qualified handgun instructor or of a judge, justice, prosecuting attorney, or assistant prosecuting attorney, as described by Section 46.15(a)(4) or (6), Penal Code, to indicate on the license the license holder's status as a qualified handgun instructor or as a judge, justice, district attorney, criminal district attorney, or county attorney. In establishing the procedure, the department shall require sufficient documentary evidence to establish the license holder's status under this subsection.

(d) In adopting the form of the license under Subsection (a), the department shall establish a procedure for the license of a federal judge, a state judge, or the spouse of a federal judge or state judge to omit the license holder's residence address and to include, in lieu of that address, the street address of the courthouse in which the license holder or license holder's spouse serves as a federal judge or state judge. In establishing the procedure, the department shall require sufficient documentary evidence to establish the license holder's status as a federal judge, a state judge, or the spouse of a federal judge or state judge.

Added by Acts 1997, 75th Leg., ch. 165, § 10.01(a), eff. Sept. 1, 1997. Amended by Acts 2007, 80th Leg., ch. 594, § 9, eff. Sept. 1, 2007; Acts 2007, 80th Leg., ch. 1222, § 1, eff. June 15, 2007; Acts 2009, 81st Leg., ch. 87, §§ 27.001(25), 27.002(6), eff. Sept. 1, 2009; Acts 2009, 81st Leg., ch. 316, § 5, eff. Sept. 1, 2009; Acts 2009, 81st Leg., ch. 1146, § 11.07, eff. Sept. 1, 2009.

§ 411.180. Notification of Denial, Revocation, or Suspension of License; Review

(a) The department shall give written notice to each applicant for a handgun license of any denial, revocation, or suspension of that license. Not later than the 30th day after the notice is received by the applicant, according to the records of the department, the applicant or license holder may request a hearing on the denial, revocation, or suspension. The applicant must make a written request for a hearing addressed to the department at its Austin address. The request for hearing must reach the department in Austin prior to the 30th day after the date of receipt of the written notice. On receipt of a request for hearing from a license holder or applicant, the department shall promptly schedule a hearing in the appropriate justice court in the county of residence of the applicant or license holder. The justice court shall conduct a hearing to review the denial, revocation, or suspension of the license. In a proceeding under this section, a justice of the peace shall act as an administrative hearing officer. A hearing under this section is not subject to Chapter 2001 (Administrative Procedure Act). A district attorney or county attorney, the attorney general, or a designated member of the department may represent the department.

(b) The department, on receipt of a request for hearing, shall file the appropriate petition in the justice court selected for the hearing and send a copy of that petition to the applicant or license holder at the address contained in departmental records. A hearing under this section must be scheduled within 30 days of receipt of the request for a hearing. The hearing shall be held expeditiously but in no event more than 60 days after the date that the applicant or license holder requested the hearing. The date of the hearing may be reset on the motion of either party, by agreement of the parties, or by the court as necessary to accommodate the court's docket.

(c) The justice court shall determine if the denial, revocation, or suspension is supported by a preponderance of the evidence. Both the applicant or license holder and the department may present evidence. The court shall affirm the denial, revocation, or suspension if the court determines that denial, revocation, or suspension is supported by a preponderance of the evidence. If the court determines that the denial, revocation, or suspension is not supported by a preponderance of the evidence, the court shall order the department to immediately issue or return the license to the applicant or license holder.

(d) A proceeding under this section is subject to Chapter 105, Civil Practice and Remedies Code, relating to fees, expenses, and attorney's fees.

(e) A party adversely affected by the court's ruling following a hearing under this section may appeal the ruling by filing within 30 days after the ruling a petition in a county court at law in the county in which the applicant or license holder resides or, if there is no county court at law in the county, in the county court of the county. A person who appeals under this section must send by certified mail a copy of the person's petition, certified by the clerk of the court in which the petition is filed, to the appropriate division of the department at its Austin headquarters. The trial on appeal shall be a trial de novo without a jury. A district or county attorney or the attorney general may represent the department.

(f) A suspension of a license may not be probated.

(g) If an applicant or a license holder does not petition the justice court, a denial becomes final and a revocation or suspension takes effect on the 30th day after receipt of written notice.

(h) The department may use and introduce into evidence certified copies of governmental records to establish the existence of certain events that could result in the denial, revocation, or suspension of a license under this subchapter, including records regarding convictions, judicial findings regarding mental competency, judicial findings regarding chemical dependency, or other matters that may be established by governmental records that have been properly authenticated.

(i) This section does not apply to a suspension of a license under Section 85.022, Family Code, or Article 17.292, Code of Criminal Procedure.

Added by Acts 1997, 75th Leg., ch. 165, § 10.01(a), eff. Sept. 1, 1997. Amended by Acts 1999, 76th Leg., ch. 1412, § 5, eff. Sept. 1, 1999.

§ 411.181. Notice of Change of Address or Name

(a) If a person who is a current license holder moves from any residence address stated on the license, if the name of the person is changed by marriage or otherwise, or if the person's status becomes inapplicable for purposes of the information required to be displayed on the license under Section 411.179, the person shall, not later than the 30th day after the date of the address, name, or status change, notify the department and provide the department with the number of the person's license and, as applicable, the person's:

(1) former and new addresses;

(2) former and new names; or

(3) former and new status.

(b) If the name of the license holder is changed by marriage or otherwise, or if the person's status becomes inapplicable as described by Subsection (a), the person shall apply for a duplicate license. The duplicate license must reflect the person's current name, residence address, and status.

(c) If a license holder moves from the address stated on the license, the person shall apply for a duplicate license.

(d) The department shall charge a license holder a fee of $25 for a duplicate license.

(e) The department shall make the forms available on request.

(f) On request of a local law enforcement agency, the department shall notify the agency of changes made under Subsection (a) by license holders who reside in the county in which the agency is located.

(g) If a license is lost, stolen, or destroyed, the license holder shall apply for a duplicate license not later than the 30th day after the date of the loss, theft, or destruction of the license.

(h) If a license holder is required under this section to apply for a duplicate license and the license expires not later than the 60th day after the date of the loss, theft, or destruction of the license, the applicant may renew the license with the modified information included on the new license. The applicant must pay only the nonrefundable renewal fee.

(i) A license holder whose application fee for a duplicate license under this section is dishonored or reversed may reapply for a duplicate license at any time, provided the application fee and a dishonored payment charge of $25 is paid by cashier's check or money order made payable to the "Texas Department of Public Safety."

Added by Acts 1997, 75th Leg., ch. 165, § 10.01(a), eff. Sept. 1, 1997. Amended by Acts 1999, 76th Leg., ch. 1189, § 15, eff. Sept. 1, 1999; Acts 2005, 79th Leg., ch. 1065, § 3, eff. Sept. 1, 2005; Acts 2007, 80th Leg., ch. 594, § 10, eff. Sept. 1, 2007; Acts 2007, 80th Leg., ch. 1222, § 2, eff. June 15, 2007; Acts 2009, 81st Leg., ch. 316, § 6, eff. Sept. 1, 2009; Acts 2009, 81st Leg., ch. 1146, § 11.08, eff. Sept. 1, 2009.

§ 411.182. Notice

(a) For the purpose of a notice required by this subchapter, the department may assume that the address currently reported to the department by the applicant or license holder is the correct address.

(b) A written notice meets the requirements under this subchapter if the notice is sent by certified mail to the current address reported by the applicant or license holder to the department.

(c) If a notice is returned to the department because the notice is not deliverable, the department may give notice by publication once in a newspaper of general interest in the county of the applicant's or license holder's last reported address. On the 31st day after the date the notice is published, the department may take the action proposed in the notice.

Added by Acts 1997, 75th Leg., ch. 165, § 10.01(a), eff. Sept. 1, 1997.

§ 411.183. Expiration

(a) A license issued under this subchapter expires on the first birthday of the license holder occurring after the fourth anniversary of the date of issuance.

(b) A renewed license expires on the license holder's birthdate, five years after the date of the expiration of the previous license.

(c) A duplicate license expires on the date the license that was duplicated would have expired.

(d) A modified license expires on the date the license that was modified would have expired.

(e) Expired.

Added by Acts 1997, 75th Leg., ch. 165, § 10.01(a), eff. Sept. 1, 1997. Amended by Acts 2005, 79th Leg., ch. 915, § 3, eff. Sept. 1, 2005.

§ 411.184. Modification

(a) To modify a license to allow a license holder to carry a handgun of a different category than the license indicates, the license holder must:

(1) complete a proficiency examination as provided by Section 411.188(e);

(2) submit to the department:

(A) an application for a modified license on a form provided by the department;

(B) evidence of handgun proficiency, in the form and manner required by the department;

(C) payment of a modified license fee of $25; and

(D) one or more photographs of the license holder that meet the requirements of the department.

(b) The director by rule shall adopt a modified license application form requiring an update of the information on the original completed application.

(c) The department may modify the license of a license holder who meets all the eligibility requirements and submits all the modification materials. Not later than the 45th day after receipt of the modification materials, the department shall issue the modified license or notify the license holder in writing that the modified license application was denied.

(d) On receipt of a modified license, the license holder shall return the previously issued license to the department.

(e) A license holder whose application fee for a modified license under this section is dishonored or reversed may reapply for a modified license at any time, provided the application fee and a dishonored payment charge of $25 is paid by cashier's check or money order made payable to the "Texas Department of Public Safety."

Added by Acts 1997, 75th Leg., ch. 165, § 10.01(a), eff. Sept. 1, 1997. Amended by Acts 2005, 79th Leg., ch. 486, § 3, eff. Sept. 1, 2005; Acts 2005, 79th Leg., ch. 1065, § 4, eff. Sept. 1, 2005; Acts 2009, 81st Leg., ch. 1146, § 11.09, eff. Sept. 1, 2009.

Section 11.27 of Acts 2009, 81st Leg., ch. 1146 provides:

"The changes in law made by Sections 411.174, 411.176, 411.177, 411.184, 411.185, 411.188, 411.1882, and 411.201(d), Government Code, as amended by this article, and by the repeal of Sections 411.175 and 411.189, Government Code, apply only to an application for the issuance, modification, or renewal of a license that is submitted to the Department of Public Safety on or after the effective date of this article. An application submitted before the effective date of this article is governed by the law in effect when the application was submitted, and the former law is continued in effect for that purpose."

§ 411.185. Renewal

(a) To renew a license, a license holder must:

(1) complete a continuing education course in handgun proficiency under Section 411.188(c) within the six-month period preceding:

(A) the date of application for renewal, for a first or second renewal; and

(B) the date of application for renewal or the date of application for the preceding renewal, for a third or subsequent renewal, to ensure that the license holder is not required to complete the course more than once in any 10–year period; and

(2) submit to the department:

(A) an application for renewal on a form provided by the department;

(B) evidence of handgun proficiency, in the form and manner required by the department;

(C) payment of a nonrefundable renewal fee as set by the department; and

(D) one or more photographs of the applicant that meet the requirements of the department.

(b) The director by rule shall adopt a renewal application form requiring an update of the information on the original completed application. The director by rule shall set the renewal fee in an amount that is sufficient to cover the actual cost to the department to renew a license. Not later than the 60th day before the expiration date of the license, the department shall mail to each license holder a written notice of the expiration of the license and a renewal form.

(c) The department shall renew the license of a license holder who meets all the eligibility requirements and submits all the renewal materials. Not later than the 45th day after receipt of the renewal materials, the department shall issue the renewal or notify the license holder in writing that the renewal application was denied.

(d) The director by rule shall adopt a procedure by which a license holder who satisfies the eligibility criteria may renew a license by mail. The materials for renewal by mail must include a form to be signed and returned to the department by the applicant that describes state law regarding:

(1) the use of deadly force; and

(2) the places where it is unlawful for the holder of a license issued under this subchapter to carry a concealed handgun.

Added by Acts 1997, 75th Leg., ch. 165, § 10.01(a), eff. Sept. 1, 1997. Amended by Acts 2007, 80th Leg., ch. 694, § 1, eff. Sept. 1, 2007; Acts 2009, 81st Leg., ch. 1146, § 11.10, eff. Sept. 1, 2009.

Section 2 of Acts 2007, 80th Leg., ch. 694 provides:

"The change in law made by this Act applies to a license that is renewed under Subchapter H, Chapter 411, Government Code, on or after the effective date [Sept. 1, 2007] of this Act."

Section 11.27 of Acts 2009, 81st Leg., ch. 1146 provides:

"The changes in law made by Sections 411.174, 411.176, 411.177, 411.184, 411.185, 411.188, 411.1882, and 411.201(d), Government Code, as amended by this article, and by the repeal of Sections 411.175 and 411.189, Government Code, apply only to an application for the issuance, modification, or renewal of a license that is submitted to the Department of Public Safety on or after the effective date of this article. An application submitted before the effective date of this article is governed by the law in effect when the application was submitted, and the former law is continued in effect for that purpose."

§ 411.186. Revocation

(a) The department shall revoke a license under this section if the license holder:

(1) was not entitled to the license at the time it was issued;

(2) made a material misrepresentation or failed to disclose a material fact in an application submitted under this subchapter;

(3) subsequently becomes ineligible for a license under Section 411.172, unless the sole basis for the ineligibility is that the license holder is charged with the commission of a Class A or Class B misdemeanor or equivalent offense, or of an offense under Section 42.01, Penal Code, or equivalent offense, or of a felony under an information or indictment;

(4) is convicted of an offense under Section 46.035, Penal Code;

(5) is determined by the department to have engaged in conduct constituting a reason to suspend a license listed in Section 411.187(a) after the person's license has been previously suspended twice for the same reason; or

(6) submits an application fee that is dishonored or reversed if the applicant fails to submit a cashier's check or money order made payable to the "Department of Public Safety of the State of Texas" in the amount of the dishonored or reversed fee, plus $25, within 30 days of being notified by the department that the fee was dishonored or reversed.

(b) If a peace officer believes a reason listed in Subsection (a) to revoke a license exists, the officer shall prepare an affidavit on a form provided by the department stating the reason for the revocation of the license and giving the department all of the information available to the officer at the time of the preparation of the form. The officer shall attach the officer's reports relating to the license holder to the form and send the form and attachments to the appropriate division of the department at its Austin headquarters not later than the fifth working day after the date the form is prepared. The officer shall send a copy of the form and the attachments to the license holder. If the license holder has not surrendered the license or the license was not seized as evidence, the license holder shall surrender the license to the appropriate division of the department not later than the 10th day after the date the license holder receives the notice of revocation from the department, unless the license holder requests a hearing from the department. The license holder may request that the justice court in the justice court precinct in which the license holder resides review the revocation as provided by Section 411.180. If a request is made for the justice court to review the revocation and hold a hearing, the license holder shall surrender the license on the date an order of revocation is entered by the justice court.

(c) A license holder whose license is revoked for a reason listed in Subsections (a)(1)–(5) may reapply as a new applicant for the issuance of a license under this subchapter after the second anniversary of the date of the revocation if the cause for revocation does not exist on the date of the second anniversary. If the cause for revocation exists on the date of the second anniversary after the date of revocation, the license holder may not apply for a new license until the cause for revocation no longer exists and has not existed for a period of two years.

(d) A license holder whose license is revoked under Subsection (a)(6) may reapply for an original or renewed license at any time, provided the application fee and a dishonored payment charge of $25 is paid by cashier's check or money order made payable to the "Texas Department of Public Safety."

Added by Acts 1997, 75th Leg., ch. 165, § 10.01(a), eff. Sept. 1, 1997. Amended by Acts 1999, 76th Leg., ch. 62, § 9.09(a), eff. Sept. 1, 1999; Acts 2005, 79th Leg., ch. 1065, § 2, eff. Sept. 1, 2005; Acts 2009, 81st Leg., ch. 1146, § 11.11, eff. Sept. 1, 2009.

Section 11.28 of Acts 2009, 81st Leg., ch. 1146 provides:

"The changes in law made by this article to Sections 411.186 and 411.187, Government Code, Article 17.292, Code of Criminal Procedure, and Section 85.022, Family Code, apply only to an administrative or judicial determination concerning the revocation or suspension of a license to carry a concealed handgun that is made on or after the effective date of this article. An administrative or judicial determination made before the effective date of this article is covered by the law in effect when the determination was made, and the former law is continued in effect for that purpose."

§ 411.187. Suspension of License

(a) The department shall suspend a license under this section if the license holder:

(1) is charged with the commission of a Class A or Class B misdemeanor or equivalent offense, or of an offense under Section 42.01, Penal Code, or equivalent offense, or of a felony under an information or indictment;

(2) fails to notify the department of a change of address, name, or status as required by Section 411.181;

(3) carries a concealed handgun under the authority of this subchapter of a different category than the license holder is licensed to carry;

(4) fails to return a previously issued license after a license is modified as required by Section 411.184(d);

(5) commits an act of family violence and is the subject of an active protective order rendered under Title 4, Family Code; or

(6) is arrested for an offense involving family violence or an offense under Section 42.072, Penal Code, and is the subject of an order for emergency protection issued under Article 17.292, Code of Criminal Procedure.

(b) If a peace officer believes a reason listed in Subsection (a) to suspend a license exists, the officer shall prepare an affidavit on a form provided by the department stating the reason for the suspension of the license and giving the department all of the information available to the officer at the time of the preparation of the form. The officer shall attach the officer's reports relating to the license holder to the form and send the form and the attachments to the appropriate division of the department at its Austin headquarters not later than the fifth working day after the date the form is prepared. The officer shall send a copy of the form and the attachments to the license holder. If the license holder has not surrendered the license or the license was not seized as evidence, the license holder shall surrender the license to the appropriate division of the department not later than the 10th day after the date the license holder receives the notice of suspension from the department unless the license holder requests a hearing from the department. The license holder may request that the justice court in the justice court precinct in which the license holder resides review the suspension as provided by Section 411.180. If a request is made for the justice court to review the suspension and hold a hearing, the license holder shall surrender the license on the date an order of suspension is entered by the justice court.

(c) The department shall suspend a license under this section:

(1) for 30 days, if the person's license is subject to suspension for a reason listed in Subsection (a)(2), (3), or (4), except as provided by Subdivision (2);

(2) for not less than one year and not more than three years if the person's license:

(A) is subject to suspension for a reason listed in Subsection (a), other than the reason listed in Subsection (a)(1); and

(B) has been previously suspended for the same reason;

(3) until dismissal of the charges, if the person's license is subject to suspension for the reason listed in Subsection (a)(1); or

(4) for the duration of or the period specified by:

(A) the protective order issued under Title 4, Family Code, if the person's license is subject to suspension for the reason listed in Subsection (a)(5); or

(B) the order for emergency protection issued under Article 17.292, Code of Criminal Procedure, if the person's license is subject to suspension for the reason listed in Subsection (a)(6).

Added by Acts 1997, 75th Leg., ch. 165, § 10.01(a), eff. Sept. 1, 1997. Amended by Acts 1999, 76th Leg., ch. 62, § 9.10(a), eff. Sept. 1, 1999; Acts 1999, 76th Leg., ch. 1412, § 6, eff. Sept. 1, 1999; Acts 2009, 81st Leg., ch. 316, § 7, eff. Sept. 1, 2009; Acts 2009, 81st Leg., ch. 1146, §§ 11.12, 12A.01, eff. Sept. 1, 2009.

Section 11.28 of Acts 2009, 81st Leg., ch. 1146 provides:

"The changes in law made by this article to Sections 411.186 and 411.187, Government Code, Article 17.292, Code of Criminal Procedure, and Section 85.022, Family Code, apply only to an administrative or judicial determination concerning the revocation or suspension of a license to carry a concealed handgun that is made on or after the effective date of this article. An administrative or judicial determination made before the effective date of this article is covered by the law in effect when the determination was made, and the former law is continued in effect for that purpose."

§ 411.188. Handgun Proficiency Requirement

(a) The director by rule shall establish minimum standards for handgun proficiency and shall develop a course to teach handgun proficiency and examinations to measure handgun proficiency. The course to teach handgun proficiency must contain training sessions divided into two parts. One part of the course must be classroom instruction and the other part must be range instruction and an actual demonstration by the applicant of the applicant's ability to safely and proficiently use the applicable category of handgun. An applicant must be able to demonstrate, at a minimum, the degree of proficiency that is required to effectively operate a handgun of .32 caliber or above. The department shall distribute the standards, course requirements, and examinations on request to any qualified handgun instructor.

(b) Only a qualified handgun instructor may administer a handgun proficiency course. The handgun proficiency course must include at least 10 hours and not more than 15 hours of instruction on:

(1) the laws that relate to weapons and to the use of deadly force;

(2) handgun use, proficiency, and safety;

(3) nonviolent dispute resolution; and

(4) proper storage practices for handguns with an emphasis on storage practices that eliminate the possibility of accidental injury to a child.

(c) The department by rule shall develop a continuing education course in handgun proficiency for a license holder who wishes to renew a license. Only a qualified handgun instructor may administer the continuing education course. The course must include:

(1) at least four hours of instruction on one or more of the subjects listed in Subsection (b); and

(2) other information the director determines is appropriate.

(d) Only a qualified handgun instructor may administer the proficiency examination to obtain or to renew a license. The proficiency examination must include:

(1) a written section on the subjects listed in Subsection (b); and

(2) a physical demonstration of proficiency in the use of one or more handguns of specific categories and in handgun safety procedures.

(e) Only a qualified handgun instructor may administer the proficiency examination to modify a license. The proficiency examination must include a physical demonstration of the proficiency in the use of one or more handguns of specific categories and in handgun safety procedures.

(f) The department shall develop and distribute directions and materials for course instruction, test administration, and recordkeeping. All test results shall be sent to the department, and the department shall maintain a record of the results.

(g) A person who wishes to obtain or renew a license to carry a concealed handgun must apply in person to a qualified handgun instructor to take the appropriate course in handgun proficiency and demonstrate handgun proficiency as required by the department.

(h) A license holder who wishes to modify a license to allow the license holder to carry a handgun of a different category than the license indicates must apply in person to a qualified handgun instructor to demonstrate the required knowledge and proficiency in that category.

(i) A certified firearms instructor of the department may monitor any class or training presented by a qualified handgun instructor. A qualified handgun instructor shall cooperate with the department in the department's efforts to monitor the presentation of training by the qualified handgun instructor. A qualified handgun instructor shall make available for inspection to the department any and all records maintained by a qualified handgun instructor under this subchapter. The qualified handgun instructor shall keep a record of all information required by department rule.

(j) The department may offer online, or allow a qualified handgun instructor to offer online, the continuing education instruction course and written section of the proficiency examination required to renew a license.

(k) A qualified handgun instructor may submit to the department a written recommendation for disapproval of the application for a license, renewal, or modification of a license, accompanied by an affidavit stating personal knowledge or naming persons with personal knowledge of facts that lead the instructor to believe that an applicant does not possess the required handgun proficiency. The department may use a written recommendation submitted under this subsection as the basis for denial of a license only if the department determines that the recommendation is made in good faith and is supported by a preponderance of the evidence. The department shall make a determination under this subsection not later than the 45th day after the date the department receives the written recommendation. The 60–day period in which the department must take action under Section 411.177(b) is extended one day for each day a determination is pending under this subsection.

Added by Acts 1997, 75th Leg., ch. 165, § 10.01(a) eff. Sept. 1, 1997. Amended by Acts 1999, 76th Leg., ch. 62, § 9.11(a), eff. Sept. 1, 1999; Acts 2009, 81st Leg., ch. 1146, §§ 5.10, 11.13, eff. Sept. 1, 2009.

Sections 5.16, 5.17, 11.27 of Acts 2009, 81st Leg., ch. 1146 provide:

"Sec. 5.16. The changes in law made by this article by the amendment of Section 411.0035, Government Code, apply only to a person first appointed to the Public Safety Commission or employed by the Department of Public Safety of the State of Texas on or after the effective date of this Act. A person first appointed or employed before the effective date of this Act is governed by the law in effect immediately before that date, and the former law is continued in effect for that purpose.

"Sec. 5.17. The changes in law made by this article by the amendment of Section 411.0195, Government Code, apply only to a complaint filed on or after the effective date of this Act. A complaint filed before the effective date of this Act is governed by the law in effect when the complaint was filed, and the former law is continued in effect for that purpose."

"Sec. 11.27. The changes in law made by Sections 411.174, 411.176, 411.177, 411.184, 411.185, 411.188, 411.1882, and 411.201(d), Government Code, as amended by this article, and by the repeal of Sections 411.175 and 411.189, Government Code, apply only to an application for the issuance, modification, or renewal of a license that is submitted to the Department of Public Safety on or after the effective date of this article. An application submitted before the effective date of this article is governed by the law in effect when the application was submitted, and the former law is continued in effect for that purpose."

§ 411.1881. Exemption From Instruction for Certain Persons

(a) Notwithstanding any other provision of this subchapter, a person may not be required to complete the range instruction portion of a handgun proficiency course to obtain or renew a concealed handgun license issued under this subchapter if the person:

(1) is currently serving in or is honorably discharged from:

(A) the army, navy, air force, coast guard, or marine corps of the United States or an auxiliary service or reserve unit of one of those branches of the armed forces; or

(B) the state military forces, as defined by Section 431.001; and

(2) has, within the five years preceding the date of the person's application for an original or renewed license, as applicable, completed a course of training in handgun proficiency or familiarization as part of the person's service with the armed forces or state military forces.

(b) The director by rule shall adopt a procedure by which a license holder who is exempt under Subsection (a) from the range instruction portion of the handgun proficiency requirement may submit a form demonstrating the license holder's qualification for an exemption under that subsection. The form must provide sufficient information to allow the department to verify whether the license holder qualifies for the exemption.

Added by Acts 2005, 79th Leg., ch. 132, § 1, eff. Sept. 1, 2005.

§ 411.1882. Evidence of Handgun Proficiency for Certain Persons

(a) A person who is serving in this state as a judge or justice of a federal court, as an active judicial officer, as defined by Section 411.201, or as a district attorney, assistant district attorney, criminal district attorney, assistant criminal district attorney, county attorney, or assistant county attorney may establish handgun proficiency for the purposes of this subchapter by obtaining from a handgun proficiency instructor approved by the Commission on Law Enforcement Officer Standards and Education for purposes of Section 1702.1675, Occupations Code, a sworn statement that:

(1) indicates that the person, during the 12–month period preceding the date of the person's application to the department, demonstrated to the instructor proficiency in the use of handguns; and

(2) designates the categories of handguns with respect to which the person demonstrated proficiency.

(b) The director by rule shall adopt a procedure by which a person described under Subsection (a) may submit a form demonstrating the person's qualification for an exemption under that subsection. The form must provide sufficient information to allow the department to verify whether the person qualifies for the exemption.

(c) A license issued under this section automatically expires on the six-month anniversary of the date the person's status under Subsection (a) becomes inapplicable. A license that expires under this subsection may be renewed under Section 411.185.

Added by Acts 2007, 80th Leg., ch. 1222, § 3, eff. June 15, 2007. Amended by Acts 2009, 81st Leg., ch. 1146, § 11.14, eff. Sept. 1, 2009.

Section 11.27 of Acts 2009, 81st Leg., ch. 1146 provides:

"The changes in law made by Sections 411.174, 411.176, 411.177, 411.184, 411.185, 411.188, 411.1882, and 411.201(d), Government Code, as amended by this article, and by the repeal of Sections 411.175 and 411.189, Government Code, apply only to an application for the issuance, modification, or renewal of a license that is submitted to the Department of Public Safety on or after the effective date of this article. An application submitted before the effective date of this article is governed by the law in effect when the application was submitted, and the former law is continued in effect for that purpose."

§ 411.189. Repealed by Acts 2009, 81st Leg., ch. 1146, § 11.25, eff. Sept. 1, 2009

§ 411.190. Qualified Handgun Instructors

(a) The director may certify as a qualified handgun instructor a person who:

(1) is certified by the Commission on Law Enforcement Officer Standards and Education or under Chapter 1702, Occupations Code, to instruct others in the use of handguns;

(2) regularly instructs others in the use of handguns and has graduated from a handgun instructor school that uses a nationally accepted course designed to train persons as handgun instructors; or

(3) is certified by the National Rifle Association of America as a handgun instructor.

(b) In addition to the qualifications described by Subsection (a), a qualified handgun instructor must be qualified to instruct persons in:

(1) the laws that relate to weapons and to the use of deadly force;

(2) handgun use, proficiency, and safety;

(3) nonviolent dispute resolution; and

(4) proper storage practices for handguns, including storage practices that eliminate the possibility of accidental injury to a child.

(c) In the manner applicable to a person who applies for a license to carry a concealed handgun, the department shall conduct a background check of a person who applies for certification as a qualified handgun instructor. If the background check indicates that the applicant for certification would not qualify to receive a handgun license, the department may not certify the applicant as a qualified handgun instructor. If the background check indicates that the applicant for certification would qualify to receive a handgun license, the department shall provide handgun instructor training to the applicant. The applicant shall pay a fee of $100 to the department for the training. The applicant must take and successfully complete the training offered by the department and pay the training fee before the department may certify the applicant as a qualified handgun instructor. The department shall issue a license to carry a concealed handgun under the authority of this subchapter to any person who is certified as a qualified handgun instructor and who pays to the department a fee of $100 in addition to the training fee. The department by rule may prorate or waive the training fee for an employee of another governmental entity.

(d) The certification of a qualified handgun instructor expires on the second anniversary after the date of certification. To renew a certification, the qualified handgun instructor must pay a fee of $100 and take and successfully complete the retraining courses required by department rule.

(d-1) The department shall ensure that an applicant may renew certification under Subsection (d) from any county in this state by using an online format to complete the required retraining courses if:

(1) the applicant is renewing certification for the first time; or

(2) the applicant completed the required retraining courses in person the previous time the applicant renewed the certificate.

(e) After certification, a qualified handgun instructor may conduct training for applicants for a license under this subchapter.

(f) If the department determines that a reason exists to revoke, suspend, or deny a license to carry a concealed handgun with respect to a person who is a qualified handgun instructor or an applicant for certification as a qualified handgun instructor, the department shall take that action against the person's:

(1) license to carry a concealed handgun if the person is an applicant for or the holder of a license issued under this subchapter; and

(2) certification as a qualified handgun instructor.

Added by Acts 1997, 75th Leg., ch. 165, § 10.01(a), eff. Sept. 1, 1997. Amended by Acts 1999, 76th Leg., ch. 62, § 9.13(a), eff. Sept. 1, 1999; Acts 1999, 76th Leg., ch. 199, § 1, eff. Sept. 1, 1999; Acts 2001, 77th Leg., ch. 1420, § 14.758, eff. Sept. 1, 2001; Acts 2009, 81st Leg., ch. 1146, §§ 5.11, 11.15, eff. Sept. 1, 2009.

Sections 5.16 and 5.17 of Acts 2009, 81st Leg., ch. 1146 provide:

"Sec. 5.16. The changes in law made by this article by the amendment of Section 411.0035, Government Code, apply only to a person first appointed to the Public Safety Commission or employed by the Department of Public Safety of the State of Texas on or after the effective date of this Act. A person first appointed or employed before the effective date of this Act is governed by the law in effect immediately before that date, and the former law is continued in effect for that purpose.

"Sec. 5.17. The changes in law made by this article by the amendment of Section 411.0195, Government Code, apply only to a complaint filed on or after the effective date of this Act. A complaint filed before the effective date of this Act is governed by the law in effect when the complaint was filed, and the former law is continued in effect for that purpose."

§ 411.191. Review of Denial, Revocation, or Suspension of Certification as Qualified Handgun Instructor

The procedures for the review of a denial, revocation, or suspension of a license under Section 411.180 apply to the review of a denial, revocation, or suspension of certification as a qualified handgun instructor. The notice provisions of this subchapter relating to denial, revocation, or suspension of handgun licenses apply to the proposed denial, revocation, or suspension of a certification of a qualified handgun instructor or an applicant for certification as a qualified handgun instructor.

Added by Acts 1997, 75th Leg., ch. 165, § 10.01(a), eff. Sept. 1, 1997.

§ 411.192. Confidentiality of Records

(a) The department shall disclose to a criminal justice agency information contained in its files and records regarding whether a named individual or any individual named in a specified list is licensed under this subchapter. Information on an individual subject to disclosure under this section includes the individual's name, date of birth, gender, race, zip code, telephone number, e-mail address, and Internet website address. Except as otherwise provided by this section and by Section 411.193, all other records maintained under this subchapter are confidential and are not subject to mandatory disclosure under the open records law, Chapter 552.

(b) An applicant or license holder may be furnished a copy of disclosable records regarding the applicant or license holder on request and the payment of a reasonable fee.

(c) The department shall notify a license holder of any request that is made for information relating to the license holder under this section and provide the name of the agency making the request.

(d) The department shall make public and distribute to the public at no cost lists of individuals who are certified as qualified handgun instructors by the department and who request to be included as provided by Subsection (e). The department shall include on the lists each individual's name, telephone number, e-mail address, and Internet website address. The department shall make the list available on the department's Internet website.

(e) An individual who is certified as a qualified handgun instructor may request in writing that the department disclose all or part of the information described by Subsection (d) regarding the individual. The department shall include all or part of the individual's information on the list as requested.

Added by Acts 1997, 75th Leg., ch. 165, § 10.01(a), eff. Sept. 1, 1997. Amended by Acts 2007, 80th Leg., ch. 172, § 1, eff. May 23, 2007; Acts 2009, 81st Leg., ch. 1146, § 6.03, eff. Sept. 1, 2009.

§ 411.193. Statistical Report

The department shall make available, on request and payment of a reasonable fee to cover costs of copying, a statistical report that includes the number of licenses issued, denied, revoked, or suspended by the department during the preceding month, listed by age, gender, race, and zip code of the applicant or license holder.

Added by Acts 1997, 75th Leg., ch. 165, § 10.01(a), eff. Sept. 1, 1997.

§ 411.194. Reduction of Fees Due to Indigency

(a) Notwithstanding any other provision of this subchapter, the department shall reduce by 50 percent any fee required for the issuance of an original, duplicate, modified, or renewed license under this subchapter if the department determines that the applicant is indigent.

(b) The department shall require an applicant requesting a reduction of a fee to submit proof of indigency with the application materials.

(c) For purposes of this section, an applicant is indigent if the applicant's income is not more than 100 percent of the applicable income level established by the federal poverty guidelines.

Added by Acts 1997, 75th Leg., ch. 165, § 10.01(a), eff. Sept. 1, 1997.

§ 411.195. Reduction of Fees for Senior Citizens

Notwithstanding any other provision of this subchapter, the department shall reduce by 50 percent any fee required for the issuance of an original, duplicate, modified, or renewed license under this subchapter if the applicant for the license is 60 years of age or older.

Added by Acts 1997, 75th Leg., ch. 165, § 10.01(a), eff. Sept. 1, 1997. Amended by Acts 2005, 79th Leg., ch. 289, § 1, eff. Sept. 1, 2005.

§ 411.1951. Waiver Or Reduction of Fees for Members or Veterans of United States Armed Forces

(a) In this section, "veteran" means a person who:

(1) has served in:

(A) the army, navy, air force, coast guard, or marine corps of the United States;

(B) the state military forces as defined by Section 431.001; or

(C) an auxiliary service of one of those branches of the armed forces; and

(2) has been honorably discharged from the branch of the service in which the person served.

(b) Notwithstanding any other provision of this subchapter, the department shall waive any fee required for the issuance of an original, duplicate, modified, or renewed license under this subchapter if the applicant for the license is:

(1) a member of the United States armed forces, including a member of the reserves, national guard, or state guard; or

(2) a veteran who, within 365 days preceding the date of the application, was honorably discharged from the branch of service in which the person served.

(c) Notwithstanding any other provision of this subchapter, the department shall reduce by 50 percent any fee required for the issuance of an original, duplicate, modified, or renewed license under this subchapter if the applicant for the license is a veteran who, more than 365 days preceding the date of the application, was honorably discharged from the branch of the service in which the person served.

Added by Acts 2005, 79th Leg., ch. 486, § 4, eff. Sept. 1, 2005. Amended by Acts 2007, 80th Leg., ch. 200, § 1, eff. Sept. 1, 2007.

§ 411.196. Method of Payment

A person may pay a fee required by this subchapter by cash, credit card, personal check, cashier's check, or money order. A person who pays a fee required by this subchapter by cash must pay the fee in person. Checks or money orders must be made payable to the "Texas Department of Public Safety." A person whose payment for a fee required by this subchapter is dishonored or reversed must pay any future fees required by this subchapter by cashier's check or money order made payable to the "Texas Department of Public Safety." A fee received by the department under this subchapter is nonrefundable.

Added by Acts 1997, 75th Leg., ch. 165, § 10.01(a), eff. Sept. 1, 1997. Amended by Acts 2005, 79th Leg., ch. 1065, § 1, eff. Sept. 1, 2005.

§ 411.197. Rules

The director shall adopt rules to administer this subchapter.

Added by Acts 1997, 75th Leg., ch. 165, § 10.01(a), eff. Sept. 1, 1997.

§ 411.198. Law Enforcement Officer Alias Handgun License

(a) On written approval of the director, the department may issue to a law enforcement officer an alias license to carry a concealed handgun to be used in supervised activities involving criminal investigations.

(b) It is a defense to prosecution under Section 46.035, Penal Code, that the actor, at the time of the commission of the offense, was the holder of an alias license issued under this section.

Added by Acts 1997, 75th Leg., ch. 165, § 10.01(a), eff. Sept. 1, 1997.

§ 411.199. Honorably Retired Peace Officers

(a) A person who is licensed as a peace officer under Chapter 1701, Occupations Code, and who has been employed full-time as a peace officer by a law enforcement agency may apply for a license under this subchapter at any time after retirement.

(b) The person shall submit two complete sets of legible and classifiable fingerprints and a sworn statement from the head of the law enforcement agency employing the applicant. A head of a law enforcement agency may not refuse to issue a statement under this subsection. If the applicant alleges that the statement is untrue, the department shall investigate the validity of the statement. The statement must include:

(1) the name and rank of the applicant;

(2) the status of the applicant before retirement;

(3) whether or not the applicant was accused of misconduct at the time of the retirement;

(4) the physical and mental condition of the applicant;

(5) the type of weapons the applicant had demonstrated proficiency with during the last year of employment;

(6) whether the applicant would be eligible for reemployment with the agency, and if not, the reasons the applicant is not eligible; and

(7) a recommendation from the agency head regarding the issuance of a license under this subchapter.

(c) The department may issue a license under this subchapter to an applicant under this section if the applicant is honorably retired and physically and emotionally fit to possess a handgun. In this subsection, "honorably retired" means the applicant:

(1) did not retire in lieu of any disciplinary action;

(2) was eligible to retire from the law enforcement agency or was ineligible to retire only as a result of an injury received in the course of the applicant's employment with the agency; and

(3) is entitled to receive a pension or annuity for service as a law enforcement officer or is not entitled to receive a pension or annuity only because the law enforcement agency that employed the applicant does not offer a pension or annuity to its employees.

(d) An applicant under this section must pay a fee of $25 for a license issued under this subchapter.

(e) A retired peace officer who obtains a license under this subchapter must maintain, for the category of weapon licensed, the proficiency required for a peace officer under Section 1701.355, Occupations Code. The department or a local law enforcement agency shall allow a retired peace officer of the department or agency an opportunity to annually demonstrate the required proficiency. The proficiency shall be reported to the department on application and renewal.

(f) A license issued under this section expires as provided by Section 411.183.

(g) A retired officer of the United States who was eligible to carry a firearm in the discharge of the officer's official duties is eligible for a license under this section. An applicant described by this subsection may submit the application at any time after retirement. The applicant shall submit with the application proper proof of retired status by presenting the following documents prepared by the agency from which the applicant retired:

(1) retirement credentials; and

(2) a letter from the agency head stating the applicant retired in good standing.

Added by Acts 1997, 75th Leg., ch. 165, § 10.01(a), eff. Sept. 1, 1997. Amended by Acts 1999, 76th Leg., ch. 25, § 1, eff. May 3, 1999; Acts 1999, 76th Leg., ch. 62, § 9.14, eff. Sept. 1, 1999; Acts 2001, 77th Leg., ch. 196, § 1, eff. Sept. 1, 2001; Acts 2009, 81st Leg., ch. 1146, § 11.16, eff. Sept. 1, 2009.

§ 411.1991. Active Peace Officers

(a) A person who is licensed as a peace officer under Chapter 1701, Occupations Code, and is employed full-time as a peace officer by a law enforcement agency may apply for a license under this subchapter. The person shall submit to the department two complete sets of legible and classifiable fingerprints and a sworn statement of the head of the law enforcement agency employing the applicant. A head of a law enforcement agency may not refuse to issue a statement under this subsection. If the applicant alleges that the statement is untrue, the department shall investigate the validity of the statement. The statement must include:

(1) the name and rank of the applicant;

(2) whether the applicant has been accused of misconduct at any time during the applicant's period of employment with the agency and the disposition of that accusation;

(3) a description of the physical and mental condition of the applicant;

(4) a list of the types of weapons the applicant has demonstrated proficiency with during the preceding year; and

(5) a recommendation from the agency head that a license be issued to the person under this subchapter.

(b) The department may issue a license under this subchapter to an applicant under this section if the statement from the head of the law enforcement agency employing the applicant complies with Subsection (a) and indicates that the applicant is qualified and physically and mentally fit to carry a handgun.

(c) An applicant under this section shall pay a fee of $25 for a license issued under this subchapter.

(d) A license issued under this section expires as provided by Section 411.183.

Added by Acts 1999, 76th Leg., ch. 62, § 9.15(a), eff. Sept. 1, 1999. Amended by Acts 2009, 81st Leg., ch. 1146, § 11.17, eff. Sept. 1, 2009.

§ 411.200. Application to Licensed Security Officers

This subchapter does not exempt a license holder who is also employed as a security officer and licensed under Chapter 1702, Occupations Code, from the duty to comply with Chapter 1702, Occupations Code, or Section 46.02, Penal Code.

Added by Acts 1997, 75th Leg., ch. 165, § 10.01(a), eff. Sept. 1, 1997. Amended by Acts 2001, 77th Leg., ch. 1420, § 14.759, eff. Sept. 1, 2001.

§ 411.201. Active and Retired Judicial Officers

(a) In this section:

(1) "Active judicial officer" means:

(A) a person serving as a judge or justice of the supreme court, the court of criminal appeals, a court of appeals, a district court, a criminal district court, a constitutional county court, a statutory county court, a justice court, or a municipal court; or

(B) a federal judge who is a resident of this state.

(2) "Retired judicial officer" means:

(A) a special judge appointed under Section 26.023 or 26.024; or

(B) a senior judge designated under Section 75.001 or a judicial officer as designated or defined by Section 75.001, 831.001, or 836.001.

(b) Notwithstanding any other provision of this subchapter, the department shall issue a license under this subchapter to an active or retired judicial officer who meets the requirements of this section.

(c) An active judicial officer is eligible for a license to carry a concealed handgun under the authority of this subchapter. A retired judicial officer is eligible for a license to carry a concealed handgun under the authority of this subchapter if the officer:

(1) has not been convicted of a felony;

(2) has not, in the five years preceding the date of application, been convicted of a Class A or Class B misdemeanor or equivalent offense;

(3) is not charged with the commission of a Class A or Class B misdemeanor or equivalent offense or of a felony under an information or indictment;

(4) is not a chemically dependent person; and

(5) is not a person of unsound mind.

(d) An applicant for a license who is an active or retired judicial officer must submit to the department:

(1) a completed application, including all required affidavits, on a form prescribed by the department;

(2) one or more photographs of the applicant that meet the requirements of the department;

(3) two complete sets of legible and classifiable fingerprints of the applicant, including one set taken by a person employed by a law enforcement agency who is appropriately trained in recording fingerprints;

(4) evidence of handgun proficiency, in the form and manner required by the department for an applicant under this section;

(5) a nonrefundable application and license fee set by the department in an amount reasonably designed to cover the administrative costs associat-

ed with issuance of a license to carry a concealed handgun under this subchapter; and

(6) if the applicant is a retired judicial officer, a form executed by the applicant that authorizes the department to make an inquiry into any noncriminal history records that are necessary to determine the applicant's eligibility for a license under this subchapter.

(e) On receipt of all the application materials required by this section, the department shall:

(1) if the applicant is an active judicial officer, issue a license to carry a concealed handgun under the authority of this subchapter; or

(2) if the applicant is a retired judicial officer, conduct an appropriate background investigation to determine the applicant's eligibility for the license and, if the applicant is eligible, issue a license to carry a concealed handgun under the authority of this subchapter.

(f) Except as otherwise provided by this subsection, an applicant for a license under this section must satisfy the handgun proficiency requirements of Section 411.188. The classroom instruction part of the proficiency course for an active judicial officer is not subject to a minimum hour requirement. The instruction must include instruction only on:

(1) handgun use, proficiency, and safety; and

(2) proper storage practices for handguns with an emphasis on storage practices that eliminate the possibility of accidental injury to a child.

(g) A license issued under this section expires as provided by Section 411.183 and, except as otherwise provided by this subsection, may be renewed in accordance with Section 411.185 of this subchapter. An active judicial officer is not required to attend the classroom instruction part of the continuing education proficiency course to renew a license.

(h) The department shall issue a license to carry a concealed handgun under the authority of this subchapter to an elected attorney representing the state in the prosecution of felony cases who meets the requirements of this section for an active judicial officer. The department shall waive any fee required for the issuance of an original, duplicate, or renewed license under this subchapter for an applicant who is an attorney elected or employed to represent the state in the prosecution of felony cases.

Added by Acts 1997, 75th Leg., ch. 165, § 10.01(a), eff. Sept. 1, 1997. Amended by Acts 2007, 80th Leg., ch. 402, § 1, eff. June 15, 2007; Acts 2007, 80th Leg., ch. 1222, § 4, eff. June 15, 2007; Acts 2009, 81st Leg., ch. 1146, § 11.18, eff. Sept. 1, 2009.

Sections 11.26 and 11.27 of Acts 2009, 81st Leg., ch. 1146 provide:

"Sec. 11.26. The changes in law made by Sections 411.171, 411.1711, 411.172, and 411.201(c), Government Code, as amended by this article, apply only to the eligibility of a person for the issuance, modification, or renewal of a license, the application for which is made on or after the effective date of this article. A holder of a license that was issued, modified, or renewed before the effective date of this article is not disqualified from holding that license solely by reason of this article.

"Sec. 11.27. The changes in law made by Sections 411.174, 411.176, 411.177, 411.184, 411.185, 411.188, 411.1882, and 411.201(d), Government Code, as amended by this article, and by the repeal of Sections 411.175 and 411.189, Government Code, apply only to an application for the issuance, modification, or renewal of a license that is submitted to the Department of Public Safety on or after the effective date of this article. An application submitted before the effective date of this article is governed by the law in effect when the application was submitted, and the former law is continued in effect for that purpose."

§ 411.202. License a Benefit

The issuance of a license under this subchapter is a benefit to the license holder for purposes of those sections of the Penal Code to which the definition of "benefit" under Section 1.07, Penal Code, applies.

Added by Acts 1997, 75th Leg., ch. 165, § 10.01(a), eff. Sept. 1, 1997.

§ 411.203. Rights of Employers

This subchapter does not prevent or otherwise limit the right of a public or private employer to prohibit persons who are licensed under this subchapter from carrying a concealed handgun on the premises of the business.

Added by Acts 1997, 75th Leg., ch. 165, § 10.01(a), eff. Sept. 1, 1997.

§ 411.204. Notice Required on Certain Premises

(a) A business that has a permit or license issued under Chapter 25, 28, 32, 69, or 74, Alcoholic Beverage Code, and that derives 51 percent or more of its income from the sale of alcoholic beverages for on-premises consumption as determined by the Texas Alcoholic Beverage Commission under Section 104.06, Alcoholic Beverage Code, shall prominently display at each entrance to the business premises a sign that complies with the requirements of Subsection (c).

(b) A hospital licensed under Chapter 241, Health and Safety Code, or a nursing home licensed under Chapter 242, Health and Safety Code, shall prominently display at each entrance to the hospital or nursing home, as appropriate, a sign that complies with the requirements of Subsection (c) other than the requirement that the sign include on its face the number "51".

(c) The sign required under Subsections (a) and (b) must give notice in both English and Spanish that it is unlawful for a person licensed under this subchapter to carry a handgun on the premises. The sign must appear in contrasting colors with block letters at least one inch in height and must include on its face the number "51" printed in solid red at least five inches in height. The sign shall be displayed in a conspicuous manner clearly visible to the public.

(d) A business that has a permit or license issued under the Alcoholic Beverage Code and that is not required to display a sign under this section may be required to display a sign under Section 11.041 or 61.11, Alcoholic Beverage Code.

(e) This section does not apply to a business that has a food and beverage certificate issued under the Alcoholic Beverage Code.

Added by Acts 1997, 75th Leg., ch. 165, § 10.01(a), eff. Sept. 1, 1997. Amended by Acts 1999, 76th Leg., ch. 62, § 9.16(a), eff. Sept. 1, 1999; Acts 1999, 76th Leg., ch. 523, § 1, eff. June 18, 1999.

§ 411.205. Requirement to Display License

If a license holder is carrying a handgun on or about the license holder's person when a magistrate or a peace officer demands that the license holder display identification, the license holder shall display both the license holder's driver's license or identification certificate issued by the department and the license holder's handgun license.

Added by Acts 1997, 75th Leg., ch. 165, § 10.01(a), eff. Sept. 1, 1997. Amended by Acts 1999, 76th Leg., ch. 62, § 9.17(a), eff. Sept. 1, 1999; Acts 2009, 81st Leg., ch. 1146, § 12A.02, eff. Sept. 1, 2009.

Section 12A.03 of Acts 2009, 81st Leg., ch. 1146 provides:

"An offense under Section 411.205, Government Code, may not be prosecuted after the effective date of this article. If, on the effective date of this article, a criminal action is pending for an offense under Section 411.205, the action is dismissed on that date. However, a final conviction for an offense under Section 411.205 that exists on the effective date of this article is unaffected by this article."

§ 411.206. Seizure of Handgun and License

(a) If a peace officer arrests and takes into custody a license holder who is carrying a handgun under the authority of this subchapter, the officer shall seize the license holder's handgun and license as evidence.

(b) The provisions of Article 18.19, Code of Criminal Procedure, relating to the disposition of weapons seized in connection with criminal offenses, apply to a handgun seized under this subsection.

(c) Any judgment of conviction entered by any court for an offense under Section 46.035, Penal Code, must contain the handgun license number of the convicted license holder. A certified copy of the judgment is conclusive and sufficient evidence to justify revocation of a license under Section 411.186(a)(4).

Added by Acts 1997, 75th Leg., ch. 165, § 10.01(a), eff. Sept. 1, 1997.

§ 411.207. Authority of Peace Officer to Disarm

(a) A peace officer who is acting in the lawful discharge of the officer's official duties may disarm a license holder at any time the officer reasonably believes it is necessary for the protection of the license holder, officer, or another individual. The peace officer shall return the handgun to the license holder before discharging the license holder from the scene if the officer determines that the license holder is not a threat to the officer, license holder, or another individual and if the license holder has not violated any provision of this subchapter or committed any other violation that results in the arrest of the license holder.

(b) A peace officer who is acting in the lawful discharge of the officer's official duties may temporarily disarm a license holder when a license holder enters a nonpublic, secure portion of a law enforcement facility, if the law enforcement agency provides a gun locker where the peace officer can secure the license holder's handgun. The peace officer shall secure the handgun in the locker and shall return the handgun to the license holder immediately after the license holder leaves the nonpublic, secure portion of the law enforcement facility.

(c) A law enforcement facility shall prominently display at each entrance to a nonpublic, secure portion of the facility a sign that gives notice in both English and Spanish that, under this section, a peace officer may temporarily disarm a license holder when the license holder enters the nonpublic, secure portion of the facility. The sign must appear in contrasting colors with block letters at least one inch in height. The sign shall be displayed in a clearly visible and conspicuous manner.

(d) In this section:

(1) "Law enforcement facility" means a building or a portion of a building used exclusively by a law enforcement agency that employs peace officers as described by Articles 2.12(1) and (3), Code of Criminal Procedure, and support personnel to conduct

the official business of the agency. The term does not include:

(A) any portion of a building not actively used exclusively to conduct the official business of the agency; or

(B) any public or private driveway, street, sidewalk, walkway, parking lot, parking garage, or other parking area.

(2) "Nonpublic, secure portion of a law enforcement facility" means that portion of a law enforcement facility to which the general public is denied access without express permission and to which access is granted solely to conduct the official business of the law enforcement agency.

Added by Acts 1997, 75th Leg., ch. 165, § 10.01(a), eff. Sept. 1, 1997. Amended by Acts 2007, 80th Leg., ch. 572, § 1, eff. Sept. 1, 2007.

§ 411.208. Limitation of Liability

(a) A court may not hold the state, an agency or subdivision of the state, an officer or employee of the state, a peace officer, or a qualified handgun instructor liable for damages caused by:

(1) an action authorized under this subchapter or a failure to perform a duty imposed by this subchapter; or

(2) the actions of an applicant or license holder that occur after the applicant has received a license or been denied a license under this subchapter.

(b) A cause of action in damages may not be brought against the state, an agency or subdivision of the state, an officer or employee of the state, a peace officer, or a qualified handgun instructor for any damage caused by the actions of an applicant or license holder under this subchapter.

(c) The department is not responsible for any injury or damage inflicted on any person by an applicant or license holder arising or alleged to have arisen from an action taken by the department under this subchapter.

(d) The immunities granted under Subsections (a), (b), and (c) do not apply to an act or a failure to act by the state, an agency or subdivision of the state, an officer of the state, or a peace officer if the act or failure to act was capricious or arbitrary.

(e) The immunities granted under Subsection (a) to a qualified handgun instructor do not apply to a cause of action for fraud or a deceptive trade practice.

Added by Acts 1997, 75th Leg., ch. 165, § 10.01(a), eff. Sept. 1, 1997. Amended by Acts 2009, 81st Leg., ch. 1146, § 11.19, eff. Sept. 1, 2009.

Section 11.29 of Acts 2009, 81st Leg., ch. 1146 provides:

"The change in law made by Section 411.208, Government Code, as amended by this article, applies only to a cause of action that accrues on or after the effective date of this article. A cause of action that accrued before the effective date of this article is governed by the law in effect immediately before the effective date of this article, and the former law is continued in effect for that purpose."

HEALTH AND SAFETY CODE

TITLE 6. FOOD, DRUGS, ALCOHOL, AND HAZARDOUS SUBSTANCES

SUBTITLE C. SUBSTANCE ABUSE REGULATION AND CRIMES

CHAPTER 481. TEXAS CONTROLLED SUBSTANCES ACT

SUBCHAPTER A. GENERAL PROVISIONS

SUBCHAPTER B. SCHEDULES

SUBCHAPTER C. REGULATION OF MANUFACTURE, DISTRIBUTION, AND DISPENSATION OF CONTROLLED SUBSTANCES, CHEMICAL PRECURSORS, AND CHEMICAL LABORATORY APPARATUS

SUBCHAPTER D. OFFENSES AND PENALTIES

SUBCHAPTER A. GENERAL PROVISIONS

§ 481.001. Short Title

This chapter may be cited as the Texas Controlled Substances Act.

Acts 1989, 71st Leg., ch. 678, § 1, eff. Sept. 1, 1989.

§ 481.002. Definitions

In this chapter:

(1) "Administer" means to directly apply a controlled substance by injection, inhalation, ingestion, or other means to the body of a patient or research subject by:

(A) a practitioner or an agent of the practitioner in the presence of the practitioner; or

(B) the patient or research subject at the direction and in the presence of a practitioner.

(2) "Agent" means an authorized person who acts on behalf of or at the direction of a manufacturer, distributor, or dispenser. The term does not include a common or contract carrier, public warehouseman, or employee of a carrier or warehouseman acting in the usual and lawful course of employment.

(3) "Commissioner" means the commissioner of public health or the commissioner's designee.

(4) "Controlled premises" means:

(A) a place where original or other records or documents required under this chapter are kept or are required to be kept; or

(B) a place, including a factory, warehouse, other establishment, or conveyance, where a person registered under this chapter may lawfully hold, manufacture, distribute, dispense, administer, possess, or otherwise dispose of a controlled substance or other item governed by this chapter, including a chemical precursor and a chemical laboratory apparatus.

(5) "Controlled substance" means a substance, including a drug, an adulterant, and a dilutant, listed in Schedules I through V or Penalty Groups 1, 1-A, or 2 through 4. The term includes the aggregate weight of any mixture, solution, or other substance containing a controlled substance.

(6) "Controlled substance analogue" means:

(A) a substance with a chemical structure substantially similar to the chemical structure of a controlled substance in Schedule I or II or Penalty Group 1, 1-A, or 2; or

(B) a substance specifically designed to produce an effect substantially similar to, or greater than, the effect of a controlled substance in Schedule I or II or Penalty Group 1, 1-A, or 2.

(7) "Counterfeit substance" means a controlled substance that, without authorization, bears or is in a container or has a label that bears an actual or simulated trademark, trade name, or other identifying mark, imprint, number, or device of a manufacturer, distributor, or dispenser other than the person who in fact manufactured, distributed, or dispensed the substance.

(8) "Deliver" means to transfer, actually or constructively, to another a controlled substance, counterfeit substance, or drug paraphernalia, regardless of whether there is an agency relationship. The term includes offering to sell a controlled substance, counterfeit substance, or drug paraphernalia.

(9) "Delivery" or "drug transaction" means the act of delivering.

(10) "Designated agent" means an individual designated under Section 481.073 to communicate a practitioner's instructions to a pharmacist.

(11) "Director" means the director of the Department of Public Safety or an employee of the department designated by the director.

(12) "Dispense" means the delivery of a controlled substance in the course of professional practice or research, by a practitioner or person acting under the lawful order of a practitioner, to an ultimate user or research subject. The term includes the prescribing, administering, packaging, labeling, or compounding necessary to prepare the substance for delivery.

(13) "Dispenser" means a practitioner, institutional practitioner, pharmacist, or pharmacy that dispenses a controlled substance.

(14) "Distribute" means to deliver a controlled substance other than by administering or dispensing the substance.

(15) "Distributor" means a person who distributes.

(16) "Drug" means a substance, other than a device or a component, part, or accessory of a device, that is:

(A) recognized as a drug in the official United States Pharmacopoeia, official Homeopathic Pharmacopoeia of the United States, official National Formulary, or a supplement to either pharmacopoeia or the formulary;

(B) intended for use in the diagnosis, cure, mitigation, treatment, or prevention of disease in man or animals;

(C) intended to affect the structure or function of the body of man or animals but is not food; or

(D) intended for use as a component of a substance described by Paragraph (A), (B), or (C).

(17) "Drug paraphernalia" means equipment, a product, or material that is used or intended for use in planting, propagating, cultivating, growing, harvesting, manufacturing, compounding, converting, producing, processing, preparing, testing, analyzing, packaging, repackaging, storing, containing, or concealing a controlled substance in violation of this chapter or in injecting, ingesting, inhaling, or otherwise introducing into the human body a controlled substance in violation of this chapter. The term includes:

(A) a kit used or intended for use in planting, propagating, cultivating, growing, or harvesting a species of plant that is a controlled substance or from which a controlled substance may be derived;

(B) a material, compound, mixture, preparation, or kit used or intended for use in manufacturing, compounding, converting, producing, processing, or preparing a controlled substance;

(C) an isomerization device used or intended for use in increasing the potency of a species of plant that is a controlled substance;

(D) testing equipment used or intended for use in identifying or in analyzing the strength, effectiveness, or purity of a controlled substance;

(E) a scale or balance used or intended for use in weighing or measuring a controlled substance;

(F) a dilutant or adulterant, such as quinine hydrochloride, mannitol, inositol, nicotinamide, dextrose, lactose, or absorbent, blotter-type material, that is used or intended to be used to increase the amount or weight of or to transfer a controlled substance regardless of whether the dilutant or adulterant diminishes the efficacy of the controlled substance;

(G) a separation gin or sifter used or intended for use in removing twigs and seeds from or in otherwise cleaning or refining marihuana;

(H) a blender, bowl, container, spoon, or mixing device used or intended for use in compounding a controlled substance;

(I) a capsule, balloon, envelope, or other container used or intended for use in packaging small quantities of a controlled substance;

(J) a container or other object used or intended for use in storing or concealing a controlled substance;

(K) a hypodermic syringe, needle, or other object used or intended for use in parenterally injecting a controlled substance into the human body; and

(L) an object used or intended for use in ingesting, inhaling, or otherwise introducing marihuana, cocaine, hashish, or hashish oil into the human body, including:

(i) a metal, wooden, acrylic, glass, stone, plastic, or ceramic pipe with or without a screen, permanent screen, hashish head, or punctured metal bowl;

(ii) a water pipe;

(iii) a carburetion tube or device;

(iv) a smoking or carburetion mask;

(v) a chamber pipe;

(vi) a carburetor pipe;

(vii) an electric pipe;

(viii) an air-driven pipe;

(ix) a chillum;

(x) a bong; or

(xi) an ice pipe or chiller.

(18) "Federal Controlled Substances Act" means the Federal Comprehensive Drug Abuse Prevention and Control Act of 1970 (21 U.S.C. Section 801 et seq.) or its successor statute.

(19) "Federal Drug Enforcement Administration" means the Drug Enforcement Administration of the United States Department of Justice or its successor agency.

(20) "Hospital" means:

(A) a general or special hospital as defined by Section 241.003 (Texas Hospital Licensing Law); or

(B) an ambulatory surgical center licensed by the Texas Department of Health and approved by the federal government to perform surgery paid by Medicaid on patients admitted for a period of not more than 24 hours.

(21) "Human consumption" means the injection, inhalation, ingestion, or application of a substance to or into a human body.

(22) "Immediate precursor" means a substance the director finds to be and by rule designates as being:

(A) a principal compound commonly used or produced primarily for use in the manufacture of a controlled substance;

(B) a substance that is an immediate chemical intermediary used or likely to be used in the manufacture of a controlled substance; and

(C) a substance the control of which is necessary to prevent, curtail, or limit the manufacture of a controlled substance.

(23) "Institutional practitioner" means an intern, resident physician, fellow, or person in an equivalent professional position who:

(A) is not licensed by the appropriate state professional licensing board;

(B) is enrolled in a bona fide professional training program in a base hospital or institutional training facility registered by the Federal Drug Enforcement Administration; and

(C) is authorized by the base hospital or institutional training facility to administer, dispense, or prescribe controlled substances.

(24) "Lawful possession" means the possession of a controlled substance that has been obtained in accordance with state or federal law.

(25) "Manufacture" means the production, preparation, propagation, compounding, conversion, or processing of a controlled substance other than

marihuana, directly or indirectly by extraction from substances of natural origin, independently by means of chemical synthesis, or by a combination of extraction and chemical synthesis, and includes the packaging or repackaging of the substance or labeling or relabeling of its container. However, the term does not include the preparation, compounding, packaging, or labeling of a controlled substance:

(A) by a practitioner as an incident to the practitioner's administering or dispensing a controlled substance in the course of professional practice; or

(B) by a practitioner, or by an authorized agent under the supervision of the practitioner, for or as an incident to research, teaching, or chemical analysis and not for delivery.

(26) "Marihuana" means the plant Cannabis sativa L., whether growing or not, the seeds of that plant, and every compound, manufacture, salt, derivative, mixture, or preparation of that plant or its seeds. The term does not include:

(A) the resin extracted from a part of the plant or a compound, manufacture, salt, derivative, mixture, or preparation of the resin;

(B) the mature stalks of the plant or fiber produced from the stalks;

(C) oil or cake made from the seeds of the plant;

(D) a compound, manufacture, salt, derivative, mixture, or preparation of the mature stalks, fiber, oil, or cake; or

(E) the sterilized seeds of the plant that are incapable of beginning germination.

(27) "Medical purpose" means the use of a controlled substance for relieving or curing a mental or physical disease or infirmity.

(28) "Medication order" means an order from a practitioner to dispense a drug to a patient in a hospital for immediate administration while the patient is in the hospital or for emergency use on the patient's release from the hospital.

(29) "Narcotic drug" means any of the following, produced directly or indirectly by extraction from substances of vegetable origin, independently by means of chemical synthesis, or by a combination of extraction and chemical synthesis:

(A) opium and opiates, and a salt, compound, derivative, or preparation of opium or opiates;

(B) a salt, compound, isomer, derivative, or preparation of a salt, compound, isomer, or derivative that is chemically equivalent or identical to a substance listed in Paragraph (A) other than the isoquinoline alkaloids of opium;

(C) opium poppy and poppy straw; or

(D) cocaine, including:

(i) its salts, its optical, position, or geometric isomers, and the salts of those isomers;

(ii) coca leaves and a salt, compound, derivative, or preparation of coca leaves; and

(iii) a salt, compound, derivative, or preparation of a salt, compound, or derivative that is chemically equivalent or identical to a substance described by Subparagraph (i) or (ii), other than decocainized coca leaves or extractions of coca leaves that do not contain cocaine or ecgonine.

(30) "Opiate" means a substance that has an addiction-forming or addiction-sustaining liability similar to morphine or is capable of conversion into a drug having addiction-forming or addiction-sustaining liability. The term includes its racemic and levorotatory forms. The term does not include, unless specifically designated as controlled under Subchapter B,[1] the dextrorotatory isomer of 3-methoxy-n-methylmorphinan and its salts (dextromethorphan).

(31) "Opium poppy" means the plant of the species Papaver somniferum L., other than its seeds.

(32) "Patient" means a human for whom or an animal for which a drug is administered, dispensed, delivered, or prescribed by a practitioner.

(33) "Person" means an individual, corporation, government, business trust, estate, trust, partnership, association, or any other legal entity.

(34) "Pharmacist" means a person licensed by the Texas State Board of Pharmacy to practice pharmacy and who acts as an agent for a pharmacy.

(35) "Pharmacist-in-charge" means the pharmacist designated on a pharmacy license as the pharmacist who has the authority or responsibility for the pharmacy's compliance with this chapter and other laws relating to pharmacy.

(36) "Pharmacy" means a facility licensed by the Texas State Board of Pharmacy where a prescription for a controlled substance is received or processed in accordance with state or federal law.

(37) "Poppy straw" means all parts, other than the seeds, of the opium poppy, after mowing.

(38) "Possession" means actual care, custody, control, or management.

(39) "Practitioner" means:

(A) a physician, dentist, veterinarian, podiatrist, scientific investigator, or other person licensed, registered, or otherwise permitted to distribute, dispense, analyze, conduct research with respect to, or administer a controlled substance in the course of professional practice or research in this state;

(B) a pharmacy, hospital, or other institution licensed, registered, or otherwise permitted to distribute, dispense, conduct research with respect to, or administer a controlled substance in the course of professional practice or research in this state;

(C) a person practicing in and licensed by another state as a physician, dentist, veterinarian, or podiatrist, having a current Federal Drug Enforcement Administration registration number, who may legally prescribe Schedule II, III, IV, or V controlled substances in that state; or

(D) an advanced practice nurse or physician assistant to whom a physician has delegated the authority to carry out or sign prescription drug orders under Section 157.0511, 157.052, 157.053, 157.054, 157.0541, or 157.0542, Occupations Code.

(40) "Prescribe" means the act of a practitioner to authorize a controlled substance to be dispensed to an ultimate user.

(41) "Prescription" means an order by a practitioner to a pharmacist for a controlled substance for a particular patient that specifies:

(A) the date of issue;

(B) the name and address of the patient or, if the controlled substance is prescribed for an animal, the species of the animal and the name and address of its owner;

(C) the name and quantity of the controlled substance prescribed with the quantity shown numerically followed by the number written as a word if the order is written or, if the order is communicated orally or telephonically, with the quantity given by the practitioner and transcribed by the pharmacist numerically;

(D) directions for the use of the drug;

(E) the intended use of the drug unless the practitioner determines the furnishing of this information is not in the best interest of the patient; and

(F) the legibly printed or stamped name, address, Federal Drug Enforcement Administration registration number, and telephone number of the practitioner at the practitioner's usual place of business.

(42) "Principal place of business" means a location where a person manufactures, distributes, dispenses, analyzes, or possesses a controlled substance. The term does not include a location where a practitioner dispenses a controlled substance on an outpatient basis unless the controlled substance is stored at that location.

(43) "Production" includes the manufacturing, planting, cultivating, growing, or harvesting of a controlled substance.

(44) "Raw material" means a compound, material, substance, or equipment used or intended for use, alone or in any combination, in manufacturing a controlled substance.

(45) "Registrant" means a person who is registered under Section 481.063.

(46) "Substitution" means the dispensing of a drug or a brand of drug other than that which is ordered or prescribed.

(47) "Official prescription form" means a prescription form that contains the prescription information required by Section 481.075.

(48) "Ultimate user" means a person who has lawfully obtained and possesses a controlled substance for the person's own use, for the use of a member of the person's household, or for administering to an animal owned by the person or by a member of the person's household.

(49) "Adulterant or dilutant" means any material that increases the bulk or quantity of a controlled substance, regardless of its effect on the chemical activity of the controlled substance.

(50) "Abuse unit" means:

(A) except as provided by Paragraph (B):

(i) a single unit on or in any adulterant, dilutant, or similar carrier medium, including marked or perforated blotter paper, a tablet, gelatin wafer, sugar cube, or stamp, or other medium that contains any amount of a controlled substance listed in Penalty Group 1-A, if the unit is commonly used in abuse of that substance; or

(ii) each quarter-inch square section of paper, if the adulterant, dilutant, or carrier medium is paper not marked or perforated into individual abuse units; or

(B) if the controlled substance is in liquid form, 40 micrograms of the controlled substance including any adulterant or dilutant.

(51) "Chemical precursor" means:

(A) Methylamine;

(B) Ethylamine;

(C) D–lysergic acid;

(D) Ergotamine tartrate;

(E) Diethyl malonate;

(F) Malonic acid;

(G) Ethyl malonate;

(H) Barbituric acid;

(I) Piperidine;

(J) N–acetylanthranilic acid;

(K) Pyrrolidine;

(L) Phenylacetic acid;

(M) Anthranilic acid;

(N) Ephedrine;

(O) Pseudoephedrine;

(P) Norpseudoephedrine; or

(Q) Phenylpropanolamine.

(52) "Department" means the Department of Public Safety.

(53) "Chemical laboratory apparatus" means any item of equipment designed, made, or adapted to manufacture a controlled substance or a controlled substance analogue, including:

(A) a condenser;

(B) a distilling apparatus;

(C) a vacuum drier;

(D) a three-neck or distilling flask;

(E) a tableting machine;

(F) an encapsulating machine;

(G) a filter, Buchner, or separatory funnel;

(H) an Erlenmeyer, two-neck, or single-neck flask;

(I) a round-bottom, Florence, thermometer, or filtering flask;

(J) a Soxhlet extractor;

(K) a transformer;

(L) a flask heater;

(M) a heating mantel; or

(N) an adaptor tube.

Acts 1989, 71st Leg., ch. 678, § 1, eff. Sept. 1, 1989. Amended by Acts 1989, 71st Leg., ch. 1100, § 5.02(b), eff. Sept. 1, 1989; Acts 1993, 73rd Leg., ch. 351, § 27, eff. Sept. 1, 1993; Acts 1993, 73rd Leg., ch. 789, § 15, eff. Sept. 1, 1993; Acts 1993, 73rd Leg., ch. 900, § 2.01, eff. Sept. 1, 1994; Acts 1997, 75th Leg., ch. 745, §§ 1, 2, eff. Jan. 1, 1998; Acts 1999, 76th Leg., ch. 145, §§ 1, 5(1), eff. Sept. 1, 1999; Acts 2001, 77th Leg., ch. 251, § 1, eff. Sept. 1, 2001; Acts 2001, 77th Leg., ch. 1188, § 1, eff. Sept. 1, 2001; Acts 2003, 78th Leg., ch. 88, § 9, eff. May 20, 2003; Acts 2003, 78th Leg., ch. 1099, § 4, eff. Sept. 1, 2003.

[1] V.T.C.A., Health & Safety Code § 481.031 et seq.

§ 481.003. Rules

(a) The director may adopt rules to administer and enforce this chapter.

(b) The director by rule shall prohibit a person in this state, including a person regulated by the Texas Department of Insurance under the Insurance Code or the other insurance laws of this state, from using a practitioner's Federal Drug Enforcement Administration number for a purpose other than a purpose described by federal law or by this chapter. A person who violates a rule adopted under this subsection commits a Class C misdemeanor.

Added by Acts 1997, 75th Leg., ch. 745, § 3, eff. Jan. 1, 1998. Amended by Acts 1999, 76th Leg., ch. 1266, § 1, eff. Sept. 1, 1999.

SUBCHAPTER B. SCHEDULES

DISPOSITION TABLE

Showing where the subject matter of provisions contained in former Subchapter B may be found in Subchapter B as amended by Acts 1997, 75th Leg., ch. 745, § 4.

Former Section	Amended Section
481.031	481.031
481.032	——
481.033	——
481.034	——
481.035	——
481.036	——
481.037	481.033
481.038	481.034
481.039	481.035
481.040	481.036

§ 481.031. Nomenclature

Controlled substances listed in Schedules I through V and Penalty Groups 1 through 4 are included by whatever official, common, usual, chemical, or trade name they may be designated.

Acts 1989, 71st Leg., ch. 678, § 1, eff. Sept. 1, 1989. Amended by Acts 1997, 75th Leg., ch. 745, § 4, eff. Jan. 1, 1998.

§ 481.032. Schedules

(a) The commissioner shall establish and modify the following schedules of controlled substances under this subchapter: Schedule I, Schedule II, Schedule III, Schedule IV, and Schedule V.

(b) A reference to a schedule in this chapter means the most current version of the schedule established or altered by the commissioner under this subchapter and published in the Texas Register on or after January 1, 1998.

Added by Acts 1997, 75th Leg., ch. 745, § 4, eff. Jan. 1, 1998. Amended by Acts 2001, 77th Leg., ch. 251, § 2, eff. Sept. 1, 2001.

§ 481.033. Exclusion From Schedules and Application of Act

(a) A nonnarcotic substance is excluded from Schedules I through V if the substance may lawfully be sold over the counter without a prescription, under the Federal Food, Drug, and Cosmetic Act (21 U.S.C. Section 301 et seq.).

(b) The commissioner may not include in the schedules:

(1) a substance described by Subsection (a); or

(2) distilled spirits, wine, malt beverages, or tobacco.

(c) A compound, mixture, or preparation containing a stimulant substance listed in Schedule II and having a potential for abuse associated with a stimulant effect on the central nervous system is excepted from the application of this chapter if the compound, mixture, or preparation contains one or more active medicinal ingredients not having a stimulant effect on the central nervous system and if the admixtures are included in combinations, quantity, proportions, or concentrations that vitiate the potential for abuse of the substance having a stimulant effect on the central nervous system.

(d) A compound, mixture, or preparation containing a depressant substance listed in Schedule III or IV and having a potential for abuse associated with a depressant effect on the central nervous system is excepted from the application of this chapter if the compound, mixture, or preparation contains one or more active medicinal ingredients not having a depressant effect on the central nervous system and if the admixtures are included in combinations, quantity, proportions, or concentrations that vitiate the potential for abuse of the substance having a depressant effect on the central nervous system.

(e) A nonnarcotic prescription substance is exempted from Schedules I through V and the application of this chapter to the same extent that the substance has been exempted from the application of the Federal Controlled Substances Act, if the substance is listed as an exempt prescription product under 21 C.F.R. Section 1308.32 and its subsequent amendments.

(f) A chemical substance that is intended for laboratory, industrial, educational, or special research purposes and not for general administration to a human being or other animal is exempted from Schedules I through V and the application of this chapter to the same extent that the substance has been exempted from the application of the Federal Controlled Substances Act, if the substance is listed as an exempt chemical preparation under 21 C.F.R. Section 1308.24 and its subsequent amendments.

(g) An anabolic steroid product, which has no significant potential for abuse due to concentration, preparation, mixture, or delivery system, is exempted from Schedules I through V and the application of this chapter to the same extent that the substance has been exempted from the application of the Federal Controlled Substances Act, if the substance is listed as an exempt anabolic steroid product under 21 C.F.R. Section 1308.34 and its subsequent amendments.

Acts 1989, 71st Leg., ch. 678, § 1, eff. Sept. 1, 1989. Amended by Acts 1993, 73rd Leg., ch. 532, § 1, eff. Sept. 1, 1993. Renumbered from V.T.C.A., Health & Safety Code § 481.037 and amended by Acts 1997, 75th Leg., ch. 745, § 4, eff. Jan. 1, 1998.

§ 481.034. Establishment and Modification of Schedules by Commissioner

(a) The commissioner shall annually establish the schedules of controlled substances. These annual schedules shall include the complete list of all controlled substances from the previous schedules and modifications in the federal schedules of controlled substances as required by Subsection (g). Any further additions to and deletions from these schedules, any rescheduling of substances and any other modifications made by the commissioner to these schedules of controlled substances shall be made:

(1) in accordance with Section 481.035;

(2) in a manner consistent with this subchapter; and

(3) with approval of the Texas Board of Health.

(b) Except for alterations in schedules required by Subsection (g), the commissioner may not make an alteration in a schedule unless the commissioner holds a public hearing on the matter in Austin and obtains approval from the Texas Board of Health.

(c) The commissioner may not:

(1) add a substance to the schedules if

the substance has been deleted from the schedules by the legislature;

(2) delete a substance from the schedules if the substance has been added to the schedules by the legislature; or

(3) reschedule a substance if the substance has been placed in a schedule by the legislature.

(d) In making a determination regarding a substance, the commissioner shall consider:

(1) the actual or relative potential for its abuse;

(2) the scientific evidence of its pharmacological effect, if known;

(3) the state of current scientific knowledge regarding the substance;

(4) the history and current pattern of its abuse;

(5) the scope, duration, and significance of its abuse;

(6) the risk to the public health;

(7) the potential of the substance to produce psychological or physiological dependence liability; and

(8) whether the substance is a controlled substance analogue, chemical precursor, or an immediate precursor of a substance controlled under this chapter.

(e) After considering the factors listed in Subsection (d), the commissioner shall make findings with respect to those factors and adopt a rule controlling the substance if the commissioner finds the substance has a potential for abuse.

(f) Repealed by Acts 2003, 78th Leg., ch. 1099, § 17.

(g) Except as otherwise provided by this subsection, if a substance is designated, rescheduled, or deleted as a controlled substance under federal law and notice of that fact is given to the commissioner, the commissioner similarly shall control the substance under this chapter. After the expiration of a 30-day period beginning on the day after the date of publication in the Federal Register of a final order designating a substance as a controlled substance or rescheduling or deleting a substance, the commissioner similarly shall designate, reschedule, or delete the substance, unless the commissioner objects during the period. If the commissioner objects, the commissioner shall publish the reasons for the objection and give all interested parties an opportunity to be heard. At the conclusion of the hearing, the commissioner shall publish a decision, which is final unless altered by statute. On publication of an objection by the commissioner, control as to that particular substance under this chapter is stayed until the commissioner publishes the commissioner's decision.

(h) Not later than the 10th day after the date on which the commissioner designates, deletes, or reschedules a substance under Subsection (a), the commissioner shall give written notice of that action to the director and to each state licensing agency having jurisdiction over practitioners.

Acts 1989, 71st Leg., ch. 678, § 1, eff. Sept. 1, 1989. Renumbered from V.T.C.A., Health & Safety Code § 481.038 and amended by Acts 1997, 75th Leg., ch. 745, § 4, eff. Jan. 1, 1998; Acts 2003, 78th Leg., ch. 1099, §§ 5, 17, eff. Sept. 1, 2003.

§ 481.035. Findings

(a) The commissioner shall place a substance in Schedule I if the commissioner finds that the substance:

(1) has a high potential for abuse; and

(2) has no accepted medical use in treatment in the United States or lacks accepted safety for use in treatment under medical supervision.

(b) The commissioner shall place a substance in Schedule II if the commissioner finds that:

(1) the substance has a high potential for abuse;

(2) the substance has currently accepted medical use in treatment in the United States; and

(3) abuse of the substance may lead to severe psychological or physical dependence.

(c) The commissioner shall place a substance in Schedule III if the commissioner finds that:

(1) the substance has a potential for abuse less than that of the substances listed in Schedules I and II;

(2) the substance has currently accepted medical use in treatment in the United States; and

(3) abuse of the substance may lead to moderate or low physical dependence or high psychological dependence.

(d) The commissioner shall place a substance in Schedule IV if the commissioner finds that:

(1) the substance has a lower potential for abuse than that of the substances listed in Schedule III;

(2) the substance has currently accepted medical use in treatment in the United States; and

(3) abuse of the substance may lead to a more limited physical or psychological dependence than that of the substances listed in Schedule III.

(e) The commissioner shall place a substance in Schedule V if the commissioner finds that the substance:

(1) has a lower potential for abuse than that of the substances listed in Schedule IV;

(2) has currently accepted medical use in treatment in the United States; and

(3) may lead to a more limited physical or psychological dependence liability than that of the substances listed in Schedule IV.

Acts 1989, 71st Leg., ch. 678, § 1, eff. Sept. 1, 1989. Renumbered from V.T.C.A., Health & Safety Code § 481.039 and amended by Acts 1997, 75th Leg., ch. 745, § 4, eff. Jan. 1, 1998.

§ 481.036. Publication of Schedules

(a) The commissioner shall publish the schedules by filing a certified copy of the schedules with the secretary of state for publication in the Texas Register not later than the fifth working day after the date the commissioner takes action under this subchapter.

(b) Each published schedule must show changes, if any, made in the schedule since its latest publication.

(c) An action by the commissioner that establishes or modifies a schedule under this subchapter may take effect not earlier than the 21st day after the date on which the schedule or modification is published in the Texas Register unless an emergency exists that necessitates earlier action to avoid an imminent hazard to the public safety.

Acts 1989, 71st Leg., ch. 678, § 1, eff. Sept. 1, 1989. Renumbered from V.T.C.A., Health & Safety Code § 481.040 and amended by Acts 1997, 75th Leg., ch. 745, § 4, eff. Jan. 1, 1998.

§ 481.037. Carisoprodol

Schedule IV includes carisoprodol.

Added by Acts 2009, 81st Leg., ch. 774, § 4, eff. June 19, 2009.

Section 5 of Acts 2009, 81st Leg., ch. 774 provides:

"The change in law made by this Act applies only to the issuance of a prescription on or after the effective date of this Act. The issuance of a prescription before the effective date of this Act is covered by the law in effect when the prescription was issued, and the former law is continued in effect for that purpose."

§§ 481.037 to 481.040. Renumbered as V.T.C.A., Health & Safety Code §§ 481.033 to 481.036 by Acts 1997, 75th Leg., ch. 745, § 4, eff. Jan. 1, 1998

SUBCHAPTER C. REGULATION OF MANUFACTURE, DISTRIBUTION, AND DISPENSATION OF CONTROLLED SUBSTANCES, CHEMICAL PRECURSORS, AND CHEMICAL LABORATORY APPARATUS

§ 481.061. Registration Required

(a) Except as otherwise provided by this chapter, a person who is not a registrant may not manufacture, distribute, prescribe, possess, analyze, or dispense a controlled substance in this state.

(b) A person who is registered by the director to manufacture, distribute, analyze, dispense, or conduct research with a controlled substance may possess, manufacture, distribute, analyze, dispense, or conduct research with that substance to the extent authorized by the person's registration and in conformity with this chapter.

(c) A separate registration is required at each principal place of business or professional practice where the applicant manufactures, distributes, analyzes, dispenses, or possesses a controlled substance. However, the director may not require separate registration for a practitioner engaged in research with a nonnarcotic controlled substance listed in Schedules II through V if the registrant is already registered under this subchapter in another capacity.

Acts 1989, 71st Leg., ch. 678, § 1, eff. Sept. 1, 1989. Amended by Acts 1997, 75th Leg., ch. 745, § 5, eff. Jan. 1, 1998.

§ 481.062. Exemptions

(a) The following persons are not required to register and may possess a controlled substance under this chapter:

(1) an agent or employee of a registered manufacturer, distributor, analyzer, or dispenser of the controlled substance acting in the usual course of business or employment;

(2) a common or contract carrier, a warehouseman, or an employee of a carrier or warehouseman whose possession of the controlled substance is in the usual course of business or employment;

(3) an ultimate user or a person in possession of the controlled substance under a lawful order of a practitioner or in lawful possession of the controlled substance if it is listed in Schedule V;

(4) an officer or employee of this state, another state, a political subdivision of this state or another state, or the United States who is lawfully engaged in the enforcement of a law relating to a controlled substance or drug or to a customs law and authorized to possess the controlled substance in the discharge of the person's official duties; or

(5) if the substance is tetrahydrocannabinol or one of its derivatives:

(A) a Texas Department of Health official, a medical school researcher, or a research program participant possessing the substance as authorized under Subchapter G; or

(B) a practitioner or an ultimate user possessing the substance as a participant in a federally approved therapeutic research program that the commissioner has reviewed and found, in writing, to contain a medically responsible research protocol.

(b) The director by rule may waive the requirement for registration of certain manufacturers, distributors, or dispensers if the director finds it consistent with the public health and safety and if the attorney general of the United States has issued a similar waiver under the Federal Controlled Substances Act.[1]

Acts 1989, 71st Leg., ch. 678, § 1, eff. Sept. 1, 1989. Amended by Acts 1997, 75th Leg., ch. 745, § 6, eff. Jan. 1, 1998; Acts 2001, 77th Leg., ch. 251, § 3, eff. Sept. 1, 2001; Acts 2001, 77th Leg., ch. 1420, § 21.001(79), eff. Sept. 1, 2001.

[1] 21 U.S.C.A. § 801 et seq.

§ 481.0621. Exceptions

(a) This subchapter does not apply to an educational or research program of a school district or a public or private institution of higher education. This subchapter does not apply to a manufacturer, wholesaler, retailer, or other person who sells, transfers, or furnishes materials covered by this subchapter to those educational or research programs.

(b) The department and the Texas Higher Education Coordinating Board shall adopt a memorandum of understanding that establishes the responsibilities of the board, the department, and the public or private institutions of higher education in implementing and maintaining a program for reporting information concerning controlled substances, controlled substance analogues, chemical precursors, and chemical laboratory apparatus used in educational or research activities of institutions of higher education.

(c) The department and the Texas Education Agency shall adopt a memorandum of understanding that establishes the responsibilities of the agency, the department, and school districts in implementing and maintaining a program for reporting information concerning controlled substances, controlled substance analogues, chemical precursors, and chemical laboratory apparatus used in educational or research activities of those schools and school districts.

Added by Acts 1989, 71st Leg., ch. 1100, § 5.02(e), eff. Sept. 1, 1989. Amended by Acts 1997, 75th Leg., ch. 165, § 6.45, eff. Sept. 1, 1997; Acts 1997, 75th Leg., ch. 745, § 7, eff. Jan. 1, 1998.

§ 481.063. Registration Application; Issuance or Denial

(a) The director may refuse to issue a registration to a person to manufacture, distribute, analyze, or conduct research with a controlled substance if the person fails or refuses to provide to the director a consent form signed by the person granting the director the right to inspect the person's controlled premises and any record, controlled substance, or other item covered by this chapter.

(b) The director may not issue a registration to a person to dispense a controlled substance unless the director receives a consent form signed by the person granting the director the right to inspect records as required by this chapter.

(c) The director shall register a person to manufacture, distribute, or analyze a controlled substance listed in Schedules II through V if:

(1) the person furnishes the director evidence that the person is registered for that purpose under the Federal Controlled Substances Act;

(2) the person has made proper application and paid the applicable fee; and

(3) the person has not been found by the director to have violated a provision of Subsection (e).

(d) The director shall register a person to dispense or conduct research with a controlled substance listed in Schedules II through V if the person:

(1) is a practitioner licensed under the laws of this state;

(2) has made proper application and paid the applicable fee; and

(3) has not been found by the director to have violated a provision of Subsection (e).

(e) An application for registration to manufacture, distribute, analyze, dispense, or conduct research with a controlled substance may be denied on a finding that the applicant:

(1) has furnished material information in an application filed under this chapter that the applicant knows is false or fraudulent;

(2) has been convicted of or placed on community supervision or other probation for:

(A) a felony;

(B) a violation of this chapter or of Chapters 482–485; or

(C) an offense reasonably related to the registration sought;

(3) has voluntarily surrendered or has had suspended, denied, or revoked a registration or application for registration to manufacture, distribute, analyze, or dispense controlled substances under the Federal Controlled Substances Act; [1]

(4) has had suspended, probated, or revoked a registration or a practitioner's license under the laws of this state or another state;

(5) has intentionally or knowingly failed to establish and maintain effective security controls against diversion of controlled substances into other than legitimate medical, scientific, or industrial channels as provided by federal regulations or laws, this chapter, or a rule adopted under this chapter;

(6) has intentionally or knowingly failed to maintain records required to be kept by this chapter or a rule adopted under this chapter;

(7) has refused to allow an inspection authorized by this chapter or a rule adopted under this chapter;

(8) has intentionally or knowingly violated this chapter or a rule adopted under this chapter; or

(9) has voluntarily surrendered a registration that has not been reinstated.

(f) The director may inspect the premises or establishment of an applicant for registration in accordance with this chapter.

(g) A registration is valid until the first anniversary of the date of issuance and may be renewed annually under rules adopted by the director, unless a rule provides for a longer period of validity or renewal.

(h) Chapter 2001, Government Code, does not apply to a denial of a registration under Subsection (e)(2)(A) or (B), (e)(3), (e)(4), or (e)(9).

(i) For good cause shown, the director may probate the denial of an application for registration. If a denial of an application is probated, the director may require the person to report regularly to the department on matters that are the basis of the probation or may limit activities of the person to those prescribed by the director, or both.

Acts 1989, 71st Leg., ch. 678, § 1, eff. Sept. 1, 1989. Amended by Acts 1989, 71st Leg., ch. 1100, § 5.02(f), eff. Sept. 1, 1989; Acts 1993, 73rd Leg., ch. 790, § 19, eff. Sept. 1, 1993; Acts 1995, 74th Leg., ch. 76, § 5.95(49), eff. Sept. 1, 1995; Acts 1997, 75th Leg., ch. 745, § 8, eff. Jan. 1, 1998; Acts 2001, 77th Leg., ch. 251, § 4, eff. Sept. 1, 2001.

[1] 21 U.S.C.A. § 801 et seq.

§ 481.064. Registration Fees

(a) The director may charge a nonrefundable fee of not more than $25 before processing an application for annual registration and may charge a late fee of not more than $50 for each application for renewal the department receives after the date the registration expires. The director by rule shall set the amounts of the fees at the amounts that are necessary to cover the cost of administering and enforcing this subchapter. Except as provided by Subsection (b), registrants shall pay the fees to the director. Not later than 60 days before the date the registration expires, the director shall send a renewal notice to the registrant at the last known address of the registrant according to department records.

(b) The director may authorize a contract between the department and an appropriate state agency for the collection and remittance of the fees. The director by rule may provide for remittance of the fees collected by state agencies for the department.

(c) The director shall deposit the collected fees to the credit of the operator's and chauffeur's license account in the general revenue fund. The fees may be used only by the department in the administration or enforcement of this subchapter.

Acts 1989, 71st Leg., ch. 678, § 1, eff. Sept. 1, 1989. Amended by Acts 1997, 75th Leg., ch. 745, § 9, eff. Jan. 1, 1998; Acts 2001, 77th Leg., ch. 251, § 5, eff. Sept. 1, 2001; Acts 2007, 80th Leg., ch. 1391, § 1, eff. Sept. 1, 2007.

§ 481.065. Authorization for Certain Activities

(a) The director may authorize the possession, distribution, planting, and cultivation of controlled substances by a person engaged in research, training animals to detect controlled substances, or designing or calibrating devices to detect controlled substances. A person who obtains an authorization under this subsection does not commit an offense involving the possession or distribution of controlled substances to the extent that the possession or distribution is authorized.

(b) A person may conduct research with or analyze substances listed in Schedule I in this state only if the person is a practitioner registered under federal law to conduct research with or analyze those substances and the person provides the director with evidence of federal registration.

Acts 1989, 71st Leg., ch. 678, § 1, eff. Sept. 1, 1989.

§ 481.066. Voluntary Surrender, Cancellation, Suspension, Probation, or Revocation of Registration

(a) The director may accept a voluntary surrender of a registration.

(b) The director may cancel, suspend, or revoke a registration, place on probation a person whose license has been suspended, or reprimand a registrant for a cause described by Section 481.063(e).

(c) The director may cancel a registration that was issued in error.

(d) The director may limit the cancellation, suspension, probation, or revocation to the particular schedule or controlled substance within a schedule for which grounds for cancellation, suspension, probation, or revocation exist.

(e) After accepting the voluntary surrender of a registration or ordering the cancellation, suspension, probation, or revocation of a registration, the director may seize or place under seal all controlled substances owned or possessed by the registrant under the authority of that registration. If the director orders the cancellation, suspension, probation, or revocation of a registration, a disposition may not be made of the seized or sealed substances until the time for administrative appeal of the order has elapsed or until all appeals have been concluded, except that the director may order the sale of perishable substances and deposit of the proceeds of the sale in a special interest-bearing account in the general revenue fund. When a surrender or cancellation, suspension, probation, or revocation order becomes final, all controlled substances may be forfeited to the state as provided under Subchapter E.

(f) The operation of a registrant in violation of this section is a public nuisance, and the director may apply to any court of competent jurisdiction for an injunction suspending the registration of the registrant.

(g) Chapter 2001, Government Code, applies to a proceeding under this section to the extent that that chapter does not conflict with this subchapter. Chapter 2001, Government Code, does not apply to a cancellation, suspension, probation, or revocation of a registration for a cause described by Section 481.063(e)(2)(A) or (B), (e)(3), (e)(4), or (e)(9).

(h) The director shall promptly notify appropriate state agencies of an order accepting a voluntary surrender or canceling, suspending, probating, or revoking a registration and the forfeiture of controlled substances.

(i) The director shall give written notice to the applicant or registrant of the acceptance of a voluntary surrender of a registration, or of the cancellation, suspension, probation, revocation, or denial of a registration. The notice shall be sent by certified mail, return receipt requested, to the most current address of the applicant or registrant contained in department files.

(j) After a voluntary surrender, cancellation, suspension, probation, revocation, or denial of a registration, on petition of the applicant or former registrant, the director may issue or reinstate the registration for good cause shown by the petitioner.

Acts 1989, 71st Leg., ch. 678, § 1, eff. Sept. 1, 1989. Amended by Acts 1997, 75th Leg., ch. 745, § 10, eff. Jan. 1, 1998; Acts 2001, 77th Leg., ch. 251, § 6, eff. Sept. 1, 2001.

§ 481.067. Records

(a) A person who is registered to manufacture, distribute, analyze, or dispense a controlled substance shall keep records and maintain inventories in compliance with recordkeeping and inventory requirements of federal law and with additional rules the director adopts.

(b) The pharmacist-in-charge of a pharmacy shall maintain the records and inventories required by this section.

(c) A record required by this section must be made at the time of the transaction that is the basis of the record. A record or inventory required by this section must be kept or maintained for at least two years after the date the record or inventory is made.

Acts 1989, 71st Leg., ch. 678, § 1, eff. Sept. 1, 1989. Amended by Acts 2001, 77th Leg., ch. 251, § 7, eff. Sept. 1, 2001.

§ 481.068. Confidentiality

(a) The director may authorize a person engaged in research on the use and effects of a controlled substance to withhold the names and other identifying characteristics of individuals who are the subjects of the research. A person who obtains the authorization may not be compelled in a civil, criminal, administrative, legislative, or other proceeding to identify the individuals who are the subjects of the research for which the authorization is obtained.

(b) Except as provided by Sections 481.074 and 481.075, a practitioner engaged in authorized medical practice or research may not be required to furnish the name or identity of a patient or research subject to the department, the director of the Texas Commission on Alcohol and Drug Abuse, or any other agency, public official, or law enforcement officer. A practitioner may not be compelled in a state or local civil, criminal, administrative, legislative, or other proceeding to furnish the name or identity of an individual that the practitioner is obligated to keep confidential.

(c) The director may not provide to a federal, state, or local law enforcement agency the name or identity of a patient or research subject whose identity could not be obtained under Subsection (b).

Acts 1989, 71st Leg., ch. 678, § 1, eff. Sept. 1, 1989. Amended by Acts 2001, 77th Leg., ch. 251, § 8, eff. Sept. 1, 2001.

§ 481.069. Order Forms

A registrant may not distribute or order a controlled substance listed in Schedule I or II to or from another registrant except under an order form. A registrant complying with the federal law concerning order forms is in compliance with this section.

Acts 1989, 71st Leg., ch. 678, § 1, eff. Sept. 1, 1989. Amended by Acts 1989, 71st Leg., ch. 1100, § 5.02(g), eff. Sept. 1, 1989.

§ 481.070. Administering or Dispensing Schedule I Controlled Substance

Except as permitted by this chapter, a person may not administer or dispense a controlled substance listed in Schedule I.

Acts 1989, 71st Leg., ch. 678, § 1, eff. Sept. 1, 1989.

§ 481.071. Medical Purpose Required Before Prescribing, Dispensing, Delivering, or Administering Controlled Substance

(a) A practitioner defined by Section 481.002(39)(A) may not prescribe, dispense, deliver, or administer a controlled substance or cause a controlled substance to be administered under the practitioner's direction and supervision except for a valid medical purpose and in the course of medical practice.

(b) An anabolic steroid or human growth hormone listed in Schedule III may only be:

(1) dispensed, prescribed, delivered, or administered by a practitioner, as defined by Section 481.002(39)(A), for a valid medical purpose and in the course of professional practice; or

(2) dispensed or delivered by a pharmacist according to a prescription issued by a practitioner, as defined by Section 481.002(39)(A) or (C), for a valid medical purpose and in the course of professional practice.

(c) For the purposes of Subsection (b), bodybuilding, muscle enhancement, or increasing muscle bulk or strength through the use of an anabolic steroid or human growth hormone listed in Schedule III by a person who is in good health is not a valid medical purpose.

Acts 1989, 71st Leg., ch. 678, § 1, eff. Sept. 1, 1989. Amended by Acts 1989, 71st Leg., ch. 1100, § 5.03(b), eff. Sept. 1, 1989; Acts 1997, 75th Leg., ch. 745, § 11, eff. Jan. 1, 1998.

§ 481.072. Medical Purpose Required Before Distributing or Dispensing Schedule V Controlled Substance

A person may not distribute or dispense a controlled substance listed in Schedule V except for a valid medical purpose.

Acts 1989, 71st Leg., ch. 678, § 1, eff. Sept. 1, 1989.

§ 481.073. Communication of Prescriptions by Agent

(a) Only a practitioner defined by Section 481.002(39)(A) and an agent designated in writing by the practitioner in accordance with rules adopted by the department may communicate a prescription by telephone. A pharmacy that receives a telephonically communicated prescription shall promptly write the prescription and file and retain the prescription in the manner required by this subchapter. A practitioner who designates an agent to communicate prescriptions shall maintain the written designation of the agent in the practitioner's usual place of business and shall make the designation available for inspection by investigators for the Texas State Board of Medical Examiners, the State Board of Dental Examiners, the State Board of Veterinary Medical Examiners, and the department. A practitioner who designates a different agent shall designate that agent in writing and maintain the designation in the same manner in which the practitioner initially designated an agent under this section.

(b) On the request of a pharmacist, a practitioner shall furnish a copy of the written designation authorized under Subsection (a).

(c) This section does not relieve a practitioner or the practitioner's designated agent from the requirement of Subchapter A, Chapter 562, Occupations Code. A practitioner is personally responsible for the actions of the designated agent in communicating a prescription to a pharmacist.

Acts 1989, 71st Leg., ch. 678, § 1, eff. Sept. 1, 1989. Amended by Acts 2001, 77th Leg., ch. 251, § 9, eff. Sept. 1, 2001; Acts 2001, 77th Leg., ch. 1420, § 14.794, eff. Sept. 1, 2001.

§ 481.074. Prescriptions

(a) A pharmacist may not:

(1) dispense or deliver a controlled substance or cause a controlled substance to be dispensed or delivered under the pharmacist's direction or supervision except under a valid prescription and in the course of professional practice;

(2) dispense a controlled substance if the pharmacist knows or should have known that the prescription was issued without a valid patient-practitioner relationship;

(3) fill a prescription that is not prepared or issued as prescribed by this chapter;

(4) permit or allow a person who is not a licensed pharmacist or pharmacist intern to dispense, distribute, or in any other manner deliver a controlled substance even if under the supervision of a pharmacist, except that after the pharmacist or pharmacist intern has fulfilled his professional and legal responsibilities, a nonpharmacist may complete the actual cash or credit transaction and delivery; or

(5) permit the delivery of a controlled substance to any person not known to the pharmacist, the pharmacist intern, or the person authorized by the pharmacist to deliver the controlled substance without first requiring identification of the person taking possession of the controlled substance, except as provided by Subsection (n).

(b) Except in an emergency as defined by rule of the director or as provided by Subsection (*o*) or Section 481.075(j) or (m), a person may not dispense or administer a controlled substance listed in Schedule II without the written prescription of a practitioner on an official prescription form that meets the requirements of and is completed by the practitioner in accordance with Section 481.075. In an emergency, a person may dispense or administer a controlled substance listed in Schedule II on the oral or telephonically communicated prescription of a practitioner. The person who administers or dispenses the substance shall:

(1) if the person is a prescribing practitioner or a pharmacist, promptly comply with Subsection (c); or

(2) if the person is not a prescribing practitioner or a pharmacist, promptly write the oral or telephonically communicated prescription and include in the written record of the prescription the name, address, department registration number,[1] and Federal Drug Enforcement Administration number of the prescribing practitioner, all information required to be provided by a practitioner under Section 481.075(e)(1), and all information required to be provided by a dispensing pharmacist under Section 481.075(e)(2).

(c) Not later than the seventh day after the date a prescribing practitioner authorizes an emergency oral or telephonically communicated prescription, the prescribing practitioner shall cause a written prescription, completed in the manner required by Section 481.075, to be delivered in person or mailed to the dispensing pharmacist at the pharmacy where the prescription was dispensed. The envelope of a prescription delivered by mail must be postmarked not later than the seventh day after the date the prescription was authorized. On receipt of the prescription, the dispensing pharmacy shall file the transcription of the telephonically communicated prescription and the pharmacy copy and shall send information to the director as required by Section 481.075.

(d) Except as specified in Subsections (e) and (f), the director, by rule and in consultation with the Texas Medical Board and the Texas State Board of Pharmacy, shall establish the period after the date on which the prescription is issued that a person may fill a prescription for a controlled substance listed in Schedule II. A person may not refill a prescription for a substance listed in Schedule II.

(d–1) Notwithstanding Subsection (d), a prescribing practitioner may issue multiple prescriptions authorizing the patient to receive a total of up to a 90–day supply of a Schedule II controlled substance if:

(1) each separate prescription is issued for a legitimate medical purpose by a prescribing practitioner acting in the usual course of professional practice;

(2) the prescribing practitioner provides written instructions on each prescription to be filled at a later date indicating the earliest date on which a pharmacy may fill each prescription;

(3) the prescribing practitioner concludes that providing the patient with multiple prescriptions in this manner does not create an undue risk of diversion or abuse; and

(4) the issuance of multiple prescriptions complies with other applicable state and federal laws.

(e) The partial filling of a prescription for a controlled substance listed in Schedule II is permissible, if the pharmacist is unable to supply the full quantity called for in a written or emergency oral prescription and the pharmacist makes a notation of the quantity supplied on the face of the written prescription or written record of the emergency oral prescription. The remaining portion of the prescription may be filled within 72 hours of the first partial filling; however, if the remaining portion is not or cannot be filled within the 72-hour period, the pharmacist shall so notify the prescribing individual practitioner. No further quantity may be supplied beyond 72 hours without a new prescription.

(f) A prescription for a Schedule II controlled substance written for a patient in a long-term care facility (LTCF) or for a patient with a medical diagnosis documenting a terminal illness may be filled in partial quantities to include individual dosage units. If there is any question about whether a patient may be classified as having a terminal illness, the pharmacist must contact the practitioner before partially filling the prescription. Both the pharmacist and the practitioner have a corresponding responsibility to assure that the controlled substance is for a terminally ill patient. The pharmacist must record the prescription on an official prescription form and must indicate on the form whether the patient is "terminally ill" or an "LTCF patient." A prescription that is partially filled and does not contain the notation "terminally ill" or "LTCF patient" is considered to have been filled in violation of this chapter. For each partial filling, the dispensing pharmacist shall record on the back of the official prescription form the date of the partial filling, the quantity dispensed, the remaining quantity authorized to be dispensed, and the identification of the dispensing pharmacist. Before any subsequent partial filling, the pharmacist must determine that the additional partial filling is necessary. The total quantity of Schedule II controlled substances dispensed in all partial fillings may not exceed the total quantity prescribed. Schedule II prescriptions for patients in a long-term care facility or patients with a medical diagnosis documenting a terminal illness are valid for a period not to exceed 60 days following the issue date unless sooner terminated by discontinuance of the medication.

(g) A person may not dispense a controlled substance in Schedule III or IV that is a prescription drug under the Federal Food, Drug, and Cosmetic Act (21 U.S.C. Section 301 et seq.) without a written, oral, or telephonically or electronically communicated prescription of a practitioner defined by Section 481.002(39)(A) or (D), except that the practitioner may dispense the substance directly to an ultimate user. A prescription for a controlled substance listed in Schedule III or IV may not be filled or refilled later than six months after the date on which the prescription is issued and may not be refilled more than five times, unless the prescription is renewed by the practitioner. A prescription under this subsection must comply with other applicable state and federal laws.

(h) A pharmacist may dispense a controlled substance listed in Schedule III, IV, or V under a written, oral, or telephonically or electronically communicated prescription issued by a practitioner defined by Section 481.002(39)(C) and only if the pharmacist determines that the prescription was issued for a valid medical purpose and in the course of professional practice. A prescription issued under this subsection may not be filled or refilled later than six months after the date the prescription is issued and may not be refilled more than five times, unless the prescription is renewed by the practitioner.

(i) A person may not dispense a controlled substance listed in Schedule V and containing 200 milligrams or less of codeine, or any of its salts, per 100 milliliters or per 100 grams, or containing 100 milligrams or less of dihydrocodeine, or any of its salts, per 100 milliliters or per 100 grams, without the prescription of a practitioner defined by Section 481.002(39)(A), except that a practitioner may dispense the substance directly to an ultimate user. A prescription issued under this subsection may not be filled or refilled later than six months after the date the prescription is issued and may not be refilled more than five times, unless the prescription is renewed by the practitioner.

(j) A practitioner or institutional practitioner may not allow a patient, on the patient's release from the hospital, to possess a controlled substance prescribed by the practitioner unless:

(1) the substance was dispensed under a medication order while the patient was admitted to the hospital;

(2) the substance is in a properly labeled container; and

(3) the patient possesses not more than a seven-day supply of the substance.

(k) A prescription for a controlled substance must show:

(1) the quantity of the substance prescribed:

(A) numerically, followed by the number written as a word, if the prescription is written; or

(B) if the prescription is communicated orally or telephonically, as transcribed by the receiving pharmacist;

(2) the date of issue;

(2–a) if the prescription is issued for a Schedule II controlled substance to be filled at a later date under Subsection (d–1), the earliest date on which a pharmacy may fill the prescription;

(3) the name, address, and date of birth or age of the patient or, if the controlled substance is prescribed for an animal, the species of the animal and the name and address of its owner;

(4) the name and strength of the controlled substance prescribed;

(5) the directions for use of the controlled substance;

(6) the intended use of the substance prescribed unless the practitioner determines the furnishing of this information is not in the best interest of the patient;

(7) the legibly printed or stamped name, address, Federal Drug Enforcement Administration registration number, and telephone number of the practitioner at the practitioner's usual place of business;

(8) if the prescription is handwritten, the signature of the prescribing practitioner; and

(9) if the prescribing practitioner is licensed in this state, the practitioner's department registration number.

(*l*) A pharmacist may exercise his professional judgment in refilling a prescription for a controlled substance in Schedule III, IV, or V without the authorization of the prescribing practitioner provided:

(1) failure to refill the prescription might result in an interruption of a therapeutic regimen or create patient suffering;

(2) either:

(A) a natural or manmade disaster has occurred which prohibits the pharmacist from being able to contact the practitioner; or

(B) the pharmacist is unable to contact the practitioner after reasonable effort;

(3) the quantity of prescription drug dispensed does not exceed a 72-hour supply;

(4) the pharmacist informs the patient or the patient's agent at the time of dispensing that the refill is being provided without such authorization and that authorization of the practitioner is required for future refills; and

(5) the pharmacist informs the practitioner of the emergency refill at the earliest reasonable time.

(*l*–1) Notwithstanding Subsection (*l*), in the event of a natural or manmade disaster, a pharmacist may dispense not more than a 30–day supply of a prescription drug, other than a controlled substance listed in Schedule II, without the authorization of the prescribing practitioner if:

(1) failure to refill the prescription might result in an interruption of a therapeutic regimen or create patient suffering;

(2) the natural or manmade disaster prohibits the pharmacist from being able to contact the practitioner;

(3) the governor has declared a state of disaster under Chapter 418, Government Code; and

(4) the Texas State Board of Pharmacy, through its executive director, has notified pharmacies in this state that pharmacists may dispense up to a 30–day supply of a prescription drug.

(*l*–2) The prescribing practitioner is not liable for an act or omission by a pharmacist in dispensing a prescription drug under Subsection (l–1).

(m) A pharmacist may permit the delivery of a controlled substance by an authorized delivery person, by a person known to the pharmacist, a pharmacist intern, or the authorized delivery person, or by mail to the person or address of the person authorized by the prescription to receive the controlled substance. If a pharmacist permits delivery of a controlled substance under this subsection, the pharmacist shall retain in the records of the pharmacy for a period of not less than two years:

(1) the name of the authorized delivery person, if delivery is made by that person;

(2) the name of the person known to the pharmacist, a pharmacist intern, or the authorized delivery person if delivery is made by that person; or

(3) the mailing address to which delivery is made, if delivery is made by mail.

(n) A pharmacist may permit the delivery of a controlled substance to a person not known to the pharmacist, a pharmacist intern, or the authorized delivery person without first requiring the identification of the person to whom the controlled substance is delivered if the pharmacist determines that an emergency exists and that the controlled substance is needed for the immediate well-being of the patient for whom the controlled substance is prescribed. If a pharmacist permits delivery of a controlled substance under this subsection, the pharmacist shall retain in the records of the pharmacy for a period of not less than two years all information relevant to the delivery known to the pharmacist, including the name, address, and date of birth or age of the person to whom the controlled substance is delivered.

(*o*) A pharmacist may dispense a Schedule II controlled substance pursuant to a facsimile copy of an official prescription completed in the manner required by Section 481.075 and transmitted by the practitioner or the practitioner's agent to the pharmacy if:

(1) the prescription is written for:

(A) a Schedule II narcotic or nonnarcotic substance for a patient in a long-term care facility (LTCF), and the practitioner notes on the prescription "LTCF patient";

(B) a Schedule II narcotic product to be compounded for the direct administration to a patient by parenteral, intravenous, intramuscular, subcutaneous, or intraspinal infusion; or

(C) a Schedule II narcotic substance for a patient with a medical diagnosis documenting a terminal illness or a patient enrolled in a hospice care program certified or paid for by Medicare under Title XVIII, Social Security Act (42 U.S.C. Section 1395 et seq.), as amended, by Medicaid, or by a hospice program that is licensed under Chapter 142, and the practitioner or the practitioner's agent notes on the prescription "terminally ill" or "hospice patient"; and

(2) after transmitting the prescription, the prescribing practitioner or the practitioner's agent:

(A) writes across the face of the official prescription "VOID—sent by fax to (name and telephone number of receiving pharmacy)"; and

(B) files the official prescription in the patient's medical records instead of delivering it to the patient.

(p) On receipt of the prescription, the dispensing pharmacy shall file the facsimile copy of the prescription and shall send information to the director as required by Section 481.075.

(q) Each dispensing pharmacist shall send all information required by the director, including any information required to complete the Schedule III through V prescription forms, to the director by electronic transfer or another form approved by the director not later than the 15th day after the last day of the month in which the prescription is completely filled.

Acts 1989, 71st Leg., ch. 678, § 1, eff. Sept. 1, 1989. Amended by Acts 1989, 71st Leg., ch. 1100, § 5.02(h), eff. Sept. 1, 1989; Acts 1991, 72nd Leg., ch. 615, § 10, eff. Sept. 1, 1991; Acts 1991, 72nd Leg., ch. 761, § 6, eff. Sept. 1, 1991; Acts 1993, 73rd Leg., ch. 351, § 28, eff. Sept. 1, 1993; Acts 1993, 73rd Leg., ch. 789, § 16, eff. Sept. 1, 1993; Acts 1997, 75th Leg., ch. 745, §§ 12, 13, eff. Jan. 1, 1998; Acts 1999, 76th Leg., ch. 145, § 2, eff. Sept. 1, 1999; Acts 2001, 77th Leg., ch. 251, § 10, eff. Sept. 1, 2001; Acts 2001, 77th Leg., ch. 1254, § 10, eff. Sept. 1, 2001; Acts 2005, 79th Leg., ch. 349, § 21(a), eff. Sept. 1, 2005; Acts 2005, 79th Leg., ch. 1345, § 44(a), eff. Sept. 1, 2005; Acts 2007, 80th Leg., ch. 535, § 1, eff. Sept. 1, 2007; Acts 2007, 80th Leg., ch. 567, § 2, eff. Sept. 1, 2007; Acts 2007, 80th Leg., ch. 1391, § 2, eff. Sept. 1, 2008; Acts 2009, 81st Leg., ch. 774, § 1, eff. June 19, 2009.

[1] Acts 2007, 80th Leg., ch. 1391, § 10(d) provides in part that the required "use of registration numbers issued by the Department of Public Safety of the State of Texas takes effect only after the department establishes a means by which pharmacies are able to electronically access and verify the accuracy of the registration numbers".

Section 2 of Acts 2007, 80th Leg., ch. 535 provides:

"The changes in law made by this Act apply to conduct that occurs on or after the effective date of this Act. Conduct that occurs before that date is governed by the law in effect when the conduct occurs, and the former law is continued in effect for that purpose."

Section 10(a) of Acts 2007, 80th Leg., ch. 1391 provides a general effective date for this act of September 1, 2007. Section 10(c) and (d) of Acts 2007, 80th Leg., ch. 1391 provides:

"(c) Except as otherwise provided by Subsection (d) of this section, the changes in law made by this Act in amending Subsection (k), Section 481.074, and Section 481.076, Health and Safety Code, and in adding Subsection (q), Section 481.074 of that code, take effect September 1, 2008. The public safety director of the Department of Public Safety of the State of Texas shall adopt any rules necessary to administer and enforce the changes in law made by those provisions not later than September 1, 2008.

"(d) The change in law made by this Act in amending Subsections (b) and (k), Section 481.074, Health and Safety Code, to require the use of registration numbers issued by the Department of Public Safety of the State of Texas takes effect only after the department establishes a means by which pharmacies are able to electronically access and verify the accuracy of the registration numbers."

Section 5 of Acts 2009, 81st Leg., ch. 774 provides:

"The change in law made by this Act applies only to the issuance of a prescription on or after the effective date of this Act. The issuance of a prescription before the effective date of this Act is covered by the law in effect when the prescription was issued, and the former law is continued in effect for that purpose."

§ 481.075. Official Prescription Program

(a) A practitioner who prescribes a controlled substance listed in Schedule II shall, except as provided by rule adopted under Section 481.0761, record the prescription on an official prescription form that includes the information required by this section.

(b) Each official prescription form must be sequentially numbered.

(c) The director shall issue official prescription forms to practitioners for a fee covering the actual cost of printing, processing, and mailing the forms at 100 a package. Before mailing or otherwise delivering prescription forms to a practitioner, the director shall print on each form the number of the form and any other information the director determines is necessary.

(d) A person may not obtain an official prescription form unless the person is a practitioner as defined by Section 481.002(39)(A) or an institutional practitioner.

(e) Each official prescription form used to prescribe a Schedule II controlled substance must contain:

(1) information provided by the prescribing practitioner, including:

(A) the date the prescription is written;

(B) the controlled substance prescribed;

(C) the quantity of controlled substance prescribed, shown numerically followed by the number written as a word;

(D) the intended use of the controlled substance or the diagnosis for which it is prescribed and the instructions for use of the substance;

(E) the practitioner's name, address, department registration number, and Federal Drug Enforcement Administration number;

(F) the name, address, and date of birth or age of the person for whom the controlled substance is prescribed; and

(G) if the prescription is issued to be filled at a later date under Section 481.074(d–1), the earliest date on which a pharmacy may fill the prescription;

(2) information provided by the dispensing pharmacist, including the date the prescription is filled; and

(3) the signatures of the prescribing practitioner and the dispensing pharmacist.

(f) Not more than one prescription may be recorded on an official prescription form, except as provided by rule adopted under Section 481.0761.

(g) Except for an oral prescription prescribed under Section 481.074(b), the prescribing practitioner shall:

(1) legibly fill in, or direct a designated agent to legibly fill in, on the official prescription form, each item of information required to be provided by the prescribing practitioner under Subsection (e)(1), unless the practitioner determines that:

(A) under rule adopted by the director for this purpose, it is unnecessary for the practitioner or the practitioner's agent to provide the patient identification number; or

(B) it is not in the best interest of the patient for the practitioner or practitioner's agent to provide information regarding the intended use of the controlled substance or the diagnosis for which it is prescribed; and

(2) sign the official prescription form and give the form to the person authorized to receive the prescription.

(h) In the case of an oral prescription prescribed under Section 481.074(b), the prescribing practitioner shall give the dispensing pharmacy the information needed to complete the form.

(i) Each dispensing pharmacist shall:

(1) fill in on the official prescription form each item of information given orally to the dispensing pharmacy under Subsection (h), the date the prescription is filled, and the dispensing pharmacist's signature;

(2) retain with the records of the pharmacy for at least two years:

(A) the official prescription form; and

(B) the name or other patient identification required by Section 481.074(m) or (n); and

(3) send all information required by the director, including any information required to complete an official prescription form, to the director by electronic transfer or another form approved by the director not later than the 15th day after the last day of the month in which the prescription is completely filled.

(j) A medication order written for a patient who is admitted to a hospital at the time the medication order is written and filled is not required to be on a form that meets the requirements of this section.

(k) Not later than the 30th day after the date a practitioner's department registration number, Federal Drug Enforcement Administration number, or license to practice has been denied, suspended, canceled, surrendered, or revoked, the practitioner shall return to the department all official prescription forms in the practitioner's possession that have not been used for prescriptions.

(*l*) Each prescribing practitioner:

(1) may use an official prescription form only to prescribe a controlled substance;

(2) shall date or sign an official prescription form only on the date the prescription is issued; and

(3) shall take reasonable precautionary measures to ensure that an official prescription form issued to the practitioner is not used by another person to violate this subchapter or a rule adopted under this subchapter.

(m) A pharmacy in this state may fill a prescription for a controlled substance listed in Schedule II issued by a practitioner in another state if:

(1) a share of the pharmacy's business involves the dispensing and delivery or mailing of controlled substances;

(2) the prescription is issued by a prescribing practitioner in the other state in the ordinary course of practice; and

(3) the prescription is filled in compliance with a written plan providing the manner in which the pharmacy may fill a Schedule II prescription issued by a practitioner in another state that:

(A) is submitted by the pharmacy to the director; and

(B) is approved by the director in consultation with the Texas State Board of Pharmacy.

(n) Repealed by Acts 1999, 76th Leg., ch. 145, § 5(2), eff. Sept. 1, 1999.

Acts 1989, 71st Leg., ch. 678, § 1, eff. Sept. 1, 1989. Amended by Acts 1989, 71st Leg., ch. 1100, § 5.02(i), eff. Sept. 1, 1989; Acts 1993, 73rd Leg., ch. 789, § 17, eff. Sept. 1, 1993; Acts 1997, 75th Leg., ch. 745, § 14, eff. Jan. 1, 1998; Acts 1999, 76th Leg., ch. 145, §§ 3, 5(2), eff. Sept. 1, 1999; Acts 2001, 77th Leg., ch. 251, § 11, eff. Sept. 1, 2001; Acts 2009, 81st Leg., ch. 774, § 2, eff. June 19, 2009.

Section 5 of Acts 2009, 81st Leg., ch. 774 provides:

"The change in law made by this Act applies only to the issuance of a prescription on or after the effective date of this Act. The issuance of a prescription before the effective date of this Act is covered by the law in effect when the prescription was issued, and the former law is continued in effect for that purpose."

§ 481.076. Official Prescription Information

(a) The director may not permit any person to have access to information submitted to the director under Section 481.074(q) or 481.075 except:

(1) an investigator for the Texas Medical Board, the Texas State Board of Podiatric Medical Examiners, the State Board of Dental Examiners, the State Board of Veterinary Medical Examiners, or the Texas State Board of Pharmacy;

(2) an authorized officer or member of the department engaged in the administration, investigation, or enforcement of this chapter or another law governing illicit drugs in this state or another state; or

(3) if the director finds that proper need has been shown to the director:

(A) a law enforcement or prosecutorial official engaged in the administration, investigation, or enforcement of this chapter or another law governing illicit drugs in this state or another state;

(B) a pharmacist or practitioner who is a physician, dentist, veterinarian, podiatrist, or advanced practice nurse or physician assistant described by Section 481.002(39)(D) and is inquiring about a recent Schedule II, III, IV, or V prescription history of a particular patient of the practitioner; or

(C) a pharmacist or practitioner who is inquiring about the person's own dispensing or prescribing activity.

(b) This section does not prohibit the director from creating, using, or disclosing statistical data about information received by the director under this section if the director removes any information reasonably likely to reveal the identity of each patient, practitioner, or other person who is a subject of the information.

(c) The director by rule shall design and implement a system for submission of information to the director by electronic or other means and for retrieval of information submitted to the director under this section and Sections 481.074 and 481.075. The director shall use automated information security techniques and devices to preclude improper access to the information. The director shall submit the system design to the Texas State Board of Pharmacy and the Texas Medical Board for review and approval or comment a reasonable time before implementation of the system and shall comply with the comments of those agencies unless it is unreasonable to do so.

(d) Information submitted to the director under this section may be used only for:

(1) the administration, investigation, or enforcement of this chapter or another law governing illicit drugs in this state or another state;

(2) investigatory or evidentiary purposes in connection with the functions of an agency listed in Subsection (a)(1); or

(3) dissemination by the director to the public in the form of a statistical tabulation or report if all information reasonably likely to reveal the identity of each patient, practitioner, or other person who is a subject of the information has been removed.

(e) The director shall remove from the information retrieval system, destroy, and make irretrievable the record of the identity of a patient submitted under this section to the director not later than the end of the 12th calendar month after the month in which the identity is entered into the system. However, the director may retain a patient identity that is necessary for use in a specific ongoing investigation conducted in accordance with this section until the 30th day after the end of the month in which the necessity for retention of the identity ends.

(f) If the director permits access to information under Subsection (a)(2) relating to a person licensed or regulated by an agency listed in Subsection (a)(1), the director shall notify and cooperate with that agency regarding the disposition of the matter before taking action against the person, unless the director determines that notification is reasonably likely to interfere with an administrative or criminal investigation or prosecution.

(g) If the director permits access to information under Subsection (a)(3)(A) relating to a person licensed or regulated by an agency listed in Subsection (a)(1), the director shall notify that agency of the disclosure of the information not later than the 10th working day after the date the information is disclosed.

(h) If the director withholds notification to an agency under Subsection (f), the director shall notify the agency of the disclosure of the information and the reason for withholding notification when the director determines that notification is no longer likely to interfere with an administrative or criminal investigation or prosecution.

(i) Information submitted to the director under Section 481.075 is confidential and remains confidential regardless of whether the director permits access to the information under this section.

(j) Repealed by Acts 1999, 76th Leg., ch. 145, § 5(3), eff. Sept. 1, 1999.

Acts 1989, 71st Leg., ch. 678, § 1, eff. Sept. 1, 1989. Amended by Acts 1995, 74th Leg., ch. 965, § 81, eff. June 16, 1995; Acts 1997, 75th Leg., ch. 745, § 15, eff. Jan. 1, 1998; Acts 1999, 76th Leg., ch. 145, §§ 4, 5(3), eff. Sept. 1, 1999; Acts 2007, 80th Leg., ch. 1391, § 3, eff. Sept. 1, 2008.

§ 481.0761. Rules; Authority to Contract

(a) The director shall consult with the Texas State Board of Pharmacy and by rule establish and revise as necessary a standardized database format that may be used by a pharmacy to transmit the information required by Sections 481.074(q) and 481.075(i) to the director electronically or to deliver the information on storage media, including disks, tapes, and cassettes.

(b) The director shall consult with the Department of State Health Services, the Texas State Board of Pharmacy, and the Texas Medical Board and by rule may:

(1) remove a controlled substance listed in Schedules II through V from the official prescription program, if the director determines that the burden imposed by the program substantially outweighs the risk of diversion of the particular controlled substance; or

(2) return a substance previously removed from Schedules II through V to the official prescription program, if the director determines that the risk of diversion substantially outweighs the burden imposed by the program on the particular controlled substance.

(c) The director by rule may:

(1) permit more than one prescription to be administered or dispensed and recorded on one prescription form for a Schedule III through V controlled substance;

(1–a) establish a procedure for the issuance of multiple prescriptions of a Schedule II controlled substance under Section 481.074(d–1);

(2) remove from or return to the official prescription program any aspect of a practitioner's or pharmacist's hospital practice, including administering or dispensing;

(3) waive or delay any requirement relating to the time or manner of reporting;

(4) establish compatibility protocols for electronic data transfer hardware, software, or format;

(5) establish a procedure to control the release of information under Sections 481.074, 481.075, and 481.076; and

(6) establish a minimum level of prescription activity below which a reporting activity may be modified or deleted.

(d) The director by rule shall authorize a practitioner to determine whether it is necessary to obtain a particular patient identification number and to provide that number on the official prescription form.

(e) In adopting a rule relating to the electronic transfer of information under this subchapter, the director shall consider the economic impact of the rule on practitioners and pharmacists and, to the extent permitted by law, act to minimize any negative economic impact, including the imposition of costs related to computer hardware or software or to the transfer of information. The director may not adopt a rule relating to the electronic transfer of information under this subchapter that imposes a fee in addition to the fees authorized by Section 481.064.

(f) The director may authorize a contract between the department and another agency of this state or a private vendor as necessary to ensure the effective operation of the official prescription program.

(g) Repealed by Acts 1999, 76th Leg., ch. 145, § 5(4), eff. Sept. 1, 1999.

Added by Acts 1997, 75th Leg., ch. 745, § 16, eff. Sept. 1, 1997. Amended by Acts 1999, 76th Leg., ch. 145, § 5(4), eff. Sept. 1, 1999; Acts 2007, 80th Leg., ch. 1391, § 4, eff. Sept. 1, 2007; Acts 2009, 81st Leg., ch. 774, § 3, eff. June 19, 2009.

Section 5 of Acts 2009, 81st Leg., ch. 774 provides:

"The change in law made by this Act applies only to the issuance of a prescription on or after the effective date of this Act. The issuance of a prescription before the effective date of this Act is covered by the law in effect when the prescription was issued, and the former law is continued in effect for that purpose."

§ 481.077. Chemical Precursor Records and Reports

(a) Except as provided by Subsection (*l*), a person who sells, transfers, or otherwise furnishes a chemical precursor to another person shall make an accurate and legible record of the transaction and maintain the record for at least two years after the date of the transaction.

(b) The director by rule may:

(1) name an additional chemical substance as a chemical precursor for purposes of Subsection (a) if the director determines that public health and welfare are jeopardized by evidenced proliferation or use of the chemical substance in the illicit manufacture of a controlled substance or controlled substance analogue; or

(2) exempt a chemical precursor from the requirements of Subsection (a) if the director determines that the chemical precursor does not jeopardize public health and welfare or is not used in the illicit manufacture of a controlled substance or a controlled substance analogue.

(b–1) If the director names a chemical substance as a chemical precursor for purposes of Subsection (a) or designates a substance as an immediate precursor, a substance that is a precursor of the chemical precursor or the immediate precursor is not subject to control solely because it is a precursor of the chemical precursor or the immediate precursor.

(c) This section and Section 481.078 do not apply to a person to whom a registration has been issued under Section 481.063.

(d) Before selling, transferring, or otherwise furnishing to a person in this state a chemical precursor subject to Subsection (a), a manufacturer, wholesaler, retailer, or other person shall:

(1) if the recipient does not represent a business, obtain from the recipient:

(A) the recipient's driver's license number or other personal identification certificate number, date of birth, and residential or mailing address, other than a post office box number, from a driver's license or personal identification certificate issued by the department that contains a photograph of the recipient;

(B) the year, state, and number of the motor vehicle license of the motor vehicle owned or operated by the recipient;

(C) a complete description of how the chemical precursor is to be used; and

(D) the recipient's signature; or

(2) if the recipient represents a business, obtain from the recipient:

(A) a letter of authorization from the business that includes the business license or comptroller tax identification number, address, area code, and telephone number and a complete description of how the chemical precursor is to be used; and

(B) the recipient's signature; and

(3) for any recipient, sign as a witness to the signature and identification of the recipient.

(e) If the recipient does not represent a business, the recipient shall present to the manufacturer, wholesaler, retailer, or other person a permit issued in the name of the recipient by the department under Section 481.078.

(f) Except as provided by Subsection (h), a manufacturer, wholesaler, retailer, or other person who sells, transfers, or otherwise furnishes to a person in this state a chemical precursor subject to Subsection (a) shall submit, at least 21 days before the delivery of the chemical precursor, a report of the transaction on a form obtained from the director that includes the information required by Subsection (d).

(g) The director shall supply to a manufacturer, wholesaler, retailer, or other person who sells, transfers, or otherwise furnishes a chemical precursor subject to Subsection (a) a form for the submission of:

(1) the report required by Subsection (f);

(2) the name and measured amount of the chemical precursor delivered; and

(3) any other information required by the director.

(h) The director may authorize a manufacturer, wholesaler, retailer, or other person to submit a comprehensive monthly report instead of the report required by Subsection (f) if the director determines that:

(1) there is a pattern of regular supply and purchase of the chemical precursor between the furnisher and the recipient; or

(2) the recipient has established a record of use of the chemical precursor solely for a lawful purpose.

(i) A manufacturer, wholesaler, retailer, or other person who receives from a source outside this state a chemical precursor subject to Subsection (a) or who discovers a loss or theft of a chemical precursor subject to Subsection (a) shall:

(1) submit a report of the transaction to the director in accordance with department rule; and

(2) include in the report:

(A) any difference between the amount of the chemical precursor actually received and the amount of the chemical precursor shipped according to the shipping statement or invoice; or

(B) the amount of the loss or theft.

(j) A report under Subsection (i) must:

(1) be made not later than the third day after the date that the manufacturer, wholesaler, retailer, or other person learns of the discrepancy, loss, or theft; and

(2) if the discrepancy, loss, or theft occurred during a shipment of the chemical precursor, include the name of the common carrier or person who transported the chemical precursor and the date that the chemical precursor was shipped.

(k) Unless the person is the holder of only a permit issued under Section 481.078(b)(1), a manufacturer, wholesaler, retailer, or other person who sells, transfers, or otherwise furnishes any chemical precursor subject to Subsection (a) or a permit holder, commercial purchaser, or other person who receives a chemical precursor subject to Subsection (a):

(1) shall maintain records and inventories in accordance with rules established by the director;

(2) shall allow a member of the department or a peace officer to conduct audits and inspect records of purchases and sales and all other records made in accordance with this section at any reasonable time; and

(3) may not interfere with the audit or with the full and complete inspection or copying of those records.

(*l*) This section does not apply to the sale or transfer of any compound, mixture, or preparation containing ephedrine, pseudoephedrine, or norpseudoephedrine that is in liquid, liquid capsule, or liquid gel capsule form.

Acts 1989, 71st Leg., ch. 678, § 1, eff. Sept. 1, 1989. Amended by Acts 1989, 71st Leg., ch. 1100, § 5.02(k), eff. Sept. 1, 1989; Acts 1997, 75th Leg., ch. 745, § 17, eff. Jan. 1, 1998; Acts 2001, 77th Leg., ch. 251, § 12, eff. Sept. 1, 2001; Acts 2003, 78th Leg., ch. 570, § 1, eff. Sept. 1, 2003; Acts 2003, 78th Leg., ch. 1099, § 6, eff. Sept. 1, 2003; Acts 2005, 79th Leg., ch. 282, § 4, eff. Aug. 1, 2005.

§ 481.0771. Records and Reports on Pseudoephedrine

(a) A wholesaler who sells, transfers, or otherwise furnishes a product containing ephedrine, pseudoephedrine, or norpseudoephedrine to a retailer shall:

(1) before delivering the product, obtain from the retailer the retailer's address, area code, and telephone number; and

(2) make an accurate and legible record of the transaction and maintain the record for at least two years after the date of the transaction.

(b) The wholesaler shall make all records available to the director in accordance with department rule, including:

(1) the information required by Subsection (a)(1);

(2) the amount of the product containing ephedrine, pseudoephedrine, or norpseudoephedrine delivered; and

(3) any other information required by the director.

(c) Not later than 10 business days after receipt of an order for a product containing ephedrine, pseudoephedrine, or norpseudoephedrine that requests delivery of a suspicious quantity of the product as determined by department rule, a wholesaler shall submit to the director a report of the order in accordance with department rule.

(d) A wholesaler who, with reckless disregard for the duty to report, fails to report as required by Subsection (c) may be subject to disciplinary action in accordance with department rule.

Added by Acts 2005, 79th Leg., ch. 282, § 5, eff. Aug. 1, 2005.

§ 481.078. Chemical Precursor Transfer Permit

(a) A person must obtain a chemical precursor transfer permit from the department to be eligible:

(1) to sell, transfer, or otherwise furnish a chemical precursor subject to Section 481.077(a) to a person in this state;

(2) to receive a chemical precursor subject to Section 481.077(a) from a source outside this state; or

(3) to receive a chemical precursor subject to Section 481.077(a) if the person, in receiving the chemical precursor, does not represent a business.

(b) The director by rule shall adopt procedures and standards for the issuance and renewal or the voluntary surrender, cancellation, suspension, probation, or revocation of:

(1) a permit for one sale, transfer, receipt, or otherwise furnishing of a chemical precursor; or

(2) a permit for more than one sale, transfer, receipt, or otherwise furnishing of a chemical precursor.

(c) A permit issued or renewed under Subsection (b)(1) is valid only for the transaction indicated on the permit. A permit issued or renewed under Subsection (b)(2) is valid for one year after the date of issuance or renewal.

(d) A permit holder must report in writing or by telephone to the director a change in the holder's business name, address, area code, and telephone number not later than the seventh day after the date of the change.

(e) The director may not issue a permit under this section unless the person applying for the permit delivers to the director a written consent to inspect signed by the person that grants to the director the right to inspect any controlled premises, record, chemical precursor, or other item governed by this chapter in the care, custody, or control of the person. After the director receives the consent, the director may inspect any controlled premises, record, chemical precursor, or other item to which the consent applies.

(f) The director may adopt rules to establish security controls and provide for the inspection of a place, entity, or item to which a chemical precursor transfer permit applies.

Added by Acts 1989, 71st Leg., ch. 1100, § 5.02(*l*), eff. Sept. 1, 1989. Amended by Acts 1997, 75th Leg., ch. 745, § 18, eff. Jan. 1, 1998; Acts 2001, 77th Leg., ch. 251, § 13, eff. Sept. 1, 2001.

§ 481.079. Repealed by Acts 1997, 75th Leg., ch. 745, § 37, eff. Jan. 1, 1998

§ 481.080. Chemical Laboratory Apparatus Record–keeping Requirements and Penalties

(a) A manufacturer, wholesaler, retailer, or other person who sells, transfers, or otherwise furnishes a chemical laboratory apparatus shall make an accurate and legible record of the transaction and maintain the record for at least two years after the date of the transaction.

(b) The director may adopt rules to implement this section.

(c) The director by rule may:

(1) name an additional item of equipment as a chemical laboratory apparatus for purposes of Subsection (a) if the director determines that public health and welfare are jeopardized by evidenced proliferation or use of the item of equipment in the illicit manufacture of a controlled substance or controlled substance analogue; or

(2) exempt a chemical laboratory apparatus from the requirement of Subsection (a) if the director determines that the apparatus does not jeopardize public health and welfare or is not used in the illicit manufacture of a controlled substance or a controlled substance analogue.

(d) This section and Section 481.081 do not apply to a person to whom a registration has been issued under Section 481.063.

(e) Before selling, transferring, or otherwise furnishing to a person in this state a chemical laboratory apparatus subject to Subsection (a), a manufacturer, wholesaler, retailer, or other person shall:

(1) if the recipient does not represent a business, obtain from the recipient:

(A) the recipient's driver's license number or other personal identification certificate number, date of birth, and residential or mailing address, other than a post office box number, from a driver's license or personal identification certificate issued by the department that contains a photograph of the recipient;

(B) the year, state, and number of the motor vehicle license of the motor vehicle owned or operated by the recipient;

(C) a complete description of how the apparatus is to be used; and

(D) the recipient's signature; or

(2) if the recipient represents a business, obtain from the recipient:

(A) a letter of authorization from the business that includes the business license or comptroller tax identification number, address, area code, and telephone number and a complete description of how the apparatus is to be used; and

(B) the recipient's signature; and

(3) for any recipient, sign as a witness to the signature and identification of the recipient.

(f) If the recipient does not represent a business, the recipient shall present to the manufacturer, wholesaler, retailer, or other person a permit issued in the name of the recipient by the department under Section 481.081.

(g) Except as provided by Subsection (i), a manufacturer, wholesaler, retailer, or other person who sells, transfers, or otherwise furnishes to a person in this state a chemical laboratory apparatus subject to Subsection (a) shall, at least 21 days before the delivery of the apparatus, submit a report of the transaction on a form obtained from the director that includes the information required by Subsection (e).

(h) The director shall supply to a manufacturer, wholesaler, retailer, or other person who sells, transfers, or otherwise furnishes a chemical laboratory apparatus subject to Subsection (a) a form for the submission of:

(1) the report required by Subsection (g);

(2) the name and number of apparatus delivered; and

(3) any other information required by the director.

(i) The director may authorize a manufacturer, wholesaler, retailer, or other person to submit a comprehensive monthly report instead of the report required by Subsection (g) if the director determines that:

(1) there is a pattern of regular supply and purchase of the apparatus between the furnisher and the recipient; or

(2) the recipient has established a record of use of the apparatus solely for a lawful purpose.

(j) A manufacturer, wholesaler, retailer, or other person who receives from a source outside this state a chemical laboratory apparatus subject to Subsection (a) or who discovers a loss or theft of such an apparatus shall:

(1) submit a report of the transaction to the director in accordance with department rule; and

(2) include in the report:

(A) any difference between the number of the apparatus actually received and the number of the apparatus shipped according to the shipping statement or invoice; or

(B) the number of the loss or theft.

(k) A report under Subsection (j) must:

(1) be made not later than the third day after the date that the manufacturer, wholesaler, retailer, or other person learns of the discrepancy, loss, or theft; and

(2) if the discrepancy, loss, or theft occurred during a shipment of the apparatus, include the name of the common carrier or person who transported the apparatus and the date that the apparatus was shipped.

(*l*) This subsection applies to a manufacturer, wholesaler, retailer, or other person who sells, transfers, or otherwise furnishes any chemical laboratory apparatus subject to Subsection (a) and to a permit holder, commercial purchaser, or other person who receives such an apparatus unless the person is the holder of only a permit issued under Section 481.081(b)(1). A person covered by this subsection:

(1) shall maintain records and inventories in accordance with rules established by the director;

(2) shall allow a member of the department or a peace officer to conduct audits and inspect records of purchases and sales and all other records made in accordance with this section at any reasonable time; and

(3) may not interfere with the audit or with the full and complete inspection or copying of those records.

Added by Acts 1989, 71st Leg., ch. 1100, § 5.02(*l*), eff. Sept. 1, 1989. Amended by Acts 1997, 75th Leg., ch. 745, § 19, eff. Jan. 1, 1998; Acts 2001, 77th Leg., ch. 251, § 14, eff. Sept. 1, 2001.

§ 481.081. Chemical Laboratory Apparatus Transfer Permit

(a) A person must obtain a chemical laboratory apparatus transfer permit from the department to be eligible:

(1) to sell, transfer, or otherwise furnish an apparatus subject to Section 481.080(a) to a person in this state;

(2) to receive an apparatus subject to Section 481.080(a) from a source outside this state; or

(3) to receive an apparatus subject to Section 481.080(a) if the person, in receiving the apparatus, does not represent a business.

(b) The director by rule shall adopt procedures and standards for the issuance and renewal or the voluntary surrender, cancellation, suspension, probation, or revocation of:

(1) a permit for one sale, transfer, receipt, or otherwise furnishing of a chemical laboratory apparatus; or

(2) a permit for more than one sale, transfer, receipt, or otherwise furnishing of a chemical laboratory apparatus.

(c) A permit issued or renewed under Subsection (b)(1) is valid only for the transaction indicated on the permit. A permit issued or renewed under Subsection (b)(2) is valid for one year after the date of issuance or renewal.

(d) A permit holder must report in writing or by telephone to the director a change in the holder's business name, address, area code, and telephone number not later than the seventh day after the date of the change.

(e) The director may not issue a permit under this section unless the person applying for the permit delivers to the director a written consent to inspect signed by the person that grants to the director the right to inspect any controlled premises, record, chemical laboratory apparatus, or other item governed by this chapter in the care, custody, or control of the person. After the director receives the consent, the director may inspect any controlled premises, record, chemical laboratory apparatus, or other item to which the consent applies.

(f) The director may by rule establish security controls and provide for the inspection of a place, entity, or item to which a chemical laboratory apparatus transfer permit applies.

Added by Acts 1989, 71st Leg., ch. 1100, § 5.02(*l*), eff. Sept. 1, 1989. Amended by Acts 1997, 75th Leg., ch. 745, § 20, eff. Jan. 1, 1998; Acts 2001, 77th Leg., ch. 251, § 15, eff. Sept. 1, 2001.

§ 481.082. Repealed by Acts 1997, 75th Leg., ch. 745, § 37, eff. Jan. 1, 1998

SUBCHAPTER D. OFFENSES AND PENALTIES

§ 481.101. Criminal Classification

For the purpose of establishing criminal penalties for violations of this chapter, controlled substances, including a material, compound, mixture, or preparation containing the controlled substance, are divided into Penalty Groups 1 through 4.

Acts 1989, 71st Leg., ch. 678, § 1, eff. Sept. 1, 1989. Amended by Acts 1989, 71st Leg., ch. 1100, § 5.02(n), eff. Sept. 1, 1989.

§ 481.102. Penalty Group 1

Penalty Group 1 consists of:

(1) the following opiates, including their isomers, esters, ethers, salts, and salts of isomers, esters, and ethers, unless specifically excepted, if the existence of these isomers, esters, ethers, and salts is possible within the specific chemical designation:

Alfentanil;

Allylprodine;

Alphacetylmethadol;
Benzethidine;
Betaprodine;
Clonitazene;
Diampromide;
Diethylthiambutene;
Difenoxin not listed in Penalty Group 3 or 4;
Dimenoxadol;
Dimethylthiambutene;
Dioxaphetyl butyrate;
Dipipanone;
Ethylmethylthiambutene;
Etonitazene;
Etoxeridine;
Furethidine;
Hydroxypethidine;
Ketobemidone;
Levophenacylmorphan;
Meprodine;
Methadol;
Moramide;
Morpheridine;
Noracymethadol;
Norlevorphanol;
Normethadone;
Norpipanone;
Phenadoxone;
Phenampromide;
Phenomorphan;
Phenoperidine;
Piritramide;
Proheptazine;
Properidine;
Propiram;
Sufentanil;
Tilidine; and
Trimeperidine;

(2) the following opium derivatives, their salts, isomers, and salts of isomers, unless specifically excepted, if the existence of these salts, isomers, and salts of isomers is possible within the specific chemical designation:

Acetorphine;
Acetyldihydrocodeine;
Benzylmorphine;
Codeine methylbromide;
Codeine–N–Oxide;
Cyprenorphine;
Desomorphine;
Dihydromorphine;
Drotebanol;
Etorphine, except hydrochloride salt;
Heroin;
Hydromorphinol;
Methyldesorphine;
Methyldihydromorphine;
Monoacetylmorphine;
Morphine methylbromide;
Morphine methylsulfonate;
Morphine–N–Oxide;
Myrophine;
Nicocodeine;
Nicomorphine;
Normorphine;
Pholcodine; and
Thebacon;

(3) the following substances, however produced, except those narcotic drugs listed in another group:

(A) Opium and opiate not listed in Penalty Group 3 or 4, and a salt, compound, derivative, or preparation of opium or opiate, other than thebaine derived butorphanol, nalmefene and its salts, naloxone and its salts, and naltrexone and its salts, but including:

Codeine not listed in Penalty Group 3 or 4;
Dihydroetorphine;
Ethylmorphine not listed in Penalty Group 3 or 4;
Granulated opium;
Hydrocodone not listed in Penalty Group 3;
Hydromorphone;
Metopon;
Morphine not listed in Penalty Group 3;
Opium extracts;
Opium fluid extracts;
Oripavine;
Oxycodone;
Oxymorphone;
Powdered opium;
Raw opium;

Thebaine; and

Tincture of opium;

(B) a salt, compound, isomer, derivative, or preparation of a substance that is chemically equivalent or identical to a substance described by Paragraph (A), other than the isoquinoline alkaloids of opium;

(C) Opium poppy and poppy straw;

(D) Cocaine, including:

(i) its salts, its optical, position, and geometric isomers, and the salts of those isomers;

(ii) coca leaves and a salt, compound, derivative, or preparation of coca leaves;

(iii) a salt, compound, derivative, or preparation of a salt, compound, or derivative that is chemically equivalent or identical to a substance described by Subparagraph (i) or (ii), other than decocainized coca leaves or extractions of coca leaves that do not contain cocaine or ecgonine; and

(E) concentrate of poppy straw, meaning the crude extract of poppy straw in liquid, solid, or powder form that contains the phenanthrine alkaloids of the opium poppy;

(4) the following opiates, including their isomers, esters, ethers, salts, and salts of isomers, if the existence of these isomers, esters, ethers, and salts is possible within the specific chemical designation:

Acetyl-alpha-methylfentanyl (N–[1–(1–methyl–2–phenethyl)–4–piperidinyl]–N–phenylacetamide);

Alpha-methylthiofentanyl (N–[1–m ethyl–2–(2–thienyl)ethyl–4–piperidinyl]–N–phenylpropanamide);

Alphaprodine;

Anileridine;

Beta-hydroxyfentanyl (N–[1–(2–hy droxy–2–phenethyl)–4–piperidinyl]–N–phenylpropanamide);

Beta–hydroxy–3–methylfentanyl;

Bezitramide;

Carfentanil;

Dihydrocodeine not listed in Penalty Group 3 or 4;

Diphenoxylate not listed in Penalty Group 3 or 4;

Fentanyl or alpha-methylfentanyl, or any other derivative of Fentanyl;

Isomethadone;

Levomethorphan;

Levorphanol;

Metazocine;

Methadone;

Methadone–Intermediate, 4–cyano–2–dimethylamino–4, 4–diphenyl butane;

3–methylfentanyl(N–[3–methyl–1–(2–phenylethyl)–4–piperidyl]–N–phenylpropanamide);

3–methylthiofentanyl(N–[3–methyl –1–(2–thienyl)ethyl–4–piperidinyl]–N–phenylpropanamide);

Moramide–Intermediate, 2–methyl–3–morpholino–1, 1–diphenyl–propane–carboxylic acid;

Para-fluorofentanyl(N–(4–fluorop henyl)–N–1–(2–phenylethyl)–4–piperidinylpropanamide);

PEPAP (1–(2–phenethyl)–4–phenyl–4–acetoxypiperidine);

Pethidine (Meperidine);

Pethidine–Intermediate–A, 4–cyano–1–methyl–4–phenylpiperidine;

Pethidine–Intermediate–B, ethyl–4–phenylpiperidine–4 carboxylate;

Pethidine–Intermediate–C, 1–methyl–4–phenylpiperidine–4–carboxylic acid;

Phenazocine;

Piminodine;

Racemethorphan;

Racemorphan;

Remifentanil; and

Thiofentanyl(N–phenyl–N–[1–(2–thienyl)ethyl–4–piperidinyl]–propanamide) ;

(5) Flunitrazepam (trade or other name: Rohypnol);

(6) Methamphetamine, including its salts, optical isomers, and salts of optical isomers;

(7) Phenylacetone and methylamine, if possessed together with intent to manufacture methamphetamine;

(8) Phencyclidine, including its salts;

(9) Gamma hydroxybutyric acid (some trade or other names: gamma hydroxybutyrate, GHB), including its salts; and

(10) Ketamine.

Acts 1989, 71st Leg., ch. 678, § 1, eff. Sept. 1, 1989. Amended by Acts 1989, 71st Leg., ch. 1100, § 5.02(n), eff. Sept. 1, 1989; Acts 1991, 72nd Leg., ch. 761, § 1, eff. Sept. 1, 1991. Amended by Acts 1997, 75th Leg., ch. 745, § 21, eff. Jan. 1, 1998; Acts 2001, 77th Leg., ch. 251, § 16, eff. Sept. 1, 2001; Acts 2001, 77th Leg., ch. 459, § 1, eff. Sept. 1, 2001; Acts 2003, 78th Leg., ch. 1099, § 7, eff. Sept. 1, 2003; Acts 2009, 81st Leg., ch. 739, § 1, eff. Sept. 1, 2009.

Section 4 of Acts 2009, 81st Leg., ch. 739 provides:

"The change in law made by this Act applies only to an offense committed on or after the effective date [Sept. 1, 2009] of this Act. An offense committed before the effective date of this Act is covered by the law in effect when the offense was committed, and the former law is continued in effect for that purpose. For purposes of this section, an offense was committed before the effective date of this Act if any element of the offense was committed before that date."

§ 481.1021. Penalty Group 1-A

Penalty Group 1-A consists of lysergic acid diethylamide (LSD), including its salts, isomers, and salts of isomers.

Added by Acts 1997, 75th Leg., ch. 745, § 22, eff. Jan. 1, 1998.

§ 481.103. Penalty Group 2

(a) Penalty Group 2 consists of:

(1) any quantity of the following hallucinogenic substances, their salts, isomers, and salts of isomers, unless specifically excepted, if the existence of these salts, isomers, and salts of isomers is possible within the specific chemical designation:

alpha-ethyltryptamine;

alpha-methyltryptamine;

4–bromo–2, 5–dimethoxyamphetamine (some trade or other names: 4–bromo–2, 5–dimethoxy–alpha–methylphenethylamine; 4–bromo–2, 5–DMA);

4–bromo–2, 5–dimethoxyphenethylamine;

Bufotenine (some trade and other names: 3–(beta-Dimethylaminoethyl)–5–hydroxyindole; 3–(2–dimethylaminoethyl)–5–indolol; N, N-dimethylserotonin; 5–hydroxy–N, N-dimethyltryptamine; mappine);

Diethyltryptamine (some trade and other names: N, N–Diethyltryptamine, DET);

2, 5–dimethoxyamphetamine (some trade or other names: 2, 5–dimethoxy–alpha–methylphenethylamine; 2, 5–DMA);

2, 5–dimethoxy–4–ethylamphetamine (trade or other name: DOET);

2, 5–dimethoxy–4–(n)–propylthiophenethylamine (trade or other name: 2C–T–7);

Dimethyltryptamine (trade or other name: DMT);

Dronabinol (synthetic) in sesame oil and encapsulated in a soft gelatin capsule in a U.S. Food and Drug Administration approved drug product (some trade or other names for Dronabinol: (a6aR–trans)–6a,7,8,10a–tetrahydro- 6,6, 9- trimethyl–3–pentyl–6H- dibenzo [b,d]pyran–1–ol or (–)–delta–9– (trans)- tetrahydrocannabinol);

Ethylamine Analog of Phencyclidine (some trade or other names: N–ethyl–1–phenylcyclohexylamine, (1– phenylcyclohexyl) ethylamine, N–(1–phenylcyclohexyl) ethylamine, cyclohexamine, PCE);

Ibogaine (some trade or other names: 7–Ethyl–6, 6, beta 7, 8, 9, 10, 12, 13–octahydro–2–methoxy–6, 9–methano–5H- pyrido [1′, 2′:1, 2] azepino [5, 4–b] indole; tabernanthe iboga.);

Mescaline;

5–methoxy–N, N-diisopropyltryptamine;

5–methoxy–3, 4–methylenedioxy amphetamine;

4–methoxyamphetamine (some trade or other names: 4–methoxy–alpha–methylphenethylamine; paramethoxyamphetamine; PMA);

1–methyl- 4–phenyl–4–propionoxypiperidine (MPPP, PPMP);

4–methyl–2, 5–dimethoxyamphetamine (some trade and other names: 4–methyl–2, 5–dimethoxy–alpha- methylphenethylamine; "DOM"; "STP");

3,4–methylenedioxy methamphetamine (MDMA, MDM);

3,4–methylenedioxy amphetamine;

3,4–methylenedioxy N-ethylamphetamine (Also known as N-ethyl MDA);

Nabilone (Another name for nabilone: (+)–trans-3–(1,1–dimethylheptyl)- 6,6a, 7,8,10,10a–hexahydro–1–hydroxy- 6, 6–dimethyl–9H–dibenzo[b,d] pyran–9–one;

N-benzylpiperazine (some trade or other names: BZP; 1–benzylpiperazine);

N–ethyl–3–piperidyl benzilate;

N–hydroxy–3,4–methylenedioxyamphetamine (Also known as N-hydroxy MDA);

4–methylaminorex;

N–methyl–3–piperidyl benzilate;

Parahexyl (some trade or other names: 3–Hexyl–1- hydroxy–7, 8, 9, 10–tetrahydro–6, 6, 9–trimethyl–6H–dibenzo [b, d] pyran; Synhexyl);

1–Phenylcyclohexylamine;

1–Piperidinocyclohexanecarbonitrile (PCC);

Psilocin;

Psilocybin;

Pyrrolidine Analog of Phencyclidine (some trade or other names: 1–(1–phenylcyclohexyl)–pyrrolidine, PCPy, PHP);

Tetrahydrocannabinols, other than marihuana, and synthetic equivalents of the substances contained in the plant, or in the resinous extractives of Cannabis, or synthetic substances, derivatives, and their isomers with similar chemical structure and pharmacological activity such as:

delta–1 cis or trans tetrahydrocannabinol, and their optical isomers;

delta–6 cis or trans tetrahydrocannabinol, and their optical isomers;

delta–3, 4 cis or trans tetrahydrocannabinol, and its optical isomers;

compounds of these structures, regardless of numerical designation of atomic positions, since nomenclature of these substances is not internationally standardized;

Thiophene Analog of Phencyclidine (some trade or other names: 1–[1–(2–thienyl) cyclohexyl] piperidine; 2–Thienyl Analog of Phencyclidine; TPCP, TCP);

1–pyrrolidine (some trade or other name: TCPy);

1–(3–trifluoromethylphenyl)piperazine (trade or other name: TFMPP); and

3,4,5–trimethoxy amphetamine;

(2) Phenylacetone (some trade or other names: Phenyl–2–propanone; P2P, Benzymethyl ketone, methyl benzyl ketone); and

(3) unless specifically excepted or unless listed in another Penalty Group, a material, compound, mixture, or preparation that contains any quantity of the following substances having a potential for abuse associated with a depressant or stimulant effect on the central nervous system:

Aminorex (some trade or other names: aminoxaphen; 2–amino–5–phenyl–2–oxazoline; 4,5–dihydro–5– phenyl–2–oxazolamine);

Amphetamine, its salts, optical isomers, and salts of optical isomers;

Cathinone (some trade or other names: 2–amino–1– phenyl–1–propanone, alpha-aminopropiophenone, 2– aminopropiophenone);

Etorphine Hydrochloride;

Fenethylline and its salts;

Lisdexamfetamine, including its salts, isomers, and salts of isomers;

Mecloqualone and its salts;

Methaqualone and its salts;

Methcathinone (some trade or other names: 2–methylamino-propiophenone; alpha–(methylamino)propriophenone; 2–(methylamino)–1–phenylpropan–1–one; alpha–N- methylaminopropriophenone; monomethylpropion; ephedrone, N- methylcathinone; methylcathinone; AL–464; AL–422; AL–463; and UR 1431);

N–Ethylamphetamine, its salts, optical isomers, and salts of optical isomers; and

N,N-dimethylamphetamine (some trade or other names: N,N,alpha–trimethylbenzeneethaneamine; N,N,alpha–trimethylphenethylamine), its salts, optical isomers, and salts of optical isomers.

(b) For the purposes of Subsection (a)(1) only, the term "isomer" includes an optical, position, or geometric isomer.

Amended by Acts 1997, 75th Leg., ch. 745, § 23, eff. Jan. 1, 1998; Acts 2001, 77th Leg., ch. 251, § 17, eff. Sept. 1, 2001; Acts 2003, 78th Leg., ch. 1099, § 8, eff. Sept. 1, 2003; Acts 2009, 81st Leg., ch. 739, § 2, eff. Sept. 1, 2009.

Section 4 of Acts 2009, 81st Leg., ch. 739 provides:

"The change in law made by this Act applies only to an offense committed on or after the effective date [Sept. 1, 2009] of this Act. An offense committed before the effective date of this Act is covered by the law in effect when the offense was committed, and the former law is continued in effect for that purpose. For purposes of this section, an offense was committed before the effective date of this Act if any element of the offense was committed before that date."

§ 481.104. Penalty Group 3

(a) Penalty Group 3 consists of:

(1) a material, compound, mixture, or preparation that contains any quantity of the following substances having a potential for abuse associated with a stimulant effect on the central nervous system:

Methylphenidate and its salts; and

Phenmetrazine and its salts;

(2) a material, compound, mixture, or preparation that contains any quantity of the following substances having a potential for abuse associated with a depressant effect on the central nervous system:

a substance that contains any quantity of a derivative of barbituric acid, or any salt of a derivative of barbituric acid not otherwise described by this subsection;

a compound, mixture, or preparation containing amobarbital, secobarbital, pentobarbital, or any salt of any of these, and one or more active medicinal ingredients that are not listed in any penalty group;

a suppository dosage form containing amobarbital, secobarbital, pentobarbital, or any salt of any of these drugs, and approved by the United States Food and Drug Administration for marketing only as a suppository;

Alprazolam;

Amobarbital;

Bromazepam;

Camazepam;

Chlordiazepoxide;

Chlorhexadol;

Clobazam;

Clonazepam;

Clorazepate;

Clotiazepam;

Cloxazolam;

Delorazepam;

Diazepam;

Estazolam;

Ethyl loflazepate;

Fludiazepam;

Flurazepam;

Glutethimide;

Halazepam;

Haloxzolam;

Ketazolam;

Loprazolam;

Lorazepam;

Lormetazepam;

Lysergic acid, including its salts, isomers, and salts of isomers;

Lysergic acid amide, including its salts, isomers, and salts of isomers;

Mebutamate;

Medazepam;

Methyprylon;

Midazolam;

Nimetazepam;

Nitrazepam;

Nordiazepam;

Oxazepam;

Oxazolam;

Pentazocine, its salts, derivatives, or compounds or mixtures thereof;

Pentobarbital;

Pinazepam;

Prazepam;

Quazepam;

Secobarbital;

Sulfondiethylmethane;

Sulfonethylmethane;

Sulfonmethane;

Temazepam;

Tetrazepam;

Tiletamine and zolazepam in combination, and its salts. (some trade or other names for a tiletamine-zolazepam combination product: Telazol, for tiletamine: 2–(ethylamino)- 2–(2–thienyl)–cyclohexanone, and for zolazepam: 4–(2- fluorophenyl)–6, 8–dihydro–1,3,8,–trimethylpyrazolo–[3,4– e](1,4)–d diazepin–7(1H)–one, flupyrazapon);

Triazolam;

Zaleplon;

Zolpidem; and

Zopiclone;

(3) Nalorphine;

(4) a material, compound, mixture, or preparation containing limited quantities of the following narcotic drugs, or any of their salts:

not more than 1.8 grams of codeine, or any of its salts, per 100 milliliters or not more than 90 milligrams per dosage unit, with an equal or greater quantity of an isoquinoline alkaloid of opium;

not more than 1.8 grams of codeine, or any of its salts, per 100 milliliters or not more than 90 milligrams per dosage unit, with one or more active, nonnarcotic ingredients in recognized therapeutic amounts;

not more than 300 milligrams of dihydrocodeinone (hydrocodone), or any of its salts, per 100 milliliters or not more than 15 milligrams per dosage unit, with a fourfold or greater quantity of an isoquinoline alkaloid of opium;

not more than 300 milligrams of dihydrocodeinone (hydrocodone), or any of its salts, per 100 milliliters or not more than 15 milligrams per dosage unit, with one or more active, nonnarcotic ingredients in recognized therapeutic amounts;

not more than 1.8 grams of dihydrocodeine, or any of its salts, per 100 milliliters or not more than 90 milligrams per dosage unit, with one or more active, nonnarcotic ingredients in recognized therapeutic amounts;

not more than 300 milligrams of ethylmorphine, or any of its salts, per 100 milliliters or not more than 15 milligrams per dosage unit, with one or more active, nonnarcotic ingredients in recognized therapeutic amounts;

not more than 500 milligrams of opium per 100 milliliters or per 100 grams, or not more than 25 milligrams per dosage unit, with one or more active, nonnarcotic ingredients in recognized therapeutic amounts;

not more than 50 milligrams of morphine, or any of its salts, per 100 milliliters or per 100 grams with one or more active, nonnarcotic ingredients in recognized therapeutic amounts; and

not more than 1 milligram of difenoxin and not less than 25 micrograms of atropine sulfate per dosage unit;

(5) a material, compound, mixture, or preparation that contains any quantity of the following substances:

Barbital;

Chloral betaine;

Chloral hydrate;

Ethchlorvynol;

Ethinamate;

Meprobamate;

Methohexital;

Methylphenobarbital (Mephobarbital);

Paraldehyde;

Petrichloral; and

Phenobarbital;

(6) Peyote, unless unharvested and growing in its natural state, meaning all parts of the plant classified botanically as Lophophora, whether growing or not, the seeds of the plant, an extract from a part of the plant, and every compound, manufacture, salt, derivative, mixture, or preparation of the plant, its seeds, or extracts;

(7) unless listed in another penalty group, a material, compound, mixture, or preparation that contains any quantity of the following substances having a stimulant effect on the central nervous system, including the substance's salts, optical, position, or geometric isomers, and salts of the substance's isomers, if the existence of the salts, isomers, and salts of isomers is possible within the specific chemical designation:

Benzphetamine;

Cathine [(+)-norpseudoephedrine];

Chlorphentermine;

Clortermine;

Diethylpropion;

Fencamfamin;

Fenfluramine;

Fenproporex;

Mazindol;

Mefenorex;

Modafinil;

Pemoline (including organometallic complexes and their chelates);

Phendimetrazine;

Phentermine;

Pipradrol;

Sibutramine; and

SPA [(–)–1–dimethylamino–1,2–diphenylethane];

(8) unless specifically excepted or unless listed in another penalty group, a material, compound, mixture, or preparation that contains any quantity of the following substance, including its salts:

Dextropropoxyphene (Alpha–(+)–4–dimethylamino– 1,2–diphenyl–3–methyl–2–propionoxybutane); and

(9) an anabolic steroid, including any drug or hormonal substance, or any substance that is chemically or pharmacologically related to testosterone, other than an estrogen, progestin, dehydroepiandrosterone, or corticosteroid, and promotes muscle growth, including the following drugs and substances and any salt, ester, or ether of the following drugs and substances:

Androstanediol;

Androstanedione;

Androstenediol;

Androstenedione;

Bolasterone;

Boldenone;

Calusterone;

Clostebol;

Dehydrochlormethyltestosterone;

Delta–1–dihydrotestosterone;

Dihydrotestosterone (4–dihydrotestosterone);

Drostanolone;

Ethylestrenol;

Fluoxymesterone;

Formebulone;

Furazabol;

13beta–ethyl–17beta–hydroxygon–4–en–3–one;

4–hydroxytestosterone;

4–hydroxy–19–nortestosterone;

Mestanolone;

Mesterolone;

Methandienone;

Methandriol;

Methenolone;

17alpha–methyl–3beta, 17 beta–dihydroxy–5alpha- androstane;

17alpha–methyl–3alpha, 17 beta–dihydroxy–5alpha- androstane;

17alpha–methyl–3beta, 17beta–dihydroxyandrost–4- ene;

17alpha–methyl–4–hydroxynandrolone;

Methyldienolone;

Methyltestosterone;

Methyltrienolone;

17alpha–methyl–delta–1–dihydrotestosterone;

Mibolerone;

Nandrolone;

Norandrostenediol;

Norandrostenedione;

Norbolethone;

Norclostebol;

Norethandrolone;

Normethandrolone;

Oxandrolone;

Oxymesterone;

Oxymetholone;

Stanozolol;

Stenbolone;

Testolactone;

Testosterone;

Tetrahydrogestrinone; and

Trenbolone.

(b) Penalty Group 3 does not include a compound, mixture, or preparation containing a stimulant substance listed in Subsection (a)(1) if the compound, mixture, or preparation contains one or more active medicinal ingredients not having a stimulant effect on the central nervous system and if the admixtures are included in combinations, quantity, proportion, or concentration that vitiate the potential for abuse of the substances that have a stimulant effect on the central nervous system.

(c) Penalty Group 3 does not include a compound, mixture, or preparation containing a depressant substance listed in Subsection (a)(2) or (a)(5) if the compound, mixture, or preparation contains one or more active medicinal ingredients not having a depressant effect on the central nervous system and if the admixtures are included in combinations, quantity, proportion, or concentration that vitiate the potential for abuse of the substances that have a depressant effect on the central nervous system.

Amended by Acts 1997, 75th Leg., ch. 745, § 24, eff. Jan. 1, 1998; Acts 2001, 77th Leg., ch. 251, § 18, eff. Sept. 1, 2001; Acts 2009, 81st Leg., ch. 739, § 3, eff. Sept. 1, 2009.

Section 4 of Acts 2009, 81st Leg., ch. 739 provides:

"The change in law made by this Act applies only to an offense committed on or after the effective date [Sept. 1, 2009] of this Act. An offense committed before the effective date of this Act is covered by the law in effect when the offense was committed, and the former law is continued in effect for that purpose. For purposes of this section, an offense was committed before the effective date of this Act if any element of the offense was committed before that date."

§ 481.105. Penalty Group 4

Penalty Group 4 consists of:

(1) a compound, mixture, or preparation containing limited quantities of any of the following narcotic drugs that includes one or more nonnarcotic active medicinal ingredients in sufficient proportion to confer on the compound, mixture, or preparation valuable medicinal qualities other than those possessed by the narcotic drug alone:

not more than 200 milligrams of codeine per 100 milliliters or per 100 grams;

not more than 100 milligrams of dihydrocodeine per 100 milliliters or per 100 grams;

not more than 100 milligrams of ethylmorphine per 100 milliliters or per 100 grams;

not more than 2.5 milligrams of diphenoxylate and not less than 25 micrograms of atropine sulfate per dosage unit;

not more than 15 milligrams of opium per 29.5729 milliliters or per 28.35 grams; and

not more than 0.5 milligram of difenoxin and not less than 25 micrograms of atropine sulfate per dosage unit;

(2) unless specifically excepted or unless listed in another penalty group, a material, compound, mixture, or preparation containing any quantity of the

narcotic drug Buprenorphine or Butorphanol or a salt of either; and

(3) unless specifically exempted or excluded or unless listed in another penalty group, any material, compound, mixture, or preparation that contains any quantity of pyrovalerone, a substance having a stimulant effect on the central nervous system, including its salts, isomers, and salts of isomers.

Amended by Acts 1997, 75th Leg., ch. 745, § 25, eff. Jan. 1, 1998; Acts 2001, 77th Leg., ch. 251, § 19, eff. Sept. 1, 2001.

§ 481.106. Classification of Controlled Substance Analogue

For the purposes of the prosecution of an offense under this subchapter involving the manufacture, delivery, or possession of a controlled substance, Penalty Groups 1, 1–A, and 2 include a controlled substance analogue that:

(1) has a chemical structure substantially similar to the chemical structure of a controlled substance listed in the applicable penalty group; or

(2) is specifically designed to produce an effect substantially similar to, or greater than, a controlled substance listed in the applicable penalty group.

Added by Acts 2003, 78th Leg., ch. 1099, § 9, eff. Sept. 1, 2003.

§ 481.107. Repealed by Acts 1993, 73rd Leg., ch. 900, § 2.07, eff. Sept. 1, 1994

§ 481.108. Preparatory Offenses

Title 4, Penal Code,[1] applies to an offense under this chapter.

Acts 1989, 71st Leg., ch. 678, § 1, eff. Sept. 1, 1989. Amended by Acts 1993, 73rd Leg., ch. 900, § 2.02, eff. Sept. 1, 1994; Acts 1995, 74th Leg., ch. 318, § 36, eff. Sept. 1, 1995.

[1] V.T.C.A., Penal Code § 15.01 et seq.

§§ 481.109, 481.110. Repealed by Acts 1991, 72nd Leg., ch. 141, § 6, eff. Sept. 1, 1991

§ 481.111. Exemptions

(a) The provisions of this chapter relating to the possession and distribution of peyote do not apply to the use of peyote by a member of the Native American Church in bona fide religious ceremonies of the church. However, a person who supplies the substance to the church must register and maintain appropriate records of receipts and disbursements in accordance with rules adopted by the director. An exemption granted to a member of the Native American Church under this section does not apply to a member with less than 25 percent Indian blood.

(b) The provisions of this chapter relating to the possession of denatured sodium pentobarbital do not apply to possession by personnel of a humane society or an animal control agency for the purpose of destroying injured, sick, homeless, or unwanted animals if the humane society or animal control agency is registered with the Federal Drug Enforcement Administration. The provisions of this chapter relating to the distribution of denatured sodium pentobarbital do not apply to a person registered as required by Subchapter C,[1] who is distributing the substance for that purpose to a humane society or an animal control agency registered with the Federal Drug Enforcement Administration.

(c) A person does not violate Section 481.113, 481.116, 481.121, or 481.125 if the person possesses or delivers tetrahydrocannabinols or their derivatives, or drug paraphernalia to be used to introduce tetrahydrocannabinols or their derivatives into the human body, for use in a federally approved therapeutic research program.

(d) The provisions of this chapter relating to the possession and distribution of anabolic steroids do not apply to the use of anabolic steroids that are administered to livestock or poultry.

Acts 1989, 71st Leg., ch. 678, § 1, eff. Sept. 1, 1989. Amended by Acts 1989, 71st Leg., ch. 1100, § 5.03(d), eff. Sept. 1, 1989.

[1] V.T.C.A., Health & Safety Code § 481.061 et seq.

§ 481.112. Offense: Manufacture or Delivery of Substance in Penalty Group 1

(a) Except as authorized by this chapter, a person commits an offense if the person knowingly manufactures, delivers, or possesses with intent to deliver a controlled substance listed in Penalty Group 1.

(b) An offense under Subsection (a) is a state jail felony if the amount of the controlled substance to which the offense applies is, by aggregate weight, including adulterants or dilutants, less than one gram.

(c) An offense under Subsection (a) is a felony of the second degree if the amount of the controlled substance to which the offense applies is, by aggregate weight, including adulterants or dilutants, one gram or more but less than four grams.

(d) An offense under Subsection (a) is a felony of the first degree if the amount of the controlled substance to which the offense applies is, by aggregate weight, including adulterants or dilutants, four grams or more but less than 200 grams.

(e) An offense under Subsection (a) is punishable by imprisonment in the Texas Department of Criminal Justice for life or for a term of not more than 99 years or less than 10 years, and a fine not to exceed $100,000, if the amount of the controlled substance to which the offense applies is, by aggregate weight, including adulterants or dilutants, 200 grams or more but less than 400 grams.

(f) An offense under Subsection (a) is punishable by imprisonment in the Texas Department of Criminal Justice for life or for a term of not more than 99 years or less than 15 years, and a fine not to exceed $250,000, if the amount of the controlled substance to which the offense applies is, by aggregate weight, including adulterants or dilutants, 400 grams or more.

Acts 1989, 71st Leg., ch. 678, § 1, eff. Sept. 1, 1989. Amended by Acts 1993, 73rd Leg., ch. 900, § 2.02, eff. Sept. 1, 1994; Acts 2001, 77th Leg., ch. 1188, § 2, eff. Sept. 1, 2001; Acts 2009, 81st Leg., ch. 87, § 25.095, eff. Sept. 1, 2009.

§ 481.1121. Offense: Manufacture or Delivery of Substance in Penalty Group 1-A

(a) Except as provided by this chapter, a person commits an offense if the person knowingly manufactures, delivers, or possesses with intent to deliver a controlled substance listed in Penalty Group 1-A.

(b) An offense under this section is:

(1) a state jail felony if the number of abuse units of the controlled substance is fewer than 20;

(2) a felony of the second degree if the number of abuse units of the controlled substance is 20 or more but fewer than 80;

(3) a felony of the first degree if the number of abuse units of the controlled substance is 80 or more but fewer than 4,000; and

(4) punishable by imprisonment in the Texas Department of Criminal Justice for life or for a term of not more than 99 years or less than 15 years and a fine not to exceed $250,000, if the number of abuse units of the controlled substance is 4,000 or more.

Added by Acts 1997, 75th Leg., ch. 745, § 26, eff. Jan. 1, 1998. Amended by Acts 2001, 77th Leg., ch. 1188, § 3, eff. Sept. 1, 2001; Acts 2009, 81st Leg., ch. 87, § 25.096, eff. Sept. 1, 2009.

§ 481.1122. Manufacture of Substance in Penalty Group 1: Presence of Child

If it is shown at the punishment phase of a trial for the manufacture of a controlled substance listed in Penalty Group 1 that when the offense was committed a child younger than 18 years of age was present on the premises where the offense was committed:

(1) the punishments specified by Sections 481.112(b) and (c) are increased by one degree;

(2) the minimum term of imprisonment specified by Section 481.112(e) is increased to 15 years and the maximum fine specified by that section is increased to $150,000; and

(3) the minimum term of imprisonment specified by Section 481.112(f) is increased to 20 years and the maximum fine specified by that section is increased to $300,000.

Added by Acts 2007, 80th Leg., ch. 840, § 1, eff. Sept. 1, 2007.

Section 3 of Acts 2007, 80th Leg., ch. 840 provides:

"The change in law made by this Act applies only to an offense committed on or after the effective date [Sept. 1, 2007] of this Act. An offense committed before the effective date of this Act is governed by the law in effect when the offense was committed, and the former law is continued in effect for that purpose. For purposes of this section, an offense was committed before the effective date of this Act if any element of the offense was committed before that date."

§ 481.113. Offense: Manufacture or Delivery of Substance in Penalty Group 2

(a) Except as authorized by this chapter, a person commits an offense if the person knowingly manufactures, delivers, or possesses with intent to deliver a controlled substance listed in Penalty Group 2.

(b) An offense under Subsection (a) is a state jail felony if the amount of the controlled substance to which the offense applies is, by aggregate weight, including adulterants or dilutants, less than one gram.

(c) An offense under Subsection (a) is a felony of the second degree if the amount of the controlled substance to which the offense applies is, by aggregate weight, including adulterants or dilutants, one gram or more but less than four grams.

(d) An offense under Subsection (a) is a felony of the first degree if the amount of the controlled substance to which the offense applies is, by aggregate weight, including adulterants or dilutants, four grams or more but less than 400 grams.

(e) An offense under Subsection (a) is punishable by imprisonment in the Texas Department of Criminal Justice for life or for a term of not more than 99 years or less than 10 years, and a fine not to exceed $100,000, if the amount of the controlled substance to which the offense applies is, by aggregate weight, including adulterants or dilutants, 400 grams or more.

Acts 1989, 71st Leg., ch. 678, § 1, eff. Sept. 1, 1989. Amended by Acts 1993, 73rd Leg., ch. 900, § 2.02, eff. Sept. 1, 1994; Acts 2001, 77th Leg., ch. 1188, § 4, eff. Sept. 1, 2001; Acts 2009, 81st Leg., ch. 87, § 25.097, eff. Sept. 1, 2009.

§ 481.114. Offense: Manufacture or Delivery of Substance in Penalty Group 3 or 4

(a) Except as authorized by this chapter, a person commits an offense if the person knowingly manufactures, delivers, or possesses with intent to deliver a controlled substance listed in Penalty Group 3 or 4.

(b) An offense under Subsection (a) is a state jail felony if the amount of the controlled substance to which the offense applies is, by aggregate weight, including adulterants or dilutants, less than 28 grams.

(c) An offense under Subsection (a) is a felony of the second degree if the amount of the controlled substance to which the offense applies is, by aggregate weight, including adulterants or dilutants, 28 grams or more but less than 200 grams.

(d) An offense under Subsection (a) is a felony of the first degree, if the amount of the controlled substance to which the offense applies is, by aggregate weight, including adulterants or dilutants, 200 grams or more but less than 400 grams.

(e) An offense under Subsection (a) is punishable by imprisonment in the Texas Department of Criminal Justice for life or for a term of not more than 99 years or less than 10 years, and a fine not to exceed $100,000, if the amount of the controlled substance to which the offense applies is, by aggregate weight, including any adulterants or dilutants, 400 grams or more.

Acts 1989, 71st Leg., ch. 678, § 1, eff. Sept. 1, 1989. Amended by Acts 1993, 73rd Leg., ch. 900, § 2.02, eff. Sept. 1, 1994; Acts 2001, 77th Leg., ch. 1188, § 5, eff. Sept. 1, 2001; Acts 2009, 81st Leg., ch. 87, § 25.098, eff. Sept. 1, 2009.

§ 481.115. Offense: Possession of Substance in Penalty Group 1

(a) Except as authorized by this chapter, a person commits an offense if the person knowingly or intentionally possesses a controlled substance listed in Penalty Group 1, unless the person obtained the substance directly from or under a valid prescription or order of a practitioner acting in the course of professional practice.

(b) An offense under Subsection (a) is a state jail felony if the amount of the controlled substance possessed is, by aggregate weight, including adulterants or dilutants, less than one gram.

(c) An offense under Subsection (a) is a felony of the third degree if the amount of the controlled substance possessed is, by aggregate weight, including adulterants or dilutants, one gram or more but less than four grams.

(d) An offense under Subsection (a) is a felony of the second degree if the amount of the controlled substance possessed is, by aggregate weight, including adulterants or dilutants, four grams or more but less than 200 grams.

(e) An offense under Subsection (a) is a felony of the first degree if the amount of the controlled substance possessed is, by aggregate weight, including adulterants or dilutants, 200 grams or more but less than 400 grams.

(f) An offense under Subsection (a) is punishable by imprisonment in the Texas Department of Criminal Justice for life or for a term of not more than 99 years or less than 10 years, and a fine not to exceed $100,000, if the amount of the controlled substance possessed is, by aggregate weight, including adulterants or dilutants, 400 grams or more.

Acts 1989, 71st Leg., ch. 678, § 1, eff. Sept. 1, 1989. Amended by Acts 1993, 73rd Leg., ch. 900, § 2.02, eff. Sept. 1, 1994; Acts 2009, 81st Leg., ch. 87, § 25.099, eff. Sept. 1, 2009.

§ 481.1151. Offense: Possession of Substance in Penalty Group 1-A

(a) Except as provided by this chapter, a person commits an offense if the person knowingly possesses a controlled substance listed in Penalty Group 1-A.

(b) An offense under this section is:

(1) a state jail felony if the number of abuse units of the controlled substance is fewer than 20;

(2) a felony of the third degree if the number of abuse units of the controlled substance is 20 or more but fewer than 80;

(3) a felony of the second degree if the number of abuse units of the controlled substance is 80 or more but fewer than 4,000;

(4) a felony of the first degree if the number of abuse units of the controlled substance is 4,000 or more but fewer than 8,000; and

(5) punishable by imprisonment in the Texas Department of Criminal Justice for life or for a term of not more than 99 years or less than 15 years and a fine not to exceed $250,000, if the number of abuse units of the controlled substance is 8,000 or more.

Added by Acts 1997, 75th Leg., ch. 745, § 26, eff. Jan. 1, 1998. Amended by Acts 2009, 81st Leg., ch. 87, § 25.100, eff. Sept. 1, 2009.

§ 481.116. Offense: Possession of Substance in Penalty Group 2

(a) Except as authorized by this chapter, a person commits an offense if the person knowingly or intentionally possesses a controlled substance listed in Penalty Group 2, unless the person obtained the substance directly from or under a valid prescription or order of a practitioner acting in the course of professional practice.

(b) An offense under Subsection (a) is a state jail felony if the amount of the controlled substance possessed is, by aggregate weight, including adulterants or dilutants, less than one gram.

(c) An offense under Subsection (a) is a felony of the third degree if the amount of the controlled substance possessed is, by aggregate weight, including adulterants or dilutants, one gram or more but less than four grams.

(d) An offense under Subsection (a) is a felony of the second degree if the amount of the controlled substance possessed is, by aggregate weight, including adulterants or dilutants, four grams or more but less than 400 grams.

(e) An offense under Subsection (a) is punishable by imprisonment in the Texas Department of Criminal Justice for life or for a term of not more than 99 years or less than five years, and a fine not to exceed $50,000, if the amount of the controlled substance possessed is, by aggregate weight, including adulterants or dilutants, 400 grams or more.

Acts 1989, 71st Leg., ch. 678, § 1, eff. Sept. 1, 1989. Amended by Acts 1993, 73rd Leg., ch. 900, § 2.02, eff. Sept. 1, 1994; Acts 2009, 81st Leg., ch. 87, § 25.101, eff. Sept. 1, 2009.

§ 481.117. Offense: Possession of Substance in Penalty Group 3

(a) Except as authorized by this chapter, a person commits an offense if the person knowingly or intentionally possesses a controlled substance listed in Penalty Group 3, unless the person obtains the substance directly from or under a valid prescription or order of a practitioner acting in the course of professional practice.

(b) An offense under Subsection (a) is a Class A misdemeanor if the amount of the controlled substance possessed is, by aggregate weight, including adulterants or dilutants, less than 28 grams.

(c) An offense under Subsection (a) is a felony of the third degree if the amount of the controlled substance possessed is, by aggregate weight, including adulterants or dilutants, 28 grams or more but less than 200 grams.

(d) An offense under Subsection (a) is a felony of the second degree, if the amount of the controlled substance possessed is, by aggregate weight, including adulterants or dilutants, 200 grams or more but less than 400 grams.

(e) An offense under Subsection (a) is punishable by imprisonment in the Texas Department of Criminal Justice for life or for a term of not more than 99 years or less than five years, and a fine not to exceed $50,000, if the amount of the controlled substance possessed is, by aggregate weight, including adulterants or dilutants, 400 grams or more.

Acts 1989, 71st Leg., ch. 678, § 1, eff. Sept. 1, 1989. Amended by Acts 1993, 73rd Leg., ch. 900, § 2.02, eff. Sept. 1, 1994; Acts 2009, 81st Leg., ch. 87, § 25.102, eff. Sept. 1, 2009.

§ 481.118. Offense: Possession of Substance in Penalty Group 4

(a) Except as authorized by this chapter, a person commits an offense if the person knowingly or intentionally possesses a controlled substance listed in Penalty Group 4, unless the person obtained the substance directly from or under a valid prescription or order of a practitioner acting in the course of practice.

(b) An offense under Subsection (a) is a Class B misdemeanor if the amount of the controlled substance possessed is, by aggregate weight, including adulterants or dilutants, less than 28 grams.

(c) An offense under Subsection (a) is a felony of the third degree if the amount of the controlled substance possessed is, by aggregate weight, including adulterants or dilutants, 28 grams or more but less than 200 grams.

(d) An offense under Subsection (a) is a felony of the second degree, if the amount of the controlled substance possessed is, by aggregate weight, including adulterants or dilutants, 200 grams or more but less than 400 grams.

(e) An offense under Subsection (a) is punishable by imprisonment in the Texas Department of Criminal Justice for life or for a term of not more than 99 years or less than five years, and a fine not to exceed $50,000, if the amount of the controlled substance possessed is, by aggregate weight, including adulterants or dilutants, 400 grams or more.

Acts 1989, 71st Leg., ch. 678, § 1, eff. Sept. 1, 1989. Amended by Acts 1993, 73rd Leg., ch. 900, § 2.02, eff. Sept. 1, 1994; Acts 2009, 81st Leg., ch. 87, § 25.103, eff. Sept. 1, 2009.

§ 481.119. Offense: Manufacture, Delivery, or Possession of Miscellaneous Substances

(a) A person commits an offense if the person knowingly manufactures, delivers, or possesses with intent to deliver a controlled substance listed in a schedule by an action of the commissioner under this chapter but not listed in a penalty group. An offense under this subsection is a Class A misdemeanor.

(b) A person commits an offense if the person knowingly or intentionally possesses a controlled substance listed in a schedule by an action of the commissioner under this chapter but not listed in a penalty group. An offense under this subsection is a Class B misdemeanor.

Acts 1989, 71st Leg., ch. 678, § 1, eff. Sept. 1, 1989. Amended by Acts 2001, 77th Leg., ch. 1188, § 6, eff. Sept. 1, 2001.

§ 481.120. Offense: Delivery of Marihuana

(a) Except as authorized by this chapter, a person commits an offense if the person knowingly or intentionally delivers marihuana.

(b) An offense under Subsection (a) is:

(1) a Class B misdemeanor if the amount of marihuana delivered is one-fourth ounce or less and the person committing the offense does not receive remuneration for the marihuana;

(2) a Class A misdemeanor if the amount of marihuana delivered is one-fourth ounce or less and the person committing the offense receives remuneration for the marihuana;

(3) a state jail felony if the amount of marihuana delivered is five pounds or less but more than one-fourth ounce;

(4) a felony of the second degree if the amount of marihuana delivered is 50 pounds or less but more than five pounds;

(5) a felony of the first degree if the amount of marihuana delivered is 2,000 pounds or less but more than 50 pounds; and

(6) punishable by imprisonment in the Texas Department of Criminal Justice for life or for a term of not more than 99 years or less than 10 years, and a fine not to exceed $100,000, if the amount of marihuana delivered is more than 2,000 pounds.

Acts 1989, 71st Leg., ch. 678, § 1, eff. Sept. 1, 1989. Amended by Acts 1993, 73rd Leg., ch. 900, § 2.02, eff. Sept. 1, 1994; Acts 2009, 81st Leg., ch. 87, § 25.104, eff. Sept. 1, 2009.

§ 481.121. Offense: Possession of Marihuana

(a) Except as authorized by this chapter, a person commits an offense if the person knowingly or intentionally possesses a usable quantity of marihuana.

(b) An offense under Subsection (a) is:

(1) a Class B misdemeanor if the amount of marihuana possessed is two ounces or less;

(2) a Class A misdemeanor if the amount of marihuana possessed is four ounces or less but more than two ounces;

(3) a state jail felony if the amount of marihuana possessed is five pounds or less but more than four ounces;

(4) a felony of the third degree if the amount of marihuana possessed is 50 pounds or less but more than 5 pounds;

(5) a felony of the second degree if the amount of marihuana possessed is 2,000 pounds or less but more than 50 pounds; and

(6) punishable by imprisonment in the Texas Department of Criminal Justice for life or for a term of not more than 99 years or less than 5 years, and a fine not to exceed $50,000, if the amount of marihuana possessed is more than 2,000 pounds.

Acts 1989, 71st Leg., ch. 678, § 1, eff. Sept. 1, 1989. Amended by Acts 1993, 73rd Leg., ch. 900, § 2.02, eff. Sept. 1, 1994; Acts 2009, 81st Leg., ch. 87, § 25.105, eff. Sept. 1, 2009.

§ 481.122. Offense: Delivery of Controlled Substance or Marihuana to Child

(a) A person commits an offense if the person knowingly delivers a controlled substance listed in Penalty Group 1, 1–A, 2, or 3 or knowingly delivers marihuana and the person delivers the controlled substance or marihuana to a person:

(1) who is a child;

(2) who is enrolled in a public or private primary or secondary school; or

(3) who the actor knows or believes intends to deliver the controlled substance or marihuana to a person described by Subdivision (1) or (2).

(b) It is an affirmative defense to prosecution under this section that:

(1) the actor was a child when the offense was committed; or

(2) the actor:

(A) was younger than 21 years of age when the offense was committed;

(B) delivered only marihuana in an amount equal to or less than one-fourth ounce; and

(C) did not receive remuneration for the delivery.

(c) An offense under this section is a felony of the second degree.

(d) In this section, "child" means a person younger than 18 years of age.

(e) If conduct that is an offense under this section is also an offense under another section of this chapter, the actor may be prosecuted under either section or both.

Acts 1989, 71st Leg., ch. 678, § 1, eff. Sept. 1, 1989. Amended by Acts 1993, 73rd Leg., ch. 900, § 2.02, eff. Sept. 1, 1994; Acts 1997, 75th Leg., ch. 745, § 27, eff. Jan. 1, 1998; Acts 2001, 77th Leg., ch. 251, § 20, eff. Sept. 1, 2001.

§ 481.123. Defense to Prosecution For Offense Involving Controlled Substance Analogue

(a) It is an affirmative defense to the prosecution of an offense under this subchapter involving the manufacture, delivery, or possession of a controlled substance analogue that the analogue:

(1) was not in any part intended for human consumption;

(2) was a substance for which there is an approved new drug application under Section 505 of the Federal Food, Drug, and Cosmetic Act (21 U.S.C. Section 355); or

(3) was a substance for which an exemption for investigational use has been granted under Section 505 of the Federal Food, Drug, and Cosmetic Act (21 U.S.C. Section 355), if the actor's conduct with respect to the substance is in accord with the exemption.

(b) For the purposes of this section, Section 505 of the Federal Food, Drug, and Cosmetic Act (21 U.S.C. Section 355) applies to the introduction or delivery for introduction of any new drug into intrastate, interstate, or foreign commerce.

Acts 1989, 71st Leg., ch. 678, § 1, eff. Sept. 1, 1989. Amended by Acts 1997, 75th Leg., ch. 745, § 28, eff. Jan. 1, 1998; Acts 2003, 78th Leg., ch. 1099, § 10, eff. Sept. 1, 2003.

§ 481.124. Offense: Possession or Transport of Certain Chemicals With Intent to Manufacture Controlled Substance

(a) A person commits an offense if, with intent to unlawfully manufacture a controlled substance, the person possesses or transports:

(1) anhydrous ammonia;

(2) an immediate precursor; or

(3) a chemical precursor or an additional chemical substance named as a precursor by the director under Section 481.077(b)(1).

(b) For purposes of this section, an intent to unlawfully manufacture the controlled substance methamphetamine is presumed if the actor possesses or transports:

(1) anhydrous ammonia in a container or receptacle that is not designed and manufactured to lawfully hold or transport anhydrous ammonia;

(2) lithium metal removed from a battery and immersed in kerosene, mineral spirits, or similar liquid that prevents or retards hydration; or

(3) in one container, vehicle, or building, phenylacetic acid, or more than nine grams, three containers packaged for retail sale, or 300 tablets or capsules of a product containing ephedrine or pseudoephedrine, and:

(A) anhydrous ammonia;

(B) at least three of the following categories of substances commonly used in the manufacture of methamphetamine:

(i) lithium or sodium metal or red phosphorus, iodine, or iodine crystals;

(ii) lye, sulfuric acid, hydrochloric acid, or muriatic acid;

(iii) an organic solvent, including ethyl ether, alcohol, or acetone;

(iv) a petroleum distillate, including naphtha, paint thinner, or charcoal lighter fluid; or

(v) aquarium, rock, or table salt; or

(C) at least three of the following items:

(i) an item of equipment subject to regulation under Section 481.080, if the person is not registered under Section 481.063; or

(ii) glassware, a plastic or metal container, tubing, a hose, or other item specially designed, assembled, or adapted for use in the manufacture, processing, analyzing, storing, or concealing of methamphetamine.

(c) For purposes of this section, a substance is presumed to be anhydrous ammonia if the substance is in a container or receptacle that is:

(1) designed and manufactured to lawfully hold or transport anhydrous ammonia; or

(2) not designed and manufactured to lawfully hold or transport anhydrous ammonia, if:

(A) a properly administered field test of the substance using a testing device or instrument designed and manufactured for that purpose produces a positive result for anhydrous ammonia; or

(B) a laboratory test of a water solution of the substance produces a positive result for ammonia.

(d) An offense under this section is:

(1) a felony of the second degree if the controlled substance is listed in Penalty Group 1 or 1-A;

(2) a felony of the third degree if the controlled substance is listed in Penalty Group 2;

(3) a state jail felony if the controlled substance is listed in Penalty Group 3 or 4; or

(4) a Class A misdemeanor if the controlled substance is listed in a schedule by an action of the commissioner under this chapter but not listed in a penalty group.

(e) If conduct constituting an offense under this section also constitutes an offense under another section of this code, the actor may be prosecuted under either section or under both sections.

(f) This section does not apply to a chemical precursor exempted by the director under Section 481.077(b)(2) from the requirements of that section.

Added by Acts 2001, 77th Leg., ch. 1188, § 7, eff. Sept. 1, 2001. Amended by Acts 2003, 78th Leg., ch. 570, § 2, eff. Sept. 1, 2003; Acts 2005, 79th Leg., ch. 282, § 6, eff. Aug. 1, 2005.

Section 4 of Acts 2003, 78th Leg., ch. 570 provides:

"The change in law made by this Act applies only to an offense committed on or after the effective date of this Act. An offense committed before the effective date of this Act is covered by the law in effect when the offense was committed, and the former law is continued in effect for that purpose. For purposes of this section, an offense was committed before the effective date of this Act if any element of the offense occurred before that date."

§ 481.1245. Offense: Possession or Transport of Anhydrous Ammonia; Use of or Tampering With Equipment

(a) A person commits an offense if the person:

(1) possesses or transports anhydrous ammonia in a container or receptacle that is not designed or manufactured to hold or transport anhydrous ammonia;

(2) uses, transfers, or sells a container or receptacle that is designed or manufactured to hold anhydrous ammonia without the express consent of the owner of the container or receptacle; or

(3) tampers with equipment that is manufactured or used to hold, apply, or transport anhydrous ammonia without the express consent of the owner of the equipment.

(b) An offense under this section is a felony of the third degree.

Added by Acts 2005, 79th Leg., ch. 282, § 7, eff. Aug. 1, 2005.

§ 481.125. Offense: Possession or Delivery of Drug Paraphernalia

(a) A person commits an offense if the person knowingly or intentionally uses or possesses with intent to use drug paraphernalia to plant, propagate, cultivate, grow, harvest, manufacture, compound, convert, produce, process, prepare, test, analyze, pack, repack, store, contain, or conceal a controlled substance in violation of this chapter or to inject, ingest, inhale, or otherwise introduce into the human body a controlled substance in violation of this chapter.

(b) A person commits an offense if the person knowingly or intentionally delivers, possesses with intent to deliver, or manufactures with intent to deliver drug paraphernalia knowing that the person who receives or who is intended to receive the drug paraphernalia intends that it be used to plant, propagate, cultivate, grow, harvest, manufacture, compound, convert, produce, process, prepare, test, analyze, pack, repack, store, contain, or conceal a controlled substance in violation of this chapter or to inject, ingest, inhale, or otherwise introduce into the human body a controlled substance in violation of this chapter.

(c) A person commits an offense if the person commits an offense under Subsection (b), is 18 years of age or older, and the person who receives or who is intended to receive the drug paraphernalia is younger than 18 years of age and at least three years younger than the actor.

(d) An offense under Subsection (a) is a Class C misdemeanor.

(e) An offense under Subsection (b) is a Class A misdemeanor, unless it is shown on the trial of a defendant that the defendant has previously been convicted under Subsection (b) or (c), in which event the offense is punishable by confinement in jail for a term of not more than one year or less than 90 days.

(f) An offense under Subsection (c) is a state jail felony.

Acts 1989, 71st Leg., ch. 678, § 1, eff. Sept. 1, 1989. Amended by Acts 1993, 73rd Leg., ch. 900, § 2.02, eff. Sept. 1, 1994.

§ 481.126. Offense: Illegal Barter, Expenditure, or Investment

(a) A person commits an offense if the person:

(1) barters property or expends funds the person knows are derived from the commission of an offense under this chapter punishable by imprisonment in the Texas Department of Criminal Justice for life;

(2) barters property or expends funds the person knows are derived from the commission of an offense under Section 481.121(a) that is punishable under Section 481.121(b)(5);

(3) barters property or finances or invests funds the person knows or believes are intended to further the commission of an offense for which the punishment is described by Subdivision (1); or

(4) barters property or finances or invests funds the person knows or believes are intended to further the commission of an offense under Section 481.121(a) that is punishable under Section 481.121(b)(5).

(b) An offense under Subsection (a)(1) or (3) is a felony of the first degree. An offense under Subsection (a)(2) or (4) is a felony of the second degree.

Acts 1989, 71st Leg., ch. 678, § 1, eff. Sept. 1, 1989. Amended by Acts 1993, 73rd Leg., ch. 900, § 2.02, eff. Sept. 1, 1994; Acts 1995, 74th Leg., ch. 318, § 37, eff. Sept. 1, 1995; Acts 2001, 77th Leg., ch. 251, § 21, eff. Sept. 1, 2001; Acts 2003, 78th Leg., ch. 712, § 1, eff. Sept. 1, 2003; Acts 2009, 81st Leg., ch. 87, § 25.106, eff. Sept. 1, 2009.

§ 481.127. Offense: Unauthorized Disclosure of Information

(a) A person commits an offense if the person knowingly gives, permits, or obtains unauthorized access to information submitted to the director under Section 481.075.

(b) An offense under this section is a state jail felony.

Acts 1989, 71st Leg., ch. 678, § 1, eff. Sept. 1, 1989. Amended by Acts 1993, 73rd Leg., ch. 900, § 2.02, eff. Sept. 1, 1994; Acts 1997, 75th Leg., ch. 745, § 29, eff. Jan. 1, 1998.

§ 481.128. Offense and Civil Penalty: Commercial Matters

(a) A registrant or dispenser commits an offense if the registrant or dispenser knowingly:

(1) distributes, delivers, administers, or dispenses a controlled substance in violation of Sections 481.070–481.075;

(2) manufactures a controlled substance not authorized by the person's registration or distributes or dispenses a controlled substance not authorized by the person's registration to another registrant or other person;

(3) refuses or fails to make, keep, or furnish a record, report, notification, order form, statement, invoice, or information required by this chapter;

(4) prints, manufactures, possesses, or produces an official prescription form without the approval of the director;

(5) delivers or possesses a counterfeit official prescription form;

(6) refuses an entry into a premise for an inspection authorized by this chapter;

(7) refuses or fails to return an official prescription form as required by Section 481.075(k);

(8) refuses or fails to make, keep, or furnish a record, report, notification, order form, statement, invoice, or information required by a rule adopted by the director; or

(9) refuses or fails to maintain security required by this chapter or a rule adopted under this chapter.

(b) If the registrant or dispenser knowingly refuses or fails to make, keep, or furnish a record, report, notification, order form, statement, invoice, or information or maintain security required by a rule adopted by the director, the registrant or dispenser is liable to the state for a civil penalty of not more than $5,000 for each act.

(c) An offense under Subsection (a) is a state jail felony.

(d) If a person commits an act that would otherwise be an offense under Subsection (a) except that it was committed without the requisite culpable mental state, the person is liable to the state for a civil penalty of not more than $1,000 for each act.

(e) A district attorney of the county where the act occurred may file suit in district court in that county to collect a civil penalty under this section, or the district attorney of Travis County or the attorney general may file suit in district court in Travis County to collect the penalty.

Amended by Acts 1993, 73rd Leg., ch. 900, § 2.02, eff. Sept. 1, 1994; Acts 1997, 75th Leg., ch. 745, § 30, eff. Jan. 1, 1998; Acts 2001, 77th Leg., ch. 251, § 22, eff. Sept. 1, 2001.

§ 481.129. Offense: Fraud

(a) A person commits an offense if the person knowingly:

(1) distributes as a registrant or dispenser a controlled substance listed in Schedule I or II, unless the person distributes the controlled substance under an order form as required by Section 481.069;

(2) uses in the course of manufacturing, prescribing, or distributing a controlled substance a registration number that is fictitious, revoked, suspended, or issued to another person;

(3) issues a prescription bearing a forged or fictitious signature;

(4) uses a prescription issued to another person to prescribe a Schedule II controlled substance;

(5) possesses, obtains, or attempts to possess or obtain a controlled substance or an increased quantity of a controlled substance:

(A) by misrepresentation, fraud, forgery, deception, or subterfuge;

(B) through use of a fraudulent prescription form; or

(C) through use of a fraudulent oral or telephonically communicated prescription; or

(6) furnishes false or fraudulent material information in or omits material information from an application, report, record, or other document required to be kept or filed under this chapter.

(b) A person commits an offense if the person knowingly or intentionally:

(1) makes, distributes, or possesses a punch, die, plate, stone, or other thing designed to print, imprint, or reproduce an actual or simulated trademark, trade name, or other identifying mark, imprint, or device of another on a controlled substance or the container or label of a container for a controlled substance, so as to make the controlled substance a counterfeit substance; or

(2) manufactures, delivers, or possesses with intent to deliver a counterfeit substance.

(c) A person commits an offense if the person knowingly or intentionally:

(1) delivers a prescription or a prescription form for other than a valid medical purpose in the course of professional practice; or

(2) possesses a prescription for a controlled substance or a prescription form unless the prescription or prescription form is possessed:

(A) during the manufacturing or distribution process;

(B) by a practitioner, practitioner's agent, or an institutional practitioner for a valid medical purpose during the course of professional practice;

(C) by a pharmacist or agent of a pharmacy during the professional practice of pharmacy;

(D) under a practitioner's order made by the practitioner for a valid medical purpose in the course of professional practice; or

(E) by an officer or investigator authorized to enforce this chapter within the scope of the officer's or investigator's official duties.

(d) An offense under Subsection (a) is:

(1) a felony of the second degree if the controlled substance that is the subject of the offense is listed in Schedule I or II;

(2) a felony of the third degree if the controlled substance that is the subject of the offense is listed in Schedule III or IV; and

(3) a Class A misdemeanor if the controlled substance that is the subject of the offense is listed in Schedule V.

(e) An offense under Subsection (b) is a Class A misdemeanor.

(f) An offense under Subsection (c)(1) is:

(1) a felony of the second degree if the defendant delivers:

(A) a prescription form; or

(B) a prescription for a controlled substance listed in Schedule II; and

(2) a felony of the third degree if the defendant delivers a prescription for a controlled substance listed in Schedule III, IV, or V.

(g) An offense under Subsection (c)(2) is:

(1) a state jail felony if the defendant possesses:

(A) a prescription form; or

(B) a prescription for a controlled substance listed in Schedule II or III; and

(2) a Class B misdemeanor if the defendant possesses a prescription for a controlled substance listed in Schedule IV or V.

Acts 1989, 71st Leg., ch. 678, § 1, eff. Sept. 1, 1989. Amended by Acts 1989, 71st Leg., ch. 1100, § 5.02(p), eff. Sept. 1, 1989; Acts 1993, 73rd Leg., ch. 900, § 2.02, eff. Sept. 1, 1994; Acts 1997, 75th Leg., ch. 745, § 31, eff. Jan. 1, 1998; Acts 2001, 77th Leg., ch. 251, § 23, eff. Sept. 1, 2001.

§ 481.130. Penalties Under Other Law

A penalty imposed for an offense under this chapter is in addition to any civil or administrative penalty or other sanction imposed by law.

Acts 1989, 71st Leg., ch. 678, § 1, eff. Sept. 1, 1989.

§ 481.131. Offense: Diversion of Controlled Substance Property or Plant

(a) A person commits an offense if the person intentionally or knowingly:

(1) converts to the person's own use or benefit a controlled substance property or plant seized under Section 481.152 or 481.153; or

(2) diverts to the unlawful use or benefit of another person a controlled substance property or plant seized under Section 481.152 or 481.153.

(b) An offense under this section is a state jail felony.

Added by Acts 1991, 72nd Leg., ch. 141, § 2, eff. Sept. 1, 1991. Amended by Acts 1993, 73rd Leg., ch. 900, § 2.02, eff. Sept. 1, 1994.

§ 481.132. Multiple Prosecutions

(a) In this section, "criminal episode" means the commission of two or more offenses under this chapter under the following circumstances:

(1) the offenses are committed pursuant to the same transaction or pursuant to two or more transactions that are connected or constitute a common scheme, plan, or continuing course of conduct; or

(2) the offenses are the repeated commission of the same or similar offenses.

(b) A defendant may be prosecuted in a single criminal action for all offenses arising out of the same criminal episode. If a single criminal action is based on more than one charging instrument within the jurisdiction of the trial court, not later than the 30th day before the date of the trial, the state shall file written notice of the action.

(c) If a judgment of guilt is reversed, set aside, or vacated and a new trial is ordered, the state may not prosecute in a single criminal action in the new trial any offense not joined in the former prosecution unless evidence to establish probable guilt for that offense was not known to the appropriate prosecution official at the time the first prosecution began.

(d) If the accused is found guilty of more than one offense arising out of the same criminal episode prosecuted in a single criminal action, sentence for each offense for which the accused has been found guilty shall be pronounced, and those sentences run concurrently.

(e) If it appears that a defendant or the state is prejudiced by a joinder of offenses, the court may order separate trials of the offenses or provide other relief as justice requires.

(f) This section provides the exclusive method for consolidation and joinder of prosecutions for offenses under this chapter. This section is not a limitation of Article 36.09 or 36.10, Code of Criminal Procedure.

Added by Acts 1991, 72nd Leg., ch. 193, § 1, eff. Sept. 1, 1991. Renumbered from V.T.C.A., Health & Safety Code § 481.131 by Acts 1991, 72nd Leg., 1st C.S., ch. 14, § 8.01(17a), eff. Nov. 12, 1991.

§ 481.133. Offense: Falsification of Drug Test Results

(a) A person commits an offense if the person knowingly or intentionally uses or possesses with intent to use any substance or device designed to falsify drug test results.

(b) A person commits an offense if the person knowingly or intentionally delivers, possesses with intent to deliver, or manufactures with intent to deliver a substance or device designed to falsify drug test results.

(c) In this section, "drug test" means a lawfully administered test designed to detect the presence of a controlled substance or marihuana.

(d) An offense under Subsection (a) is a Class B misdemeanor.

(e) An offense under Subsection (b) is a Class A misdemeanor.

Added by Acts 1991, 72nd Leg., ch. 274, § 1, eff. Sept. 1, 1991. Renumbered from V.T.C.A., Health & Safety Code § 481.131 by Acts 1991, 72nd Leg., 1st C.S., ch. 14, § 8.01(17b), eff. Nov. 12, 1991.

§ 481.134. Drug-Free Zones

(a) In this section:

(1) "Minor" means a person who is younger than 18 years of age.

(2) "Institution of higher education" means any public or private technical institute, junior college, senior college or university, medical or dental unit, or other agency of higher education as defined by Section 61.003, Education Code.

(3) "Playground" means any outdoor facility that is not on the premises of a school and that:

(A) is intended for recreation;

(B) is open to the public; and

(C) contains three or more play stations intended for the recreation of children, such as slides, swing sets, and teeterboards.

(4) "Premises" means real property and all buildings and appurtenances pertaining to the real property.

(5) "School" means a private or public elementary or secondary school or a day-care center, as defined by Section 42.002, Human Resources Code.

(6) "Video arcade facility" means any facility that:

(A) is open to the public, including persons who are 17 years of age or younger;

(B) is intended primarily for the use of pinball or video machines; and

(C) contains at least three pinball or video machines.

(7) "Youth center" means any recreational facility or gymnasium that:

(A) is intended primarily for use by persons who are 17 years of age or younger; and

(B) regularly provides athletic, civic, or cultural activities.

(b) An offense otherwise punishable as a state jail felony under Section 481.112, 481.113, 481.114, or 481.120 is punishable as a felony of the third degree, and an offense otherwise punishable as a felony of the second degree under any of those sections is punishable as a felony of the first degree, if it is shown at the punishment phase of the trial of the offense that the offense was committed:

(1) in, on, or within 1,000 feet of premises owned, rented, or leased by an institution of higher learning, the premises of a public or private youth center, or a playground; or

(2) in, on, or within 300 feet of the premises of a public swimming pool or video arcade facility.

(c) The minimum term of confinement or imprisonment for an offense otherwise punishable under Section 481.112(c), (d), (e), or (f), 481.113(c), (d), or (e), 481.114(c), (d), or (e), 481.115(c)–(f), 481.116(c), (d), or (e), 481.117(c), (d), or (e), 481.118(c), (d), or (e), 481.120(b)(4), (5), or (6), or 481.121(b)(4), (5), or (6) is increased by five years and the maximum fine for the offense is doubled if it is shown on the trial of the offense that the offense was committed:

(1) in, on, or within 1,000 feet of the premises of a school, the premises of a public or private youth center, or a playground; or

(2) on a school bus.

(d) An offense otherwise punishable under Section 481.112(b), 481.113(b), 481.114(b), 481.115(b), 481.116(b), 481.120(b)(3), or 481.121(b)(3) is a felony of the third degree if it is shown on the trial of the offense that the offense was committed:

(1) in, on, or within 1,000 feet of any real property that is owned, rented, or leased to a school or school board, the premises of a public or private youth center, or a playground; or

(2) on a school bus.

(e) An offense otherwise punishable under Section 481.117(b), 481.119(a), 481.120(b)(2), or 481.121(b)(2) is a state jail felony if it is shown on the trial of the offense that the offense was committed:

(1) in, on, or within 1,000 feet of any real property that is owned, rented, or leased to a school or school board, the premises of a public or private youth center, or a playground; or

(2) on a school bus.

(f) An offense otherwise punishable under Section 481.118(b), 481.119(b), 481.120(b)(1), or 481.121(b)(1) is a Class A misdemeanor if it is shown on the trial of the offense that the offense was committed:

(1) in, on, or within 1,000 feet of any real property that is owned, rented, or leased to a school or school board, the premises of a public or private youth center, or a playground; or

(2) on a school bus.

(g) Subsection (f) does not apply to an offense if:

(1) the offense was committed inside a private residence; and

(2) no minor was present in the private residence at the time the offense was committed.

(h) Punishment that is increased for a conviction for an offense listed under this section may not run concurrently with punishment for a conviction under any other criminal statute.

Added by Acts 1993, 73rd Leg., ch. 888, § 1, eff. Sept. 1, 1993. Amended by Acts 1995, 74th Leg., ch. 260, § 39, eff. May 30, 1995; Acts 1995, 74th Leg., ch. 318, § 38, eff. Sept. 1, 1995; Acts 1997, 75th Leg., ch. 1063, § 9, eff. Sept. 1, 1997; Acts 2003, 78th Leg., ch. 570, § 3, eff. Sept. 1, 2003; Acts 2009, 81st Leg., ch. 452, §§ 1, 2, eff. Sept. 1, 2009.

Section 3 of Acts 2009, 81st Leg., ch. 452 provides:

"The change in law made by this Act applies only to an offense committed on or after the effective date [Sept. 1, 2009] of this Act. An offense committed before the effective date of this Act is covered by the law in effect when the offense was committed, and the former law is continued in effect for that purpose. For purposes of this section, an offense was committed before the effective date of this Act if any element of the offense was committed before that date."

§ 481.135. Maps as Evidence of Location or Area

(a) In a prosecution under Section 481.134, a map produced or reproduced by a municipal or county engineer for the purpose of showing the location and boundaries of drug-free zones is admissible in evidence and is prima facie evidence of the location or boundaries of those areas if the governing body of the municipality or county adopts a resolution or ordinance approving the map as an official finding and record of the location or boundaries of those areas.

(b) A municipal or county engineer may, on request of the governing body of the municipality or county, revise a map that has been approved by the governing body of the municipality or county as provided by Subsection (a).

(c) A municipal or county engineer shall file the original or a copy of every approved or revised map approved as provided by Subsection (a) with the county clerk of each county in which the area is located.

(d) This section does not prevent the prosecution from:

(1) introducing or relying on any other evidence or testimony to establish any element of an offense for which punishment is increased under Section 481.134; or

(2) using or introducing any other map or diagram otherwise admissible under the Texas Rules of Evidence.

Added by Acts 1993, 73rd Leg., ch. 888, § 3, eff. Sept. 1, 1993. Amended by Acts 2005, 79th Leg., ch. 728, § 9.004, eff. Sept. 1, 2005.

§ 481.136. Offense: Unlawful Transfer or Receipt of Chemical Precursor

(a) A person commits an offense if the person sells, transfers, furnishes, or receives a chemical precursor subject to Section 481.077(a) and the person:

(1) does not hold a chemical precursor transfer permit as required by Section 481.078 at the time of the transaction;

(2) does not comply with Section 481.077 or 481.0771;

(3) knowingly makes a false statement in a report or record required by Section 481.077, 481.0771, or 481.078; or

(4) knowingly violates a rule adopted under Section 481.077, 481.0771, or 481.078.

(b) An offense under this section is a state jail felony, unless it is shown on the trial of the offense that the defendant has been previously convicted of an offense under this section or Section 481.137, in which event the offense is a felony of the third degree.

Added by Acts 1997, 75th Leg., ch. 745, § 32, eff. Jan. 1, 1998. Amended by Acts 2001, 77th Leg., ch. 251, § 24, eff. Sept. 1, 2001; Acts 2005, 79th Leg., ch. 282, § 8, eff. Aug. 1, 2005.

§ 481.137. Offense: Transfer of Precursor Substance for Unlawful Manufacture

(a) A person commits an offense if the person sells, transfers, or otherwise furnishes a chemical precursor subject to Section 481.077(a) with the knowledge or intent that the recipient will use the chemical precursor to unlawfully manufacture a controlled substance or controlled substance analogue.

(b) An offense under this section is a felony of the third degree.

Added by Acts 1997, 75th Leg., ch. 745, § 32, eff. Jan. 1, 1998. Amended by Acts 2001, 77th Leg., ch. 251, § 25, eff. Sept. 1, 2001.

§ 481.138. Offense: Unlawful Transfer or Receipt of Chemical Laboratory Apparatus

(a) A person commits an offense if the person sells, transfers, furnishes, or receives a chemical laboratory apparatus subject to Section 481.080(a) and the person:

(1) does not have a chemical laboratory apparatus transfer permit as required by Section 481.081 at the time of the transaction;

(2) does not comply with Section 481.080;

(3) knowingly makes a false statement in a report or record required by Section 481.080 or 481.081; or

(4) knowingly violates a rule adopted under Section 481.080 or 481.081.

(b) An offense under this section is a state jail felony, unless it is shown on the trial of the offense that the defendant has been previously convicted of an offense under this section, in which event the offense is a felony of the third degree.

Added by Acts 1997, 75th Leg., ch. 745, § 32, eff. Jan. 1, 1998. Amended by Acts 2001, 77th Leg., ch. 251, § 26, eff. Sept. 1, 2001.

§ 481.139. Offense: Transfer of Chemical Laboratory Apparatus for Unlawful Manufacture

(a) A person commits an offense if the person sells, transfers, or otherwise furnishes a chemical laboratory apparatus with the knowledge or intent that the recipient will use the apparatus to unlawfully manufacture a controlled substance or controlled substance analogue.

(b) An offense under Subsection (a) is a felony of the third degree.

Added by Acts 1997, 75th Leg., ch. 745, § 32, eff. Jan. 1, 1998. Amended by Acts 2001, 77th Leg., ch. 251, § 27, eff. Sept. 1, 2001.

§ 481.140. Use of Child in Commission of Offense

(a) If it is shown at the punishment phase of the trial of an offense otherwise punishable as a state jail felony, felony of the third degree, or felony of the second degree under Section 481.112, 481.1121, 481.113, 481.114, 481.120, or 481.122 that the defendant used or attempted to use a child younger than 18 years of age to commit or assist in the commission of the offense, the punishment is increased by one degree, unless the defendant used or threatened to use force against the child or another to gain the child's assistance, in which event the punishment for the offense is a felony of the first degree.

(b) Notwithstanding Article 42.08, Code of Criminal Procedure, if punishment for a defendant is increased under this section, the court may not order the sentence for the offense to run concurrently with any other sentence the court imposes on the defendant.

Added by Acts 2001, 77th Leg., ch. 786, § 1, eff. June 14, 2001.

§ 481.141. Manufacture or Delivery of Controlled Substance Causing Death or Serious Bodily Injury

(a) If at the guilt or innocence phase of the trial of an offense described by Subsection (b), the judge or jury, whichever is the trier of fact, determines beyond a reasonable doubt that a person died or suffered serious bodily injury as a result of injecting, ingesting, inhaling, or introducing into the person's body any amount of the controlled substance manufactured or delivered by the defendant, regardless of whether the controlled substance was used by itself or with another substance, including a drug, adulterant, or dilutant, the punishment for the offense is increased by one degree.

(b) This section applies to an offense otherwise punishable as a state jail felony, felony of the third degree, or felony of the second degree under Section 481.112, 481.1121, 481.113, 481.114, or 481.122.

(c) Notwithstanding Article 42.08, Code of Criminal Procedure, if punishment for a defendant is increased under this section, the court may not order the sentence for the offense to run concurrently with any other sentence the court imposes on the defendant.

Added by Acts 2003, 78th Leg., ch. 712, § 2, eff. Sept. 1, 2003.

SUBCHAPTER E. FORFEITURE

§ 481.151. Definitions

In this subchapter:

(1) "Controlled substance property" means a controlled substance, mixture containing a controlled substance, controlled substance analogue, counterfeit controlled substance, drug paraphernalia, chem-

ical precursor, chemical laboratory apparatus, or raw material.

(2) "Controlled substance plant" means a species of plant from which a controlled substance listed in Schedule I or II may be derived.

(3) "Summary destruction" or "summarily destroy" means destruction without the necessity of any court action, a court order, or further proceedings.

(4) "Summary forfeiture" or "summarily forfeit" means forfeiture without the necessity of any court action, a court order, or further proceedings.

Amended by Acts 1991, 72nd Leg., ch. 141, § 1, eff. Sept. 1, 1991; Acts 2001, 77th Leg., ch. 251, § 28, eff. Sept. 1, 2001; Acts 2007, 80th Leg., ch. 152, § 1, eff. May 21, 2007.

§ 481.152. Seizure, Summary Forfeiture, and Summary Destruction of Controlled Substance Plants

(a) Controlled substance plants are subject to seizure and summary forfeiture to the state if:

(1) the plants have been planted, cultivated, or harvested in violation of this chapter;

(2) the plants are wild growths; or

(3) the owners or cultivators of the plants are unknown.

(b) Subsection (a) does not apply to unharvested peyote growing in its natural state.

(c) If a person who occupies or controls land or premises on which the plants are growing fails on the demand of a peace officer to produce an appropriate registration or proof that the person is the holder of the registration, the officer may seize and summarily forfeit the plants.

(d) If a controlled substance plant is seized and forfeited under this section, a court may order the disposition of the plant under Section 481.159, or the department or a peace officer may summarily destroy the property under the rules of the department.

Acts 1989, 71st Leg., ch. 678, § 1, eff. Sept. 1, 1989. Amended by Acts 1991, 72nd Leg., ch. 141, § 1, eff. Sept. 1, 1991; Acts 2007, 80th Leg., ch. 152, §§ 2, 3, eff. May 21, 2007.

§ 481.153. Seizure, Summary Forfeiture, and Summary Destruction of Controlled Substance Property

(a) Controlled substance property that is manufactured, delivered, or possessed in violation of this chapter is subject to seizure and summary forfeiture to the state.

(b) If an item of controlled substance property is seized and forfeited under this section, a court may order the disposition of the property under Section 481.159, or the department or a peace officer may summarily destroy the property under the rules of the department.

Amended by Acts 1991, 72nd Leg., ch. 141, § 1, eff. Sept. 1, 1991; Acts 2007, 80th Leg., ch. 152, §§ 4, 5, eff. May 21, 2007.

§ 481.154. Rules

(a) The director may adopt reasonable rules and procedures, not inconsistent with the provisions of this chapter, concerning:

(1) summary forfeiture and summary destruction of controlled substance property or plants;

(2) establishment and operation of a secure storage area;

(3) delegation by a law enforcement agency head of the authority to access a secure storage area; and

(4) minimum tolerance for and the circumstances of loss or destruction during an investigation.

(b) The rules for the destruction of controlled substance property or plants must require:

(1) more than one person to witness the destruction of the property or plants;

(2) the preparation of an inventory of the property or plants destroyed; and

(3) the preparation of a statement that contains the names of the persons who witness the destruction and the details of the destruction.

(c) A document prepared under a rule adopted under this section must be completed, retained, and made available for inspection by the director.

Amended by Acts 1991, 72nd Leg., ch. 141, § 1, eff. Sept. 1, 1991; Acts 2007, 80th Leg., ch. 152, § 6, eff. May 21, 2007.

§§ 481.155, 481.156. Repealed by Acts 1989, 71st Leg., 1st C.S., ch. 12, § 6, eff. Oct. 18, 1989

§ 481.157. Repealed by Acts 1989, 71st Leg., 1st C.S., ch. 12, § 6, eff. Oct. 18, 1989; Acts 1991, 72nd Leg., ch. 14, § 198, eff. Sept. 1, 1991

§ 481.158. Repealed by Acts 1989, 71st Leg., 1st C.S., ch. 12, § 6, eff. Oct. 18, 1989

§ 481.159. Disposition of Controlled Substance Property or Plant

(a) If a district court orders the forfeiture of a controlled substance property or plant under Chapter 59, Code of Criminal Procedure, or under this code, the court shall also order a law enforcement agency to:

(1) retain the property or plant for its official purposes, including use in the investigation of offenses under this code;

(2) deliver the property or plant to a government agency for official purposes;

(3) deliver the property or plant to a person authorized by the court to receive it;

(4) deliver the property or plant to a person authorized by the director to receive it for a purpose described by Section 481.065(a); or

(5) destroy the property or plant that is not otherwise disposed of in the manner prescribed by this subchapter.

(b) The district court may not require the department to receive, analyze, or retain a controlled substance property or plant forfeited to a law enforcement agency other than the department.

(c) In order to ensure that a controlled substance property or plant is not diluted, substituted, diverted, or tampered with while being used in the investigation of offenses under this code, law enforcement agencies using the property or plant for this purpose shall:

(1) employ a qualified individual to conduct qualitative and quantitative analyses of the property or plant before and after their use in an investigation;

(2) maintain the property or plant in a secure storage area accessible only to the law enforcement agency head and the individual responsible for analyzing, preserving, and maintaining security over the property or plant; and

(3) maintain a log documenting:

(A) the date of issue, date of return, type, amount, and concentration of property or plant used in an investigation; and

(B) the signature and the printed or typed name of the peace officer to whom the property or plant was issued and the signature and the printed or typed name of the individual issuing the property or plant.

(d) A law enforcement agency may contract with another law enforcement agency to provide security that complies with Subsection (c) for controlled substance property or plants.

(e) A law enforcement agency may adopt a written policy with more stringent requirements than those required by Subsection (c). The director may enter and inspect, in accordance with Section 481.181, a location at which an agency maintains records or controlled substance property or plants as required by this section.

(f) If a law enforcement agency uses a controlled substance property or plant in the investigation of an offense under this code and the property or plant has been transported across state lines before the forfeiture, the agency shall cooperate with a federal agency in the investigation if requested to do so by the federal agency.

(g) Under the rules of the department, a law enforcement agency head may grant to another person access to a secure storage facility under Subsection (c)(2).

(h) A county, justice, or municipal court may order forfeiture of a controlled substance property or plant, unless the lawful possession of and title to the property or plant can be ascertained. If the court determines that a person had lawful possession of and title to the controlled substance property or plant before it was seized, the court shall order the controlled substance property or plant returned to the person, if the person so desires. The court may only order the destruction of a controlled substance property or plant that is not otherwise disposed of in the manner prescribed by Section 481.160.

(i) If a controlled substance property or plant seized under this chapter was forfeited to an agency for the purpose of destruction or for any purpose other than investigation, the property or plant may not be used in an investigation unless a district court orders disposition under this section and permits the use of the property or plant in the investigation.

Acts 1989, 71st Leg., ch. 678, § 1, eff. Sept. 1, 1989. Amended by Acts 1989, 71st Leg., 1st C.S., ch. 12, § 5(a), eff. Oct. 18, 1989; Acts 1991, 72nd Leg., ch. 141, § 1, eff. Sept. 1, 1991.

§ 481.160. Destruction of Excess Quantities

(a) If a controlled substance property or plant is forfeited under this code or under Chapter 59, Code of Criminal Procedure, the law enforcement agency that seized the property or plant or to which the property or plant is forfeited may summarily destroy the property or plant without a court order before the disposition of a case arising out of the forfeiture if the agency ensures that:

(1) at least five random and representative samples are taken from the total amount of the property or plant and a sufficient quantity is preserved to provide for discovery by parties entitled to discovery;

(2) photographs are taken that reasonably depict the total amount of the property or plant; and

(3) the gross weight or liquid measure of the property or plant is determined, either by actually weighing or measuring the property or plant or by estimating its weight or measurement after making dimensional measurements of the total amount seized.

(b) If the property consists of a single container of liquid, taking and preserving one representative sample complies with Subsection (a)(1).

(c) A representative sample, photograph, or record made under this section is admissible in civil or criminal proceedings in the same manner and to the same extent as if the total quantity of the suspected controlled substance property or plant was offered in evidence, regardless of whether the remainder of the property or plant has been destroyed. An inference or presumption of spoliation does not apply to a property or plant destroyed under this section.

(d) If hazardous waste, residuals, contaminated glassware, associated equipment, or by-products from illicit chemical laboratories or similar operations that create a health or environmental hazard or are not capable of being safely stored are forfeited, those items may be disposed of under Subsection (a) or may be seized and summarily forfeited and destroyed by a law enforcement agency without a court order before the disposition of a case arising out of the forfeiture if current environmental protection standards are followed.

(e) A law enforcement agency seizing and destroying or disposing of materials described in Subsection (d) shall ensure that photographs are taken that reasonably depict the total amount of the materials seized and the manner in which the materials were physically arranged or positioned before seizure.

(f) Repealed by Acts 2005, 79th Leg., ch. 1224, § 19(2).

Acts 1989, 71st Leg., ch. 678, § 1, eff. Sept. 1, 1989. Amended by Acts 1989, 71st Leg., ch. 1100, § 5.02(r), eff. Sept. 1, 1989; Acts 1991, 72nd Leg., ch. 14, § 199, eff. Sept. 1, 1991; Acts 1991, 72nd Leg., ch. 141, § 1, eff. Sept. 1, 1991; Acts 1991, 72nd Leg., ch. 285, § 2, eff. Sept. 1, 1991; Acts 1997, 75th Leg., ch. 745, § 33, eff. Jan. 1, 1998; Acts 2001, 77th Leg., ch. 251, § 29, eff. Sept. 1, 2001; Acts 2005, 79th Leg., ch. 1224, § 19(2), eff. Sept. 1, 2005.

SUBCHAPTER F. INSPECTIONS, EVIDENCE, AND MISCELLANEOUS LAW ENFORCEMENT PROVISIONS

§ 481.181. Inspections

(a) The director may enter controlled premises at any reasonable time and inspect the premises and items described by Subsection (b) in order to inspect, copy, and verify the correctness of a record, report, or other document required to be made or kept under this chapter and to perform other functions under this chapter. For purposes of this subsection, "reasonable time" means any time during the normal business hours of the person or activity regulated under this chapter or any time an activity regulated under this chapter is occurring on the premises. The director shall:

(1) state the purpose of the entry;

(2) display to the owner, operator, or agent in charge of the premises appropriate credentials; and

(3) deliver to the owner, operator, or agent in charge of the premises a written notice of inspection authority.

(b) The director may:

(1) inspect and copy a record, report, or other document required to be made or kept under this chapter;

(2) inspect, within reasonable limits and in a reasonable manner, the controlled premises and all pertinent equipment, finished and unfinished drugs, other substances, and materials, containers, labels, records, files, papers, processes, controls, and facilities as appropriate to verify a record, report, or document required to be kept under this chapter or to administer this chapter;

(3) examine and inventory stock of a controlled substance and obtain samples of the controlled substance;

(4) examine a hypodermic syringe, needle, pipe, or other instrument, device, contrivance, equipment, control, container, label, or facility relating to a possible violation of this chapter; and

(5) examine a material used, intended to be used, or capable of being used to dilute or adulterate a controlled substance.

(c) Unless the owner, operator, or agent in charge of the controlled premises consents in writing, the director may not inspect:

(1) financial data;

(2) sales data other than shipment data; or

(3) pricing data.

Acts 1989, 71st Leg., ch. 678, § 1, eff. Sept. 1, 1989. Amended by Acts 2003, 78th Leg., ch. 1099, § 11, eff. Sept. 1, 2003.

§ 481.182. Evidentiary Rules Relating to Offer of Delivery

For the purpose of establishing a delivery under this chapter, proof of an offer to sell must be corroborated by:

(1) a person other than the person to whom the offer is made; or

(2) evidence other than a statement of the person to whom the offer is made.

Acts 1989, 71st Leg., ch. 678, § 1, eff. Sept. 1, 1989. Amended by Acts 2003, 78th Leg., ch. 1099, § 12, eff. Sept. 1, 2003.

§ 481.183. Evidentiary Rules Relating to Drug Paraphernalia

(a) In considering whether an item is drug paraphernalia under this chapter, a court or other authority shall consider, in addition to all other logically relevant factors, and subject to rules of evidence:

(1) statements by an owner or person in control of the object concerning its use;

(2) the existence of any residue of a controlled substance on the object;

(3) direct or circumstantial evidence of the intent of an owner or other person in control of the object to deliver it to a person whom the person knows or should reasonably know intends to use the object to facilitate a violation of this chapter;

(4) oral or written instructions provided with the object concerning its use;

(5) descriptive material accompanying the object that explains or depicts its use;

(6) the manner in which the object is displayed for sale;

(7) whether the owner or person in control of the object is a supplier of similar or related items to the community, such as a licensed distributor or dealer of tobacco products;

(8) direct or circumstantial evidence of the ratio of sales of the object to the total sales of the business enterprise;

(9) the existence and scope of uses for the object in the community;

(10) the physical design characteristics of the item; and

(11) expert testimony concerning the item's use.

(b) The innocence of an owner or other person in charge of an object as to a direct violation of this chapter does not prevent a finding that the object is intended or designed for use as drug paraphernalia.

Acts 1989, 71st Leg., ch. 678, § 1, eff. Sept. 1, 1989. Amended by Acts 2003, 78th Leg., ch. 1099, § 13, eff. Sept. 1, 2003.

§ 481.184. Burden of Proof; Liabilities

(a) The state is not required to negate an exemption or exception provided by this chapter in a complaint, information, indictment, or other pleading or in any trial, hearing, or other proceeding under this chapter. A person claiming the benefit of an exemption or exception has the burden of going forward with the evidence with respect to the exemption or exception.

(b) In the absence of proof that a person is the duly authorized holder of an appropriate registration or order form issued under this chapter, the person is presumed not to be the holder of the registration or form. The presumption is subject to rebuttal by a person charged with an offense under this chapter.

(c) This chapter does not impose a liability on an authorized state, county, or municipal officer engaged in the lawful performance of official duties.

Acts 1989, 71st Leg., ch. 678, § 1, eff. Sept. 1, 1989. Amended by Acts 2003, 78th Leg., ch. 1099, § 14, eff. Sept. 1, 2003.

§ 481.185. Arrest Reports

(a) Each law enforcement agency in this state shall file monthly with the director a report of all arrests made for drug offenses and quantities of controlled substances seized during the preceding month. The agency shall make the report on a form provided by the director and shall provide the information required by the form.

(b) The director shall publish an annual summary of all drug arrests and controlled substances seized in the state.

Acts 1989, 71st Leg., ch. 678, § 1, eff. Sept. 1, 1989.

§ 481.186. Cooperative Arrangements

(a) The director shall cooperate with federal and state agencies in discharging the director's responsibilities concerning traffic in controlled substances and in suppressing the abuse of controlled substances. The director may:

(1) arrange for the exchange of information among government officials concerning the use and abuse of controlled substances;

(2) cooperate in and coordinate training programs concerning controlled substances law enforcement at local and state levels;

(3) cooperate with the Federal Drug Enforcement Administration and state agencies by establishing a centralized unit to accept, catalog, file, and collect statistics, including records on drug-dependent persons and other controlled substance law offenders in this state and, except as provided by Section 481.068, make the information available for federal, state, and local law enforcement purposes; and

(4) conduct programs of eradication aimed at destroying wild or illegal growth of plant species from which controlled substances may be extracted.

(b) In the exercise of regulatory functions under this chapter, the director may rely on results, information, and evidence relating to the regulatory functions of this chapter received from the Federal Drug Enforcement Administration or a state agency.

Acts 1989, 71st Leg., ch. 678, § 1, eff. Sept. 1, 1989. Amended by Acts 2003, 78th Leg., ch. 1099, § 15, eff. Sept. 1, 2003.

SUBCHAPTER G. THERAPEUTIC RESEARCH PROGRAM

§ 481.201. Research Program; Review Board

(a) The Texas Board of Health may establish a controlled substance therapeutic research program for the supervised use of tetrahydrocannabinols for medical and research purposes to be conducted in accordance with this chapter.

(b) If the Texas Board of Health establishes the program, the board shall create a research program review board. The review board members are appointed by the Texas Board of Health and serve at the will of the board.

(c) The review board shall be composed of:

(1) a licensed physician certified by the American Board of Ophthalmology;

(2) a licensed physician certified by the American Board of Internal Medicine and certified in the subspecialty of medical oncology;

(3) a licensed physician certified by the American Board of Psychiatry;

(4) a licensed physician certified by the American Board of Surgery;

(5) a licensed physician certified by the American Board of Radiology; and

(6) a licensed attorney with experience in law pertaining to the practice of medicine.

(d) Members serve without compensation but are entitled to reimbursement for actual and necessary expenses incurred in performing official duties.

Acts 1989, 71st Leg., ch. 678, § 1, eff. Sept. 1, 1989.

§ 481.202. Review Board Powers and Duties

(a) The review board shall review research proposals submitted and medical case histories of persons recommended for participation in a research program and determine which research programs and persons are most suitable for the therapy and research purposes of the program. The review board shall approve the research programs, certify program participants, and conduct periodic reviews of the research and participants.

(b) The review board, after approval of the Texas Board of Health, may seek authorization to expand the research program to include diseases not covered by this subchapter.

(c) The review board shall maintain a record of all persons in charge of approved research programs and of all persons who participate in the program as researchers or as patients.

(d) The Texas Board of Health may terminate the distribution of tetrahydrocannabinols and their derivatives to a research program as it determines necessary.

Acts 1989, 71st Leg., ch. 678, § 1, eff. Sept. 1, 1989.

§ 481.203. Patient Participation

(a) A person may not be considered for participation as a recipient of tetrahydrocannabinols and their derivatives through a research program unless the person is recommended to a person in charge of an approved research program and the review board by a physician who is licensed by the Texas State Board of Medical Examiners and is attending the person.

(b) A physician may not recommend a person for the research program unless the person:

(1) has glaucoma or cancer;

(2) is not responding to conventional treatment for glaucoma or cancer or is experiencing severe side effects from treatment; and

(3) has symptoms or side effects from treatment that may be alleviated by medical use of tetrahydrocannabinols or their derivatives.

Acts 1989, 71st Leg., ch. 678, § 1, eff. Sept. 1, 1989.

§ 481.204. Acquisition and Distribution of Controlled Substances

(a) The Texas Board of Health shall acquire the tetrahydrocannabinols and their derivatives for use in the research program by contracting with the National Institute on Drug Abuse to receive tetrahydrocannabinols and their derivatives that are safe for human consumption according to the regulations adopted by the institute, the Food and Drug Administration, and the Federal Drug Enforcement Administration.

(b) The Texas Board of Health shall supervise the distribution of the tetrahydrocannabinols and their derivatives to program participants. The tetrahydrocannabinols and derivatives of tetrahydrocannabinols may be distributed only by the person in charge of the research program to physicians caring for program participant patients, under rules adopted by the Texas Board of Health in such a manner as to prevent unauthorized diversion of the substances and in compliance with all requirements of the Federal Drug Enforcement Administration. The physician is responsible for dispensing the substances to patients.

Acts 1989, 71st Leg., ch. 678, § 1, eff. Sept. 1, 1989.

§ 481.205. Rules; Reports

(a) The Texas Board of Health shall adopt rules necessary for implementing the research program.

(b) If the Texas Board of Health establishes a program under this subchapter, the commissioner shall publish a report not later than January 1 of each odd-numbered year on the medical effectiveness of the use of tetrahydrocannabinols and their derivatives and any other medical findings of the research program.

Acts 1989, 71st Leg., ch. 678, § 1, eff. Sept. 1, 1989.

SUBCHAPTER H. ADMINISTRATIVE PENALTY

§ 481.301. Imposition of Penalty

The department may impose an administrative penalty on a person who violates Section 481.061, 481.066, 481.067, 481.069, 481.074, 481.075, 481.077, 481.0771, 481.078, 481.080, or 481.081 or a rule or order adopted under any of those sections.

Added by Acts 2007, 80th Leg., ch. 1391, § 5, eff. Sept. 1, 2007.

§ 481.302. Amount of Penalty

(a) The amount of the penalty may not exceed $1,000 for each violation, and each day a violation continues or occurs is a separate violation for purposes of imposing a penalty. The total amount of the penalty assessed for a violation continuing or occurring on separate days under this subsection may not exceed $20,000.

(b) The amount shall be based on:

(1) the seriousness of the violation, including the nature, circumstances, extent, and gravity of the violation;

(2) the threat to health or safety caused by the violation;

(3) the history of previous violations;

(4) the amount necessary to deter a future violation;

(5) whether the violator demonstrated good faith, including when applicable whether the violator made good faith efforts to correct the violation; and

(6) any other matter that justice may require.

Added by Acts 2007, 80th Leg., ch. 1391, § 5, eff. Sept. 1, 2007.

§ 481.303. Report and Notice of Violation and Penalty

(a) If the department initially determines that a violation occurred, the department shall give written notice of the report to the person by certified mail, registered mail, personal delivery, or another manner of delivery that records the person's receipt of the notice.

(b) The notice must:

(1) include a brief summary of the alleged violation;

(2) state the amount of the recommended penalty; and

(3) inform the person of the person's right to a hearing on the occurrence of the violation, the amount of the penalty, or both.

Added by Acts 2007, 80th Leg., ch. 1391, § 5, eff. Sept. 1, 2007.

§ 481.304. Penalty to be Paid or Informal Hearing Requested

(a) Before the 21st day after the date the person receives notice under Section 481.303, the person in writing may:

(1) accept the determination and recommended penalty; or

(2) make a request for an informal hearing held by the department on the occurrence of the violation, the amount of the penalty, or both.

(b) At the conclusion of an informal hearing requested under Subsection (a), the department may modify the amount of the recommended penalty.

(c) If the person accepts the determination and recommended penalty, including any modification of the amount, or if the person fails to timely respond to the notice, the director by order shall approve the determination and impose the recommended penalty.

Added by Acts 2007, 80th Leg., ch. 1391, § 5, eff. Sept. 1, 2007.

§ 481.305. Formal Hearing

(a) The person may request a formal hearing only after participating in an informal hearing.

(b) The request must be submitted in writing and received by the department before the 21st day after the date the person is notified of the decision from the informal hearing.

(c) If a timely request for a formal hearing is not received, the director by order shall approve the determination from the informal hearing and impose the recommended penalty.

(d) If the person timely requests a formal hearing, the director shall refer the matter to the State Office of Administrative Hearings, which shall promptly set a hearing date and give written notice of the time and place of the hearing to the director and to the person. An administrative law judge of the State Office of Administrative Hearings shall conduct the hearing.

(e) The administrative law judge shall make findings of fact and conclusions of law and promptly issue to the director a proposal for a decision about the occurrence of the violation and the amount of any proposed penalty.

(f) If a penalty is proposed under Subsection (e), the administrative law judge shall include in the proposal for a decision a finding setting out costs, fees, expenses, and reasonable and necessary attorney's fees incurred by the state in bringing the proceeding. The director may adopt the finding and impose the costs, fees, and expenses on the person as part of the final order entered in the proceeding.

Added by Acts 2007, 80th Leg., ch. 1391, § 5, eff. Sept. 1, 2007.

§ 481.306. Decision

(a) Based on the findings of fact, conclusions of law, and proposal for a decision, the director by order may:

(1) find that a violation occurred and impose a penalty; or

(2) find that a violation did not occur.

(b) The notice of the director's order under Subsection (a) that is sent to the person in the manner provided by Chapter 2001, Government Code, must include a statement of the right of the person to judicial review of the order.

Added by Acts 2007, 80th Leg., ch. 1391, § 5, eff. Sept. 1, 2007.

§ 481.307. Options Following Decision: Pay or Appeal

Before the 31st day after the date the order under Section 481.306 that imposes an administrative penalty becomes final, the person shall:

(1) pay the penalty; or

(2) file a petition for judicial review of the order contesting the occurrence of the violation, the amount of the penalty, or both.

Added by Acts 2007, 80th Leg., ch. 1391, § 5, eff. Sept. 1, 2007.

§ 481.308. Stay of Enforcement of Penalty

(a) Within the period prescribed by Section 481.307, a person who files a petition for judicial review may:

(1) stay enforcement of the penalty by:

(A) paying the penalty to the court for placement in an escrow account; or

(B) giving the court a supersedeas bond approved by the court that:

(i) is for the amount of the penalty; and

(ii) is effective until all judicial review of the order is final; or

(2) request the court to stay enforcement of the penalty by:

(A) filing with the court a sworn affidavit of the person stating that the person is financially unable to pay the penalty and is financially unable to give the supersedeas bond; and

(B) sending a copy of the affidavit to the director by certified mail.

(b) Following receipt of a copy of an affidavit under Subsection (a)(2), the director may file with the court, before the sixth day after the date of receipt, a contest to the affidavit. The court shall hold a hearing on the facts alleged in the affidavit as soon as practicable and shall stay the enforcement of the penalty on finding that the alleged facts are true. The person who files an affidavit has the burden of proving that the person is financially unable to pay the penalty or to give a supersedeas bond.

Added by Acts 2007, 80th Leg., ch. 1391, § 5, eff. Sept. 1, 2007.

§ 481.309. Collection of Penalty

(a) If the person does not pay the penalty and the enforcement of the penalty is not stayed, the penalty may be collected.

(b) The attorney general may sue to collect the penalty.

Added by Acts 2007, 80th Leg., ch. 1391, § 5, eff. Sept. 1, 2007.

§ 481.310. Decision by Court

(a) If the court sustains the finding that a violation occurred, the court may uphold or reduce the amount of the penalty and order the person to pay the full or reduced amount of the penalty.

(b) If the court does not sustain the finding that a violation occurred, the court shall order that a penalty is not owed.

Added by Acts 2007, 80th Leg., ch. 1391, § 5, eff. Sept. 1, 2007.

§ 481.311. Remittance of Penalty and Interest

(a) If the person paid the penalty and if the amount of the penalty is reduced or the penalty is not upheld by the court, the court shall order, when the court's judgment becomes final, that the appropriate amount plus accrued interest be remitted to the person before the 31st day after the date that the judgment of the court becomes final.

(b) The interest accrues at the rate charged on loans to depository institutions by the New York Federal Reserve Bank.

(c) The interest shall be paid for the period beginning on the date the penalty is paid and ending on the date the penalty is remitted.

Added by Acts 2007, 80th Leg., ch. 1391, § 5, eff. Sept. 1, 2007.

§ 481.312. Release of Bond

(a) If the person gave a supersedeas bond and the penalty is not upheld by the court, the court shall order, when the court's judgment becomes final, the release of the bond.

(b) If the person gave a supersedeas bond and the amount of the penalty is reduced, the court shall order the release of the bond after the person pays the reduced amount.

Added by Acts 2007, 80th Leg., ch. 1391, § 5, eff. Sept. 1, 2007.

§ 481.313. Administrative Procedure

A proceeding to impose the penalty is considered to be a contested case under Chapter 2001, Government Code.

Added by Acts 2007, 80th Leg., ch. 1391, § 5, eff. Sept. 1, 2007.

§ 481.314. Disposition of Penalty

The department shall send any amount collected as a penalty under this subchapter to the comptroller for deposit to the credit of the general revenue fund.

Added by Acts 2007, 80th Leg., ch. 1391, § 5, eff. Sept. 1, 2007.

CHAPTER 482. SIMULATED CONTROLLED SUBSTANCES

Section

§ 482.001. Definitions

In this chapter:

(1) "Controlled substance" has the meaning assigned by § 481.002 (Texas Controlled Substances Act).

(2) "Deliver" means to transfer, actually or constructively, from one person to another a simulated controlled substance, regardless of whether there is an agency relationship. The term includes offering to sell a simulated controlled substance.

(3) "Manufacture" means to make a simulated controlled substance and includes the preparation of the substance in dosage form by mixing, compounding, encapsulating, tableting, or any other process.

(4) "Simulated controlled substance" means a substance that is purported to be a controlled substance, but is chemically different from the controlled substance it is purported to be.

Acts 1989, 71st Leg., ch. 678, § 1, eff. Sept. 1, 1989.

§ 482.002. Unlawful Delivery or Manufacture with Intent to Deliver; Criminal Penalty

(a) A person commits an offense if the person knowingly or intentionally manufactures with the intent to deliver or delivers a simulated controlled substance and the person:

(1) expressly represents the substance to be a controlled substance;

(2) represents the substance to be a controlled substance in a manner that would lead a reasonable person to believe that the substance is a controlled substance; or

(3) states to the person receiving or intended to receive the simulated controlled substance that the person may successfully represent the substance to be a controlled substance to a third party.

(b) It is a defense to prosecution under this section that the person manufacturing with the intent to deliver or delivering the simulated controlled substance was:

(1) acting in the discharge of the person's official duties as a peace officer;

(2) manufacturing the substance for or delivering the substance to a licensed medical practitioner for use as a placebo in the course of the practitioner's research or practice; or

(3) a licensed medical practitioner, pharmacist, or other person authorized to dispense or administer a controlled substance, and the person was acting in the legitimate performance of the person's professional duties.

(c) It is not a defense to prosecution under this section that the person manufacturing with the intent to deliver or delivering the simulated controlled substance believed the substance to be a controlled substance.

(d) An offense under this section is a state jail felony.

Acts 1989, 71st Leg., ch. 678, § 1, eff. Sept. 1, 1989. Amended by Acts 1993, 73rd Leg., ch. 900, § 2.03, eff. Sept. 1, 1994.

§ 482.003. Evidentiary Rules

(a) In determining whether a person has represented a simulated controlled substance to be a controlled substance in a manner that would lead a reasonable person to believe the substance was a controlled substance, a court may consider, in addition to all other logically relevant factors, whether:

(1) the simulated controlled substance was packaged in a manner normally used for the delivery of a controlled substance;

(2) the delivery or intended delivery included an exchange of or demand for property as consideration for delivery of the substance and the amount of the consideration was substantially in excess of the reasonable value of the simulated controlled substance; and

(3) the physical appearance of the finished product containing the substance was substantially identical to a controlled substance.

(b) Proof of an offer to sell a simulated controlled substance must be corroborated by a person other than the offeree or by evidence other than a statement of the offeree.

Acts 1989, 71st Leg., ch. 678, § 1, eff. Sept. 1, 1989.

§ 482.004. Summary Forfeiture

A simulated controlled substance seized as a result of an offense under this chapter is subject to summary forfeiture and to destruction or disposition in the same manner as is a controlled substance property under Subchapter E, Chapter 481. [1]

Acts 1989, 71st Leg., ch. 678, § 1, eff. Sept. 1, 1989. Amended by Acts 1991, 72nd Leg., ch. 141, § 3, eff. Sept. 1, 1991.

[1] V.T.C.A., Health & Safety Code § 481.151 et seq.

§ 482.005. Preparatory Offenses

Title 4, Penal Code,[1] applies to an offense under this chapter.

Added by Acts 1995, 74th Leg., ch. 318, § 39, eff. Sept. 1, 1995.

[1] V.T.C.A., Penal Code § 15.01 et seq.

CHAPTER 483. DANGEROUS DRUGS

SUBCHAPTER A. GENERAL PROVISIONS

§ 483.0001. Short Title

This Act may be cited as the Texas Dangerous Drug Act.

Added by Acts 1993, 73rd Leg., ch. 789, § 18, eff. Sept. 1, 1993.

§ 483.001. Definitions

In this chapter:

(1) "Board" means the Texas State Board of Pharmacy.

(2) "Dangerous drug" means a device or a drug that is unsafe for self-medication and that is not included in Schedules I through V or Penalty Groups 1 through 4 of Chapter 481 (Texas Controlled Substances Act). The term includes a device or a drug that bears or is required to bear the legend:

(A) "Caution: federal law prohibits dispensing without prescription" or "Rx only" or another legend that complies with federal law; or

(B) "Caution: federal law restricts this drug to use by or on the order of a licensed veterinarian."

(3) "Deliver" means to sell, dispense, give away, or supply in any other manner.

(4) "Designated agent" means:

(A) a licensed nurse, physician assistant, pharmacist, or other individual designated by a practitioner to communicate prescription drug orders to a pharmacist;

(B) a licensed nurse, physician assistant, or pharmacist employed in a health care facility to whom the practitioner communicates a prescription drug order; or

(C) a registered nurse or physician assistant authorized by a practitioner to carry out a prescription drug order for dangerous drugs under Subchapter B, Chapter 157, Occupations Code. [1]

(5) "Dispense" means to prepare, package, compound, or label a dangerous drug in the course of professional practice for delivery under the lawful order of a practitioner to an ultimate user or the user's agent.

(6) "Manufacturer" means a person, other than a pharmacist, who manufactures dangerous drugs.

The term includes a person who prepares dangerous drugs in dosage form by mixing, compounding, encapsulating, entableting, or any other process.

(7) "Patient" means:

(A) an individual for whom a dangerous drug is prescribed or to whom a dangerous drug is administered; or

(B) an owner or the agent of an owner of an animal for which a dangerous drug is prescribed or to which a dangerous drug is administered.

(8) "Person" includes an individual, corporation, partnership, and association.

(9) "Pharmacist" means a person licensed by the Texas State Board of Pharmacy to practice pharmacy.

(10) "Pharmacy" means a facility where prescription drug or medication orders are received, processed, dispensed, or distributed under this chapter, Chapter 481 of this code, and Subtitle J, Title 3, Occupations Code. [2] The term does not include a narcotic drug treatment program that is regulated by Chapter 466, Health and Safety Code.

(11) "Practice of pharmacy" means:

(A) provision of those acts or services necessary to provide pharmaceutical care;

(B) interpretation and evaluation of prescription drug orders or medication orders;

(C) participation in drug and device selection as authorized by law, drug administration, drug regimen review, or drug or drug-related research;

(D) provision of patient counseling;

(E) responsibility for:

(i) dispensing of prescription drug orders or distribution of medication orders in the patient's best interest;

(ii) compounding and labeling of drugs and devices, except labeling by a manufacturer, repackager, or distributor of nonprescription drugs and commercially packaged prescription drugs and devices;

(iii) proper and safe storage of drugs and devices; or

(iv) maintenance of proper records for drugs and devices. In this subdivision, "device" has the meaning assigned by Subtitle J, Title 3, Occupations Code; [2] or

(F) performance of a specific act of drug therapy management for a patient delegated to a pharmacist by a written protocol from a physician licensed by the state under Subtitle B, Title 3, Occupations Code. [3]

(12) "Practitioner" means a person licensed:

(A) by the Texas State Board of Medical Examiners, State Board of Dental Examiners, Texas State Board of Podiatric Medical Examiners, Texas Optometry Board, or State Board of Veterinary Medical Examiners to prescribe and administer dangerous drugs;

(B) by another state in a health field in which, under the laws of this state, a licensee may legally prescribe dangerous drugs;

(C) in Canada or Mexico in a health field in which, under the laws of this state, a licensee may legally prescribe dangerous drugs; or

(D) an advanced practice nurse or physician assistant to whom a physician has delegated the authority to carry out or sign prescription drug orders under Section 157.0511, 157.052, 157.053, 157.054, 157.0541, or 157.0542, Occupations Code.

(13) "Prescription" means an order from a practitioner, or an agent of the practitioner designated in writing as authorized to communicate prescriptions, or an order made in accordance with Subchapter B, Chapter 157, Occupations Code, [1] or Section 203.353, Occupations Code, to a pharmacist for a dangerous drug to be dispensed that states:

(A) the date of the order's issue;

(B) the name and address of the patient;

(C) if the drug is prescribed for an animal, the species of the animal;

(D) the name and quantity of the drug prescribed;

(E) the directions for the use of the drug;

(F) the intended use of the drug unless the practitioner determines the furnishing of this information is not in the best interest of the patient;

(G) the name, address, and telephone number of the practitioner at the practitioner's usual place of business, legibly printed or stamped; and

(H) the name, address, and telephone number of the licensed midwife, registered nurse, or physician assistant, legibly printed or stamped, if signed by a licensed midwife, registered nurse, or physician assistant.

(14) "Warehouseman" means a person who stores dangerous drugs for others and who has no control

over the disposition of the drugs except for the purpose of storage.

(15) "Wholesaler" means a person engaged in the business of distributing dangerous drugs to a person listed in Sections 483.041(c)(1)–(6).

Acts 1989, 71st Leg., ch. 678, § 1, eff. Sept. 1, 1989. Amended by Acts 1989, 71st Leg., ch. 1100, §§ 5.03(h), 5.04(b), eff. Sept. 1, 1989; Acts 1991, 72nd Leg., ch. 14, § 200, eff. Sept. 1, 1991; Acts 1991, 72nd Leg., ch. 237, § 10, eff. Sept. 1, 1991; Acts 1991, 72nd Leg., ch. 588, § 26, eff. Sept. 1, 1991; Acts 1993, 73rd Leg., ch. 351, § 29, eff. Sept. 1, 1993; Acts 1993, 73rd Leg., ch. 789, § 18, eff. Sept. 1, 1993; Acts 1995, 74th Leg., ch. 965, §§ 6, 82, eff. June 16, 1995; Acts 1997, 75th Leg., ch. 1095, § 18, eff. Sept. 1, 1997; Acts 1997, 75th Leg., ch. 1180, § 22, eff. Sept. 1, 1997; Acts 2001, 77th Leg., ch. 112, § 6, eff. May 11, 2001; Acts 2001, 77th Leg., ch. 1254, § 11, eff. Sept. 1, 2001; Acts 2001, 77th Leg., ch. 1420, § 14.795, eff. Sept. 1, 2001; Acts 2003, 78th Leg., ch. 88, § 10, eff. May 20, 2003; Acts 2005, 79th Leg., ch. 1240, § 54, eff. Sept. 1, 2005.

[1] V.T.C.A., Occupations Code § 157.051 et seq.

[2] V.T.C.A., Occupations Code § 551.001 et seq.

[3] V.T.C.A., Occupations Code § 151.001 et seq.

§ 483.002. Rules

The board may adopt rules for the proper administration and enforcement of this chapter.

Acts 1989, 71st Leg., ch. 678, § 1, eff. Sept. 1, 1989.

§ 483.003. Board of Health Hearings Regarding Certain Dangerous Drugs

(a) The Texas Board of Health may hold public hearings in accordance with Chapter 2001, Government Code to determine whether there is compelling evidence that a dangerous drug has been abused, either by being prescribed for nontherapeutic purposes or by the ultimate user.

(b) On making that finding, the Texas Board of Health may limit the availability of the abused drug by permitting its dispensing only on the prescription of a practitioner described by Section 483.001(12)(A), (B), or (D).

Acts 1989, 71st Leg., ch. 678, § 1, eff. Sept. 1, 1989. Amended by Acts 1995, 74th Leg., ch. 76, § 5.95(49), eff. Sept. 1, 1995; Acts 1997, 75th Leg., ch. 1180, § 23, eff. Sept. 1, 1997; Acts 2001, 77th Leg., ch. 112, § 7, eff. May 11, 2001.

§ 483.004. Commissioner of Health Emergency Authority Relating to Dangerous Drugs

If the commissioner of health has compelling evidence that an immediate danger to the public health exists as a result of the prescription of a dangerous drug by practitioners described by Section 483.001(12)(C), the commissioner may use the commissioner's existing emergency authority to limit the availability of the drug by permitting its prescription only by practitioners described by Section 483.001(12)(A), (B), or (D).

Acts 1989, 71st Leg., ch. 678, § 1, eff. Sept. 1, 1989. Amended by Acts 2001, 77th Leg., ch. 112, § 8, eff. May 11, 2001.

SUBCHAPTER B. DUTIES OF PHARMACISTS, PRACTITIONERS, AND OTHER PERSONS

§ 483.021. Determination by Pharmacist on Request to Dispense Drug

(a) A pharmacist who is requested to dispense a dangerous drug under a prescription issued by a practitioner shall determine, in the exercise of the pharmacist's professional judgment, that the prescription is a valid prescription. A pharmacist may not dispense a dangerous drug if the pharmacist knows or should have known that the prescription was issued without a valid patient-practitioner relationship.

(b) A pharmacist who is requested to dispense a dangerous drug under a prescription issued by a therapeutic optometrist shall determine, in the exercise of the pharmacist's professional judgment, whether the prescription is for a dangerous drug that a therapeutic optometrist is authorized to prescribe under Section 351.358, Occupations Code.

Acts 1989, 71st Leg., ch. 678, § 1, eff. Sept. 1, 1989. Amended by Acts 1991, 72nd Leg., ch. 588, § 27, eff. Sept. 1, 1991; Acts 2001, 77th Leg., ch. 1254, § 12, eff. Sept. 1, 2001; Acts 2001, 77th Leg., ch. 1420, § 14.796, eff. Sept. 1, 2001.

§ 483.022. Practitioner's Designated Agent; Practitioner's Responsibilities

(a) A practitioner shall provide in writing the name of each designated agent as defined by Section 483.001(4)(A) and (C), and the name of each healthcare facility which employs persons defined by Section 483.001(4)(B).

(b) The practitioner shall maintain at the practitioner's usual place of business a list of the designated agents or healthcare facilities as defined by Section 483.001(4).

(c) The practitioner shall provide a pharmacist with a copy of the practitioner's written authorization for a designated agent as defined by Section 483.001(4) on the pharmacist's request.

(d) This section does not relieve a practitioner or the practitioner's designated agent from the requirements of Subchapter A, Chapter 562, Occupations Code. [1]

(e) A practitioner remains personally responsible for the actions of a designated agent who communicates a prescription to a pharmacist.

(f) A practitioner may designate a person who is a licensed vocational nurse or has an education equivalent to or greater than that required for a licensed vocational nurse to communicate prescriptions of an advanced practice nurse or physician assistant authorized by the practitioner to sign prescription drug orders under Subchapter B, Chapter 157, Occupations Code. [2]

Acts 1989, 71st Leg., ch. 678, § 1, eff. Sept. 1, 1989. Amended by Acts 1991, 72nd Leg., ch. 14, § 201, eff. Sept. 1, 1991; Acts 1991, 72nd Leg., ch. 237, § 11, eff. Sept. 1, 1991; Acts 1993, 73rd Leg., ch. 789, § 19, eff. Sept. 1, 1993; Acts 1999, 76th Leg., ch. 428, § 4, eff. Sept. 1, 1999; Acts 2001, 77th Leg., ch. 1420, § 14.797, eff. Sept. 1, 2001.

[1] V.T.C.A., Occupations Code 562.001 et seq.

[2] V.T.C.A., Occupations Code 157.051 et seq.

§ 483.023. Retention of Prescriptions

A pharmacy shall retain a prescription for a dangerous drug dispensed by the pharmacy for two years after the date of the initial dispensing or the last refilling of the prescription, whichever date is later.

Acts 1989, 71st Leg., ch. 678, § 1, eff. Sept. 1, 1989.

§ 483.024. Records of Acquisition or Disposal

The following persons shall maintain a record of each acquisition and each disposal of a dangerous drug for two years after the date of the acquisition or disposal:

(1) a pharmacy;

(2) a practitioner;

(3) a person who obtains a dangerous drug for lawful research, teaching, or testing purposes, but not for resale;

(4) a hospital that obtains a dangerous drug for lawful administration by a practitioner; and

(5) a manufacturer or wholesaler registered with the commissioner of health under Chapter 431 (Texas Food, Drug, and Cosmetic Act).

Acts 1989, 71st Leg., ch. 678, § 1, eff. Sept. 1, 1989.

§ 483.025. Inspections; Inventories

A person required to keep records relating to dangerous drugs shall:

(1) make the records available for inspection and copying at all reasonable hours by any public official or employee engaged in enforcing this chapter; and

(2) allow the official or employee to inventory all stocks of dangerous drugs on hand.

Acts 1989, 71st Leg., ch. 678, § 1, eff. Sept. 1, 1989.

§ 483.026. Repealed by Acts 1989, 71st Leg., ch. 1100, § 5.03(h), eff. Sept. 1, 1989

SUBCHAPTER C. CRIMINAL PENALTIES

§ 483.041. Possession of Dangerous Drug

(a) A person commits an offense if the person possesses a dangerous drug unless the person obtains the drug from a pharmacist acting in the manner described by Section 483.042(a)(1) or a practitioner acting in the manner described by Section 483.042(a)(2).

(b) Except as permitted by this chapter, a person commits an offense if the person possesses a dangerous drug for the purpose of selling the drug.

Text of subsec. (c) effective until Sept. 1, 2010

(c) Subsection (a) does not apply to the possession of a dangerous drug in the usual course of business or practice or in the performance of official duties by the following persons or an agent or employee of the person:

(1) a pharmacy licensed by the board;

(2) a practitioner;

(3) a person who obtains a dangerous drug for lawful research, teaching, or testing, but not for resale;

(4) a hospital that obtains a dangerous drug for lawful administration by a practitioner;

(5) an officer or employee of the federal, state, or local government;

(6) a manufacturer or wholesaler licensed by the Department of State Health Services under Chapter 431 (Texas Food, Drug, and Cosmetic Act);

(7) a carrier or warehouseman;

(8) a home and community support services agency licensed under and acting in accordance with Chapter 142;

(9) a licensed midwife who obtains oxygen for administration to a mother or newborn or who obtains a dangerous drug for the administration of prophylaxis to a newborn for the prevention of ophthalmia neonatorum in accordance with Section 203.353, Occupations Code; or

(10) a salvage broker or salvage operator licensed under Chapter 432.

Text of subsec. (c) effective Sept. 1, 2010

(c) Subsection (a) does not apply to the possession of a dangerous drug in the usual course of business or practice or in the performance of official duties by the following persons or an agent or employee of the person:

(1) a pharmacy licensed by the board;

(2) a practitioner;

(3) a person who obtains a dangerous drug for lawful research, teaching, or testing, but not for resale;

(4) a hospital that obtains a dangerous drug for lawful administration by a practitioner;

(5) an officer or employee of the federal, state, or local government;

(6) a manufacturer or wholesaler licensed by the Department of State Health Services under Chapter 431 (Texas Food, Drug, and Cosmetic Act);

(7) a carrier or warehouseman;

(8) a home and community support services agency licensed under and acting in accordance with Chapter 142;

(9) a licensed midwife who obtains oxygen for administration to a mother or newborn or who obtains a dangerous drug for the administration of prophylaxis to a newborn for the prevention of ophthalmia neonatorum in accordance with Section 203.353, Occupations Code;

(10) a salvage broker or salvage operator licensed under Chapter 432; or

(11) a certified laser hair removal professional under Subchapter M,[1] Chapter 401, who possesses and uses a laser or pulsed light device approved by and registered with the department and in compliance with department rules for the sole purpose of cosmetic nonablative hair removal.

(d) An offense under this section is a Class A misdemeanor.

Acts 1989, 71st Leg., ch. 678, § 1, eff. Sept. 1, 1989. Amended by Acts 1989, 71st Leg., ch. 1100, § 5.03(f), eff. Sept. 1, 1989; Acts 1993, 73rd Leg., ch. 16, § 2, eff. April 2, 1993; Acts 1993, 73rd Leg., ch. 789, § 20, eff. Sept. 1, 1993; Acts 1995, 74th Leg., ch. 307, § 2, eff. Sept. 1, 1995; Acts 1995, 74th Leg., ch. 318, § 41, eff. Sept. 1, 1995; Acts 1997, 75th Leg., ch. 1095, § 19, eff. Sept. 1, 1997; Acts 1997, 75th Leg., ch. 1129, § 2, eff. Sept. 1, 1997; Acts 2001, 77th Leg., ch. 265, § 9, eff. May 22, 2001; Acts 2001, 77th Leg., ch. 1420, § 14.798, eff. Sept. 1, 2001; Acts 2005, 79th Leg., ch. 1240, § 55, eff. Sept. 1, 2005; Acts 2009, 81st Leg., ch. 303, § 2, eff. Sept. 1, 2010.

[1] V.T.C.A., Health and Safety Code § 401.501 et seq.

§ 483.042. Delivery or Offer of Delivery of Dangerous Drug

(a) A person commits an offense if the person delivers or offers to deliver a dangerous drug:

(1) unless:

(A) the dangerous drug is delivered or offered for delivery by a pharmacist under:

(i) a prescription issued by a practitioner described by Section 483.001(12)(A) or (B);

(ii) a prescription signed by a registered nurse or physician assistant in accordance with Subchapter B, Chapter 157, Occupations Code; [1] or

(iii) an original written prescription issued by a practitioner described by Section 483.001(12)(C); and

(B) a label is attached to the immediate container in which the drug is delivered or offered to be delivered and the label contains the following information:

(i) the name and address of the pharmacy from which the drug is delivered or offered for delivery;

(ii) the date the prescription for the drug is dispensed;

(iii) the number of the prescription as filed in the prescription files of the pharmacy from which the prescription is dispensed;

(iv) the name of the practitioner who prescribed the drug and, if applicable, the name of the registered nurse or physician assistant who signed the prescription;

(v) the name of the patient and, if the drug is prescribed for an animal, a statement of the species of the animal; and

(vi) directions for the use of the drug as contained in the prescription; or

(2) unless:

(A) the dangerous drug is delivered or offered for delivery by:

(i) a practitioner in the course of practice; or

(ii) a registered nurse or physician assistant in the course of practice in accordance with Subchapter B, Chapter 157, Occupations Code; [1] and

(B) a label is attached to the immediate container in which the drug is delivered or offered to be delivered and the label contains the following information:

(i) the name and address of the practitioner who prescribed the drug, and if applicable, the name and address of the registered nurse or physician assistant;

(ii) the date the drug is delivered;

(iii) the name of the patient and, if the drug is prescribed for an animal, a statement of the species of the animal; and

(iv) the name of the drug, the strength of the drug, and directions for the use of the drug.

(b) Subsection (a) does not apply to the delivery or offer for delivery of a dangerous drug to a person listed in Section 483.041(c) for use in the usual course of business or practice or in the performance of official duties by the person.

(c) Proof of an offer to sell a dangerous drug must be corroborated by a person other than the offeree or by evidence other than a statement by the offeree.

(d) An offense under this section is a state jail felony.

(e) The labeling provisions of Subsection (a) do not apply to a dangerous drug prescribed or dispensed for administration to a patient who is institutionalized. The board shall adopt rules for the labeling of such a drug.

(f) Provided all federal requirements are met, the labeling provisions of Subsection (a) do not apply to a dangerous drug prescribed or dispensed for administration to food production animals in an agricultural operation under a written medical directive or treatment guideline from a veterinarian licensed under Chapter 801, Occupations Code.

Acts 1989, 71st Leg., ch. 678, § 1, eff. Sept. 1, 1989. Amended by Acts 1989, 71st Leg., ch. 1100, § 5.03(g), eff. Sept. 1, 1989; Acts 1993, 73rd Leg., ch. 287, § 34, eff. Sept. 1, 1993; Acts 1993, 73rd Leg., ch. 789, § 21, eff. Sept. 1, 1993; Acts 1993, 73rd Leg., ch. 900, § 2.04, eff. Sept. 1, 1994; Acts 1995, 74th Leg., ch. 965, § 7, eff. June 16, 1995; Acts 1997, 75th Leg., ch. 1180, § 24, eff. Sept. 1, 1997; Acts 1999, 76th Leg., ch. 1404, § 1, eff. Sept. 1, 1999; Acts 2001, 77th Leg., ch. 1420, § 14.799, eff. Sept. 1, 2001.

[1] V.T.C.A., Occupations Code § 157.051 et seq.

§ 483.043. Manufacture of Dangerous Drug

(a) A person commits an offense if the person manufactures a dangerous drug and the person is not authorized by law to manufacture the drug.

(b) An offense under this section is a state jail felony.

Acts 1989, 71st Leg., ch. 678, § 1, eff. Sept. 1, 1989. Amended by Acts 1993, 73rd Leg., ch. 900, § 2.05, eff. Sept. 1, 1994.

§ 483.044. Repealed by Acts 1989, 71st Leg., ch. 1100, § 5.03(h), eff. Sept. 1, 1989

§ 483.045. Forging or Altering Prescription

(a) A person commits an offense if the person:

(1) forges a prescription or increases the prescribed quantity of a dangerous drug in a prescription;

(2) issues a prescription bearing a forged or fictitious signature;

(3) obtains or attempts to obtain a dangerous drug by using a forged, fictitious, or altered prescription;

(4) obtains or attempts to obtain a dangerous drug by means of a fictitious or fraudulent telephone call; or

(5) possesses a dangerous drug obtained by a forged, fictitious, or altered prescription or by means of a fictitious or fraudulent telephone call.

(b) An offense under this section is a Class B misdemeanor unless it is shown on the trial of the defendant that the defendant has previously been convicted of an offense under this chapter, in which event the offense is a Class A misdemeanor.

Acts 1989, 71st Leg., ch. 678, § 1, eff. Sept. 1, 1989.

§ 483.046. Failure to Retain Prescription

(a) A pharmacist commits an offense if the pharmacist:

(1) delivers a dangerous drug under a prescription; and

(2) fails to retain the prescription as required by Section 483.023.

(b) An offense under this section is a Class B misdemeanor unless it is shown on the trial of the defendant that the defendant has previously been convicted of an offense under this chapter, in which event the offense is a Class A misdemeanor.

Acts 1989, 71st Leg., ch. 678, § 1, eff. Sept. 1, 1989.

§ 483.047. Refilling Prescription Without Authorization

(a) Except as authorized by Subsection (b), a pharmacist commits an offense if the pharmacist refills a prescription unless:

(1) the prescription contains an authorization by the practitioner for the refilling of the prescription,

and the pharmacist refills the prescription in the manner provided by the authorization; or

(2) at the time of refilling the prescription, the pharmacist is authorized to do so by the practitioner who issued the prescription.

(b) A pharmacist may exercise his professional judgment in refilling a prescription for a dangerous drug without the authorization of the prescribing practitioner provided:

(1) failure to refill the prescription might result in an interruption of a therapeutic regimen or create patient suffering;

(2) either:

(A) a natural or manmade disaster has occurred which prohibits the pharmacist from being able to contact the practitioner; or

(B) the pharmacist is unable to contact the practitioner after reasonable effort;

(3) the quantity of drug dispensed does not exceed a 72-hour supply;

(4) the pharmacist informs the patient or the patient's agent at the time of dispensing that the refill is being provided without such authorization and that authorization of the practitioner is required for future refills; and

(5) the pharmacist informs the practitioner of the emergency refill at the earliest reasonable time.

(c) An offense under this section is a Class B misdemeanor unless it is shown on the trial of the defendant that the defendant has previously been convicted under this chapter, in which event the offense is a Class A misdemeanor.

Acts 1989, 71st Leg., ch. 678, § 1, eff. Sept. 1, 1989. Amended by Acts 1993, 73rd Leg., ch. 789, § 22, eff. Sept. 1, 1993.

§ 483.048. Unauthorized Communication of Prescription

(a) An agent of a practitioner commits an offense if the agent communicates by telephone a prescription unless the agent is designated in writing under Section 483.022 as authorized by the practitioner to communicate prescriptions by telephone.

(b) An offense under this section is a Class B misdemeanor unless it is shown on the trial of the defendant that the defendant has previously been convicted of an offense under this chapter, in which event the offense is a Class A misdemeanor.

Acts 1989, 71st Leg., ch. 678, § 1, eff. Sept. 1, 1989.

§ 483.049. Failure to Maintain Records

(a) A person commits an offense if the person is required to maintain a record under Section 483.023 or 483.024 and the person fails to maintain the record in the manner required by those sections.

(b) An offense under this section is a Class B misdemeanor unless it is shown on the trial of the defendant that the defendant has previously been convicted of an offense under this chapter, in which event the offense is a Class A misdemeanor.

Acts 1989, 71st Leg., ch. 678, § 1, eff. Sept. 1, 1989.

§ 483.050. Refusal to Permit Inspection

(a) A person commits an offense if the person is required to permit an inspection authorized by Section 483.025 and fails to permit the inspection in the manner required by that section.

(b) An offense under this section is a Class B misdemeanor unless it is shown on the trial of the defendant that the defendant has previously been convicted of an offense under this chapter, in which event the offense is a Class A misdemeanor.

Acts 1989, 71st Leg., ch. 678, § 1, eff. Sept. 1, 1989.

§ 483.051. Using or Revealing Trade Secret

(a) A person commits an offense if the person uses for the person's advantage or reveals to another person, other than to an officer or employee of the board or to a court in a judicial proceeding relevant to this chapter, information relating to dangerous drugs required to be kept under this chapter, if that information concerns a method or process subject to protection as a trade secret.

(b) An offense under this section is a Class B misdemeanor unless it is shown on the trial of the defendant that the defendant has previously been convicted of an offense under this chapter, in which event the offense is a Class A misdemeanor.

Acts 1989, 71st Leg., ch. 678, § 1, eff. Sept. 1, 1989.

§ 483.052. Violation of Other Provision

(a) A person commits an offense if the person violates a provision of this chapter other than a provision for which a specific offense is otherwise described by this chapter.

(b) An offense under this section is a Class B misdemeanor, unless it is shown on the trial of the defendant that the defendant has previously been convicted of an offense under this chapter, in which event the offense is a Class A misdemeanor.

Acts 1989, 71st Leg., ch. 678, § 1, eff. Sept. 1, 1989.

§ 483.053. Preparatory Offenses

Title 4, Penal Code,[1] applies to an offense under this subchapter.

Added by Acts 1995, 74th Leg., ch. 318, § 40, eff. Sept. 1, 1995.

[1] V.T.C.A., Penal Code § 15.01 et seq.

SUBCHAPTER D. CRIMINAL AND CIVIL PROCEDURE

§ 483.071. Exceptions; Burden of Proof

(a) In a complaint, information, indictment, or other action or proceeding brought for the enforcement of this chapter, the state is not required to negate an exception, excuse, proviso, or exemption contained in this chapter.

(b) The defendant has the burden of proving the exception, excuse, proviso, or exemption.

Acts 1989, 71st Leg., ch. 678, § 1, eff. Sept. 1, 1989.

§ 483.072. Uncorroborated Testimony

A conviction under this chapter may be obtained on the uncorroborated testimony of a party to the offense.

Acts 1989, 71st Leg., ch. 678, § 1, eff. Sept. 1, 1989.

§ 483.073. Search Warrant

A peace officer may apply for a search warrant to search for dangerous drugs possessed in violation of this chapter. The peace officer must apply for and execute the search warrant in the manner prescribed by the Code of Criminal Procedure.

Acts 1989, 71st Leg., ch. 678, § 1, eff. Sept. 1, 1989.

§ 483.074. Seizure and Destruction

(a) A dangerous drug that is manufactured, sold, or possessed in violation of this chapter is contraband and may be seized by an employee of the board or by a peace officer authorized to enforce this chapter and charged with that duty.

(b) If a dangerous drug is seized under Subsection (a), the board may direct an employee of the board or an authorized peace officer to destroy the drug. The employee or authorized peace officer directed to destroy the drug must act in the presence of another employee of the board or authorized peace officer and shall destroy the drug in any manner designated as appropriate by the board.

(c) Before the dangerous drug is destroyed, an inventory of the drug must be prepared. The inventory must be accompanied by a statement that the dangerous drug is being destroyed at the direction of the board, by an employee of the board or an authorized peace officer, and in the presence of another employee of the board or authorized peace officer. The statement must also contain the names of the persons in attendance at the time of destruction, state the capacity in which each of those persons acts, be signed by those persons, and be sworn to by those persons that the statement is correct. The statement shall be filed with the board.

Acts 1989, 71st Leg., ch. 678, § 1, eff. Sept. 1, 1989. Amended by Acts 1991, 72nd Leg., ch. 237, § 12, eff. Sept. 1, 1991.

§ 483.075. Injunction

The board may institute an action in its own name to enjoin a violation of this chapter.

Acts 1989, 71st Leg., ch. 678, § 1, eff. Sept. 1, 1989.

§ 483.076. Legal Representation of Board

(a) If the board institutes a legal proceeding under this chapter, the board may be represented only by a county attorney, a district attorney, or the attorney general.

(b) The board may not employ private counsel in any legal proceeding instituted by or against the board under this chapter.

Acts 1989, 71st Leg., ch. 678, § 1, eff. Sept. 1, 1989.

CHAPTER 485. ABUSABLE VOLATILE CHEMICALS

SUBCHAPTER A. GENERAL PROVISIONS

SUBCHAPTER A. GENERAL PROVISIONS

§ 485.001. Definitions

In this chapter:

(1) "Abusable volatile chemical " means:

(A) a chemical, including aerosol paint, that:

(i) is packaged in a container subject to the labeling requirements concerning precautions against inhalation established under the Federal Hazardous Substances Act (15 U.S.C. Section 1261 et seq.), as amended, and regulations adopted under that Act and is labeled with the statement of principal hazard on the principal display panel "VAPOR HARMFUL" or other labeling requirement subsequently established under that Act or those regulations;

(ii) when inhaled, ingested, or otherwise introduced into a person's body, may:

(a) affect the person's central nervous system;

(b) create or induce in the person a condition of intoxication, hallucination, or elation; or

(c) change, distort, or disturb the person's eyesight, thinking process, balance, or coordination; and

(iii) is not:

(a) a pesticide subject to Chapter 76, Agriculture Code, or to the Federal Environmental Pesticide Control Act of 1972 (7 U.S.C. Section 136 et seq.), as amended;

(b) a food, drug, or cosmetic subject to Chapter 431 or to the Federal Food, Drug, and Cosmetic Act (21 U.S.C. Section 301 et seq.), as amended; or

(c) a beverage subject to the Federal Alcohol Administration Act (27 U. S.C. Section 201 et seq.), as amended; or

(B) nitrous oxide that is not:

(i) a pesticide subject to Chapter 76, Agriculture Code, or to the Federal Environmental Pesticide Control Act of 1972 (7 U.S.C. Section 136 et seq.), as amended;

(ii) a food, drug, or cosmetic subject to Chapter 431 or to the Federal Food, Drug, and Cosmetic Act (21 U.S.C. Section 301 et seq.), as amended; or

(iii) a beverage subject to the Federal Alcohol Administration Act (27 U.S.C. Section 201 et seq.), as amended.

(2) "Aerosol paint" means an aerosolized paint product, including a clear or pigmented lacquer or finish.

(3) "Board" means the Texas Board of Health.

(4) "Commissioner" means the commissioner of health.

(5) "Deliver" means to make the actual or constructive transfer from one person to another of an abusable volatile chemical, regardless of whether there is an agency relationship. The term includes an offer to sell an abusable volatile chemical.

(6) "Delivery" means the act of delivering.

(7) "Department" means the Texas Department of Health.

(8) "Inhalant paraphernalia" means equipment or materials of any kind that are intended for use in inhaling, ingesting, or otherwise introducing into the human body an abusable volatile chemical. The term includes a tube, balloon, bag, fabric, bottle, or other container used to concentrate or hold in suspension an abusable volatile chemical or vapors of the chemical.

(9) "Sell" includes a conveyance, exchange, barter, or trade.

Acts 1989, 71st Leg., ch. 678, § 1, eff. Sept. 1, 1989. Amended by Acts 2001, 77th Leg., ch. 1463, § 2, eff. Sept. 1, 2001.

§ 485.002. Rules

The board may adopt rules necessary to comply with any labeling requirements concerning precautions against inhalation of an abusable volatile chemical established under the Federal Hazardous Substances Act (15 U.S.C. Section 1261 et seq.), as amended, or under regulations adopted under that Act.

Added by Acts 2001, 77th Leg., ch. 1463, § 2, eff. Sept. 1, 2001.

SUBCHAPTER B. SALES PERMITS AND SIGNS

§ 485.011. Permit Required

A person may not sell an abusable volatile chemical at retail unless the person or the person's employer holds, at the time of the sale, a volatile chemical sales permit for the location of the sale.

Acts 1989, 71st Leg., ch. 678, § 1, eff. Sept. 1, 1989. Renumbered from V.T.C.A., Health & Safety Code § 485.012 and amended by Acts 2001, 77th Leg., ch. 1463, § 2, eff. Sept. 1, 2001.

§ 485.012. Issuance and Renewal of Permit

(a) To be eligible for the issuance or renewal of a volatile chemical sales permit, a person must:

(1) hold a sales tax permit that has been issued to the person;

(2) complete and return to the department an application as required by the department; and

(3) pay to the department the application fee established under Section 485.013 for each location at which an abusable volatile chemical may be sold by the person holding a volatile chemical sales permit.

(b) The board shall adopt rules as necessary to administer this chapter, including application procedures and procedures by which the department shall give each permit holder reasonable notice of permit expiration and renewal requirements.

(c) The department shall issue or deny a permit and notify the applicant of the department's action not later than the 60th day after the date on which the department receives the complete application and appropriate fee. If the department denies an application, the department shall include in the notice the reasons for the denial.

(d) A permit issued or renewed under this chapter is valid for one year from the date of issuance or renewal.

(e) A permit is not valid if the permit holder has been convicted more than once in the preceding year of an offense committed:

(1) at a location for which the permit is issued; and

(2) under Section 485.031, 485.032, or 485.033.

(f) A permit issued by the department is the property of the department and must be surrendered on demand by the department.

(g) The department shall prepare an annual roster of permit holders.

(h) The department shall monitor and enforce compliance with this chapter.

Acts 1989, 71st Leg., ch. 678, § 1, eff. Sept. 1, 1989. Amended by Acts 1991, 72nd Leg., ch. 14, § 203, eff. Sept. 1, 1991. Renumbered from V.T.C.A., Health & Safety Code § 485.013 and amended by Acts 2001, 77th Leg., ch. 1463, § 2, eff. Sept. 1, 2001.

§ 485.013. Fee

The board by rule may establish fees in amounts not to exceed $25 for the issuance of a permit under this chapter.

Added by Acts 2001, 77th Leg., ch. 1463, § 2, eff. Sept. 1, 2001.

§ 485.014. Permit Available for Inspection

A permit holder must have the volatile chemical sales permit or a copy of the permit available for inspection by the public at each location where the permit holder sells an abusable volatile chemical.

Acts 1989, 71st Leg., ch. 678, § 1, eff. Sept. 1, 1989. Amended by Acts 2001, 77th Leg., ch. 1463, § 2, eff. Sept. 1, 2001.

§ 485.015. Refusal to Issue or Renew Permit

A proceeding for the failure to issue or renew a volatile chemical sales permit under Section 485.012 or for an appeal from that proceeding is governed by the contested case provisions of Chapter 2001, Government Code.

Acts 1989, 71st Leg., ch. 678, § 1, eff. Sept. 1, 1989. Amended by Acts 1995, 74th Leg., ch. 76, § 5.95(49), eff. Sept. 1, 1995; Acts 2001, 77th Leg., ch. 1463, § 2, eff. Sept. 1, 2001.

§ 485.016. Disposition of Funds; Education and Prevention Programs

(a) The department shall account for all amounts received under Section 485.013 and send those amounts to the comptroller.

(b) The comptroller shall deposit the amounts received under Subsection (a) in the state treasury to the credit of the general revenue fund to be used only by the department to:

(1) administer, monitor, and enforce this chapter; and

(2) finance statewide education projects concerning the hazards of abusable volatile chemicals and the prevention of inhalant abuse.

Acts 1989, 71st Leg., ch. 678, § 1, eff. Sept. 1, 1989. Amended by Acts 1991, 72nd Leg., ch. 14, § 204, eff. Sept. 1, 1991; Acts 2001, 77th Leg., ch. 1463, § 2, eff. Sept. 1, 2001.

§ 485.017. Signs

A business establishment that sells an abusable volatile chemical at retail shall display a conspicuous sign, in English and Spanish, that states the following:

It is unlawful for a person to sell or deliver an abusable volatile chemical to a person under 18 years of age. Except in limited situations, such an offense is a state jail felony.

It is also unlawful for a person to abuse a volatile chemical by inhaling, ingesting, applying, using, or possessing with intent to inhale, ingest, apply, or use a volatile chemical in a manner designed to affect the central nervous system. Such an offense is a Class B misdemeanor.

Acts 1989, 71st Leg., ch. 678, § 1, eff. Sept. 1, 1989. Amended by Acts 2001, 77th Leg., ch. 1463, § 2, eff. Sept. 1, 2001.

§ 485.018. Prohibited Ordinance and Rule

(a) A political subdivision or an agency of this state may not enact an ordinance or rule that requires a business establishment to display an abusable volatile chemical, other than aerosol paint, in a manner that makes the chemical accessible to patrons of the business only with the assistance of personnel of the business.

(b) This section does not apply to an ordinance or rule that was enacted before September 1, 1989.

Added by Acts 1991, 72nd Leg., ch. 14, § 205, eff. Sept. 1, 1991. Amended by Acts 2001, 77th Leg., ch. 1463, § 2, eff. Sept. 1, 2001; Acts 2009, 81st Leg., ch. 1130, § 28, eff. Sept. 1, 2009.

§ 485.019. Restriction of Access to Aerosol Paint

(a) A business establishment that holds a permit under Section 485.012 and that displays aerosol paint shall display the paint:

(1) in a place that is in the line of sight of a cashier or in the line of sight from a workstation normally continuously occupied during business hours;

(2) in a manner that makes the paint accessible to a patron of the business establishment only with the assistance of an employee of the establishment; or

(3) in an area electronically protected, or viewed by surveillance equipment that is monitored, during business hours.

(b) This section does not apply to a business establishment that has in place a computerized checkout system at the point of sale for merchandise that alerts the cashier that a person purchasing aerosol paint must be over 18 years of age.

(c) A court may issue a warning to a business establishment or impose a civil penalty of $50 on the business establishment for a first violation of this section. After receiving a warning or penalty for the first violation, the business establishment is liable to the state for a civil penalty of $100 for each subsequent violation.

(d) For the third violation of this section in a calendar year, a court may issue an injunction prohibiting the business establishment from selling aerosol paint for a period of not more than two years. A business establishment that violates the injunction is liable to the state for a civil penalty of $100, in addition to any other penalty authorized by law, for each day the violation continues.

(e) If a business establishment fails to pay a civil penalty under this section, the court may issue an injunction prohibiting the establishment from selling aerosol paint until the establishment pays the penalty, attorney's fees, and court costs.

(f) The district or county attorney for the county in which a violation of this section is alleged to have occurred, or the attorney general, if requested by the district or county attorney for that county, may file suit for the issuance of a warning, the collection of a penalty, or the issuance of an injunction.

(g) A penalty collected under this section shall be sent to the comptroller for deposit in the state treasury to the credit of the general revenue fund.

(h) This section applies only to a business establishment that is located in a county with a population of 75,000 or more.

Added by Acts 1997, 75th Leg., ch. 593, § 4, eff. Sept. 1, 1997. Amended by Acts 2001, 77th Leg., ch. 1463, § 2, eff. Sept. 1, 2001.

SUBCHAPTER C. CRIMINAL PENALTIES

§ 485.031. Possession and Use

(a) A person commits an offense if the person inhales, ingests, applies, uses, or possesses an abusable volatile chemical with intent to inhale, ingest, apply, or use the chemical in a manner:

(1) contrary to directions for use, cautions, or warnings appearing on a label of a container of the chemical; and

(2) designed to:

(A) affect the person's central nervous system;

(B) create or induce a condition of intoxication, hallucination, or elation; or

(C) change, distort, or disturb the person's eyesight, thinking process, balance, or coordination.

(b) An offense under this section is a Class B misdemeanor.

Acts 1989, 71st Leg., ch. 678, § 1, eff. Sept. 1, 1989. Amended by Acts 2001, 77th Leg., ch. 1463, § 2, eff. Sept. 1, 2001.

§ 485.032. Delivery to a Minor

(a) A person commits an offense if the person knowingly delivers an abusable volatile chemical to a person who is younger than 18 years of age.

(b) It is a defense to prosecution under this section that:

(1) the abusable volatile chemical that was delivered contains additive material that effectively discourages intentional abuse by inhalation; or

(2) the person making the delivery is not the manufacturer of the chemical and the manufacturer of the chemical failed to label the chemical with the statement of principal hazard on the principal display panel "VAPOR HARMFUL" or other labeling requirement subsequently established under the Federal Hazardous Substances Act (15 U.S.C. Section 1261 et seq.), as amended, or regulations subsequently adopted under that Act.

(c) It is an affirmative defense to prosecution under this section that:

(1) the person making the delivery is an adult having supervisory responsibility over the person younger than 18 years of age and:

(A) the adult permits the use of the abusable volatile chemical only under the adult's direct supervision and in the adult's presence and only for its intended purpose; and

(B) the adult removes the chemical from the person younger than 18 years of age on completion of that use; or

(2) the person to whom the abusable volatile chemical was delivered presented to the defendant an apparently valid Texas driver's license or an identification certificate, issued by the Department of Public Safety of the State of Texas and containing a physical description consistent with the person's appearance, that purported to establish that the person was 18 years of age or older.

(d) Except as provided by Subsections (e) and (f), an offense under this section is a state jail felony.

(e) An offense under this section is a Class B misdemeanor if it is shown on the trial of the defendant that at the time of the delivery the defendant or the defendant's employer held a volatile chemical sales permit for the location of the sale.

(f) An offense under this section is a Class A misdemeanor if it is shown on the trial of the defendant that at the time of the delivery the defendant or the defendant's employer:

(1) did not hold a volatile chemical sales permit but did hold a sales tax permit for the location of the sale; and

(2) had not been convicted previously under this section for an offense committed after January 1, 1988.

Acts 1989, 71st Leg., ch. 678, § 1, eff. Sept. 1, 1989. Amended by Acts 1993, 73rd Leg., ch. 900, § 2.06, eff. Sept. 1, 1994. Renumbered from V.T.C.A., Health & Safety Code § 485.033 and amended by Acts 2001, 77th Leg., ch. 1463, § 2, eff. Sept. 1, 2001.

§ 485.033. Inhalant Paraphernalia

(a) A person commits an offense if the person knowingly uses or possesses with intent to use inhalant paraphernalia to inhale, ingest, or otherwise introduce into the human body an abusable volatile chemical in violation of Section 485.031.

(b) A person commits an offense if the person:

(1) knowingly:

(A) delivers or sells inhalant paraphernalia;

(B) possesses, with intent to deliver or sell, inhalant paraphernalia; or

(C) manufactures, with intent to deliver or sell, inhalant paraphernalia; and

(2) at the time of the act described by Subdivision (1), knows that the person who receives or is intended to receive the paraphernalia intends that it be used to inhale, ingest, apply, use, or otherwise introduce into the human body a volatile chemical in violation of Section 485.031.

(c) An offense under Subsection (a) is a Class B misdemeanor, and an offense under Subsection (b) is a Class A misdemeanor.

Acts 1989, 71st Leg., ch. 678, § 1, eff. Sept. 1, 1989. Amended by Acts 1991, 72nd Leg., ch. 14, § 206, eff. Sept. 1, 1991. Renumbered from V.T.C.A., Health & Safety Code § 485.034 and amended by Acts 2001, 77th Leg., ch. 1463, § 2, eff. Sept. 1, 2001.

§ 485.034. Failure to Post Sign

(a) A person commits an offense if the person sells an abusable volatile chemical in a business establishment and the person does not display the sign required by Section 485.017.

(b) An offense under this section is a Class C misdemeanor.

Acts 1989, 71st Leg., ch. 678, § 1, eff. Sept. 1, 1989. Renumbered from V.T.C.A., Health & Safety Code § 485.035 and amended by Acts 2001, 77th Leg., ch. 1463, § 2, eff. Sept. 1, 2001.

§ 485.035. Sale Without Permit

(a) A person commits an offense if the person sells an abusable volatile chemical in violation of Section 485.011 and the purchaser is 18 years of age or older.

(b) An offense under this section is a Class B misdemeanor.

Acts 1989, 71st Leg., ch. 678, § 1, eff. Sept. 1, 1989. Renumbered from V.T.C.A., Health & Safety Code § 485.036 and amended by Acts 2001, 77th Leg., ch. 1463, § 2, eff. Sept. 1, 2001.

§ 485.036. Proof of Offer to Sell

Proof of an offer to sell an abusable volatile chemical must be corroborated by a person other than the offeree or by evidence other than a statement of the offeree.

Acts 1989, 71st Leg., ch. 678, § 1, eff. Sept. 1, 1989. Renumbered from V.T.C.A., Health & Safety Code § 485.037 and amended by Acts 2001, 77th Leg., ch. 1463, § 2, eff. Sept. 1, 2001.

§ 485.037. Summary Forfeiture

An abusable volatile chemical or inhalant paraphernalia seized as a result of an offense under this chapter is subject to summary forfeiture and to destruction or disposition in the same manner as controlled substance property under Subchapter E, Chapter 481.[1]

Added by Acts 1991, 72nd Leg., ch. 141, § 5, eff. Sept. 1, 1991. Renumbered from V.T.C.A., Health & Safety Code § 485.038 and amended by Acts 2001, 77th Leg., ch. 1463, § 2, eff. Sept. 1, 2001.

[1] V.T.C.A., Health & Safety Code § 481.151 et seq.

§ 485.038. Preparatory Offenses

Title 4, Penal Code,[1] applies to an offense under this subchapter.

Added by Acts 1995, 74th Leg., ch. 318, § 43, eff. Sept. 1, 1995. Renumbered from V.T.C.A., Health & Safety Code § 485.039 by Acts 2001, 77th Leg., ch. 1463, § 2, eff. Sept. 1, 2001.

[1] V.T.C.A., Penal Code § 15.01 et seq.

§ 485.039. Renumbered as V.T.C.A., Health & Safety Code § 485.038 by Acts 2001, 77th Leg., ch. 1463, § 2, eff. Sept. 1, 2001

SUBCHAPTER D. ADMINISTRATIVE PENALTY

§ 485.101. Imposition of Penalty

(a) The department may impose an administrative penalty on a person who sells abusable glue or aerosol paint at retail who violates this chapter or a rule or order adopted under this chapter.

(b) A penalty collected under this subchapter shall be deposited in the state treasury in the general revenue fund.

Added by Acts 1999, 76th Leg., ch. 1411, § 6.01, eff. Sept. 1, 1999.

§ 485.102. Amount of Penalty

(a) The amount of the penalty may not exceed $1,000 for each violation, and each day a violation continues or occurs is a separate violation for purposes of imposing a penalty. The total amount of the penalty assessed for a violation continuing or occurring on separate days under this subsection may not exceed $5,000.

(b) The amount shall be based on:

(1) the seriousness of the violation, including the nature, circumstances, extent, and gravity of the violation;

(2) the threat to health or safety caused by the violation;

(3) the history of previous violations;

(4) the amount necessary to deter a future violation;

(5) whether the violator demonstrated good faith, including when applicable whether the violator made good faith efforts to correct the violation; and

(6) any other matter that justice may require.

Added by Acts 1999, 76th Leg., ch. 1411, § 6.01, eff. Sept. 1, 1999.

§ 485.103. Report and Notice of Violation and Penalty

(a) If the department initially determines that a violation occurred, the department shall give written notice of the report by certified mail to the person.

(b) The notice must:

(1) include a brief summary of the alleged violation;

(2) state the amount of the recommended penalty; and

(3) inform the person of the person's right to a hearing on the occurrence of the violation, the amount of the penalty, or both.

Added by Acts 1999, 76th Leg., ch. 1411, § 6.01, eff. Sept. 1, 1999.

§ 485.104. Penalty to be Paid or Hearing Requested

(a) Within 20 days after the date the person receives the notice sent under Section 485.103, the person in writing may:

(1) accept the determination and recommended penalty of the department; or

(2) make a request for a hearing on the occurrence of the violation, the amount of the penalty, or both.

(b) If the person accepts the determination and recommended penalty or if the person fails to respond to the notice, the commissioner by order shall approve the determination and impose the recommended penalty.

Added by Acts 1999, 76th Leg., ch. 1411, § 6.01, eff. Sept. 1, 1999.

§ 485.105. Hearing

(a) If the person requests a hearing, the commissioner shall refer the matter to the State Office of Administrative Hearings, which shall promptly set a hearing date and give written notice of the time and place of the hearing to the person. An administrative law judge of the State Office of Administrative Hearings shall conduct the hearing.

(b) The administrative law judge shall make findings of fact and conclusions of law and promptly issue to the commissioner a proposal for a decision about the occurrence of the violation and the amount of a proposed penalty.

Added by Acts 1999, 76th Leg., ch. 1411, § 6.01, eff. Sept. 1, 1999.

§ 485.106. Decision by Commissioner

(a) Based on the findings of fact, conclusions of law, and proposal for a decision, the commissioner by order may:

(1) find that a violation occurred and impose a penalty; or

(2) find that a violation did not occur.

(b) The notice of the commissioner's order under Subsection (a) that is sent to the person in accordance with Chapter 2001, Government Code, must include a statement of the right of the person to judicial review of the order.

Added by Acts 1999, 76th Leg., ch. 1411, § 6.01, eff. Sept. 1, 1999.

§ 485.107. Options Following Decision: Pay or Appeal

Within 30 days after the date the order of the commissioner under Section 485.106 that imposes an administrative penalty becomes final, the person shall:

(1) pay the penalty; or

(2) file a petition for judicial review of the commissioner's order contesting the occurrence of the violation, the amount of the penalty, or both.

Added by Acts 1999, 76th Leg., ch. 1411, § 6.01, eff. Sept. 1, 1999.

§ 485.108. Stay of Enforcement of Penalty

(a) Within the 30-day period prescribed by Section 485.107, a person who files a petition for judicial review may:

(1) stay enforcement of the penalty by:

(A) paying the penalty to the court for placement in an escrow account; or

(B) giving the court a supersedeas bond approved by the court that:

(i) is for the amount of the penalty; and

(ii) is effective until all judicial review of the commissioner's order is final; or

(2) request the court to stay enforcement of the penalty by:

(A) filing with the court a sworn affidavit of the person stating that the person is financially unable to pay the penalty and is financially unable to give the supersedeas bond; and

(B) sending a copy of the affidavit to the commissioner by certified mail.

(b) If the commissioner receives a copy of an affidavit under Subsection (a)(2), the commissioner may file with the court, within five days after the date the copy is received, a contest to the affidavit. The court shall hold a hearing on the facts alleged in the affidavit as soon as practicable and shall stay the enforcement of the penalty on finding that the alleged facts are true. The person who files an affidavit has the burden of proving that the person is financially unable to pay the penalty or to give a supersedeas bond.

Added by Acts 1999, 76th Leg., ch. 1411, § 6.01, eff. Sept. 1, 1999.

§ 485.109. Collection of Penalty

(a) If the person does not pay the penalty and the enforcement of the penalty is not stayed, the penalty may be collected.

(b) The attorney general may sue to collect the penalty.

Added by Acts 1999, 76th Leg., ch. 1411, § 6.01, eff. Sept. 1, 1999.

§ 485.110. Decision by Court

(a) If the court sustains the finding that a violation occurred, the court may uphold or reduce the amount of the penalty and order the person to pay the full or reduced amount of the penalty.

(b) If the court does not sustain the finding that a violation occurred, the court shall order that a penalty is not owed.

Added by Acts 1999, 76th Leg., ch. 1411, § 6.01, eff. Sept. 1, 1999.

§ 485.111. Remittance of Penalty and Interest

(a) If the person paid the penalty and if the amount of the penalty is reduced or the penalty is not upheld by the court, the court shall order, when the court's judgment becomes final, that the appropriate amount plus accrued interest be remitted to the person within 30 days after the date that the judgment of the court becomes final.

(b) The interest accrues at the rate charged on loans to depository institutions by the New York Federal Reserve Bank.

(c) The interest shall be paid for the period beginning on the date the penalty is paid and ending on the date the penalty is remitted.

Added by Acts 1999, 76th Leg., ch. 1411, § 6.01, eff. Sept. 1, 1999.

§ 485.112. Release of Bond

(a) If the person gave a supersedeas bond and the penalty is not upheld by the court, the court shall order, when the court's judgment becomes final, the release of the bond.

(b) If the person gave a supersedeas bond and the amount of the penalty is reduced, the court shall order the release of the bond after the person pays the reduced amount.

Added by Acts 1999, 76th Leg., ch. 1411, § 6.01, eff. Sept. 1, 1999.

§ 485.113. Administrative Procedure

A proceeding to impose the penalty is considered to be a contested case under Chapter 2001, Government Code.

Added by Acts 1999, 76th Leg., ch. 1411, § 6.01, eff. Sept. 1, 1999.

CHAPTER 486. OVER–THE–COUNTER SALES OF EPHEDRINE, PSEUDOEPHEDRINE, AND NORPSEUDOEPHEDRINE

SUBCHAPTER A. GENERAL PROVISIONS

§ 486.001. Definitions

(a) In this chapter:

(1) "Commissioner" means the commissioner of state health services.

(2) "Council" means the State Health Services Council.

(3) "Department" means the Department of State Health Services.

(4) "Ephedrine," "pseudoephedrine," and "norpseudoephedrine" mean any compound, mixture, or preparation containing any detectable amount of that substance, including its salts, optical isomers, and salts of optical isomers. The term does not include any compound, mixture, or preparation that is in liquid, liquid capsule, or liquid gel capsule form.

(5) "Sale" includes a conveyance, exchange, barter, or trade.

(b) A term that is used in this chapter but is not defined by Subsection (a) has the meaning assigned by Section 481.002.

Added by Acts 2005, 79th Leg., ch. 282, § 9, eff. Aug. 1, 2005.

§ 486.002. Applicability

This chapter does not apply to the sale of any product dispensed or delivered by a pharmacist according to a prescription issued by a practitioner for a valid medical purpose and in the course of professional practice.

Added by Acts 2005, 79th Leg., ch. 282, § 9, eff. Aug. 1, 2005.

§ 486.003. Rules

The council shall adopt rules necessary to implement and enforce this chapter.

Added by Acts 2005, 79th Leg., ch. 282, § 9, eff. Aug. 1, 2005.

§ 486.004. Fees

(a) The department shall collect fees for:

(1) the issuance of a certificate of authority under this chapter; and

(2) an inspection performed in enforcing this chapter and rules adopted under this chapter.

(b) The commissioner by rule shall set the fees in amounts that allow the department to recover the biennial expenditures of state funds by the department in:

(1) reviewing applications for the issuance of a certificate of authority under this chapter;

(2) issuing certificates of authority under this chapter;

(3) inspecting and auditing a business establishment that is issued a certificate of authority under this chapter; and

(4) otherwise implementing enforcing this chapter.

(c) Fees collected under this section shall be deposited to the credit of a special account in the general revenue fund and appropriated to the department to implement and enforce this chapter.

Added by Acts 2005, 79th Leg., ch. 282, § 9, eff. Aug. 1, 2005.

§ 486.005. Statewide Application and Uniformity

(a) To ensure uniform and equitable implementation and enforcement throughout this state, this chapter constitutes the whole field of regulation regarding over-the-counter sales of products that contain ephedrine, pseudoephedrine, or norpseudoephedrine.

(b) This chapter preempts and supersedes a local ordinance, rule, or regulation adopted by a political subdivision of this state pertaining to over-the-counter sales of products that contain ephedrine, pseudoephedrine, or norpseudoephedrine.

(c) This section does not preclude a political subdivision from imposing administrative sanctions on the holder of a business or professional license or permit issued by the political subdivision who engages in conduct that violates this chapter.

Added by Acts 2005, 79th Leg., ch. 282, § 9, eff. Aug. 1, 2005.

SUBCHAPTER B. OVER–THE–COUNTER SALES

§ 486.011. Sales by Pharmacies

A business establishment that operates a pharmacy licensed by the Texas State Board of Pharmacy may engage in over-the-counter sales of ephedrine, pseudoephedrine, and norpseudoephedrine.

Added by Acts 2005, 79th Leg., ch. 282, § 9, eff. Aug. 1, 2005.

§ 486.012. Sales by Establishments Other Than Pharmacies; Certificate of Authority

(a) A business establishment that does not operate a pharmacy licensed by the Texas State Board of Pharmacy may engage in over-the-counter sales of ephedrine, pseudoephedrine, or norpseudoephedrine only if the establishment holds a certificate of authority issued under this section.

(b) The department may issue a certificate of authority to engage in over-the-counter sales of ephedrine, pseudoephedrine, and norpseudoephedrine to a business establishment that does not operate a pharmacy licensed by the Texas State Board of Pharmacy if the establishment:

(1) applies to the department for the certificate in accordance with department rule; and

(2) complies with the requirements established by the department for issuance of a certificate.

(c) The department by rule shall establish requirements for the issuance of a certificate of authority under this section. The rules must include a consideration by the department of whether the establishment:

(1) complies with the requirements of the Texas State Board of Pharmacy for the issuance of a license to operate a pharmacy;

(2) sells a wide variety of healthcare products; and

(3) employs sales techniques and other measures designed to deter the theft of products containing ephedrine, pseudoephedrine, or norpseudoephedrine and other items used in the manufacture of methamphetamine.

(d) The department may inspect or audit a business establishment that is issued a certificate of authority under this section at any time the department determines necessary.

Added by Acts 2005, 79th Leg., ch. 282, § 9, eff. Aug. 1, 2005.

§ 486.013. Restriction of Access to Ephedrine, Pseudoephedrine, and Norpseudoephedrine

A business establishment that engages in over-the-counter sales of products containing ephedrine, pseudoephedrine, or norpseudoephedrine shall:

(1) if the establishment operates a pharmacy licensed by the Texas State Board of Pharmacy, maintain those products:

(A) behind the pharmacy counter; or

(B) in a locked case within 30 feet and in a direct line of sight from a pharmacy counter staffed by an employee of the establishment; or

(2) if the establishment does not operate a pharmacy licensed by the Texas State Board of Pharmacy, maintain those products:

(A) behind a sales counter; or

(B) in a locked case within 30 feet and in a direct line of sight from a sales counter continuously staffed by an employee of the establishment.

Added by Acts 2005, 79th Leg., ch. 282, § 9, eff. Aug. 1, 2005.

§ 486.014. Prerequisites to Sale

Before completing an over-the-counter sale of a product containing ephedrine, pseudoephedrine, or norpseudoephedrine, a business establishment that engages in those sales shall:

(1) require the person making the purchase to:

(A) display a driver's license or other form of identification containing the person's photograph and indicating that the person is 16 years of age or older; and

(B) sign for the purchase;

(2) make a record of the sale, including the name of the person making the purchase, the date of the purchase, and the item and number of grams purchased; and

(3) take actions necessary to prevent a person who makes over-the-counter purchases of one or more products containing ephedrine, pseudoephedrine, or norpseudoephedrine from obtaining from the establishment in a single transaction more than:

(A) two packages of those products; or

(B) six grams of ephedrine, pseudoephedrine, norpseudoephedrine, or a combination of those substances.

Added by Acts 2005, 79th Leg., ch. 282, § 9, eff. Aug. 1, 2005.

§ 486.015. Maintenance of Records

The business establishment shall maintain each record made under Section 486.014(2) until at least the second anniversary of the date the record is made and shall make each record available on request by the department or the Department of Public Safety.

Added by Acts 2005, 79th Leg., ch. 282, § 9, eff. Aug. 1, 2005.

SUBCHAPTER C. ADMINISTRATIVE PENALTY

§ 486.021. Imposition of Penalty

The department may impose an administrative penalty on a person who violates this chapter.

Added by Acts 2005, 79th Leg., ch. 282, § 9, eff. Aug. 1, 2005.

§ 486.022. Amount of Penalty

(a) The amount of the penalty may not exceed $1,000 for each violation, and each day a violation continues or occurs is a separate violation for purposes of imposing a penalty. The total amount of the penalty assessed for a violation continuing or occurring on separate days under this subsection may not exceed $20,000.

(b) The amount shall be based on:

(1) the seriousness of the violation, including the nature, circumstances, extent, and gravity of the violation;

(2) the threat to health or safety caused by the violation;

(3) the history of previous violations;

(4) the amount necessary to deter a future violation;

(5) whether the violator demonstrated good faith, including when applicable whether the violator made good faith efforts to correct the violation; and

(6) any other matter that justice may require.

Added by Acts 2005, 79th Leg., ch. 282, § 9, eff. Aug. 1, 2005.

§ 486.023. Report and Notice of Violation and Penalty

(a) If the department initially determines that a violation occurred, the department shall give written notice of the report by certified mail to the person.

(b) The notice must:

(1) include a brief summary of the alleged violation;

(2) state the amount of the recommended penalty; and

(3) inform the person of the person's right to a hearing on the occurrence of the violation, the amount of the penalty, or both.

Added by Acts 2005, 79th Leg., ch. 282, § 9, eff. Aug. 1, 2005.

§ 486.024. Penalty to be Paid or Hearing Requested

(a) Before the 21st day after the date the person receives notice under Section 486.023, the person in writing may:

(1) accept the determination and recommended penalty; or

(2) make a request for a hearing on the occurrence of the violation, the amount of the penalty, or both.

(b) If the person accepts the determination and recommended penalty or if the person fails to respond to the notice, the commissioner by order shall approve the determination.

Added by Acts 2005, 79th Leg., ch. 282, § 9, eff. Aug. 1, 2005.

§ 486.025. Hearing

(a) If the person requests a hearing, the commissioner shall refer the matter to the State Office of Administrative Hearings, which shall promptly set a hearing date and give written notice of the time and place of the hearing to the person. An administrative law judge of the State Office of Administrative Hearings shall conduct the hearing.

(b) The administrative law judge shall make findings of fact and conclusions of law and promptly issue to the commissioner a proposal for a decision about the occurrence of the violation and the amount of a proposed penalty.

Added by Acts 2005, 79th Leg., ch. 282, § 9, eff. Aug. 1, 2005.

§ 486.026. Decision

(a) Based on the findings of fact, conclusions of law, and proposal for a decision, the commissioner by order may:

(1) find that a violation occurred and impose a penalty; or

(2) find that a violation did not occur.

(b) The notice of the commissioner's order under Subsection (a) that is sent to the person in the manner provided by Chapter 2001, Government Code, must include a statement of the right of the person to judicial review of the order.

Added by Acts 2005, 79th Leg., ch. 282, § 9, eff. Aug. 1, 2005.

§ 486.027. Options Following Decision: Pay or Appeal

Before the 31st day after the date the order under Section 486.026 that imposes an administrative penalty becomes final, the person shall:

(1) pay the penalty; or

(2) file a petition for judicial review of the order contesting the occurrence of the violation, the amount of the penalty, or both.

Added by Acts 2005, 79th Leg., ch. 282, § 9, eff. Aug. 1, 2005.

§ 486.028. Stay of Enforcement of Penalty

(a) Within the period prescribed by Section 486.027, a person who files a petition for judicial review may:

(1) stay enforcement of the penalty by:

(A) paying the amount of the penalty to the court for placement in an escrow account; or

(B) giving the court a supersedeas bond approved by the court that:

(i) is for the amount of the penalty; and

(ii) is effective until all judicial review of the order is final; or

(2) request the court to stay enforcement of the penalty by:

(A) filing with the court an affidavit of the person stating that the person is financially unable to pay the penalty and is financially unable to give the supersedeas bond; and

(B) sending a copy of the affidavit to the commissioner by certified mail.

(b) Following receipt of a copy of an affidavit under Subsection (a)(2), the commissioner may file with the court, before the sixth day after the date of receipt, a contest to the affidavit. The court shall hold a hearing on the facts alleged in the affidavit as soon as practicable and shall stay the enforcement of the penalty on finding that the alleged facts are true. The person who files an affidavit has the burden of proving that the person is financially unable to pay the penalty or to give a supersedeas bond.

Added by Acts 2005, 79th Leg., ch. 282, § 9, eff. Aug. 1, 2005.

§ 486.029. Collection of Penalty

(a) If the person does not pay the penalty and the enforcement of the penalty is not stayed, the penalty may be collected.

(b) The attorney general may sue to collect the penalty.

Added by Acts 2005, 79th Leg., ch. 282, § 9, eff. Aug. 1, 2005.

§ 486.030. Decision by Court

(a) If the court sustains the finding that a violation occurred, the court may uphold or reduce the amount of the penalty and order the person to pay the full or reduced amount of the penalty.

(b) If the court does not sustain the finding that a violation occurred, the court shall order that a penalty is not owed.

Added by Acts 2005, 79th Leg., ch. 282, § 9, eff. Aug. 1, 2005.

§ 486.031. Remittance of Penalty and Interest

(a) If the person paid the penalty and if the amount of the penalty is reduced or the penalty is not upheld by the court, the court shall order, when the court's judgment becomes final, that the appropriate amount plus accrued interest be remitted to the person before the 31st day after the date that the judgment of the court becomes final.

(b) The interest accrues at the rate charged on loans to depository institutions by the New York Federal Reserve Bank.

(c) The interest shall be paid for the period beginning on the date the penalty is paid and ending on the date the penalty is remitted.

Added by Acts 2005, 79th Leg., ch. 282, § 9, eff. Aug. 1, 2005.

§ 486.032. Release of Bond

(a) If the person gave a supersedeas bond and the penalty is not upheld by the court, the court shall order, when the court's judgment becomes final, the release of the bond.

(b) If the person gave a supersedeas bond and the amount of the penalty is reduced, the court shall order the release of the bond after the person pays the reduced amount.

Added by Acts 2005, 79th Leg., ch. 282, § 9, eff. Aug. 1, 2005.

§ 486.033. Administrative Procedure

A proceeding to impose the penalty under this subchapter is considered to be a contested case under Chapter 2001, Government Code.

Added by Acts 2005, 79th Leg., ch. 282, § 9, eff. Aug. 1, 2005.

TRANSPORTATION CODE

TITLE 7. VEHICLES AND TRAFFIC

SUBTITLE I. ENFORCEMENT OF TRAFFIC LAWS

CHAPTER 705. ALLOWING DANGEROUS DRIVER TO BORROW MOTOR VEHICLE

§ 705.001. Allowing Dangerous Driver to Borrow Motor Vehicle; Offense

(a) A person commits an offense if the person:

(1) knowingly permits another to operate a motor vehicle owned by the person; and

(2) knows that at the time permission is given the other person's license has been suspended as a result of a:

(A) conviction of an offense under:

(i) Section 49.04, Penal Code;

(ii) Section 49.07, Penal Code, if the offense involved operation of a motor vehicle; or

(iii) Article 6701*l*–1, Revised Statutes, as that law existed before September 1, 1994; or

(B) failure to give a specimen under:

(i) Chapter 724; or

(ii) Chapter 434, Acts of the 61st Legislature, Regular Session, 1969 (Article 6701*l*–5, Vernon's Texas Civil Statutes), as that law existed before September 1, 1995.

(b) An offense under this section is a Class C misdemeanor.

Acts 1995, 74th Leg., ch. 165, § 1, eff. Sept. 1, 1995.

SUBTITLE J. MISCELLANEOUS PROVISIONS

CHAPTER 724. IMPLIED CONSENT

SUBCHAPTER A. GENERAL PROVISIONS

§ 724.001. Definitions

In this chapter:

(1) "Alcohol concentration" has the meaning assigned by Section 49.01, Penal Code.

(2) "Arrest" includes the taking into custody of a child, as defined by Section 51.02, Family Code.

(3) "Controlled substance" has the meaning assigned by Section 481.002, Health and Safety Code.

(4) "Criminal charge" includes a charge that may result in a proceeding under Title 3, Family Code.[1]

(5) "Criminal proceeding" includes a proceeding under Title 3, Family Code.[1]

(6) "Dangerous drug" has the meaning assigned by Section 483.001, Health and Safety Code.

(7) "Department" means the Department of Public Safety.

(8) "Drug" has the meaning assigned by Section 481.002, Health and Safety Code.

(9) "Intoxicated" has the meaning assigned by Section 49.01, Penal Code.

(10) "License" has the meaning assigned by Section 521.001.

(11) "Operate" means to drive or be in actual control of a motor vehicle or watercraft.

(12) "Public place" has the meaning assigned by Section 1.07, Penal Code.

Acts 1995, 74th Leg., ch. 165, § 1, eff. Sept. 1, 1995. Amended by Acts 1997, 75th Leg., ch. 1013, § 31, eff. Sept. 1, 1997.

[1] V.T.C.A., Family Code § 51.01 et seq.

§ 724.002. Applicability

The provisions of this chapter that apply to suspension of a license for refusal to submit to the taking of a specimen (Sections 724.013, 724.015, and 724.048 and Subchapters C and D) apply only to a person arrested for an offense involving the operation of a motor vehicle or watercraft powered with an engine having a manufacturer's rating of 50 horsepower or above.

Acts 1995, 74th Leg., ch. 165, § 1, eff. Sept. 1, 1995. Amended by Acts 2001, 77th Leg., ch. 444, § 7, eff. Sept. 1, 2001.

§ 724.003. Rulemaking

The department and the State Office of Administrative Hearings shall adopt rules to administer this chapter.

Acts 1995, 74th Leg., ch. 165, § 1, eff. Sept. 1, 1995.

SUBCHAPTER B. TAKING AND ANALYSIS OF SPECIMEN

§ 724.011. Consent to Taking of Specimen

(a) If a person is arrested for an offense arising out of acts alleged to have been committed while the person was operating a motor vehicle in a public place, or a watercraft, while intoxicated, or an offense under Section 106.041, Alcoholic Beverage Code, the person is deemed to have consented, subject to this chapter, to submit to the taking of one or more specimens of the person's breath or blood for analysis to determine the alcohol concentration or the presence in the person's body of a controlled substance, drug, dangerous drug, or other substance.

(b) A person arrested for an offense described by Subsection (a) may consent to submit to the taking of any other type of specimen to determine the person's alcohol concentration.

Acts 1995, 74th Leg., ch. 165, § 1, eff. Sept. 1, 1995. Amended by Acts 1997, 75th Leg., ch. 1013, § 32, eff. Sept. 1, 1997.

§ 724.012. Taking of Specimen

(a) One or more specimens of a person's breath or blood may be taken if the person is arrested and at the request of a peace officer having reasonable grounds to believe the person:

(1) while intoxicated was operating a motor vehicle in a public place, or a watercraft; or

(2) was in violation of Section 106.041, Alcoholic Beverage Code.

(b) A peace officer shall require the taking of a specimen of the person's breath or blood under any of the following circumstances if the officer arrests the person for an offense under Chapter 49, Penal Code, involving the operation of a motor vehicle or a watercraft and the person refuses the officer's request to submit to the taking of a specimen voluntarily:

(1) the person was the operator of a motor vehicle or a watercraft involved in an accident that the officer reasonably believes occurred as a result of the offense and, at the time of the arrest, the officer reasonably believes that as a direct result of the accident:

(A) any individual has died or will die;

(B) an individual other than the person has suffered serious bodily injury; or

(C) an individual other than the person has suffered bodily injury and been transported to a hospital or other medical facility for medical treatment;

(2) the offense for which the officer arrests the person is an offense under Section 49.045, Penal Code; or

(3) at the time of the arrest, the officer possesses or receives reliable information from a credible source that the person:

(A) has been previously convicted of or placed on community supervision for an offense under Section 49.045, 49.07, or 49.08, Penal Code, or an offense under the laws of another state containing elements substantially similar to the elements of an offense under those sections; or

(B) on two or more occasions, has been previously convicted of or placed on community supervision for an offense under Section 49.04, 49.05, 49.06, or 49.065, Penal Code, or an offense under the laws of another state containing elements substantially similar to the elements of an offense under those sections.

(c) The peace officer shall designate the type of specimen to be taken.

(d) In this section, "bodily injury" and "serious bodily injury" have the meanings assigned by Section 1.07, Penal Code.

Acts 1995, 74th Leg., ch. 165, § 1, eff. Sept. 1, 1995. Amended by Acts 1997, 75th Leg., ch. 1013, § 33, eff. Sept. 1, 1997; Acts 2003, 78th Leg., ch. 422, § 1, eff. Sept. 1, 2003; Acts 2009, 81st Leg., ch. 1348, § 18, eff. Sept. 1, 2009.

Section 20(b) of Acts 2009, 81st Leg., ch. 1348 provides:

"The changes in law to Chapters 521 and 524 and Section 724.012, Transportation Code, and Section 13, Article 42.12, Code of Criminal Procedure, apply only to an offense committed on or after the effective date [Sept. 1, 2009] of this Act. An offense committed before the effective date of this Act is covered by the law in effect when the offense was committed, and the former law is continued in effect for that purpose. For purposes of this section, an offense was committed before the effective date of this Act if any element of the offense was committed before that date."

§ 724.013. Prohibition on Taking Specimen if Person Refuses; Exception

Except as provided by Section 724.012(b), a specimen may not be taken if a person refuses to submit to the taking of a specimen designated by a peace officer.

Acts 1995, 74th Leg., ch. 165, § 1, eff. Sept. 1, 1995.

§ 724.014. Person Incapable of Refusal

(a) A person who is dead, unconscious, or otherwise incapable of refusal is considered not to have withdrawn the consent provided by Section 724.011.

(b) If the person is dead, a specimen may be taken by:

(1) the county medical examiner or the examiner's designated agent; or

(2) a licensed mortician or a person authorized under Section 724.016 or 724.017 if there is not a county medical examiner for the county.

(c) If the person is alive but is incapable of refusal, a specimen may be taken by a person authorized under Section 724.016 or 724.017.

Acts 1995, 74th Leg., ch. 165, § 1, eff. Sept. 1, 1995.

§ 724.015. Information Provided by Officer Before Requesting Specimen

Before requesting a person to submit to the taking of a specimen, the officer shall inform the person orally and in writing that:

(1) if the person refuses to submit to the taking of the specimen, that refusal may be admissible in a subsequent prosecution;

(2) if the person refuses to submit to the taking of the specimen, the person's license to operate a motor vehicle will be automatically suspended, whether or not the person is subsequently prosecuted as a result of the arrest, for not less than 180 days;

(3) if the person is 21 years of age or older and submits to the taking of a specimen designated by the officer and an analysis of the specimen shows the person had an alcohol concentration of a level specified by Chapter 49, Penal Code, the person's license to operate a motor vehicle will be automatically suspended for not less than 90 days, whether or not the person is subsequently prosecuted as a result of the arrest;

(4) if the person is younger than 21 years of age and has any detectable amount of alcohol in the person's system, the person's license to operate a motor vehicle will be automatically suspended for not less than 60 days even if the person submits to the taking of the specimen, but that if the person submits to the taking of the specimen and an analysis of the specimen shows that the person had an alcohol concentration less than the level specified by Chapter 49, Penal Code, the person may be subject to criminal penalties less severe than those provided under that chapter;

(5) if the officer determines that the person is a resident without a license to operate a motor vehicle in this state, the department will deny to the person the issuance of a license, whether or not the person is subsequently prosecuted as a result of the arrest, under the same conditions and for the same periods that would have applied to a revocation of the

person's driver's license if the person had held a driver's license issued by this state; and

(6) the person has a right to a hearing on the suspension or denial if, not later than the 15th day after the date on which the person receives the notice of suspension or denial or on which the person is considered to have received the notice by mail as provided by law, the department receives, at its headquarters in Austin, a written demand, including a facsimile transmission, or a request in another form prescribed by the department for the hearing.

Acts 1995, 74th Leg., ch. 165, § 1, eff. Sept. 1, 1995. Amended by Acts 1997, 75th Leg., ch. 1013, § 34, eff. Sept. 1, 1997; Acts 2001, 77th Leg., ch. 444, § 8, eff. Sept. 1, 2001.

§ 724.016. Breath Specimen

(a) A breath specimen taken at the request or order of a peace officer must be taken and analyzed under rules of the department by an individual possessing a certificate issued by the department certifying that the individual is qualified to perform the analysis.

(b) The department may:

(1) adopt rules approving satisfactory analytical methods; and

(2) ascertain the qualifications of an individual to perform the analysis.

(c) The department may revoke a certificate for cause.

Acts 1995, 74th Leg., ch. 165, § 1, eff. Sept. 1, 1995.

§ 724.017. Blood Specimen

(a) Only a physician, qualified technician, chemist, registered professional nurse, or licensed vocational nurse may take a blood specimen at the request or order of a peace officer under this chapter. The blood specimen must be taken in a sanitary place.

(b) If the blood specimen was taken according to recognized medical procedures, the person who takes the blood specimen under this chapter, the facility that employs the person who takes the blood specimen, or the hospital where the blood specimen is taken is immune from civil liability for damages arising from the taking of the blood specimen at the request or order of the peace officer or pursuant to a search warrant as provided by this chapter and is not subject to discipline by any licensing or accrediting agency or body. This subsection does not relieve a person from liability for negligence in the taking of a blood specimen. The taking of a specimen from a person who objects to the taking of the specimen or who is resisting the taking of the specimen does not in itself constitute negligence and may not be considered evidence of negligence.

(c) In this section, "qualified technician" does not include emergency medical services personnel.

(d) A person whose blood specimen is taken under this chapter in a hospital is not considered to be present in the hospital for medical screening or treatment unless the appropriate hospital personnel determine that medical screening or treatment is required for proper medical care of the person.

Acts 1995, 74th Leg., ch. 165, § 1, eff. Sept. 1, 1995. Amended by Acts 2009, 81st Leg., ch. 1348, § 19, eff. Sept. 1, 2009.

§ 724.018. Furnishing Information Concerning Test Results

On the request of a person who has given a specimen at the request of a peace officer, full information concerning the analysis of the specimen shall be made available to the person or the person's attorney.

Acts 1995, 74th Leg., ch. 165, § 1, eff. Sept. 1, 1995.

§ 724.019. Additional Analysis by Request

(a) A person who submits to the taking of a specimen of breath, blood, urine, or another bodily substance at the request or order of a peace officer may, on request and within a reasonable time not to exceed two hours after the arrest, have a physician, qualified technician, chemist, or registered professional nurse selected by the person take for analysis an additional specimen of the person's blood.

(b) The person shall be allowed a reasonable opportunity to contact a person specified by Subsection (a).

(c) A peace officer or law enforcement agency is not required to transport for testing a person who requests that a blood specimen be taken under this section.

(d) The failure or inability to obtain an additional specimen or analysis under this section does not preclude the admission of evidence relating to the analysis of the specimen taken at the request or order of the peace officer.

(e) A peace officer, another person acting for or on behalf of the state, or a law enforcement agency is not liable for damages arising from a person's request to have a blood specimen taken.

Acts 1995, 74th Leg., ch. 165, § 1, eff. Sept. 1, 1995.

SUBCHAPTER C. SUSPENSION OR DENIAL OF LICENSE ON REFUSAL OF SPECIMEN

§ 724.031. Statement Requested on Refusal

If a person refuses the request of a peace officer to submit to the taking of a specimen, the peace officer shall request the person to sign a statement that:

(1) the officer requested that the person submit to the taking of a specimen;

(2) the person was informed of the consequences of not submitting to the taking of a specimen; and

(3) the person refused to submit to the taking of a specimen.

Acts 1995, 74th Leg., ch. 165, § 1, eff. Sept. 1, 1995.

§ 724.032. Officer's Duties for License Suspension; Written Refusal Report.

(a) If a person refuses to submit to the taking of a specimen, whether expressly or because of an intentional failure of the person to give the specimen, the peace officer shall:

(1) serve notice of license suspension or denial on the person;

(2) take possession of any license issued by this state and held by the person arrested;

(3) issue a temporary driving permit to the person unless department records show or the officer otherwise determines that the person does not hold a license to operate a motor vehicle in this state; and

(4) make a written report of the refusal to the director of the department.

(b) The director must approve the form of the refusal report. The report must:

(1) show the grounds for the officer's belief that the person had been operating a motor vehicle or watercraft powered with an engine having a manufacturer's rating of 50 horsepower or above while intoxicated; and

(2) contain a copy of:

(A) the refusal statement requested under Section 724.031; or

(B) a statement signed by the officer that the person refused to:

(i) submit to the taking of the requested specimen; and

(ii) sign the requested statement under Section 724.031.

(c) The officer shall forward to the department not later than the fifth business day after the date of the arrest:

(1) a copy of the notice of suspension or denial;

(2) any license taken by the officer under Subsection (a);

(3) a copy of any temporary driving permit issued under Subsection (a); and

(4) a copy of the refusal report.

(d) The department shall develop forms for notices of suspension or denial and temporary driving permits to be used by all state and local law enforcement agencies.

(e) A temporary driving permit issued under this section expires on the 41st day after the date of issuance. If the person was driving a commercial motor vehicle, as defined by Section 522.003, a temporary driving permit that authorizes the person to drive a commercial motor vehicle is not effective until 24 hours after the time of arrest.

Acts 1995, 74th Leg., ch. 165, § 1, eff. Sept. 1, 1995. Amended by Acts 2001, 77th Leg., ch. 444, § 9, eff. Sept. 1, 2001.

§ 724.033. Issuance by Department of Notice of Suspension or Denial of License

(a) On receipt of a report of a peace officer under Section 724.032, if the officer did not serve notice of suspension or denial of a license at the time of refusal to submit to the taking of a specimen, the department shall mail notice of suspension or denial, by first class mail, to the address of the person shown by the records of the department or to the address given in the peace officer's report, if different.

(b) Notice is considered received on the fifth day after the date it is mailed.

Acts 1995, 74th Leg., ch. 165, § 1, eff. Sept. 1, 1995. Amended by Acts 1999, 76th Leg., ch. 1409, § 5, eff. Sept. 1, 1999.

§ 724.034. Contents of Notice of Suspension or Denial of License

A notice of suspension or denial of a license must state:

(1) the reason and statutory grounds for the action;

(2) the effective date of the suspension or denial;

(3) the right of the person to a hearing;

(4) how to request a hearing; and

(5) the period in which a request for a hearing must be received by the department.

Acts 1995, 74th Leg., ch. 165, § 1, eff. Sept. 1, 1995.

§ 724.035. Suspension or Denial of License

(a) If a person refuses the request of a peace officer to submit to the taking of a specimen, the department shall:

(1) suspend the person's license to operate a motor vehicle on a public highway for 180 days; or

(2) if the person is a resident without a license, issue an order denying the issuance of a license to the person for 180 days.

(b) The period of suspension or denial is two years if the person's driving record shows one or more alcohol-related or drug-related enforcement contacts, as defined by Section 524.001(3), during the 10 years preceding the date of the person's arrest.

(c) A suspension or denial takes effect on the 40th day after the date on which the person:

(1) receives notice of suspension or denial under Section 724.032(a); or

(2) is considered to have received notice of suspension or denial under Section 724.033.

Acts 1995, 74th Leg., ch. 165, § 1, eff. Sept. 1, 1995. Amended by Acts 1997, 75th Leg., ch. 165, § 30.163, eff. Sept. 1, 1997; Acts 1997, 75th Leg., ch. 1013, § 35, eff. Sept. 1, 1997; Acts 2001, 77th Leg., ch. 444, § 10, eff. Sept. 1, 2001.

SUBCHAPTER D. HEARING

§ 724.041. Hearing on Suspension or Denial

(a) If, not later than the 15th day after the date on which the person receives notice of suspension or denial under Section 724.032(a) or is considered to have received notice under Section 724.033, the department receives at its headquarters in Austin, in writing, including a facsimile transmission, or by another manner prescribed by the department, a request that a hearing be held, the State Office of Administrative Hearings shall hold a hearing.

(b) A hearing shall be held not earlier than the 11th day after the date the person is notified, unless the parties agree to waive this requirement, but before the effective date of the notice of suspension or denial.

(c) A request for a hearing stays the suspension or denial until the date of the final decision of the administrative law judge. If the person's license was taken by a peace officer under Section 724.032(a), the department shall notify the person of the effect of the request on the suspension of the person's license before the expiration of any temporary driving permit issued to the person, if the person is otherwise eligible, in a manner that will permit the person to establish to a peace officer that the person's license is not suspended.

(d) A hearing shall be held by an administrative law judge employed by the State Office of Administrative Hearings.

(e) A hearing shall be held:

(1) at a location designated by the State Office of Administrative Hearings:

(A) in the county of arrest if the county has a population of 300,000 or more; or

(B) in the county in which the person was alleged to have committed the offense for which the person was arrested or not more than 75 miles from the county seat of the county of arrest if the population of the county of arrest is less than 300,000; or

(2) with the consent of the person requesting the hearing and the department, by telephone conference call.

(f) The State Office of Administrative Hearings shall provide for the stenographic or electronic recording of a hearing under this subchapter.

(g) An administrative hearing under this section is governed by Sections 524.032(b) and (c), 524.035(e), 524.037(a), and 524.040.

Acts 1995, 74th Leg., ch. 165, § 1, eff. Sept. 1, 1995. Amended by Acts 1997, 75th Leg., ch. 165, § 30.164, eff. Sept. 1, 1997; Acts 2001, 77th Leg., ch. 444, § 11, eff. Sept. 1, 2001.

§ 724.042. Issues at Hearing

The issues at a hearing under this subchapter are whether:

(1) reasonable suspicion or probable cause existed to stop or arrest the person;

(2) probable cause existed to believe that the person was:

(A) operating a motor vehicle in a public place while intoxicated; or

(B) operating a watercraft powered with an engine having a manufacturer's rating of 50 horsepower or above while intoxicated;

(3) the person was placed under arrest by the officer and was requested to submit to the taking of a specimen; and

(4) the person refused to submit to the taking of a specimen on request of the officer.

Acts 1995, 74th Leg., ch. 165, § 1, eff. Sept. 1, 1995. Amended by Acts 2001, 77th Leg., ch. 444, § 12, eff. Sept. 1, 2001.

§ 724.043. Findings of Administrative Law Judge

(a) If the administrative law judge finds in the affirmative on each issue under Section 724.042, the suspension order is sustained. If the person is a resident without a license, the department shall continue to deny to the person the issuance of a license for the applicable period provided by Section 724.035.

(b) If the administrative law judge does not find in the affirmative on each issue under Section 724.042, the department shall return the person's license to the person, if the license was taken by a peace officer under Section 724.032(a), and reinstate the person's license or rescind any order denying the issuance of a license because of the person's refusal to submit to the taking of a specimen under Section 724.032(a).

Acts 1995, 74th Leg., ch. 165, § 1, eff. Sept. 1, 1995. Amended by Acts 2001, 77th Leg., ch. 444, § 13, eff. Sept. 1, 2001.

§ 724.044. Waiver of Right to Hearing

A person waives the right to a hearing under this subchapter and the department's suspension or denial is final and may not be appealed if the person:

(1) fails to request a hearing under Section 724.041; or

(2) requests a hearing and fails to appear, without good cause.

Acts 1995, 74th Leg., ch. 165, § 1, eff. Sept. 1, 1995.

§ 724.045. Prohibition on Probation of Suspension

A suspension under this chapter may not be probated.

Acts 1995, 74th Leg., ch. 165, § 1, eff. Sept. 1, 1995.

§ 724.046. Reinstatement of License or Issuance of New License

(a) A license suspended under this chapter may not be reinstated or a new license issued until the person whose license has been suspended pays to the department a fee of $125 in addition to any other fee required by law. A person subject to a denial order issued under this chapter may not obtain a license after the period of denial has ended until the person pays to the department a fee of $125 in addition to any other fee required by law.

(b) If a suspension or denial under this chapter is rescinded by the department, an administrative law judge, or a court, payment of the fee under this section is not required for reinstatement or issuance of a license.

(c) Each fee collected under this section shall be deposited to the credit of the Texas mobility fund.

Acts 1995, 74th Leg., ch. 165, § 1, eff. Sept. 1, 1995. Amended by Acts 2001, 77th Leg., ch. 444, § 14(b), eff. Sept. 1, 2001; Acts 2003, 78th Leg., ch. 1325, § 11.09, eff. Sept. 1, 2003.

§ 724.047. Appeal

Chapter 524 governs an appeal from an action of the department, following an administrative hearing under this chapter, in suspending or denying the issuance of a license.

Acts 1995, 74th Leg., ch. 165, § 1, eff. Sept. 1, 1995.

§ 724.048. Relationship of Administrative Proceeding to Criminal Proceeding

(a) The determination of the department or administrative law judge:

(1) is a civil matter;

(2) is independent of and is not an estoppel as to any matter in issue in an adjudication of a criminal charge arising from the occurrence that is the basis for the suspension or denial; and

(3) does not preclude litigation of the same or similar facts in a criminal prosecution.

(b) Except as provided by Subsection (c), the disposition of a criminal charge does not affect a license suspension or denial under this chapter and is not an estoppel as to any matter in issue in a suspension or denial proceeding under this chapter.

(c) If a criminal charge arising from the same arrest as a suspension under this chapter results in an acquittal, the suspension under this chapter may not be imposed. If a suspension under this chapter has already been imposed, the department shall rescind the suspension and remove references to the suspension from the computerized driving record of the individual.

Acts 1995, 74th Leg., ch. 165, § 1, eff. Sept. 1, 1995. Amended by Acts 1997, 75th Leg., ch. 1013, § 36, eff. Sept. 1, 1997.

For application provisions of Acts 1997, 75th Leg., ch. 1013, see notes following V.T.C.A., Transportation Code § 724.001.

SUBCHAPTER E. ADMISSIBILITY OF EVIDENCE

§ 724.061. Admissibility of Refusal of Person to Submit to Taking of Specimen

A person's refusal of a request by an officer to submit to the taking of a specimen of breath or blood, whether the refusal was express or the result of an intentional failure to give the specimen, may be introduced into evidence at the person's trial.

Acts 1995, 74th Leg., ch. 165, § 1, eff. Sept. 1, 1995.

§ 724.062. Admissibility of Refusal of Request for Additional Test

The fact that a person's request to have an additional analysis under Section 724.019 is refused by the officer or another person acting for or on behalf of the state, that the person was not provided a reasonable opportunity to contact a person specified by Section 724.019(a) to take the specimen, or that reasonable access was not allowed to the arrested person may be introduced into evidence at the person's trial.

Acts 1995, 74th Leg., ch. 165, § 1, eff. Sept. 1, 1995.

§ 724.063. Admissibility of Alcohol Concentration or Presence of Substance

Evidence of alcohol concentration or the presence of a controlled substance, drug, dangerous drug, or other substance obtained by an analysis authorized by Section 724.014 is admissible in a civil or criminal action.

Acts 1995, 74th Leg., ch. 165, § 1, eff. Sept. 1, 1995. Amended by Acts 1997, 75th Leg., ch. 165, § 30.165, eff. Sept. 1, 1997.

§ 724.064. Admissibility in Criminal Proceeding of Specimen Analysis

On the trial of a criminal proceeding arising out of an offense under Chapter 49, Penal Code, involving the operation of a motor vehicle or a watercraft, or an offense under Section 106.041, Alcoholic Beverage Code, evidence of the alcohol concentration or presence of a controlled substance, drug, dangerous drug, or other substance as shown by analysis of a specimen of the person's blood, breath, or urine or any other bodily substance taken at the request or order of a peace officer is admissible.

Acts 1995, 74th Leg., ch. 165, § 1, eff. Sept. 1, 1995. Amended by Acts 1997, 75th Leg., ch. 1013, § 37, eff. Sept. 1, 1997.

CHAPTER 729. OPERATION OF MOTOR VEHICLE BY MINOR

§ 729.001. Operation of Motor Vehicle by Minor in Violation of Traffic Laws; Offense

(a) A person who is younger than 17 years of age commits an offense if the person operates a motor vehicle on a public road or highway, a street or alley in a municipality, or a public beach in violation of any traffic law of this state, including:

(1) Chapter 502, other than Section 502.282 or 502.412;

(2) Chapter 521, other than an offense under Section 521.457;

(3) Subtitle C,[1] other than an offense punishable by imprisonment or by confinement in jail under Section 550.021, 550.022, 550.024, or 550.025;

(4) Chapter 601;

(5) Chapter 621;

(6) Chapter 661; and

(7) Chapter 681.

(b) In this section, "beach" means a beach bordering on the Gulf of Mexico that extends inland from the line of mean low tide to the natural line of vegetation bordering on the seaward shore of the Gulf of Mexico, or the larger contiguous area to which the public has acquired a right of use or easement to or over by prescription, dedication, or estoppel, or has retained a right by virtue of continuous right in the public since time immemorial as recognized by law or custom.

(c) An offense under this section is punishable by the fine or other sanction, other than confinement or imprisonment, authorized by statute for violation of the traffic law listed under Subsection (a) that is the basis of the prosecution under this section.

Acts 1995, 74th Leg., ch. 165, § 1, eff. Sept. 1, 1995. Amended by Acts 1997, 75th Leg., ch. 165, § 30.167, eff. Sept. 1, 1997; Acts 1997, 75th Leg., ch. 167, § 30.167, eff. Sept. 1, 1997; Acts 1997, 75th Leg., ch. 822, § 1, eff. Sept. 1, 1997; Acts 1997, 75th Leg., ch. 1086, § 40, eff. Sept. 1, 1997; Acts 1999, 76th Leg., ch. 1477, § 36, eff. Sept. 1, 1999; Acts 2003, 78th Leg., ch. 283, § 58, eff. Sept. 1, 2003.

[1] V.T.C.A., Transportation Code § 541.001 et seq.

§ 729.002. Operation of Motor Vehicle by Minor Without License

(a) A person who is younger than 17 years of age commits an offense if the person operates a motor vehicle without a driver's license authorizing the operation of a motor vehicle on a:

(1) public road or highway;

(2) street or alley in a municipality; or

(3) public beach as defined by Section 729.001.

(b) An offense under this section is punishable in the same manner as if the person was 17 years of age or older and operated a motor vehicle without a license as described by Subsection (a), except that an offense under this section is not punishable by confinement or imprisonment.

Acts 1995, 74th Leg., ch. 165, § 1, eff. Sept. 1, 1995. Amended by Acts 1997, 75th Leg., ch. 1086, § 43, eff. Sept. 1, 1997; Acts 1999, 76th Leg., ch. 1477, § 37, eff. Sept. 1, 1999.

INDEX

Abbreviations

Gov .... Government Code
H & S .... Health and Safety Code
Pen .... Penal Code
Tran .... Transportation Code